# BEYOND MYTHS & LEGENDS:
## A NARRATIVE HISTORY OF TEXAS

# BEYOND MYTHS & LEGENDS:
## A NARRATIVE HISTORY OF TEXAS

## Sixth Edition

Kenneth W. Howell
Blinn College

Keith J. Volanto
Collin College

F. Todd Smith
University of North Texas

Charles D. Grear
Central Texas College

Jennifer S. Lawrence
Tarrant County College

Design and Production: Abigail Press
Typesetting: Abigail Press
Typeface: AGaramond
Cover Art: Sam Tolia

**BEYOND MYTHS & LEGENDS:**
**A NARRATIVE HISTORY OF TEXAS**

Sixth Edition, 2020
Printed in the United States of America
Translation rights reserved by the publisher
ISBN 1-890919-98-5  13-digit 978-1-890919-98-6

Copyright @ by Abigail Press Inc., 2050 Middleton Dr., Wheaton, IL 60189

All rights reserved. No part of the material protected by the copyright notice may be reproduced or utilized in any form or by any means, electronic or mechanical, including photocopy, recording, or any information storage and retrieval system, without permission in writing from the publisher.

# CONTENTS IN BRIEF

**Chapter One**
    The Native Americans of Texas to 1684 — 1

**Chapter Two**
    Texas Under Spanish Rule, 1684-1821 — **29**

**Chapter Three**
    The Northern Province of Mexico, 1821-1835 — **61**

**Chapter Four**
    Revolutionary Texas: The Birth of the Republic, 1835-1836 — **85**

**Chapter Five**
    Forging a New Nation, 1836-1845 — **111**

**Chapter Six**
    The 28th State in the Union, 1845-1861 — **133**

**Chapter Seven**
    Texas During the Civil War, 1861-1865 — **163**

**Chapter Eight**
    Reconstruction in Texas: The Unfinished Civil War, 1865-1874 — **189**

**Chapter Nine**
    Economic and Political Reforms, 1874-1890 — **217**

**Chapter Ten**
    The Populist Movement, 1890-1900 — **247**

**Chapter Eleven**
    Society and Culture, 1874-1900 — **269**

**Chapter Twelve**
    The Progressive Era and WWI, 1900-1919 — **299**

**Chapter Thirteen**
    The Rise of Urbanization, Expanding Opportunities, and the Invisible Empire, 1920-1929 — **325**

**Chapter Fourteen**
    The Great Depression and the New Deal, 1929-1940 — **355**

**Chapter Fifteen**
   World War II and Texas, 1941-1945     **385**

**Chapter Sixteen**
   On the Threshold of Modernization, 1945-1959     **411**

**Chapter Seventeen**
   The Turbulent Decade: Reform and Reaction, 1960-1972     **441**

**Chapter Eighteen**
   A Transitional Decade, 1972-1979     **465**

**Chapter Nineteen**
   Complex Times, 1980-1994     **493**

**Chapter Twenty**
   The Dawn of a New Century, 1995-2020     **521**

**Appendix I**     **555**
**Appendix II**     **558**
**Index**     **560**

# TABLE OF CONTENTS

| | |
|---|---|
| **Maps and Illustrations** | xvii |
| **Preface** | xx |

**Chapter One**
**The Native Americans of Texas to 1684** — 1

| | |
|---|---|
| **Prelude: A Migratory Crossroads—History, Archaeology, and Science** | 1 |
| Into the Western Hemisphere | 2 |
| Paleolithic Era | 3 |
| Archaic Period | 5 |
| The Atakapas, Karankawas, and Coahuiltecans | 6 |
| Woodland Indians, the Agricultural Revolution, and the Mississippian Cultural Tradition | 8 |
| The Caddos and the Wichitas | 10 |
| Pueblo Cultural Tradition, the Jumanos, and the Apaches | 13 |
| Spanish Explorers, Diseases, and Horses | 14 |
| Lipan Apaches, Comanches, and Tonkawas | 17 |
| Spaniards, Franciscans, and the Kingdom of the Tejas | 20 |
| **Afterward: A More Important Question** | 21 |
| **Myth & Legend—The First Texans: The Debate Continues** | 22 |
|    Suggestions for Further Reading | 24 |
|    Identification | 25 |
|    Multiple Choice | 25 |
|    True/False | 27 |
|    Matching | 27 |
|    Essay Questions | 28 |

**Chapter Two**
**Texas Under Spanish Rule, 1684-1821** — 29

| | |
|---|---|
| **Prelude: An Early American Treks through Spanish Texas—Zebulon Pike's Expedition** | 29 |
| French Interlopers and the Spanish Response | 30 |
| The Permanent Occupation of Spanish Texas | 34 |
| Spanish Settlements in Texas to Mid-Century | 37 |
| French Louisiana and the Norteño Alliance | 38 |
| Franciscan Missionary Efforts among the Texas Native Americans | 39 |
| Spanish Accession of Louisiana and the Reorganization of Texas | 41 |
| Spanish Texas during the Late Eighteenth Century | 45 |
| Spanish Texas and the United States | 46 |
| Revolution and War in Texas | 49 |
| The Final Years of Spanish Texas | 50 |
| **Afterward: After Pike—Changes to the Texas Landscape** | 53 |
| **Myth & Legend—The Lady in Blue** | 54 |
|    Suggestions for Further Reading | 56 |
|    Identification | 57 |

|   |   |
|---|---|
| Multiple Choice | 57 |
| True/False | 59 |
| Matching | 59 |
| Essay Questions | 60 |

## Chapter Three
## The Northern Province of Mexico, 1821-1835     61

| | |
|---|---|
| **Prelude: The Solution is Simple—Invite the Europeans** | 61 |
| The Origins of Austin's Colony | 63 |
| The Shaping of Mexican Texas | 65 |
| Early Empresarios and the Fredonian Rebellion | 66 |
| Texas Becomes an Anglo-Protestant Province | 68 |
| The Law of April 6, 1830 and the Anahuac Rebellion | 71 |
| Requests for Separate Statehood | 72 |
| Native Americans in the 1830s | 75 |
| Texas in 1834 | 77 |
| **Afterward: The Results of Tadeo Ortiz de Ayala's Failed Policy** | 77 |
| **Myth & Legend—Multiculturalism in Early Texas** | 78 |
|    Suggestions for Further Reading | 80 |
|    Identification | 81 |
|    Multiple Choice | 81 |
|    True/False | 83 |
|    Matching | 83 |
|    Essay Questions | 84 |

## Chapter Four
## Revolutionary Texas: The Birth of the Republic, 1835-1836     85

| | |
|---|---|
| **Prelude: A Texan Remembers the Victory at the Battle of San Jacinto** | 85 |
| Outbreak of the War | 87 |
| The Consultation of 1835 | 90 |
| "Remember the Alamo!" | 91 |
| Creation of the Republic of Texas | 93 |
| "Remember Goliad!" | 94 |
| The Runaway Scrape | 95 |
| The Battle of San Jacinto | 96 |
| Native Americans and the Texas Revolution | 99 |
| Impact of the Texas Revolution | 102 |
| **Afterward: New Questions Arise for the Republic** | 102 |
| **Myth & Legend—The Yellow Rose of Texas** | 103 |
|    Suggestions for Further Reading | 106 |
|    Identification | 107 |
|    Multiple Choice | 107 |
|    True/False | 109 |
|    Matching | 109 |
|    Essay Questions | 110 |

**Chapter Five**
**Forging a New Nation, 1836-1845** ............................................. 111

    **Prelude: The Killough Massacre** ............................................. 111
    Problems with the Republic ...................................................... 112
    The Provincial Government of the Republic of Texas ............. 113
    Houston's First Administration ................................................ 115
    Lamar's Administration ............................................................ 117
    Houston's Second Administration ............................................ 121
    Annexation to the United States .............................................. 124
    **Afterward: The Cherokee War** .............................................. 125
    **Myth & Legend—The Legend of Sam Houston: His True Intentions**
        **for Texas** ............................................................................. 126
        Suggestions for Further Reading ........................................ 128
        Identification ....................................................................... 129
        Multiple Choice .................................................................. 129
        True/False ............................................................................ 130
        Matching ............................................................................. 131
        Essay Questions .................................................................. 132

**Chapter Six**
**The 28th State in the Union, 1845-1861** ................................... 133

    **Prelude: The Façade of the Alamo** ....................................... 133
    Problems with Statehood .......................................................... 134
    New Mexico-Texas Boundary Dispute and the Compromise of 1850 ... 138
    Advantages of Statehood ........................................................... 141
    Ethnic Groups and Slaves in Texas ........................................... 141
    Social Classes ............................................................................. 146
    Texas Social and Cultural Life .................................................. 148
    Texas Politics in the 1850s ......................................................... 150
    Texas Secession .......................................................................... 151
    **Afterward: The Evolving Interpretations of the Alamo** ....... 155
    **Myth & Legend—Slavery as a Benevolent Institution** ......... 156
        Suggestions for Further Reading ........................................ 158
        Identification ....................................................................... 159
        Multiple Choice .................................................................. 159
        True/False ............................................................................ 160
        Matching ............................................................................. 161
        Essay Questions .................................................................. 162

**Chapter Seven**
**Texas During the Civil War, 1861-1865** ................................... 163

    **Prelude: The Story of Britton "Britt" Johnson** ..................... 163
    Initial Actions of Texans ........................................................... 164
    Why Did They Fight ................................................................. 165
    Preparation for War ................................................................... 166

| | |
|---|---|
| Fighting East of the Mississippi River | 166 |
| The Invasion of New Mexico | 168 |
| Fighting in the Trans-Mississippi Theater | 170 |
| Desertion and the Last Battle of the Civil War | 176 |
| The Texas Home Front | 177 |
| Texas Women during the War | 178 |
| Internal Dissent | 179 |
| Defending the Frontier | 180 |
| The End of the War | 181 |
| **Afterward: Searching for Britton "Britt" Johnson** | 181 |
| **Myth & Legend—Divided Loyalties: Texans and the Confederacy** | 182 |
| Suggestions for Further Reading | 184 |
| Identification | 185 |
| Multiple Choice | 185 |
| True/False | 186 |
| Matching | 187 |
| Essay Questions | 188 |

## Chapter Eight
### Reconstruction in Texas: The Unfinished Civil War, 1865-1874 — 189

| | |
|---|---|
| **Prelude: The Assassination of J. N. Baughman, 1874** | 189 |
| Presidential Reconstruction | 191 |
| The Arrival of Federal Troops | 192 |
| The Bureau of Refugees, Freedmen, and Abandoned Lands | 193 |
| The Provisional Government | 195 |
| Congressional Reconstruction | 200 |
| Constitutional Convention of 1868-1869 | 201 |
| Violence and Guerilla Warfare | 204 |
| Governor Edmund J. Davis and the Republican State Government | 206 |
| The End of Republican Government in Texas | 208 |
| How Should We Remember the Reconstruction Era? | 208 |
| **Afterward: The Failures of Reconstruction in Texas** | 209 |
| **Myth & Legend—Texas Under the Terrible Carpetbaggers** | 210 |
| Suggestions for Further Reading | 212 |
| Identification | 213 |
| Multiple Choice | 213 |
| True/False | 215 |
| Matching | 215 |
| Essay Questions | 216 |

## Chapter Nine
### Economic and Political Reforms, 1874-1890 — 217

| | |
|---|---|
| **Prelude: John Henry Kirby—The Paul Bunyan of East Texas** | 217 |
| Railroad Development and Its Impact on Texans | 219 |
| Other Leading Industries | 219 |
| Labor Unions | 221 |
| Agriculture: The Mainstay of the Economy | 224 |

| | |
|---|---|
| Texas Ranches and Ranchers—the Cattle Industry | 225 |
| Democratic Reign in State Politics | 228 |
| Agrarian Organizations and Challenges to Democratic Hegemony | 236 |
| Conclusions | 239 |
| **Afterward: Troubled Times for the Paul Bunyan of Texas** | 239 |
| Myth & Legend—African Americans and Voting in the Late Nineteenth Century | 240 |
|     Suggestions for Further Reading | 242 |
|     Identification | 243 |
|     Multiple Choice | 243 |
|     True/False | 245 |
|     Matching | 245 |
|     Essay Questions | 246 |

## Chapter Ten
### The Populist Movement, 1890-1900    247

| | |
|---|---|
| **Prelude: The *Southern Mercury*: Voice of the Populist Movement in Texas** | 247 |
| Foundations of the People's Party | 248 |
| Governor Hogg and the Democratic Response to Populism | 253 |
| The Elections of 1892: A Promising Start | 256 |
| The Elections of 1894: Sustained Hopes | 258 |
| The Elections of 1896: The Final Curtain Call | 259 |
| Populist Women | 260 |
| The End of the Movement | 260 |
| **Afterward: The *Southern Mercury*'s Fall from Stardom** | 261 |
| Myth & Legend—Women's Political Participation in the Late Nineteenth Century | 262 |
|     Suggestions for Further Reading | 264 |
|     Identification | 265 |
|     Multiple Choice | 265 |
|     True/False | 267 |
|     Matching | 267 |
|     Essay Questions | 268 |

## Chapter Eleven
### Society and Culture, 1874-1900    269

| | |
|---|---|
| **Prelude: The Making of a Texas Baptist Legend—Benajah Harvey Carroll** | 269 |
| Population Demographics | 270 |
| Living and Working Conditions | 271 |
| Urban Growth | 273 |
| Health | 273 |
| Entertainment | 276 |
| Religion | 277 |
| Education | 278 |
| Women | 280 |

| | |
|---|---|
| Lawlessness and the Texas Rangers | 281 |
| The Final Destruction of the Plains Indians | 283 |
| The Trials and Tribulations of African Americans | 286 |
| Mexican Americans and European Immigrants | 287 |
| Literature and the Arts | 289 |
| Conclusion | 290 |
| **Afterward: The Legacy of a Baptist Legend** | 291 |
| **Myth & Legend—African-American Landownership in Texas During the Decades Following the Civil War** | 292 |
| Suggestions for Further Reading | 294 |
| Identification | 295 |
| Multiple Choice | 295 |
| True/False | 296 |
| Matching | 297 |
| Essay Questions | 298 |

**Chapter Twelve**
**The Progressive Era and WWI, 1900-1919** — 299

| | |
|---|---|
| **Prelude: Spindletop—The Beginning of King Oil** | 299 |
| Texas: Population and Economic Demographics | 302 |
| Urban Growth and the Galveston Plan | 304 |
| Texas Politics: Early Progressive Era | 306 |
| Texas and World War I | 311 |
| Women and the Vote | 313 |
| Minorities and the Progressive Movement | 314 |
| The Drive for Prohibition | 316 |
| **Afterward: The Bequests of Spindletop—The Oil Industry in Texas** | 317 |
| **Myth & Legend—A Strange Tale from the Galveston Hurricane of 1900** | 318 |
| Suggestions for Further Reading | 320 |
| Identification | 321 |
| Multiple Choice | 321 |
| True/False | 323 |
| Matching | 323 |
| Essay Questions | 324 |

**Chapter Thirteen**
**The Rise of Urbanization, Expanding Opportunities, and the Invisible Empire, 1920-1929** — 325

| | |
|---|---|
| **Prelude: The All-Woman Supreme Court** | 325 |
| Economic Developments: Industry and Agriculture | 327 |
| Farm Women | 328 |
| Tejanos | 329 |
| African Americans | 330 |
| The Growing Cities and Urbanization | 332 |
| J. Frank Norris and the Rise of Fundamentalism | 333 |
| The "Invisible Empire" Appears in Texas | 336 |

| | |
|---|---|
| Klan Violence and Reaction | 338 |
| Governor Pat Neff | 339 |
| The Klan Enters Politics | 340 |
| The Klan Seeks the Governorship | 342 |
| Governor Miriam Ferguson | 344 |
| Governor Dan Moody | 346 |
| **Afterward: The Beginning of a Slow Ascent** | 347 |
| **Myth & Legend—The 1920s as the "Roaring Twenties"** | 348 |
| Suggestions for Further Reading | 350 |
| Identification | 351 |
| Multiple Choice | 351 |
| True/False | 353 |
| Matching | 353 |
| Essay Question | 354 |

## Chapter Fourteen
### The Great Depression and the New Deal, 1929-1940 — 355

| | |
|---|---|
| **Prelude: The New London School Explosion** | 355 |
| Arrival of the Great Depression | 356 |
| Governor Ross Sterling | 357 |
| The East Texas Oil Boom | 357 |
| The "Cotton Holiday" Plan | 359 |
| The Return of the Fergusons | 360 |
| Texas Influence on the New Deal | 361 |
| Immediate Relief Efforts | 362 |
| Work Relief | 363 |
| A New Deal for Youth | 365 |
| Agricultural Recovery | 367 |
| Agricultural Aid and Reform | 370 |
| Industry and Labor | 371 |
| State and National Politics | 373 |
| Evaluation of the New Deal | 377 |
| **Afterward: A Town Recovers—A Memory Endures** | 377 |
| **Myth & Legend—The New Deal as Socialism Forced Upon Reluctant Texans** | 378 |
| Suggestions for Further Reading | 380 |
| Identification | 381 |
| Multiple Choice | 381 |
| True/False | 383 |
| Matching | 383 |
| Essay Question | 384 |

## Chapter Fifteen
### World War II and Texas, 1941-1945 — 385

| | |
|---|---|
| **Prelude: Frank Fujita, Jr.—A Japanese Texan Prisoner of the Empire of the Rising Sun** | 385 |

| | |
|---|---|
| The Roots of War | 387 |
| Synopsis of the War | 388 |
| Texas Military Installations | 390 |
| Texans in Uniform | 391 |
| Wartime Voluntarism | 394 |
| The Texas Wartime Economy | 396 |
| Wartime Politics | 399 |
| The "Greatest Generation" Returns Home | 403 |
| **Afterward: Liberation** | 403 |
| **Myth & Legend—Texan Doris Miller Shot Down Numerous Japanese Planes During Pearl Harbor Raid** | 404 |
| Suggestions for Further Reading | 406 |
| Identification | 407 |
| Multiple Choice | 407 |
| True/False | 409 |
| Matching | 409 |
| Essay Question | 410 |

**Chapter Sixteen**
**On the Threshold of Modernization, 1945-1959** — 411

| | |
|---|---|
| **Prelude: The Texas City Disaster** | 411 |
| Postwar Manufacturing | 412 |
| Changes in Agriculture | 414 |
| Postwar Urbanization and Suburbanization | 415 |
| Tejano Civil Rights Activism during the 1950s | 417 |
| African American Civil Rights Activism during the 1950s | 421 |
| Texas Politics during the Beauford Jester Years | 425 |
| Governor Allan Shivers | 428 |
| Politics during the Late-1950s | 432 |
| Into the 1960s | 433 |
| **Afterward: Learning from Tragedy** | 433 |
| **Myth & Legend—Lyndon Johnson Stole the 1948 Democratic Party Nomination for a U.S. Senate Seat from Coke Stevenson** | 434 |
| Suggestions for Further Reading | 436 |
| Identification | 437 |
| Multiple Choice | 437 |
| True/False | 439 |
| Matching | 439 |
| Essay Question | 440 |

**Chapter Seventeen**
**The Turbulent Decade: Reform and Reaction, 1960-1972** — 441

| | |
|---|---|
| **Prelude: The Marshall Sit-In Movement** | 441 |
| Early 1960s Texas Politics | 443 |
| Early 1960s Civil Rights Activism | 444 |
| The Kennedy Assassination | 446 |

| | |
|---|---|
| Johnson's Great Society and the Vietnam War | 449 |
| Black Political Gains and Late-1960s Activism | 451 |
| Tejano Activism during the 1960s | 453 |
| Governor Connally and Late-1960s State Politics | 455 |
| **Afterward: Vindication** | 457 |
| **Myth & Legend—Members of a Vast Conspiracy Killed President John Kennedy in Dallas** | 458 |
| Suggestions for Further Reading | 460 |
| Identification | 461 |
| Multiple Choice | 461 |
| True/False | 463 |
| Matching | 463 |
| Essay Question | 464 |

## Chapter Eighteen
## A Transitional Decade, 1972-1979 — 465

| | |
|---|---|
| **Prelude: Tom Landry—Texas Sports Icon** | 465 |
| The Sharpstown Scandal | 466 |
| Texans and Watergate | 467 |
| Post-Sharpstown Politics | 468 |
| Constitutional Convention | 471 |
| La Raza Unida Party | 472 |
| Women's Rights and Political Representation | 473 |
| Oil Growth in the 1970s | 475 |
| Growth of New Industries | 477 |
| Ranching and Farming | 478 |
| Texas in Literature, Television, and Film | 479 |
| The Influence of Texas Musicians | 480 |
| The Rise of Major League Sports in Texas | 482 |
| A Decade in Transition | 485 |
| **Afterward: Tom Landry Finally Wins the "Big One"—and Many More** | 485 |
| **Myth & Legend—Myth of the Citizen-Legislator** | 486 |
| Suggestions for Further Reading | 488 |
| Identification | 489 |
| Multiple Choice | 489 |
| True/False | 491 |
| Matching | 491 |
| Essay Question | 492 |

## Chapter Nineteen
## Complex Times, 1980-1994 — 493

| | |
|---|---|
| **Prelude: The Waco Siege** | 493 |
| Texas and National Politics | 495 |
| 1980s State Politics: White, Clements, and Education Reform | 499 |
| Ann Richards and Early 1990s State Politics | 503 |

| | |
|---|---|
| Decline in the Oil Industry | 506 |
| The North American Free Trade Agreement | 506 |
| Post-Cold War Base Closures | 507 |
| The Growing Tech Industry | 508 |
| Environmental Issues | 509 |
| The Death of the SWC and the Ongoing Allure of Texas Football | 510 |
| Two Texas Tragedies—Stevie Ray Vaughan and Selena | 511 |
| The Emergence of a New Texas | 512 |
| **Aftermath: Apocalypse in Waco** | 513 |
| **Myth & Legend—Myth of the Oil Industry** | 514 |
|     Suggestions for Further Reading | 516 |
|     Identification | 517 |
|     Multiple Choice | 517 |
|     True/False | 519 |
|     Matching | 519 |
|     Essay Question | 520 |

## Chapter Twenty
## The Dawn of a New Century, 1995-2020 — 521

| | |
|---|---|
| **Prelude: A Terrorist Attack in Texas** | 521 |
| Politics During the Bush Years | 522 |
| Early Twenty-first Century Texas Politics | 525 |
| Public Transportation and Infrastructure | 532 |
| A Home for High-Tech Industries | 533 |
| The Enron Scandal | 533 |
| Tourism, Sports, and Entertainment | 535 |
| Education | 539 |
| Criminal Justice Issues | 540 |
| Mixing of Cultures | 541 |
| Immigration | 543 |
| A Series of Catastrophes | 544 |
| Economic Ups and Downs | 545 |
| **Aftermath: The War Abroad Hits Home** | 547 |
| **Myth & Legend—Myth of the Cowboy Culture** | 548 |
|     Suggestions for Further Reading | 550 |
|     Identification | 551 |
|     Multiple Choice | 551 |
|     True/False | 552 |
|     Matching | 552 |
|     Essay Question | 554 |
| **Appendix I** | 555 |
| **Appendix II** | 558 |
| **Index** | 560 |

# Maps and Illustrations

## MAPS

The Beringia Land Bridge  3
Regions of Texas  9
Major Rivers of Texas  12
Indian Tribes of Texas  15
Early Spanish Exploration  16
LaSalle in Texas  32
Spanish Missions and Presidios 1682-1722  36
Spanish Missions and Presidios 1746-1762  41
North America Before 1763  42
North America After 1763  43
The Neutral Ground  49
The Filibusterers  51
Boundary Treaties, 1818-19  53
Mexican Texas in Early 1830s  67
Revolutionary Battles in 1835  89
Military Battles of 1835  91
Military Battles of 1836  94
Battle of San Jacinto  97
Towns of the Republic of Texas 1836-1845  114
Conflicts on the Texas and Mexico Frontier  123
Louisiana Purchase  135
Missouri Compromise  136
Boundary dispute between Mexico and Texas, 1846  138
U.S. Army Forts in Texas 1849  140
Results of the Secession Referendum, February 23, 1861  153
Trans-Mississippi Theater of the American Civil War  167
Arizona and New Mexico Battles  168
Missouri, Arkansas and Louisiana Battles  171
Civil War Military Battles  175
Railroad Track by 1870  220
Railroad Track by 1890  221
Cattle and Railroads  227

## ILLUSTRATIONS

Clovis Point   4
Comanche Indian Village   19
Mission San Jose   37
Antonio López de Santa Anna   73
The Alamo   92
Sam Houston   121
Hardin R. Runnels   150
Ben McCulloch   170
Gen. Gordon Granger, and Capt. Charles Griffin   193
Freedmen's Bureau   194
Governor Elisha M. Pease and Governor James Webb Throckmorton   199
The Union as it was The Lost Cause, worse than slavery   205
River boy poles the heavy logs   222
Richard Coke   229
Richard Bennett Hubbard, Jr.   231
Agricultural and Mechanical College, Texas   232
Austin, Texas   235
Texas farm renter   249
African Americans at Work in the Cotton Field   250
Texas tenant farmer   251
James S. Hogg   254
Cotton field at the Baptist Orphanage   272
Jack Johnson   277
Fort Davis, Texas   284
Victorio, Apache Chief   285
Henry Flipper   287
Dallas Cotton Mill Girls   302
Port Arthur Oil Gusher   304
Galveston Hurricane 1900   305
Young Boy Selling Newspapers   331
Thomas G. McLeod and Pat Neff   339
Senator Morris Sheppard   342
Mrs. Miriam Ferguson   343
Huey Long   359
Franklin D. Roosevelt and John Nance Garner   361
Tom Connally   362
WPA poster   364
NYA Project   366
Dust Storm Approaching Spearman, Texas   368
Dust Storm in Amarillo   369
Governor James V Allred and Texas Rangers   373
General MacArthur, FDR, and Admiral Nimitz   389
Fort Sam Houston, Texas   390
Doris Miller   392

Oveta (Culp) Hobby   395
Civil Service Worker, Mrs. Virginia Davis   397
Lyndon B. Johnson Campaigning for the 1941 U.S. Senate   400
Lady Bird Johnson at Austin Hotel during 1941 Campaign   401
LULAC meeting   418
Dr. Hector P. García   419
Latino civil rights leaders   419
Representative Henry B. Gonzalez   421
Katy Depot   422
San Antonio bus   425
Governor Allan Shivers and Chinese Optimist Club   429
Swearing in of Lyndon B. Johnson as President, Air Force One   448
Signing of Civil Rights Act of 1964   450
Protest Vigil at the Alamo   451
Martin Luther King, Jr. talks with President Lyndon B. Johnson   452
Attorney and Professor José Ángel Gutierrez   454
Governor John B. Connally and President Lyndon B. Johnson   455
Representative Barbara Jordan   473
Line of Cars at Gas Station   475
Ross Perot, May 2, 1980   476
Former First Lady Rosalynn Carter with Waylon Jennings   480
Houston Astrodome   483
Texas Rangers Ballpark, Arlington, TX 484
Vice President H.W. Bush, President Ronald Reagan, and Soviet General Secretary Gorbachev   496
Ross Perot, January 24, 1990   497
Inauguration of Ann Richards   502
President H.W. Bush with Son, George W. Bush, in Rangers' Locker Room   504
NASA space shuttle   509
Senator Kay Bailey Hutchison   529
Texas Rangers Baseball   535

# PREFACE

Since the publication of the Fifth Edition of *Beyond Myths and Legends: A Narrative History of Texas*, my co-authors have received many valuable suggestions from colleagues and friends for improving this volume. As always, we have attempted to incorporate their valuable insights into the Sixth Edition, improving the overall merits of our book. While there are other Texas history textbooks, I contend that *Beyond Myths and Legends* provides the most balanced view of Texas's past, including coverage of the state's early trials and tribulations as well as the challenges facing the people of Texas in the twentieth and twenty-first centuries. Though there are substantial revisions to the Sixth Edition, my co-authors and I have remained devoted to our original mission of providing a comprehensive history of the state, while at the same time, producing a book that is affordable for students.

Though many attributes of this edition remain the same, scholars and students familiar with *Beyond Myths and Legends* will immediately notice changes to the first four chapters. Dr. F. Todd Smith, Professor of History at the University of North Texas, has done a masterful job of writing these chapters, providing students a richer and deeper understanding of Texas's indigenous cultures, the arrival of Europeans, the eras of Spanish and Mexican Texas, and the Texas Revolution. Some will notice that we have dropped Dr. James Smallwood's name from the list of authors in this edition. Dr. Smallwood was the original author of the first four chapters. Since Dr. Smith has rewritten those chapters, I decided that it was no longer appropriate to carry Dr. Smallwood's name forward with this edition. My co-authors and I will be forever grateful to Jim for all his support and his contributions to the earlier editions of *Beyond Myths and Legends*. This work would not have been possible without his early efforts and guidance. As is often the case with new editions, the authors have updated the content throughout the textbook in accordance with new interpretations and evidence. In additions to Dr. Smith's revisions, Dr. Charles Grear and Dr. Jennifer Lawrence have added new materials to their respective chapters.

Despite changes to *Beyond Myths and Legends*, the book has maintained its same basic format. The authors believe that this layout provides an effective and efficient way to deliver information to the students. The "Prelude" and "Afterward" sections provide a brief vignette at the beginning and end of each chapter, capturing the attention and imagination of the reader. Each Prelude provides a unique perspective on historical content covered more fully within the chapter, while the Afterward brings the vignette full circle by placing the brief story in historical context and foreshadowing events to come in the subsequent chapter. We have also retained many of the other features of the textbook as well, such as the inclusion of numerous maps and images, which provide students with a visual context for understanding the events covered in the chapters. In addition, the "Myth & Legend" boxes at the end of each chapter were left in place. The Myth & Legend sections provide students the opportunity to experience how public memory sometimes deviates from the historical record. Furthermore, we have kept the "Suggested for Further Reading" sections, which provides students with an updated list of scholarly works related to key topics covered within the chapters. Finally, and perhaps most importantly, we have retained the review questions at the end of each chapter, a valuable tool that provides students an effective way to monitor their comprehension of the content.

Over the years, it has been an honor and a pleasure to work with my fellow co-authors. I have also enjoyed working closely with Phyllis Botterweck, the owner and director of Abigail Press. The authors of this textbook are a select group of Texas history scholars, whose expertise and devotion to the historical field have enhanced the merits of this work from its inception. Phyllis has been, and continues to be, the driving force behind this work, and we have all benefitted from her expertise as an editor and her unwavering commitment to making this one of the best Texas history textbooks on the market. If not for her guidance, this *Beyond Myths and Legends* would not have survived to a Sixth Edition. Together, we have made every effort possible to provide students with an enjoyable, informative, and accurate account of Texas's remarkable history. In general, the authors wish the students success in all their academic endeavors. More specifically, we hope they enjoy their journey through time as they read our narrative of the Lone Star State.

Kenneth W. Howell
March 26, 2020

# The Native Americans of Texas to 1684

*Prelude: A Migratory Crossroads—History, Archaeology, and Science*

If one thing is certain about the first Americans (as well as the first Texans), nobody knows exactly how or when they arrived. Even after decades of debate, modern scholars are no closer to answering this great mystery. Some scholars claim that between 12,000 and 20,000 years ago, the indigenous peoples crossed a land bridge that formed between Siberia and Alaska when sea levels were significantly lower because water had become glacially locked during the last world-wide ice age. This migration across the land bridge is commonly referred to as the Beringian Land Bridge theory. Scholars who support this explanation claim that ancestors of the indigenous peoples were originally from Asia and used the land bridge to cross into North America and eventually migrate to the interior of the continent.

Other scholars promote what is referred to as the Solutrean Theory, asserting that the ancestors of the indigenous peoples were from present-day Western Europe. This hypothesis posits that the early settlers to the Americas traveled by sea, finding their way to eastern regions of North America. These academics base their theory on the fact that Clovis point arrowheads found in North America are similar to arrowheads found in present-day Spain. Additionally, scholars claim that genetic markers in Native American DNA are more similar to Europeans than to Siberians. The Solutrean Theory is not widely accepted by scientists who study the origins of Native American culture groups in the Americas. Furthermore, there is a lack of firm evidence to support the theory.

Another group of scholars support the Pacific Ocean migration theory. Anthropological evidence suggests that American Indian cultures in South America are similar to those found in Polynesia and Australia. According to this theory, early migrants coming into the Americas arrived by boat, crossing the Pacific Ocean. While this theory lacks hard evidence, scholars cite that the Kennewick Man is the missing link that proves their claim. The Kennewick Man are the skeletal remains of a Paleo-Indian found on the bank of the Columbia River in Kennewick, Washington, in 1996. Using modern technology, facial reconstruction of the Kennewick Man bears a striking resemblance to indigenous peoples of Japan.

## 2  Beyond Myths and Legends

*Recent DNA studies have linked the indigenous population in the Americas with people of ancient Siberia. Using mitochondrial DNA as a reference, the supporters of the Beringian Land Bridge theory have modified their earlier claims. These scholars now believe that the Beringian land mass was home to the ancestors of early migrants for approximately 15,000 years. As the glaciers began to erode in the northwestern part of North America, these early peoples moved further into the interior of the continent. Though archaeological data is still lacking, some scholars claim that DNA evidence supports their theory that the ancestors of Native Americans migrated from Asia. Future archaeological finds will hopefully bring more clarity to this debate.*

Although Europeans first established permanent settlements in Texas approximately four hundred years ago, humans had inhabited the region for at least one hundred centuries prior to their arrival. These first Texans, who came to be known as Native Americans or Indians, adapted to various changes in climate, establishing successful and complex cultures within the different geographical regions they settled. These diverse groups of people, speaking a multitude of languages, adopted various methods that allowed them to survive, raise families, establish religious beliefs, and pass their acquired knowledge to succeeding generations. Some groups raised food crops in fertile river valleys, while others hunted animals and gathered wild fruits and nuts along the Gulf Coast and westward into the interior. The various tribes arranged themselves advantageously; some traveled in small nomadic bands, while others remained sedentary in populous villages. Although warfare was not uncommon, it was rarely destructive. In fact, many of the indigenous peoples of Texas cooperated with one another and established extensive trade networks across vast distances. All embraced various creation myths and engendered beliefs about what occurred following death. By the time that Europeans arrived in North America, the first Texans had been prosperous and thriving for over a millennium.

### Into the Western Hemisphere

Although it is not certain when the first human beings set foot in the Western Hemisphere, nor from where they came or how they arrived here, the general consensus among scholars is that humans migrated to North America sometime between 12,000 and 40,000 years ago. Most scholars also agree that humans became fully evolved members of the species *Homo sapiens* in East Africa from 100,000 to 200,000 years ago. About 60,000 years ago—in the midst of the most recent Ice Age—some humans began to leave Africa in small bands to pursue big game such as woolly mammoths. During this epoch, which began 90,000 years ago and lasted approximately 80,000 years, much of the ocean's water became trapped in glaciers, dropping sea levels to the point that a land bridge opened between eastern Asia and western Alaska, through which most researchers believe humans began passing into the Western Hemisphere beginning about 40,000 years ago. Over the course of the next three hundred centuries, these migrants spread throughout North and South America, until the Ice Age ended about 10,000 years ago, refilling the oceans, and isolating the peoples of the Western and Eastern Hemispheres.

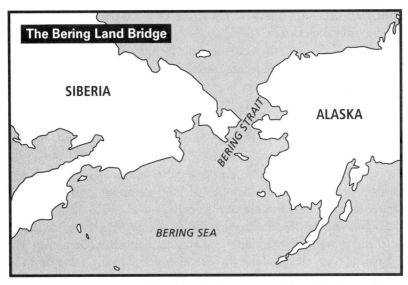

Texas has played its own role in the development of thought about the peopling of the Americas. During the 1950s, the bones of a woman, dubbed "Midland Minnie," by the archaeologists who unearthed them in Midland County of modern-day West Texas. The discovery caused a stir within the scholarly community when her age was initially estimated at 37,000 years, making her remains the oldest ever found in the Western Hemisphere. However, recent studies suggest that the bones may only be 12,000 years old. Thus, the earliest evidence of humans in Texas so far is about 10,000 B.C., though some archaeologists think this date could be pushed back several thousand years. No matter which date is more accurate, the landscape of Midland Minnie's Texas was very different from our own in the twenty-first century. Much of the terrain was cool, wet, and green, with vast forests growing tall under regular rainfall. Grasslands covered the high plains of West Texas, making it an American version of the East African Serengeti, as herds of giant bison, woolly mammoths, small horses, camels, and sloths roamed throughout the region, providing ample game for the arriving hunting and gathering humans. While we will never know what these earliest Texans called themselves, anthropologists and ethnohistorians refer to them as Paleoindians. The prefix *paleo* was derived from the Greek adjective *palaios*, meaning "old."

## Paleolithic Era

These first Texans lived by following large herd animals, particularly mammoths and giant bison—tasks performed predominantly by men. Although women might assist in these hunts, they primarily performed a myriad of other important tasks such as gathering local plants, separating tissue from animal hides, drying meat, and cooking meals while also packing and unpacking equipment, crafting clothes and blankets, and tending to young children. Since they followed the herds, Paleoindians lived in small bands of forty to fifty members, an organizational structure that served as the basic social and political unit of these hunter-gatherers and essentially was one big extended family. Often on the move, Paleoindians lived in caves, underneath rock overhangs, and in small man-made shelters. Their nomadic lifestyle meant traveling light, therefore the acquisition of property was limited. Thus, class structures and the development of specialized skills among the Paleoindians were basically nonexistent.

Though limited to tools and weapons made from rocks, woods, and bones, Paleoindians in Texas made important technological advances that propelled their societies forward. About 11,500 years ago, they began creating a distinct and efficient spear point that archaeologists labeled the Clovis point, because the first one found was embedded in mammoth bones at Blackwater Draw near the town of Clovis, New Mexico. These spear points predominated in Texas for five hundred years, and the people who used them relied heavily on mammoths for food and clothing. Then, between 10,000 and 11,000 years ago, the Paleoindians of the region made yet another technological leap that dramatically improved their hunting skills. They created a more efficient spear point, smaller but wider and more deadly, which became known as the Folsom point, named after its initial discovery near Folsom, New Mexico, among the bones of a giant bison. Although Paleoindians obtained flint for both the Clovis and Folsom points from numerous places, one of the best quarries was situated along the Canadian River in the Texas Panhandle near present-day Amarillo, at a place now known as Alibates National Monument. With the new Folsom technology, the Paleoindians of Texas became expert hunters, often driving herds of giant buffalo over cliffs before butchering them with the improved spear points. They also began to fashion different points for other animals such as deer, rabbits, and rodents.

Around this same time period, between 8,000 and 13,000 years ago, the Ice Age ended as the climate became warmer and dryer. During that 5,000-year span, as the grassland habitat shrank and water became scarcer, all of the giant mammals of the Great Plains became extinct. In addition to the climate change, Paleoindians helped contribute to the extinction of the mammoths, giant bison, horses, camels, and other great mammals due to their expert hunting methods. By about 5,000 years ago, with the disappearance of giant herd mammals, a dwarfed species of bison (the modern buffalo) that possessed a faster reproductive time and other traits better adapted to the new conditions evolved as a new, fully formed plains species. In the meantime, the disappearance of the large mammals and the change in the climate forced the Paleoindians to diversify their lifestyle, making them more dependent on foraging and smaller game. In turn, this brought about a flourishing of Native American culture, and a new era that anthropologists call the Archaic Period.

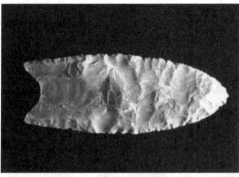

**Clovis Point**

## Archaic Period

During the long Archaic Period, which began about eight thousand years ago, the climate of Texas became hotter and drier, pushing many tribes to move off the plains and relocate in more hospitable regions of modern-day Texas. Unlike their predecessors, the Archaic Indians tended to remain in their own territory, where they learned how to survive and thrive in their own particular region by diversifying their diet according to the landscape. Like Paleoindians, the Archaic peoples lived in small family units, though the band sizes got larger as they attained better knowledge of their surrounding environment and the population grew. Most still lived in caves and rock shelters, but a few Texas Indians built small huts of brush and mulch.

Due to technological innovations and the increased, surer supply of food, there was a population explosion among the Texas Indians during the Archaic period. Men improved their hunting skills by developing the *atlatl,* a spear-thrower device that provided greater leverage and velocity. Toward the end of the Archaic period, around 600 A.D., Texas Indians developed the bow and arrow, increasing their hunting efficiency exponentially. They also continued to improve their spear and arrow points, while fashioning axes, knives, scrapers, weights, and drills from stone. Using these new tools, men expertly hunted the smaller animals that proliferated after the Ice Age. Natives located near the Gulf Coast survived by fishing and hunting water birds. They also enjoyed shellfish and oysters. In East and South Texas, Archaic Indians hunted deer, rabbits, and turkeys, while Plains bands relied upon buffalo. Also, women increasingly became important in Native cultures. They gathered the seeds, roots, nuts, and berries that provided most of the food eaten by Archaic peoples. Using mortar holes cut in rock, women ground various plants and nuts to a pulp and used rock ovens to bake the meal into bread-like cakes. Additionally, women learned to use natural fibers to make ropes, sandals, mats, and most importantly, they produced baskets used to carry their increased supply of goods. In order to obtain goods that could not be found in their own territory, Archaic Indians developed trade networks throughout Texas and beyond. They also domesticated dogs, employing them to aid in the hunt excursions as well as using them to transport bulky items when moving from one location to the next.

With a more diverse food supply, Archaic peoples enjoyed what might be labeled in today's language as leisure time. During such periods, they developed specialized talents and skills. For example, savvy hunters studied the animals, and as their hunting successes grew, so did their status. This allowed the hunter to exert some measure of authority in the ever-enlarging band. He was not yet a "chief," but he could be considered somewhat of a headman or band leader. While some people became expert toolmakers and others learned to fashion baskets, a few Archaic men and women learned the medicinal properties of various plants and became healers. At some point, healers who worked with plants began to think there was a close relationship between their medicinal and spiritual properties, for the Archaic peoples believed that the world was filled with both helpful and malevolent gods and spirits. Healing a person came to consist of using not only plants, but also rituals, chants, and prayers, which also might be employed to try and bring rain, attract animals for the hunt, or even foretell the future. In Texas, these rituals might incorporate mind-altering plants such as mescal beans, peyote, yaupon leaves, and tobacco. If successful in both the medicinal and the spiritual realm, a priest-healer might gain tremendous power and become a "shaman." Accordingly, Archaic shamans located near the confluence of the Pecos and Rio Grande rivers—most particularly at Seminole Canyon in Val Verde County—painted huge pictographs and carved petroglyphs on rocks of various mammals in order to obtain hunting prowess from the animal's spirit. At the same time, they came to believe in human spirits and an afterlife, demonstrated by the scores of Archaic burial sites that have been uncovered by archaeologists. Common to virtually all these burials was the loving care bestowed upon the dead and the items and utensils that were placed inside the graves to be used in the spirit world.

For some Indian tribes living in Texas, the Archaic Period ended approximately two thousand years ago, leading toward a new epoch known as the Woodland Era. On the other hand, most of the people living along the Gulf Coast and westward toward the interior of Texas maintained a lifestyle similar to the Archaic Period well into the seventeenth century.

**The Atakapas, Karankawas, and Coahuiltecans**

Three groups of Texas Indians still possessed an Archaic-style culture when newcomers from the Eastern Hemisphere arrived in Texas at the beginning of the sixteenth century. Europeans had the least amount of direct contact with the group called the Atakapas, thus less is known about them than any other indigenous Texan tribe. The Atakapas were an Atakapan-speaking group—the language is a part of the Tunican stock spoken throughout much of Southern Louisiana—who lived along the Gulf Coast from Galveston Bay eastward towards the Mississippi River. Their territory in Texas also stretched about one hundred miles inland up the Sabine, Neches, and Trinity River valleys. At least four separate groups comprised the Atakapas by the beginning of the eighteenth century. The Atakapas proper, lived along the lower reaches of the Sabine River, while the Akokisas ranged to the west around Galveston Bay. The Bidais and the Deadoses lived north of the Akokisas between the Neches and the Trinity. The word "Atakapa" comes from the Choctaw language and means "eaters of men," implying the practice of cannibalism. This interpretation is misleading as little direct evidence bolsters the claim of Atakaps engaging in cannibalism. In fact, most Texas Indians, as well as many throughout North America, practiced a form of ritual cannibalism, in which bits of one's enemies were eaten to gain positive spiritual power over them.

The Atakapas lived as fishermen, hunters, and gatherers who never took up agriculture. They spent most of their time along the coast spearfishing and collecting oysters and birds' eggs. They used canoes but only in the bays and streams, not out in the open ocean. The Atakapas occasionally moved inland to hunt in the forests and prairies for deer and buffalo, while the women forged for wild potatoes and other vegetables and fruits. However, the Atakapas obtained their best supply of meat, oils, and hides from alligators, using oil extracted from the animal as repellent for mosquitoes and the hides for clothing and shelter coverings. They lived in small bands often on the move, residing in small lodges made of bent limbs covered with deer, buffalo, and alligator skins.

Little is known about the culture of the Atakapas except that they sported tattoos and wore body paint. Men wore breechlouts or went naked, while women wore skirts of moss and grasses or animal hides. Even less is known about their society, politics, and religion. Like most hunter-gatherers, the Atakapas lived in small bands that often hunted separately but might join others at various times. Certainly there was no paramount chief, nor were there social rankings and political hierarchy. Nevertheless, seniors took precedence over juniors, and an older man generally presided over each band. Shamans, using herbs and rituals, handled the religious ceremonies of the Atakapas, and dances were integral ceremonies in which men danced while the women sang. Reflecting the importance of the sea, bays, and rivers to their material culture, the Atakapas believed that they had emerged from the ocean in large oyster shells and had survived a large deluge by moving upland.

Living southwestward along the Gulf Coast of Texas from Galveston Bay to Corpus Christi Bay were the Karankawas, a tribe similar in culture to the Atakapas, but a group that spoke a different language, one that seems to have been a dialect of Coahuiltecan. The Karankawas lived among five main tribal divisions. The Cocos were the most northeastern group, living primarily along the lower reaches of the Trinity and Brazos Rivers. The Carancaguases made their camps southwest of the Cocos, around Matagorda Bay. The Cujanes were located near San Antonio Bay, along the lower San Antonio and Guadalupe Rivers, while the Coapites lived westward near Aransas Bay. The southernmost Karankawa tribe, the Copanes, roamed the area between Copano Bay and the mouth of the Nueces River.

The five tribes shared the same Karankawan language and had similar manners and customs. The Karankawas were unusually tall; men frequently attained statures approaching six feet and were noted for their strong and robust physiques. Like most Texas Indians, the Karankawas painted and tattooed their bodies and also pierced the nipples of each breast and lower lip with small pieces of cane. Similar to the Atakapas, they warded off mosquitoes by smearing their bodies with a mixture of dirt and alligator or shark grease. Karankawa men usually went naked, or wore just a deerskin breechclout; the women wore skirts of Spanish moss or animal skin that reached their knees.

The Karankawa method of subsistence dictated that the members of the five different tribes arrange themselves into groups of only a few hundred people. As with most nomadic tribes, each group was a separate political entity. Leadership was divided between a civil chief, usually a tribal elder, and a war chief, a younger man probably appointed by the civil chief. The bands spent the fall and winter along the shoreline and estuaries of the Gulf Coast, where they fished and hunted deer. In the spring, the Karankawas divided into smaller bands of about fifty people and moved inland to establish camps along the rivers and creeks that emptied into the coastal bays. In these prairie riverine camps, located no more than thirty miles from the shore, the Karankawa women and children spent the summer collecting the fruits of various plants such as mustang grape, prickly pear cactus, and persimmon, while the men hunted buffalo and deer. The Karankawan bands relocated when the local resources had been exhausted, usually after a few weeks at the camp. To facilitate mobility, the Karankawas lived in portable wigwams that consisted of a willow pole frame covered with animal skins and rush mats, structures large enough to accommodate seven or eight people. They crafted light baskets and pottery, lining both with asphaltum, a natural tar substance found along Gulf Coast beaches. Their principal means of transportation was a dugout canoe, made by hollowing out the trunk of a large tree.

The third group of Texas Indians that maintained an Archaic lifestyle have come to be known as the Coahuiltecans, who consisted of perhaps six hundred different bands living in the interior of Texas and northern Mexico, stretching from the Colorado River southward across the Rio Grande. Sharing a common dialect, each independent band consisted of between one hundred and three hundred individuals. Among the many Coahuiltecans, several major divisions stand out. In Texas, three bands of Payayas lived where San Antonio is today. To their southeast, between the Guadalupe and San Antonio Rivers, resided the Aranamas and Tamiques.

The numerous bands of Coahuiltecans seasonally migrated throughout one of the harshest regions in North America, eking out a marginal existence by collecting nuts and fruits, mainly prickly pear cactus and pecans. The men also hunted deer, and tribal members captured small reptiles. Constantly on the move, the Coahuiltecans constructed low, circular huts by placing reed mats and hides over bent saplings. The only container the Coahuiltecans had was either a woven bag or a flexible basket. Spending most of the year under the hot Texas sun, Coahuiltecan men were nude much of the time, and the women wore deerskin skirts. Like the more successful Karankawas, the Coahuiltecans formed small bands of patrilineal (tracing the family line only through the father) kinship groups led by a headman with limited authority.

Due to the lack of agricultural possibilities in their respective regions, the Atakapas, Karankawas, and Coahuiltecans maintained a nomadic, hunting and gathering Archaic way of life well into the 1500s. However, about two thousand years ago, Caddoan-speaking Indians living in the eastern forests of Texas, introduced a new lifestyle based on the cultivation of food crops. This development resulted in yet another population explosion, and the creation of a village culture characterized by a sedentary way of life, the establishment of hierarchy, the creation of earthen burial mounds, the appearance of pottery, and participation in long-distance trade networks. Scholars have designated this period as the Woodland Era.

## Woodland Indians, the Agricultural Revolution, and the Mississippian Cultural Tradition

The Woodland Tradition originated about 2,500 years ago in the wet, forested region of Eastern North America before being transmitted a few centuries later to Northeast Texas, the westernmost extension of the Eastern Woodlands. A Woodland culture, called the Adena culture, emerged in the Ohio River Valley around 500 B.C. and exerted a tremendous influence on all the peoples then living throughout the Eastern Woodlands. The Adena planted squash gardens, lived in small villages of round, thatch-roofed houses, baked pottery, built small burial mounds over their dead, and participated in long-distance trade. About 200 B.C., a religious movement, called the Hopewell Complex, took hold amongst the Adena and spread to virtually all Woodland peoples, including the Caddoans of Northeast Texas. The Hopewell Complex, which lasted until about 500 A.D., was characterized by the honoring of the dead. Burial mounds became larger, but more important was the variety, amount, and beauty of items now interred with the dead, many objects obtained from trading networks throughout North America. Evidence of Hopewell Complex burials has been found in Northeast Texas along the Neches, Sabine, and Red Rivers. By 500 A.D., the Caddoan-speaking Indians of Northeast Texas had also learned to make pottery, first introduced into the region by Louisiana tribes of the Tchefuncte and Marksville varieties of Woodland culture that had learned the skill nearly

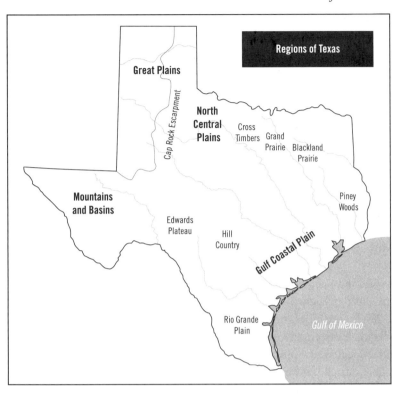

one thousand years earlier. By 500 A.D., the Caddoans clearly had transformed from the Archaic Period to the Woodland.

Initially, the Caddoans planted small gardens of squash to supplement their basic diet of meat while gathering fruits and nuts. However, in the eighth century A.D., two new foods—corn and beans—entered Texas, paving the way for a full-scale agricultural revolution two hundred years later. Corn was first domesticated in Mexico almost six thousand years ago, and beans followed a couple millennia later. Another two thousand years transpired before Native Americans dwelling in New Mexico began planting the two crops and finally, around 700 A.D., corn and beans made their way across the plains to Northeast Texas. By 900 A.D., corn, beans, and squash—the "American triad"—had become the lifeblood of the Caddoans of Northeast Texas, as well as for most of the Indians of Eastern North America. Over time, the natives perfected the cultivation of all three crops together. The men would initially clear the forest through the use of fire before the women planted crops amid the blackened, fertilized soil. Corn would be planted first. Once the corn sprouted, bean and squash seeds were added. As the corn grew tall, the beans used the cornstalk as a pole, while the squash covered the ground, keeping down weeds and erosion. It was a fortuitous match, for the beans, rich in nitrogen, replaced the nutrients in the soil that had been depleted by the corn.

As corn, beans, and squash spread throughout the Eastern Woodlands, economics, religion, trade, and politics all contributed to bring about the rise of what scholars call the Mississippian cultural tradition. After 700 A.D., with surer food supplies, large populations coalesced along the major river systems, particularly the Mississippi and its tributaries. Within 500 years, large cities holding thousands of people, complete with houses, markets, plazas, earthen mounds, workshops, temples, and cemeteries had arisen first at Cahokia in Illinois, and then throughout the Southeast, from modern-day Spiro, Oklahoma to Moundville, Alabama, and Etowah, Georgia. At the same time, medium-size settlements of several hundred people also grew up along smaller rivers and streams. These villages might also have ceremonial mounds, plazas, and temples. A theocratic form of government arose among the agricultural societies of the Southeast in which priest-chiefs gained prestige, status, and the power to control the common people. Society became ranked into hierarchical divisions, physically reinforced by the construction of huge flat-topped earthen mounds, upon which the new noble class of priest-chiefs resided. The Mississippian cultural tradition reached its peak of sophistication during the thirteenth and fourteenth centuries as the veneration of the agricultural priest-chiefs reached its height. However, by about 1350, probably due to climate change, the cities began to decline and mound building came to an end.

**The Caddos and the Wichitas**

Caddoan-speaking people—who eventually established tribes that came to be known as the Caddos and the Wichitas—were full-fledged participants in the Mississippian cultural tradition, developing cities, towns, and villages throughout the western edge of the Eastern Woodlands between the Trinity and Arkansas Rivers. Although the largest mound complex was located at Spiro on the Arkansas River near today's Oklahoma-Arkansas border, others dotted the landscape, including one located in Northeast Texas near Nacogdoches, at Caddo Mounds State Historic Site. Their geographical locale allowed the Caddoans to be the most productive farmers in the region, and the surplus food raised in their fields led to the development of a sophisticated political and religious system dominated by a hereditary elite.

Led by a chief known as the *caddí*, a well-defined hierarchy held complete political power in the settlement. The *caddí* presided over a well-defined chain of command that carried out his orders with, according to a Spanish missionary, "peace and harmony and absolute lack of quarrels." Each *caddí* had four to eight principal aides called *canahas*, who in turn had a number of *chayas* to assist them. Policy meetings were held in a large public assembly house located near the dwelling of the *caddí*. *Tammas*, or town criers, performed the function of policing the tribe, keeping people in order and at work by whipping all idlers with a stick. These clearly defined lines of authority allowed the Caddoans to function smoothly. The offices of government were held by a hereditary, aristocratic elite that was accorded certain forms of deference and respect. There were even specially raised seats in each house that could be occupied only by this elite class, who were also served first at public functions and had menial services performed for them. The only way common tribal members could gain prestige was by distinguishing themselves in battle and being awarded the status of *amayxoya*.

A religious leader, called the *xinesí*, presided over several communities that supported him materially and treated him with great reverence. The *xinesí* provided blessings for the planting of crops and construction of houses and presided over various feasts and ceremonies. The office was hereditary, carrying tremendous veneration and respect. The tribal members catered to all the *xinesí's* wants and needs. The commands that he issued were, in the words of a Spanish priest, "more strictly obeyed by these Indians than the ten commandments are observed by Christians."

As with all aspects of their society, the religion of the Caddoans was well-defined. The supreme deity was called *Ahahayo*, which means "Father above." The Caddoans believed that *Ahahayo* had created everything and that he rewarded good and punished evil. Communication between *Ahahayo* and the tribe was carried out through the *xinesi*, who was in charge of keeping a perpetual fire in a temple near his own house in which two divine children called *coninisi* were said to reside. Except on special occasions, only the *xinesi* was allowed to enter their house, and it was through the *coninisi* that he learned the wishes of *Ahahayo*.

A more numerous but lesser class of priests or shamans—called *connas*—existed below the *xinesi*. They were male and female healers who attempted to cure the sick or wounded by using a variety of methods, including spells and incantations, for the Caddoans believed that sickness was caused by the witchcraft of enemy tribes. The *connas* also developed great knowledge of the medicinal herbs that abounded in the forest, information that allowed them to have great success in helping the ill. The *connas* performed many other religious duties as well, the most important of which was presiding over burials. The Caddoans believed that a person's soul went up to the sky and entered the House of Death, presided over by *Ahahayo*. Here, all were required to wait until all the Caddo souls had been gathered together, at which time the whole tribe would enter another world to live anew. All the Caddoan people were entitled to enter the House of Death; only enemies of the tribe were sent to the house of *texino*, the devil to be punished.

Agriculture determined the arrangement of the Caddoan living quarters. They lived in scattered dwellings near their fields, all of which were grouped around a central village where the elites lived. Temple mounds serving as ceremonial centers, dominated the villages. Several families—about twenty people—occupied each Caddo house, well-constructed dwellings of grass and reeds resembling a haystack. Although both men and women planted corn, beans, and squash in the spring, during the summer men hunted for deer, bear, and small game in the surrounding forest, and the women tended the fields and collected wild fruits and nuts. Due to the important role that women played in food production, the Caddoans—like most agricultural peoples in early Texas—were matrilineal, meaning that they traced their lineage only through the mother's family, who were responsible for the raising of the children. After harvesting the crops in the fall, the men went on extensive winter hunts, sometimes heading west to stalk buffalo. Expert craftsmen fashioned bows made of the pliable Osage orange wood and also made some of the finest pottery in North America. The Caddoans traded these items, in addition to salt and food products, north to the great mound-building chiefdom and population center at Cahokia and west to the Pueblo villages in New Mexico. Living at the crossroads of four major trails where the Eastern Woodlands met the Great Plains, the Caddoans relied heavily on trade.

The Caddoans lived in this manner for nearly four hundred years before the drought of the fourteenth century caused decline, abandonment of Spiro, and dispersal throughout the region. One group, the Caddos, coalesced in the area where Texas, Oklahoma, Arkansas, and Louisiana come together, and formed three loose confederacies, still dominated by the political-religious, hereditary elite. The Kadohadacho confederacy was established along the bend of the Red River, just upstream from modern-day Texarkana. The least populous of the three Caddoan confederacies, the Natchitoches, was located farther down the Red River in Louisiana. To the west, located along the upper reaches

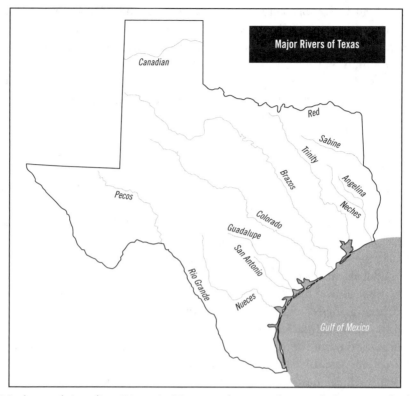

of the Neches and Angelina Rivers in Texas, and centered around the Nacogdoches village, were the Hasinais, the largest and most prestigious of the Caddo confederacies. The Hasinais were also known as the "Tejas," a term taken from the Caddoan word *techas*, meaning "friend." Thus, many Indians of the region alluded to the great Kingdom of the Tejas when speaking about the Hasinais.

Whereas the Caddos were able to maintain their Mississippian lifestyle and well-defined hierarchy by establishing sedentary villages in the fourteenth and fifteenth centuries, their linguistic kinsmen, the Wichitas, followed a different path. As the Mississippian tradition broke down in the 1300s, the Wichitas moved westward up the Arkansas and Red Rivers onto the Great Plains, where they relied much more on buffalo hunting than the Caddos. To maximize their productive capabilities, the Wichitas adopted a semi-sedentary lifestyle. In the spring and summer, they lived in fixed, extended villages along the river valleys, where they planted crops. The Wichitas spaced their grass lodges—which were very similar to the Caddo dwellings—at about fifty foot intervals, and between them built open-sided edifices to dry and store meat and food. In the fall, after the crops had been harvested, the entire group headed west for the annual winter hunt. During this period, when men hunted among the buffalo herds, Wichita families lived in portable tipis made of skins. On the hunt, women skinned the buffalo and smoked the meat; on returning to their village in the spring, they tanned the hides and fashioned them into blankets and robes. Women also made earthenware pots and other cooking utensils, as well as deerskin and wolfskin pouches for storage.

To facilitate their farming and hunting lifestyle, the Wichitas arranged themselves in numerous independent villages that often stretched for miles. Each village was headed by a principal chief and a subordinate, both chosen by the men on the basis of physical prowess and leadership abilities. The chief's power was not absolute, however, and the warriors could remove him at any time. A council of the entire tribe, including women, debated important matters. Solutions to problems were reached by consensus, and dissenters were free to join other villages rather than adhere to decisions they opposed. The egalitarian nature of the Wichita political system stood in marked contrast to the hierarchy maintained by the Caddos. Wichita religion also differed from the Caddos in that it did not revolve around an authority figure such as the *xinesí*. Instead, various shamanistic societies, open to anyone who cared to join, paid homage to the important deities by performing certain ceremonies and dances.

Although there were many distinct Wichita villages, the tribe consisted of three major groups at the beginning of the sixteenth century. The Taovayas resided along the Great Bend of the Arkansas River in Kansas, while the Tawakonis lived near the confluence of the Canadian and Arkansas Rivers in Oklahoma. The third Wichita group, the Kichais, established villages along the Red River upstream from their linguistic relatives, the Kadohadachos. In the eighteenth century, all three of the Wichita groups would migrate southward toward Central Texas, one of the most notable tribe being a Tawakoni group called the Wacos, who established their village on the Brazos River near the site of the city that now bears their name.

## Pueblo Cultural Tradition, the Jumanos, and the Apaches

While the Mississippian cultural tradition was reaching prominence on the eastern side of the Southern Plains, so too were sophisticated corn-based cultures rising on the western side that would play an important role in Texas. Corn appeared in the Southwest as early as 1000 B.C., eventually leading to the flourishing of a culture known as Anasazi around 900 A.D., at the same time that the Mississippian tradition was hitting its stride on the eastern side of the plains. At places such as Chaco Canyon and Mesa Verde in northwestern New Mexico and southwestern Colorado, the Anasazis used their corn-based wealth to build towns of huge multi-leveled apartment buildings. The Anasazis became renowned for their bread made of corn, their beautiful pottery, turquoise jewelry, and clothing made of cotton and feathers. In the fourteenth century, just as the Mississippian tradition was breaking down, drought caused the Anasazis to abandon their towns and move eastward across the Continental Divide into the Rio Grande Valley of northern New Mexico. There, the various independent groups reestablished the Anasazi lifestyle—now known as the Puebloan cultural tradition—by building smaller towns complete with many-roomed adobe houses surrounded by irrigated fields of corn.

Whereas the heartland of Puebloan culture lay in the area between Albuquerque and Taos in northern New Mexico, some native groups migrated down the Rio Grande and formed clusters of hamlets and villages near present-day El Paso. Others continued even farther down the river, where they constructed several large Puebloan-style towns at La Junta, the juncture of the Rio Grande and the Conchos River, in the vicinity of Big Bend. Known by the Spaniards as the Jumanos, little is known about who they were or what language they spoke. Some Jumano groups lived along the Rio Grande in houses made of adobe or grass and farmed corn, beans, and squash, while others roamed between the Rio Grande and the Pecos hunting buffalo and living in tipis. One of the most common things mentioned about the Jumanos is that they painted or tattooed stripes on their faces.

The most important thing about the Jumanos is that they were great travelers who, between the fifteenth and seventeenth centuries, were able to tie the Mississippian Caddoans and the New Mexican Puebloans together through trade and exchange. The Jumanos annually brought buffalo meat and hides to the Pueblo towns of the upper Rio Grande, where they acquired, among other items, cotton blankets and turquoise nuggets. They next would travel eastward across the Southern Plains to exchange these items with the Caddoans of East Texas, principally the Hasinais, in return for Osage orange bows and the exquisite Caddo pottery.

Little is known about the Jumanos because they were eventually supplanted on the Southern Plains by the Apaches—Athabaskan-speakers who had migrated southward to present-day New Mexico and West Texas during the thirteenth and fourteenth centuries. The buffalo-hunting Apaches, like their fellow Athabaskans, the Navajos, were attracted to New Mexico by the wealth of the farming Puebloans, with whom they traded and also raided. The Apaches were divided into small, nomadic bands of a few hundred people, with each group led by a chief who gained his position through displays of bravery and wisdom. The role of chief, however, was mostly advisory, as the Apaches had no mechanism for enforcing authority beyond the use of peer pressure. They lived in portable buffalo-skin tipis and used buffalo hides for blankets and clothing. The Apaches quickly entered into trading agreements with the various Pueblo villages of New Mexico, providing them with buffalo products such as dried meat and skins in return for vegetables, blankets, pottery, and turquoise. The Apaches also stole as much as they could from the Pueblos, the main prize being women and children, in order to maintain and expand their population levels. Many Native American men practiced warfare not only to demonstrate their bravery, but also to obtain women and children who they would ultimately adopt as full members of the tribe. Often, the Puebloans would retaliate against the Apaches in the same manner for the same purpose, thus, both groups were bonded to some extent through ties of kinship.

**Spanish Explorers, Diseases, and Horses**

The lifestyles of Native Americans began to change dramatically in the sixteenth century with the arrival of Europeans to North America. In 1492 the Italian explorer, Christopher Columbus, sailed across the Atlantic Ocean from Spain to the Caribbean, ushering in the Spanish settlement of the region over the following two decades. By 1520, the Spaniards had developed a firm understanding of the geography of the Caribbean and the Gulf of Mexico, as well as their relation to the Atlantic Ocean. Soon thereafter, news traveled throughout the Spanish world that Hernán Cortés, one of the original settlers of Cuba, had successfully invaded the Aztec empire of mainland Mexico and had taken possession of its capital, Tenochtitlán, bringing enormous riches to himself and to a few of his followers. The conquest of Mexico set off dozens of Spanish expeditions throughout the Western Hemisphere in search of indigenous empires comparable to that of the Aztecs.

Three of these expeditions passed through what would become the province of Texas. The first, led by Pánfilo de Narváez, sailed from Spain in June 1527 and landed on the coast of Florida near Tampa Bay in April 1528, after first stopping at Spanish Caribbean posts in Hispaniola and Cuba. Leaving his ships and traversing by land up the west coast of Florida, hostile Indians forced Narváez and his party to construct five rafts on which

they hoped to float safely toward Mexico. By November 1528, all five of the vessels had miraculously landed on the Texas Gulf Coast between Corpus Christi Bay and Galveston Bay. Soon thereafter, most of the four hundred expedition members were either killed or enslaved by the coastal Karankawa Indians. In 1534, the royal treasurer of the expedition, Alvar Núñez Cabeza de Vaca, and three other survivors escaped together and, after traveling across south Texas and northern Mexico, reached fellow Spaniards north of Mexico City.

Learning of the Narváez expedition's fate following Cabeza de Vaca's arrival in Mexico City, Hernando de Soto, a veteran of the Spanish conquest of Nicaragua and Peru, sought and received permission to search for Indian kingdoms in Florida, what the Spaniards then defined as the land between Delaware Bay and the Pánuco River in Mexico. De Soto's fleet of ten ships left Spain in April 1538 and, after stopping first in Cuba to gather more supplies, landed in Tampa Bay in May 1539. Three years later, after wreaking havoc among the Indian chiefdoms of the North American Southeast, De Soto died near present-day Memphis on the Mississippi River in May 1542. De Soto's field marshal, Luís de Moscoso y Alvarado, took command of the three hundred or so surviving Spaniards, who agreed to give up their search for riches and attempt to reach Mexico by traveling overland. Heading west from the Mississippi, the Spaniards crossed the Red River and entered Texas near present-day Texarkana. Continuing on through the densely populated territory of the Caddo Indians, who unwillingly supplied the Spaniards with food, Moscoso reached the Trinity River in October. After the Caddos informed Moscoso that the Indian groups to the west had no settled towns and did not practice agriculture, the Spaniards retreated to the Mississippi River, where they built boats and floated out to sea, reaching the safety of Mexico the following year.

Cabeza de Vaca's return to Mexico also inspired the third Spanish expedition that passed through Texas in the first half of the sixteenth century. In March 1540, Francisco Vázquez de Coronado left Mexico with a few hundred Spaniards and Indian allies and

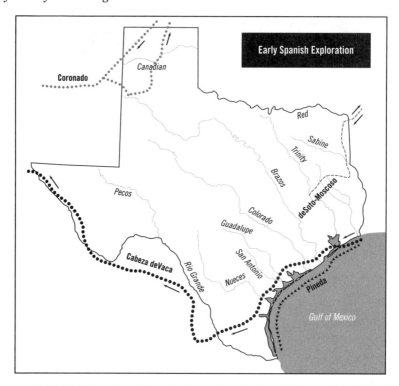

headed toward the Rio Grande, where he hoped to find wealthier Indian kingdoms than those in Mexico. Coronado, however, was disappointed in the New Mexico he encountered later that year, for the adobe Pueblo Indian villages located along the Rio Grande near Taos contained little of value to the Spaniards. Learning of a great Indian kingdom called Quivira to the east, in 1541, Coronado led his force across eastern New Mexico into the Texas panhandle, where they encountered the nomadic Apache Indians as well as sighting their first buffalo. Continuing northeastward, Coronado reached the eastern edge of Quivira, located along the Arkansas River in present-day Kansas, in July 1541. Instead of golden cities, Coronado found only the grass huts and cornfields of the Wichita Indians and thus disheartened, headed back to New Mexico and onward to Old Mexico soon thereafter.

Although it would be another century and a half before the Spaniards permanently settled in Texas, these initial forays, along with the Spanish colonization of New Mexico in the early seventeenth century, would introduce two things to the Native Americans that would change their lives dramatically: disease and horses. A series of diseases began to affect the Native Americans almost immediately following the Spanish arrival on the mainland. Because of their isolation from the Eastern Hemisphere, the natives lacked immunity to the sicknesses that existed across the Atlantic Ocean. European diseases with the ability to diffuse in advance of direct transmission, such as typhus, plague, and smallpox, caused great population loss and cultural disruption among the Texas tribes. Epidemics of smallpox, measles, and cholera decreased population fertility, and sporadic infections killed those born between outbreaks. Some tribes lost as much as 95 percent of their population. Following the introduction of European diseases into the region in the early sixteenth century, at least eight recorded epidemic "events" occurred in Texas over the course of the next two hundred years.

Epidemics caused some tribes to disappear, while others were forced to change their lifestyle in response to population losses. Because of the great demographic and economic changes brought on by the European presence in North America, remaining tribal groups often altered themselves culturally to forge unity with other bands in a process known as ethnogenesis. Threatened tribes created new communities tied together by intermarriage, adaptation of language, and the emergence of a new culture, effectively reinventing themselves in order to adapt to the new reality. Over time almost all of the Native American groups in the region went through the process of ethnogenesis in order to adjust to a growing European population presence.

The Texas Indians were forced to adapt not only to disease, but also to horses. The Spaniards established the colony of New Mexico in 1598, centered among the Puebloan villages and brought many equines with them. By the end of the seventeenth century, the local Indians had acquired many of the animals either by seizing wild mustangs or by poaching them from the newcomers. Flourishing in the open, arid country, the horse became a Southern Plains competitor with the buffalo for grass and added to the hunting abilities of the natives, increasing their range and ease of travel. Horses quickly became a commodity in the villages of most tribes, an item that brought wealth and power to the owners. By the time that the Europeans returned to Texas in the early eighteenth century, most of the Texas Indians—including some newcomers—had to some extent incorporated the horse into daily life. In fact, a few tribes completely changed their mode of living because of the possibilities afforded by the Old World animal.

**Lipan Apaches, Comanches, and Tonkawas**

The Apaches were the first Texas people to successfully adapt to the horse. Through their contact with the Puebloans, the Apaches had become familiar with Spanish horses by the middle of the seventeenth century. Mimicking the Puebloans and the Spaniards, the Apaches mounted horses and found that they greatly added to their hunting success. Horses also increased the Apaches' range and raiding efficiency, and the tribe obtained even more Spanish animals through forays along the entire northern frontier of New Spain. Apache warriors also acquired horses by trading with the Spaniards of New Mexico for Indian slaves. The decimation of the Puebloans, due to disease, made the Spaniards desperate for manpower, and they sought other captives to use as slaves, even though Indian bondage was officially illegal in the Spanish empire. One Apache group, the Lipans, took advantage of this situation and moved eastward toward Central Texas, where they raided other tribes, particularly the Jumanos. The Lipans acquired Indian captives and sold them for Spanish horses and firearms in the underground market that had been established in New Mexico by Spanish smugglers. The raiding allowed Lipan warriors to add to their possessions, while affording them honor and status, recognition that depended upon success in battle.

The Lipan Apaches, whose near monopoly of the possession of horses allowed them to dominate the Southern Plains during the latter decades of the seventeenth century, were actually an amalgamation of peoples from different tribes. The success of the Lipan Apaches after their acquisition of the horse drew shattered groups toward them and their way of life. Various Apache groups combined with Coahuiltecan bands from the lower Rio Grande, and with the Jumanos—who had been decimated by disease earlier in the century—to form the Lipans. The group's new power, however, forced other Native Americans to acquire horses and challenge Apache control. By 1680, on the eve of Spanish settlement of Texas, the tribes who had been victimized by Lipan Apache slave raids, like the Wichitas and Caddos, had incorporated the horse into their cultures through trade, theft, or seizure of mustangs. Along the Gulf Coast and southward toward the Rio Grande, the Karankawas, Atakapas, and Coahuiltecans adopted horses to a much lesser extent than the other tribes.

The Apaches' success also attracted tribes from outside the area, most importantly the Shoshonean Comanches, whose adoption of the horse eventually made them the dominant Native American group of the region. The Comanches emerged from the Rocky Mountains and migrated to the Southern Plains in the late seventeenth century. In this new region, they learned the art of horsemanship, and by the early 1700s they had successfully wrested control of the Southern Plains from the Lipans, who were driven deeper into Central Texas, establishing themselves between the Pecos River and the Hill Country. The Comanches quickly took possession of the area where New Mexico, Texas, Colorado, Oklahoma, and Kansas come together, a region particularly well-suited to obtaining and raising horses. Tribal members used their equines to hunt buffalo, whose products provided for most of their needs. They ate buffalo meat, used easily portable buffalo-skin tipis for shelter, and utilized buffalo skins for clothes and blankets. Due to the size of their horse herds, the Comanches had to break camp and move fairly often in order to obtain forage for their animals. Also needing someone to tend to their ever-expanding horse herds, the Comanches often made raids upon other tribes—and eventually, Europeans—in order to obtain women and children. Young boys were employed to take care of the horses, while women were used to have and raise children, in addition to doing all the work necessary for the maintenance of the camp, as well as dressing buffalo robes to be used as trade items. Eventually, all the kidnapped women and children would be adopted into the tribe as full-fledged Comanches.

Clearly, the Comanche lifestyle revolved around the acquisition of the horse and pursuit of the buffalo. Their nomadism caused the Comanches to adopt a fluid structure, allowing band size and leadership to change with necessity. The knowledge that all of the Comanche individuals were one of the *nuhmuhnuh*, or "people," allowed them to forge tight bonds, while maintaining an extremely flexible system. The Comanches divided into small bands, each led by a peace chief chosen on the basis of leadership abilities. His authority was limited to internal matters and he could only give advice. A council of men sought to reach a consensus on important matters. If anyone disagreed with a decision, they were free to join another group.

While peace chiefs and their councils provided direction for the internal workings of the group, war chiefs led the warriors in actions that defined what it meant to be a Comanche male: hunting, fighting, and raiding. Comanche success depended on the ability to obtain horses—often through theft—in order to hunt buffalo. The best way for a Comanche man to obtain wealth, honor, and status was through warfare and the plundering of horses, as well as the capturing of women and children from their enemies. Horses were a medium of exchange to the Comanche—an individual could obtain women, weapons, and other necessities of life through ownership of horses. The most successful warriors obtained status through their actions and attracted other followers into battle, leading to the acquisition of more horses and increased opportunities for a

**Photograph shows reproduction of George Catlin's drawing of a Comanche Indian village near the Red River, 1830s. Photo credit: UTSA's Institute of Texan Cultures**

prestigious standing within one's band. Comanche men gained glory by dying in battle, but death at the hands of the enemy also demanded the vengeance of the living, which only escalated the constant raiding and plundering. Due to the heightened importance of warfare, Comanche men formed military societies that reinforced the martial ethos of the tribe. Ultimately, this aggressive behavior allowed the Comanches to become the predominant tribe in Texas and throughout the Southern Plains.

As the Comanches established their empire during the eighteenth century, they divided into five major divisions stretching all the way from Central Texas, north to the Arkansas River, and westward to the Sangre de Cristo Mountains of New Mexico. The Penatekas became the largest and southernmost Comanche group, establishing themselves well into Texas, roaming west of the Cross Timbers between the Guadalupe and Trinity Rivers. To their north, along the Red River ranged the Noconis. The Kotsotekas lived further north, in modern-day Oklahoma. The Kwahadis lived to the west in the Texas Panhandle region and the Llano Estacado of New Mexico, while the Yamparikas roamed the region between the Canadian and Arkansas Rivers in westernmost Oklahoma and Kansas. All these divisions, particularly the Penatekas, would have an enormous impact upon Texas.

Another new tribe to Texas, the Tonkawas, also came to orient their culture, like the Lipan Apaches and the Comanches, toward equestrian nomadism. By the late seventeenth century, the Tonkawan cultural group began the process of ethnogenesis when a number of native groups who roamed the Southern Plains between the Rio Grande and the Arkansas River came together as a result of the changes wrought by the European intrusion. Ultimately, the tribe consisted of the Tonkawan-speaking Tancagues and May-eyes, as well as the intermingled Coahuiltecan Ervipiames and Caddoan Yojuanes. Pressured by the Lipan Apaches from the west, the Tonkawas settled in Central Texas in the Post-Oak Savannah region, bordered by the Hill Country and the Piney Woods, between the Colorado and Trinity Rivers.

Like other nomadic tribes, the Tonkawas lived in politically autonomous bands, headed by separate civil and war chiefs. Reflecting the diverse origins of the group, Tonkawan society was divided into thirteen matrilineal clans. Individual membership in the clans cut across band divisions and bound the tribe together. Unlike the Apaches and Comanches, the Tonkawas hunted deer more than buffalo, adding small mammals, birds, reptiles, fish, and shellfish to their diets. In addition to game, the Tonkawas also ate a large assortment of plant foods, including herbs, roots, fruits, and seeds. Rather than living in buffalo-skin tipis, the Tonkawas constructed small, conical huts covered with brush or hides. Animal skins provided the scant clothing worn by Tonkawa men and women. Males wore earrings, necklaces, and other ornaments of shell, bone, and feathers, and both males and females tattooed their bodies.

By the late seventeenth century, the Spanish and the French would begin to make permanent settlements, ultimately creating the colonies of Texas and Louisiana, causing the various Indian groups to dramatically alter their lifestyles yet again.

**Spaniards, Franciscans, and the Kingdom of the Tejas**

Following the Spanish incursions into Texas in the first half of the sixteenth century, the character of the Spanish effort in the Western Hemisphere changed dramatically. Having subjugated most of the wealthy Indian kingdoms in America through military force, in 1573 the Spanish Crown issued the Royal Orders for New Discoveries, giving missionaries the central role in the exploration and pacification of new lands. Preaching the holy Gospel to heathens theoretically became the principal purpose for new discoveries and settlement in America. Pacification rather than conquest would be the new order of the day, and missionaries, their expenses paid by the Crown, were to enter new lands before all others. The Royal Orders particularly benefited the Order of St. Francis, whose members had worked to seek Christian converts since the thirteenth century. The first Franciscans had come to America in 1493 and had been successful in converting the Indians of central Mexico following the conquest. By the late sixteenth century, however, the Crown cut costs by replacing the Franciscans with secular clergy—nonmonastic priests—and transformed the missions into self-supporting diocesan parishes. Dislodged from the settled region of central Mexico, the Franciscans were given the opportunity to move into fringe areas in North America that were marginal to the economic life of the Spanish empire and minister to the Indians without much competition from civilians, soldiers, or secular priests. As a result, over the course of the following century the Franciscans successfully transformed Florida and New Mexico into colonies whose main purpose was the evangelization of the indigenous tribes, while always being on the lookout for new tribes to evangelize.

In 1650 Spanish officials in New Mexico learned of a great Indian kingdom to the east called the "Tejas…that was very large and contained many people." They were also told that the "Tejas have native princes or chiefs to govern them. They plant and gather their crops of corn; their lands are fertile." In 1675 Spanish Franciscan missionaries on the Rio Grande heard of a nation to the northeast, "a populous…people, and so extensive that those who give detailed reports of them do not know where it ends…The people of that nation, which they call Tejas…live under an organized government, congregated in their towns [and] governed by a *cacique* who is named the Great Lord, as they call the one who rules them all, who they say resides in the interior. They have houses made of wood, cultivate the soil, plant maize and other crops, wear clothes, and punish misdemeanors, especially theft."

Reports of a tribe as culturally advanced and as well organized as the Hasinais excited the Franciscan missionaries immensely. They reasoned that the tribe, because it was sedentary and agriculturally inclined, could be as easily converted to Catholicism as the Pueblos of New Mexico. The bishop of Guadalajara recommended that the Franciscans establish four missions among the Coahuiltecans near the Rio Grande, thus making it easier for the Spaniards to reach their ultimate goal, the rich and powerful Tejas. As the Franciscans were seeking out the Hasinais, the tribe was also attempting to establish direct contact with the Spaniards. In 1683 the Hasinais sent two messengers to the Jumanos asking them to get in touch with the Franciscans to ask that missionaries be sent to their country. As a result, a Jumano chief contacted the Franciscans and told them of the request from the "great kingdom of the Tejas." In 1684, just as Spanish officials in New Spain began to discuss plans to send soldiers and missionaries to the province of Tejas to investigate the promising possibilities of an alliance with the Hasinais, settlers from France landed in Matagorda Bay, further spurring the Spaniards' desire to reach this relatively unexplored region.

### *Afterward: A More Important Question*

*While scholars may not agree when or how the first Americans arrived in North America, they are certain what happened to their descendants. They became the victims of European conquest. Beginning with the arrival of the first Europeans, Native Americans suffered centuries of atrocities and devastating epidemics that forever changed their cultures. For Native Americans in Texas, these changes began with the arrival of the Spaniards and continued until the last tribes were subdued along the Red River in the late nineteenth century.*

# Myth & Legend

### The First Texans: The Debate Continues

*In a gravel quarry near the small towns of Malakoff and Trinidad in Henderson County, a mystery was born in Texas archaeology during the 1930s. At this location in 1929, quarry workers unearthed a large boulder that seemingly had been hand-carved into the shape of a man's head. The artifact weighed approximately 100 pounds. Later, in 1935 and 1939, workers found two additional heads, one weighing approximately 60 pounds, the other about 135 pounds. The finds puzzled scholars because the facial characteristics of the boulders were most unlike those of any Native Americans who had lived in the region. Furthermore, the faces did not resemble the earliest Europeans who explored eastern Texas. What people do those heads represent? Although some experts have convincingly debunked the legend of the "Malakoff Man," calling them an elaborate hoax, many laypeople and some scholars still believe in the authenticity of the heads.*

*Even if the Malakoff heads are a hoax and are the basis of an enduring myth, the "artifacts" force scholars to think about the earliest inhabitants of North America and Texas. Two questions are particularly important: Where did these peoples come from? How did they travel to the Americas? To answer these questions, Thor Heyerdahl, a Norwegian ethnographer, combined scholarly knowledge with adventurism when he built the watercraft* **Con-Tiki** *according to the technology available to the ancient Polynesians. Setting sail from the coast of Peru with a small crew, Heyerdahl piloted the small boat on a 101-day, 4,300-mile trip across the Pacific Ocean before hitting a reef near Raroia in the Tuamotu Islands, a chain of atolls in French Polynesia, on August 7, 1947. The expedition proved that Polynesians had the boat-building capacity to have reached the Americas. Many years later, in 1969-1970, Heyerdahl supervised the construction of the* **Ra**, *a reed boat similar to ones that ancient Egyptians built. He intended to prove that they could also have reached the Americas. After clearing the Mediterranean Sea and spending several weeks sailing across the Atlantic Ocean, the tail of the* **Ra** *began dragging in the water, and the expedition had to be abandoned. Heyerdahl studied his failure and found the cause of it. Egyptians used ropes made of hemp to lift the tail by tying it to another part of the boat. Not understanding the significance of the rope, Heyerdahl did not include it, a mistake he remedied when he supervised the building of the* **Ra II**. *A success, the* **Ra II** *made landfall on the Caribbean island of Barbados, a voyage proving that Egyptians and other ancient peoples from North Africa could have reached the Americas.*

*The idea that Egyptians might have come to the Americas is highlighted by the presence of pyramids in the Americas. For example, both the Aztecs and the Mayas, among other New World Indians, built step-pyramids similar to the ones tourists of today's Egypt can see if they journey west of the Nile River. Interestingly, the Caddos of East Texas built stair-stepped, rectangular, flat-topped hills on a plain known as Mound Prairie in Cherokee County and in other areas nearby. Well to the north, other Indians built the Spiro Mounds in today's eastern Oklahoma. Such construction causes one's imagination to wonder if different peoples from such diverse places as Egypt and Texas had common origins. Did the East Texas mound-builders have knowledge of their heritage and ancient relations? Why else build structures so similar? At this time, no evidence exists that links the two cultures together, but the pyramids seem to suggest a possible connection between the Egyptians and the early inhabitants of the Americas.*

*In 1989, author Barry Fell published a book that he entitled* **America B.C.: Ancient Settlers in the New World.** *He made the case that various peoples in the past journeyed to North America, including the ancient Celts of Europe. It is also possible that 11th century Vikings may have reached the Texas-Oklahoma region. Well known were the voyages of Eric the Red and Leif Erickson that reached America's northeast Atlantic shores. Less well known is that searchers discovered what could be Viking runes (characters of an ancient alphabet) written on a stone slab found in Le Flore County, Oklahoma, near Heavener. When translated, the runes said, simply, "Sun Dail Vally." If the runes are legitimate, just as Vikings used the Arkansas River to reach Oklahoma, one could conclude that they may have also used it and the Red River to explore areas of East-Northeast Texas.*

*Some scholars believe that the Americas and possibly Texas could have been reached by Africans, Phoenicians, and perhaps even the Chinese. Such trips, if they happened, would predate Columbus's arrival to the Americas by several centuries. Regardless, at this time, scholars only have various plausible theories to suggest how the first people arrived to North America and Texas. Perhaps, future discoveries will reveal how and why these people came to the Western Hemisphere. Until then, we can only speculate and perpetuate the myths centered on their arrival.*

## Suggestions for Further Reading

Anderson, Gary Clayton. *The Indian Southwest, 1580-1830: Ethnogenesis and Reinvention.* Norman: University of Oklahoma Press, 1999.

Aten, Lawrence E. *Indians of the Upper Texas Coast.* New York: Academic Press, 1983.

Barr, Juliana. *Peace Came in the Form of a Woman.* The University of North Carolina Press, 2007.

Carlson, Paul H. *The Plains Indians.* College Station: Texas A&M University Press, 1998.

Carter, Cecile Elkins. *Caddo Indians: Where We Come From.* Norman: University of Oklahoma Press, 1995.

Chipman, Donald E. and Harriet Denise Joseph. *Spanish Texas, 1519-1821* Austin: University of Texas Press, 2010.

Ewers, John C. "The Influence of Epidemics on the Indian Populations and Cultures in Texas." *Plains Anthropologist* 18 (May 1973): 104-155.

Hämäläinen, Pekka. *The Comanche Empire.* New Haven: Yale University Press, 2008.

Hickerson, Parrott, *Jumano: Hunters and Traders of the South Plains.* Austin: University of Texas Press, 1994.

Hudson, Charles. *Knights of Spain, Warriors of the Sun: Hernando de Soto and the South's Ancient Chiefdoms* Athens: University of Georgia Press, 1997.

John, Elizabeth A.H. *Storms Brewed in Other Men's Worlds: The Confrontation of Indians, Spanish, and French in the Southwest, 1540-1795* College Station: Texas A&M University Press, 1975.

Kavanagh, Thomas. *The Comanches: A History, 1706-1875*, University of Nebraska Press 1999.

Kessell, John L. *Spain in the Southwest: A Narrative History of Colonial New Mexico, Arizona, Texas and California* Norman: University of Oklahoma Press, 2002.

La Vere, David. *A History of the Indians in Texas.* College Station: Texas A&M University Press, 2004.

___, *Life Among the Texas Indians: The WPA Narratives.* College Station: Texas A&M University Press, 1998.

Myers, Sandra L. *Native Americans of Texas.* Boston: American Press, 1981.

Newcomb, W. W. *The Indians of Texas from Prehistory to Modern Times.* Austin: University of Texas Press, 1961.

Newkumet, Vynol Beaver. *Hasinai: Traditional History of the Caddo Confederacy.* College Station: University of Texas A&M Press, 1988.

Perttula, Timothy K. *The Caddo Nation: Archaeological & Ethnohistoric Perspectives.* Austin: University of Texas Press, 1994.

Ricklis, Robert A. *The Karankawa Indians of Texas.* Austin: University of Texas Press, 1996.

Schilz, Thomas. *Lipan Apaches in Texas.* El Paso: Texas Western Press, 1987.

Smith, F. Todd. *The Caddo Indians: Tribes at the Convergence of Empires, 1542-1854.* Texas A&M University Press, 2000.

___, *The Wichita Indians: Traders of Texas and the Southern Plains, 1540-1945.* Texas A&M University Press, 2000.

Weber, David J. *Spanish Frontier in North America, 1512-1821* New Haven: Yale University Press, 1992.

**IDENTIFICATION:** Briefly describe each term.

Midland Minnie
Folsom Point
Petroglyphs
Archaic Period
Agricultural Revolution
Spiro, Oklahoma
ethnogenesis
Wichitas
Tonkawas
Apaches
Pueblos
Comanches
Cabeza de Vaca
Luis de Moscoso
Spanish horses

**MULTIPLE CHOICE:** Choose the correct response.

1. Which giant mammal of the Great Plains survived the end of the Ice Age?
    A. Dwarf bison
    B. Horse
    C. Woolly Mammoth
    D. Camel

2. Which of the tribes listed below are Karankawas?
    A. Caddos
    B. Coahuiltecans
    C. Cocos
    D. Comanches

3. The Mississippian Cultural Tradition began where?
    A. Spiro, Oklahoma
    B. Cahokia, Illinois
    C. Moundville, Alabama
    D. Etowah, Georgia

4. The term "Tejas" means friend in which Native American language?
    A. Shoshonean
    B. Athabaskan
    C. Tunican
    D. Caddoan

5. The Pueblo Indians live in which river valley?
   A. Red
   B. Colorado
   C. Rio Grande
   D. Brazos

6. The Tonkawas lived in what region of Texas?
   A. Gulf Coast
   B. Great Plains
   C. Central Texas
   D. Trans-Pecos

7. All of the tribes listed below were Plains Indians EXCEPT:
   A. the Comanches
   B. the Apaches
   C. the Atakapas
   D. the Jumanos

8. All terms listed below are Caddo confederacies EXCEPT:
   A. Kadohadacho
   B. Natchitoches
   C. Nacogdoches
   D. Hasinai

9. Which of the following Spanish explorers landed on the coast of Texas?
   A. Hernán Cortes
   B. Juan de Oñate
   C. Pánfilo de Narvaez
   D. Christopher Columbus

10. The 1573 Royal Order for New Discoveries gave which group the central role in the exploration and settlement of new lands?
   A. Soldiers
   B. Missionaries
   C. Government Officials
   D. Explorers

**TRUE/FALSE:** Indicate whether each statement is true or false.

1. Paleoindians of Texas farmed corn, beans, and squash.

2. Archaic Indians developed the *atlatl* and the bow and arrow.

3. The Karankawa Indians of Coastal Texas were most like the Caddos of East Texas.

4. The Mississippian cultural tradition began first in Etowah, Georgia.

5. The Caddos of East Texas were led by a chief known as the *caddí*.

6. The Jumano Indians conducted trade between the Pueblos and the Caddos.

7. The Spanish explorer, Francisco Coronado, landed on the Texas Gulf Coast.

8. Comanche lifestyle revolved around the acquisition of the horse and pursuit of buffalo.

9. The Atakapa Indians lived on the Great Plains of Texas.

10. Wichitas and Caddos lived in houses made of grass.


**MATCHING:** Match the response in column A with the item in column B.

1. Paleoindians
2. Coahuiltecans
3. "American triad"
4. *xinesí*
5. Wacos
6. Apaches
7. Hernando de Soto
8. *nuhmuhnuh*
9. Kingdom of Tejas
10. La Junta

A. Spanish explorer
B. Comanche people
C. Caddo priest
D. Jumano settlement
E. Archaic Indians
F. Corn, beans, and squash
G. Hasinai Indians
H. Clovis Point
I. South Texas and Northern Mexico
J. Wichita tribe

**ESSAY QUESTIONS:**

1. Explain the major characteristics among the Native Americans during the Archaic Period, and list which groups in Texas maintained those characteristics into the modern era.

2. Discuss the Agricultural Revolution and the introduction of the Mississippian cultural tradition to Texas, noting which tribes adapted to this tradition.

3. Discuss the early Spanish explorations of Texas, explaining where they went, and what changes they brought to the province as a result of their travels.

4. Explain the importance of the horse to the Plains Indians, and list which groups in Texas profited most from the introduction of horses.

# Chapter 2

# *Texas Under Spanish Rule, 1684-1821*

*Prelude: An Early American Treks through Spanish Texas—Zebulon Pike's Expedition*

*In February 1807, Spanish troops arrested Zebulon Pike and the members of his American expedition near the upper Rio Grande. Following their capture, the American explorers were taken on a long journey through New Mexico and across Texas to the Louisiana border, where they were freed and warned not to return. Along the journey, Pike recorded what he saw in his personal diary. This proved to be the only record that the expedition was able to bring back to the United States, because Spanish soldiers confiscated the rest of the group's maps and other notes.*

*Approximately ten months prior, Pike set out on his government-sponsored mission to locate the headwaters of the Arkansas River and to explore Spanish borderlands. Pike failed to locate the source of the Arkansas in the southern Rocky Mountains, but he did gaze upon the majestic summit that would later be named Pike's Peak in his honor. After traveling throughout Colorado, Pike's expedition turned southward, hoping to reach one of the tributaries of the Rio Grande. Unfortunately for the expedition, Pike miscalculated the group's position and led them instead across the Sangre de Cristo Mountains into New Mexico, where they were taken into custody by Spanish troops in February 1807. Pike reportedly asked the captain of the Spanish dragoons, "What, this is not the Red River?" His Spanish captor supposedly replied, "No, Sir! The Rio del Norte." There is little doubt that the Spanish officer was unimpressed by Pike's navigation skills. Pike and his men were escorted to Santa Fe, the capital of New Mexico, before being ushered south to the Spanish provincial capital of Chihuahua for further questioning.*

*The Spanish authorities were concerned that Pike was an American spy sent by the United States government to explore troop strength in Spain's northern frontier and gathering information on the resources available in the borderlands. After a lengthy interrogation, Spanish officials deemed that Pike was not a direct threat to their sovereignty and ordered a military escort to conduct him back home through the provinces of Coahuila and Texas along the Old San Antonio Road to the American post at the old French town of Natchitoches in Louisiana.*

*Though the members of Pike's Expedition were treated well during their captivity, Spanish troops confiscated all of the notes and maps compiled by the explorer. Despite the fact that the Spaniards had taken his papers, Pike was able to hide and retain a small personal diary and was very observant of his surroundings: The Spanish could not confiscate nor erase his memories of the landscape. Based on his brief diary entries and his memories, Pike published an account of what he witnessed in Texas, providing valuable information about the Texas landscape for future American settlers. For the most part, he was impressed with Mexico's northern province of Tejas, known today as Texas. He wrote of the region's fertile soil, plentiful grasslands, and of the elegance and charming manners of the Tejanos. He wrote of conversations with leading men, revealing that they were primarily interested in three main topics— money, horses, and women. He recorded that these men often talked of opening trade with the United States. They were especially interested in trading cattle and horses on the open market in New Orleans. Pike even confessed that the Tejanas (Spanish women in Texas) were most agreeable to him. He reported that they fascinated him with their short skirts and their high-heeled shoes, and silk shawls covering their faces, "but from under which you frequently see peeping large, sparkling black eyes." According to the images that Pike created with his pen, Texas was a Garden of Eden that lay just across the border from the United States.*

Although French explorers from Canada made initial contact with the Hasinais before the Spanish Franciscans arrived in the late 1600s, Spain would eventually establish the colony of Texas in the early eighteenth century. For many decades thereafter, however, Texas lay isolated at the far northern end of Spain's hemisphere-wide empire with Spanish imperial officials primarily focused upon their wealthier conquests in Mexico and Peru. As occurred in the Spanish colonies of Florida and California, Texas was settled by a small number of soldiers and priests for defensive and religious purposes, rather than for economic gain. Throughout the history of Spanish Texas, actual power remained in the hands of the region's Native Americans, who allied themselves commercially and militarily with whichever country controlled the well populated, economically dynamic province of Louisiana. France initially founded the colony in the early 1700s, with the aggressive, expansionist United States ultimately assuming dominion over Louisiana a century later. By the time Mexico gained independence from Spain in 1821, Texas lay in ruins due to the destruction caused by a disastrous revolution and war, opening the province up to American settlement during the Mexican era.

**French Interlopers and the Spanish Response**

France began to establish colonies in the Western Hemisphere more than a century after Spain, with settlers first approaching Louisiana moving southward from Canada during the reign of the nation's first Bourbon ruler, Henry IV. In 1603, the French Crown granted monopoly companies the right to settle in Acadia, along the Bay of Fundy (in between present-day Maine and Nova Scotia), and in New France along the St. Lawrence River, where they built Quebec and Montreal. By 1670, French traders had traversed the vast Great Lakes region and established a post at Green Bay along the shores of Lake

Michigan. From there, they portaged across the watershed and entered streams flowing southwestward toward a great river that the Indians called the Mississippi. When word of the river filtered back to New France, French officials chose Louis Jolliet, a talented surveyor and cartographer, along with Jesuit priest Jacques Marquette, to lead an expedition to ascertain whether the Mississippi flowed into the Gulf of Mexico. In May 1673, the two explorers embarked in canoes from Canada along with five other Frenchmen and, two months later, reached the villages of the Quapaw Indians, located along the Mississippi near the mouth of the Arkansas River. After the Quapaws confirmed that the river flowed into the gulf, Jolliet and Marquette decided to return to New France rather than continue downstream to report their findings to French officials.

Although Jolliet requested permission to establish a settlement in the Mississippi Valley, that privilege was granted to René-Robert Cavelier, sieur de La Salle. In preparation for his project, over the next few years La Salle established a chain of posts from Lake Ontario to the Mississippi River. Finally, in January 1682, La Salle, along with a party of Frenchmen and Algonquian Indians, proceeded down the Mississippi and reached the Gulf of Mexico by early April. Near the river's mouth, La Salle conducted a ceremony by which he claimed possession of the country he called, "Louisiana," for Louis XIV. Although La Salle had determined conclusively that the Mississippi entered the Gulf of Mexico, he mistakenly calculated that the river's mouth was located far to the southwest of its actual location. La Salle's miscalculation would soon prove fatal to himself and hundreds of other Frenchmen, while also prodding Spanish officials to begin occupying Texas.

The aggressive, expansion-minded Louis XIV accepted La Salle's proposal to establish a settlement upstream from the Mississippi's mouth. In the summer of 1684, La Salle left France with one hundred soldiers and nearly three hundred colonists in four ships. The ill-fated expedition was plagued from the start, mainly as a result of La Salle's insecurity and paranoia, which caused him to quarrel incessantly with the expedition's naval commander, Taneguy Le Gallois Beaujeu, during the Atlantic crossing. When the flotilla reached the French Caribbean island of Saint-Domingue—present-day Haiti—in September, the leaders' disagreement allowed Spanish privateers to capture one ship and caused numerous other members of the expedition to desert. Continuing on with the remaining three ships, the French expedition arrived at Matagorda Bay in early 1685, halfway down the Texas coast between present-day Galveston and Corpus Christi. Although initially certain that he was at the Mississippi River's mouth, by the time La Salle finally accepted his error a few months later, the French party was stranded. Beaujeu had returned to France in the lead ship, and the other two vessels, *L'Aimable* and *La Belle*, had run aground and sunk, along with precious supplies, in Matagorda Bay.

After constructing a temporary site for the remaining colonists a few miles inland from the bay on Garcitas Creek, La Salle concluded that their only hope for survival lay in his ability to locate the actual Mississippi River and ascend it to the French post that he and his lieutenant, Henri de Tonti, had founded on the Illinois River. In April 1686, the increasingly volatile La Salle set out to find the Mississippi along with about twenty men. A few months later, the Hasinai Indians, eager for trade ties with Europeans, welcomed the French stragglers into their East Texas villages. The Hasinais agreed to lead the party eastward toward the Mississippi, but the mercurial La Salle became ill and the French group returned to the settlement on Garcitas Creek with the intention of returning to East Texas the following year.

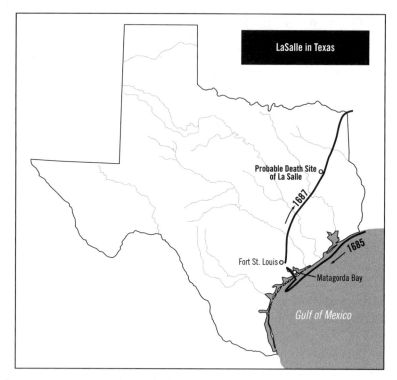

Sickness, starvation, and attacks by the local Karankawa Indians reduced the Garcitas Creek settlement to fewer than fifty people by January 1687, when La Salle made another attempt to reach the Mississippi. Along with seventeen men, La Salle left the coast and headed northeastward toward the Hasinais. Before reaching the tribe, however, quarreling broke out within the group, and La Salle and a few others were killed. The remnants of the French party continued on to the Hasinai villages, where half of the party decided to remain among the tribe, while the other contingent continued on to the Mississippi. Hasinai guides took the French group to the Kadohadacho villages along the Red River, and from there they were led to the Arkansas Post, a small French trading facility that Tonti had recently established among the Quapaws. Ultimately, the French party ascended the Mississippi, made it to Canada, and returned safely to France.

Due in part, to the outbreak of war with England, the French made no attempt to send a vessel for the two dozen remaining colonists, who survived until early 1689, when the Karankawas killed all but a few children. Although the French effort in the late seventeenth century did not result in permanent settlement, the various travelers' positive encounters with the Caddos and Quapaws did pave the way for the establishment of trading alliances and friendship when some Frenchmen returned a few years later.

The French intrusion into their claimed territory forced Spanish officials to initiate a response ultimately leading to the Spanish occupation of Texas. Learning of the French incursion into Spanish waters from the captured Frenchmen who had deserted La Salle at Saint-Domingue, officials in New Spain undertook a large-scale search to find and destroy the intruders. Beginning in 1686, the Spaniards sent out five maritime expeditions and six overland parties seeking La Salle's outpost. Finally, in early 1689, an expedition led by Alonso de León left Mexico and discovered the ransacked French settlement on Garcitas Creek and a couple of survivors, who informed the Spaniards that Karankawa Indians had killed most of the French colonists. After burying the remaining French cannons, de León and his Franciscan associate, Damián Massanet, encountered representatives from the Hasinai Indians who, assuming that the Spaniards were French allies of La Salle, invited them to establish a trading post at their East Texas villages. The Spaniards, who had been hearing tales of the "great kingdom of the Tejas" for nearly a quarter of a century, incorrectly thought the Hasinais had asked them to establish a mission in their midst. This misunderstanding would plague the Spanish effort among the Hasinais from the start.

Back in New Spain, de León and Massanet received permission to return to East Texas with one hundred soldiers and five Franciscan friars from the missionary Colegio de la Santa Cruz in Querétaro in order to bring Christianity to the Hasinais and to ensure there was no longer a French presence in the area. Traveling first to Garcitas Creek to burn all remnants of La Salle's settlement, in May 1690 the Spaniards were greeted by the Nabedaches, the westernmost Hasinai group, at their village located along the Neches River. Eager to cement an alliance with the visitors, the Nabedaches allowed the Franciscans to establish a mission called San Francisco de los Tejas, near their settlement. To service other Hasinais, the Franciscans founded a second mission, Santísimo Nombre de María, the following year about five miles east, at the Neches Indian village. Finding no sign of the French, and misinformed about the Hasinais' desire for Christianity, de León returned to Mexico in late 1690, leaving only a small number of soldiers behind with the Franciscan priests.

Relations between the Franciscans and the Hasinais became tense soon after de León's departure. The Indians had invited the foreigners to their villages in order to acquire a military alliance and access to trade goods and weapons, only to watch the Spanish military contingent retire to Mexico and find that the Franciscans refused to provide them with guns or ammunition. Unlike the missionaries in New Mexico, the Franciscans among the Hasinais were isolated and had almost no support system on which to rely; thus the Indians had little respect for the friars and refused to succumb to their clumsy indoctrination efforts. An epidemic, brought on by a Franciscan who died of smallpox, swept through the country in early 1691 and exacerbated the strained relations between the Hasinais and the priests. By the time that the sickness had run its course in March 1691, four hundred or so Hasinais and three thousand members of the other Caddo tribes had died.

Despite their unhappiness with the Franciscans, the Hasinais allowed a Spanish expedition of fifty soldiers and ten priests, led by Domingo Terán de los Ríos, to enter their villages in August 1691. Optimistic officials in New Spain had ordered Terán to accompany the Franciscans to East Texas in order to establish more missions among the Hasinais and their Kadohadacho allies. However, the Hasinais' sullen attitude toward the Spaniards during their five-month stay in Caddo country forced Terán to abandon attempts to construct new churches and caused all but three Franciscans—along with a few lay brothers and soldiers—to accompany the troops when they headed back to Mexico in January 1692. The Hasinais' enmity for the Spaniards did not decrease following Terán's departure, as yet another epidemic swept through East Texas in the summer. The Hasinais tolerated the Franciscans' presence for another year, until October 1693 when the Nabedache *caddí* informed the friars that his people would kill them if they did not leave immediately. Choosing survival over martyrdom, the Franciscans buried the church ornaments, set fire to the two missions, and headed to the nearest Spanish settlement at Monclova in northern Mexico, which they reached the following February. Thus, the flurry of activities that had occurred in Texas over the course of a decade came to an end. The Spanish attempt to win over the Hasinais by peaceful conversion to Christianity had failed, and the tribe's experience with the French had made the Indians more desirous of establishing a military and commercial partnership with the Gallic visitors.

## The Permanent Occupation of Spanish Texas

France's second (ultimately successful) effort to establish the colony of Louisiana near the Mississippi's mouth compelled Spain to establish a permanent presence in Texas during the second decade of the eighteenth century. Landing first on the Gulf Coast at Biloxi and Mobile in 1699, French settlement of Louisiana was hampered by the outbreak of the War of Spanish Succession in 1702, initiated when Louis XIV installed his Bourbon grandson on the Spanish throne, vacated by the death of the final Habsburg ruler. As the war wound down in 1712, the financially troubled Louis XIV ceded control of Louisiana to Antoine Crozat, a wealthy financier. Preferring to remain in Paris, Crozat appointed Antoine de la Mothe, sieur de Cadillac, as governor with the explicit goal of making Louisiana more economically productive.

Cadillac realized soon after assuming the governorship that, because neither Crozat nor the king was willing to provide funds to populate Louisiana with French settlers or African slaves, trade with Native Americans and with colonists in New Spain would be the only possible way to make the venture profitable. Thus, Cadillac decided to initiate trade with Mexico and with the Indian tribes situated on Louisiana's western flank, through the reestablishment of the Spanish missions among the Hasinais of East Texas. The French governor seized upon this strategy after receiving a letter from a Spanish Franciscan, Father Francisco Hidalgo, who had labored at the failed Hasinai missions in the 1690s. In spite of that experience, Hidalgo had continued to be enthusiastic about missionary work on the frontier and had helped found the Franciscan mission of San Juan Bautista on the southern bank of the Rio Grande in 1700, about thirty miles downstream from present-day Eagle Pass. Hidalgo addressed Cadillac as a fellow Catholic, asking him to help save Hasinai souls, either directly through the establishment of French missions or indirectly by inspiring Spanish officials to rebuild their stations to prevent Gallic occupation. Interpreting the Franciscan's religious invitation as an opening to create a market for French goods in East Texas, Cadillac ordered Louis Juchereau de Saint-Denis, a Canadian who had arrived in Louisiana in 1700, to establish a trading post on the colony's western boundary along the Red River.

In early 1714, St. Denis, along with twenty-four Frenchmen and five boatloads of merchandise, traveled up the Red River to the villages of the Natchitoches Indians, with whom the French had been trading for over a decade. Eager to establish French traders and soldiers permanently nearby, Natchitoches tribesmen assisted St. Denis in constructing living quarters for the Frenchmen and two warehouses for the safekeeping of merchandise. Having laid the foundations of the French town of Natchitoches, St. Denis soon traveled to East Texas, distributed presents to the Hasinais, and managed to persuade the tribal leaders to ask for the return of Spanish missionaries. He explained that, because Spain and France had recently become allies, the French now recognized the Spanish claim to Hasinai territory and therefore, despite the wishes of the tribe, his people could not settle there. The Canadian convinced the Hasinais that having the Spaniards as well as the French nearby would be advantageous, as the tribe would share in the profitable trade that promised to develop. To convince the Spaniards to return, however, the Hasinais had to once again play upon the Franciscans' desire to convert the natives to Christianity. Therefore, Hasinai leaders agreed to accompany St. Denis to the nearest Spanish establishment at San Juan Bautista.

Upon his arrival at the presidio in July 1714, St. Denis explained to the commandant, Diego Ramón, that he was responding to Father Hidalgo's letter and only sought to assist the Spaniards in rebuilding missions among the Hasinais. Ramón initially placed St. Denis under house arrest before sending him on to Mexico City for interrogation. Following months of discussions, the Spanish bureaucrats answered Hidalgo's prayers by deciding to reoccupy East Texas in order to resume the conversion efforts among the Hasinais, but they thwarted St. Denis's commercial schemes by declaring French trade with Mexico illegal.

Realizing that the Franciscans and soldiers in East Texas would most likely be dependent on French merchandise in spite of the law, St. Denis agreed to assist the Spaniards in reestablishing missions among the Hasinais. In April 1716, the Canadian led Captain Domingo Ramón (Diego's son), twenty-five Spanish soldiers, and two groups of Franciscan missionaries—one from the Colegio de la Santa Cruz de Querétaro and the other from the Colegio de Nuestra Señora de Guadalupe de Zacatecas—back to the Hasinai country. When they entered East Texas in late June, the Hasinais, in conformity with St. Denis's desires, allowed the Spaniards to establish four missions among their villages, as well as an accompanying presidio. In order to halt the French at the Red River, Ramón also established a mission approximately fifteen miles west of Natchitoches at the Adaes Indian village. The Franciscans founded yet another mission at the Ais Indian village, just west of the Sabine River. All in all, Spaniards placed six missions—split equally between the Franciscans from Querétaro and Zacatecas—in an attempt to instruct the natives in Christianity and Hispanic civilization while securing the frontier from the French.

Although far better supported than the first Franciscan effort among the Hasinais in the 1690s, the missions established by Ramón faced many similar problems. Not only were they located four hundred miles from the nearest Spanish settlements on the Rio Grande, the Hasinais showed little desire to accept the Catholic faith and refused to provide food for the soldiers and priests. As a result, Spanish officials in Mexico City appointed Martín de Alarcón as governor of Texas and directed him to lead an expedition to create a mission, presidio and civilian settlement along the San Antonio River as a halfway post to East Texas. In May 1718, Alarcón, along with seventy-two persons, including soldiers, Franciscan missionaries from Querétaro, and ten families recruited in northern Mexico, founded Mission San Antonio de Valero—ultimately known as the Alamo—for the Coahuiltecan Indians living nearby. Presidio San Antonio de Béxar was established a mile west of the mission to house the soldiers, while the civilians constructed their homes around the fort. Soon thereafter, Zacatecan Franciscans founded a second mission, San José, a few miles downstream from the original San Antonio settlements.

Although Alarcón traveled on to East Texas in 1718, he disappointed the priests living among the Hasinais by not bringing more soldiers or settlers to the region. The missions continued to struggle until 1719, when a short war—inspired by events in Europe—broke out between France and Spain, forcing the Spaniards to abandon East Texas altogether and fall back to San Antonio. Though officials in Spain and Mexico City

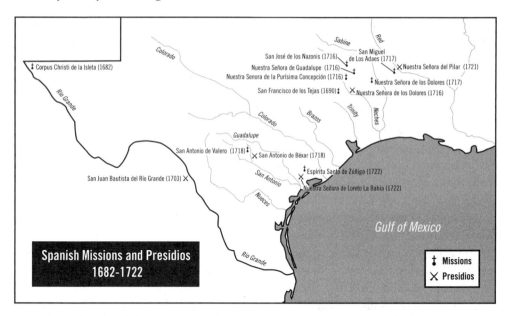

soon thereafter decided to reoccupy the region, it was not until peace had been signed in March 1721 that the Marqués de San Miguel de Aguayo, a wealthy resident of Coahuila, crossed the Rio Grande at the head of an expedition designed to resupply Texas with five hundred men and enormous herds of horses, cattle, sheep, and goats. After reinforcing the small Spanish outpost of San Antonio, Aguayo headed to East Texas and reestablished the presidio and the four abandoned missions among the Hasinais. Aguayo continued eastward to restore the mission at the Ais town and added a presidio to the mission at the newly named Los Adaes, which would remain the official capital of Spanish Texas for the next half century. The Rio Hondo, a small stream between Los Adaes and Natchitoches, served as the boundary with French Louisiana.

Leaving over one hundred soldiers in East Texas, Aguayo headed south and initiated construction of a mission for the Karankawas and Coahuiltecans, along with a nearby presidio to guard the Texas coast at Matagorda Bay, both of which would be commonly known as La Bahía (literally, "the bay"). By the time he returned to Coahuila in May 1722, Aguayo had successfully anchored Spanish Texas at three vital points—Los Adaes, La Bahía, and San Antonio.

Within a decade, however, the Spanish presence on the Louisiana border had diminished greatly, making San Antonio the main focus of Texas. Although Aguayo had placed the Franciscans in East Texas, the Hasinais remained aloof from the priests' conversion efforts. Brigadier General Pedro de Rivera y Villalón visited the Hasinai country in 1727 while conducting an inspection tour of northern Mexico, and found that the Indians had not gathered at any of the four missions. Rivera was even more disturbed by the close ties the Hasinais maintained with the French at Natchitoches, and he recognized the futility of maintaining two presidios in East Texas. Therefore, in 1729 the viceroy of New Spain accepted Rivera's recommendations and ordered the abandonment of the presidio among the Hasinais and the reduction of the number of troops at the remaining three forts in Texas. Two years later, the Queréteran missionaries, who had been left unprotected by the military withdrawal, abandoned their three missions among the Hasinais and retreated to San Antonio, bringing the total number of missions there to five. Only the mission run

**Front exterior of church, Mission San Jose, 1927, photographed in San Antonio, Texas.
Photo credit: UTSA's Institute of Texan Cultures**

by the Franciscan fathers of Zacatecas, located near the Nacogdoches village, remained among the Hasinais, along with the two missions for the Ais and the Adaes.

**Spanish Settlements in Texas to Mid-Century**

Although Spanish officials tried to induce settlers to move from Mexico to Texas in the early eighteenth century, the province's isolation and lack of economic promise failed to attract many colonists. The only newcomers to Texas were fifty-five people who arrived in San Antonio in 1731 from the impoverished, Spanish-controlled Canary Islands that lay off the coast of Africa. These so-called *Isleños* founded the villa of San Fernando de Béxar, separate from the presidio and the missions, and formed a municipal government—the first and only civilian government in Spanish Texas. Much to the chagrin of the original soldier-settlers, the *Isleños* were granted rights to the irrigated farmlands that they had established near the presidio during the previous decade. The Canary Islanders also clashed with the Franciscans, who refused to allow them to hire Indian laborers from the missions or sell foodstuffs to the presidio, an exclusive privilege that the friars maintained. The priests, *Isleños*, and the descendants of the community's first Hispanic settlers carried on a running feud over the valley's limited resources, until intermarriage and common interests eventually united both factions of townfolk at mid-century. By then, San Antonio's population stood at nearly six hundred non-Indians.

Although the number of Spanish troops in East Texas had been reduced in 1729, the Hispanic population of the region grew to four hundred people—called Adaeseños—by the middle of the eighteenth century. Most were former soldiers who, along with their families, established farms and ranches among the three Franciscan missions and the presidio. Despite the efforts of the Adaeseños to feed the priests and soldiers of East Texas, the latter groups were forced to purchase food and manufactured goods from the well-supplied French in Natchitoches. The mission-presidial complex of La Bahía, which was moved to its final destination on the lower reaches of the San Antonio River in 1749, contained about half as many Spaniards as East Texas, most of whom were also ex-soldiers who raised foodstuffs and livestock for their own consumption.

**French Louisiana and the Norteño Alliance**

In the meantime, the French expanded their settlements in Louisiana, founding New Orleans in 1718 as the capital of their colony, which encompassed the entire Lower Mississippi Valley and its nearly ten thousand people by mid-century. The population of Natchitoches grew to over six hundred residents, many of whom were involved in providing Texas Indians with manufactured goods. Following the establishment of trade with the Natchitoches Indians in 1714, the Caddos allowed the French to set up trading posts at the Yatasi village on Bayou Pierre about fifty miles northwest of town, and at the Kadohadacho villages further up the Red River. From these posts, French traders circumvented the limited Spanish presence in East Texas to barter with many other tribes, most particularly the Hasinais and the Wichitas.

To gain greater access to French trade goods and to escape the attacks from their Siouan Osage enemies in Missouri, the Wichitas moved south from Oklahoma into northern Texas in the early eighteenth century. By the 1750s, the Tawakonis had moved from the Arkansas Valley to form villages near the Kichais in the area between the Sabine and Red Rivers in East Texas. The Taovayas established the most important Wichita settlement at a place that would become one of the landmark villages of the Southern Plains for the next half century. The excellent site that they chose was located along the Red River, just west of the thin sliver of forest known as the Western Cross Timbers. On the south bank of the river, in present-day Montague County, Texas, the Taovayas constructed an impressive fort with a twelve-foot high stockade, surrounded by a deep trench. French traders flocked to the village (which was the farthest point upstream that could be reached by boat) to exchange goods with the Taovayas. The Wichitas also cemented a profitable alliance with the Penateka Comanches who lived to the west, and the Taovayas established themselves as middlemen in the lucrative trade between the Comanches and the French. The Comanches not only became trading partners of the Wichitas, the two tribes also formed a military alliance aimed at the Lipan Apaches and the Osages. Whereas the Osages were well supplied with weapons from French traders from Illinois, the Lipans increasingly found themselves outgunned by the Comanches and Wichitas. Therefore, the two tribes constantly preyed upon the Apaches for slaves, selling mainly women and children to French traders who distributed them throughout Louisiana and the West Indies. The alliance the French traders formed along the Red River with the Caddos, Wichitas, and Comanches—who the Spaniards grouped together as the Norteños, or the Northern tribes—proved to be the most powerful force in Texas throughout the 1700s and into the early nineteenth century.

## Franciscan Missionary Efforts among the Texas Native Americans

Whereas the French won the favor of most Native Americans in Texas through trade, the Spanish Franciscans continued fruitlessly to convert the province's Indians to Christianity. Well supplied with French goods, no Hasinai, Ais, or Adaes Indian ever agreed to live in any of the three Zacatecan missions in East Texas. Although a few Karankawas were initially attracted to the mission at La Bahía, they abandoned it in 1723 after killing the Spanish presidio commander. The Coahuiltecans were the only Indian group of the region attracted to the Franciscans' inducements. Poverty and pressure from Lipan Apache raiders combined to cause the Coahuiltecans to seek refuge in the missions at San Antonio and La Bahía. These missions, particularly the five located at San Antonio, greatly improved the economic well-being of the Coahuiltecans because the priests taught the Indians how to divert water from the San Antonio River to irrigate their newly established fields. Very quickly, the mission Indians produced enough corn, beans, and squash to supply not only themselves but also to sell to the nearby soldiers and settlers. Cattle herds offered a second food source for the Coahuiltecans, and each mission set up outlying ranches where herders tended the animals. The Indians also learned how to weave, and they began to produce cotton and woolen clothes and blankets.

Despite the economic success of the missions, the Coahuiltecan population declined throughout the eighteenth century. The Franciscans housed the former nomads in closely concentrated quarters, which exacerbated the spread of epidemic diseases. Infant mortality rates were high under such conditions. The amount of work that the Indians were expected to perform was far greater than what hunters and gatherers normally expended. As a consequence, they often ran away, resulting in the priests and soldiers resorting to forceful methods in order to keep the natives in the fields. Given the high child mortality rate and the continued problem with runaways, the population at the missions could not sustain itself. To maintain them, the priests had to continually recruit more Coahuiltecans. By the middle of the century, however, very few Coahuiltecans survived outside the mission walls of San Antonio and La Bahía, and their numbers continued to fall.

While the Coahuiltecan population declined, the number of cattle, horses, and mules in the mission ranches—as well as those of the settlers at San Antonio—increased dramatically. An intense period of drought in the first two decades of the eighteenth century had caused the great buffalo herds to disappear from the region south of the San Antonio River, just as the Spaniards settled in Texas. Their cattle thrived in the absence of buffalo, which were kept from returning to the area by the spread of mesquite. Whereas buffalo refused to forage on mesquite, Spanish cattle and horses fattened up on the plant and their population grew tremendously. By the 1760s, at least twenty thousand head of cattle roamed the open ranges between San Antonio and La Bahía. Actually, the numerous Spanish livestock affected the Texas Indians much more than the Spaniards ever did. Some Indian groups raided the Spanish cattle herds to replace the buffalo as a food source, while others poached horses to enrich their own herds or to sell to the French in Louisiana who were desperate for mounts. Nonetheless, the Franciscans continued to hope that some of these Indians could be compelled to accept mission life.

The availability of Spanish livestock, combined with the effects of disease and Lipan Apache pressure, caused members of a number of different tribes—mainly Tonkawas,

Atakapas, and Karankawas—to come together in a community located in the middle Brazos River Valley. From this settlement, which the Spaniards called *Ranchería Grande*, men stole livestock from the nearby Spanish ranches. The Indians consumed the beef, but exchanged the horses with the French in Louisiana. The success of *Ranchería Grande*, however, attracted even more Apache raiders. In hope of gaining protection from the Lipans, the Indians on the Brazos requested that the Spanish authorities establish a mission for them in 1745. The Spaniards responded by erecting three missions—one for each tribe—and a presidio along the San Xavier River (presently called the San Gabriel River) in 1748-49. Lipan warriors, however, attacked the missions almost immediately after their opening, making it apparent to the tribesmen that the Spaniards could not offer any meaningful protection from the Apaches. Most of the Indians left the San Gabriel missions soon thereafter, forcing the Franciscans to abandon the empty establishments in 1756.

The Franciscans persisted in trying to induce Indians to settle among them, despite the failure on the San Xavier. In 1754 they established a new mission for the Karankawas, Nuestra Señora del Rosario, about four miles up the San Antonio River from the settlement at La Bahía. Whereas a few Karankawas occasionally visited the station to receive food and gifts, and two hundred or so agreed to be baptized in the first fifteen years of its existence, the majority of tribesmen avoided Mission Rosario, preferring to remain near the coast. The Franciscans had even less success with the mission that they founded for the Atakapas near the mouth of the Trinity River in 1756. No Indians settled at the mission, which was situated in a malarial lowland with unpotable water. The Spaniards abandoned the station after fourteen useless years.

The most spectacular missionary failure, and the one that best illuminates the weakness of the Spanish position in Texas, was the Franciscan effort to bring Christianity to the Lipan Apaches. The Apaches had begun making raids upon San Antonio to steal livestock almost as soon as the town was founded in 1718. For the next three decades, the Lipans and Spaniards fought occasionally as the Indians sporadically assaulted the missions and civilian settlements, to which the presidial soldiers responded with punitive expeditions. By 1749, however, incessant Comanche and Wichita slave raiding forced the beleaguered Apaches to negotiate a peace treaty at San Antonio, and their conduct toward Béxar improved accordingly. Continued attacks by the Norteños, however, induced the Apaches to ask their ally to establish a mission and presidio in their country in hope of gaining protection from their enemies. The Spaniards responded by constructing a mission-presidial complex for the Apaches along the San Saba River northwest of San Antonio in 1757.

Although the Lipans desired Spanish military protection, they had no intention of being reduced to mission life or to accept Christianity. While a few Apaches visited the mission as they passed through the area on their way north to hunt buffalo, none agreed to give up their nomadic lifestyle. The Norteños, meanwhile, believed that the mission would provide the Lipans with a safe refuge from which to make retaliatory attacks. Therefore, in March 1758, two thousand Norteño warriors, half of whom were carrying French guns, gathered near the mission on the San Saba. The Norteños, led by a fully armed Comanche chief dressed in a French army officer's uniform, surrounded the mission and forced the priests to let them inside the walls. After the native troops found that there were no Apaches present, they turned on the Spaniards, killing eight (including two Franciscans, one of whom they decapitated), and set fire to the mission.

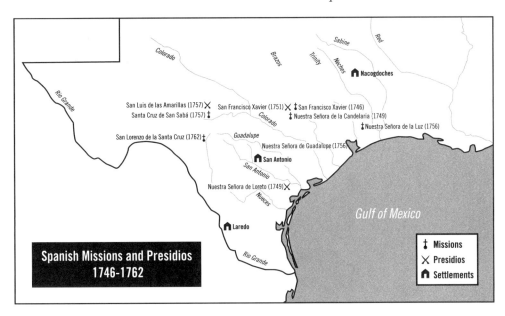

The brutal attack caused the Spaniards to seek retribution against the Norteños. In August 1759 Colonel Diego Ortiz Parrilla led an expedition of five hundred Spanish troops and Lipan and Coahuiltecan allies out from the San Saba. Two months later, Ortiz Parrilla's troops attacked the Norteños at the Taovaya town on the Red River. The well-armed natives outnumbered the Spanish-Indian force, however, and Ortiz Parrilla's men could not penetrate the Taovayas' palisaded village, over which flew a French flag. The stunned Spanish colonel was forced to retreat to the San Saba River after suffering heavy casualties. Realizing that the Apaches feared coming to the area, in 1762 the Franciscans abandoned the mission and constructed two others for the Lipans, jointly known as El Cañon, on the headwaters of the Nueces River. The Indians avoided these missions as well, and the Spaniards discontinued El Cañon and the presidio on the San Saba nine years later.

**Spanish Accession of Louisiana and the Reorganization of Texas**

By the 1760s, the Native Americans in Texas had endured the presence of Europeans in their midst for over half a century, and almost all had come to prefer the French and their trade goods over the Spaniards and their religion. Nonetheless, in 1763, the Indians lost their French ally when, as a result of their defeat in the Seven Years' War, France ceded Louisiana to Spain and turned over their possessions east of the Mississippi River to Great Britain. It became crucial to the natives of Texas, as well as to the merchants of Louisiana, that Spain continue their liberal French trading policies and not adopt the ineffectual Franciscan methods. Without weapons, the Texas Indians—in particular, the Norteños, who were seen as the enemies of Spain—would be at the mercy of the Osage Indians, who lived in present-day Missouri and Arkansas and had access to British traders, now poised on the east bank of the Mississippi River. Other merchants, mainly Frenchmen, simply crossed the river illegally and ascended the Arkansas River to provide the Osages with weapons and manufactured goods in exchange for furs, as well as for horses and Indian slaves plundered from the Texas tribes. The Osages particularly targeted the Caddos

**North America Before 1763**

- English Claims
- French Claims
- Spanish Claims

and Wichitas on their raids. Unable to defend themselves adequately, the Tawakonis and Kichais retreated southward during the decade, establishing settlements in the Trinity and Brazos river valleys, including a landmark village at Waco.

Ultimately, Spain adopted a modified form of the French trading policies, by making peace with their heretofore Norteño enemies, and abandoning, for the most part, the missionary effort among the tribes. The Spaniards, however, put these policies into effect in a piecemeal fashion that took nearly two decades to complete. Matters were complicated by the fact that Spain administered Louisiana and Texas separately; the Captaincy-General of Havana controlled Louisiana, while Texas remained under the jurisdiction of the Viceroyalty of New Spain. In 1769, Louisiana governor Alejandro O'Reilly realized that the only way to win the allegiance of the Indians was to forgo missionary efforts and to follow French methods. Tribes that had been French allies, however, would now have to pledge an oath of fidelity to Spain. In return, the Spanish government would provide the tribe with annual presents and would designate distinguished leaders as chiefs, dignified by decorative medals. Although O'Reilly utilized French trading policies, he made significant modifications, forcing the tribes to deal only with licensed traders and forbidding them to deal in Native American slaves and livestock. In early 1770, the Kadohadachos along the Red River became the first group to transfer their allegiance from France to Spain when tribal representatives met in Natchitoches with Athanase de Mézières, the newly appointed commandant of the post. De Mézières was a Frenchman who had lived in Natchitoches since the 1740s and was a widower of the daughter of the town's founder, St. Denis. He had traded extensively with all the Caddo tribes and had advised Governor O'Reilly to adopt French methods of dealing with the Indians.

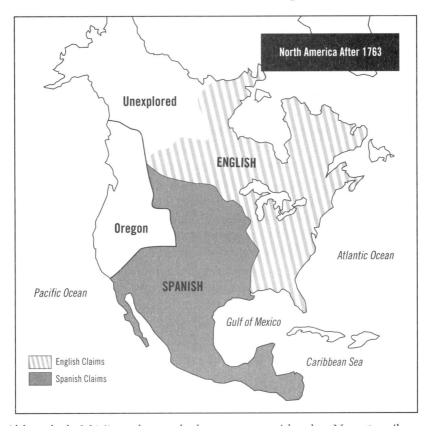

Although de Mézières also reached agreements with other Norteño tribes such as the Hasinais and the Wichitas, in addition to the Tonkawas and Atakapas, whole-scale Spanish changes in Texas—part of the empire-wide Bourbon Reforms—greatly complicated relations between the Indians and the Euroamericans of the colony. In 1767, the energetic new king of Spain, Charles III, sent the Marqués de Rubí to Texas to inspect the situation there and make recommendations for improvements. As a result of Rubí's report, the king issued the Regulation of 1772, a document designed to dramatically transform the way that Spain administered Texas. Realizing that most of the province's Indians had not responded to the ministrations of the Franciscan friars, the new rules mandated the adoption of the system that Spain now employed in Louisiana—that of dealing with the Indians principally through trade and gifts. Therefore, the Regulation of 1772 called for the abandonment of all missions and presidios in Texas, except those at San Antonio and La Bahía. Now that the French threat was gone, the king saw no need to maintain the capital at Los Adaes, so it, along with the four hundred settlers then living in East Texas, was moved to San Antonio. In addition, the regulations called for making peace with the Norteños at the expense of breaking the Apache alliance.

In early 1773, Viceroy Antonio María de Bucareli y Ursúa ordered the governor of Texas, Juan María Vicencio, Barón de Ripperdá, to bring about the immediate closure of the presidio and missions in East Texas and the prompt removal of the Adaeseño settlers. Whereas the isolated priests left the three missions without complaint, the Adaeseños protested the forced evacuation of their homes and the abandonment of their crops and livestock, which they were not given enough time to round up before their removal. Nonetheless, most of them followed the lead of Antonio Gil Ibarvo and accompanied the Spanish soldiers back to San Antonio in the summer of 1773. Immediately upon his arrival in Béxar, however, Gil Ibarvo traveled to Mexico City, where he convinced Viceroy Bucareli to permit the settlers to return to East Texas—but only as far as the Trinity River—in order to maintain friendly relations with the Hasinais and to make sure that British settlers from east of the Mississippi did not occupy the area. As a result, later that year Gil Ibarvo and a few of his compatriots founded the town of Nuestra Señora del Pilar de Bucareli where the road between San Antonio and Los Adaes crossed the Trinity River.

The town of Bucareli prospered for the first four years of its existence, with fifty families establishing residences there. Comanche raids and flooding, however, forced the colonists to abandon the settlement in early 1779 and move eastward to the site of the abandoned mission at Nacogdoches. Following lengthy discussions, Spanish officials gave the relocation their formal approval in October 1779, naming Antonio Gil Ibarvo the new captain of the militia and lieutenant governor of Nacogdoches. Soon thereafter, he began construction of a large house—now referred to as the Old Stone Fort—which served as a commissary, trading post, and his personal home. Gil Ibarvo also established an informal system of granting land verbally. By the early 1780s, about four hundred people lived in and around Nacogdoches, where they raised cattle and foodstuffs for their own consumption.

Although the Spaniards followed the king's orders and abandoned all of the missions and presidios except for those at San Antonio and La Bahía the year after the orders were issued, it took much longer to complete the peace process with the Norteños, and to initiate warfare against the Apaches. Spanish administrators in Mexico were unable to forget the massacre on the San Saba River and blocked de Mézières' efforts to negotiate a treaty with the Comanches. Things began to change in 1776 when viceregal control over Indian affairs in Texas was superseded by the creation of a new administrative unit, called the *Provincias Internas*. Consisting of all the northern provinces of New Spain (including Texas, but not Louisiana), the *Provincias Internas* was detached from the viceroy's jurisdiction and brought under the control of a commandant general who reported directly to the king. Free to deal with the Indians as he pleased, in 1778 the commandant authorized de Mézières to establish peace and trade with the Norteños in order to launch a campaign, in conjunction with Spanish troops, against the Lipan Apaches. The following year, however, Charles III vetoed the plan because of Spain's entry in the struggle against Great Britain that emerged from the American War of Independence. Following the end of the war with England in 1783, Texas governor Domingo Cabello resumed efforts to establish peace through trade with the Norteños and to isolate the Lipan Apaches. Assisted by French traders from Louisiana, finally, in October 1785, Comanche and Wichita headmen met with Cabello in San Antonio and reached the accord that both groups had been trying to achieve for a decade. Each party agreed to peace, and the Spaniards promised to distribute annual gifts and send traders to the Comanche and Wichita villages.

The Spaniards also encouraged the Norteños to make war upon the Apaches. Over the course of the next few years, Norteño warriors constantly attacked the Lipans in their homelands west and south of San Antonio. In late 1789, Spanish troops launched an offensive against the Apaches, assisted by Comanches and Wichitas. On January 9, 1790, the Spanish-Norteño force surprised a large Lipan village on Soledad Creek, a small tributary of the Medina River, and killed sixty Apaches, while capturing a large number of women and children in addition to nearly eight hundred horses. Following the rout on

Soledad Creek, well-armed Norteño warriors continued to pursue the beleaguered Lipans until finally, in April 1793, the Apaches entered into a treaty with Spanish officials in San Antonio. In return for agreeing to peace and refraining from stealing livestock, the Lipan leaders were granted the right to trade with the Spaniards, as long as they remained south of the Nueces River.

Just as relations between the Norteños, Lipan Apaches, and the Spaniards stabilized by the end of the century, the Karankawas also ended their hostilities. By the end of the 1780s, the constant warfare with the Spaniards had begun to weigh heavily upon the Karankawan groups. The situation was becoming particularly dangerous now that the innocuous Coahuiltecans had disappeared from the region, thus depriving the Karankawas of a buffer between themselves and the threatening Apache and Comanche raiders. Therefore, in 1794, groups of Cocos and Carancaguases gathered around the empty Mission Rosario, while other Karankawas agreed to settle at the final mission that the Franciscans had recently established in Texas, Nuestra Señora del Refugio. While only a few Indians spent the entire year at the two missions, many Karankawas incorporated the settlements into their way of life as yet another source of sustenance, as they traveled from the coast to the interior throughout the year. Although the Spanish officials and Franciscan priests disapproved of this casual approach to mission life, they realized that the stations promoted friendly relations, resulting in a peaceful understanding finally existing with the Karankawas during the final decades of Spanish Texas.

## Spanish Texas during the Late Eighteenth Century

By 1783, the non-Indian population of Spanish Texas had doubled—mainly through natural increase—to reach twenty-five hundred individuals, still concentrated in three settlements. The capital, San Antonio, was the largest of the Texas towns. The presidio counted about three hundred soldiers and their dependents, while the civilian population stood at twelve hundred men, women, and children. About six hundred people, two-thirds being civilians, lived at La Bahía, while another four hundred or so resided around the civilian village of Nacogdoches. About half of the settlers—known as Tejanos—were considered Spaniards (most of them creoles, born in America), while the other half had some form of Spanish, Indian, and African parentage. There were only twenty slaves of African descent in all of Texas. Males made up just over half of the population. Although women did not have equal status with men, Spanish laws and traditions gave them rights not generally accorded women in other societies. For example, Spanish law included the concepts of separate and community property, meaning that unmarried women who owned property, maintained title to that property even after marriage, and that married women shared equally in the ownership of property acquired after entering the bonds of matrimony. Community property could not be sold without the consent of both husband and wife.

Due to the lack of economic opportunities in Texas prior to the outbreak of the American Revolution, most of the civilians raised foodstuffs and livestock for their own consumption. Countless head of cattle and horses—nominally owned by the Franciscan missions—continued to roam on the open range between San Antonio and La Bahía. During the American Revolutionary War, however, the Spanish governor of Louisiana, Bernardo de Gálvez, initiated the famed Texas tradition of the cattle drive by allowing

Tejanos to send their cattle eastward across the border to feed his troops. Between 1779 and 1783, ten to fifteen thousand head of cattle were driven along a trail leading from La Bahía to Nacogdoches, across the Sabine River to Natchitoches, and then on to Opelousas, Louisiana. Texas vaqueros herded the cattle, and soldiers from several presidios served as escorts, thereby providing invaluable assistance to Gálvez, as his troops defeated the British at Baton Rouge, Mobile, and Pensacola.

Galvez's importation of cattle from Texas, along with the establishment of peace with the province's Indians, spurred the development of the private ranching industry in Texas during the late eighteenth century, especially as the numbers of Coahuiltecans at the missions continued to decline. In the late 1780s, Governor Rafael Martínez Pacheco organized two roundups and the branding of all unclaimed cattle roaming downstream from San Antonio. Neither roundup involved the participation of any of the Béxar missions and their Indians, as they were unable to field enough men or horses to do the job. Although the missions at La Bahía were involved, the roundups indicated the predominance of privately owned ranches over those belonging to the missions. Although the Franciscans had pioneered ranching in Texas, by the last quarter of the eighteenth century the absence of Indians had rendered the Béxar missions incapable of rounding up a single stray or mustang.

The lack of Coahuiltecans at Béxar forced Fray Francisco López, president of the Texas missions, to recommend in 1792 that the Valero mission be completely secularized, and that the administration of affairs for the other four missions be passed along to officials appointed by the government. Secularization meant that the government would be relieved of all financial responsibility for the religious establishments at San Antonio. The few mission Indians residing at those locations would henceforth become Spanish citizens with tax-paying obligations rather than continuing as wards of the state. The following year, viceregal officials in Mexico City ordered the complete secularization of San Antonio de Valero, followed the next year with a command to partially secularize the four remaining missions. Two missions were permanently closed, with its few Indians in residence transferred to the other two sites.

**Spanish Texas and the United States**

The incredibly slow growth of Spanish Texas—the Tejano population rose only to just over three thousand individuals by 1810—opened up the province to incursions (legal and illegal) by Anglo (or English speaking) Protestants from the newly-independent United States. Following the end of the American War for Independence in 1783—in which the United States acquired all the territory east of the Mississippi River except Florida, which reverted to Spanish control—Anglo Protestant settlers poured across the Appalachian Mountains into Kentucky and Tennessee, increasing the populations of those two states to 300,000 (one-fifth of them slaves) by 1800. Spain's ability to forestall the westward movement of Anglo-Americans across the Mississippi River was hindered by its 1795 defeat by French forces in the war caused by the outbreak of the French Revolution. This loss forced Spanish diplomats to abandon their claims to the northern part of American Mississippi Territory, which actually belonged to Spanish Florida, thus allowing Anglo Protestants from the United States to overwhelm the rich, agricultural district of Natchez, from where the first Americans began entering Texas in the 1790s.

Spain's loss to France also diminished ties between the mother country and its American allies. As result, the legal flow of Indian trade items to Texas necessary to maintain the alliance with the Norteños, light during the best of times, slowed to a trickle. Although Spanish officials in Texas did their best to ensure that the all-powerful Comanches received trade goods, they found it nearly impossible to supply the Wichitas and Caddos with enough weapons to defend themselves from the marauding Osages. An ample supply of illegal goods, however, existed among the Anglo Protestant traders in Natchez and elsewhere east of the Mississippi River, and the Indians of the region defied their Spanish allies by eagerly tapping into these sources.

Beginning in the 1790s, Anglos from horse poor Natchez traveled to the Texas plains to capture mustangs from the huge wild herds roaming near the Wichita villages. The first of these men to cross into Spanish lands, Philip Nolan of Belfast, Ireland, legally entered Texas from Natchez in 1791 with a passport obtained from the Spanish governor of Louisiana. Nolan established relations with the Wichitas and realized that, in addition to obtaining wild horses in Texas, he might supplement his income by providing the desperate tribes with trade goods. Nolan again received a passport to make legal trips into Texas in 1794 and 1797, and on both occasions he conducted illegal commerce with the Wichitas. In October 1800, however, Nolan and thirty Anglos entered Texas without passports and established a camp on a tributary of the Brazos River, upstream from the Tawakoni villages, and began rounding up mustangs. In March 1801, Spanish troops from Nacogdoches angered the Wichitas by locating the camp, killing Nolan, and capturing most of his men, who were later tried and imprisoned in Chihuahua, Mexico. However, a few of Nolan's associates who escaped to Mississippi were intent on returning to Texas to trade with the Wichitas and capture more horses.

The 1803 American purchase of Louisiana from France—which had acquired the province, on paper, from Spain in 1800—created great tension between the U.S. and Spain along the Louisiana-Texas frontier, because France had sold the huge expanse of territory without formally defining its western border. Thus, the boundary between Louisiana and Texas became subject to various interpretations, the most extreme being that of President Thomas Jefferson, who held that the border was the Rio Grande. Understandably, Spain scoffed at this claim, interpreting the line to be just a few miles west of the Red River, where it had been when France controlled Louisiana in the early eighteenth century. Since the situation was so tenuous, Spanish and American officials understood that the loyalty of the native tribes along the border would be crucial in any boundary determination. The Norteños were particularly central to this dispute because American officials held that the tribes formerly allied to France were now under their jurisdiction. Representatives of both nations realized that trade was crucial to win the tribes' favor. Despite the Spaniards' comprehension of the situation, their lack of resources and general ineffectualness would prove no match for the wealthy and energetic Americans in winning the Indians' allegiances.

American officials immediately took actions to provide the Norteños with the trade goods they desired upon taking possession of Natchitoches in early 1804. President Jefferson appointed John Sibley as the United States Indian agent for the region, who subsequently sent traders up the Red River with goods and American flags to the Kadohadacho and Taovaya villages while dispatching invitations to the Hasinais and Comanches of Texas to visit him at Natchitoches to initiate commerce. All three of the Norteño tribes welcomed Sibley's efforts and began providing the Americans with much-needed horses in exchange for metal goods and weapons. Upon the establishment of an official United States Indian trading post at Natchitoches in early 1806, the American commercial advantage over the Spaniards on the Louisiana-Texas frontier became complete.

In the meantime, President Jefferson began to arrange an exploratory venture—similar to the concurrent Lewis and Clark expedition on the Missouri River—along the Red River in order to more firmly establish the United States' claims along the border. Jefferson chose Major Thomas Freeman, an Irish-born surveyor, and Peter Custis, a doctoral student at the University of Pennsylvania, to ascend to the source of the Red River in an attempt to define the border between Louisiana and Texas. The Freeman-Custis expedition—consisting of three boats, twenty-one soldiers, and a black servant—entered the Red River in April 1806, doubled their numbers upon reaching Natchitoches the following month, and headed upriver once more in early June. Two weeks later, the Americans met with Dehahuit, the Kadohadacho chief, and promised that the United States would protect them and supply their wants in the future. The Kadohadacho leader gladly accepted this pledge and ordered three tribesmen to guide the expedition on to the Taovaya village.

Spanish officials, however, saw the expedition as an invasion of Texas and dispatched Lieutenant Colonel Simon Herrera and one thousand troops to the Red River to stop the Americans. On the way, the Spanish force passed through the Kadohadacho village on Caddo Lake, where Herrera brusquely tore down the American flag that was flying above it, informing Dehahuit that the town lay on Spanish soil. A couple of weeks later, the overwhelming Spanish force met Freeman and Custis on the Red River, and the expedition was obliged to retreat. Upon hearing the news of the expedition's fate, the American territorial governor of Louisiana, William C.C. Claiborne, sent a letter to Herrera protesting the Spanish troops' having stopped the expedition on U.S. soil and their having committed "another outrage" by chopping down the American flag in the Kadohadacho village. Lieutenant Colonel Herrera dismissed Claiborne's claims, asserting that the Indian town was not on American soil "and on the contrary the place which they inhabit is very far from it and belongs to Spain." Tensions between the two countries continued to mount, but war was averted in November 1806 when American General James Wilkinson and Herrera struck a deal, known as the Neutral Ground Agreement. The accord established a demilitarized zone between Louisiana and Texas that, though claimed by both countries, would remain ungoverned and unoccupied by Spain and the United States. This agreement remained in force until 1821, by which time the neutral zone had become a notorious home to fugitive slaves, outlaws, smugglers, and squatters from the United States, as well as a staging ground for filibustering expeditions into Texas.

The Freeman-Custis expedition and Spain's reaction served only to propel the Norteños further toward the Americans. Two weeks after the expedition was repelled, Dehahuit met with Claiborne in Natchitoches and accepted the governor's claim that the Kadohadachos were now subjects of the United States. Although the Spaniards had stopped the expedition before it could reach the Taovaya village, in the fall of 1806 Agent Sibley took advantage of the Neutral Ground Agreement and sent traders up the Red River, where they met and exchanged goods with Wichita and Comanche tribesmen. Texas Indians and the United States drew even closer in August 1807 when Sibley held a grand council at Natchitoches with the Caddos, Wichitas, and Comanches. Sibley addressed a gathering of the visiting headmen, inviting the Indians to deposit their goods

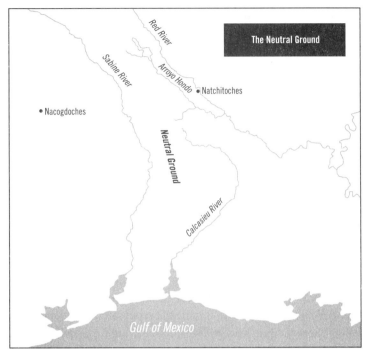

at Natchitoches and to accept American traders in their villages regardless of which side of the border they lived on. As a result of the grand council, the Taovayas welcomed Anthony Glass, a Natchez merchant familiar with the exploits of Nolan and his cronies, into their village the following summer. Glass and his men spent the fall and winter on the Red River obtaining horses and exchanging goods with various Comanche and Wichita headmen. By 1808, it had become clear that ample trade goods and skilled diplomacy had won over the Red River Caddoans, as well as many Comanches, to the American side of the boundary dispute.

**Revolution and War in Texas**

Although conflict had been avoided between Spain and the United States on the Louisiana-Texas frontier, a new round of fighting in Europe would soon throw Texas into even more turmoil. Following a brief lull in the wars of the French Revolution, in 1803, France—with Napoleon Bonaparte now crowned as emperor—and Great Britain resumed their struggle, with Austria, Prussia, and Russia soon joining the anti-Napoleonic coalition. After defeating Austria and Prussia and signing an armistice with Russia, Napoleon invaded Spain in February 1808, forced Carlos IV to abdicate, and placed his brother, Joseph Bonaparte, on the Spain throne.

Taking advantage of the chaos and confusion caused by Napoleon's invasion, a group of wealthy Mexican creoles decided the time was right to declare independence from Spain. In September 1810, a popular insurgency led by Father Miguel Hidalgo y Costilla broke out in Querétaro, about two hundred miles north of Mexico City. Hidalgo and his associates hoped to free Mexico from Spanish rule by advancing a radical agenda that called for social and economic justice, including the abolition of slavery with death to slaveowners who refused to free their chattel. The conspirators assembled a peasant army consisting of Mexicans, Indians, and mestizos who sacked the important mining town of Guanajuato in September 1810, exacting vengeance on the lives and property of the wealthy citizenry. The horrifying specter of social revolution sent a wave of fear through the upper classes of New Spain and quickly undermined much creole support for the revolutionaries. Nonetheless, Hidalgo's force was not thwarted until January 1811, when royalist forces won a decisive victory outside Mexico City. Hidalgo and other rebel leaders were eventually captured and executed, their heads being displayed on poles throughout the countryside.

News of the Hidalgo revolt spread northward to Texas, where sympathizers of the rebellion, led by Juan Bautista de las Casas, seized power in the province by orchestrating uprisings in San Antonio and Nacogdoches. By March 1811, however, royalists overthrew las Casas and effectively regained control of the province. A few rebels, most notably Bernardo Gutiérrez de Lara, a rancher and merchant from northern Mexico, slipped across the international border into Louisiana and traveled to Washington. Arriving at the capital in December 1811, Gutiérrez met with President James Madison and Secretary of State James Monroe who, while not officially approving of his call for the overthrow of Spanish Texas, provided him with money and transportation to New Orleans. Louisiana governor Claiborne then sent the rebel to Natchitoches in the company of William Shaler, a special agent charged with monitoring his activities. Arriving on the Louisiana-Texas frontier in April 1812, Gutiérrez, with Shaler's full support, began to gather volunteers for an invasion of Texas.

By August, Gutiérrez had assembled more than one hundred so-called filibusterers, most of them Anglos like Augustus William Magee, a West Point graduate and former lieutenant in the United States Army who entered Texas at the head of the self-styled Republican Army of the North. The force quickly captured Nacogdoches, where not a single civilian nor Indian answered the Spanish commander's appeal for volunteers to defend the town. The republicans then headed to La Bahía near the Texas coast and took control of the presidio there without a struggle, before finding themselves placed under a siege during which Magee died. After several weeks, the republicans lifted the siege, drove the royalist forces back to San Antonio, defeated them in battle, and forced their surrender on April 2. After Gutierrez approved the execution of a group of officials a few days later, including Governor Manuel Salcedo and Lieutenant Colonel Herrera, the rebels proclaimed the independence of Texas and promulgated its first constitution. Republicans' glory was short-lived, however, for a large, well-disciplined royalist army, commanded by Joaquín de Arredondo, marched upon San Antonio and crushed the unorganized republican mob in August at the Battle of Medina. The victors then unleashed a wave of vengeance in Texas, using confiscation, detention, and execution to restore royal authority. The royalists did their work so thoroughly that all of the residents of Nacogdoches and East Texas abandoned their homes and ranches and fled to Louisiana for safety, while the populations of La Bahía and San Antonio were severely reduced. Following a century of existence, the disastrous civil war in Texas returned the Spanish colony almost exclusively to Indian hands.

## The Final Years of Spanish Texas

Spanish Texas lay in ruins in the aftermath of the warfare that shook the colony between 1811 and 1813. Less than two thousand Tejanos remained in the province, three-fourths

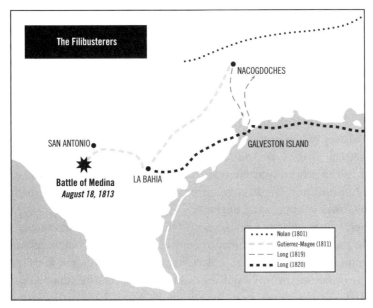

of whom lived near San Antonio, while the rest huddled around La Bahía. One observer lamented that in the second decade of the nineteenth century, Texas "had advanced at an amazing rate toward ruin and destruction," and that the country's resources had been drained of "everything that could sustain human life." Inept Spanish administration of the province did not help the desperate situation. In the four years following Arredondo's victory over the republicans, a succession of five interim governors ruled Texas. Finally, in 1817 Antonio Martínez began a term that proved to be the last for Spanish governors.

With the colony in tatters, the few Spaniards in Texas could hardly defend themselves from the many Indian tribes that turned hostile now that Spain could not provide them with the trade goods they desired. Induced by American traders on the Red River and in Louisiana to provide them with livestock, the Comanches, Wichitas, Lipan Apaches, and Tonkawas turned their attention to the great horse and cattle herds that still roamed throughout South Texas, initiating the most intense Indian warfare the Spaniards in the colony had experienced in three decades. Competition for livestock, combined with a drought that reduced the number of buffalo in Texas, caused the Comanches and Wichitas to wage war against the Tonkawas. Due to incessant Norteño pressure, the Tonkawas made peace with the Spaniards in 1818 and agreed that, in return for goods and protection, the tribe would assist the Tejanos in their battles against the Comanches, Wichitas, and Lipans—a policy that the Tonkawas would continue to follow for another half century.

Although disease had greatly reduced the population of the Caddos, Atakapas, Karankawas, and Coahuiltecans over the course of the eighteenth century, tribes from the United States took advantage of Spanish weakness and moved into the vacant lands of East Texas in the early 1800s. Following the Louisiana Purchase in 1803, a group of Muskhogean-speaking agricultural Native Americans asked and received permission from the Spaniards to relocate to the heavily forested region located one hundred miles south of Nacogdoches—soon to be called the "Big Thicket." By 1810, nearly one thousand Native Americans, led by the Alabamas and Coushattas, had established villages between the Neches and Trinity Rivers, in the territory of the nearly extinct Atakapas. Different groups of Native American refugees moved from the United States to the northeastern section of Texas following Arredondo's victory and the abandonment of Nacogdoches. Kickapoos, Delawares, and Shawnees, Algonquian speakers originally from Pennsylvania and Ohio, established villages southwest of the Red River's bend. The Cherokees, of Iroquoian linguistic stock, were emigrants who had originally lived in the southeastern Appalachian highlands of Georgia and Tennessee. Led by a chief named Duwali, the Cherokees established farms and ranches along the upper reaches of the Sabine, Neches, and Angelina River valleys within thirty miles or so north of Nacogdoches, near the few remaining Hasinai villages. By 1820, about two thousand emigrant Native Americans—more than a few of whom were literate English speakers—had settled in the relatively empty area of northeastern Texas, determined to carve out new lives for themselves based upon farming, stock-raising, and hunting.

Although a few hundred Tejanos reestablished their farms and ranches near Nacogdoches late in the decade, official Spanish control in East Texas remained minimal. Jean Laffitte, a pirate based in Louisiana, took advantage of the situation and moved his base of smuggling operations from Grand Terre in American-patrolled waters to Galveston Island in 1816. At the same time, Americans in New Orleans continued to support filibustering expeditions into Texas in hopes that they might result in the United States obtaining possession of the undeveloped province. Ignoring strong protests by Spanish diplomats, United States officials allowed Francisco Xavier Mina to purchase supplies and recruit a number of American soldiers in New Orleans for his badly organized invasion of Texas, which was defeated by Spanish royalists in April 1817. Following Mina's failure, President Monroe sent former Secretary of War George Graham to Galveston to try and win Laffitte's support for the American annexation of the Texas coast as far as Rio Grande. Graham's negotiations with Laffitte had come to nothing by October 1818, by which time Secretary of State John Quincy Adams began to consider seizing Galveston in an attempt to pressure Spain into ceding Texas to the United States.

The situation in Spanish West Florida—which General Andrew Jackson had invaded in 1818, taking possession of the Pensacola and defeating bands of marauding Seminole Indians—caused Adams to give up this idea, which even he realized was extreme. As a result of Jackson's invasion, on February 22, 1819, Adams and Spain's ambassador to the United States, Luis de Onís, signed the treaty that bears their names, in which Spain ceded Florida to the United States. In return, Adams relinquished his demand for Texas, drawing the boundary between the province and Louisiana at the Sabine River, only a few miles west of the former border between the Spanish and French territories. The two ministers continued to draw the boundary between Spain and the United States westward up the Red and Arkansas Rivers, then moving due west to the Pacific along the 42nd parallel, the northern border of Spanish California. Two years to the day after it had first been signed, on February 22, 1821, the treaty was formally ratified by Spain and the United States.

Although the Adams-Onís Treaty gave the United States complete possession over most of the Gulf South region, a few Americans were angry that the agreement had not included Texas. Therefore, in the spring of 1819 a Natchez merchant named James Long followed in the illustrious footsteps of other filibusterers by organizing an expedition designed to wrest control of Texas from the Spanish royalists. With about three hundred followers, Long occupied Nacogdoches in June 1819 and held it for a few months before Spanish troops drove him back to Louisiana. The following year, Long established a new

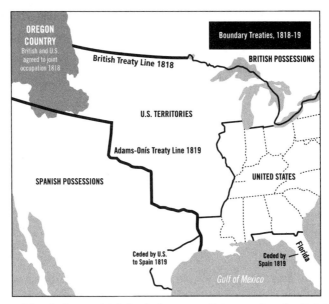

base on Galveston Island, from which he led an expedition against La Bahía in the fall of 1821. This time Spanish troops captured Long and sent him to Mexico City, where he died in captivity six months later. Although Long's efforts, like those of other filibusterers in Texas, had ended in abject failure, it would not be long before other Anglo Protestants from the United States would follow his lead and take possession of the province, ultimately resulting in Texas independence and, eventually, American statehood.

### *Afterward: After Pike—Changes to the Texas Landscape*

*Not long after he left Texas, the land that Pike so admired lay in ruins. During the Mexican independence movement against Spain in the 1810s, the northern provinces became the target of American filibusters. By 1820, the population of Texas had been reduced by half. Spanish authorities realized that unless something was done, they would lose the territory to their aggressive neighbors to the east. Failing to attract settlers to the northern provinces from central Mexico, Spanish officials became receptive to an idea proposed by Moses Austin, an entrepreneur who had past business dealings with the Spanish government in connection with lead mines that he and his family operated in Missouri. Austin proposed in 1820 to settle three hundred families in Texas if the Spanish government would provide him with a large grant of land. For Mexican officials, Austin's proposal solved one problem but created another. Three hundred families would help develop the northern provinces, but they could also potentially open the flood gates of American immigration, legal and illegal, into Texas. In 1821, with no other solutions available to them, Spanish officials granted Austin two hundred thousand acres of rich Texas land, setting a chain of event in place that would end with Texas independence and ultimately result in the United States taking ownership of Texas in 1845.*

# Myth & Legend

### The Lady in Blue

*The remarkable young Spanish nun, who became known as the "Lady in Blue," was born María Coronel y Arana on April 2, 1602, in Ágreda, Castile, north of Madrid. Religiously devout as a child, she took her chastity vow at the age of eight. Also religious, her aristocratic parents converted their castle into a convent and took their religious vows as a monk and a nun in 1618. On February 2, 1620, María became a nun of the Sisters of St. Clare (also known as Poor Clares). Their habits (regularly worn clothing) were white, covered with a blue mantle or cloak. Young María took the name María de Jesús de Agreda. A mystic and a writer, she wrote several tracts that have survived into the modern age, including* **Divine History of the Virgin Mother of God** *and* **Mystical City of God.**

*According to legend, between 1620 and 1631, María entered cataleptic trances and had otherworldly dreams (or hallucinations) wherein she had an out-of-body experience in which she supposedly traveled to strange, wild lands where she taught the Catholic religion and where she converted equally strange people to Christianity.*

*The strange people whom Sister María encountered consisted of two Indian tribes, the Caddos of East Texas and the Jumanos of West Texas. Between 1621 and 1629, numerous missionaries—working in East and West Texas and in today's New Mexico—encountered Indians who spoke no Spanish but described in their own language Sister María's visits. They carried crosses that were sacred to them, and they knew and practiced Catholic rituals. As well, they had Catholic alters in their villages, and they could repeat Catholic liturgy in their own language.*

*The natives told the early missionaries that the woman who visited them wore blue, taught them about Christianity, and told them to be kind to white-skinned people who would one day come among them.*

*Similar to the accounts of earlier missionaries, Father Damián Massanet reported in 1690 that the Tejas (Caddos) in East Texas told him that according to their oral history, a beautiful woman "came down from the hills," talked in their native language, and converted them to Christianity. They described the clothing the missionary wore that was most accurate about the habits of the Poor Clares: the "Lady in Blue" wore a white habit that was covered by a blue mantle. Soon, blue became the favorite (almost sacred) color of the Caddos. Father Massanet reported that one of the leaders of the tribe asked him for some blue baize to make a shroud for his mother when she died. The leader told Massanet that his mother and other elders remembered María's visits to their tribe. The Indians he visited confirmed the stories the earlier missionaries had heard. They told him that they already knew a missionary like him would come among them and that their lady told them to welcome such missionaries.*

*After reading Massanet's report, Fray Alonzo de Benavides attempted to solve the mystery of the "Lady in Blue." He managed to find a painting depicting a Poor Clare nun in her habit of white with blue mantle. He showed it to numerous older Indians who had earlier* verified that they had seen Sister María face-to-face. "Is this your lady?" Alonzo asked. They said no. They told him that the colors were right but that the nun depicted in the painting was old and somewhat rotund; whereas, their lady was young and beautiful.

After Fray Alonzo sent his report to Spain, an official went to the Poor Clare convent in Ágreda and asked if anyone was familiar with the "Lady in Blue." Now Mother María de Jesús de Ágreda—leader of the Poor Clare nuns—said that, indeed, she was the "Lady in Blue." The official could scarcely believe her because Poor Clare, over the years, had remained a cloistered order, the members of which never left the convent. To solve the mystery, Alonzo, himself, visited Mother María. In an interview, she told him in detail about the customs of the tribes she visited and even described their clothing. She gave him the names of various Indian tribes and their leaders. Alonzo heard enough to convince him that Mother María had indeed visited the Indians. While this story seems strange, it is the type of legend and myth that fills the annals of Texas history.

Logically speaking, we can find other potential explanations for María's "out-of-body experiences" that are somewhat less mystical and more grounded in reality. First, when just seven years old, María reportedly saw a play based on "The New World Unveiled by Christopher Columbus," written by playwright Lope de Vega. Apparently from that time forward, María felt a great missionary zeal to journey to the New World and Christianize the native peoples. However, because of her age and gender, she was not permitted to travel. Thus, she decided to devote her life to Christ as a nun. The fact that María saw this play is extremely important to her story. She would have gained some knowledge of the people in the New World even if the information represented in the play was not completely accurate. Additionally, the incident reveals that stories of the Americas circulated freely through her hometown. Because Ágreda was located between Castile and Aragon, an untold number of writers, journeymen, and adventurers would have passed near María's home. As a result, María could have found out all that she needed to know about the Americas without any real difficulty. It seems certain that her childhood desires to travel to the New World would have fueled María's thirst for knowledge of a region in the world that she could only visit in dreams.

Second, María was a controversial figure who challenged the norms of the Catholic Church. As such, many leading church leaders would have sought to either excommunicate her or at least censor her writings and teachings. In fact, María became such a disturbance that she was forced to endure an on-going investigation of the Spanish Inquisition beginning in 1635 and lasting until 1650. Undoubtedly, one reason she survived the inquiry was her close association with King Felipe IV.

These basic facts lead us to a possible explanation for the story of the "Lady in Blue." Given the nature of María's problems with the church, it is likely that her supporters, including the King of Spain, crafted the story to prevent her from suffering dire hardships at the hands of the Spanish Inquisition. After all, if her story was corroborated on both sides of the Atlantic Ocean, the inquisitors would have found it difficult to cast doubts on her religious beliefs, especially given her reputation as a missionary spirit in the American Southwest. For all practical purposes, the Spanish Inquisition would have found María virtually untouchable, because she had become one of God's chosen saints.

## Suggestions for Further Reading

Anderson, Gary Clayton. *The Indian Southwest, 1580-1830: Ethnogenesis and Reinvention* Norman: University of Oklahoma Press, 1999.

Britten, Thomas. *The Lipan Apaches: People of Wind and Lightning* Albuquerque: University of New Mexico Press, 2009.

Castaneda, Carlos E. *Our Catholic Heritage in Texas, 1519-1936.* (7 vols.) Austin: Von Boeckmann-Jones Co., 1936-1958.

Chipman, Donald E. and Harriet Denise Joseph. *Spanish Texas, 1519-1821* Austin: University of Texas Press, 2010.

de la Teja, Jesus F., *San Antonio de Bexar: A Community in New Spain's Northern Frontier.* Albuquerque: University of New Mexico Press, 1995.

Foster, William C. *Spanish Expeditions into Texas, 1689-1768* Austin: University of Texas Press, 1995.

Jackson, Jack. *Los Mesteños: Spanish Ranching in Texas, 1721-1821.* College Station: University of Texas A&M Press, 1986.

Jackson, Jack, and William C. Foster, eds. *Imaginary Kingdom: Texas as Seen by the Rivera and Rubí Military Expeditions, 1727 and 1767* (Austin: Texas State Historical Association, 1995).

John, Elizabeth. *Storms Brewed in Other Men's Worlds: The Confrontation of Indians, Spanish, and France in the Southwest, 1540-1795.* College Station: University of Texas A&M Press, 1975.

Jones, Oakah L. *Los Paisanos: Spanish Settlers on the Northern Frontier of New Spain.* Norman: University of Oklahoma Press, 1979.

Kessell, John L. *Spain in the Southwest: A Narrative History of Colonial New Mexico, Arizona, Texas and California* Norman: University of Oklahoma Press, 2002.

La Vere, David. *A History of the Indians of Texas.* College Station: Texas A&M Press, 2004.

Moorhead, Max L. *The Presidio: Bastion of the Spanish Borderlands.* Norman: University of Oklahoma Press, 1975.

Owsley, Frank L., and Gene A. Smith. *Filibusters and Expansionists: Jeffersonian Manifest Destiny, 1800-1821* Tuscaloosa: University of Alabama Press, 1997.

Pike, Zebulon M. *An Account of Expeditions to the Sources of the Mississippi, and Through the Western Parts of Louisiana, to the Sources of the Arkansaw, Kans, La Platte, and Pierre Juan, Rivers; Performed by Order of the Government of the United States during the Years 1805, 1806, and 1807. And a Tour Through the Interior Parts of New Spain, When Conducted Through These Provinces, by Order of The Captain-General in the Year 1807.* Philadelphia: C. & A. Conrad, & Co., 1810.

Smith, F. Todd. *The Caddo Indians: Tribes at the Convergence of Empires, 1542-1854* College Station: Texas A&M University Press, 1995.

___. *The Wichita Indians: Traders of Texas and the Southern Plains, 1540-1845* College Station: Texas A&M University Press, 2000.

Weber, David. *The Spanish Frontier in North America.* New Haven: Yale University Press, 1992.

Weddle, Robert S. *The French Thorn: Rival Explorers in the Spanish Sea.* College Station, University of Texas A&M Press, 1991.

**IDENTIFICATION:** Briefly describe each term.

René Robert Cavelier, Sieur de La Salle
Alonso de León
Martín de Alarcón
Los Adaes
Taovayas
San Gabriel Missions
The Norteños
Antonio Gil Ibarvo
Nuestra Señora del Refugio
Philip Nolan
John Sibley
Neutral Ground Agreement
Joaquín de Arredondo
Duwali
Adams-Onís Treaty



**MULTIPLE CHOICE:** Choose the correct response.

1. La Salle and the French landed at which bay on the Texas coast?
    A. Galveston Bay
    B. Matagorda Bay
    C. Corpus Christi Bay
    D. None of the above

2. The Franciscan missions in San Antonio served which tribe of Indians?
    A. Caddos
    B. Karankawas
    C. Coahuiltecans
    D. Atakapas

3. Louis Juchereau de St. Denis founded which settlement in Louisiana?
    A. Natchitoches
    B. Nacogdoches
    C. New Orleans
    D. Shreveport

4. The Indian group known as the Norteños consisted of all of the tribes below EXCEPT:
    A. Comanches
    B. Lipan Apaches
    C. Wichitas
    D. Caddos

5. The Franciscans established missions on all the rivers listed below EXCEPT:
   A. Brazos
   B. San Antonio
   C. San Saba
   D. Neches

6. The Regulation of 1772 was issued following the inspection tour of which Spaniard?
   A. Marqués de San Miguel de Aguayo
   B. Alonso de León
   C. Pedro de Rivera y Villalón
   D. Marqués de Rubí

7. Mission Nuestra Señora del Refugio was established for which Indian group?
   A. Tonkawas
   B. Tawakonis
   C. Comanches
   D. Karankawas

8. The first cattle drives originating in Texas headed to which province?
   A. New Mexico
   B. Coahuila
   C. Louisiana
   D. Oklahoma

9. The Freeman-Custis expedition explored which Texas river?
   A. Rio Grande
   B. Colorado
   C. Sabine
   D. Red

10. Which Indian tribe migrated to Texas from the United States in the 1800s?
    A. Chickasaws
    B. Creeks
    C. Cherokees
    D. Seminoles

**TRUE/FALSE:** Indicate whether each statement is true or false.

1. The Hasinai/Tejas Indians responded favorably to the Spanish Franciscans' missionary efforts.

2. Martin de Alarcón established the settlement of San Antonio in 1718.

3. The *Isleños* who settled at San Antonio originally came for the Cape Verde Islands.

4. The Norteños were trading partners and military allies of the French in Louisiana.

5. The Regulation of 1772 called for the Franciscans to reinforce the East Texas missions.

6. Spanish women in Texas were not allowed to keep their property once they married.

7. The Neutral Ground Agreement was established in 1806 between Spain and France.

8. Joaquín de Arredondo led the Republican Army of the North into Texas in 1812.

9. The Alabama and Coushatta Indians established villages in the Big Thicket in the early 1800s.

10. James Long fought to defend the Louisiana-Texas border established by the Adams-Onís Treaty.


**MATCHING:** Match the response in column A with the item in column B.

1. Joliet
2. Sieur de Cadillac
3. Coahuiltecans
4. Mission San Antonio de Valero
5. Comanches
6. Nuestra Señora del Rosario
7. Gil Ibarvo
8. Athanase de Mézières
9. Simon Herrera
10. Duwali

A. The Alamo
B. Cherokee chief
C. San Antonio missions
D. Natchitoches
E. Nacogdoches
F. Neutral Ground Agreement
G. Marquette
H. Karankawas
I. Treaty of 1785
J. Louisiana governor

**ESSAY QUESTIONS:**

1. Discuss the establishment of Spanish missions in San Antonio. Was the mission system a success or failure in San Antonio.

2. Discuss the trade established between the French in Louisiana and the Indians of Texas. Which tribes were involved and what items were exchanged?

3. Discuss the economic and social development of Texas under Spanish rule.

4. Discuss the various American intrusions into Texas in the late 1700s and early 1800s.

# The Northern Province of Mexico, 1821-1835

*Prelude: The Solution is Simple—Invite the Europeans*

*By the mid-1820s, Mexican officials became increasingly concerned about developments taking place in Texas. With or without the help of empresarios, Anglo-Americans and their slaves had migrated to the Mexican province in large numbers. Before the end of the decade, Anglo settlers not only outnumbered Mexican residents, but most of the American migrants refused to assimilate into Mexican society. The potential dangers to Mexican sovereignty became clear in Nacogdoches in 1826, when Americans in the area participated in the infamous Fredonian Rebellion. Following the Anglos' rebellion, General Manuel de Mier y Terán traveled throughout Texas examining conditions in the Mexican province. The general reported back to his superiors that the Mexican government could not depend on the loyalty of the American settlers who had moved into Texas. Mier y Terán would eventually make a series of recommendations to prevent further immigration from the United States. His suggestions were relatively simple: He called for the strengthening of existing presidios (Mexican fortifications) and the creation of new military garrisons in East Texas. In an effort to weaken United States commercial influence in Texas, he urged the increase of coastal trade between Texas and Mexico, and he suggested that European and Mexican colonists be persuaded to move into Texas to counter the growing American influence. Mier y Terán's recommendations would become the foundation for the Law of April 6, 1830.*

*Mexican authorities created a new government office, director of colonization, to enforce the Law of April 6, 1830. The first director was General Mier y Terán who held the office until July 1832, under the conservative administration of President Anastasio Bustamante. With a change in administration in Mexico City, the more liberal President Valentín Gómez Farías appointed Tadeo Ortiz de Ayala as director of colonization in August 1833. The new director had first-hand knowledge of the United States, Texas, and Europe, having traveled to these distant lands. He was also well versed in the problems and issues related to colonization of Mexico. Ironically, despite political differences, Mier y Terán and Ortiz held similar views when it came to solving the immigration crisis in Texas. Both men believed that counter-colonization was the key to saving Texas for Mexico, but each approached the task from a different perspective. Mier y Terán argued that Mexican settlers should be sent to Texas to offset* the effects of Anglos' migration into the province, while Ortiz believed it would be preferable to resettle Europeans in Texas.

Unfortunately for Ortiz, Mexico did not hold the same allure for European immigrants as it did for Americans. Apparently, Europeans avoided coming to Mexico because of the constant presence of political instability, a poor economy, religious intolerance, and ethnic tensions. Ortiz understood the nature of these problems and concluded that the only way to entice Europeans to Texas was for the federal government to develop new policies regarding immigration. Ortiz called on the government to initiate and finance widespread political, economic, and social reforms, including the acceptance of religious toleration, financial support to cover transportation cost, and the issuance of supplies such as food, tools, and other provisions needed for a fresh start in a new land. In accordance with the Law of April 6, 1830, such assistance had already been offered to Mexican settlers who would move to the northern frontier, but Ortiz suggested extending these privileges to Europeans as well. Unfortunately, the Ortiz proposal could not have come at a worst time. Mexico was suffering from a failed economy and continued political turmoil. Reformers found it difficult to pass any legislation in this unstable environment.

Despite his best efforts, Ortiz did not live long enough to see his ideas become a reality. Ortiz had received his appointment as director of colonization in August 1833, shortly after returning to Mexico City from a trip to Texas. He quickly made plans to return to the northern provinces but was delayed in the port city of Veracruz because of personal financial matters. The delay proved unfortunate as Ortiz died in the great cholera outbreak of that year. Even if Ortiz had lived, his plans to increase European colonization would have gone unfulfilled; it seems reasonable to assume that the instability and financial problems of the Mexican government would have prevented Mexican officials from funding the expensive programs that Ortiz had recommended.

Although Spanish royalists had quelled most of the unrest in Mexico by the end of the Napoleonic Wars in 1815, political instability in Spain led to outright independence in 1821. During the period in which Joseph Bonaparte sat on the throne of Spain, Ferdinand VII (the son of the abdicated king, Carlos IV) served as a unifying symbol to the Spanish citizens throughout Iberia and in the Western Hemisphere. The Central Junta at Seville governed in his name, but in 1812 a Spanish parliament met in Cádiz and wrote a constitution that limited the monarch's absolute power. Following principles championed during the American and French Revolutions, the liberals at Cádiz created a constitutional monarchy in which the king derived his power from the people, all of whom would be equal before the law. Upon his restoration to the throne in 1814, however, Ferdinand immediately dismissed the parliament, threw out the Constitution of 1812, and set out to destroy liberalism in Spain and America. His attempt to restore absolutism drew opposition at home and in Mexico, leading to a revolt by the Spanish army in 1820 that forced him to reinstate the Constitution of 1812 and reconvene the parliament.

Alarmed, conservative creoles in New Spain, who had envisioned a nation retaining the basic foundations of the colonial era but with themselves presiding over the society, determined that independence was preferable to living under a liberal rule that might well encourage the lower classes to challenge the social order. Agustín de Iturbide, the ranking royalist military commander, surfaced as the leader of this conservative faction. In the summer of 1821, Iturbide proposed to Vicente Guerrero, head of the main republican forces, the signing of an agreement to make Mexico an independent, constitutional monarchy with full protections for the Catholic Church and equal treatment under the law for Spaniards and creoles. This Plan de Iguala gained widespread support across Mexico, and the viceroy, seeing that opposition was hopeless, accepted it by signing the Treaty of Córdoba on August 24, 1821. At that point, Spanish Texas became Mexican Texas.

Finally free from the yoke of Spain, Mexico confronted the task of forming its own national government. Unfortunately, two antagonistic factions arose with different rationales for governing. One group, the Centralist Conservatives, included most of the landed aristocracy, military leaders and church officials, all of whom were favored by the Spanish government during colonial times. This faction sought not only to perpetuate their power by favoring a strong national government, but also to preserve the old economic and social order. Federalist Liberals, on the other hand, wished to mold a republic based on the precepts of the Constitution of 1812, promoting egalitarian ideals while diminishing the powers of the Church and the military, as well as establishing the state governments as a counterweight to the national government in Mexico City. For decades after independence, Mexico remained in flux politically while Centralists and Federalists vied for political control of their country. Iturbide, a Centralist Conservative at heart, took advantage of the chaos of Mexican politics by establishing himself as emperor in May 1822. Nine months later, however, a Federalist Liberal military commander named Antonio López de Santa Anna denounced him in the Plan de Casa Mata, and Iturbide was removed from power, opening the path for the creation of a federalist republic in Mexico. This liberal dream finally came to fruition in October 1824 with the promulgation of the Federal Constitution of the United States of Mexico.

**The Origins of Austin's Colony**

In the meantime, officials in Mexico had opened the door to American immigration into Texas, in part as a means of keeping the empty province from being annexed by the United States. In January 1821, Spanish officials in Texas had agreed to a proposal put forth by an American named Moses Austin, allowing him to establish a settlement in Texas. Born in Connecticut in 1761, Austin moved to Virginia in 1789 and for a short time thrived as a merchant and lead smelter. In 1797, following the failure of his businesses in Virginia, Austin secured a grant from the Spanish government to establish a lead mine in present-day Missouri, then a part of what was known as Upper Louisiana. Although he amassed sizeable wealth through his endeavors, Austin lost his fortune in the wake of economic turmoil caused by the War of 1812 and the Panic of 1819. At this point Austin conceived the idea of establishing an Anglo-American colony in Texas, hoping to recover his wealth through real estate transactions.

Austin traveled to San Antonio in December 1820, only to have Governor Antonio Martinez rebuff his colonization scheme. Before returning to Missouri, however, Austin encountered a respected San Antonio resident of Dutch ancestry whom he had met two decades before, the self-styled Baron de Bastrop. Austin's old friend intervened and persuaded Martinez to accept a proposal calling for the American to settle three hundred families in Texas and to create a town at the mouth of the Colorado River. Realizing that the Spanish hold on Texas was threatened by its lack of population, officials in Mexico agreed to the proposal in January 1821. However, before Austin could put his newly approved plan into action, he died five months later back home in Missouri.

Upon Moses Austin's death in June 1821, his son, Stephen Fuller Austin, assumed responsibility for the contract and began to make plans to establish a colony in Texas. Stephen F. Austin was born in Virginia in 1793 and moved with his father to Missouri later in the decade. He studied for two years at Transylvania University in Lexington, Kentucky, entered the family business, and served nearly five years in the territorial legislature of Missouri. When the Panic of 1819 ruined the Austin family financially, he lived briefly in Arkansas before moving on to New Orleans in 1820.

The next year, somewhat reluctantly at first, Stephen F. Austin took up his father's Texas project. He journeyed to San Antonio, landing in August 1821 just as news arrived that Mexico had gained independence from Spain. Throughout the rest of the year, Austin inspected the area near the mouths of the Colorado and the Brazos Rivers, and welcomed a few of the first settlers to his colony. In March 1822, however, Governor Martinez received word that national officials of the newly independent Mexico no longer recognized Austin's colonization contract. Compelled to press his claim in the nation's capital, Austin traveled to Mexico City. He arrived there in time to witness Iturbide's coronation as emperor in July, but was forced to wait until January 1823 before the passage of an Imperial Colonization Law that confirmed Austin's grant. Under its terms, each family in his colony would receive a *sitio* (or league) of land (4,428 acres) if they were stock raisers or a *labor* (177 acres) if they planned to farm. The land had to be occupied within two years and the settlers were supposed to be Catholic. The issue of slavery was somewhat unclear, but the law's provision that slave children were to be freed at age fourteen implied that settlers could bring bondspeople with them. Austin would receive for his services as *empresario* (land agent) twenty-two leagues (97,416 acres) from the government and a fee of sixty dollars from each family of colonists plus twelve and a half cents per acre for each league granted. Public lands in the United States cost ten times that amount during this period, thus ensuring that Austin would have little problem obtaining settlers for his fledgling colony.

While Austin was in Mexico, immigrants from the United States continued to move into his colony, defined as lying between the Lavaca and San Jacinto Rivers. Upon returning to Texas in the summer of 1823, he established the capital of the colony on the Brazos River, calling it San Felipe de Austin. From there, Austin and the Baron de Bastrop, who served as land commissioner, gave land titles to settlers, explained to them their responsibilities, and urged unity. In January 1824, Austin issued a set of law codes based upon a practical mix of Spanish and American legal concepts. By later that year, Austin had essentially fulfilled his contract, as the "Old Three Hundred" families—the original Anglo settlers of Texas—had established farms and ranches in the colony.

Austin's success in obtaining a land grant in Texas stood in opposition to attempts by the recently arrived Cherokees to gain clear title to their settlements. In November 1822, Richard Fields, the Cherokee war chief—who also handled diplomatic negotiations—traveled to San Antonio with twenty or so tribesmen and met with the new governor of Texas, José Felix Trespalacios. Fields was only one-eighth Cherokee but gained his important position by being literate in English, French, and Spanish. Arguing that his tribe could assist the Mexicans in dealing with the hostile Comanches and Wichitas, Fields concluded an agreement with the governor that gave the Cherokees official permission to settle in Texas. Realizing that the treaty was not valid without higher approval, Trespalacios sent Fields on to Mexico City to gain an audience with Emperor Iturbide. Although the Fields delegation was unable to meet with Iturbide before he was ousted as emperor in March 1823, upon their return to Texas the Cherokees acted as if the Trespalacios-Fields agreement was fully in force. Soon thereafter, the Cherokees formed an alliance with all the emigrant tribes in northeastern Texas, and Fields began to act as spokesman for the Delawares, Shawnees, and Kickapoos, as well as for his own people.

**The Shaping of Mexican Texas**

Whereas Austin had peopled his colony under the provisions of the Imperial Colonization Law of January 1823, Iturbide's government fell two months later, and Mexico began the process of transforming from an empire to a republic. With Iturbide removed from office, Mexican leaders gathered to write a constitution. In the meantime, on August 18, 1824, the Mexican congress passed the National Colonization Law, which left the individual states of Mexico with complete control over immigration and the disposal of public lands. The legislation instructed the states, however, to remain within the limits of the yet to be promulgated national constitution. Even though general sentiment in Mexico scorned human bondage, the law did not directly prohibit the importation of slaves or outlaw slavery.

Two months later, on October 4, 1824, the congress promulgated a Federal Constitution of the United States of Mexico, a victory for the Liberals in that it resembled the United States Constitution, while borrowing items from the Spanish Constitution of 1812. The main feature of the Constitution of 1824 was its federalism, granting each of the nineteen Mexican states control over their internal affairs while diluting the power of the central government. This feature had been a goal of Texas's sole representative at the constitutional convention, Juan Erasmo Seguín of San Antonio. Seguín worked to have provisions included in the constitution that were beneficial to his native San Antonio and to the Anglos living in Texas, for he believed that more immigration and capital from the United States would help the new republic develop economically, while at the same time preventing the United States from annexing the province. Against Seguín's wishes, Mexican officials united Texas with Coahuila as a single state (Coahuila y Texas) within the nation's federal system. Seguín, however, succeeded in having the constitution include provisions that would allow for Texas to petition for separate statehood at a future date, as well as providing a loose interpretation of the requirement that settlers must be Catholic, while broadly defining the nature of slavery in Texas by allowing settlers to possess "indentured servants."

Mexico's federal system greatly enhanced the importance of the state government of Coahuila y Texas. With its capital at Saltillo, located over three hundred miles to the south of San Antonio, the state legislature had one representative from thinly populated Texas and ten from Coahuila. Acting as a legislative as well as constituent body while it wrote a state constitution, the Coahuila y Texas legislature passed a vitally important Colonization Law on March 25, 1825. This act, following the outlines of Iturbide's law in 1823, offered settlers a league and a *labor* of land for less than one hundred dollars in fees, which could be paid over six years with nothing due for the first four. Empresarial contracts were to run for six years and became void if one hundred families had not been settled in the colony by that time. Successful empresarios were to receive five leagues of grazing land and five *labores* of farm land for each one hundred families they resettled into their colony. Settlers agreed to become Mexican citizens and practicing Catholics. Another act passed by the state legislature in 1825 separated Texas from the rest of Coahuila for administrative purposes and called for the state governor in Saltillo to appoint a political chief to reside in San Antonio and take primary responsibility for the government there. The act also designated the Nueces River as the line dividing the Department of Texas from Coahuila. Finally, the state legislature completed the writing of a constitution for the state of Coahuila y Texas in 1827. The constitution divided Texas into four municipalities: Béxar, Goliad (La Bahía renamed with an anagram of Hidalgo), San Felipe de Austin, and Nacogdoches. Each municipality was governed by a four-man council called an *ayuntamiento*, which had responsibility for local roads, buildings, and taxes. An *alcalde*, an official who combined the powers of mayor, sheriff, and judge, presided over the *ayuntamiento*. Adult male citizens elected the *alcalde* and the members of the *ayuntamiento*.

**Early Empresarios and the Fredonian Rebellion**

While Mexican Texas took shape constitutionally and politically, Austin and other empresarios, most of them Anglo Protestants from the United States, brought in thousands of colonists. Between 1821 and 1835, a total of forty-one empresarial contracts were signed, permitting over thirteen thousand families to come to Texas. Whereas most of the empresarios did not come close to fulfilling their contracts, three of the earliest land agents were among the most successful. Stephen F. Austin, the original empresario, received four additional contracts calling for a total of seventeen hundred more families, and extending the boundaries of his colony into central Texas beyond present Austin and Waco. Although never fulfilling any of these contracts to the letter or actually expanding much farther northwest than his original colony, Austin succeeded in bringing nearly fifteen hundred families to Texas by 1835. Texas's second empresario, Martín de León, actually received his grant before the passage of the Colonization Law of 1825. The previous year, the provisional government in San Antonio granted the Mexican-born de León the right to settle forty-one Mexican families on the lower Guadalupe River and found a town to be named for Guadalupe Victoria, a hero of the independence movement. De León brought all the Mexican families to his colony, in addition to welcoming more than one hundred Anglo Protestant and Irish Catholic families onto his lands before his death in 1833. Green DeWitt, a native of Kentucky, received a contract to settle four hundred families in a colony located adjacent to de León's and Austin's grants. Establishing his capital at Gonzalez, fifty miles up the Guadalupe River from Victoria, DeWitt was only able to settle about one hundred fifty families in his colony before his contract expired in 1831.

Although there were disputes between DeWitt and de León due to the poorly defined boundaries of their respective colonies, Haden Edwards proved to be the most problematic of all the various empresarios of Texas, causing trouble for the province's Mexicans, Anglos, and Native Americans alike. A native Virginian who had relocated to Kentucky, Edwards received a contract allowing him to settle eight hundred families in East Texas

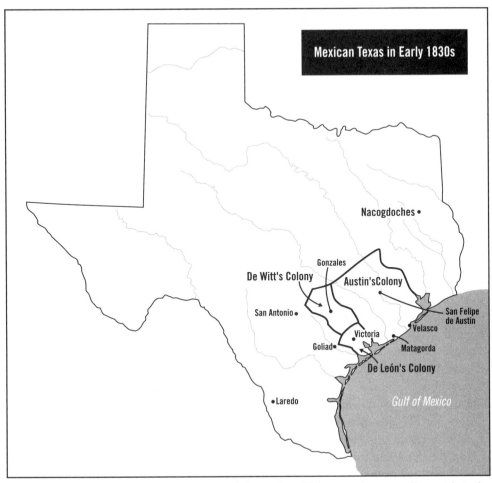

around Nacogdoches, an area teeming with long-time Tejano settlers as well as with Indians, led by the Cherokees and their emigrant allies.

Edwards arrived in Nacogdoches in September 1825 and immediately issued a decree ordering all residents to produce titles to their lands. Old settlers protested, but the empresario ignored their complaints and then made matters worse in December by certifying the election of his son-in-law as alcalde of Nacogdoches. The old settlers appealed to José Antonio Saucedo, the political chief in San Antonio, who overturned the election in March 1826 because most of the Edwards supporters were unqualified to vote due to not yet owning land. Soon thereafter, the government officials, objecting to his actions and the tone of his correspondence with them, nullified Edwards's empresarial contract. In November, Edwards responded by leading a group of thirty-six settlers to Nacogdoches, where they arrested the alcalde, the commander of the town's small Mexican garrison, and other officials. The following month, Edwards and his cronies declared independence from Mexico and proclaimed their colony to be "the Republic of Fredonia." Seeking to gain military support for the rebellion, Edwards signed a treaty with the Cherokee diplomat, Richard Fields, awarding the tribe and its allies title to all lands lying north of Nacogdoches. The revolt collapsed, however, early in 1827 when the more successful, Anglo colonists denounced the affair and Austin led his colony's militia, along with Mexican officials, to Nacogdoches to suppress it. Angered that Fields had threatened the Cherokees' claims in Texas, Chief Duwali had the diplomatic leader executed. In return for Duwali's assistance, the Mexican government rewarded him with a lieutenant colonel's commission. Despite Austin's display of loyalty to Mexico, the Fredonian Rebellion heightened Mexican concerns that further American immigration might dissolve the fledgling republic's hold on Texas.

**Texas Becomes an Anglo Protestant Province**

By the end of Mexico's first decade of independence, approximately ten thousand Anglos lived in Texas, most of whom had come from the southern portion of the United States. Initially they arrived from the states closest to Texas—Louisiana, Arkansas, Mississippi, and Missouri—but increasingly they journeyed from older states such as Georgia and Virginia as well. New arrivals from the upper South tended to move into northern Texas and those from the lower South into southern areas of the province, establishing a pattern that held throughout the next century. Nearly all of the Southern-born colonists in Texas were Protestants, unwilling to comply with the requirement that they convert to Catholicism. Most immigrants lived on land acquired through empresarios, although a good many, especially in northeast Texas along the Red River and in East Texas around San Augustine, had illegally entered on their own. Regardless of how they arrived, the great majority came in family units, lured by cheap land on which they supported themselves as small, self-dependent farmers, planting gardens and raising hogs and cattle.

Although subsistence remained the first priority, a trend toward cash-crop agriculture also developed very quickly. Farmers in Austin's colony produced six hundred bales of cotton by 1827, and other colonists followed suit as quickly as they could. Cotton production depended on African slavery, which in turn provided the strongest link between Texas and the American South. Enslaved Africans had existed in New Spain but had never become truly important anywhere outside Veracruz, and certainly not on the northern frontier. During the final decade of Spanish Texas, only thirty slaves lived in Nacogdoches, while less than ten toiled in San Antonio and La Bahía. American colonists made slavery an institution of significance in Texas from the beginning, in part because they saw it as an economic necessity. No family could clear enough land or provide enough labor to move beyond subsistence agriculture, and free labor could not be hired where land was so inexpensive. Therefore, the only way to raise the cash crop of cotton was through slave labor, workers who could be owned and controlled. Most Texas immigrants were Southerners who had generations of experience with slavery and held racist views that allowed them to see nothing wrong with the practice of whites owning blacks in order to profit from their labor. Any moral qualms that may have remained were mitigated by a belief in the Christianizing and civilizing benefits of the institution. Some of the first settlers in Austin's colony, including the empresario himself, were slaveholders. As early as January 1822, Jared E. Groce brought ninety slaves from Georgia to Austin's grant and established a cotton plantation on the Brazos. A census enumeration from 1825 shows nearly four hundred fifty slaves out of a total of eighteen hundred people residing in Austin's colony, and the empresario's law code provided the legal means necessary to protect slavery.

Regardless of its economic potential, however, slavery faced opposition in Mexico. Officials throughout Mexico considered slavery an evil but recognized the rights of property and the need for economic development, so they took a stand on the institution that was negative enough to alarm the Anglo Protestant colonists but too weak to prevent its growth. For example, Iturbide's Colonization Law of 1823, which applied only to Austin's first colony, permitted slavery but called for emancipation of Texas-born slave children when they reached the age of fourteen. In 1824, the national constituent congress prohibited the importation of slaves into Mexico, but the colonization law and constitution it adopted the same year did not mention slavery, thus seemingly leaving the issue up to the individual states. Although the Colonization Law of 1825 passed by Coahuila y Texas said nothing important about slavery, Article 13 of the state constitution of 1827 clearly stated that no one shall be born a slave in the state and prohibited the further introduction of bondspeople into the province. In September 1827, the legislature enacted a law to put this statute into effect, thus signaling the end of slavery in Texas in the near future.

These actions confirmed the worst fears of many Anglo Protestant immigrants to Texas, including the most important empresario, Stephen F. Austin. While he occasionally made statements critical of slavery, overall Austin continuously worked to ensure immigrants the opportunity to bring slaves into the province and keep them for life. Austin unsuccessfully opposed Article 13 of the 1827 state constitution, but in early 1828 settlers found a way around its restrictions. In March, the *ayuntamiento* of San Felipe de Austin sent a suggestion to the state legislature stating that slaves would be "freed," then brought into Texas and held indefinitely as indentured servants working to pay their former masters for freedom. Austin endorsed the proposal, and José Antonio Navarro, a representative from Texas, introduced it in the state legislature, which formally adopted the policy in May 1828, thus assuring the continued growth of slavery in Texas. The following year, however, President Vicente Guerrero issued a decree in September emancipating all slaves throughout Mexico. The political chief at San Antonio, Ramón Múzquiz, appealed to the governor at Saltillo to have Texas exempted from the decree because it threatened the development of the province. President Guerrero responded to this appeal by issuing another decree in December, exempting Texas from the general emancipation. By the beginning of 1830, when it seemed that the slavery issue had finally been settled in the interests of the Anglo Protestant immigrants, the ten thousand or so newcomers to Texas owned more than one thousand slaves.

At this point, the aggressive, slave-owning Anglo Protestants threatened to overwhelm the province's four thousand or so Tejano Catholics. Most of the Tejanos lived in San Antonio, Goliad, and Victoria or on ranches in their vicinity. Nacogdoches also had a sizeable Mexican population, as did Laredo, although that town at the time was technically part of Coahuila rather than Texas. Mexico had no more success than Spain in persuading settlers to move to the northern frontier, so population growth among Tejanos had mainly occurred during the decade through natural increase rather than immigration. A few wealthy ranchers, such as José Antonio Navarro and Juan Erasmo Seguín, constituted the powerful elite of Tejano society, while most of the population consisted of poor folk who worked in some manner for the great landowners. Many of the Tejano elite dreamed of a dynamic, capitalistic northern Mexico that would build an expanding economy based on trade with the United States and the growth of cotton, thus they supported the Anglos' efforts to protect slavery in the province. On the other hand, they did not wish to lose control to the Anglo Protestant immigrants, who generally showed little respect for their traditions and thought of themselves as racially superior as well. The independent Tejanos were also interested in maintaining political control of their province, and opposed efforts of the central government in Mexico City, and even the state government in Saltillo, to harness their power.

The Anglo settlers of Texas also thought themselves to be racially superior to the province's Native Americans. Like their southern kinsmen in the United States, they began taking steps in the 1820s to remove the Indians from their ancestral lands in order to establish farms, ranches, and cotton plantations. Whereas the Lipan Apaches and Penateka Comanches entered into peace treaties with the Mexican government in 1822 and, for the most part, remained well to the west of the newly established empresarial colonies, the Karankawas and Tonkawas resided within the confines of Austin's colony, as well as on the periphery of DeWitt's and de León's colonies. Although the Brazos and Trinity River villages of the Wacos, Tawakonis, and Kichais were located more than one hundred miles above the colonies of Austin and DeWitt, these three Wichita tribes were also greatly impacted by the newcomers. The chaos of Mexican politics in the 1820s left Austin virtually in charge of dealing with the Indians in the region, and he adopted different policies for handling the Karankawas, Tonkawas, and Wichitas. Unfortunately for all three of the tribes, the end result was disaster.

Austin was most interested in the Karankawas, since the tribe occupied the all-important coastal region of his colony, controlling the mouths of the Brazos and Colorado Rivers. The empresario set the tone for relations with the Karankawas immediately upon encountering them for the first time while on his survey of Texas in 1821. Austin subsequently warned his colonists that the Karankawas were "universal enemies to man," adding, without any evidence, that they were cannibals who "frequently feast on the bodies of their victims." He prophesized that the approach of the Anglo settlers "will be the signal of their extermination for there will be no way of subduing them but extermination." This attitude, shared by most of the colonists, quickly led to the outbreak of violence between the Anglos and the Karankawas, resulting in the full realization of Austin's prediction concerning the tribe's disappearance.

Anglo settlers clashed with the Karankawas almost immediately upon their arrival, accusing the Indians of theft and murder. In 1824, Austin led an armed force of ninety men against the Karankawas and forced them to take refuge with the Franciscans at La Bahía. The priests brokered a deal in which, in return for peace, the Karankawas agreed to abandon the lower Brazos and Colorado and remain west of the Guadalupe River. Many Karankawas, however, stayed in their homeland, becoming fair game for Austin's colonists who began to attack them on sight until a second peace settlement was arranged in 1827. The surviving Karankawas moved down the Gulf Coast of Texas, where their numbers continued to decline over the next few years. In little more than a half decade, the Karankawas had been pushed off their ancestral lands between Galveston Bay and Matagorda Bay.

At the same time that the Anglos initiated warfare against the Karankawas, the settlers laid the foundation for an alliance with the Tonkawas, who lived along the upper reaches of the Austin and DeWitt grants between the Brazos and Guadalupe River. Learning that the Tonkawas had just recently formed an alliance with the Spaniards aimed at the Comanches and Wichitas, in April 1824 Austin also entered into an agreement with their leaders. In return for annual gifts of food, trade goods, and arms, the Tonkawas agreed to remain north of the Anglo settlements and act as auxiliaries against the colonists' enemies, namely the Wichita groups located farther inland. The following year the Tonkawas came to the aid of Austin and his settlers following a series of Waco and Tawakoni raids upon the colony. Tonkawa warriors joined with Austin's militia units—the antecedents of the Texas Rangers—to track down and kill the Waco and Tawakoni raiders. In 1826, Austin's forces, along with a group of Tonkawa scouts, invaded the territory of the Wichitas, forcing the Wacos and Tawakonis to temporarily abandon their Brazos River villages, bringing an end to their raids for a couple of years. Neither the peace with the Wichitas, nor the alliance with the Tonkawas, would last into the next decade, as Texas increasingly became an Anglo Protestant province.

**The Law of April 6, 1830 and the Anahuac Rebellion**

The Fredonian Rebellion, and the aggressive behavior of the Anglo Protestant newcomers in Texas, heightened concerns in Mexico that further American immigration might dissolve the nation's hold on the province. In order to evaluate how the national government might best deal with the situation in Texas, Mexican officials dispatched Manuel de Mier y Terán, a high-ranking military officer and trained engineer, to the north. Crossing into Texas in 1828, Mier y Terán found that Anglo Protestants now dominated the province, particularly in the eastern section where Nacogdoches had essentially become an American town. He also noted that the immigrants generally resisted obeying the colonization laws and that they had a negative view of Mexicans, thus there was little hope that the newcomers could be assimilated into the Mexican Catholic culture. Upon returning to Mexico City in 1829, Mier y Terán prepared a formal report on his inspection, bluntly stating that unless further immigration from the United States was suspended, Mexico would lose Texas to its northern neighbor.

Political instability in Mexico, however, delayed a quick response to Mier y Terán's alarming report. President Manuel Gómez Pedraza, a Conservative centralist elected in 1828, was overthrown in April 1829 by supporters of Vicente Guerrero, the Liberal federalist who had previously served as vice president. Eight months later, another coup removed Guerrero and replaced him with Vice President Anastasio Bustamante, a Conservative who sought to weaken the states and strengthen the central government. With the support of the new president, the Mexican congress responded to Mier y Terán's report by passing the Law of April 6, 1830. This act prohibited further immigration from the United States, ended all empresarial contracts not yet fulfilled, outlawed bringing slaves to Texas under any guise, and called for the collection of customs duties on imports and exports. Stepping up their initiative, the conservatives reinforced the presidios at San Antonio, Goliad, and Nacogdoches with soldiers and commissioned the building of more garrisons, among the most important being Velasco, at the mouth of the Brazos River, and Anahuac, founded on Galveston Bay. Situated near the Gulf Coast, these two forts were to discourage the infiltration of illegal immigrants by sea.

The passage of the Law of April 6, 1830, which threatened the position of the Anglo slaveholders in Texas, led to the formation of a radical faction of men, known as the "War Party." Led by such immigrants as James Bowie, Branch T. Archer, and William Barrett Travis, their party helped sway public opinion among the Texans in favor of armed resistance against Mexico and, ultimately, for a call for outright independence. The War Party initially focused their efforts against Colonel John D. Bradburn, an Anglo mercenary serving the Mexican army and the Centralists, who was placed in charge of establishing the post at Anahuac in October 1830. After objecting to Bradburn's actions in collecting customs and suppressing smuggling, Anglo settlers turned violent in June 1832 after the colonel arrested Travis when he used a ruse to try and secure the release of two runaway slaves that Bradburn had in protective custody. When Bradburn refused to release Travis, Anglo Protestants from the area assembled and marched on the Anahuac garrison. Following a short skirmish, the attackers stopped short to await reinforcements before commencing a wider conflict. Instead of fighting, the War Party issued a document known as the Turtle Bayou Resolutions on June 13, 1832, which argued that their actions at Anahuac were not a rebellion but a demand for their constitutional rights as Mexican citizens. Soon thereafter, the tense situation was diffused when the Mexican authorities recalled Bradburn and released Travis from jail. While bloodshed had been avoided at Anahuac, the episode led to deaths on both sides at the newly installed presidio at Velasco. Before the situation at Anahuac had been settled, about one hundred Anglo settlers had traveled to the mouth of the Brazos to obtain a cannon for use in opposing Bradburn. Colonel Domingo de Ugartachea, the commander at Velasco, tried to stop the force, and a battle broke out resulting in the deaths of seven Anglo rebels and five Mexican soldiers, the first casualties of the undeclared revolution.

**Requests for Separate Statehood**

Despite the violence, the War Party failed to garner widespread popular support among the Anglo Protestant immigrants to Texas. Instead, a "Peace Party" emerged, led by Austin, which preferred to work for solutions to settlers' grievances through established political channels. In August 1832, the *ayuntamiento* of San Felipe de Austin called for a convention, which met there on October 1. Fifty-eight delegates—all Anglos except one—attended and elected Austin as president of the consultation. They drafted a petition asking that Texas be exempted from customs duties for another three years and that the ban on immigration from the United States in the Law of April 6, 1830, be lifted. They also requested that Texas should be separated from Coahuila. Nothing came of the Convention of 1832, primarily because Ramón Múzquiz, the political chief at San Antonio, declared that the petition lacked legality. Under Mexican law, petitions of this type could only come from *ayuntamientos*, not from conventions.

Undeterred, Austin persuaded his Tejano friends in San Antonio to draft a reform petition to the state legislature. In late 1832, leading citizens of Béxar, among them Juan Nepumenco Seguín (son of Juan Erasmo Seguín) and José María Balmaceda, met in their own consultation. The Béxareños criticized interference by the national government in state colonization and contended that the Law of April 6, 1830 threatened to dissuade useful capitalists from moving to Texas. They further demanded bilingual administrators, more judges, better militia protection from hostile Indians, and certain tax exemptions for businesses. The *ayuntamientos* of Goliad, Nacogdoches, and San Felipe endorsed the Tejanos' petition, and Political Chief Múzquiz submitted it to the governor, explaining that the petition was designed to remedy a situation that might otherwise lead the Anglos to try and separate Texas from Coahuila. What the Tejanos wanted, he assured the governor, were reforms, not the creation of their own state. They understood that should Texas become a separate state with its own legislature, the Anglo Protestant immigrants, who already outnumbered the native Mexicans, would dominate politics.

**Antonio López de Santa Anna, between 1850 and 1876. Photo credit: Library of Congress**

Since little had come out of the 1832 convention, another was held at San Felipe de Austin in April of the following year. This second convention, however, was not controlled by Austin and older, moderate settlers, but by men like William Wharton, who were more recent arrivals willing to take stronger stances against Mexico. Wharton, whom Austin had defeated for the presidency of the 1832 convention, presided this time. A new resident of the province, Sam Houston, represented Nacogdoches at the Convention of 1833, supporting Wharton and the more aggressive colonists. Born in Virginia in 1793, Houston moved with his family to Tennessee at an early age, and then ran away from home and lived with a band of Cherokee for several years. Joining the United States Army during the War of 1812, Houston served under Andrew Jackson, suffering near-fatal wounds fighting against the Creek Indians at the Battle of Horseshoe Bend in 1814. He studied law and then, as a protégé of Jackson, was elected governor of Tennessee only to resign in 1829 following the breakup of his marriage. After three aimless years with the Cherokees, during which he gave in completely to his weakness for alcohol, Houston moved to Texas in 1832. At the Convention of 1833, Houston joined with Wharton, David G. Burnet, and others, to put forth a petition asking for a repeal of the Law of April 6, 1830, and for separate statehood for Texas. Upon adjourning, the second consultation entrusted Juan Erasmo Seguín, Stephen F. Austin, and James B. Miller, a Kentucky-born doctor who had come to Texas in 1829, with taking the grievances to Mexico City. Seguín and Miller could not make the trip, however, so Austin made the long journey to the capital alone.

Austin had reason to be optimistic that the petition put forth by the Convention of 1833 might be adopted by the national government, because Antonio López de Santa Anna, a Liberal Federalist, had been elected as president of Mexico in January 1833. Back in favor, the Liberals in Coahuila y Texas immediately arranged for the state legislature to petition the national government for the repeal of the Law of April 6, 1830. Now they had more helpful allies in Mexico City, among them Vice President Valentín Gómez Farías who assisted Santa Anna's election to the presidency and served as acting chief executive when the president retired to his Veracruz hacienda. Another important Federalist ally, Lorenzo de Zavala, a legislator from Yucatán, also worked in favor of repeal, as he held interests in Texas lands for which he sought settlers from the United States. In November 1833, these men succeeded in convincing the national congress to revoke the portion of the Law of April 6, 1830 that limited the immigration of settlers from the United States, effective six months later.

Despite this action, the national government refused to separate Texas from Coahuila. When Mexican officials discovered letters that Austin had previously written in a moment of despair, encouraging the people of Texas to move forward with the creation of a separate state government and declare their independence from Coahuila, regardless of the federal government's decision, Farías ordered his arrest and imprisoned him in Mexico City. For three months beginning in February 1834, Austin was held in solitary confinement. Two Texas lawyers, Patrick Jack and Peter Grayson, then arrived at the capital to take up the case, arguing that Austin was being held without an indictment or a decision as to what law had been violated, let alone having a trial. Thanks to their efforts and numerous appeals from *ayuntamientos* in Texas, Austin was allowed to post bail and leave prison on Christmas Day, 1834. He had spent nearly a year in jail, and another eight months would pass before he could obtain amnesty and return home.

During his long absence, though, developments had generally favored Texas. Throughout 1834, the state legislature of Coahuila y Texas passed several important reforms. A liberal land law allowed Anglos to buy directly from the state on generous terms. English became an official language in the state, and its citizens received the right to trial by jury, a practice unique in all of Mexico. The legislature also divided Texas into three departments—Béxar, Brazos, and Nacogdoches—and accordingly increased its representation from one to three seats. These reforms seemed to demonstrate the general ineffectiveness of the Law of April 6, 1830. Since Mexican officials had not been strict in interpreting the provisions of the decree, Anglo Protestant settlers from the United States had continued to come into those colonies whose empresarios had imported the minimum one hundred families by the time the law had been enacted. In addition, two empresario groups from Ireland persisted in their efforts to complete contracts they had acquired in the late 1820s. James McGloin and John McMullen brought several Irish Catholic families to the mouth of the Nueces River in 1831 and founded San Patricio, while James Power and James Hewetson located Irish settlers near Mission Refugio.

At the same time, the Galveston Bay and Texas Land Company, a land-speculating corporation from the United States that the empresarios Joseph Vehlein, David G. Burnet, and Lorenzo de Zavala had commissioned to complete their contracts, continued to advertise the availability of property in Texas, despite the passage of the Law of April 6, 1830. Thus, the company sold invalid land certificates to several European families who, not being Americans, were ultimately accepted by Mexican officials and allowed to settle in Texas. In 1825 Robert Leftwich had received an empresarial contract to settle lands situated northwest of Austin's grant, but no one colonized them until the early 1830s, when a Tennessean named Sterling C. Robertson took over the contract for what was called the Texas Association of Nashville, Tennessee. Robertson successfully settled numerous families on his grant while the immigration law had been in effect. Finally, many Anglo Protestant immigrants from the United States simply migrated illegally to Texas between 1830 and 1834.

**Native Americans in the 1830s**

The Anglos' success in obtaining land came at the expense of the province's Native Americans. Realizing the difficulty of preventing American immigration into Texas, Mier y Terán had hoped to temper the tide of illegal settlement by providing the emigrant Indians of East Texas with title to their lands. While in Nacogdoches on his tour of Texas in 1828, Mier y Terán had been visited by emissaries from the east Texas tribes—including the Cherokees, Delawares, Shawnees, and Alabama-Coushattas--who he opined were equal, if not superior in character to many of the American settlers he encountered. Therefore, in the summer of 1831, following an Alabama-Coushatta request for a land grant, Mier y Terán put in motion the process by which the East Texas emigrant tribes might gain secure possession of their territory. In July, he instructed José María Letona, the governor of Coahuila y Texas, to award a concession of land to the Alabama-Coushattas and have the boundaries of their holdings surveyed. A month later, he ordered the governor to put the Cherokees and their allies in possession of a fixed tract of land between the Trinity and Sabine Rivers.

Just as it seemed that the emigrant tribes might finally secure legal title to their lands, events conspired to deny them once again. In July 1832, Mier y Terán, despondent over his failure to check American immigration into Texas, committed suicide. Governor Letona died of yellow fever in the same year. Vicente Filisola, Mier y Terán's successor as commanding general of the Eastern Interior Provinces, did not follow through on his predecessor's plan to obtain land for the East Texas Indians, for the Mexican government had awarded him an empresarial grant on lands where the Cherokees lived. As a result, the Indians' petition for land stalled before receiving approval from the national government.

Although the Alabama-Coushattas gave up their attempts to obtain legal rights to the land, the Cherokees continued moving forward. In July 1833, Chief Duwali traveled to San Antonio and asked Miguel Arciniega, interim political chief of Béxar, to follow through on the grant of land promised them two years before. The following month Duwali traveled to Monclova and met with the new governor of Coahuila y Texas, Juan Martín de Veramendi. After listening to Duwali's argument, Veramendi judged that, although the Cherokees were not to be moved from their lands, the Indians were living on General Filisola's grant, and that no determination pertaining to their status could be made until his empresarial contract expired. Despite the Cherokees' efforts, the East Texas Indians had yet to obtain clear title to their lands as the end of the Mexican era approached.

In the meantime, most of the emigrant tribes tried to secure their lands by joining with American settlers and Mexican troops in attacking the Wichitas and Comanches in Central Texas. Ironically, the Mexican army, which had been reinforced after the Law of April 6, 1830 in order to contain American immigration, directed many of the campaigns against the two tribes. As a result of their efforts, the Mexican forces succeeded in reducing the Indian threat to Texas settlers, opening up the region to even greater numbers of illegal American immigrants. The numerous Anglos, in turn, eventually decided to remove the Indians from Texas as well as trying to wrest control of the province from Mexico altogether. By 1835, many original inhabitants of Texas had been driven from the lands that they had so securely possessed just a decade before.

The Wichita tribes were the first to feel the wrath of the Texas forces. Throughout 1828 and 1829 Austin encouraged the Cherokees and their allies to attack the Wacos and Tawakonis in their villages on the Brazos River, resulting in great loss of life, as well as horses and supplies. Finally, in August 1830 the military commandant of Texas, Colonel Antonio Elosúa, ordered Captain Nicasio Sánchez to lead a force to the Brazos to assault the Wacos and Tawakonis. Alerted that the Mexican force was approaching, the two Wichita tribes quickly harvested their corn crops and abandoned their villages. Sánchez, finding both towns empty, destroyed the Waco and Tawakoni towns by ordering his men to burn all the houses and supporting structures, as well as confiscating their remaining stored supplies. Following the destructive Sánchez campaign, the Wacos permanently abandoned their villages and retreated farther up the Brazos to join the Taovayas, who were in the process of moving north of the Red River and out of Texas. Most of the Wacos settled in villages along the upper Brazos and near the mouth of the Wichita River. A few Wacos joined the Taovayas, who eventually settled in a village near present Lawton, Oklahoma, where they would remain for the following two decades. Over the course of the following four years, Mexican troops and Anglo militia groups consistently attacked the remaining Tawakonis on the Brazos, as well as the Kichais on the Trinity, ultimately driving them northwestward toward the Red River, far from any Anglo settlements, by 1835.

With the defeat and removal of most of the Wichita tribes from Central Texas, Mexican officials in 1832 ordered a campaign against the Comanches. Assisted by the emigrant tribes, as well as Lipan Apache and Tonkawa auxiliaries, Mexican forces attacked Comanche villages located west of the Colorado River. Despite the assault upon Comanche towns, the Mexicans and their allies were unable to dislodge the mobile Penatekas, and warriors continued to raid throughout Coahuila y Texas over the next two years. At the same time, however, Penateka leaders began to negotiate a peace treaty with the Mexican authorities. In the summer of 1833, and again in 1834, Comanche chiefs traveled to San Antonio to discuss a truce. In February 1835, a party of nearly four hundred Comanches arrived in Béxar to return horses and mules that had been stolen by young tribesmen. As a result of these peaceful demonstrations, Martín Perfecto de Cos, the new commanding general of the Eastern Interior Provinces, met with three hundred Comanches in Matamoros in August 1835, and the two parties agreed to end their hostilities. On the eve of the Texas Revolution, the largest and most powerful Native American group in Texas had once again entered into a peace treaty with the Mexican forces that controlled the province.

Although the Mexican troops failed to remove the powerful Comanches from Texas, their soldiers succeeded in driving the beleaguered Karankawas even farther from the various empresarial grants. Beginning in 1830, de León's colonists petitioned the Mexican government to punish the starving Karankawas for repeated thefts of their livestock. As a result, Mexican army assaults reduced the Karankawas to a group of only two hundred who lived in the lowlands around Refugio. Free from the threat of Karankawa and Wichita hostilities, Anglos from Austin's and DeWitt's colonies went ahead and forced their erstwhile Tonkawa allies from their midst. Denied access to the buffalo-laden plains by the Comanches, the famished Tonkawas began to steal livestock and corn from the Anglo colonies. As a result, settlers from both colonies attacked the Tonkawas and forced them to move northwest of San Antonio by 1835. Within a decade and a half of the founding of Austin's colony, the Anglos, with the assistance of Mexican troops and the emigrant tribes, had completely driven the original Karankawa, Tonkawa, and Wichita inhabitants from the region. Future settlers in Texas over the course of the next twenty-five years would follow the example set by their predecessors and remove most of the remaining Indians from the province.

**Texas in 1834**

Concerns over conditions in Texas led national officials in Mexico City to authorize yet another investigative mission to province in 1834. Colonel Juan Nepomuceno Almonte spent several months in Texas during the summer of 1834 and prepared a detailed report. Almonte estimated that the province had a population of 21,000 non-Indians—4,000 in the Department of Béxar, 8,000 in Brazos, and 9,000 in Nacogdoches. Béxar had no slaves, while the other two departments had one thousand each. Although his statistics demonstrated the ever-increasing control of the Anglo Protestants, Almonte found the political situation generally quiet and suggested that stability in the government of Mexico would maintain calm in Texas. Austin, still out of prison on bond in Mexico City but much encouraged by the reforms of 1834, agreed and decided that separate statehood could wait. Few observers considered revolution imminent in Texas at the beginning of 1835, but Santa Anna's return from retirement in April 1835 and the dictatorial actions he took soon thereafter, set the process in motion through which Texas would gain its independence one year later.

*Afterward: The Results of Tadeo Ortiz de Ayala's Failed Policy*

*In mid-November 1833, a month after Oritz's death, the Mexican Senate rescinded the anti-immigration clause of the Law of April 6, 1830. Two prominent Mexican officials, Lorenzo de Zavala and José Antonio Mexía, were among the legislators who owned land in Texas and who worked to reverse the federal policies. De Zavala and Mexía both had business connections with American financiers and wanted immigrants from the United States to settle on lands that they held.*

*No new director of colonization followed Ortiz. Tensions continued to grow between the Mexican government and the Anglo-American settlers in Texas. These tensions would eventually result in revolution despite the effort of men like Tadeo Ortiz de Ayala who attempted to dilute the American's influence in the frontier regions of his country.*

# Myth & Legend

**Multiculturalism in Early Texas**

*In truth, Texas has always had a multicultural society, even though some Texas history texts targeting the public schools leave readers with the thought that white Americans, who came from the South, were the authors of all the great achievements in Texas history.*

*To understand the diverse past of Texas, one need not look much beyond the plaques at the Alamo that identify those (whose identities could be confirmed) who died during the epic battle there. At least eight Tejanos died inside the walls of the old Spanish mission as did many Europeans, including six men from England, nine from Ireland, one from Denmark, four from Scotland, two from Germany, and one from Spain. There were likely other Tejanos and Europeans, whose identities can not be validated, but the point is clear—the defenders of the Alamo represented the diversity of Texas at that time.*

*On May 27, 1965, the Texas Legislature created the Institute of Texan Cultures (located in San Antonio), an act that began the state's participation in HemisFair '68. The HemisFair '68 was the first officially designated world fair held in the American Southwest. The international exposition was hosted in 1968 in San Antonio, and the theme of the fair was "The Confluence of Civilizations in the Americas." The legislators wanted to display exhibits celebrating all the ethnic groups and racial groups that had contributed mightily to the development of the Lone Star State. Toward that end, they approved plans to build a substantial structure to house all the displays. Thus, the Institute of Texan Cultures was born. Built at the high tide of the Civil Rights Movement, the project had the support of President Lyndon B. Johnson, a native Texan, supporting the project with federal funds. Unlike some HemisFair '68 activities, the Institute became a permanent fixture and is now attached to the University of Texas at San Antonio. Not exactly a museum, the Institute operates much like one. Even today, long after the Hemis-Fair ended, one can view various displays that celebrate multiculturalism in Texas. This is important because visitors at the Institute are reminded that even before Texas was a Republic, multiculturalism was a vital part of Texas's heritage. These displays highlight the achievements of many cultural groups, including Czech, Slovak, German, Pole, Tejano, African American, and Native Americans.*

*Prior to Texas becoming a republic, emigrants from a variety of foreign countries came to Mexican Texas, adding to the Indian and Tejano populations that were already extant. Between 1821 and 1835, the Mexican government gave forty-one empresarios grants of land on which to settle immigrants. Although Mexico gave a majority of such contracts to Anglos from the United States, other groups emigrated as well, a movement that lasted well beyond the Texas Revolution. Each group in the ethnic mix brought their own unique culture with them when they settled. Consequently, diversity came early to Texas: diversity in religion, in languages, in social institutions, in world views, in education, in ancient traditions and festivals (still observed), and even in choice of food and preparation of that food. Most historians hold that anytime two different groups meet, civilization advances, for the two share such things as trade goods and, more important, they learn from each other. Knowledge advances as civilizations incorporate new groups.*

*To acknowledge the diversity in the state, the Institute of Texan Cultures has published extensively on the different groups that have contributed to the history of Texas, including the Institute's series titled "Texans All." This series includes: **The Indian Texans, The Mexican Texans, The European Texans, The African Texans, and The Asian Texans**. These books are a wealth of knowledge for anyone wanting to know more about the foreign immigrants of Texas.*

## Suggestions for Further Reading

Anna, Timothy E. *Forging Mexico, 1821-1835* Lincoln: University of Nebraska Press, 1998.
Anderson, Gary Clayton. *The Conquest of Texas: Ethnic Cleansing in the Promised Land, 1820-1875* Norman: University of Oklahoma Press, 2005.
Barker, Eugene C. *The Life of Stephen F. Austin: Founder of Texas, 1793-1836.* Nashville and Dallas: Cokesbury Press, 1925.
Campbell, Randolph B. *An Empire for Slavery: The Peculiar Institution in Texas.* Baton Rouge: Louisiana State University Press, 1989.
_____. *Gone to Texas: A History of the Lone Star State* New York: Oxford University Press, 2012.
Cantrell, Gregg. *Stephen F. Austin: Empresario of Texas.* New Haven: Yale University Press, 1999.
Crimm, Ana Carolina Castillo. *De León: A Tejano Family History* Austin: University of Texas Press, 2003.
Davis, Graham. *Land! Irish Pioneers in Mexican and Revolutionary Texas* College Station: Texas A&M University Press, 2002.
Everett, Dianna. *The Texas Cherokees: A People Between Two Fires, 1819-1840* Norman: University of Oklahoma Press, 1990.
Gracy, David B. II. *Moses Austin: His Life.* San Antonio: Trinity University Press, 1988.
Haley, James L. *Sam Houston* Norman: University of Oklahoma Press, 2002.
Henson, Margaret S. *Lorenzo D. Zavala.* Fort Worth: Texas Christian University Press, 1996.
Himmel, Kelly F. *The Conquest of the Karankawas and Tonkawas, 1821-1859* College Station: Texas A&M University Press, 1999.
Jackson, Jack. *Indian Agent: Peter Ellis Bean in Mexican Texas* College Station: Texas A&M University Press, 2005.
Kelley, Sean. *Los Brazos de Dios: A Plantation Society in the Texas Borderlands, 1821-1865* Baton Rouge: Louisiana State University Press, 2010.
Lukes, Edward A. *DeWitt Colony of Texas.* Austin: Jenkins, 1976.
Smith, F. Todd. *From Dominance to Disappearance: The Indians of Texas and the Near Southwest, 1786-1859* Lincoln: University of Nebraska Press, 2005.
Tijerina, Andres A. *Tejanos and Texas under the Mexican Flag, 1821-1836.* College Station: Texas A&M Press, 1994.
Torget, Andrew J. *Seeds of Empire: Cotton, Slavery, and the Transformation of the Texas Borderlands, 1800-1850* Chapel Hill: University of North Carolina Press, 2015.
Weber, David J. *The Mexican Frontier, 1821-1846: The American Southwest Under Mexico.* Albuquerque: University of New Mexico Press, 1982.

**IDENTIFICATION:** Briefly describe each term.

Centralist Conservatives
Federalist Liberals
Moses Austin
Stephen F. Austin
Coahuila y Texas Colonization Law
Fredonian Rebellion
Martin de León
Richard Fields
Anglo Protestants
Slavery in Texas
Waco Village
Law of April 6, 1830
Anahuac
Juan Erasmo Seguín
Antonio Lopez de Santa Anna

**MULTIPLE CHOICE:** Choose the correct response.

1. All of the following groups favored the Centralist EXCEPT:
   A. Landed Aristocracy
   B. Military Leaders
   C. Church Officials
   D. Guadalupe Victoria

2. Moses Austin lived in all of the following states EXCEPT:
   A. Connecticut
   B. Virginia
   C. Tennessee
   D. Missouri

3. Stephen F. Austin's Colony was situated between which Texas rivers?
   A. Sabine and Neches
   B. Brazos and Trinity
   C. Colorado and Guadalupe
   D. Lavaca and San Jacinto

4. All of the following men received empresarial contracts EXCEPT:
   A. Sam Houston
   B. Green DeWitt
   C. Haden Edwards
   D. Martín de León

5. All of the following Indian tribes were allies with the Cherokees EXCEPT:
   A. Wichitas
   B. Shawnees
   C. Kickapoos
   D. Delawares

6. The Law of April 6, 1830 was the result of whose report?
   A. Vicente Guerrero
   B. Anastasio Bustamante
   C. Antonio Lopez de Santa Anna
   D. Manuel de Mier y Terán

7. The Turtle Bayou Resolutions were issued after the outbreak of violence at which town?
   A. Galveston
   B. Anahuac
   C. San Felipe de Austin
   D. Victoria

8. Sam Houston was the former governor of which state?
   A. Virginia
   B. Alabama
   C. Kentucky
   D. Tennessee

9. The state legislature of Coahuila y Texas divided Texas into which three departments?
   A. Béxar, Goliad, and Nacogdoches
   B. Béxar, Brazos, and Nacogdoches
   C. Goliad, Brazos, and Nacogdoches
   D. Béxar, Goliad, and Brazos

10. In 1834, Juan Nepomuceno Almonte estimated the population of Texas was:
    A. 10,000 non-Indians and 5,000 slaves
    B. 21,000 non-Indians and 5,000 slaves
    C. 21,000 non-Indians and 2,000 slaves
    D. 10,000 non-Indians and 2,000 slaves

**TRUE/FALSE:** Indicate whether each statement is true or false.

1. Mexican independence resulted in a united nation.

2. Stephen F. Austin encouraged an alliance with the Karankawa Indians.

3. Mexican land grants in Texas were cheaper than those in the United States.

4. Haden Edwards was the leader of the Fredonian Rebellion.

5. Stephen F. Austin consistently opposed slavery in Texas.

6. The Law of April 6, 1830 sought to curtail immigration from the United States.

7. John D. Bradburn led the fight against the Mexicans at Anahuac.

8. Sam Houston was a delegate to Stephen F. Austin's consultation of 1833.

9. The Comanche Indians made peace with Mexican officials in the early 1830s.

10. Most American who immigrated to Texas were from the South.


**MATCHING:** Match the response in column A with the item in column B.

1. Agustín de Iturbide
2. "Old Three Hundred"
3. Juan Erasmo Seguín
4. Goliad
5. Haden Edwards
6. Jared E. Groce
7. William B. Travis
8. Convention of 1833
9. Sterling C. Robertson
10. San Patricio

A. William Wharton
B. Irish empresarial grant
C. Emperor of Mexico
D. War Party member
E. La Bahía
F. Texas Association of Nashville, Tennessee
G. Austin Colony settlers
H. Tejano delegate
I. Fredonian Rebellion
J. Texas slaveholder

**ESSAY QUESTIONS:**

1. Compare and contrast the Centralist Conservatives and Federalist Liberals and their views on governing independent Mexico.

2. Explain the empresarial system in Texas and discuss the successes or failures of the various empresarios.

3. Discuss the slavery question as it pertained to the central Mexican government, the state legislature of Coahuila y Texas, and the Anglo Protestant settlers of Texas.

4. Discuss the situation of the Native Americans of Texas during the Mexican period, paying particular attention to the Cherokees, Wichitas, Karankawas, and Tonkawas.

# Revolutionary Texas: The Birth of the Republic, 1835-1836

**Prelude: A Texan Remembers the Victory at the Battle of San Jacinto**

*On April 21, 1836, Texans won their independence from Mexico by defeating Santa Anna's forces at the Battle of San Jacinto. Undoubtedly, this was the most important victory in the Texas Revolution. Texas Secretary of War Thomas J. Rusk was an eyewitness and participant in the Battle of San Jacinto. As such, Rusk recorded his observations of the battle in a report that he sent to David G. Burnet, the ad interim president of Texas. Rusk wrote:*

> Sir: I have the honor to communicate to you a brief account of a general engagement with the army of Santa Anna at this place, on the 21st instant. Our army, under the command of General Houston, arrived here on the 20th instant. The enemy, a few miles off at Washington, appraised of our arrival, committed some depredations upon private property, and commenced their line of march to this point. They were unconscious of our approach until our standard was planted on the banks of the San Jacinto. Our position was a favorable one for battle. On the noon of the 20th, the appearance of our foe was hailed with enthusiasm. The enemy (marched in good order, took a position in front of our encampment, on an eminence within cannon-shot, where they planted their only piece of artillery, a brass nine-pounder; and then arrayed their cavalry and infantry a short distance on the right, under the shelter of a skirt of woods. In a short time they commenced firing upon us; their cannon in front, their infantry on the left, and their cavalry changing their position on the right. A charge was (made on the left of our camp by their infantry, which was promptly repelled by a few shots from our artillery, which forced them to retire . . . .
>
> The attack ceased; the enemy retired and formed in two skirts of timber, and remained in that position, occasionally opening their fire upon us, until just before sunset, when they attempted to draw off their forces. The artillery and cavalry were removed to other points. Colonel Sherman, with sixty of our cavalry, charged upon theirs, consisting of upward of one hundred, killing and wounding several. Their infantry came to the assistance of their cavalry, and opened upon us an incessant fire for ten or fifteen minutes . . . . This terminated the movements of the day.

> Early next morning, about nine o'clock, the enemy received a reinforcement of 500 men, under the command of General Martin Perfecto de Cos, which increased their force to fourteen or fifteen hundred men. It was supposed that an attack upon our encampment would now be made; and, having a good position, we stationed our artillery, and disposed of the forces, so as to receive the enemy to the best advantage. At three o'clock, however, the foe, instead of showing signs of attack, was evidently engaged in fortifying. We determined, therefore, immediately to assail him; and, in half an hour, we were formed in four divisions; the first, intended as our right wing, composed of the regulars under Colonel Millard, and the second division, under command of Colonel Sidney Sherman, formed our left wing. A division, commanded by Colonel Burleson, formed our center. Our two six-pounders, under the command of Colonel Hockley, Captains Isaac N. Moreland and Stillwell, were drawn upon the right of the center division. The cavalry, under the command of Colonel Mirabeau B. Lamar, formed upon our right. At the command to move forward, all the divisions advanced in good order and high spirits. On arriving within reach of the enemy, a heavy fire was opened, first with their artillery on our cavalry. A general conflict now ensued. Orders were given to charge. Colonel Sherman's division moved up, and drove the enemy from the woods occupied by them on their right wing. At the same moment, Colonel Burleson's division, together with the regulars, charged upon and mounted the breastworks of the enemy, and drove them from their cannon, our artillery, the meanwhile, charging up and firing upon them with great effect. The cavalry, under Colonel Lamar, at the same time fell on them with great fury and great slaughter. Major-General Houston acted with great gallantry, encouraging his men to the attack, and heroically charging, in front of the infantry, within a few yards of the enemy, receiving at the same time a wound in the leg.
>
> The enemy soon took to flight, officers and all, some on foot and some on horseback. In ten minutes after the firing of the first gun, we were charging through the camp, and driving them before us. They fled in confusion and dismay down the river, followed closely by our troops for four miles. Some of them, took the prairie, and were pursued by our cavalry; others were shot in attempting to swim the river; and in a short period the sanguinary conflict was terminated by the surrender of nearly all who were not slain in the combat. . . . This glorious achievement is attributed, not to superior force, but to the valor of our soldiers and the sanctity of our cause. Our army consisted of 750 effective men. This brave band achieved a victory as glorious as any on the records of history, and the happy consequences will be felt in Texas by succeeding generations. It has saved the country from a yoke of bondage; and all who mingled in it are entitled to the special munificence of government, and the heart-felt gratitude of every lover of liberty. . . .
>
> Thomas J. Rusk, Secretary of War.

With their victory at San Jacinto, the Texans had secured their independence. The road to freedom had been paved with many hardships and failures, but through it all the people of Texas endured.

## The Outbreak of War

Although tensions between the Mexican government and the Anglo settlers of Texas had been simmering since at least early 1827, it was not until after Antonio López de Santa Anna resumed control of Mexico that war actually erupted. In April 1835, Santa Anna removed his acting president, Valentín Gómez Farías, whose liberalism had thoroughly alienated the Catholic Church and the established military. Resurfacing as a reactionary, Santa Anna abolished the Constitution of 1824 and held elections for a new congress composed of Conservatives who supported the powers of the army and the Church. In October 1835, the new congress took steps to create a Centralist state in Mexico by dissolving all state legislatures and turning the former states into military departments, over which presidential appointees would now govern.

The dissolution of federalism produced revolts in several Mexican states. Zacatecas opposed the new order most resolutely, but Santa Anna crushed the rebellion unmercifully, allowing his soldiers to brutalize the state's citizens, killing thousands. The people in Yucatán also broke with the government at this time, managing to retain their separatism until 1846. Meanwhile, in Monclova (which had become the capital of Coahuila y Texas in 1833), liberal politicians denounced Santa Anna's new government in the summer of 1834. The legislature refused to obey Centralist orders, and in March and April of 1835 it passed two laws designed to raise money for resisting Santa Anna. The decrees authorized the governor to sell up to four hundred leagues of public land in order to obtain funds to fight the Centralists, and they designated another four hundred leagues with which to compensate militiamen willing to take up arms against hostile Indians. A few Anglo Texans in Monclova acquired grants during the crisis by promising to raise and equip one thousand-man companies on these lands. Fearing that these militias might be used against the central government, Colonel Domingo de Ugartechea, now the principal commandant in Béxar, called upon General Martín Perfecto de Cos to muster reinforcements. Cos, the commanding general of the northeastern Mexican states, relayed the request to President Santa Anna.

Responding to reports that Mexico was preparing to send troops into Texas, Anglo settlers near Anahuac, the scene of the 1832 disturbances, took matters into their own hands and made the town the focal point for renewed difficulties in 1835. In the spring, Captain Antonio Tenorio triggered hostilities when he arrived in Anahuac with a small detachment of troops and orders to reestablish the customhouse there. Local residents accused Tenorio of collecting higher duties than usual and responded by smuggling and refusing to provide supplies for the Mexican soldiers. Tensions between Tenorio and local residents reached a climax in June when William Travis, a leader in the original Anahuac uprising, raised a party of between twenty-five and fifty armed volunteers who descended upon the town and forced Tenorio to surrender, allowing his forty or so troops safe passage to San Antonio. Although the old grievance regarding import tariffs was the immediate cause behind the assault on Anahuac, Travis and other members of the War Party, the small group who had favored a strong stance since 1832, hoped the episode would rally people in support of their desire for Texan independence from Mexico. However, committees of correspondence, which had organized in early summer 1835, still held divided views on what stand Texas should take in its relationship with Mexico.

On the other hand, General Cos and Colonel Ugartechea believed that the Anahuac incident represented the beginning of a revolt. Therefore, the two military commanders announced in early August that additional troops would soon be sent to Texas and asked Anglo officials to arrest some of the leading troublemakers, including Travis. News of the impending military occupation and the request for arrests drove the various committees of correspondence to take a more defiant stance. Leaders and local communities resolved not to surrender any fugitives to the authorities, plus they also called for a "Consultation" of representatives from across Texas to meet and discuss further actions. The likelihood of unified Texan resistance increased in early September when Stephen F. Austin arrived home after his long stay, much of it in prison, in Mexico City. Although never a radical, Santa Anna's dictatorial actions caused Austin to throw his prestige behind the call for the Consultation. A growing number of Texans followed his lead and began to support the War Party, couching their protest in conservative terms, picturing Mexico and Santa Anna as the aggressor in the conflict.

Meanwhile, General Cos arrived on the Texas coast in late September with five hundred men, determined to arrest the ringleaders of the revolt and bring Texas back under control. After reinforcing the presidio at Goliad, Cos headed toward San Antonio to take command of the Mexican troops in Texas. Before he could reach Béxar, however, the first skirmish of the Texas Revolution occurred in Gonzalez, on the Guadalupe River east of San Antonio. On September 29, Lieutenant Francisco de Castañeda and one hundred troops arrived at Gonzalez to request the transfer of a cannon that Mexican authorities had earlier provided the settlers for protection from Comanche raiders. Unable to cross the rain-swollen Guadalupe, Castañeda was forced to shout his request for the cannon across the torrent to the local residents. Over the course of the next two days, an army of Texan volunteers converged on Gonzalez determined to resist the Mexican troops, electing John H. Moore as their commander. A member of one of the first Anglo families to arrive in Texas, Moore had settled on the upper Colorado River in 1821, making a reputation for himself as an effective militia leader directing campaigns against the Indians in his region. On October 2, Moore ordered the Texan force to attack Castañeda's camp, employing the very artillery piece in question, now draped with a white banner bearing a picture of the cannon along with the combative phrase "COME AND TAKE IT." Outnumbered and without orders from Colonel Ugartechea to engage in battle, Castañeda retreated soon thereafter back to San Antonio with the loss of a couple of men. Once word of the victory at Gonzalez spread, volunteers from other Texan settlements rushed to join the men who had defended the cannon. A week later, a group of volunteers from Matagorda led by George M. Collinsworth, a Mississippian who had settled near Brazoria in 1832, met little Mexican resistance in taking possession of the fort at Goliad. In addition to obtaining a cache of weapons recently left behind by General Cos, the capture of Goliad isolated the Mexican forces at San Antonio, ensuring that they could not be resupplied or reinforced from the sea.

Most of the victorious party at Goliad immediately marched to Gonzalez to find that Stephen F. Austin had been elected commander of all the volunteers. With about four hundred men under his command, Austin marched the ragtag bunch to the outskirts of San Antonio, where they made camp on Salado Creek, five miles east of town. Although General Cos had more than twice as many troops at his disposal than the Texans, Austin decided to move his base of operations closer to the town and dispatched a force of nearly

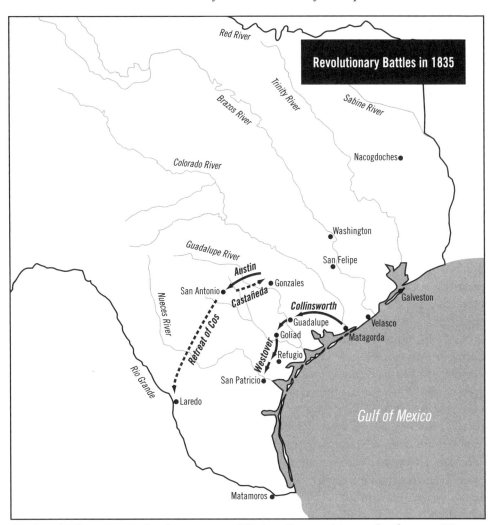

one hundred men to probe the area near Mission Concepción south of town. He gave command to Jim Bowie, the famed Arkansas knife-fighter who had come to Texas in 1828 and married into a wealthy Béxar family. Bowie was assisted by James W. Fannin, a Georgian who had attended West Point for two years in the 1820s before dropping out. Fannin brought his family to Texas in 1834 and soon got involved in an illegal African slave-trading venture. He was one of the few men in the province with any formal military training, so Texans looked to him for leadership even though he had no experience in actual command. In late October, Bowie and Fannin's men overwhelmed Mexican troops and took possession of Mission Concepción, allowing Austin to besiege his opponents at Béxar.

In mid-November, Austin was sent on a diplomatic mission to the United States, and the men elected Edward Burleson, a veteran Indian fighter from North Carolina, to command the army. Burleson decided to abandon the siege for the winter, but Ben Milam convinced him to allow volunteers to try and take the town. A native of Kentucky, Milam had come to Texas by 1818, participated in James Long's filibustering expedition, engaged in mining and land speculation during the 1820s, and gotten into trouble in Mexico in 1835 because of his association with federalists in Coahuila. He escaped to Texas in time to join the force that captured Goliad in October and then linked up with the volunteers at Béxar. On December 5, Milam attacked with three hundred men, which included a group of Tejanos led by Juan Seguín. Isolated from reinforcements for his army, Cos's men desperately tried to defend Béxar house-by house in a series of close-order combat engagements. Though Milam had been killed by a sniper during the fighting, his men pressed their assault, finally forcing Cos to surrender on December 9. After taking full possession of San Antonio, the Texans allowed Cos to withdraw his defeated force across the Rio Grande.

**The Consultation of 1835**

While the events at San Antonio were transpiring, fifty-eight delegates from a dozen Texas communities assembled in San Felipe de Austin to hold the meeting that has come to be known as the Consultation of 1835. Although the delegates did not represent all of Texas—none came from Béxar, Goliad, or Victoria—those present generally came from the established Anglo leadership of the province. Meeting between November 3 and November 14, they elected Branch T. Archer, a Virginian, as president of the Consultation and, after lengthy discussion, declared their commitment to federalism as embodied in the Constitution of 1824. By this strategy, the delegates hoped to win support from liberals in Mexico and gain time in which to acquire assistance from the United States. Actually, the Texans demonstrated their desire for independence by creating a provisional government with a general legislative council to be composed of representatives from the various settlements, and electing Henry Smith, a Kentuckian, as governor. Among other things, the Consultation empowered the new government to seek funds to finance the expected war with Mexico, and dispatched Austin, Archer, and William H. Wharton—a Tennessee lawyer who had moved to Texas in 1827 and married Jared Groce's daughter—to the United States for that purpose. They also selected Sam Houston as commander of a new regular Texas army.

Although the Texans had successfully come together to force the Mexican army to abandon San Antonio and to create a provisional government, the political and military situation soon descended into chaos. Most of the volunteer army at Bexar returned to their homes, leaving only one hundred soldiers in San Antonio under the command of Colonel James C. Neill—a North Carolinian who came to Texas in 1831 after having fought the Creeks with Sam Houston at the Battle of Horseshoe Bend—who concentrated his force at the remnants of Mission San Antonio de Bexar, the Alamo. About four hundred other soldiers joined a troop organized by Fannin at Goliad that planned to attack the Mexican city of Matamoros on the lower Rio Grande. Ultimately, General Houston was able to convince Fannin and his men to call off the disorganized expedition and remain at Goliad. While Texan military operations degenerated into factionalized foolishness, civilian government deteriorated into such confusion and dissension that in December 1835 the general council called for the election of men to meet in early March 1836 for the purpose of adopting an interim government and framing a new constitution. Before the convention could meet, however, Governor Smith and the general legislative council clashed over key issues such as the creation of a regular army and whether or not to declare independence from Mexico. Smith suspended the general council, which retaliated by removing Smith from office. Neither recognized the legality of the other's

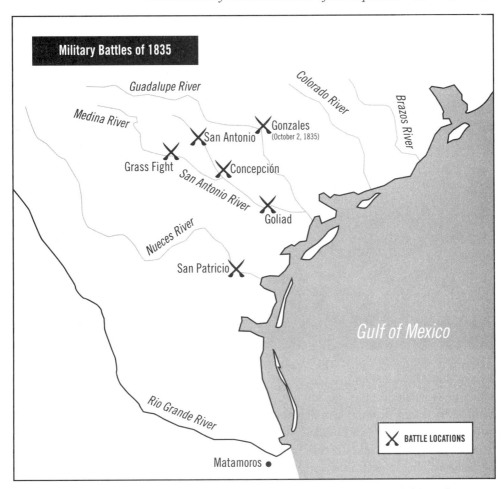

action, and for all practical purposes Texas ceased to have a government by mid-January 1836.

**"Remember the Alamo!"**

In the meantime, Antonio López de Santa Anna had determined to crush the rebellion in Texas and issued a decree on December 30 declaring that all foreigners (mainly immigrants from the United States) captured in arms against the Mexican government would be treated as pirates and executed. He also put together an army of six thousand men that crossed the Rio Grande on February 16, en route to San Antonio, determined to carry out that proclamation. The following day, General José Urrea led a force of five hundred cavalrymen into Texas from Matamoros, headed toward Goliad. Defenses at Santa Anna's first objective, San Antonio, had been centered at the Alamo mission, reinforced in early 1836 by Colonel Neill with cannons captured from General Cos. Desperate for reinforcements since he only had about one hundred men, Neill welcomed Jim Bowie and thirty men who arrived in late January. Bowie had come to deliver Sam Houston's orders to remove all military equipment from Béxar, destroy the Alamo, and retreat to Gonzalez. Impressed by Neill's defensive preparations, however, Bowie convinced Governor Smith that the Alamo should be held instead. Smith responded by ordering Travis, a recruiting

**The Alamo, San Antonio, Texas**

officer at San Felipe at the time, to raise a company and reinforce the Alamo. Reluctantly, because he feared that the fort did not have enough men or supplies, Travis gathered twenty-nine volunteers and headed for San Antonio, arriving on February 3. Five days later a small group of volunteers from Tennessee entered the Alamo under the leadership of celebrated Tennessee frontiersman and former congressman Davy Crockett. Like Neill and Houston, Crockett had fought under fellow Tennessean, Andrew Jackson and had gone on to serve three terms in Congress. Losing re-election to his seat in Washington in 1835, Crockett told his constituents that they could "go to Hell, and I would go to Texas."

Soon after Crockett arrived, changes in command occurred. Colonel Neill left the Alamo on February 11 due to illness in his family and turned over command to Travis. Many of the men, however, preferred Bowie. The two leaders avoided trouble by agreeing to act as joint commanders, an arrangement that held until Bowie became too ill to serve and turned over full control to Travis on February 24. The day before, however, Santa Anna had entered San Antonio with a force of nearly twenty-five hundred men and had begun to lay siege to the Alamo. On the second day of the siege, Travis sent Captain Albert Martin to Gonzalez with a plea for reinforcements. In response, thirty-three men from Gonzalez made their way into the Alamo under cover of early morning darkness on March 1, raising the number of defenders to nearly two hundred men. Two days later James Bonham daringly rode into the Alamo in broad daylight to announce that Fannin and his four hundred men from Goliad would not be coming to the aid of Travis. Fannin had actually marched his army toward San Antonio on February 28, but bad weather and the approach of General Urrea's cavalry had convinced him to return to Goliad.

Finally, after two weeks of besiegement, on March 6 Santa Anna commanded his troops to attack the Alamo, with orders to take no prisoners. The attack began just before dawn against four different points on the mission's perimeter walls.. By the time that the Texans became aware of the Mexican advance, their troops were already within musket range. Using cannon fire and long rifles, the Alamo's defenders felled the lead Mexican soldiers responsible for positioning the ladders that would allow the attackers to scale the mission's defenses. Nonetheless, the attack continued, and the Texans began to lose men as well. Travis was one of the first to die, shot in the head after exposing himself above the wall to fire at the Mexican infantry. The attackers reached the walls and huddled under them in confusion until a few climbed over the north wall and opened a door that permitted free access to the interior. Once the walls had been penetrated, the Texans withdrew to the chapel and barracks on the east side of the fort. Using the defenders' cannon to blast their way into the barracks and chapel, the fighting became hand-to-hand. The battle came to an end after about thirty minutes, with most of the Texans killed, except for seven men, including Crockett, who were captured and executed soon thereafter. A few women, children, and a slave of Travis survived. Though estimates of Mexican casualties have varied, the assault cost Santa Anna more than two hundred deaths and total casualties of at least four hundred men.

Although there was no strategic need to attack or defend the Alamo, the fort's fall benefited the Texas cause in several ways. First, the destruction of the Alamo woke up Texans who did not strongly support the revolution to the fact that their survival hung in the balance. Second, the story of fighting to the last man stirred the imaginations and increased support for Texas in the United States. Third, the battle weakened Santa Anna's army and provided a rallying cry—"Remember the Alamo"—for Texans during the remainder of the war. Finally, by delaying the Mexican invasion for more than two weeks, the Alamo defenders gave the convention that met on March 1 an opportunity to declare independence and organize a temporary government for Texas. At last, leaders clarified the purpose of the revolution and brought a bit of order out of political chaos.

## Creation of the Republic of Texas

Elections for the convention scheduled to meet at Washington-on-the-Brazos had taken place on February 1, a full month before the fall of the Alamo. Voters tended to reject men associated with the Consultation and sent younger, even more recent arrivals who favored decisive action. Nearly half of the fifty-nine delegates had lived in Texas for less than two years and only two—José Antonio Navarro and José Francisco Ruiz—were natives. When the delegates convened on March 1, Santa Anna's invasion had crystallized sentiment in favor of separation from Mexico. As a result, on the following day, the convention adopted a declaration of independence without debate. Written by George C. Childress, a Tennessean who had been in Texas less than eight months, the document was patterned on the American Declaration of Independence. It argued that Mexican violations of the 1824 Constitution had caused the revolt, necessitating the separation and creation of Texas as a sovereign, independent republic as being a matter of "self-preservation."

Having declared independence, the convention turned to creating an army and a government for their republic. On March 4, with only one negative vote, the delegates named Sam Houston commander in chief of the entire Texan army, volunteers and regulars alike. Two days later, Houston left the convention and traveled to Gonzalez to take

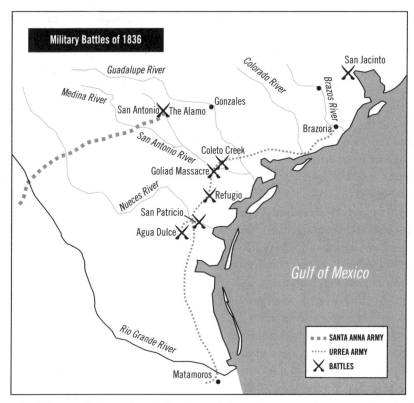

command of the small force that had gathered there in preparation to relieve the Alamo, in the unlikely event that proved possible. The convention remained in session until March 17 and wrote a constitution for the Republic of Texas. Modeled on the United States Constitution, it varied from that document mainly in restricting the power of the government. Representatives served one-year terms, while senators and the president served for three years, with the executive prohibited from succeeding himself. Reflecting the overwhelming dominance of Southerners in Texas, the constitution guaranteed that people held as slaves in Texas would remain in servitude and that future immigrants to the republic could bring slaves with them. Furthermore, no free black could live in Texas without the approval of Congress, and any slave freed without the legislature's approval had to leave the republic. As a last step before adjourning, the convention chose leaders of an interim government to operate until regular elections could be held. New Jersey native, David G. Burnet—one of the few Texas revolutionary leaders from the North—became the first president, and Lorenzo de Zavala, a federalist refugee from Yucatán, was named vice president.

## "Remember Goliad!"

Despite the declaration of independence and the creation of a constitution, the fate of the revolution lay in the hands of the Texas military. General Houston began his ride to Gonzalez on March 6 not knowing that the Alamo had fallen that very morning. Santa Anna, in the aftermath of his overwhelming victory at San Antonio, was determined to make the Texans pay as dearly for their rebellion as Joaquín de Arredondo had done to the Republican Army of the North in 1813. Thus, the Mexican commander devised a three-pronged movement across Texas. General Antonio Gaona was to swing north and proceed to Nacogdoches, while General José Urrea's cavalry was to continue its advance up the coast toward Galveston. Santa Anna would remain with the main Mexican force, commanded by General Vicente Filisola, as it headed eastward toward Gonzalez and San Felipe de Austin. Houston arrived in Gonzalez on March 11, whereupon he learned the fate of Alamo. Assuming command of the four hundred or so volunteers gathered there under the leadership of Edward Burleson, Houston sent a message to Colonel Fannin, ordering him to fall back from Goliad to Victoria with his force of four hundred men. Two days later, after learning that the main Mexican army was advancing rapidly upon Gonzalez, Houston decided to abandon the town and head east toward the Colorado River.

Whereas General Houston chose to immediately retreat in the face of the overwhelming force headed his way, Colonel Fannin hesitated and remained at Goliad for a few days after receiving the order to move to Victoria. At first, he was waiting for the return of several detachments that he had sent out to evacuate settlers near Refugio. After several days Fannin learned that Urrea's cavalry, aided by loyalist Tejanos, had killed or dispersed these detachments, but then he took another day preparing for the retreat to Victoria. Finally, Fannin's army moved out of Goliad on the morning of March 19. Moving at a slow pace because the commander insisted on using wagons drawn by oxen to haul cannons and muskets, the troops covered only six miles before halting to rest in the middle of a prairie. Soon thereafter, Urrea's force caught up with the Texans, forcing Fannin to form his men into a hollow square defensive formation. Although the Mexican cavalry could not break the defensive formation, by nightfall the Texans were short of food, water, and ammunition.

At dawn on the following day, Fannin learned that Urrea had brought up reinforcements during the night, leaving him no choice but to surrender. Urrea ordered Colonel Nicolás de la Portilla to march the Texan prisoners back to Goliad and confine them in the old presidio. Urrea proceeded to Victoria and sent a message to Santa Anna recommending clemency for Fannin and his men. The dictator, however, commanded Colonel Portilla to execute the prisoners, an order that was carried out on Palm Sunday, March 27. After separating the prisoners into four groups, the Mexican troops marched them out of town, halted the columns and opened fire. Lancers then butchered most of those who were not killed immediately in the volley. More than three hundred men died, while nearly thirty escaped and took word of the massacre eastward to Houston's retreating army. Back at the fort, guards executed Fannin and forty other wounded prisoners from his command. General Houston used news from Goliad to inflame his soldiers, while sympathy for the revolution increased dramatically in the United States once word of a second massacre of their American brethren in Texas crossed the Sabine River.

**The Runaway Scrape**

As General Houston continued to retreat eastward toward the Colorado River with his ragtag army, some of his men began to grumble that they had volunteered to fight rather than run, a complaint that would only increase over the next month. When the army reached the Colorado River on March 17, they found their retreat complicated by a large collection of civilians gathered there. Word of the Alamo's fall had caused such panic among the Texan settlers that many hurriedly threw whatever belongings they could onto any available means of conveyance and headed toward the safety of Louisiana and the United States. Fearful of the Mexican army and hearing unfounded rumors of an alliance between Santa Anna and the Indians, the stragglers clogged the few roads—muddied by incessant spring rains—and fought for places on ferries at the rivers during what came to be known as the "Runaway Scrape." At the Colorado, Houston had the army aid the refugees in crossing the river, then move over to the east bank itself and remain for two days while the civilians carried on eastward to the Brazos River.

Soon thereafter, Houston learned the demoralizing news of Fannin's surrender at Goliad, leaving his army the only Texas force in the field. Houston also found out that the provisional government, frightened by the advancing Mexican armies, had fled from Washington-on-the-Brazos to Harrisburg on Buffalo Bayou. Despite the protests of many of his soldiers, Houston continued to retreat, intending to keep his army intact and wait for Santa Anna to make a mistake. Arriving at San Felipe on March 28, Houston decided to move northward about twenty miles along the west bank of the Brazos River to the plantation of Jared Groce. Houston knew that he could use the steamboat *Yellow Stone*, which was at Groce's estate, to cross the flooded river and be in a position to continue retreating toward Harrisburg to join the provisional government. Before he could leave San Felipe for Groce's plantation, however, Houston faced a mutiny in his army, as Captains Mosely Baker and Wylie Martin refused to abandon the town and began to talk about choosing a new leader. Houston quelled the rebellion by allowing Baker to remain at San Felipe to defend the crossing of the river and sent Martin downstream to Fort Bend to do the same. Juan Seguín's cavalry, which had helped cover the retreat from Gonzalez, stayed with Baker at San Felipe.

On March 30, the Texan army reached Groce's land, where they settled down to rest and train, much to the dismay of President David Burnet, who ordered the general to engage the enemy, a command that Houston refused to consider. Santa Anna reached San Felipe a week later, only to find that Houston was to the north at Groce's plantation, while the government was to the southeast at Harrisburg. Needing to traverse the Brazos but bothered by Baker's small force guarding the crossing, Santa Anna led most of his force down the river toward Fort Bend, where they captured a ferry and moved east of the river unopposed. Outflanked, Baker and Martin retreated and rejoined Houston's army, which crossed to the east bank of the Brazos via steamboat on April 12 and headed toward Harrisburg. Santa Anna, choosing to capture the provisional government and deal with Houston's army later, made a major blunder by leaving most of his troops at the Brazos, and took less than one thousand men toward Harrisburg. The Mexican force arrived on April 15 and learned that Burnet and the others had already fled to New Washington on Galveston Bay. Assuming that Houston was continuing on toward Louisiana, Santa Anna pursued the government officials, who barely escaped capture as they manned boats headed for Galveston Island.

## The Battle of San Jacinto

On April 18, Houston reached Harrisburg and discovered from a captured Mexican courier that Santa Anna had divided his army, finally providing him with the opportunity he had been waiting for. Acting quickly, Houston left behind more than two hundred men

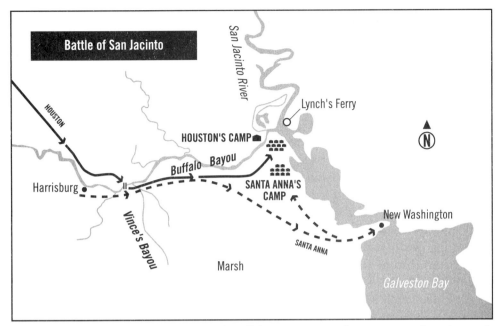

who were too sick to travel, and crossed Buffalo Bayou, intending to move along its south bank in order to put his army in front of Santa Anna's when it turned back north from Galveston Bay. Pushing his men to the limit during the night of April 19-20, Houston reached Lynch's Ferry on the San Jacinto River in the morning before the Mexicans arrived, after he burned New Washington and turned northward. The Texan army made camp underneath the trees lining Buffalo Bayou, forcing Santa Anna's army to cross an open prairie in front of Houston's men sheltered in the timber, in order to reach the ferry and rejoin his troops waiting at the Brazos River. Following a brief fight on April 20 that failed to dislodge the Texans, Santa Anna withdrew to the south and made camp less than a quarter mile from Houston's troops, in an area surrounded by marshes and water on the east and south, providing him no room to retreat.

Some of Houston's men, seeing the withdrawal and believing that they could turn it into a rout, demanded an immediate attack. Houston approved a request by their leader, Lt. Colonel Sidney Sherman and allowed sixty or so mounted riflemen to go out and reconnoiter the field but gave strict orders that they should not get within range of the Mexicans' guns or to provoke an attack. Sherman, like many officers within the Texan army, disobeyed orders, drew fire from the Mexicans and charged their line with his cavalry. Sherman's troops soon found themselves in danger of being overrun by Mexican lancers when they dismounted to reload their rifles. However, the Texan cavalry managed to withdraw with only minor casualties, thanks especially to the heroism of Mirabeau Buonaparte Lamar, a recently arrived volunteer from Georgia. In the aftermath of the failed attack and Sherman's disobedience, Houston gave Lamar command of the cavalry and promoted him from private to the rank of colonel.

Having learned that General Cos had arrived overnight with more than five hundred troops, bringing Santa Anna's strength to approximately thirteen hundred men, Houston decided to attack on April 21. Houston, however, did not assemble his army for battle until early in the afternoon, convincing Santa Anna—who planned to make his own attack the following day—that the Texans were using the day to rest. Therefore, it came as a complete surprise when, a little before four o'clock in the afternoon, Houston's force of nearly one thousand troops (enlarged by newly recruited volunteers from Texas and the United States, as well as a detachment of Tejanos led by Seguín) approached Santa Anna's army, many of whom were asleep. With Houston on horseback and in the lead, the Texans quietly advanced across the prairie with two recently arrived cannons nicknamed the "Twin Sisters," which had been donated by the people of Cincinnati, Ohio.

Two hundred yards from the enemy line, the Twin Sisters began firing upon the Mexican troops, using musket balls, horseshoes, and broken glass as ammunition. The shocked Mexicans responded with their own concerted volley, most of which went over the heads of the Texans, who were marching through a depression in the prairie at that point. Houston, however, was struck in the left leg, just above his ankle, shattering his tibia. Nonetheless, he stayed on his horse and commanded his men to attack once they were within twenty yards of the Mexican line. After delivering one organized volley, the Texan troops charged while screaming "Remember the Alamo! Remember Goliad!" Employing pistols and knives, and using their muskets as clubs, the Texans took control of the field in less than twenty minutes. The Mexican army, by this time already deserted by Santa Anna, became disorganized and gave ground, with the Texans chasing the troops as they fled into the river and the marsh, slaughtering them well past dusk, despite the efforts of the wounded Sam Houston to stop them. Altogether, in the stunning Battle of San Jacinto, the Texans killed more than six hundred Mexican troops and captured another seven hundred at a cost of only eight dead and thirty wounded.

In spite of the great victory, Houston knew the war might continue if Santa Anna managed to escape to the Brazos to assume command of the main force of Mexican troops waiting at Fort Bend. A search party, however, discovered Santa Anna the next day dressed as a common soldier but addressed by other captured Mexicans as "El Presidente." Many of the Texan troops wanted to execute Santa Anna in revenge for the Alamo and Goliad, but Houston knew that the president was worth a great deal alive and nothing dead. He protected the Mexican leader and forced him to sign an armistice calling for an end to the fighting and ordering the retreat of his three armies back to Mexico. During their withdrawal, the Mexican army under the command of General Filisola suffered immensely due to a shortage of provisions and from foundering in a "sea of mud" for two weeks due to heavy rains. As a result, the troops ignored orders from the Mexican government to remain in Texas, pushing on to the supplies and rest that awaited them across the Rio Grande in Matamoros.

In spite of his wound, Houston remained near the battlefield for two weeks after April 21, protecting Santa Anna and waiting for the government leaders to arrive. President Burnet and a few others finally got to San Jacinto on May 4 and quickly transported Santa Anna by boat to Velasco, near the mouth of the Brazos, to negotiate a formal treaty. In return for sparing his life and allowing him to return to Mexico, on May 14, Santa Anna signed the Treaty of Velasco that publicly brought an end to the war and provided that all Mexican armies would move south of the Rio Grande. In a secret provision of the treaty, however, Santa Anna promised to use his influence to have the government of Mexico recognize the independence of Texas with the boundary at the Rio Grande. These treaties originated Texas's claim that the Rio Grande was its southern border, although the province had never previously extended south of the Nueces River.

**Native Americans and the Texas Revolution**

Although Native Americans in Texas did not play an active, significant role in the events of the Texas Revolution, the possibility that they might become involved weighed heavily on the minds of the participants, particularly among the Texan rebels. The Indians of coastal and central Texas had little to do with the events that unfolded in late 1835, as most of the tribesmen preferred to stay out of the way of the opposing forces. The Tonkawas and Lipan Apaches remained in the safety of their Hill Country villages west of San Antonio, while the Penateka Comanches continued to honor the peace agreement they had made with Mexican officials in August 1835. However, in October, a few Karankawas took advantage of the unrest between the Texans and the Mexican troops at Gonzalez and crossed east of the Guadalupe River to prey upon the settlers' cattle. In response, Thomas G. Western, future superintendent of Indian affairs for the Republic of Texas, led a rebel commission to ensure the neutrality of the Karankawas and to convince them to retreat to the San Antonio River. Following initial talks, on October 29, Karankawa tribesmen gathered about twenty miles downstream from Goliad and entered "into a firm and lasting peace" with the Texans. Following the signing of the treaty, the Karankawas retreated farther down the coast where they remained, out of harm's way, for the rest of the struggle. Soon thereafter, almost all of the few surviving Karankawas abandoned Texas to take refuge near the mouth of the Rio Grande.

The emigrant Indians of east Texas, as well as the native Caddo tribes, however, found themselves in the midst of a situation that was dangerous on one hand, while offering the possibility of obtaining the land grants they had desired for more than a decade on the other. Both the Mexicans and the Texans hoped to entice the Indians to join their cause. Although few of the warriors actually wanted to get involved in the fight between the opposing forces, Cherokee Chief Duwali, self-appointed spokesman for the tribes, understood that he might manipulate the situation to the Indians' advantage by offering his men's services—as well as those of the other East Texas tribes—to whichever side chose to recognize their claims to land in Texas. However, this was an extremely complicated endeavor. The Indians realized that the Mexican government would probably be more favorable to their claims than the Texans, but the tribes could not be sure that Santa Anna would be victorious. Duwali, therefore, was forced to play a duplicitous game, pledging the Indians' allegiance to both Mexican and Texan representatives, depending upon which side seemed to be closest to victory.

In September 1835, Duwali initiated his diplomatic efforts by traveling to San Antonio to meet with Colonel Domingo de Ugartachea. At the conference, the officer attempted to enlist the Indians of East Texas in the fight against the rebellious Texans. Ugartechea did not offer the Indians a guarantee to their lands, however, so Duwali returned to his Cherokee village, where he held a general council of the emigrant tribes of Texas as well as with the Hasinais. The group concluded that it would be in their best interests to cultivate a friendship with the revolutionaries, believing that the Mexicans in the province would have difficulty defeating the more numerous Texans. In mid-October, Duwali met with Texan agents and assured them that the Cherokees and their allies would remain peaceful if the rebels granted them territory.

Upon the advice of the agents, the newly formed Consultation agreed to give land to the Indians, albeit a smaller tract than the tribes desired. On November 13, every member of the Consultation signed a declaration stating that the Texans recognized the Cherokee claim to lands from the San Antonio road northward to the Sabine River, between the Neches on the west and the Angelina on the east. In late December, a commission headed by Sam Houston initiated treaty negotiations with the Cherokees. Two months later, on February 23, 1836, Duwali and a few other tribal leaders entered into an agreement with the commissioners in the name of the "Cherokees and their associated bands," even though no member of the other East Texas tribes were present at the signing of the treaty. The Cherokee spokesmen compromised and accepted the Texan offer of the tract of land they had been assigned three months earlier, despite their protests that the Mexican government had acknowledged in 1833 that the claim stretched west of the Neches all the way to the Trinity. In return for the grant, the Indians were required to maintain peace with the Texans, give up all outside land claims, and move within the boundaries of the reservation by November 1836. Although the various tribes—Kickapoos, Shawnees, Delawares, and Hasinais—living near the land grant might have agreed to the terms of the treaty, it is doubtful whether the Alabama-Coushattas, whose villages lay much farther to the south, would have done so.

At the same time that Duwali and the Cherokees were negotiating with the Texans, representatives of the Mexican government increased their efforts to convince the East Texas Indians to join forces with them. In February 1836, as he crossed the Rio Grande at the head of six thousand Mexican troops, Santa Anna noted that the Cherokees "held a solemn promise from [his] government to give them lands." He suggested that if they were placated, they could be "used to good advantage." Soon thereafter, General Cos commissioned Eusebio Cortinez as Indian agent and instructed him to raise a troop of East Texas Indians to fight the rebels. Cortinez met with Duwali at his village and informed the Cherokee chief of the approaching Mexican army. Realizing that the Mexicans might be holding the upper hand in Texas, Duwali agreed to Cortinez's request that the Cherokees attack Nacogdoches and set fire to the town if called to do so. Having pledged his tribes' support to both sides of the struggle in Texas, Duwali and the Cherokees now sat back and waited to see who would win.

The Mexican government also commissioned Manuel Flores to enlist Kadohadacho warriors to fight against the Texan revolutionaries. In July 1835, United States officials had forced Kadohadacho leaders to sell their lands in Louisiana and Arkansas and move west across the border into Mexican Texas within one year. Throughout the fall and winter, the main body of the Kadohadachos had remained quietly in their villages near the Louisiana-Texas border awaiting their first annuity payment before moving to Texas. Flores, who was a resident of the area and longtime friend of the tribe, met with the Kadohadachos in February 1836 and promised them money and "free plunder" if they would attack the Texans, who he shrewdly characterized as being Americans. Flores's cajoling influenced the uncertain Kadohadacho Chief Tarshar to lead most of the tribe's warriors into Texas along with the Mexican agent. The Kadohadachos passed Flores's offer on to the Hasinais and the various Wichita tribes, all of whom then gathered at the forks of the Trinity River to judge the progress of Santa Anna's army.

As events in Texas quickly unfolded over the next month and a half, most of the province's Indians observed the dangerous situation from positions of safety. For a short time, everything seemed to indicate that the Indians should join with the Mexicans. The convention that created the Republic of Texas in early March chose David G. Burnet—an empresario whose lapsed grant had conflicted with the Cherokee lands—as president, and the provisional government took no action to ratify the Treaty of February 23, 1836. Following the Mexican victories at the Alamo and at Goliad, as the remaining Texas troops under Houston retreated eastward, the general sent a delegation to ask the nearby Alabamas and Coushattas for assistance. Like the other Texas tribes, however, both groups preferred to stay out of the fray and neither the Alabamas nor the Coushattas committed warriors to the fight.

As Santa Anna's large army hotly pursued Houston's retreating forces, rumors of an imminent attack by the Cherokees and the Kadohadachos were rife among the fleeing settlers. When Duwali advised a few Nacogdoches settlers that they were in danger due to the approaching Mexican army, some Texans mistook his warning as a threat. A report soon spread that the Cherokees were in their villages "with very hostile feelings [against the Texans], and in a state of preparation for war." Others believed that the Kadohadachos, in the wake of the fall of the Alamo, were leading a force of Indians, estimated at seventeen hundred warriors, from the forks of the Trinity to pillage the emptied settlements of East Texas. As a result of these unfounded rumors, the Texans appealed to the Untied States for help in containing the Indians, citing an 1831 treaty with Mexico in which each country pledged to keep the tribes within its territory from crossing the border. On March 20, John T. Mason of Nacogdoches addressed an urgent dispatch to the commander of American troops at Fort Jesup near Natchitoches, begging him to send a messenger to the Indians in Texas from the United States, "particularly to the Caddoes, to make them keep quiet." Continued pleas caused General Edmund P. Gaines, the officer in charge of American troops along the Louisiana-Texas frontier, to order fourteen companies to move to the border and encamp on the east bank of the Sabine. General Gaines sent messengers to notify the Cherokees and Kadohadachos that their active involvement in the war in Texas would not be tolerated. He also dispatched soldiers to the Kadohadacho villages to investigate Manuel Flores's activities among the tribe.

Even though none of the Kadohadachos, or any of the tribes of East Texas, joined the Mexican forces or attacked the Texans on their own, American and Texan officials continued to be suspicious of the Indians even after General Houston defeated Santa Anna's army at San Jacinto. General Gaines notified U.S. Secretary of War Lewis Cass in early June that he believed the Kadohadachos and Cherokees were "disposed to keep up appearances of a pacific disposition…until a more favorable change occurs in the affairs of those pretended friends." A few Kadohadacho warriors reinforced these suspicions in June by joining with the Wichitas to attack the residents of Robertson's Colony, located on the Brazos River upstream from Austin's Colony. Although most of the Caddo had peacefully returned to their villages in East Texas and Louisiana, this raid, coupled with a rumor that another large Mexican force was headed toward Texas, caused General Gaines to order his troops across the border to occupy Nacogdoches in July. Many of the citizens of the newly independent nation of Texas suspected the tribes of favoring the Mexicans and did not trust the many tribesmen who continued to live in their midst after the fighting was over. It would be only a matter of time before the Texans drove nearly all of the Indians out of East Texas.

**Impact of the Texas Revolution**

Not only did the Texas Revolution and the victory over the Mexican Army at the Battle of the San Jacinto result in Texan independence, these events ultimately led to the Civil War and the abolition of slavery in the United States. In the aftermath of San Jacinto and the establishment of the Republic of Texas, Mexico disavowed the Treaties of Velasco and warned that war with the United States would be the result of an American annexation of Texas. Although northern opposition due to the slavery issue kept Texas from joining the United States until 1845, the Mexican War erupted, nevertheless, the following year. The Americans emerged victorious in 1848, and Mexico was forced to cede its northern territories of California and New Mexico to the United States. The question of slavery in these newly acquired lands immediately divided the country, causing the intense polarization over the following decade that resulted in the outbreak of the Civil War in 1861 and the northern triumph and slavery's eradication in 1865. How different would the history of the United States be if Santa Anna had defeated Sam Houston at the Battle of San Jacinto, and Texas had remained under the control of Mexico?

*Afterward: New Questions Arise for the Republic*

*At the end of his report on the Battle of San Jacinto, Thomas J. Rusk poetically reflected on what motivated the Texans when they rushed the Mexican army's position. He wrote:*

> *The sun was sinking in the horizon as the battle commenced; but, at the close of the conflict, the sun of liberty and independence rose in Texas, never, it is to be hoped, to be obscured by the clouds of despotism. We have read of deeds of chivalry, and perused with ardor the annals of war; we have contemplated, with the highest emotions of sublimity, the loud roaring thunder, the desolating tornado, and the withering simoom of the desert; but neither of these, nor all, inspired us with emotions like those felt on this occasion. The officers and men seemed inspired by a like enthusiasm. There was a general cry which pervaded the ranks: "Remember the Alamo!" "Remember La Bahía!" These words electrified all. "Onward!" was the cry. The unerring aim and irresistible energy of the Texas army could not be withstood. It was freemen fighting against the minions of tyranny and the results proved the inequality of such a contest.*

*Though the Texans had won their independence, keeping it would become the new challenge. For a decade after the end of the Revolution, Texans faced many choices and potential problems: Should they join the United States? Should they remain an independent republic? Could they defend themselves from their Mexican neighbors who did not recognize their independence? Could they survive hostile Native Americans who attacked frontier settlers as they moved westward? Could they survive internal divisions? These and other questions would soon be answered as Texans struggled with their independence through the late 1830s and early 1840s.*

# Myth & Legend

**The Yellow Rose of Texas**

*The "Yellow Rose of Texas," which remains shrouded in mystery even today, refers to both a person and a song. Both the song and the woman, who supposedly is the subject of the song's lyrics, remains one of the most controversial and least understood legends in Texas history. This topic has even proved elusive to the authors of this book, who have strived to piece together the story of the myth and legend of the "Yellow Rose" in earlier editions. To the best of our knowledge, we now present the account of Emily D. West and her role at the Battle of San Jacinto in its correct form, but we are sure that her story will remain controversial.*

*In brief, the song has evolved over a long period of time with different interpretative meanings associated with each stage of its evolutionary development. The earliest published lyrics known to exist at this time emerged as part of minstrels performed in Philadelphia in the early 1850s. This early version of the song's lyrics describe an African-American male's unrequited love for a young woman, traditionally believed to be mulatto, because the term "yellow" was commonly used to describe people of mixed race in the mid-nineteenth century. Who the man and the women portrayed in the lyrics are unknown, as neither were identified by name. Even the name of the song writer is unknown. It is likely that the early version of "The Yellow Rose of Texas" was simply a rendition of other popular songs of the era, such as "The Virginia Rose-Bud," "The Rose of Alabama," and "The Rose of Baltimore." The first known time that the song was copyrighted as stand-alone sheet music was September 2, 1858, when Firth, Pond, and Company of New York, a music store in New York City, published a collection of twenty-two popular songs performed by Edwin P. Christy's minstrel group, known simply as Christy's Minstrels. Over the next eight decades, the song was performed by numerous musicians and was included in a variety of different popular music collections. With each publication, the song endured various transformations. At one point the song was associated with yellow flowers, which became a popular symbol among Texans. In fact, the symbol was so closely aligned to the state of Texas that politicians used the image of yellow flowers as part of their political campaigns. For example, Governor James Hogg reportedly adorned his lapel with a yellow rose pin during his 1892 gubernatorial campaign. Even as late as the 1950s and 1960s, politicians made political capital out the popular image of "The Yellow Rose of Texas." In 1956, the theme song of the Democratic Party was based on a version of the song. Also, leading politicians, such as Dwight Eisenhower, John F. Kennedy, Lyndon Johnson, Ralph Yarborough, and Allen Shivers, used the image of the yellow rose as part of their campaign strategies when in Texas. As a status symbol of Texas pride, the "Yellow Rose of Texas" was often performed at public gatherings as a patriotic gesture to the state. One of the most significant transformations to the song came in the early 1930s, when white songwriters changed the original lyrics to make them racially neutral, an indication that whites now viewed the song as a description of the unidentified woman's beauty, rather than her race. This was a trend that continued well into the 1960s.*

However, the greatest transformation to the song came in 1961, when "The Yellow Rose of Texas" became associated with Texans' victory at the Battle of San Jacinto. It was at that time, some lay historians and researchers began to assert that the woman, who was the subject of the song, might possibly be connected to the individual mentioned in William Bollaert's account of his travels in Texas between 1842 and 1844. According to Bollaert, Sam Houston had personally told him that the success of the Texas Army in the Battle of San Jacinto was related in part to the actions of a slave girl, known only as Emily. Houston supposedly revealed that a young mulatto girl named Emily was in Santa Anna's tent when the battle at San Jacinto erupted. The inference being that the two were engaged in some form of sexual relations that distracted the Mexican general long enough to ensure a breakdown in command of the Mexican forces, resulting in the Texans' victory.

But just who was Emily? Traditionally, folklorists, lay historians and music aficionados have referred to the young woman as Emily Morgan, a slave of Colonel James Morgan. However, primarily through the research efforts of Jeffrey Dunn, James Lutzweiler, and Margaret Henson, the woman who was mentioned in Bollaert's travel account had been identified as Emily D. West, a free woman who Colonel Morgan hired as an indentured servant to work for him for a period of one year. Also, Dunn and Lutzweiler have convincingly argued that there is absolutely no evidence to suggest a connection between the song "The Yellow Rose of Texas" and Emily. Naturally, their work came as a shock to some in the scholarly community, especially to those scholars and researchers who claimed that the song and Emily were definitively linked. Despite such controversies, it does ap- pear that the facts, as represented by Dunn and Lutzweiler, are indeed correct.

Less clear now is the question of whether Emily D. West was actually in the company of General Santa Anna at the beginning of the Battle of San Jacinto, and if she truly played a significant role in aiding the Texans' cause. One historical interpretation argues that during the Texas Revolution, James Morgan supposedly helped sustain Sam Houston's army with fruits, grains, and cattle. From Morgan's Point, a parcel of land that extended into the San Jacinto Bay, Morgan loaded the needed supplies onto flatboats, shipping the foodstuffs to Houston by a water route. Having earned the general's trust, Houston commissioned Morgan a colonel in the Texas Army and sent him to Galveston to guard Texas refugees and government officials who were preparing to make their escape by sea should the approaching Mexican army turn toward their position. In order to make sure supplies continued to reach Houston's men, Morgan allegedly left Emily behind to oversee the operations of the flatboats. By April 18, 1836, General Santa Anna's army moved his men into position to attack Houston's troops. It was at this time that he captured Emily and a young mulatto boy named Turner while they were loading one of the flatboats destined for Houston's troops. According to legend, Santa Anna was immediately attracted to Emily. After seizing the supplies intended for Houston's men, Santa Anna reportedly ordered Turner to lead a scouting party to Houston's location. Emily convinced her young friend, however, to escape when opportunity presented itself and to find Houston, informing the Texas commander that the Mexican troops were in the area. Turner did as he was told. As a result, Houston prepared his men to attack the Mexican army now camped on the *plains of the San Jacinto River. On April 21, while Houston made final preparations for his attack, General Santa Anna was allegedly in the company of Emily in his personal tent. Being distracted by his female companion, the Mexican general neglected his military duties, allowing his army to fall victim to Houston's surprise attack on their position. In part, according to this account, the Texas victory at San Jacinto was made possible by the flirtatious efforts of Emily.*

*Emily West survived the battle and made her way back to New Washington, the settlement that James Morgan had established near Morgan's Point. Soon afterwards, Colonel Morgan returned to the settlement and, upon learning of Emily's role in the decisive battle, provided her with money and a passport to New York. However, no records exist of Morgan's actions. Still, even today, the heroic acts of Emily are celebrated by the Knights of the Yellow Rose on April 21 at the site of the famous battle.*

*While the events surrounding Emily's role at the Battle of San Jacinto has been told in various versions over the decades, the basic facts have remained fairly consistent. But is this story more myth than reality? Some Texas historians refute that the event even took place, claiming that Santa Anna in all probability was too exhausted from military actions he had overseen the day before to concern himself with Emily. The Mexican general and his troops had engaged the Texans in a brief skirmish on April 20, and they had been up all night building barricades in anticipation of Houston's attack. The following day the Mexican troops had stood guard into the early afternoon waiting for an engagement with Houston's men. By mid-afternoon, the Mexican troops would have been utterly exhausted, and as the sun began to move closer to the horizon, they lowered their guard, believing Houston had decided against an assault on their position. According to these scholars, this accounted more for why the Mexicans lost the battle than does Santa Anna's indiscretions and dereliction of duty.*

*Still other scholars claim that it was possible that Emily West was, indeed, in Santa Anna's tent when the Texans charged the Mexicans at San Jacinto. The views of those who support this opinion argue that William Bollaert's travel journal, based on Sam Houston's own account, accurately reflect Emily's role at San Jacinto. Based on the evi- dence that exists, it does seem probable that Emily West was in the Mexican camp during the Battle of San Jacinto.*

*Whether she was in Santa Anna's tent will remain the subject of debate. It is just as likely that the story was fueled by stereotypes that Anglos had of Mexicans. Anglos labeled Mexican men as sexually promiscuous and immoral, and it is likely that they circulated the story of the "Yellow Rose" as a way to show that Mexican men could not control their sexual desires even in the face of an imminent peril. Thus, Anglos would have contributed Santa Anna's loss to his uncontrollable desire to fulfill his sexual needs. Regardless, it is certain that the "Yellow Rose" was not the sole factor contributing to the defeat of Santa Anna's forces at San Jacinto. Instead, the Mexican defeat primarily resulted from Santa Anna's overconfidence and his disregard for proper military protocol. Despite the famous myth of the "Yellow Rose," Santa Anna deserves most of the credit for the Texans' victory.*

## Suggestions for Further Reading

Anna, Timothy E. *Forging Mexico, 1821-1835* Lincoln: University of Nebraska Press, 1998.
Anderson, Gary Clayton. *The Conquest of Texas: Ethnic Cleansing in the Promised Land, 1820-1875* Norman: University of Oklahoma Press, 2005.
Barr, Alwyn. *Texans in Revolt: The Battle for San Antonio.* Austin: University of Texas Press, 1990.
Binkley, William C. *The Texas Revolution.* Baton Rouge: Louisiana State University Press, 1952; reprint, Austin: Texas State Historical Association, 1979.
Brands, H. W. *Lone Star Nation: The Epic Story of the Battle for Texas Independence.* New York: Doubleday, 2004.
Crimm, Ana Carolina Castillo. *De León: A Tejano Family History* Austin: University of Texas Press, 2003.
Davis, Graham. *Land! Irish Pioneers in Mexican and Revolutionary Texas* College Station: Texas A&M University Press, 2002.
Dimmick, Gregg, *Sea of Mud: The Retreat of the Mexican Army after San Jacinto, An Archeological Investigation.* Austin: Texas State Historical Association, 2006.
Everett, Dianna. *The Texas Cherokees: A People Between Two Fires, 1819-1840* Norman: University of Oklahoma Press, 1990.
Haley, James L. *Sam Houston* Norman: University of Oklahoma Press, 2002.
Hardin, Stephen L. *Texan Iliad: A Military History of the Texas Revolution.* Austin: University of Texas Press, 1994.
Himmel, Kelly F. *The Conquest of the Karankawas and Tonkawas, 1821-1859* College Station: Texas A&M University Press, 1999.
Jackson, Jack. *Indian Agent: Peter Ellis Bean in Mexican Texas* College Station: Texas A&M University Press, 2005.
Jones, Oakah L. *Santa Anna.* New York: Twayne, 1968.
Kelley, Sean. *Los Brazos de Dios: A Plantation Society in the Texas Borderlands, 1821-1865* Baton Rouge: Louisiana State University Press, 2010.
Lack, Paul D. *The Texas Revolutionary Experience: A Political and Social History.* College Station: Texas A&M Press, 1992.
Lord, Walter. *A Time to Stand.* New York: Harper, 1961; 2d ed. Lincoln: University of Nebraska Press, 1978.
McDonald, Archie P. *Travis.* Austin: Jenkins, 1976.
Pohl, James W. *The Battle of San Jacinto.* Austin: Texas State Historical Association, 1989.
Pruett, Jakie L. and Everett B. Cole. *Goliad Massacre: A Tragedy of the Texas Revolution.* Austin: Eakin Press, 1985.
Smith, F. Todd. *From Dominance to Disappearance: The Indians of Texas and the Near Southwest, 1786-1859* Lincoln: University of Nebraska Press, 2005.
Tinkle, Lon. *13 Days to Glory: The Siege of the Alamo.* New York: McGraw-Hill, 1958.
Torget, Andrew J. *Seeds of Empire: Cotton, Slavery, and the Transformation of the Texas Borderlands, 1800-1850* Chapel Hill: University of North Carolina Press, 2015.
Vigness, David M. *The Revolutionary Decades: The Saga of Texas, 1810-1836.* Austin: Steck-Vaughan, 1965.

**IDENTIFICATION:** Briefly describe each term.

Domingo de Ugartechea
"COME AND TAKE IT"
Jim Bowie
Ben Milam
Consulation of 1835
James Fannin
David Crockett
David G. Burnet
Runaway Scrape
Mirabeau Buonaparte Lamar
Twin Sisters
"Sea of Mud"
Treaty of Velasco
Cherokees and associated bands
Manuel Flores



**MULTIPLE CHOICE:** Choose the correct response.

1. Santa Anna's dictatorial actions caused rebellions in the following Mexican states EXCEPT:
   A. Coahuila y Texas
   B. Nuevo León
   C. Zacatecas
   D. Yucatan

2. The first skirmish of the Texas Revolution occurred in which town?
   A. Goliad
   B. Gonzalez
   C. San Antonio
   D. Victoria

3. The Consultation of 1835 selected who to command the Texas army?
   A. Jim Bowie
   B. William B. Travis
   C. Sam Houston
   D. James Fannin

4. The Mexican general who surrendered in San Antonio was:
   A. Domingo de Ugartechea
   B. Vicente de Filisola
   C. Martín Perfecto de Cos
   D. Santa Anna

5. David Crockett came to the Alamo from what state?
   A. Kentucky
   B. Louisiana
   C. Arkansas
   D. Tennessee

6. José de Urrea defeated the Texan forces at which battle?
   A. The Alamo
   B. San Jacinto
   C. Goliad
   D. Gonzalez

7. The delegates at the Texas Convention of 1836:
   A. Declared the independence of Mexico
   B. Named Burnet interim president
   C. Wrote a constitution
   D. All of the above

8. The Texan army decided to fight at San Jacinto because:
   A. Santa Anna had divided his army
   B. The Texan troops refused to continue their retreat
   C. The Texan troops outnumbered the Mexicans
   D. None of the above

9. In the Treaty of Velasco, Santa Anna agreed to all of the following EXCEPT:
   A. End the war
   B. Texas independence
   C. Southern boundary at the Nueces River
   D. All of the above

10. The Cherokee Treaty of February 1836 granted the Indians lands between which rivers?
    A. Sabine and Neches
    B. Neches and Angelina
    C. Trinity and Angelina
    D. Trinity and Brazos

**TRUE/FALSE:** Indicate whether each statement is true or false.

1. In 1835, Santa Anna created a Federalist state in Mexico.

2. John H. Moore led the Texan troops at Gonzalez.

3. The Consultation of 1835 declared Texan independence from Mexico.

4. James C. Neill prepared the defenses at the Alamo.

5. The constitution of the Republic of Texas allowed the president to succeed himself.

6. Texans forces under Fannin executed three hundred Mexican soldiers at Goliad.

7. In the "Runaway Scrape" Texan civilians headed north to Oklahoma.

8. The "Twin Sisters" were cannons that helped the Texans at San Jacinto.

9. Mexican troops under General Filisola continued to fight after the Battle of San Jacinto.

10. Cherokee warriors fought with the Texans at San Jacinto.

**MATCHING:** Match the response in column A with the item in column B.

1. Branch T. Archer
2. George C. Childress
3. William B. Travis
4. James Fannin
5. Lorenzo de Zavala
6. Vicente Filisola
7. Mirabeau Buonaparte Lamar
8. *Yellow Stone*
9. Duwali
10. Manuel Flores

A. The Alamo
B. Goliad
C. Mexican Indian agent
D. Texan Declaration of Independence
E. Consultation of 1835
F. Texas Vice-President
G. Cherokee chief
H. Texas cavalry commander
I. "Sea of Mud"
J. Steamboat

**ESSAY QUESTIONS:**

1. Explain Santa Anna's efforts to centralize the Mexican government and discuss the political responses of the Texans through March 1836.

2. Discuss the first phase of the military aspect of the Texas Revolution from October 1835 through December 1835.

3. Discuss the second phase of the military aspect of the Texas Revolution from January 1836 through April 1836.

4. Discuss the actions of the Cherokee Indians from October 1835 through April 1836.

# Chapter 5

# *Forging a New Nation, 1836-1845*

***Prelude: The Killough Massacre***

*In the years after the Texas Revolution, waves of new settlers reached the recently founded republic. Though the conflict ended, tension between the Republic of Texas, supporters of Mexico, and Native Americans remained high. Texans needed to increase its population to better defend its borders and maintain its land claims, Mexican supporters wanted to bring the nascent country back into Mexico, and Indians sought to stem the tide of settlers encroaching on their lands. One particular group of settlers, collectively known as the Killoughs, would find themselves in the middle of this rising tension when they became victims of the largest Native American raid on settlers in East Texas.*

*On Christmas Eve 1837, seven interrelated families from Talladega County, Alabama arrived under the leadership of Isaac Killough, Sr., and settled seven miles northwest of Jacksonville. Controversy surrounded their land claim since 1836 when President Sam Houston ceded the area to the Cherokee in a treaty, only to have the Republic of Texas Congress overturn the deal. Killough family members purchased plots and shortly began clearing the land, planting crops, and building houses. By August of 1838, when the cornfields were ready for harvest, news arrived at the Killough homesteads of an impending insurgency of resentful Mexicans and Indians. Led by Vincente Córdova, former **alcalde** (mayor) of Nacogdoches, the insurgents, coordinating with Mexican officials on the Rio Grande, contrived to retake Texas. Fearing Córdova's Rebellion, the Killough families along with other neighbors fled to Nacogdoches for safety. Luckily, the rebellion never materialized, and General Thomas J. Rusk and his militia scattered the remnants of the insurgency.*

*With the imminent threat gone, the Killoughs returned to harvest their crops in late September. Still leery of an attack, they carried their guns into the fields. On October 5, with the harvest nearly complete, the men returned to the fields after lunch unarmed. Indian raiders attacked the defenseless homesteaders, killing or carrying off eighteen of the settlers, including Isaac Killough, Sr. who was shot eighteen times in his front yard. Survivors hid for the rest of the day and started a three-day, forty-mile trek to Fort Lacy, travelling only at night to avoid other marauders. Once safely within the confine of the fort, they told the story of loved ones murdered and taken into captivity.*

*News of the Killough Massacre spread quickly, and once again Rusk led volunteers in pursuit. When the Texan forces arrived at Fort Houston, near present-day Palestine, the Indian band had been sighted at an old Kickapoo village near Frankston. Rusk pushed his force toward the camp and attacked at dawn. Texans killed eleven of the raiders, running off the rest. Soon after the skirmish, survivors and militiamen debated the composition of the marauders. Rusk's men claimed that the band were Indians from various nations including Cherokees, Caddos, and Coushattas, along with runaway slaves and disgruntled Mexicans. Survivors swore that one of the raiders was a white man disguised as an Indian. Some even claimed they recognized him as a former neighbor from Alabama. This assertion was never confirmed along with other conspiracy theories that claim there was only one Indian in the group and the rest were whites and Mexicans.*

The conclusion of the Texas Revolution with the signing of the Treaties of Velasco started a new era in the history of the Lone Star State. While Texans remained optimistic about their future prospects, many of them questioned what would happen to their new Republic in the days and months ahead. Would the United States annex their newly formed Republic? How long could their independent Republic continue to exist if the United States refused to annex it? Could the Texas government protect its people and property from Indian and Mexican raids? How would the rest of the world view the tiny Republic? How was Texas going to raise money to support itself and pay off its debts that were incurred during the revolution? For almost ten years, Texans struggled to answer these questions. In the end, their answers helped to shape their views of the world and helped to forge a unique cultural identity.

**Problems with the Republic**

Following the Battle of San Jacinto, Texans wondered if their newly created Republic would survive. One of the most daunting problems confronting Texas was financial stability. As a result of the revolution, the Republic of Texas's treasury was empty. The Republic had no money to aid those who lost everything during the runaway scrape, to fund government expenses, and to retire its $1.25 million debt. The government's only real asset was land, but most Texans realized that the land would bring minimal revenues to the government in the short term, especially considering that land prices would remain low in order to entice new settlers to the region. Thus, Texans would have to find other more profitable ways to fund its newly formed government.

Foreign diplomacy was another obstacle. Texas lay in a state of political limbo at the conclusion of the revolution since it had not received official recognition as a sovereign nation by any foreign powers, including Mexico. As a result, Texas voters in their first public election overwhelmingly approved the idea of annexation to the United States. Despite Texans enthusiasm for annexation, members of the United States Congress reacted with caution—fearful that annexation would possibly lead to war with Mexico.

Following the Battle of San Jacinto, the Mexican military still stationed at Matamoros threatened to invade Texas and reclaim its northern territory. Fortunately for the citizens of Texas, the Mexican army did not immediately attack because of political turmoil in Mexico City.

Equally problematic for Texans was the fact that they still held President Antonio López de Santa Anna as a prisoner of war. Texan soldiers who wanted revenge for the massacres at the Alamo and Goliad demanded his execution. Others, however, warned that, if they killed Santa Anna, Mexican officials would retaliate by ordering the execution of Anglo prisoners who had been captured during the war and still held as prisoners. The Texas government eventually sent the Mexican president to the United States' capital where he met with President Andrew Jackson before being set free, returning back to Mexico aboard an American naval vessel.

**The Provisional Government of the Republic of Texas**

Following their victory at San Jacinto, Texans operated under the provisional government that delegates had created in the convention at Washington-on-the-Brazos. The delegates decided that the provisional government would remain in place until voters of an independent Texas could fill the offices with duly elected officials. Elections would be held in accordance with the constitution, which had also been drafted at Washington-on-the-Brazos and was based loosely on the United States Constitution. The Texas Constitution of 1836 stipulated that the newly elected president would serve for two years and that all succeeding presidents would serve three-year terms. Another interesting aspect of the Texas constitution was that it clearly defined term limits for presidents and members of congress. While the presidents could serve more than one term, they could not serve consecutive terms. Also, individuals who were elected to the House of Representatives could only serve a one-year term, and senators could only serve three terms in office. Furthermore, it was very difficult to amend the constitution because of the numerous steps involved. First, members of congress had to approve all proposed amendments. Second, the following elected congress had to approve the amendment. Finally, the congress presented it to the people through a referendum to complete the process. Essentially, it took several years to ratify an amendment under the Republic of Texas's constitution.

The elections for the permanent government were held on September 3, 1836. Also on the ballot were other issues of importance to the new Republic, including the ratification of the Texas Constitution of 1836 and a proposal to seek annexation with the United States. Similar to the United States, Texas's government was a federal system that placed more authority with the central government. The Texas government consisted of three branches—executive, legislative, and judicial—that were regulated by a system of checks and balances. With little resistance, Texas voters overwhelmingly approved the new constitution. Furthermore, voters approved the proposal for annexation, and they elected Sam Houston the first official president of Texas. Houston appointed officials who had lengthy careers in the United States before coming to Texas: men such as Stephen F. Austin, Mirabeau Lamar, Thomas J. Rusk, and Henry Smith. The approval of annexation and Houston's appointment of experienced politicians reflected the influence that new immigrants from the United States had in the founding of the fledging Republic.

114  *Beyond Myths and Legends*

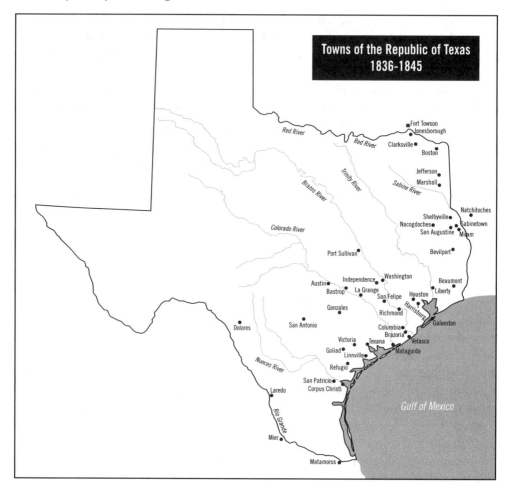

In the days leading up to the election, three front-runners emerged in the race for the first president of Texas. One of the most obvious choices was Stephen F. Austin, the father of Texas. Another was Henry Smith, who had served as governor under the 1835 Consultation. Smith did not fare well in the election because his abrasive personality had alienated many voters. The final candidate, General Sam Houston, entered the race late because he had been in New Orleans recovering from the wound he received during the Battle of San Jacinto. A popular figure of the Texas Revolution, Houston easily won the race, receiving 80 percent of the vote. His status as a hero of the revolution garnered him the votes of soldiers who had served with him and the votes of citizens who credited the hero of San Jacinto with winning the revolution. Austin undoubtedly was disappointed but realized that his time as the leading figure of Texas had passed. That point was reiterated to him when the revolutionary government had sent him away during the war as a diplomat to the United States. According to the constitution, the inauguration of the president-elect was to take place in December, but David G. Burnet, the president of the provisional government, wanting out of his responsibilities, called for the inauguration of the new first president of the Republic of Texas to take place in October. With no objections, Sam Houston took office two months early, ushering in a new chapter in Texas history.

## Houston's First Administration

In the fall of 1836, President Houston took charge of the permanent government at Columbia, Texas (present-day West Columbia). Without an established capital, the president designated the fledgling town of Houston on Buffalo Bayou as the new home for the government. President Houston soon realized that his administration faced many "daunting tasks," the most important included filling cabinet positions, securing foreign recognition, establishing financial stability, quelling defense problems, instituting a policy for peace with Indians on the frontier, and creating land policy. The first order of business for the president was establishing a cabinet. Being the first elected president, Houston was shrewd in his appointments. He crossed political lines when he included both his supporters and his opponents in nominations for the cabinet. The new president named Henry Smith, secretary of the treasury; James Pinckney Henderson, attorney general; Thomas J. Rusk, secretary of war; and Stephen F. Austin, secretary of state, whose term abruptly ended when he died of pneumonia on December 27, 1836. Houston's actions gave his administration both credibility and harmony because he included the most prominent prewar political factions into the government, adhering to the maxim—keep your friends close, but your enemies even closer.

The first priority of the Houston administration was securing foreign recognition for Texas. Even after Houston's election, Texas had not received diplomatic recognition from a single nation, especially not from Mexico. Although Santa Anna signed the Treaties of Velasco, no politician in the Mexican government would ratify the treaty, which left Texas in a precarious position. Without recognition, the Republic could neither establish credit for foreign loans nor legitimately sell its public lands—both situations that severely restricted the credibility of the new government. Additionally, without Mexico's official recognition of Texas's independence, annexation would prove elusive. Although President Andrew Jackson supported the annexation of Texas, he did not force the issue. Since Texas's constitution protected the institution of slavery, the annexation of a slaveholding republic potentially threatened to tear the United States apart. Jackson feared that Northerners would view annexation as a larger conspiracy to add a new slave state to the South. Additionally, he realized that annexation might lead to war with Mexico, especially considering the Mexican government did not recognize Texas independence. The president, therefore, avoided the issue of Texas until his final days in office when he became the first foreign leader to grant the Republic of Texas diplomatic recognition. European countries, including France, Great Britain, Holland, and Belgium, soon followed the United States' lead by acknowledging the sovereignty of the new Republic. However, Mexican officials continued in their refusal to formally recognize Texas as an independent country. Instead, Mexico maintained that Texas was simply a state in rebellion, a state that it planned to reclaim at the first available opportunity. In fact, the only reason that a Mexican army did not then cross the Rio Grande to reclaim its northern province was the continued political turmoil in Mexico City.

The second priority of President Sam Houston was the financial security of the Republic. With the government deep in debt, congress quickly passed several acts that imposed taxes on imported goods, property, and livestock. Although these acts generated some revenue for the government, the ripple effect of the Panic of 1837, a major economic depression in the United States, hampered their effectiveness because fewer products entered the Republic, and it remained difficult to secure loans. Next, the government tried to cover its expenses by printing promissory notes (paper money). With little gold or silver backing, the value of the promissory notes soon declined as inflation gripped the Republic. In some cases the value of the promissory notes were devalued by as much as 90 percent, making them virtually worthless. With Houston's administration at risk of complete failure, he began cutting the cost of government wherever possible. His first cut in expenditures was a reduction in the Texas army, reducing its military strength from approximately 2,000 soldiers to a mere 600 men. The only compensation he could offer to the discharged servicemen was money to return to New Orleans or 1,280 acres of land if they chose to remain in Texas. Other measures to cut spending included the use of diplomacy with Native Americans instead of campaigning against them. Despite Houston's fiscal actions, the Republic maintained a public debt of approximately two million dollars at the end of his first term.

Defense of the fledgling nation was another priority of President Houston. When he took office, the congress had authorized a regular army of 3,600 men, a militia larger than the actual number of males in the Republic, and a small navy to protect its coast and commerce. After Houston reduced the size of the army, the country relied heavily on the militia. Militias were volunteer soldiers who normally were very unreliable and extremely reluctant to travel far from their homes to pursue their enemy. Though this solution saved the government money, it was very inefficient in combating Indian raids. Realizing the shortcoming of the militia against Native Americans on the vast frontier, in May 1837 the government created the legendary law enforcement force, the Texas Rangers. Initially, the Rangers were not an elite police force; instead, it consisted of citizens who volunteered for a specific mission or campaign. Usually the campaign involved pursuing the Indian raiders after they struck residences on the frontier. At the conclusion of the campaign, the men simply returned home without any further responsibility. Though this was the typical Texas Rangers' career, some men actually patrolled the frontier, replicating the Tejano militia system that existed before Texas independence.

Directly related to the defense of Texas was President Houston's Indian policy. With the large debt, Houston could not afford to allow the army to campaign against marauding Indians. Instead, the president initiated a policy of peace toward Native Americans. He viewed this solution as cheaper and more humane. Besides saving money, the time that Houston had lived with the Cherokees, taking an Indian wife, and becoming an adopted member of the nation all influenced his policy of peace. Though Houston believed fervently in peace, most Texans wanted to exterminate the Native Americans who threatened their way of life and restricted their opportunities to settle land to the west.

Land policy was another major issue that President Houston's administration addressed. Texas was short on cash but big on land, so this asset was used to Texas's advantage. The Republic encouraged immigration by giving away land to attract settlers from the United States. This population increase strengthened Texas both physically and economically. More people within its borders meant more individuals to defend the Republic and more economic activity and, thus, more tax-payers. The concept of giving away land was not new to Texas since the interim government had similar policies offering land to men volunteering for the army during the revolution: 640 acres to heads of families and 320 acres to single men. Houston's administration increased the land apportioned to people in the Republic. The government gave any family living in the Republic as of March 2, 1836 one league and one labor of land to the heads of families—approximately 4,605 acres. Families who settled in Texas between March 2, 1836 and October 4, 1836 received 1,280 acres. To attract new settlers, Houston authorized the government to give 640 acres for families and veterans and 320 acres for individuals, with the stipulation that the people live on the property for three years and improve the land before being granted official title to the acreage. The government implemented this stipulation to prevent land speculators from acquiring the land without any intentions of living on it and selling the plot later for profit. Houston's land policy attracted many settlers to Texas, inspiring the "GTT" movement in the United States during the Panic of 1837. Americans experiencing economic troubles in the east simply marked GTT on their homes, "Gone to Texas," and moved west to start life anew in the Republic.

Houston concluded his term as president of the Republic after two years, as stipulated in the constitution. He could not run for reelection because the constitution forbade the president from succeeding himself. Without any true political parties in Texas, just factions similar to those in the United States before the 1830s, politics revolved around Sam Houston, the most famous figure in the government. Politicians were either pro-Houston or anti-Houston. The leader of the opposition was Vice President Mirabeau Lamar. When he ran for president in 1838, Lamar criticized Houston's inability to relieve the debt of Texas. During the election, Houston supporters could not find anybody to run against Lamar, because most of their supporters were too young and their two leading candidates, Peter W. Grayson and James Collinsworth, both died before the election. Peter W. Grayson, who suffered from periodic bouts of mental illness, committed suicide by fatally shooting himself while on a trip to Knoxville, Tennessee. Apparently, besides suffering from reoccurring mental problems, a Louisville woman whom Grayson had long courted turned down his proposal of marriage. James Collinsworth, the first chief justice of Texas, also met with an untimely death when he fell, or possibly jumped, from the deck of a steamboat in Galveston Bay after a week of heavy drinking. Some assumed that he committed suicide, but there was no evidence of such claims.

## Lamar's Administration

Mirabeau Buonaparte Lamar's rise to power differed from Houston's. Raised in Georgia and well-educated, he established several presses across his native state. Lamar did not arrive in Texas until just before the battle of San Jacinto, when he enlisted as a private. Within three months, he received promotions to major general. His political ambition was to establish Texas as the next great power in North America. Lamar's desire directly influenced his administration. He entered the presidential office with several agendas, including repairing the continuing financial crisis, establishing an education system, establishing foreign policy, instituting a policy of extermination for Indians on the frontier, and improving upon Houston's land policy. Lamar's administration changed many of the policies established by Houston.

One of Lamar's first orders of business was to move the capital of Texas to the frontier town of Austin. He wanted to remove the capital from the Houston supporters' stronghold in the Houston/Galveston area. Also, Lamar promoted his policy of expansion by placing the government in a central location of the Republic to encourage settlement on the frontier. Just like the city of Houston, Austin emerged from a sparsely settled land into a city overnight. It became the sixth and final capital city of Texas.

Another major change that Lamar initiated in Texas was the establishment of a public education system. Though in 1840 the Methodist Church independently established Rutersville College, a coeducational college and the first institution of higher learning in Texas in Rutersville, Texas (near La Grange), Lamar's background as journalist and poet influenced his promotion of education in Texas. Because of the Republic's financial strains, Lamar did not have the cash available to start a public education system. Using the only asset Texas had—land—the government parceled out four leagues of land in each county to sell. The revenue generated by the land sales was then used to establish schools within that county. Also during Lamar's tenure, the government set aside fifty leagues of land to establish two universities. The first institution of higher education chartered and established by the Republic was Texas Baptist Educational Society in Independence, Texas, present-day Baylor University. The other university chartered became the University of Texas in Austin. Unlike Baylor University, the University of Texas did not actually exist as an institution until 1883. Evident in the establishment of Protestant universities in Texas was further expansion and diversification of Christianity. Clearly, Lamar's policies on education had a major impact on Texas, which remains evident even today.

Driven to establish the next powerful country in North America, Lamar deviated from Houston's foreign policy. Instead of seeking annexation with the United States, Lamar wanted to maintain independence. He quickly withdrew the treaty requesting annexation and increased the size of the Texas navy by half a dozen ships. Additionally, he made concessions towards Mexico to recognize the sovereignty of Texas. The first attempt in 1839, Texas Secretary of State Barnard E. Bee received authorization to pay Mexico five million dollars for the recognition of Texas's independence and to establish the border between the two countries at the Rio Grande. Though Federalists in Mexico appeared friendly to the idea, Bee never officially met with the Mexican government. Diplomatically, by refusing to recognize Bee's presence, Mexican officials sent the implied message that they still did not recognize Texas independence. Not deterred, Lamar sent James Treat in late 1839, but again Mexico refused to address the issue. In 1841 James Webb led a third mission to gain recognition from Mexico, but the result was the same as the previous two attempts.

Although these attempts to gain Mexico's diplomatic recognition failed, Lamar wanted to promote the power of the Republic of Texas by expanding its territory to the west. On June 20, 1841, Lamar authorized a trading and military expedition of 320 men under the command of Hugh McLeod to Santa Fe, in present-day New Mexico. Lamar's objectives in what became known as the Santa Fe Expedition included Mexican recognition of Texas's control of the region, attempting to block the western expansion of the United States, gaining recognition of the Rio Grande as the Republic's western border, and diverting the trade between Missouri and its southern neighbor to itself, thus building up its own economy. The Santa Fe Expedition experienced problems from the beginning of their thousand mile march. Inclement weather combined with sporadic Indian attacks hampered and weakened their force. Compounding the situation, the citizens of Santa Fe did not give the weary travelers a warm reception. Upon entering Santa Fe, the weak, thirsty, and hungry Texans immediately surrendered to Mexican soldiers garrisoned in the important trade city. Mexican soldiers of Santa Fe then escorted the Texan force to Mexico City. The government eventually released them, and the men made their way back to Texas. Lamar's ambitious expedition to make Texas the next great nation in North America increased the debt of the Republic, sparked a new conflict with Mexico, caused the Texas congress to censure him, and convinced congressmen to consider impeaching him. Failure of the Santa Fe Expedition embarrassed Texans for years to come; yet, it did not keep Texas from making several more attempts to capture the region.

Another aspect of Lamar's administration that differed greatly from Houston's was his policy towards Native Americans. The second president had no intentions of establishing peace treaties with Texas tribes. Instead, he viewed Native Americans as a major obstacle to Anglo expansion and agriculture. To combat Indians, Lamar lavishly spent money by increasing the size of the army and the number of frontier fortifications to stage expeditions driving Native Americans from the Republic. Lamar used more money with his Indian policy than Houston had spent during his entire administration. Alternating Indian policies between Houston and Lamar left many tribes in precarious positions. The Karankawas were almost forced to dissolve as a tribe because Texans began encroaching onto their coastal hunting grounds. Lamar removed the Caddos from East Texas only to have them return after he left office.

The Cherokee people experienced some of the harshest treatments. In February 1836, under the ad interim government, Houston had recognized Cherokee land in East Texas. The first congress rejected the ad interim government treaty because the treaty was never ratified. Congress then proceeded to give the land to David G. Burnet who had an empresario contract for the land and had already introduced Anglo settlers to it. Duwali (Chief Bowles), the Cherokee leader, knew he had the support of Houston to resolve the situation, but Lamar's election dispelled any hope. The new president felt that the Cherokee were involved in a multi-tribal conspiracy to destroy the Republic and dealt with the situation harshly. Lamar called for the removal of the Cherokees from East Texas, telling them either to leave peacefully or face the government's might. Chief Duwali did not back down from his claims to the Cherokee land despite the threats from Lamar. When the Texas army arrived to remove the tribe, the Native Americans resisted. The result was the Battle of the Neches, which took place in present-day Van Zandt County. In the battle the Cherokees suffered a sound defeat and the death of Chief Duwali. Lamar forced the survivors to remove themselves to the Indian Territory or to Mexico. The most sinister part of Lamar's actions was that he sent Chief Duwali's hat and sword to Houston, a hat that the former president had given as a gift to the Cherokee leader.

Lamar's desire to conquer Native Americans was not restricted to East Texas but was also applied to the Comanche and Apache on the western frontier. To protect their way of life, tribes raided frontier settlers to steal their possessions and to drive them back. The Nations routinely broke the treaties they had made with Sam Houston because of the decentralized nature of the tribes. If one tribe did not agree with the treaty established for the Nation, they did not feel bound by it. Initially, Texans contested the western tribes using Ranger tactics. Though it annoyed the tribes, the "strike and pursue" tactics of the Rangers proved ineffective. In 1840, the Comanche decided that diplomacy was necessary, and Lamar took advantage of their offer. The Texas government began employing a strategy of dividing the tribes by offering peace treaties or removal to reservations to some so that Texas could focus its resources on conquering other tribes.

The first major step involved negotiations on March 19, 1840, at the Council House in San Antonio. At the meeting, Texans planned to negotiate the release of several white captives, mostly women and children who had been taken in earlier Comanche raids along the frontier. But when the Comanche delegation arrived, they brought only one captive with them, a young girl named Matilda Lockhart. When Lockhart informed the Texans that the Comanche had tortured her and the other captives and that the Comanche intended to ransom the other white prisoners one at a time, talks between the two parties deteriorated. At that point, Texas soldiers entered the Council House and informed the Comanche negotiators that they were going to be held as prisoners until the other white captives were released. The chief of the Comanche party jumped to his feet and called for help from his tribesmen outside of the building. A gun battle erupted between the two parties, resulting in the death of thirty Comanche warriors and five women and children. This event became known as the Council House Fight. In retaliation, the Comanche, who were stationed a few miles outside of San Antonio, tortured and killed all of their prisoners and launched a new wave of attacks on frontier settlements. In August 1840, approximately one thousand Comanche warriors raided Victoria and Linnville. Rangers under Benjamin McCulloch struck and pursued the Comanche raiders, delivering them two major defeats, the most famous at Plum Creek near present-day Lockhart. Even after their success, Texans maintained the pressure. The most legendary encounter between the Comanche and Texas Rangers occurred during this time. Comanche warriors caught John Coffee "Jack" Hays alone and off guard near the summit of Enchanted Rock, north of Fredericksburg. Surrounded and out-numbered with only his rifle and a pair of Colt revolvers, which utilized a new technology unfamiliar to the Comanche, Hays successfully defended himself and secured a place in the lore of the Texas Rangers. Despite some successes, Indian relations during Lamar's presidency proved to be expensive and created more problems than they resolved.

During his term Lamar's land policies produced more immigration than the efforts of Sam Houston. Texans looked to their past to attract settlers through empresarios, which was very similar to the practice during Mexican rule. The empresarios actively recruited settlers for the Republic of Texas from the United States, France, and Germany. To acquire a contract and establish a colony, the empresarios had to recruit 200 families in three years. Just like the laws governing immigration to Texas during Houston's administration, the colonists received 320 acres per single man and 640 acres per family in the colony as compensation for services rendered, including land surveys and title applications. Empresarios normally collected half of a colonist's grant for themselves. Additionally, for every 100 families that the agents settled in their colonies, they received ten segments of the finest land from the Republic. The most successful colonies included Peters Colony in North Texas, which attracted approximately 2,200 families from the American mid-west and the upper South; Castro's Colonies in the Rio Grande Valley and southwest of San Antonio, which settled 2,100 families from the border region of France and Germany; and the Fisher-Miller Grant, which settled a large number of German, Dutch, Swiss, Danish, Swedish, and Norwegian immigrants on the frontier in the Hill Country including Fredericksburg and New Braunfels. The impact of both Houston's and Lamar's policies pushed the frontier west to present-day Dallas, Waco, and Corpus Christi and increased the population of the Republic from 40,000 in 1836 to 142,000 in 1847.

Sam Houston,
President of Texas,
1836-1838, 1841-1844;
Democratic Senator from
Texas, 1846-1859.
Photo credit:
Library of Congress

Lamar's tenure had mixed successes, but his greatest failure involved the fiscal stability of the nation. During his election Lamar criticized Houston for not resolving the debt and pledged to establish credit for the country. Instead Lamar significantly added to Texas's debt. He relied on the same sources of revenue that had been established by Houston's administration, while spending more on the defense of the Republic. Lamar, with his poor financial policies combined with the other failures of his administration, took a leave of absence during the last year of his term. He went to his home in Richmond, Texas, and busied himself with managing his plantation. When his presidential term ended, Lamar had increased the debt of Texas to nearly seven million dollars, up from two million dollars at the conclusion of Houston's presidency. Sam Houston did not hesitate to criticize Lamar—throughout Houston's term as congressman from San Augustine County—on almost every issue, such as the moving of the Republic's capital, the fiscal irresponsibility of the administration, and the embarrassing Santa Fe Expedition that cost the Republic significant money and lives. Lamar's failures hampered any chances that the anti-Houston candidate, David G. Burnet, had during the presidential election in 1841. With little opposition, Houston easily won a second term as the president of Texas.

## Houston's Second Administration

Entering his second term Sam Houston faced even more problems than he did in the first. With the future of Texas even more tenuous, Houston tried to assure the survival of the Republic. Some of his main concerns included, once again, the financial stability of Texas and conciliation with Mexico. With Texas on the verge of financial collapse and foreign invasion, Houston worked to make certain that his second term was not the last of the still-fledgling Republic.

To fix the finances of a nearly bankrupt nation, Houston employed an even more aggressive fiscal policy than he pursued during his first term. His first actions included cutting government activities and costs, including eliminating several positions in the government, reducing the salaries of congressmen, and overturning many of the laws approved by Lamar's administration, such as the printing of extra money and the pursuit of foreign loans. Houston still reduced the government's budget by pursuing peace treaties and establishing trade with Native Americans, such as the treaty at Tehuacana Creek, in present-day McLennan County. The treaties significantly reduced the number and the ferocity of the Indian depredations, but Texas never experienced a "true peace" with their Native American population. Houston's peace policy with the Native Americans allowed him to shrink the Republic's budget even further by reducing the military to approximately fifty to sixty Texas Rangers. When on occasion an Indian raid did occur, local militias were responsible for defending their homesteads. The most controversial cut that Houston made was to sell the navy to pay off some of the Republic's debt. However, faced with the vulnerability from the sea and no protection for Texas merchant vessels, the citizens of Galveston blocked the sale of the ships and spared the small Texas navy. Houston's fiscal policies, though drastic, reduced the spending of the government to only $600,000 throughout his entire second term. Though Houston made a noble attempt, the debt of the Texas government continued to plague the Republic until annexation, when the debt reached ten million dollars.

Problems with Mexico emerged quickly during Houston's second term. Still denying the sovereignty of Texas, President Santa Anna ordered General Rafael Vásquez to capture San Antonio in February 1842 in retaliation for Lamar's Santa Fe Expedition. On March 5, the Mexican Army captured the Alamo city and raised the Mexican flag, temporarily claiming the territory for Mexico. After two days, the army left with their flag for Mexico. Soon thereafter, another Mexican expedition under the command of General Adrián Woll captured San Antonio again. This time the soldiers took sixty prisoners from San Antonio with them. As the Mexican forces retreated, Texan citizens rallied to reclaim the city. Though the two expeditions had limited success, the deep psychological impact in the minds of Texans was significant.

Now their Republic appeared vulnerable to Mexican attack, the government too weak to defend its people, and the sovereignty of Texas threatened. Houston responded by ordering General Alexander Somervell to lead a force of Texans to drive the Mexican army across the Rio Grande and to patrol the border. The general recruited approximately 750 men for what became known as the Somervell Expedition. The Texas force reached the border town of Laredo in early December 1842 without any confrontation from Mexican soldiers. Bored with the occupation of Laredo, 185 men deserted the expedition and returned to their homes. Somervell then ordered the remainder of his force, now just over 500 men, to march down to the Mexican town of Guerrero. After capturing the town, Somervell realized the futility of occupying the city or of continuing further into Mexico, so he ordered the disbandment of the expedition. Many Texans in the expedition expressed their discontent over Somervell's orders by refusing to leave. Only 189 men followed the general back to Texas.

Revenge remained in the hearts of the 308 Texans who remained in Guerrero. The men organized themselves under the leadership of William Fisher for an unauthorized counter-offensive and rescue mission of the San Antonio prisoners, which became known as the Mier Expedition. Some famous Texans participated in this raid on the Mexican town of Mier. Men such as future Civil War generals Thomas J. Green and Benjamin McCulloch led small detachments of Texas Rangers down the Rio Grande and captured with little opposition the border town on December 23. Unbeknownst to the small Texas force, a Mexican force of over 2,000 men was nearby. The Mexican soldiers attacked the Texans on Christmas Day. Low on food, water, and ammunition, the Texans surrendered the following day, believing that the Mexican government would treat them as prisoners of war. Unfortunately, Mexican officials considered the Texans in the Mier Expedition to be criminals and Santa Anna ordered that the soldiers escort them to Mexico City for execution.

While en route to Mexico City, the Texans escaped when they reached the Mexican city of Salado, only to get lost and be recaptured seven days later. During this escape, only three men were able to make their way back to Texas. The other 176 Texans were taken back to Salado with orders given to the Mexican soldiers to execute the prisoners. Foreign ministers in Mexico City successfully pressured Mexican officials to modify the orders, which called for the execution of only one out of every ten Texans. To help decide which soldiers the Mexicans should execute, the Texans had to draw beans out of a pot. In the pot were 159 white beans and 17 black beans. If a soldier drew a white bean, the

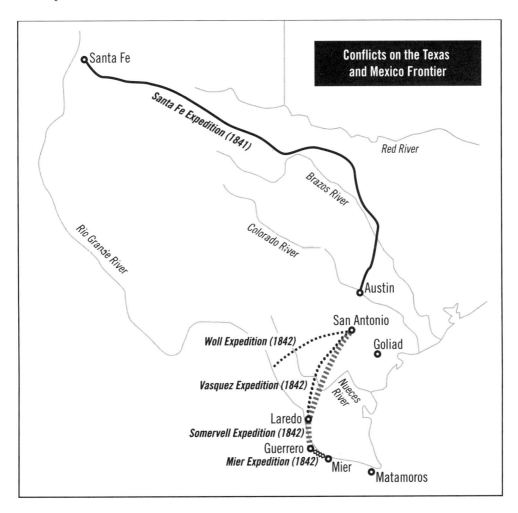

Mexican guards spared their life, but those who drew black beans had to face the firing squad. This process of drawing lots to determine who lived and who died became known as the "black bean episode." Mexican soldiers lined up the seventeen men who drew the black beans against a wall, blindfolded them, and executed them by firing squad. The remaining soldiers became prisoners in Mexico City alongside the captives from Woll's expedition in San Antonio. Over the next two years, numerous Texans escaped from their Mexican prison, and finally the Texas government negotiated the periodic release of others. Santa Anna released the last of the Texas prisoners on September 16, 1844. Although Houston never authorized the Mier Expedition, he received criticism for the event that further strained relations between Texas and Mexico.

**Annexation to the United States**

After the Mier Expedition, a sense of uncertainty reverberated throughout the Republic. Texans began realizing that any dream of remaining an independent country would be more difficult than they could imagine. These concerns renewed Texas's endeavor to seek annexation with the United States. The United States received the initial attempt by Sam Houston in 1837 with disfavor due to the slavery issue and concerns that it could lead to a war with Mexico. In 1843, Houston led a political maneuver to coerce the United States into proposing annexation. That spring he arranged a meeting with Mexican officials to discuss an armistice between Texas and Mexico. Supporting the armistice were the British chargé d'affaires to Texas and the British minister to Mexico. The British officials hoped that their assistance in the armistice would strengthen the diplomatic and economic relationship between Great Britain and Texas. Houston sought similar overtures with France. Essentially in this endeavor Sam Houston established important relationships with England and France in order to capture the United States' attention.

Now motivated by manifest destiny, the idea that divine providence guided the physical and political expansion of the country, the United States wanted to spread its land claims to the Pacific Ocean. When news of these relationships reached the United States, American politicians feared that, if European powers had any influence over Texas, such influence could hamper the United States' plans to reach the Pacific and destroy the vision of manifest destiny. With these small gestures, Houston made the United States take notice of Texas and brought annexation back into the mainstream discussions. Politicians such as John C. Calhoun clamored to make Texas a state, and presidential candidate James K. Polk made annexation a part of his election platform. Amid the controversy, President John Tyler sent Secretary of State Abel Upshur to Texas to negotiate annexation. Houston agreed and sent his own representative, Isaac Van Zandt, who with Upshur drafted a treaty of annexation. On June 8, 1844, the United States Senate rejected the treaty for a variety of reasons, but primarily the Senate wanted to wait until after the presidential elections in the fall to make such a major decision.

The issue remained dormant until Polk won the U.S. presidency in the 1844 elections, which Tyler interpreted as public approval for expansion and the annexation of Texas. With renewed effort and urgency to add Texas to the United States before his term expired, Tyler resolved to annex the Republic through a joint resolution. There were some differences between resolutions and treaties, making Texas unique to other states joining the Union. With a resolution, Texas skipped the territorial stage so that the

United States did not have to appoint a governor of the territory. Also, Texas maintained control of all its public lands, retained the right to split into as many as four additional states because of its immense size, and was responsible for its public debt. By implementing a joint resolution, Tyler made it easier to annex Texas because he only needed a majority of the congressional votes to approve the resolution instead of the usual two-thirds. This was fortunate because the resolution barely passed Congress. In his final act as president, Tyler approved the resolution, and Andrew Jackson Donelson was ordered to Texas to urge the acceptance of the offer. First, the recently elected president of Texas, Anson Jones, called for a special session of Congress in June 1845 to approve the resolution. After passing with little resistance, Texas held a constitutional convention to draft a state constitution to present to the citizens for approval in a public referendum. The Texas electorate overwhelmingly accepted the state constitution in October, and weeks later the U.S. Congress ratified it. On December 29, 1845, the Republic of Texas officially ended as Texas and became the Lone Star State. Two months later, Anson Jones, presided over a symbolic annexation ceremony during the inauguration of the new Texas state governor, James Pinckney Henderson. After a brief address, Jones concluded his speech with the words "The final act in this great drama is now performed; the Republic of Texas is no more," before lowering the flag of the Republic of Texas one last time.

Texas now belonged to the brotherhood of states after nearly ten years of struggling to keep their nation in existence. The era became one of the most colorful in Texas history. Under the leadership of legendary Texans, the Republic had endured numerous adversities. From its difficulties with annexation to the United States to the conflicts with Mexico and Native Americans, Texas persevered throughout its efforts to become the next great power in North America. The development of the Texas Rangers during this era created the origins of one of the greatest legendary law enforcement organizations in the world. Texas experienced some of its greatest achievements, such as the attraction of new settlers, and some of its greatest humiliations with the Santa Fe and Mier Expeditions.

### Afterward: The Cherokee War

*The Killough Massacre was the final chapter of the tensions among the Tejanos, Indians, and Anglo settlers in East Texas. Unfortunately the tension among the Cherokee continued, and the Cherokee War began just the following year. During the 1930s, the Works Progress Administration placed a stone obelisk on the site of the killings, and the Texas State Historical Commission dedicated an historical marker in 1965. The descendants of the Killough families hold a reunion every June in Jacksonville, TX.*

# Myth & Legend

### The Legend of Sam Houston: His True Intentions for Texas

*Why did Samuel Houston come to Texas? Did he cross the Red River from the Indian Territory (presently Oklahoma) to salvage his political career? Or perhaps, President Andrew Jackson, a long time friend of Houston, sent him to find a way to annex the Mexican region to the United States. Many historians have debated this subject without establishing a consensus. Because sources provide limited answers to the question of why Houston came to Texas, numerous myths have emerged in an effort to explain Houston's journey and his actions after arriving in Mexican Texas. Most of them center upon Houston's desire to come to Texas for a fresh start on life. But evidence seems to suggest that his ties to President Jackson may have facilitated his trip to Mexico's northern province.*

*Born March 2, 1793, in Rockbridge County, Virginia, Houston entered a growing family that already had four sons. Unfortunately for Houston, his father died after his thirteenth birthday. The family soon thereafter moved to Eastern Tennessee where his older brothers ran the family farm and a mercantile store. The loss of his father combined with moving to Tennessee caused turmoil in Houston's life. To make sense of the changes around him, he sought guidance in father figures. Unfortunately, his brothers' heavy-handed treatment of him was not what he desired. Houston left home while still a teenager to live among the Cherokee in Georgia. The tribal Chief Oolooteka adopted Houston, becoming a father figure to the wayward teen. With guidance his adopted father helped the young man mature. At age eighteen, Houston left the Cherokees to seek other opportunities.*

*Shortly after Houston left his Cherokee home, the War of 1812 broke out. Like most young men of his generation, Houston enthusiastically joined the army, serving under the notorious Gen. Andrew Jackson of Tennessee. With his charisma and personal courage he quickly rose through the ranks of Gen. Jackson's army. In the battle of Horseshoe Bend, Houston received three near-fatal wounds while leading an assault that inspired all the men that witnessed it. His heroics even caught the attention and admiration of General Jackson. Soon Houston and Jackson developed a close relationship. Houston found another adopted father, one with great influence in America.*

*For the rest of Houston's life he faithfully served both of his adopted fathers. He assisted Oolooteka and the tribe during their forced migration to the Indian Territory, protecting them from the harsh treatment of the undisciplined militia that led them to their new home. Houston also helped Jackson in his political endeavors. For his loyalty, the general rewarded him with military rank and support for government offices in the state of Tennessee, including the governorship. By the end of the 1820s Houston's star shined brightly in the United States, but that all came to an abrupt halt when his marriage to Eliza Allen fell apart just eleven weeks after the newlyweds had exchanged vows. It is unknown to scholars why Eliza left him; scholars speculate that she loved another and only married Houston because her father insisted. Once married, she could not live with her decision. Regardless, the divorce was social and political disaster for Houston. He promptly resigned the governorship and hid from his calamity with Oolooteka. During this self-imposed exile from Anglo society the only person from the East he corresponded with was Jackson.*

*After several years of drowning his sorrows with alcohol, Houston returned to American society only to further damage his political career. During a visit to Washington, D.C., Houston beat William Stanbery, a representative from Ohio, with a cane for making critical comments towards him and Jackson. His actions ostracized him from Washington society but endeared him more to Jackson.*

*Following his trial for assaulting Stanbery, Houston arrived in Texas on December 2, 1832. This moment vexes historians since his intentions are unclear. When entering Mexico, he carried with him an American passport that identified him as an official United States envoy to the Comanche Indians. It seems unlikely that Houston was sent to Mexico to talk with the Comanches, especially considering that he never held council with them. More likely, Houston was sent to Texas as part of President Jackson's plan to annex the region to the United States. Once in Texas, Houston received 4,000 acres from Stephen F. Austin making it appear that he looked to renew his fortunes. Additionally within three months of his arrival he attended a convention to call for separation of Texas from Coahuila, an act that would have given Anglos almost complete control over the province of Texas. During the meeting he sided with a small number of men that called for annexation to the United States. Immediately after the convention's adjournment, Houston traveled to Louisiana where he sent a report to Jackson on his activities. Houston's call for annexation never waned even after Texas gained its independence.*

*During both of his terms as president of Texas, Houston constantly pushed for annexation, an act that was finally achieved in 1846 when the Lone Star State officially joined the United States. The prominence he gained in Texas allowed Houston ultimately to revive his political career. The ever loyal Houston appeared to be doing the bidding of his adopted father, Andrew Jackson, but the revival of his political career also suggests that Houston acted out of his own self interest. With limited documentation explaining Houston's true intensions for coming to Texas, scholars will likely continue to debate the issue*

## Suggestions for Further Reading

Binkley, William C. *The Expansionist Movement in Texas, 1836-1850*. New York: Da Capo Press, 1970.

Conner, Seymour V. *Adventure in Glory.* Austin: Steck-Vaughn, 1965.

Everert, Dianna. *The Texas Cherokees: A People between Two Fires*. Norman: University of Oklahoma Press, 1990.

Haley, James L. *Sam Houston*. Norman: University of Oklahoma Press, 2004.

Haynes, Sam W. *Soldiers of Misfortune: The Somervell and Mier Expedition*. Austin: University of Texas Press, 1990.

Pletcher, David M. *The Diplomacy of Annexation: Texas Oregon, and the Mexican War.* Columbia: University of Missouri Press, 1973.

Reichstein, Andreas V. *Rise of the Lone Star: The Making of Texas*. College Station: Texas A&M University Press, 1989.

Schmitz, Joseph William. *Texan Statecraft, 1836-1845*. San Antonio: Naylor, 1941.

Siegel, Stanley. *A Political History of the Texas Republic, 1836-1845*. Austin: University of Texas Press, 1956.

Silbey, Joel H. *Storm Over Texas: The Annexation Controversy and the Road to Civil War.* New York: Oxford University Press, 2005.

Smith, F. Todd. *The Wichita Indians: Traders of Texas and the Southern Plains, 1540-1845.* College Station: Texas A&M University Press, 2000.

Spellman, Paul N. *Forgotten Texas Leader: Hugh McLeod and the Texan Santa Fe Expedition.* College Station: Texas A&M University Press, 1999.

Weems, John Edward. *Dream of Empire: A Human History of the Republic of Texas, 1836-1846.* New York: Simon & Schuster, 1971.

**IDENTIFICATION:** Briefly describe each term.

James K. Polk
Mier Expedition
Santa Fe Expedition
Texas Rangers
Battle of the Neches
Annexation
League and Labor of Land
Duwali
"Black Bean Episode"
Anson Jones
Plum Creek
John "Jack" Coffee Hays
Somervell Expedition
Antonio Lopez de Santa Anna
Joint Resolution

**MULTIPLE CHOICE:** Choose the correct response.

1. During the Republic era, which of the following were NOT elected president?
   A. Anson Jones
   B. Sam Houston
   C. Stephen F. Austin
   D. Mirabeau Lamar

2. Who was elected the first president of Texas?
   A. Anson Jones
   B. Sam Houston
   C. Stephen F. Austin
   D. Mirabeau Lamar

3. What was the issue that prevented the United States from annexing Texas?
   A. It was east of the Mississippi River
   B. Slavery
   C. Economic depression
   D. Frontier protection

4. Which best describes the Texas Rangers?
   A. An elite police organization
   B. A professional military force
   C. Men that enlisted for a specific campaign
   D. Part of the Texas Army

5. What best describes Houston's policy towards Native Americans:
   A. Diplomatic
   B. Militaristic
   C. Harsh
   D. All the above

6. Who won the presidential election of 1838?
   A. Sam Houston
   B. Mirabeau Lamar
   C. Anson Jones
   D. James Collinsworth

7. Lamar's policy toward annexation to the United States is best described as:
   A. Rejecting it because of his imperialistic desires
   B. Sought it to pay off the debt of Texas
   C. Sought it for frontier defense
   D. He was apathetic towards joining the United States

8. Lamar moved the Texas capital to:
   A. San Antonio
   B. Austin
   C. Columbus
   D. Houston

9. Lamar concluded his final year as president:
   A. Getting Texas out of debt
   B. At war with Mexico
   C. Orchestrating annexation to the United States
   D. At home because of his many failures

10. Which United States president sought a joint resolution to annex Texas?
    A. Andrew Jackson
    B. Anson Jones
    C. John Tyler
    D. James K. Polk

**TRUE/FALSE:** Indicate whether each statement is true or false.

1. Majority of the officials in the government of the Republic of Texas first had political experience in the United States.

2. All the presidents of Texas served three year terms.

3. Throughout the Republic era, Texas had a significant debt.

4. Sam Houston refused to give land away to settlers.

5. Americans were united in their desire to annex Texas.

6. Lamar established an aggressive policy toward Native Americans.

7. Anson Jones opposed annexation to the United States.

8. Mexico refused to recognize the sovereignty of Texas.

9. Texas soldiers were successful with the Santa Fe Expedition.

10. Houston adopted harsh policies to reduce the debt of the Republic.


**MATCHING:** Match the response in column A with the item in column B.

1. John "Jack" Coffee Hays
2. Cherokees
3. Comanche
4. Council House Massacre
5. Linnville and Victoria Raid
6. Santa Fe Expedition
7. Somervell Expedition
8. Mier Expedition
9. Sam Houston
10. Mirabeau Lamar

A. Prominent Texas Ranger during the Republic era
B. The only two time president in Texas history
C. Unfriendly Native Americans in West Texas
D. A diplomatic meeting between Comanche and Texans that ended in the slaughtering of the Native Americans at the meeting
E. Texas's successful attempt to run the Mexican Army across the Rio Grande
F. Comanche raids resulting in the death of Anglo settlers on the frontier
G. An unauthorized military expedition into Mexico, resulting in the death of many of the men
H. Friendly Native Americans in East Texas
I. The second president of Texas and founder of the first publically sponsored education system
J. Texas's failed attempt to capture eastern New Mexico

**ESSAY QUESTIONS:**

1. Why did Texas seek foreign recognition?

2. How successful was Texas as an independent country?

3. Compare and contrast the administrations of Sam Houston and Mirabeau Lamar. Which of the two presidents was the most successful? Explain why.

4. Why were some Americans reluctant to annex Texas? What eventually convinced the United States Congress to seriously consider adding Texas as a state?

# The 28th State in the Union, 1845-1861

***Prelude: The Façade of the Alamo***

*Texas has many symbols, ranging from its distinctive shape of its boundaries to the various flags that have represented its development, the most noteworthy being the "Lone Star" and "Come and Take It" flags. These representations appear on a variety of businesses products ranging from beer bottles in the United States to motels in Europe. One symbol, the façade of the Alamo chapel, transcends all others in its appeal. By the 1950s, it became a national emblem of unity during the Cold War. The story of its development, from a war-torn chapel to its current iconic step-shaped architectural design, parallels the rise of Texas's myths and legends.*

*Historians are not certain how the builders of the Mission San Antonio de Valero (Alamo) designed the façade of the chapel. By time the Texans took control of the Alamo complex, the façade and the roof were in ruins. The Battle of the Alamo inspired the Texas forces to gain their independence in the Battle of San Jacinto, thus making the complex known as the "Cradle of Texas Liberty." Despite this title, the buildings, damaged from the fighting, remained dilapidated. Interestingly, this is the first time it became a "traveler's curiosity," as people began to visit the place to tour the most tangible and popular representation of the Texas Revolution. Upon leaving the complex, visitors usually took away pieces of the buildings as mementos. Throughout the Republic period, the Alamo remained abandoned and neglected despite the Catholic Church's ownership of the property. Illustrations and daguerreotypes from this time show a crumbling building with a flat top and significant damage to the corners.*

*Within a few years, the United States annexed Texas and declared government ownership of the Alamo, turning the site into a military headquarters and supply depot. From here, all frontier fortifications in the state had to report. For a time, the U.S. Army used the chapel as a stable for military horses. In 1849, the army improved the grounds and repaired all the buildings. The first improvements to the chapel included a traditional slanted wooden roof while maintaining the decorative pillars and faux mantle on the front, which became an unfortunate consequence since a wooden roof on a limestone building was not esthetically appeasing. To hide the unsightly roof, the army engineers constructed the now famous façade with the stepped sides and rounded top. Consequently, this unintended design became the basis for the internationally recognized symbol of the Lone Star State within the next few decades.*

*The military maintained ownership of the Alamo complex until 1876. Ownership of the complex fell into private hands for the next four years and used as part of a grocery store. Appalled by these dramatic changes to the Alamo, concerned Texans founded the Alamo Monument Association in 1879 to preserve the site. Due to their efforts, the state of Texas purchased the Alamo chapel for $65,000 and turned over custodianship to the city of San Antonio. The River City cared for the buildings until January 25, 1905, when the state legislature approved a resolution obliging the governor to purchase the remainder of the property and buildings occupied by businesses. Additionally, the governor agreed to transfer ownership of the entire complex to the Daughters of the Republic of Texas (DRT), an organization created to honor the men and women who fought for the independence of the Lone Star nation. The DRT worked with the San Antonio Conservation Society to clean up and preserve the Alamo, restoring the building from its decrepit state. With their efforts, they created a garden area and a plaza, focusing most of their attention on the chapel, but controversy soon enveloped the future of the Alamo. Commercial interests quickly threatened the property, forcing the local leader of the DRT, Adina De Zavala, to barricade herself in one of the buildings, drawing national attention to San Antonio. Soon thereafter, the first motion picture of the Battle of the Alamo, "The Immortal Alamo," (1911) was released, inspiring a new influx of visitors. However, it was the famed director D. W. Griffith's depiction in "Martyrs of the Alamo: The Birth of Texas" (1915) that transmitted the image of the façade across the nation and around the world.*

After the celebrations over the Lone Star State's official annexation to the United States died out in late February 1846, troubles emerged that would seal North America's fate. The years of early statehood brought Texas to the national stage of United States politics and subjected the state to the major events that led to the American Civil War. From its annexation to the secession crisis, the state of Texas experienced dramatic changes. Annexation brought both hardships and benefits such as war with Mexico and more protection from Native Americans on the frontier. Along with statehood came a flood of migrants from the United States and immigrants from Europe and Mexico who influenced the class stratification and the social and cultural life of Texas. These changes languished among the political developments of secession and Sam Houston's feeble attempt to dissuade his state from seceding and joining the Confederate states. The initial fifteen years of Texas's statehood with the United States proved to be tumultuous. Then the state plunged into the Civil War, leaving the fate of Texas uncertain in the early spring of 1861. The impending Civil War determined the next path for the Lone Star State.

**Problems with Statehood**

Texas's honeymoon with the United States was short-lived, especially on the issue of slave labor. Slavery, the matter that blocked Texas's immediate annexation after the Texas Revolution, was the single greatest problem facing the United States in 1846. Fear of spreading the institution into new territories and allowing slave states to join the United States inhibited the annexation of Texas and further expansion in the southwest. When Texas entered the union, fears and concerns exploded as several events transpired that brought

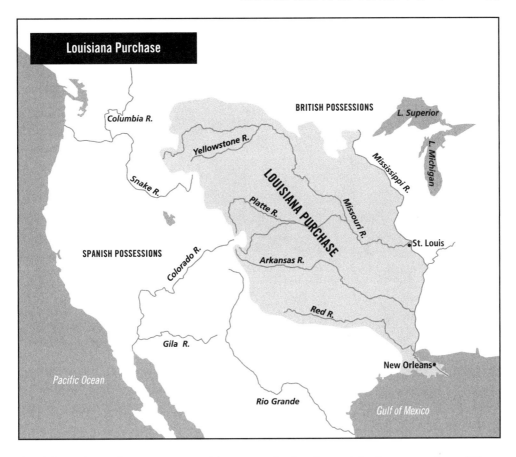

the debate about the institution of slavery to the forefront. The incorporation of Texas into the United States was unique. Texas was the first slave state largely outside of the Louisiana Purchase and ceded land since the Treaty of Paris 1783. Abolitionists were concerned that slavery would spread across the west and perpetuate into the future. The United States previously relied on the Northwest Ordinances of the 1780s to grant statehood. Before the United States granted statehood, a region had to meet criteria for statehood, such as an established government, a bill of rights, and a population that was equal to or greater than the least populated of the original thirteen states. During this process, the region held the status of territory. This precedence continued outside of the Old Northwest when new territory was acquired with the Louisiana Purchase—all the land acquired from the French, which is usually defined as the watershed for the Mississippi River in the Trans-Mississippi. Since the purchased territory contained significant land in the South, slavery became a major issue. The United States addressed this issue with the passage of the Missouri Compromise, which resolved the issue of incorporating slave states by limiting the amount of territory in which slavery could exist and established the precedence that, for every slave state admitted to the Union, a free state must join as well and vice versa. The admission of Texas was unique during the time because it was mostly outside of the Louisiana Purchase and, therefore, not covered by the Missouri Compromise or the Northwest Ordinances. One interesting aspect about the annexation of Texas was that it met all the criteria for statehood and received admission to the Union while skipping the requisite territorial stage. The an-

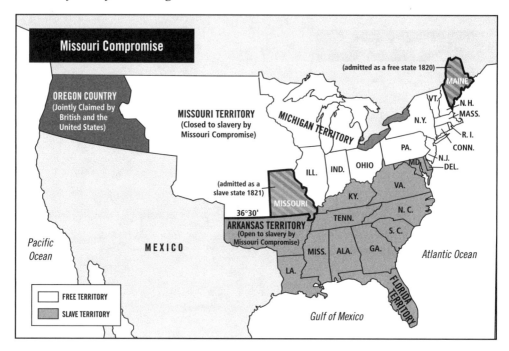

nexation of Texas created the opportunity for southern slave owners to push for further territory to expand their institution. Slavery was a major issue that the United States faced before Texas joined the country, but afterwards the issue remained the greatest subject of debate.

A more immediate problem that Texas and the United States faced early in 1846 was an international conflict with Mexico. The annexation of Texas and the United States' desire to expand its territory under the banner of manifest destiny contributed to strained relations between the U.S. and Mexico. President James K. Polk sparked a quarrel with Mexico when he sent John Slidell to contact the Mexican government to negotiate a settlement on the boundary between Texas and its southern neighbor at the Rio Grande, to negotiate the purchase of northern California, and to settle American claims against Mexico. The greatest issue was the disputed border between Texas and Mexico, which the Mexican government claimed was the Nueces River, a claim that the Texans flatly refused, stating that the real boundary was the Rio Grande. Consequently, the region in dispute became known as the "Nueces Strip." Not willing to admit that Texas was no longer a Mexican state nor to sell any part of their country, Mexican politicians viewed the annexation and Polk's attempt to negotiate with them over territory as a direct insult. With Mexican officials refusing to respond to these requests, Polk gradually realized that politicians in Mexico would not negotiate the sale of a single square foot of territory because they risked losing their political offices. On January 13, 1846, before Slidell returned, Polk ordered General Zachary Taylor and his army stationed at Corpus Christi to advance to the mouth of the Rio Grande to secure what they claimed as the border of Texas. The Mexican government viewed Polk's order as an act of war and ordered troops in Matamoros to attack the American force. In late April, Mexican troops crossed the Rio Grande and attacked the United States soldiers killing and wounding several Americans. On May 11, Polk asked Congress for a declaration war against Mexico, creating a controversy in which abolitionists accused the president of intentionally starting the war so he could capture northern California for the United States. With war declared by Congress on May 13, the United States made plans to invade northern Mexico. Given the location of their state, Texans played a major role in the invasion.

When the Mexican-American War (1846-1848) began, approximately 5,000-7,000 Texans volunteered to defend Texas and fight for their newly-adopted country, most serving in Taylor's army in northern Mexico. Some of the most notable Texans included Colonel John Coffee Hays, who gained a reputation in the state for his numerous exploits against the Comanche as a Texas Ranger. Hays's fame increased during the war when he led a regiment of Texas Mounted Rifles in the capture of Monterrey, Mexico. Major Benjamin McCulloch, another Texas Ranger, commanded a spy company that contributed to the American victory at Buena Vista, Mexico. Though men from the regular army accused the Texans of committing numerous atrocities, including murder, theft, and destruction of property, it was their physical appearance that captured the most attention. Many of the Texans who served in Taylor's army looked the part of the rugged frontiersmen with unkempt cloths, heavily bearded faces, and the appearance of uneducated barbarians. Unfortunately, when men from other states returned home after the war, they took these very opinions of Texans with them, opinions which lasted for several decades.

As the war progressed, the U.S. Army formed an expeditionary force under General Winfield Scott that landed at Vera Cruz. Scott planned to invade the interior of the country and capture Mexico City and Antonio López de Santa Anna, the president of Mexico. Once the capital city and the president were under his control, he would force a peace treaty that would cede northern Mexico to the United States. The only significant group of Texans that served under Scott was organized by Hays who formed a special ranger unit. His men protected Scott's communication and supply lines from Mexican partisans. Texans treated the partisans mercilessly causing the Mexican civilians to dub Hays's men as "los Tejanos diablos" (the Texas Devils). Scott's force eventually captured Mexico City and accomplished all their goals with the signing of the Treaty of Guadalupe-Hidalgo (1848). The treaty settled the dispute over the boundary of Texas, establishing it at the Rio Grande, and gave the United States possession of lands in northern Mexico, which included New Mexico, Arizona, Nevada, Utah, California, and parts of Colorado and Wyoming.

Even before the fighting ended in Mexico, hostility over slavery heated up again over concern about the future of the territories acquired from the Mexican American War. Earlier, in 1846, a freshman representative from Pennsylvania, David Wilmot, introduced an amendment to an appropriations bill to fund the war. The amendment proposed to outlaw slavery in all the territories acquired from Mexico as a result of the war. The amendment passed the House but failed in the Senate, where Southerners had an equal number of votes. Wilmot's direct challenge to the future spread of slavery in the United States deepened the rift between the North and South. Controversy over the expansion of slavery into the American Southwest continued in the years after the war, with Texas once again becoming a central character.

## New Mexico-Texas Boundary Dispute and the Compromise of 1850

Though the Mexican-American War settled the border dispute between Texas and Mexico, the issue of slavery continued to plague the United States. At the outbreak of the war, the United States Army sent a force to occupy New Mexico and to establish a civil government. Texas Governor James Pinckney Henderson protested to Secretary of State James Buchanan that he viewed these actions as a direct challenge to the state's western border claims of the Rio Grande based on the Treaties of Velasco, which ended the Texas Revolution. The southwest, including Texas's border claims of parts of present-day New Mexico, Colorado, and Wyoming, became a battleground between Texans—as well as most Southerners—and Free-Soilers over the status of whether the territory should be open or closed to the further expansion of slavery. Texas aided the South's cause by strengthening its claim to the Rio Grande being its western border by organizing Santa Fe County in 1848. Civilian and military leaders in New Mexico rejected Texas's attempts to claim the land by petitioning the United States government for recognition as federal territory. Even after Henderson left office, Texas politicians fought to acquire New Mexico. Texas Governor Peter H. Bell reacted to New Mexico's petition by requesting that a military unit be organized to occupy Texas's claimed lands and that Robert S. Neighbors—an Indian agent who established reservations in the state and a Texas commissioner

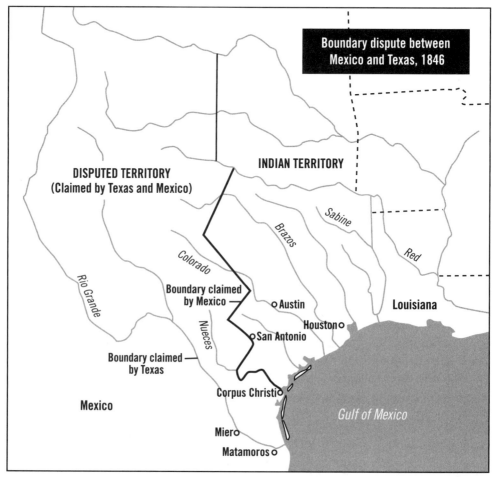

that organized El Paso County—be sent to organize four counties in the disputed region. Residents in New Mexico did not cooperate with Neighbor's attempt to organize the counties, and they continued their protest over being incorporated into Texas.

The border controversy kept Texas in the national spotlight in the late 1840s. Before Texas could organize a military force, the crisis deepened after New Mexico initiated a bid for statehood by ratifying a constitution, which included within its borders the contested territory of the new state. President Millard Fillmore reinforced New Mexico's claims by sending more federal soldiers to the territory with orders to resist any incursion by Texas forces. This instantly created outrage in the South whose leaders publicly supported Governor Bell and pledged military support if Texas did invade New Mexico. The dispute between Texas and New Mexico reached the national stage when congress attempted to resolve this volatile issue. Several congressmen, including Henry Clay and Stephen Douglas, introduced bills to settle the border dispute, including one that proposed that Texas should be split into four separate states. The compromise bills also addressed other major sectional issues, ranging from the annexation of California and the Texas border to popular sovereignty and fugitive slave laws. Success for the border dispute came as part of a series of laws known as the Compromise of 1850 when Senator James A. Pierce introduced a bill that appeased both Texas and New Mexico. The bill offered to settle the border dispute by setting the border of Texas at its modern boundary. In return, Texas would receive $10 million dollars, which would enable the state to pay off its debt incurred when Texas was an independent republic. Congress passed and President Fillmore signed the bill, along with the other components of the Compromise and sent it to Texas for approval. Though some Texans resisted, the public ratified the compromise settlement in a special election by a margin of three to one. Other components of the Compromise of 1850 addressed the growing sectional crisis, and although neither the North nor the South completely agreed with the compromise, it temporarily appeased the growing concern over the expansion of slavery.

Similar to the Compromise of 1850, the Kansas-Nebraska Act divided the nation further. Designed by Illinois Senator Stephen A. Douglas, it called for the creation of the Kansas and Nebraska territories for settlers. Employing the concept of popular sovereignty, voters could determine if slavery would be allowed or not to encourage settlement. The act essentially dissolved the Missouri Compromise allowing pro- and anti-slavery supporters to stream into the territories, and violence ensued. Disgusted with the idea, Senator Sam Houston vehemently opposed the act. He believed that removing the Missouri Compromise was "fatal to the future harmony and well-being of the country." He later prophesied that union or disunion depended upon this decision and that a Free-Soiler be elected in 1860. With the election the South would "go down in the unequal contest, in a sea of blood and smoking ruin." Houston's strong stance against the Kansas-Nebraska Act precipitated his fall in popularity, particularly with the Democrats. In 1855, the Texas legislature passed a resolution that publicly pronounced "that the Legislature approves the course of Thomas J. Rusk in voting for the Kansas-Nebraska Act and disproves the course of Sam Houston in voting against it." The Legislature, controlled by Democrats, essentially informed Houston that they would not reappoint him senator and did not support him in his failed 1857 gubernatorial race. With his senatorial term not expiring until 1859, Houston returned to Washington, D.C. wearing his famed jaguar skin vest. He conveniently called it leopard, "because

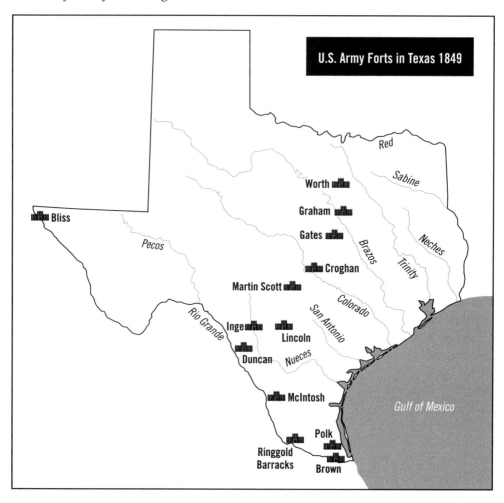

the scriptures says 'a leopard cannot change his spots'" symbolically protesting the Kansas-Nebraska Act.

Throughout the 1850s, individuals from the South remained focused on the preservation of chattel bondage. Southerners hoped to maintain slavery by forming secret societies for the purpose of creating a southern slave empire. The most prominent of these was the Knights of the Golden Circle (KGC). Seen as a precursor to the Ku Klux Klan, the KGC was a vehicle of southern manifest destiny. Founded by George Bickley in 1855, the KGC wanted to "take up the line of march," to "take possession of states of Tamaulipas, Neuava [sic] Leon, Coahuila, and Chihuahua, and of them organize a Government, thereby forming . . . a nucleus around which our valiant Knights would soon rally" in order to expand the borders of the United States and extend slavery into Latin America. Under Bickley's leadership, the KGC wanted to establish Havana, Cuba, as the center of a slave empire that would reach for 1,200 miles in every direction. The empire would include the Old South, all of Central America, and the northern tip of South America so that the South could control "the cotton lands of Mexico" and "the rich resources of Mexico and South American States." Though primarily a southern organization, Texas was critical to the Knights' cause, prompting the secret order to make their headquarters in San Antonio.

## Advantages of Statehood

Annexation led to many problems for Texas and the United States, but the Lone Star State received some major benefits. The most obvious advantage for Texas was the arrival of the United States Army on the Texas frontier. Before statehood, the inefficiency of the Texas army created an era marked by constant Indian raids and Mexican expeditions into the region. As soon as Texas joined the United States, the U.S. Army took responsibility for the protection of the Lone Star State. The Mexican-American War settled the disputes along the Mexican border, temporarily allowing the military to focus its attention on the protection of the Texas frontier. During the early years of statehood, the army established a network of self-sufficient and supportive fortifications on the frontier to combat Native Americans. The chain of military outposts started in South Texas with Fort Brown in Brownsville and extended west to Fort Bliss in El Paso and north to Fort Worth. With other forts in between, the military created a formidable defense for the frontier settlers of Texas.

Problems emerged though as Anglo settlers began to quickly encroach on Native American lands and soon outpaced the army's ability to build all the fortifications necessary to protect them and the ever-expanding frontier. Starting in 1851, the military established a new chain of fortifications over one hundred miles to the west of the original line. Though the U.S. Army's chain of fortifications was effective, Indian raids continued to occur. Texans reacted to these depredations by increasing support for the Texas Rangers and by organizing militias from volunteers living in frontier counties. The militiamen sometimes created more problems than they resolved. Ill-trained, the militias often attacked the wrong Indian camps, and they found it difficult to get along with army regulars serving on the frontier. To ease tensions and to protect the more friendly Indians in the regions, the United States government established four Indian reservations in Texas: the Brazos Indian Reservation in present-day Graham, Texas; the Comanche Indian Reservation on the Clear Forks of the Brazos River; another that never was completed in the Trans-Pecos for the Mescalero Apaches and the Lipan Apaches; and the Alabama-Coushatta Reservation. The former three reservations were eventually dissolved, and the inhabitants were moved to the Indian Territory in present-day Oklahoma in 1859. The most successful reservation was the Alabama-Coushatta Indian Reservation in Polk County, Texas, where the descendants of the two tribes remain today and still govern themselves.

## Ethnic Groups and Slaves in Texas

In the early nineteenth century it was common throughout the South to find "GTT" (Gone To Texas) marked on the doors of vacant houses. Texas symbolized a land of new opportunities for many Americans as well as for immigrants from foreign countries. Though people migrated to Texas prior to 1845, the state experienced a major influx of new people after annexation. From 1850 to 1860, the Texas population increased 184 percent—from 212,592 to 604,215. Anglos from across the United States came to Texas, and slaveholders from the South brought with them their human property. Among the new settlers were individuals and families from foreign countries, the largest numbers immigrating from Mexico, Germany, along with significant numbers of Wends (a Slavic group from the eastern part of Germany), Czechoslovakia, Poland, England, and Ireland.

This hugely diverse group of people who settled Texas left a lasting impact on the culture of the state.

Anglo Americans from all parts of the country migrated to Texas, but the majority were families from the South. Southerners tended to settle in lands that resembled the regions they left because they already possessed the specific skills to farm that certain type of land as well as the proper tools to be successful in their endeavors. Consequently, people from one state would tend to concentrate in one particular area of Texas. A general pattern developed where people from Tennessee settled in the blackland prairie of North Texas; Louisianans in the counties bordering the Gulf of Mexico; Georgians in the plantation districts in northeast Texas; Alabamans in the inland counties to the east of the resettled Tennesseans; Mississippians in western South-Central Texas, and Kentuckians in North Texas. Individuals and families from northern states also settled in Texas, primarily in North Texas where there were very few slave plantations. Within each of these regions, the migrants established themselves and brought with them their culture and way of life, with southern planters establishing cotton and sugar plantations in eastern and southeastern Texas and Northerners relying on subsistence and wheat farming in the northern region of the state.

Thousands of slaves accompanied southern planters and farmers as they migrated to Texas. Slavery had existed in Texas when it was still a part of the Republic of Mexico, but it is during early statehood that the institution saw its largest growth. When Texas entered the United States, approximately 30,505 slaves lived in the state. On the eve of the Civil War, the number of slaves increased to over 183,000—approximately a third of the total population. Most slaves lived in eastern and southeastern Texas where the majority of the slaveholders had established cotton and sugar plantations.

The treatment of the slaves in Texas was similar to that in the other southern states. Most slaves worked as field hands from sun up to sun down, with a significant minority working as house servants, craftsmen, and herdsmen. About 6 percent of the bondsmen lived and worked in urban centers as mechanics, domestic servants, and general laborers. Treatment of slaves in Texas resembled that of other southern states since the slaveholders still controlled their slaves with violence and threats to break up families. Generally, slaveowners provided their bondsmen with adequate food, clothing, and shelter to protect their investment in human property. Food consisted mainly of corn and salted pork; though rich in calories, it lacked sufficient vitamins and minerals. To supplement their diet, slaves raised their own food, including sweet potatoes and green vegetables. They also fished and hunted when their masters allowed. Clothing provided the slaves was made of inexpensive uncomfortable material but was sufficient to protect them from the elements. Slave quarters generally consisted of a small log cabin with little to no furnishings other than a bed with a fireplace for cooking and for warmth in the winter. The harsh conditions that African Americans endured led many to resist their condition, for example, by playing dumb to fool the master or by the decisive form of resistance—escape. Though slaveowners in other southern states worried about bondsmen escaping north through the underground railroad, Texans' concerns turned southward with slaves crossing the border into Mexico to gain their freedom. Some also escaped to the Indian Nations to the north.

Slaves endured a life of humiliation and hard work, but many aspects of their lives allowed them to endure an existence in bondage. Their family was crucial to the social lives of slaves especially in their quarters. At the end of the work day, slaves had relative freedom in their homes, where their family was the center of their social life and a unique African-American culture burgeoned. Family life extended to marriage and producing children. Though slave marriages were not recognized by law, masters encouraged their slaves to marry and to establish families of their own because it increased the number of slaves in their possession. More important, family life and kin provided the support that the bondsmen needed to endure their ordeal, and slaves with familial ties to the plantation made them less likely to run away. Religion also played a major role in the lives of slaves. Most religious expression involved the Christian teachings of a loving God and the hope that after death they would be reunited with their lost family members in a heaven where slavery did not exist. In instances when slaves felt the slaveholders were excessively oppressive, bondsmen employed nonviolent resistance to slow the work pace, such as breaking tools, using songs to communicate to other field hands to set a slower tempo, and pretending to not understand what the slave driver asked of them. The institution of slavery in Texas never reached the same size as the rest of the cotton states in the South, but its growth during this time period demonstrated its importance to the future of the state.

Other ethnic groups, such as the Tejanos, experienced numerous changes after statehood. A majority of the Tejano population still resided in the Rio Grande Valley, but despite the large number of Anglo migrants, Hispanics spread their settlements further north to the Nueces River. The number of people of Mexican origin increased from 14,000 in 1850 to 23,200 by 1860. The status of Tejanos changed once again after the annexation of Texas, especially with the outbreak of the Mexican American War. With the United States at war with Mexico, those of Mexican descent in Texas immediately came under suspicion. Land-hungry Anglos used the war to increase their antagonism toward Hispanic communities by confiscating their lands. Many Tejanos did not have any legal land claims to the property on which they lived and worked. Anglos who wanted that real estate challenged their land claims by forcing Hispanic landowners to defend themselves in Anglo courts, which almost exclusively ruled against Tejanos. Other reasons factored into the ill treatment of Hispanics. Migrants from other regions of the United States brought with them to Texas their racial and religious prejudices. Newcomers were not as knowledgeable or understanding of the cultural differences between themselves and Tejanos as those who had lived in the Lone Star State prior to the Texas Revolution. Resentment of a different culture, especially the celebration of Catholic holidays, contributed to many migrants' acts of violence. Additionally, the Hispanic racial view of African Americans conflicted with Anglo desires. Many Tejanos did not approve of human bondage and freely fraternized with African Americans. Anglos, especially slaveowners, interpreted these actions, in some cases correctly, to mean that all Hispanics aided slaves in escaping to Mexico.

Some Anglos viewed Tejanos as economic competition, especially in ranching. By taking away their lands, whites were able to eliminate the Hispanics' ability to contend in the cattle market. The competition over economic opportunities is most evident in the "Cart Wars." In 1857, Anglos wanted to join the Tejano-dominated transporting business of carting goods from the coast to the interior of the state. Viewing Tejanos as their major obstacle to starting their new business, whites began destroying carts, stealing their freight, and attacking Hispanic teamsters. Not wanting to lose their way of life, Tejanos began to fight back by creating a national and international sensation about this issue. Acting upon orders from the U.S. secretary of state to resolve the situation, Governor Elisha M. Pease authorized a militia force to protect the Anglo teamsters. Essentially, the Texas government restricted Tejanos from carting goods from the coast until the Civil War, when demand increased allowing both races to profit.

Resentment towards Anglos grew among the Tejano population before the Civil War. In 1859 Juan Cortina in South Texas emerged as a champion for Tejanos. Cortina served in the Mexican Army during the war with the United States and railed against the Texans' treatment of Hispanics living near the border with Mexico. His resentment began after the Mexican-American War when his family lost their land in Brownsville. Eventually, Cortina's animosity led to a self-proclaimed war against white Texans. The war began after Cortina saved an elderly Tejano ranch hand, who at one time had worked for Cortina, by shooting the white marshal who was beating the worker. Now a wanted man, Cortina escaped to Mexico but returned two months later with a group of men determined to avenge the atrocities on Mexican people by Anglo settlers. When he entered Brownsville, Cortina and his followers screamed "Death to Americans" and "Viva Mexico" and attacked any Anglo they could find, killing two white men. This demonstration rallied the local Tejano population to his cause, increasing his numbers, and caught the attention of officials in Texas and the United States. The Texas Rangers and the U.S. Army were sent to South Texas to quell the uprising. Facing overwhelming numbers, Cortina retreated into Mexico until the United States turned its attention to the secession crisis unfolding in late 1860.

One of the few bastions of power left for Tejanos was in the city of Laredo. Since the city was near the frontier and far from the main routes of trade, Anglos did not have as much interest in the area and, thus, made no challenges to the land claims. Laredo flourished under the leadership of businessman and rancher Santos Benavides, who served as *alcalde* and mayor of the city under both the Mexican and Texas governments. Tejanos enjoyed more freedom in Laredo than anywhere else in Texas. Nevertheless, Tejanos during early statehood experienced a time of hardship spurred on by the continued racism of Anglos in Texas.

Other groups of non-Americans lived in Texas during statehood, such as Germans and other European immigrants, who had been arriving on the shores of Texas even before the Republic era. During statehood there was an explosion of new immigrants from across the Atlantic Ocean with Germans being the most significant of them. During the Republic era the Fischer-Miller Land Grant in the Texas Hill Country was set aside for Germans wanting to settle in North America. Germans wanting to start a new life arrived but often were unable to reach or settle on the land grant because they were too poor to make the trip and because the area was deep in the frontier and occupied by hostile Indians. Instead of settling on the land grant, Germans founded numerous cities on the land between the coast and the Hill Country, the most significant of which was New Braunfels, located between Austin and San Antonio.

At the end of the 1840s, a new wave of German immigrants, escaping the European Revolutions of 1848 and compulsory military service, made their way to Texas. Commonly called the Greens, they were content to live in relative isolation in the sparsely settled Hill Country. By the time the Greens arrived, the U.S. Army had mostly abated the Indian threat there and pushed the frontier farther west of the region. Most Greens settled in the frontier settlements of Fredericksburg and Comfort to maintain their home culture in isolation.

Both the Germans arriving before the Texas Revolution and those arriving afterwards suffered persecution from Anglo Texans. Germans brought with them more than just their culture but also abolitionist ideas, which produced conflict with Southerners. Germans did not accept the institution of slavery, except for a handful of people in the San Antonio and New Braunfels areas. Compounding the stress of abolitionists in Texas was the Germans' efficiency in producing more crops on smaller plots of land than their native counterparts could on larger land tracts, unconsciously implying that farmers could succeed without the use of slaves. The recent Green immigrants, though isolated, felt greater discrimination than those who had lived longer in the Lone Star State. The primary reason was their antislavery position and their resistance to assimilate into southern culture. Despite these conflicts, Germans had a significant impact on Texas society, including the promotion of public education, as well as the introduction of rifle clubs, gymnastics, and breweries.

Other groups of Europeans made Texas their home during this period. Polish immigrants were a small ethnic group in Texas that has a long and interesting history in the state. Individual Poles immigrated to Texas during the first half of the nineteenth century. The first large-scale Polish immigration was in 1854 when over 100 families settled in Texas. They left Europe looking for political, economic, and social freedom. Similar to the German Greens, the Poles escaped the oppression of occupying rulers in Upper Silesia because of the failed attempts at revolution in 1848. Other reasons included the depressed economy from the flood of the Oder River in the summer of 1854, inflation of food prices by the Crimean War, conscription in the Prussian Army, and cholera and typhus outbreaks during the 1840s and 1850s. When the families settled near San Antonio, Panna Maria, and Bandera, they brought their Polish culture, national identity, and Catholic religion with them. Czech settlers in Texas began populating Central Texas in 1851 in isolated rural communities, and by 1861, approximately 700 resided in Texas. A combination of their recent arrival and their isolation allowed Czech settlers to maintain their distinctive culture. The Wends were another Central European ethnic group who immigrated to Texas in the 1850s. They were a small isolated Slavic group from eastern Germany, virtually cut off from other Slavs. Fear of the influence of German culture on their children, in addition to political, economic, and social oppression, pressured the slavic group to leave Europe. In 1854, approximately 500 Wends sailed to Texas and settled in Serbia, Texas, an isolated rural community in Lee County. Swedish immigration began in 1848. Like other recent European immigrants, Swedes maintained their culture, especially their abolitionist beliefs, that viewed the plantation system as similar to the "feudal estates" in Europe. The ability of all these ethnic groups to maintain their culture and heritage still impacts Texas, as evidenced in the local architecture, cuisine, and flourishing cultural festivals.

The migration of Southerners and foreigners to Texas in the decades before the Civil War dramatically altered the composition of the population, making it far different than the rest of the South. By 1860, the population of Texas reached 604,000. Only a quarter of this number (153,000) could call Texas their birthplace, while a third (201,000) of the residents were southern born. A very small fraction of Texans, 4 percent (24,000), came from the North, and a little over 7 percent (43,000) were foreign-born. Of the foreign-born, half were Germans, a quarter were Mexicans, and the last quarter consisted of Irish, French, English, and a mix of people from Eastern Europe. The last third of the population (182,000) were slaves. No other state in the entire South had such a large number of immigrants.

**Social Classes**

The explosion of the Texas population after annexation changed the social stratification of the state. Southerners were the most influential group that changed Texas society, making it resemble the South. The major social classes during early statehood were planters, farmers, the urban population, poor whites, and free blacks. Like the South, there were clear distinctions between the groups, but they all relied on one another for different reasons. Each group significantly contributed to the social, economic, and political life of the Lone Star State.

The planters in Texas, like those in the South, comprised the upper class. Most planters who established themselves in the Lone Star State were the younger sons of wealthy southern families or were upwardly mobile slaveholders whose only opportunity to increase their wealth was through purchasing inexpensive but fertile land in Texas. The newly arrived planters pursued the lifestyle that they had known growing up: a large house, European furniture, fine clothes, servants, and social gatherings to display their wealth. The transplantation of southern social norms made Texas culturally a southern state.

Additionally, the growing numbers of planters in Texas after statehood profoundly changed the state's economy. Based more on cotton, Texas produced almost 60,000 bales of cotton a year by 1850. Ten years later the production increased to over 400,000 bales. This increase in production allowed plantation owners to quickly become the leaders in their communities and the state, because the wealth that they generated permitted leisure time for political activities. Approximately a quarter of the Anglo families owned slaves, and 3 percent of the families could consider themselves true planters, owning more than twenty slaves. Sixty owners held more than one hundred bondsmen. Only 5 percent of the families were considered small planters with ten to nineteen slaves. The majority of the slaveowners in the state held fewer than ten slaves. Nevertheless, the 25 percent of the Texas population that owned people in bondage controlled almost three quarters of the wealth in the state.

Farmers composed most of the Texas population before and during statehood. All farmers owned land, and most relied on subsistence farming to support themselves and their families. Most farm families had gardens to grow herbs and spices for their daily cooking, tobacco, and cotton to sell for cash to purchase goods they did not generate themselves. Many of the farms ranged from 120 to 160 acres, with only 20 to 60 acres under cultivation and the rest of the acreage to support cattle, pigs, and other livestock. Some farmers primarily focused on raising livestock. In the late 1840s and 1850s, Texas farmers made several cattle drives to Ohio, Illinois, Iowa, and California, increasing the value of livestock in the Lone Star State from just over $10 million in 1850 to $43 million by 1860. Farmers lived a spartan lifestyle, had very few possessions, and worked from sunup to sundown, but most still dreamed of owning slaves to advance their social standing and to have the ability to generate more income through the sale of cotton.

Texas maintained its reputation as a rural region during early statehood, but the state's urban centers soon experienced some growth. The increase in the state's population, along with some technological advancement, increased the number and size of towns in Texas. Urban areas served as trading and service centers for Texans since cities held the largest number of merchants, professionals, and craftsmen while providing opportunities for migrants and immigrants to find work as laborers. Some slaveholders in cities used slaves as laborers to produce goods. Texas cities were primarily located in the eastern half of the state with the largest concentration along the gulf coast and in East Texas.

The largest city in Texas during this time was San Antonio, a major trade center with a population around 8,000, followed by Galveston, Houston, and Austin. The key to urban growth after annexation was railroads. Though numerous companies made plans to lay tracks across the state, the only area that experienced any development was the region between Houston and Galveston. Galveston was the largest port in Texas and the source of storing and exporting agricultural products from planters. Additionally, imported goods that arrived in Galveston were shipped to Houston by steamship and distributed to the rest of the state. Traders wanted to quicken the shipment of cargo between the two cities, so businessmen courted investors, mostly from Holland and France, to build a railroad, which was later called the Galveston, Houston and Henderson Railroad. With very few tracks outside of the Houston area, the rest of the state relied heavily on roads to transport goods. Though the number of Texans living in the cities increased because of the migration of people from other states and foreign countries, only 3.6 percent of the Texas population resided in urban centers of more than 2,500 people. Compared to the rest of the United States, Texas's urban centers developed at a very slow pace. By 1860, Texas had twenty-one small towns, whereas Iowa, which had not been settled as long, gained statehood after Texas and had over one hundred small towns. Texans, like most Southerners, resisted urbanization because profitability of cash crops and their investments in human property kept them tied to their landholdings.

Landless and living on the fringes of society were poor whites. Considered lower class, most poor whites were either frontiersmen or people living on poor land in East Texas. Frontiersmen eked out a dangerous existence of subsistence farming and ranching during the hostile Indians in West Texas. The number of frontiersmen in 1860 was well below 5 percent of the total population that lived in West Texas. Poor whites in East Texas had a tough existence. Most did not own the ground on which they lived and, in many cases, rented land or shared the land with others, attempting to generate enough wealth to purchase land of their own. Others worked as overseers on local plantations, day laborers for farmers, and clerks in small towns. Most poor whites aspired to climb the social ladder, which many did. Others either remained on the lowest rung of society willingly, or simply moved on to other places once their opportunities disappeared, or farmed on lands of others creating an early system of sharecropping.

The least populous group of Texans during this time period was free blacks. Census records of 1850 and 1860 listed only 400 free blacks in the state. Many laws existed in Texas to restrict the number of African Americans living in the state outside of bondage, the most common forbidding free blacks to reside in the state without permission of the state congress. Resentment towards these freedmen existed because they represented the idea that African Americans had the ability to live in freedom and that they would unsettle the numerous slaves in the state. Because free blacks presented a potential threat to the institution of slavery, white Texans treated them in the same manner as bondsmen. Free blacks found that freedom in Texas during early statehood was little different from slavery.

**Texas Social and Cultural Life**

The influx in the Texas population from across North America and Europe changed the social and cultural life of the new state. Impacted were women, family life, religion, education, and violence, all of which affected the lives of every Texan. The way Texans viewed themselves and the way they lived changed their social and cultural life. All these aspects of Texas society existed before annexation, but with the increased population, especially its diversity, these features became more pronounced. The importance of these cultural and societal aspects still exists today.

That Texas was a frontier state influenced the role of women. Like most frontier regions, the state was a male-dominated society. Men outnumbered women. In 1850 there were 15,704 more men than women, and in 1860 there were 36,000 more. The state's status as a frontier region influenced this disparity, since it was easier for single men to settle the frontier than to have to care for a family. Additionally, the low number of women and the democratic effects of frontier life gave women some rights rarely granted in other non-frontier states, such as not forfeiting personal property to their husband upon marriage. Women also had the right to divorce but were not assured guardianship of their children.

Even though women had freedoms rarely seen in other states, Texas was still a male-dominated society that restricted the role of women, especially since they could not vote or sit on juries. The main responsibility of Texas women was to care for the household and the children. Women also provided food for the household from the small family garden planted near the family's home. Childbearing and rearing were difficult, dangerous and emotional experiences for women. Mortality rates were extremely high for both mothers and infants. In the years after birth, the danger of infants dying remained high, which forced the parents to normally wait two years before naming their child, calling the newborn simply "it," "baby," or "our little visitor." Lives of Texas women were difficult, having to balance survival with providing for their family.

Another influence on Texas society during early statehood included religion. In the years before statehood, harsh conditions of a frontier state made survival more important than religion. Texas quickly gained a reputation as a rough and "sinful" region. During the early years of statehood, Texas experienced the influx of migrants, which led to the establishment of more churches and the introduction of new denominations. The most prominent denominations, from largest to smallest, were Methodists, Baptists, Presbyterians, Catholics, and Episcopalians. Compared to the religious movements of the North, which empowered people to improve their communities, churches in Texas resembled the focus of southern clergymen who emphasized that individuals needed to recognize their imperfections and improve them by developing a personal relationship with God. Additionally, ministers in Texas, like their southern counterparts, preached how important slavery was for the community and for the bondsmen, since the institution cared for the "child-like" Africans who, according to the clergymen, could not survive in America without the paternal guidance provided by their masters. Messages like this allowed Texans and Southerners to reconcile the institution of slavery with their religious beliefs.

Churches provided institutions of higher learning with an emphasis on training ministers. Though the different denominations established numerous colleges and universities, only a few still exist today. The most prominent and oldest university, established by Baptists in 1845 in the town of Independence, was "Old Baylor." Later, officials relocated the university in 1887 to its current location in Waco, Texas. Other institutions included Austin College established by Presbyterians in 1849 in Huntsville, later removed to Sherman in 1852. Affiliated with the Methodist Church, the Chappell Hill Male and Female Institution opened its doors around 1850. Six years later its name changed to Chappell Hill Female College with the chartering of the all-male Soule College in the same town. Financial troubles and yellow fever epidemics depleted enrollment influencing the Methodist Church in 1871 to establish Southwestern University in Georgetown, outside of the areas infected by the fever. Soule College finally closed its doors in 1888 and Chappell Hill Female College moved to its campus, only to continue until 1912. Lastly, Saint Mary's University created by Marianists, a division of Catholics devoted to the Virgin Mary and Christian education, established a campus in downtown San Antonio in 1852. With growing enrollment the university purchased a seventy-five acre plot in West Heights, far from downtown at that time, and eventually moved its operations there, where it remains today.

The state made attempts to sponsor a public education system in Texas by establishing funds and land grants for schools. Most of these measures failed to completely materialize during early statehood. Few "common" schools opened their doors, but some exceptions existed. An institution for the handicapped, mainly deaf and blind people, began serving the public in 1857, and the state legislature set aside three million acres of public land for the creation of a public university in 1858. Destined to be the University of Texas, the institution did not officially open its doors until 1883. The foundation of a public education system in Texas began during early statehood but would not see statewide success until the late nineteenth century.

Education could not stem the tide of violence in Texas. Frontier life combined with the institution of slavery made society in the Lone Star State extremely violent. Living on the frontier entailed surviving many different challenges. Indian attacks were always a concern for settlers on the frontier since they were encroaching upon the lands of the Comanche and other tribes. Being far removed from any government authority, frontier families had to guard themselves from lawlessness through vigilantism. Without any form of protection, frontiersmen issued their own form of justice against anyone who created problems in their communities, usually executing the perpetrators by hanging or shooting them. The institution of slavery contributed to violence in the state through its harsh punishments of the slaves or those who aided in their escape.

Southern culture, tied to slavery, also introduced dueling in Texas where men would settle a dispute through an elaborate ceremony that ended in the men shooting guns at one another. One famous duel in Texas was between Dr. Chauncey Goodrich, an army surgeon, and Levi L. Laurens, a reporter fresh from New York and the recipient of a mortal shot from the doctor. Additionally, duels with the famed Bowie knife were common in the 1830s and 1840s. Though the upper class disapproved of this violence, they

Hardin R. Runnels, Governor of Texas, 1857-1859. Photo credit: UTSA's Institute of Texan Cultures

rarely pursued justice in these fights unless of course, a person of a lower status killed a prominent person in their community. Violence in Texas contributed to its reputation as a place that contained a dangerous breed of people.

**Texas Politics in the 1850s**

National issues such as the Compromise of 1850 influenced the Lone Star State, but internal politics made the decade politically exciting. New parties and factions emerged. The Whig Party, born out of opposition to President Andrew Jackson and the Democrats who followed him, began to make inroads into East Texas, North Texas, and urban centers through the support of planters, professionals, and merchants. Though successful on the local level, the influence of the party was brief because it never took a firm stance on the issue of slavery, thus discouraging supporters. The American Party, better known as the Know-Nothings, emerged. Sponsoring a nativist platform, the Know-Nothings had major conflicts with the large German and Hispanic populations within the state. Even though nativist feelings permeated the United States and Texas, the party dissolved quickly because it refused to take a stand on slavery. Both parties had success on the local level, but the Democratic Party still dominated state politics.

Though all the governors during the decade were Democrats, divisions within the party over secession created tension across the state. The first governor impacted by the split was Governor Elisha M. Pease. He represented the traditional politics in the state, which was Unionism, the desire to remain a part of the United States. During his two terms from 1853 to 1857, his fiscal policy helped pay off the state debt and established the financial foundation that Texas would later use to finance its public schools and colleges. Challenging Pease and the Unionists were wealthy planters from the lower South who supported secession. During the gubernatorial election of 1857, many Unionists were divided by Know-Nothings and Whigs, allowing Hardin R. Runnels, a Secessionist Democrat, to defeat the Unionist Democrat Sam Houston. Runnels's victory allowed the "fire-eaters" (people who called for the immediate secession of Texas to protect slavery) to have a platform to promote their ideas. Initially, this created much concern across the state since the thought of seceding from the Union worried Texans. Sam Houston used the tension to win the gubernatorial election in 1859, landing a major victory for the Unionist Democrats. The victory was only temporary, for news arrived that Louis T. Wigfall, a staunch fire-eater, had won a seat in the state senate. Conflict over the future of the Texas's union with United States continued at the turn of the new decade. Events both internal and external to the state impacted the decision of Texans to leave the Union.

**Texas Secession**

As the 1850s drew to a close, the conflict over slavery and the future of Texas and the United States reached its breaking point. Though many events contributed to secession, agitation began to climax with John Brown's raid on Harpers Ferry, Virginia. On October 16, 1859, Brown with twenty other men attempted to start an armed slave revolt by capturing guns in the armory at Harpers Ferry and distributing the weapons to local slaves. Brown hoped to incite a slave uprising that would purge the South of slavery. Though the U.S. Army foiled Brown's plan and the state of Virginia later tried and executed the radical abolitionist for treason, Southerners believed that the institution of slavery was in danger and reacted strongly against any abolitionist attack, real or imaginary.

The first perceived threat to slavery in Texas after Brown's raid came in the summer of 1860. It was a hot and dry summer with temperatures reaching 114 degrees. During the searing heat and drought, a series of fires erupted around Dallas and were called the "Texas Troubles." The first fire ignited on July 8, 1860, in Dallas, and two hours later fires began to spring up in Denton. On the same day, buildings and farms in Black Jack Grove, Milford, Pilot Point, Ladonia, Millwood, Jefferson, Waxahachie, and Honey Grove burst into flames. The "Texas Troubles" created excitement, concern, and fear across the state as far as Guadalupe County in Texas and extending to Florida in the South.

Texans immediately searched for answers to the mysterious fires. A few individuals blamed the fires on a new type of phosphorus match that spontaneously ignited, which store owners and shoppers confirmed later after witnessing the matches burst into flames as they sat on the shelf. Despite this logical explanation, many Texans jumped to the conclusion that the "Texas Troubles" were part of a plot to incite a slave insurrection. Texans and Southerners alike believed that northern Republicans organized and orchestrated the fires because they thought slaves did not have the mental capacity to arrange such an elaborate event. Eventually, Texans concluded that the culprits of the fires were northern Methodist ministers. The punishment for the fires was death to all those found guilty. From July to September of 1860, the hanging of abolitionists and slaves became a frequent event, as the fires continued through the rest of the summer. After the fires died out, sentiments toward breaking away from the Union increased throughout Texas and the rest of the South as the news of the events spread throughout the nation.

In 1860 widespread notoriety of the "Texas Troubles" created political chaos in the United States and Texas and influenced the presidential election of that year. Feeling pressured, Southerners viewed any presidential candidate in the election who did not strongly support slavery as an enemy to the South. The target of concern was the Republican Party's candidate Abraham Lincoln. Texans feared that Lincoln would restrict slavery from territories in the southwest and that he would ignore the state's frontier defense. After the Democratic Party nominated two men for president, the only acceptable candidate was John Breckinridge, a Southerner and avid supporter of slavery. On November 6, 1860, Election Day, Texans cast 47,561 votes for Breckinridge, which was 75 percent of the total votes. Breckinridge won every county in the state except for three on the frontier that favored John Bell, the candidate for the Constitutional Union Party, who received 15,402 votes. In the end, the candidate whom Texas and the South feared the most, Abraham Lincoln, won the election even though his name did not even appear on the ballots of most southern states. Since Southerners believed that Lincoln's election represented the greatest threat to slavery, South Carolina decided to secede from the Union on December 20, 1860. The rest of the states in the lower South quickly followed South Carolina's lead, forming the Confederate States of America.

Texas left the Union, but its path to the Confederacy differed from that of the other southern states. While the majority of Texas politicians favored secession, they had to overcome the opposition of Governor Sam Houston, who was an avid Unionist. To call for a convention to vote on secession, the state legislature, the only government body that had the power to call such a meeting, needed to be in session. Since the state legislature was not in session, the only person who could call for a special session was Governor Houston, who refused to do so. Secessionists attempted to circumvent Houston's authority by announcing that there would be an election on January 8, 1861, for representatives for an extralegal convention to discuss leaving the United States. The planned meeting was to be held in Austin on January 28. Secessionists argued that urgency outweighed the governor and outweighed legality. Houston reacted to this challenge of his authority by calling the state legislature to a special session on January 21 to cut off the extralegal maneuver of the secessionists and to attempt to maintain some political authority over the unfolding situation. During the special legislative session, the secessionists won approval to have a convention to discuss secession. Upset about the turn of events, Houston stalled their decision by asking that any decision made for secession at the convention should be presented and should be approved by the people of Texas in a special referendum. The secessionists agreed to Houston's concession.

The Secession Convention commenced on January 28, 1861, with 177 representatives from across the Lone Star State. Delegates quickly drafted an ordinance of secession that called for the repeal of the annexation ordinance of 1845 and for the return of Texas's status as a sovereign state. Though secessionists were the clear majority, a vocal group of prominent Texans opposed leaving the Union. Men in this group included

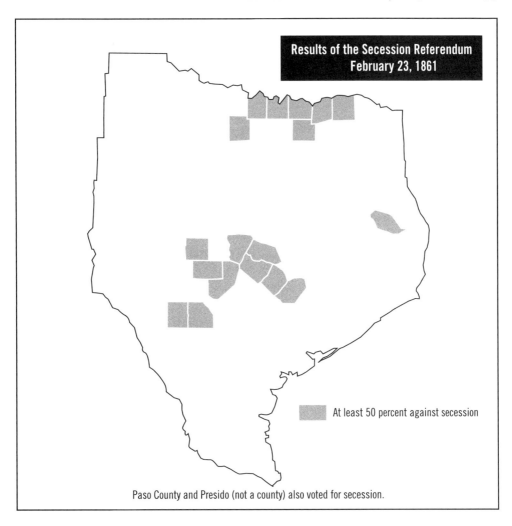

Governor Sam Houston, Congressman Andrew Jackson Hamilton, State Senator James W. Throckmorton, and the German newspaper editor from Galveston, Ferdinand Flake. Though these men attempted to delay the vote, the delegates presented the ordinance to the legislature for approval on February 1. The Ordinance of Secession passed in the state legislature 166 to 8, and the delegates hastily scheduled a referendum for February 23 to enact the ordinance. The secession convention remained in session until February 4. During this time, it chose seven delegates to proceed to the interim capital of the Confederacy at Montgomery, Alabama, once the voters approved secession. Additionally, it created a fifteen-person committee on public safety, which, once Texans approved secession, had authority to seize control of all the national government's property in the state.

Prior to the referendum going before the people, the committee sent three commissioners to the military headquarters of the U.S. Army in Texas at San Antonio. There the commissioners negotiated with General David E. Twiggs, the seventy-two-year old commander of the Department of Texas. Twiggs, a Southerner himself from Georgia, without consulting officials in Washington, D.C., agreed upon the passage of the referendum to surrender the army and all federal property in the state, including guns and supplies, to the Texans. In return, Twiggs asked that his men be allowed to leave the state honorably. His decision was extremely controversial, especially since he refused to put the agreement in writing, a move that left the Texans in a desperate situation were the government to relieve Twiggs of his duties. Soon after the Texans established the pact with Twiggs, a delegate learned that the United States government in fact planned to replace the general with a strong Unionist.

The change in commanders concerned the secessionists. As a result, Texans immediately mobilized to force Twiggs to surrender his command before the people approved the referendum. In Seguin, the famous Texan Benjamin McCulloch, veteran of the Texas Revolution and a Texas Ranger, organized approximately 400 men. With the help of the Knights of the Golden Circle, McCulloch and his men moved on San Antonio to force the surrender of the federal property in the city and to order all federal posts to do likewise. In a bloodless assault on the Alamo, the headquarters of the U.S. Army in Texas, McCulloch forced Twiggs to turn over $3 million worth of military supplies and forced over two thousand federal soldiers from across the frontier to surrender and to leave the state on February 16, 1861. Even though Texas had not officially seceded from the United States, it was now in open rebellion.

While McCulloch and his men occupied San Antonio, Unionists mobilized to keep Texas in the Union. Its diverse population assured that not everyone in the state supported secession. One of the strongest held beliefs of Texas Unionists was that secession would abolish slavery instead of preserving the institution. If the South was defeated, the United States would abolish slavery. In response to this threat, secessionists published an "Address to the People" in English, Spanish, and German to convince the public that it was in their best interest to support them in the referendum. After the government tallied up the votes from the referendum, the secessionists won by a margin of 45,154 to 14,747 votes and had the support of 104 counties out of the 122 in the state. Virtually all of Texas supported the secessionists because most of the population relied on slavery and had ties to the South through migration. Most opposition to the referendum came from northern and central western counties. North Texas contained a large population of people from the North and upper South, areas that tended to support the Union. People living on the frontier in central western Texas relied heavily on the army to protect them from Indian raids. Also, the Germans who settled in the Hill Country had experienced war in Europe and came to the United States to escape the horrors of warfare. The fate of Texas was now in the hands of traitors to the United States.

Once the people approved secession, members of the Secession Convention reassembled on March 5, 1861, to pass an ordinance that united Texas with the Confederate States of America. Governor Houston continued to resist the actions of the secessionists. He suggested that, instead of joining the other southern states, Texas should unfurl "once again her Lone Star banner and maintaining her position among the independent nations of the earth." Inferring that Texas should remain neutral and that the state should maintain its independence by becoming a republic once again. Houston also argued for Manifest Destiny, "The same spirit of enterprise that founded a Republic here, will carry her institutions Southward (Mexico) and Westward." Essentially, let's invade Mexico instead of joining the Confederacy. Abraham Lincoln twice offered Houston military support to keep him in office but he refused, because he was not "willing to deluge the capital of Texas with the blood of Texans, merely to keep one poor old man in a position for a few days longer, in a position that belongs to the people." Houston's action failed when Texas officially became the seventh star on the Confederate flag. On March 14, delegates who resented Houston's resistance passed a resolution that required all "state officers to take an oath of loyalty." Houston refused, and the delegates ordered him to meet them at the capital on March 16. The hero of San Jacinto did not appear. Instead, he was whittling a pine stick in the basement of the capital building. At the appointed time, the secretary of the convention called out Houston's name three times without reply. The convention then declared the governor's office vacant and elevated Lieutenant Governor Edward Clark to the position two days later. These actions made the future of Texas uncertain and ended the long and colorful political career of Sam Houston. The former general, president of Texas, senator, and governor left the governor's mansion and moved to Huntsville, Texas, where he died on July 26, 1863, at the age of seventy. Over Houston's protests, Texas had linked its fate with the other southern states and the institution of slavery. In the months after leaving Austin, Houston accurately prophesized, "The soil of our beloved South will drink deep the precious blood of our sons and brethren. . . . The die has been cast by your secession leaders and you must ere long reap the fearful harvest of conspiracy and revolution."

The years of early statehood brought Texas to the forefront of politics and the events of the United States. From its annexation to the secession crisis, Texas changed dramatically. Annexation brought to the Lone Star State both hardships and benefits through war with Mexico and protection on the frontier. Along with statehood came a flood of migrants from the United States and immigrants from Europe and Mexico who influenced class stratification and the social and cultural life of Texas. Political developments included secession and Sam Houston's feeble attempt to keep the Lone Star State from seceding and joining the Confederacy. The fate of Texas remained uncertain in the early spring of 1861. Only the impending Civil War would determine the next path of the Lone Star State.

### Afterward: The Evolving Interpretations of the Alamo

*Over the years, the Alamo grew to symbolize the Texas Revolution, but during the Cold War it emerged as a powerful icon of national identity. During this period, the 1959 John Wayne film "The Alamo" was released, with the Texans representing the democratic Americans resisting the encroachment of the communist Soviets, characterized by the Mexican soldiers. Once again, the Alamo rose in popularity and garnered an international appeal with numerous European businesses named after the landmark and images of the church adorning the walls of buildings in those countries. Additionally, foreign dignitaries have visited the complex ranging from Nazi sailors in the 1930s to prime ministers from Great Britain, the Netherlands, Israel, Canada and leaders of the Soviet Union and Ireland. Celebrities also have graced the Alamo including numerous presidents, sports heroes, war veteran groups, and prominent American political leaders. Though the wooden roof has since been replaced with cement, the simple act of hiding an unsightly improvement transformed a simple chapel into an internationally renowned symbol of freedom.*

# Myth & Legend

### Slavery as a Benevolent Institution

*Among the myths of the past is the falsehood about how slaveholders treated their slaves. According to apologists for human bondage, owners were most benevolent. Indeed, even slavers who sailed along the western coast of Africa and captured black people were benevolent because they started the process of civilizing and bringing the blessings of Christianity to a "heathen" people who lived on the uncivilized "Dark Continent," despite the truth that many civilizations called Africa home. Just a few examples of how Texas's slaveholders treated their bondsmen dispel the myth of the benevolence of owners.*

*During the Civil War Alex Simpson drove his slaves from Georgia to Texas to eliminate the possibility that his human property could fall into Yankee hands. His property walked all the way during the winter months. Many nights they slept in snow. When some slaves failed to maintain the pace that Simpson set, he made an example of one woman who lagged. He shot and killed her. Once in Texas, he settled on a farm near Austin. To guard against runaways who might try to run for Mexico, he branded his slaves. At first, he did not allow his slaves to build their own quarters. Instead, he worked them all day and chained them to trees at night. He made them subsist on meals of green corn and raw meat. After the war, he refused to free his slaves. The authorities finally released his human property after they inspected his farm when vigilantes lynched Simpson for horse theft.*

*In similar stories Eli Medlock and Andy Anderson commented on the way their owners abused them. A slave of Logan Stroud, Medlock reported that his mistress almost killed him by setting a bull dog after him because he took some plums and ate them. Only after he had sustained severe bites on his chest did his master's son save him by calling off the dog. Anderson said that his first master treated him benevolently but that his second one whipped him until he had scars.*

*A planter in Smith County, Texas, one Briscoe treated his slaves savagely, especially when dealing with returned runaways. Authorities found and returned a slave known only as "Old Charlie," after which Briscoe whipped him. Additionally, Briscoe held a burning pine torch over the stretched out slave, allowing burning pitch to drop all over his body. "Old Charlie" soon expired because of the beating and the burns. Also in Smith County, a white jury convicted another slave (named Charles) of stealing property worth $20 and sentenced him to 300 lashes with a leather strap.*

*The more opponents of slavery challenged the South's "Peculiar Institution," the more harshly some whites treated their bondspeople. During the Civil War, the mistress of Harriet Robinson flogged her daily, saying that "your master's out fighting and losing blood trying to save you from the Yankees, so you can get yours here." When Robinson's master returned, he ordered all beatings stopped, but he did so only because he feared Yankee retribution.*

*Other slaves mentioned that whippings after 1860 substantially increased, with the most severe lashings reserved for slaves whom informers said spoke favorably about the Yankees and Abraham Lincoln. Not satisfied with floggings, one Texas master punished his bondspeople by nailing them to trees by their ears. One slave named "Dol" faced worse punishment. During the Civil War he learned of President Lincoln's Emancipation Proclamation; whereupon, Dol decided that he should be free. Later, facing punishment for an infraction, Dol rebelled when his master was about to whip him, after which his master shot him dead.*

*Black women and under-aged girls faced a fate unlike male slaves. Many were forced to breed when they reached child-rearing age. If a female did not find a mate and begin producing more human property, her owner would force one on her. Also a problem for black women, many white men in the South, Texas included, believed they could take liberties with the bodies of female slaves of any age. Stories of forcible rape abound, as do accounts of female slaves having children of mixed white-black heritage. In his history* **Before the Mayflower**, *the journalist/historian Lerone Bennett studies the records and came away estimating that 70 percent of today's black population has at least one white ancestor. Forcible rape explains part of the total.*

*The stories of abuse mentioned above are not exceptions. Brutality was widespread throughout the South, including Texas.*

## Suggestions for Further Reading

Baum, Dale. *The Shattering of Texas Unionism: Politics in the Lone Star State During the Civil War and Reconstruction.* Baton Rouge: Louisiana State University Press, 1998.

Biesele, Rudolph Leopold. *The History of the German Settlements in Texas, 1831-1861.* Austin, TX: Von Boeckmann- Jones, Co., 1930.

Binkley, William C. *The Expansionist Movement in Texas, 1836-1850.* New York: Da Capo Press, 1970.

Boswell, Angela. *Her Act and Deed: Women's Lives in a Rural Southern County, 1837-1873.* College Station: Texas A&M University Press, 2001.

Buenger, Walter L. *Secession and the Union in Texas.* Austin: University of Texas Press, 1984.

Campbell, Randolph B. *An Empire for Slavery: The Peculiar Institution in Texas, 1821-1865.* Baton Rouge: Louisiana State University Press, 1989.

Carroll, Mark M. *Homesteads Ungovernable: Families, Sex, Race, and the Law in Frontier Texas, 1823-1860.* Austin: The University of Texas, 2001.

DeLeon, Arnoldo. *The Tejano Community, 1836-1900.* Albuquerque: University of New Mexico Press, 1982.

Eby, Frederick. *The Development of Education in Texas.* New York: The Macmillan Co., 1925.

Jordan, Terry. *German Seed in Texas Soil.* Austin: University of Texas Press, 1966.

Lathrop, Barnes F. *Migration Into East Texas 1835-1860: A Study from the United States Census.* Austin: The Texas State Historical Association, 1949.

Lowe, Richard G. and Randolph B. Campbell. *Planters and Plain Folk: Agriculture in Antebellum Texas.* Dallas, TX: Southern Methodist University Press, 1987.

Machann, Clinton and James W. Mendle. *Krásná Amerika: A Study of the Texas Czechs, 1851-1939.* Austin: Eakin Press, 1983.

Smith, F. Todd. *From Dominance to Disappearance: The Indians of Texas and the Near Southwest, 1786-1859,* Lincoln: University of Nebraska Press, 2005.

Wheeler, Kenneth W. *To Wear a City's Crown: The Beginnings of Urban Growth in Texas, 1836-1865.* Cambridge: Harvard University Press, 1968.

**IDENTIFICATION:** Briefly describe each term.

Sam Houston
Mexican-American War
Texas Troubles
"Nueces Strip"
New Mexico Border Controversy
"GTT"
David Twiggs
"Cart Wars"
Juan Cortina
Elisha M. Pease
Hardin R. Runnels
Benjamin McCulloch
James W. Throckmorton
Ordinance of Secession
Secession Convention

**MULTIPLE CHOICE:** Choose the correct response.

1. Most Texans served in the _____ during the Mexican-American War:
   A. Gen. Zachary Taylor's army in northern Mexico
   B. Gen. Winfield Scott's expeditionary force in central Mexico
   C. Eastern Theater
   D. Navy

2. What settled the Texas-New Mexico Border Controversy?
   A. The Compromise of 1850
   B. Texas invaded New Mexico
   C. New Mexico invaded Texas
   D. Texas-New Mexico Border Conference of 1849

3. What was the most obvious benefit for Texas after annexation?
   A. Another war with Mexico
   B. Slavery
   C. Economic expansion
   D. Frontier protection

4. Which of these people immigrated to Texas?
   A. Germans
   B. Mexicans
   C. Wends
   D. Czechs
   E. All the above

5. The largest social class in Texas were:
   A. Planters in East Texas
   B. Farmers
   C. Slaves
   D. Poles settlers on the Texas coast

6. What percentage of Texas families owned slaves?
   A. 10 percent
   B. 25 percent
   C. 75 percent
   D. 90 percent

7. During early statehood, which of the following was NOT a major city?
   A. San Antonio
   B. Dallas
   C. Houston
   D. Galveston

8. Which of the following colleges were NOT established in Texas during or before early statehood?
   A. Baylor University
   B. Austin College
   C. University of Texas
   D. St. Mary's University

9. What impact did the presidential election of 1860 have on Texas?
   A. No real impact since the majority of Texans voted for Abraham Lincoln
   B. Upset Texans but had no long-term affect
   C. Pushed many Texans to call for the state to secede from the union
   D. Texans started a war with Mexico

10. How did Texas secede from the United States?
    A. Popular Referendum
    B. State politicians decided
    C. It had no choice because other southern states voted it out
    D. Secession Convention

**TRUE/FALSE:** Indicate whether each statement is true or false.

1. The annexation of Texas was the catalyst for the Mexican-American War.

2. The chain of fortifications on the Texas frontier stopped all Indian raids.

3. During early statehood, the population of Texas increased more than 100 percent.

4. Relations between Anglos and Tejanos during early statehood improved.

5. German "Greens" settled mostly on the Texas frontier.

6. During early statehood Texas ceased to be a violent region.

7. Texas was dominated by the Democratic Party.

8. Unionist Democrats called for secession in 1860.

9. Sam Houston opposed secession.

10. Germans and Tejanos generally supported secession.

**MATCHING:** Match the response in column A with the item in column B.

1. John Coffee Hays
2. Knights of the Golden Circle
3. Know Nothings
4. German "Greens"
5. German "Greys"
6. Elisha M. Pease
7. Hardin R. Runnels
8. "Texas Troubles"
9. Sam Houston
10. David E. Twiggs

A. U.S. Army commander that surrendered the federal property in the state
B. Prominent Texas commander in the Mexican-American War
C. Secret society that wanted to establish a southern slave empire
D. A secretive political party that promoted anti-immigrant policies
E. German immigrants in the second wave that settled in Texas
F. German immigrants in the first wave that settled in Texas
G. Unionist Democrat governor of Texas
H. Secessionist Democrat governor of Texas
I. A series of fires in Texas that were blamed on northern Unionists
J. Governor of Texas during the Secession Crisis

**ESSAY QUESTIONS:**

1. What role did slaves play in Texas society?

2. What impact did the migration and immigration into Texas have on the state?

3. The admission of Texas sparked several controversies. Identify three and explain fully the impact they had on both Texas and the United States.

4. During early statehood the composition of the Texas population changed dramatically. Identify three ethnic groups in the state and explain fully the cultural contributions of each group.

# Chapter 7

# Texas During the Civil War, 1861-1865

**Prelude: The Story of Britton "Britt" Johnson**

*Most historians describe the Civil War as a series of battles fought by large armies in the eastern states. Forgotten are the stories of those left behind to carry on their day-to-day lives or, in the case of Texas, to protect their families from Indian raids. Though Native Americans initiated only a handful of forays during the war, much fewer than anyone could have had imagined, the Elm Creek Raid launched one of the most epic stories in Texas history—that of Britton "Britt" Johnson. Though not commonly known, Johnson's hardships and adventures remained hidden in plain sight through a famed movie starring John Wayne.*

*Britt Johnson was brought to the Republic of Texas from Tennessee as the property of Moses Johnson who owned land in Peters Colony, located in North Texas. Unlike most slaves, Britt held the title of foremen on the Johnson Ranch and had received some education since he could read, write, and solve basic math problems. Additionally, Moses permitted him unlimited movement about the region, and the freedom to own horses and cattle. Unfortunately for Britt, on October 13, 1864, he was away from the ranch when several hundred Kiowa and Comanche raided Elm Creek, northwest of Fort Belknap, near the present-day city of Graham. After the raiders killed two settlers, including Johnson's son, they captured Elizabeth Ann Fitzpatrick, her son and granddaughters, along with Britt's wife and two other children. Confederates under the command of James G. Bourland's Border Regiment, organized by the state to defend the frontier, sent a company to pursue the marauders, but their rescue was thwarted when the men rode into an ambush, leaving five dead and several wounded. Johnson returned to the ranch to find his son murdered and the rest of his family taken. Moses gave Britt permission to leave the ranch to search for his family. He visited several Texas forts and eventually searched through numerous Indian Reservations in the Indian Territory (present-day Oklahoma). Johnson went as far as to live with the Comanche for several months before ransoming his family in June 1865. Other sources credit Comanche Chief Asa Harvey for their ransom and release to Indian agents through ongoing peace talks. Eventually Johnson was reunited with his family. Five months later, United States troops rescued the last survivor, Mrs. Fitzpatrick.*

*Upon Johnson's return to Texas with his family, the Civil War had concluded and emancipation was proclaimed. Freed from bondage, he moved his family to Weatherford in Parker*

*County where his legend preceded him. Johnson had gained fame as the man who searched for his kidnapped family and returned them home safely. Using his newfound fame, Johnson gained freight contracts and started a successful shipping business, moving supplies and goods between Weatherford and Fort Griffin (near present-day Abilene).*

As secession became a reality and civil war loomed on the horizon, the future of the newly formed Confederacy remained uncertain. Like other southern states, Texas was immediately burdened with the task of organizing a new state government and sending delegates to Montgomery, Alabama, the location of the temporary Confederate capital. In April 1861, Texans were consumed with these endeavors when Confederate artillerymen fired the first shots of the war at Fort Sumter in Charleston Harbor, South Carolina. In the aftermath of Fort Sumter, Texans began to prepare for war by enlisting in the Confederate army. Before the war's end, some traveled to distant battlefronts east of the Mississippi River, while others remained closer to home, serving in various regiments in the Trans-Mississippi West. Not all Texans supported the Confederacy. Most of the dissenters chose simply to remain neutral, but a determined few left the state to join the Union army. Though the Lone Star State escaped the ravages of war, its people were forever changed by the events that transpired between 1861 and 1865.

**Initial Actions of Texans**

In the war, the first priority of Texans was the defense of the frontier and their international border. When General David Twiggs removed all federal forces and abandoned the fortifications on the frontier and the border with Mexico, Texans needed to organize themselves to fill the vacuum created by their departure. The first two military regiments organized after secession were the First and Second Texas Mounted Rifles. Henry McCulloch organized the First Mounted Rifles on March 4, 1861 to defend the Texas frontier from Comanche attacks. The other unit, under the command of Colonel John "Rip" Ford, occupied key positions along the Rio Grande from Fort Brown near the Gulf Coast to Fort Bliss in far West Texas to defend Texas from Mexican bandits such as Juan Cortina. These Texans enlisted in an effort to protect the state from the only immediate threats to their security at that time. After the attack on Fort Sumter in South Carolina on April 12, 1861, Texans organized regiments to fight for the Confederacy. On May 9, 1861, the first land engagement almost occurred west of San Antonio. The Battle of Adams Hill, though no real fighting occurred, pitted the United States troops vacating Fort Bliss, Fort Quitman, and Fort Davis against some prominent Confederates including Earl Van Dorn, John Robert Baylor, and James Duff. The soldiers were to report to General Twiggs in San Antonio, but Confederate troops confronted them near the town of Castroville, near the San Lucas Springs. Neither side wanted to spill blood, so the United States troops surrendered to Van Dorn. The Confederates allowed them safe passage to San Antonio where they gave up their arms and other public property. If there had been fighting, it would have preceded major fighting in Virginia by more than a month and a half.

## Why Did They Fight

The initial group of young Texans that volunteered to fight in the Confederate army did so for many reasons, the obvious one being a sense of martial duty to their country and state, evidenced by a variety of factors. Many of the men who enlisted were young and looking for excitement and an opportunity to prove their manhood, thereby establishing themselves in their communities. Others believed they were upholding the martial traditions of Texas, focusing on and often reciting the exploits of the men in the Texas battle for independence and the numerous conflicts with Indians in the state's history. Confederate President Jefferson Davis lauded the Texas soldiers by associating them with the men from the Texas Revolution, "The troops from other states have their reputation to gain. The sons of the defenders of the Alamo have theirs to maintain." Lee once boasted about his Texas brigade, "Never mind the raggedness, the enemy never sees the backs of my Texans." On a darker note, when Texans marched through other states, they were "respected as Texans, but it seems the people here have a different idea about Texans than they should." Captain Robert Voight, a German immigrant to Texas, noted, "They seem to think we are half-wild savages as long as they don't know us, but when we get to know them better, they sometimes even admire the fact that we can read and write."

Religion in the Civil War provided many answers to fighting soldiers. Some of the men's concerns included the role God played in their lives and the war, whether they could be good Christians and kill the enemy, and when death might take them and what the end of their life would be like. All these issues had a direct influence on why the men enlisted, continued to fight, and were able to bear the stress of being soldiers. Samuel S. Watson of the 1st Texas Infantry explained to a friend how Christianity helped him. "The righteous have many promises of protection left on record for them. I would earnestly recommend to you the Christian religion," Watson wrote. "It will help you bear up under your troubles here in this world, and fit you for everlasting happiness in the world to come." Similarly, A. J. Nelson, a Swedish immigrant fighting in Waul's Texas Legion, wrote to his brother August in their native language, "Do not grieve for me but [ill.] yourselves that the Lord had protected me as long as He has. I trust in the Lord's power that He will continue to save and protect me so I again may see you here in life." Texans, like many other soldiers, turned to religion to find the strength to continue fighting in the war.

A significant number of men, particularly recent arrivals to Texas, enlisted to protect the homes and family members whom they left behind east of the Mississippi River. Many other men fought for the Confederacy to defend the concept of "states rights," which was another way Southerners expressed their desire to protect their civil liberties to own and work people in bondage—slavery.

Regardless of popular myths, the primary reason Texans volunteered to risk their lives was to defend the institution of slavery. Charles DeMorse, editor of the Clarksville *Northern Standard* and later colonel of the Twenty-ninth Texas Cavalry, wrote about his and many Texans' feelings on slavery in his newspaper. "We want more slaves—we need them . . . We care nothing for . . . slavery as an abstraction—but we desire the practicality, the increase of our productions; the increase of the comforts and wealth of the populations; and if slavery, or slave labor, or Negro Apprentice labor ministers to this, why that is what we want." Another Texas soldier, Layfette Orr of the Twelfth Texas Cavalry, wrote to his brothers Henry and Robert late in the war asserting that white Southerners should "never give it up, and bee [sic] put on an [equal] footing with the negros."

By the beginning of the Civil War, the citizens of Texas relied heavily on the institution of slavery either directly or indirectly. Those who owned slaves relied directly on bondsmen to gain or maintain their wealth and status in the state. On the other hand, many non-slave owners relied indirectly on the large plantations, which drove the region's economy, since the large slave-owning plantations bought food from yeomen farmers and lumber from local mills. With the perceived threat to slavery by the election of Abraham Lincoln and the approaching war, Texans fought to protect their slave society.

**Preparation for War**

As Texans formed companies to fight in the Confederate army, they began to recognize the severe shortcomings in their preparation and the unique aspects of Texas soldiers. Like men from other southern states, not all the Texans' uniforms looked alike. This was especially evident in the Trans-Mississippi Department. Soldiers brought items such as blankets, socks, shoes, and hats from their homes, but, more times than not, volunteers brought almost everything. Most men wore whatever they had, ranging from flannel hunting shirts to home-spun pants of almost every possible color. A few Texans relished in their uniqueness when it came to uniforms, such as Captain Sam Richardson of W. P. Lane Rangers who wore leopard-skin pants.

Of all the different branches in the army, Texans most desired to serve in cavalry units. Governor Edward Clark summed up the Texans' desire for mounted service. "The predilection of Texans for cavalry service . . . is so powerful that they are unwilling, in many instances, to engage in service of any other description, unless required by actual necessity." One Texas soldier explained that Texans preferred cavalry service because in 1860 their state was such a wide-open space that they never walked anywhere. Since Texans cherished horsemanship and desired to be viewed as cavaliers of old, few wanted to be relegated to walking in the infantry—a branch that many believed provided fewer opportunities through which to gain honor. Texans' preference for cavalry is apparent in the number of Texas units in the different branches of the military. In 1861, Texas raised sixteen regiments, three battalions, and three independent companies of cavalry compared to seven regiments and four battalions of infantry—about two and a half cavalry units to every infantry organization. Texas was the only state in the Civil War to have more cavalry units than infantry.

**Fighting East of the Mississippi River**

When the C.S.A. made its initial call for men to enlist to defend its newly-formed nation, Texas was on the western flank of the Confederacy, far removed from the Eastern Theater of the war where major battles were erupting. This scenario gave Texans a greater number of options where they could fight. They could fight in any of the three main theaters (Eastern, Western, or Trans-Mississippi), on the Texas coast, the frontier, the Mexican border, and in the West. A clear majority of the men enlisted in units in the Trans-Mississippi, but the most famous Texas units fought east of the Mississippi River. The smallest percentage of Texans fought in the Eastern Theater of the war.

Only three Texas regiments, the First, Fourth, and Fifth Texas Infantry—part of Hood's Texas Brigade—fought east of the Appalachian Mountains and became the most famous of all the Lone Star State's units. These men fought in every engagement in the region with the exception of the first land battle of the Civil War at Manassas, Virginia. During the course of the war, the men of Hood's Texas Brigade developed a reputation as the hardest fighting and most dependable units in the Army of Northern Virginia. Initially commanded by the former senator from Texas, Louis T. Wigfall, the unit gained its fame and name under the leadership of General John Bell Hood. The Texans became a beloved group of men in General Robert E. Lee's army for their courage and reliability in battle. Lee once commented, "Never mind the raggedness, the enemy never sees the backs of my Texans." Sadly their reputations proved to be their curse since their casualty rate for the war was 61 percent. When Lee surrendered his army at Appomattox Court House, Virginia, the brigade consisted of only 600 of the 4,400 men who had filled the ranks throughout the war. Far from home, the men of Hood's Texas Brigade, though only a small percentage of Lee's army, contributed significantly to the mythology surrounding Texas's fighting soldiers.

In the Western Theater, the region between the Appalachian Mountains and the Mississippi River, a larger number of Texans participated in many important battles. Through the course of the war, Texans fought hard in this theater but felt the sting of defeat more than victory. Early in the war, the Seventh Texas Infantry participated in the defense of Fort Donelson in Tennessee, only to be captured by General Ulysses S. Grant in February 1862 and imprisoned at Camp Douglas, Illinois, for nine months. Fort Donelson had a significant impact on the Texas home front. A Texan noted, "There is a good deal of excitement at this place at this tie about the late fight in Kentucky and Tennessee." In the months after the battle, seventeen Texas cavalry and infantry regiments formally organized and joined the Confederate army. Two months later, the Confederacy almost gained a major victory on the first day at the Battle of Shiloh. But the death of the highest ranking Texan in the Confederate army, General Albert Sidney Johnston, and the last-minute reinforcements of Union troops snatched the victory away from the Southerners.

168  *Beyond Myths and Legends*

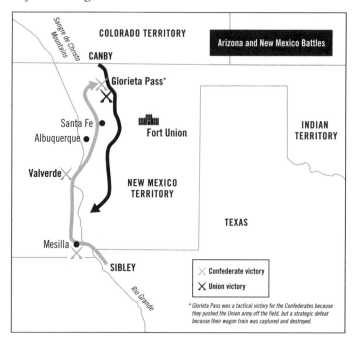

*Glorieta Pass was a tactical victory for the Confederates because they pushed the Union army off the field, but a strategic defeat because their wagon train was captured and destroyed.

Participating in the fighting at Shiloh was the most famous Texas unit in the theater, the Eighth Texas Cavalry, more commonly known as Terry's Texas Rangers.

The greatest threat to Texans in the Western Theater occurred in 1863 when Grant laid siege to Vicksburg, Mississippi. At stake was control of the entire Mississippi River. If the Union army controlled the river, then the Texans could potentially be cut off from most of the Confederate states. Because of this importance, most Texans in the theater focused on the defense of Vicksburg, but their effort was futile. The capture of the city led to the imprisonment of the Second Texas Infantry and Waul's Texas Legion and left the Trans-Mississippi cut off from the rest of the Confederacy. Though the defeat cast a shadow of doubt on the southern cause, Texans continued to fight the Union army, and they even contributed to several major Confederate victories, including the battle of Chickamauga. In the end, however, Texans fighting for the Confederacy continued experiencing defeat after defeat. Through a final attempt to defend their theater, a large number of Texans, including Terry's Texas Rangers, defended Atlanta, Georgia, only to be defeated again. This was a major blow to the Confederacy, but Texans continued fighting until the end of the war, even participating in an attack on Franklin and Nashville. Though defeated, many Texans refused to concede to the Union army; instead, some units such as Terry's Texas Rangers never formally surrendered. They simply went home to Texas.

**The Invasion of New Mexico**

Even though most of the glory and honor in the Civil War went to the men who fought east of the Mississippi River, the bulk of Texas soldiers defended the Trans-Mississippi Theater. The main concern of these Texans was the actual defense of the state, and with few exceptions, they were successful. Unlike their counterparts in the Western Theater, Texans in the Trans-Mississippi Theater won almost all their battles. From the outset of the war, they prepared their state for attack by reinforcing strong relationships with Indians who allied with the Confederacy. Colonel William C. Young's Eleventh Texas Cavalry went to the Indian Territory (in present-day Oklahoma) to strengthen the defenses of their Indian allies and to guard against a Union invasion of North Texas. Additionally, Texans began building coastal fortifications to defend their port cities. Some Texans even took advantage of the war to invade New Mexico.

The invasion of New Mexico began with the activities of Lieutenant Colonel John R. Baylor of the Second Texas Mounted Rifles. Baylor, headquartered in El Paso, commanded approximately half of the regiment, which guarded the northern half of the Rio Grande. With his small force, he advanced into the Arizona Territory (present-day southern New Mexico) and captured the town of Mesilla on the Rio Grande. After his force occupied the town, Baylor declared all of Arizona to be a territory of the Confederacy. Though it sounds significant, the Confederacy did not venture much further into the claimed territory, which extended all the way to eastern California. However, this minor victory encouraged Texans and the Confederacy to launch a grander expedition into the West to gain more territory.

Before the war, General Henry Hopkins Sibley commanded a force of U.S. soldiers campaigning against the Navajo Indians in the New Mexico Territory. When the Civil War began, the native Louisianan sided with the South and formulated a plan to capture the territory he had defended before the war. At the first opportunity, Sibley met with Confederate President Jefferson Davis and shared his plan of conquering New Mexico. After reading reports of Baylor's easy success in the West and hearing the plan of a man who knew the territory, the president agreed to the venture. Sibley's plan was to take a small force of Texas cavalrymen to conquer the New Mexico Territory and add it to the Confederacy. Though historians disagree, there is strong evidence that Sibley wanted to extend Confederate territory in the Southwest all the way to California. T. T. Teel of Sibley's brigade wrote, "As soon as the Confederate army should occupy the Territory of New Mexico an army of advance would be organized and 'on to San Francisco' would be the watch word." By conquering this territory, the Confederacy would break the Union naval blockade of their ports by transporting goods into the southern states through Pacific ports. These viable trade routes would make the Confederacy a trans-continental nation and would improve its chances of gaining foreign recognition and aid.

Sibley organized three Texas cavalry regiments in San Antonio for his expedition—the Fourth, Fifth, and Seventh Texas Mounted Volunteers. In October 1861 Sibley's force left the Alamo city for New Mexico. Once there, Sibley named his force "the Army of New Mexico" and reinforced his Texans with sympathetic Arizona "spy companies." After a brief delay to reorganize his force and to send out scouting parties, Sibley advanced on Union fortifications in New Mexico. During the Confederate delay, Union Colonel Edward R. S. Canby, commander of the Military Department of New Mexico, consolidated his regular U.S. forces with ill-trained New Mexico and Colorado volunteers to stop the Confederate advance. The ill-trained troops hampered Canby's defense of New Mexico, as Sibley and the Texans defeated his army near Fort Craig at the Battle of Valverde.

Sibley's victory opened the way for the Texans to advance up the Rio Grande to capture Albuquerque and Santa Fe and to continue to Fort Union. Sibley remained in Albuquerque, sending Lt. Col. William R. Scurry forward to lead the attack on Fort Union, located a hundred miles northeast of Santa Fe. While passing through the Sangre de

Ben McCulloch, Indian fighter, Texas Ranger, and brigadier general in the army of the Confederate States of America, c. 1860
Photo credit: UTSA's Institute of Texan Cultures

Christo Mountains, Scurry's command defeated a Union force at Glorieta Pass. Though victorious in all their battles, the Army of New Mexico suffered a major loss when a Union raiding party captured their supply train. The army was now deep into New Mexico and without food or supplies. Realizing the seriousness of the situation, Sibley called off the expedition and ordered his men to retreat—unfortunately for the men, that was a disaster. The Texans were forced to live off a land that did not have enough sustenance for all the men and their horses to survive. Retreating through the Jornada del Muerta in New Mexico, Private Collard described the land as being so harsh that for a "jack rabbit to cross it would have to take his vi[c]tuals with him." This condition forced the retreat to become unorganized, and it also forced individual self-reliance. Sibley's force gradually returned to San Antonio in the summer of 1862, disorganized and fewer in number. In time, they recovered from the brutal experience. The ill-fated campaign to capture New Mexico would be the Texans' last attempt to invade their western neighbor.

**Fighting in the Trans-Mississippi Theater**

Early in the war, President Davis appointed Ben McCulloch as commander of the Indian Territory to work in a coalition with the Confederacy's Indian allies. Headquartered in Little Rock, Arkansas, McCulloch quickly organized a Confederate army of the West with troops from Arkansas, Louisiana, and Texas. Against McCulloch's protests, he received an order to cooperate with General Sterling Price's invasion to regain control of Missouri, McCulloch's native state. The expedition proved to be fruitful for the Confederates when on August 10, 1861, they won a major victory against the controversial Union general Nathaniel Lyon at Wilson's Creek.

The following spring, Davis appointed General Earl Van Dorn as the new commander of the joint McCulloch and Price army. Van Dorn, an aggressive commander, conceived of an ambitious plan to capture St. Louis and possibly attack Southern Illinois.

Naturally, McCulloch opposed the plan but followed the orders given to him. The expedition culminated on March 7, 1862, in the Battle of Pea Ridge in northwest Arkansas. In the fighting, McCulloch and other high-ranking officers were killed, leaving the Confederate army disoriented. The resulting defeat forced Van Dorn to retreat but, more importantly, forced the Confederates in the Trans-Mississippi to go on the defensive during the summer and fall of 1862 and forced Texans to focus more on their coastal defenses.

With the Union army checked to the west and north of the Lone Star State, the only vulnerable section of Texas was its 400-mile-long coastline. Most Texans believed that Galveston would be the logical choice for the Union to attack and were surprised in mid-August 1862 when five ships appeared off the coast of Corpus Christi. The Union flotilla bombarded the city and even captured Mustang Island, but the attempt proved futile as the Union soldiers were forced from the island. It proved to be only the first of many attempts to capture Texas port cities.

On October 4, 1862, the Northern navy and army captured Galveston, the largest port city in Texas and the most important port in the state because Galveston had access to railroads leading to Houston and to the interior of the state. Before the Union ships appeared, General Paul O. Hébert, commander of the District of Texas, ordered Texas troops to remove all the heavy cannons in the city to locations inland. Hébert feared that the coastal defenders could not prevent a Union landing and that the weapons would be

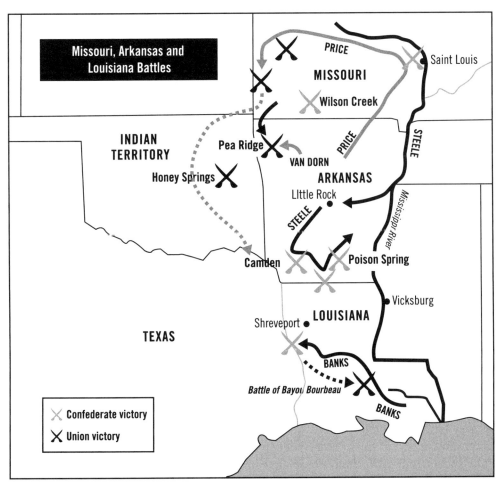

lost if such an invasion occurred. When the Union commander arrived with four ships in Galveston Bay, the Confederates asked for a four-day truce to allow the citizens of the island an opportunity to leave before 150 Union soldiers occupied the city. Hébert's reputation never recovered from this mistake, and he was quickly replaced in November by the more aggressive General John B. Magruder, affectionately called Prince John by his men because of his dapper appearance. General Magruder immediately made plans to recapture the city. The Confederates launched their attack in the early morning of New Year's Day 1863. Approximately 2,000 men, many veterans from the failed New Mexico Expedition, crossed over the railroad bridge that connected the city to the mainland. Once on Galveston Island, the Texans launched a 500-man assault on the Union soldiers' barracks at the opposite side of the island near the bayside wharf. Union troops successfully repelled this assault when six federal gunboats fired large cannons into the attackers' ranks.

As the tide of battle began to turn on the island, two Confederate cottonclads (so named because the boats' only protection were cotton bales on their decks) approached the bay. Without the aid of heavy deck guns, the Confederates used the makeshift vessels to ram and board the Union ships in the bay. Initially, the naval engagement was one-sided since the heavy guns on the Union ships could reach the Confederate flotilla from a greater distance. Though both ships were severely crippled, the Confederates were able to overtake the *Harriet Lane,* forcing the Union sailors onboard to surrender. Confusion thereafter abounded on the other Union gunboats when the *Harriet Lane* fell into Confederate hands. One ship ran aground, and the remaining vessels fled to New Orleans, abandoning the Northern soldiers stationed at the bayside wharf and forcing them to surrender. The recapturing of Galveston proved to be a complete success for the Texans, and they wasted no time in quickly reinforcing the island with the heavy cannons that Hébert had earlier removed. Much to the Texans' relief, the Union navy never attempted to take that port again.

Though 1863 started off well for the Trans-Mississippi Theater, it quickly turned disastrous. In January, a large number of Texans received orders to move to Fort Hindman, more commonly called the Arkansas Post. The post was an earthen fort on the Arkansas River near its confluence with the Mississippi River. Shortly after the Texans' arrival, a large Union force appeared with support from riverboats to attack the Confederates. Soon after the fighting started, the Southern soldiers surrendered and were taken to Ohio. The defeat at Arkansas Post left Arkansas exposed to Union forces, which captured and controlled most of the state, including the state's capital, Little Rock.

Even more damaging to Confederate forces in the Trans-Mississippi Theater was the fall of the river port Vicksburg, Mississippi, on July 4, 1863, essentially giving the Union military complete control of the Mississippi River and effectively isolating the entire Trans-Mississippi region from the rest of the Confederate states. From that point until the end of the war, the Trans-Mississippi Theater became known as "Kirby Smithdom," named after Edmund Kirby Smith, the Confederate commander who virtually became the sole authority of the region west of the Mississippi River. Adding to their misfortunes, Confederate forces in the Indian Territory suffered a major defeat at the Battle of Honey Springs. The loss forced the combined Texan and Indian division to retreat to the southern part of the territory, bringing with them the families of their Indian allies. The Indians suffered greatly, especially considering that circumstances forced them to become dependent on the Confederate government, an institution that was practically non-existent west of the Mississippi River.

As the summer ended in 1863, Texas looked more vulnerable than at any previous time during the war. Not only did the Union army control most of Arkansas and the Indian Territory, but in early September the Union navy launched a major attack on the Texas-Louisiana border at Sabine Pass. Strategically, Sabine Pass was important because of its connection to the railroad system from Beaumont to Houston. If captured, Union troops would be able to control the entire region. Union General Nathaniel P. Banks of Massachusetts planned to land a large force of infantry near Fort Griffin, the Confederate fortification at Sabine Pass, overwhelming the enemy troops stationed there, and to secure the mouth of the Sabine River for the Union. Banks was confident that his plan would succeed, especially considering that Union troops had landed at the same location in 1862 and had destroyed the fortification with relative ease.

At the time of the attack, Fort Griffin contained only six guns and 42 men. Commanding the fort was Lieutenant Richard "Dick" Dowling, an Irish immigrant who had meticulously prepared his men for this event. In the weeks leading up to the battle, the Texans had practiced firing their guns and had staked out the ranges of their fire in the Sabine River. With little effort they could pour lethal fire into an approaching enemy ship. On the morning of September 8, 1863, the men got their opportunity as Union vessels ventured up the pass to fire on the inland fort with their large guns, while other ships landed troops nearby. As soon as the gunboats got within range of Dowling's guns, they opened fire with accurate shots that wreaked havoc on the sailors and their commanders. In the panic that ensued, Union commanders lost control of the fleet. In less than an hour, Dowling's men disabled two gunboats and captured 350 Union prisoners. The remaining transports and gunboats retracted to the safety of New Orleans. Dowling and his artillerymen celebrated their lopsided victory. Banks's attempt to control southeast Texas had been a complete failure and embarrassed the inept general.

Though thwarted in this attempt, Banks made two more attempts to capture Texas during the next year. In the years that followed the war, Jefferson Davis often referred to the Union defeat at Sabine Pass as the "Thermopylae of the Civil War."

Texans had very little time to waste when Banks made his second attack on the Lone Star State in the fall, which was known as the Texas Overland Expedition. Banks made an ill-planned invasion of Texas through southern Louisiana. The main objective was unclear because the commander of the expedition, General William B. Franklin, had the option of capturing the Houston-Galveston region or infiltrating Shreveport up the Red River Valley and into Northeast Texas. The Union army failed to achieve either of their goals. General Tom Green's Cavalry, containing men from the New Mexico campaign, and General John George Walker's Texas Division, better known as "Walker's Greyhounds," soundly defeated the expedition at the Battle of Bayou Bourbeau.

Though Texans had repulsed two Union invasions earlier in 1863, with the closing of the year came doubt about the security of the state. In November, Union forces began moving into South Texas, making their first landfall at Brazos Santiago, a town on Brazos Island at the mouth of the Rio Grande. Alarmed by the invasion and the approach of the Union fleet, General Hamilton Bee, who had recently replaced John S. Ford as commander in South Texas, recognized the weaknesses of the defenses at Brownsville. Rather than allow the city to fall into the enemy's hands, General Bee ordered the evacuation of Brownsville and the destruction of all surplus supplies. Meeting little resistance, the Northern soldiers advanced along the coast as far as Corpus Christi and Matagorda and as far north on the Rio Grande as Roma (in present-day Starr County) by the end of the year.

At the beginning of 1864 South Texas seemed a lost cause. Making matters worse, expecting a federal assault on the coast between the Sabine and Brazos Rivers, Magruder deployed nearly 5,000 soldiers to that region. However, Magruder did not forsake South Texas. Instead, he turned to Ford, then serving as head of recruitment in the state, to raise an army to retake Brownsville and to repel the enemy from Texas soil. By mid-March, Ford had filled his ranks and departed from San Antonio for Brownsville. En route to South Texas, Ford learned of the Union attack at Laredo.

Confronting the invasion of Laredo by Northern soldiers was Colonel Santos Benavides, a local Tejano rancher and businessman who was the highest ranking Mexican American in the Confederate army. Benavides and his Tejano force successfully defended the city and repelled the Union forces. Upon hearing of Benavides's victory, Ford moved his forces to the border town and advanced south along the Rio Grande. Much to his surprise, Ford never encountered any Northern troops because Banks had removed them from the region to participate in a more elaborate campaign to capture the Lone Star State. Only after Ford entered Brownsville unopposed on July 30 did he finally realize that the enemy had departed from South Texas.

Union soldiers evacuated South Texas upon Banks's orders to participate in the Red River Campaign—his final attempt to invade Texas. General Banks's third and final plan was his most elaborate. He led a force of 27,000 men and had the support of gunboats in the brown water navy (that is, naval units that operated on inland water ways). Banks planned to advance up the Red River to capture the Trans-Mississippi army headquarters at Shreveport, Louisiana. From there, he planned to advance into East Texas. Coordinating with Banks was another army in Arkansas, commanded by General Frederick Steele, whose goal was to leave Fort Smith and Little Rock with 10,000 soldiers and to rendezvous at Shreveport. The campaign had two primary objectives. First, the Union commander wanted to disrupt Confederate operations in the Trans-Mississippi Theater. Second, Banks wanted to seize the estimated 150,000 bales of cotton in the region and ship it to the cotton-starved New England textile mills.

Confronting this large Union force was General Richard Taylor with approximately 7,000 soldiers, including Walker's Division and Tom Green's Texans. Initially, the campaign favored Banks's forces, as Taylor and his men retreated in front of the larger Union force advancing up the Red River. However, as Taylor retreated, his force gained valuable reinforcements. With more men in his ranks, Taylor positioned his army at Mansfield where the tide of the campaign turned. On April 6, 1864, at Natchitoches, Banks divided his forces, ordering his infantry to march on the road that led to Mansfield and the gunboats to continue advancing up the river. Banks based his decision on a report from a Louisiana planter who lived on the river. The planter deceivingly told the Union general that the road along the river ended just past Mansfield. The man cautioned General Banks that, if his men continued to march up the road, their advance would soon come to an end. Unknown to Banks, the road alongside the Red River continued unobstructed to Shreveport. The planter had simply lied to the Union officer to keep the soldiers from destroying his plantation and stealing his cotton. The general's decision to divide his forces led directly to the demise of his expedition since his infantry lost the protection of the large guns on the boats.

Two days later on April 8, Banks's army approached Mansfield and found Taylor's Confederate force prepared for battle. Banks's army suffered a humiliating defeat, losing a large number of cannons, wagons, and horses and over 2,000 men killed, wounded, or captured. Banks and his men retreated that night to Pleasant Hill, where the following afternoon the Confederates attacked. Though there was no clear victor at Pleasant Hill, after nightfall Banks ordered his men to retreat back towards the river, abandoning the campaign. The Union gunboats on the Red River experienced problems of their own. As they attempted to advance up the river, Confederates diverted the flow of the river upstream into a bayou, causing a dramatic drop in the water level of the river and the near stranding of the Union boats. Thanks to some clever engineering, the Union navy built a series of wing dams that allowed enough water to accumulate for the boats to float across exposed obstacles.

Further north in Arkansas, General Steele's forces did not fare better. Confederates blocked Steele's advance to Shreveport outside of Camden, Arkansas. With few supplies Steele ordered his men to forage for food and fodder in the vicinity, only to face opposition at every turn. The most notable conflict between Confederates and one of Steele's foraging parties occurred on April 18 at Poison Spring where a southern force consisting of Texans and the Confederacy's Indian allies routed the party and massacred the African-American Union troops who were captured during the course of the battle. Low on supplies and discouraged after receiving information that Banks's column abandoned the campaign, Steele retreated his forces to Little Rock, Arkansas.

As a result of the failed Red River campaign, Confederate forces had to contend with a large population of Union prisoners of war. Many of the captured Union soldiers were escorted to Camp Ford on the outskirts of Tyler, Texas, the largest prisoner camp west of

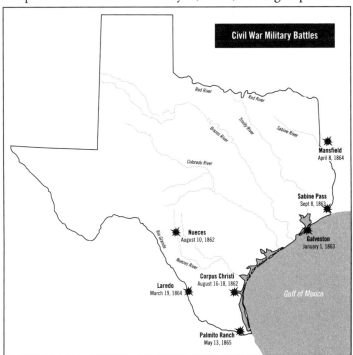

the Mississippi. A lull in the fighting followed Banks's failed campaign, providing Texas an opportunity to launch raids into Union-held territories, specifically into Indian Territory (present-day Oklahoma). In September 1864 a force of Texans under the leadership of Brigadier General Richard Montgomery Gano and the Confederacy's Indian allies commanded by Brigadier General Stand Watie raided into northeastern Indian Territory. The goal of these raiders was to capture Union supplies en route to Fort Gibson, to provide food and supplies to the soldiers and a large number of Indian refugees in southern Indian Territory and northern Texas, and to deny the Union occupation force these supplies in an effort to force them to leave the region or to prevent them from launching an attack into North Texas. While the Confederates marched through the Indian Territory, a captured Union soldier informed them that a major supply train was on its way to Fort Gibson. The Texas and Indian force confronted the train at Cabin Creek and captured or destroyed over $1.5 million of supplies ($75 million in today's currency). The Battle of Cabin Creek was the last battle in Indian Territory, and it forced the Union army to withdraw soldiers from Fort Gibson, effectively eliminating the threat to North Texas.

**Desertion and the Last Battle of the Civil War**

Myths perpetuated by Texas Civil War veterans maintain that Texas soldiers stood bravely in the face of the enemy and never deserted the army. The reality, however, is that Texans throughout the war deserted their posts. While many men simply deserted because they were unable to handle the horrors of combat, others abandoned the Confederacy because they grew tired of circumstances beyond their control. For example, some men left the army due to the military's failure to provide proper provisions. Without supplies and food, the men became vulnerable to the elements and their enemies. Some returned home after receiving letters from loved ones about problems at home, such as the hardship of harvesting the crops, the death of a family member, or the unbearable loneliness of their spouses and children. Such letters pulled the heartstrings of the men, motivating some to return home at their first opportunity. Conscription also played a part. Men forced into the army often resented military life and felt no real motivation to fight. These men usually left the army at their first opportunity or when they could no longer bear the burden of military service. The most unique reason why Texans deserted was the loss of their horses. As the war progressed and the Confederate army no longer had the means to maintain a large cavalry force, commanders ordered numerous cavalry units to dismount. Discouraged over losing their horses, Texans simply deserted and returned home, or they joined dismounted cavalry regiment in hopes of regaining their status as cavalrymen again.

By early 1865 with reports of defeats east of the Mississippi combined with frustrations of a war-time society, Texans began to believe that defeat was inevitable. Soldiers began to desert in larger numbers and to plan for life after the war. The only interruption to their plans as 1865 progressed was the final battle of the Civil War at Palmito Ranch near Brownsville. On May 13, John "Rip" Ford's men defeated the Union forces in the battle, but Ford saw the inevitable defeat of the Confederacy and soon thereafter arranged an armistice with the Union commander in Brownsville. Many Texans followed Ford's lead, dissolving their units. Though the war had not officially ended in the Trans-Mississippi Theater, General Edmund Kirby Smith quickly found himself to be a commander without an army.

## The Texas Home Front

The Texas home front differed from the majority of the Confederate states. Compared to other southern states, citizens experienced fewer hardships, the loss of property was minimal, and no major battles took place in the state. The greatest problems faced by Texans throughout the war were the death of their soldiers, internal dissent, and the constant threat of Indian raids that settlers faced on the frontier. Being isolated from major military engagements spared Texas of the horrors of war, but it also created unique situations to which Texans had to adapt.

Since there was no real invasion of Texas, the economy of the state did not truly suffer. An advantage the Lone Star State had over the other southern states blockaded by the Union navy was its border with Mexico. Being so close to Mexico provided Texas cotton growers an opportunity to get their crop safely to the international market. Planters would cart their cotton from Brownsville to Bagdad, Mexico, on the mouth of the Rio Grande where stevedores loaded the bales on a steamboat. From Bagdad the cotton was taken outside the reach of the Union blockade to the international market. Texans continued to ship cotton across the border into Mexico even after General Banks captured Brownsville in the fall of 1863; they simply moved their base of operations to Laredo. After unloading the cotton at Bagdad, merchants filled their carts with military supplies, luxury items, and medicine and returned inland.

Though the border trade was the safest means of trafficking contraband, Texas also utilized blockade runners. The centers of the blockade-running activity were at the ports of Galveston and Corpus Christi. At the start of the war, the Union navy was relatively small, allowing blockade runners to enter and to leave Texas ports virtually unscathed. As the war progressed, running the blockade became more difficult, especially when Union troops temporarily occupied the state's major ports.

Similar to the economy, the institution of slavery in Texas was not directly impacted by the war. Life on plantations and farms basically continued as it did during antebellum times. As the war progressed, General Paul O. Hébert requested that slaveowners lend their slaves to the military to build coastal fortifications. This idea was not very popular among owners who saw the proposition as risking their investment in bondsmen to exposure and injury. However, the need for military fortifications along the southern coast prompted the Confederate Congress in March 1863 to pass legislation that allowed the military to conscript slaves for up to sixty days, with the $15 per month compensation being given to the owners. In Texas, John Magruder expanded this impressment when in July of the same year he established the Labor Bureau, which forced slaves to work on constructing military fortifications, to drive carts loaded with cotton to Mexico, and to build the stockade for Camp Ford.

Another interesting phenomenon involving slaves in Texas during the war concerned refugee slaves. When Union troops reached the doorsteps of slaveowners in Missouri, Louisiana, and Arkansas, they fled to Texas with their slaves, not wanting to risk losing their property to the Northern soldiers. Approximately 50,000 refuged slaves were brought to the Lone Star State during the war. Though this dramatic increase in the number of bondsmen did not have an impact on the institution of slavery, the situation created friction between the slaveowners and plain folk (those who did not own slaves). Not wanting to risk their escaping to Mexico or to lose them to another invading army, most slaveowners resettled in the Brazos River Valley. After the war, approximately 60 percent of the bondsmen remained in the Lone Star State and the Brazos River Valley, which led directly to outbreaks of violence, such as the "Millican Race Riot," in the area immediately after the war.

Though Texas was not the home of major Civil War battles and campaigns, the death of the states' young men had a tremendous impact. Very few people escaped the pain of losing relatives, loved ones, or neighbors. Historians have estimated that over half of the military-age men in Texas served in the war. Approximately 20 to 25 percent of these men died in the war, more than half of those to disease because the majority of soldiers came from farms or isolated rural communities where exposure to disease and unsanitary conditions was limited. An estimated 15,000 Texans died in the war out of a total population of about 600,000. Children lost their fathers, parents lost their sons, wives lost their husbands, and friends lost each other in a war to protect the institution of slavery.

**Texas Women During the War**

Early in the war, women enthusiastically supported the Confederacy. They encouraged men to enlist in the army, sometimes threatening romantic rejection if they did not participate. As the units organized, mothers, wives, sisters, and sweethearts contributed to the war effort by supplying their men with socks, shirts, blankets, homemade uniforms, and other supplies that they would need in the fight to come. When the men prepared to leave for distant fronts, the women often prepared a festive banquet for the departing men. The event would culminate with a leading woman or a veteran of the Texas Revolution giving a speech and the ladies presenting a battle flag that they made to the men. The most prominent instance involved Fannie Wigfall, wife of former senator from Texas and first commander of the Texas Brigade, Louis T. Wigfall. Fannie sewed the brigades battle flag, using pieces from two of her silk dresses, one she had not previously worn and the other her own wedding dress. During the flag presentation ceremony in Virginia, Jefferson Davis, president of the Confederacy, dedicated the flag to the brigade in the name of Wigfall's fifteen-year-old daughter Lula.

Though in many cases the departure of the men was emotionally painful, the hardships that women experienced intensified after the men left. Loneliness and melancholy were commonplace among women as they saw their men and boys marching off to war. Additional problems emerged as the war became protracted, such as managing farms, plantations, and slaves without their husbands and sons. They soon felt vulnerable, especially the women on the frontier who lived with constant threats of Indian attacks. Most troubling to Texas women was the persistent fear that their loved ones would be killed in the war. Regardless of these fears, life at home continued, and women took on more responsibilities to maintain a sense of normalcy. The new responsibilities raised expectations across the state for Texas women, as they now participated in the legal system, suing and being sued, petitioning for divorces, and probating the estates of deceased husbands and family members. By wars end, Texas society viewed women in a new light having endured the rigors of war on the home front and proving that they could take on the traditional roles of their husbands and fathers.

## Internal Dissent

The Texas home front was not always supportive of the war and the men in the Confederate army. Among the Texas population were different groups of "Unionists Confederates." Though common within every southern state, Texas with its diverse population had a significant number of Unionists. The first signs of these dissenters appeared during the secession convention in 1861. Some men who opposed secession during the convention, like James W. Throckmorton, later changed their minds supporting the South once Texas had joined the Confederacy. Others, like Edmund J. Davis and John L. Hayes, joined the U.S. Army and fought to restore their state's proper relations within the Union. Davis and Hayes organized and led the First and Second Texas Cavalry Regiments. The majority of their regiments' service was in Louisiana and Texas. Both regiments saw action at the Battle of Palmito Ranch, the last battle of the war.

A unique characteristic of Davis and Hayes's regiments was that both commands had a large contingent of Tejanos and Mexican nationals serving in their units. Almost a third of the nearly 3,000 soldiers were of Hispanic descent. Hispanic soldiers enlisted for several reasons, but most of the enlistees sought revenge against white Texans who had cheated them of their ancestral lands during the antebellum period. A few Hispanics joined the military for purely economic motives. These enlistees looked forward to obtaining clothes, guns, food, pay, and a saddle with tack from the U.S. Army.

Not all Texas Unionists joined the U.S. military. In North Texas a large group of Unionists formed the Peace Party in October 1862 as a response to the passage of the conscription act that forced young men to serve in the Confederate army. Most of the Unionist activities took place in Cooke County and the surrounding area, where a few members of the Peace Party planned to raid local arsenals and promote a general uprising. When local Confederate sympathizers and officials uncovered these plans, they ordered Colonel James G. Bourland and his state troops to arrest over 150 people whom they suspected of being involved in the plot. State troops escorted the prisoners to Gainesville, Texas, where the people of the city organized a "citizens' court" that was overseen by Bourland and Colonel William C. Young, who was on sick leave from the Eleventh Texas Cavalry. The court found seven of the Unionist leaders guilty of treason and immediately sentenced them to death. Before the disbandment of the court, the community lynched fourteen additional Unionists and killed two more who attempted to escape from the authorities. The violence in Gainesville escalated in the ensuing months when a group of pro-Union men were accused of assassinating Colonel Young, an event that led to the execution of nineteen more "traitors." It was never proven that these men murdered Colonel Young. Likely, he was killed by bandits. When the bloodshed finally ended, forty-two people had lost their lives. The story of these killings in North Texas spread across both the North and the South, leaving the Confederacy embarrassed about its mishandling of dissenters and fortified the Union's accusations of southern barbarism. Remembered as the great hanging at Gainesville, the event proved to be one of the greatest wartime atrocities towards American citizens in United States history.

Dissent among the Texas populace did not end in North Texas. Months earlier, German immigrants on the frontier in the Hill Country formed their own pro-Union organization, the Union Loyal League, to protect themselves from Indian depredations and to avoid Confederate conscription. Many Texas Germans had immigrated to the Hill

Country in 1848 to avoid the turmoil of revolution in their home country. As such, they were weary of conflict and simply desired to be left alone. Their attempt to evade the service in the Confederate military led to suspicion among Texas officials. After months of harassment by Texans to join the Confederate army, sixty-one members of the league under the leadership of Frederick "Fritz" Tegener decided to escape to Mexico, an act seen as treason. Ninety-one Confederate partisan rangers commanded by Lieutenant Colin D. McRae pursued the fleeing Germans. On August 10, 1862, McRae's rangers attacked the Unionists on the banks of the Nueces River, just twenty miles from Fort Clark. During what became known as the Battle of Nueces, McRae's men killed nineteen Germans while taking nine prisoners of war. The captives were men who were severely wounded and could not retreat with the rest of their company. The prisoners soon met a gruesome fate. The Confederate troops executed them in the hours following the battle. Those Germans who managed to escape crossed the border into Mexico. Many of them later enlisted in the Union army in New Orleans. In 1865 after the war's end, relatives of the fallen Germans returned to the battleground and gathered the bones of their murdered loved ones and countrymen. They interred the bones at Comfort, Texas, on the site of the "Treue de Union" monument that commemorates the German Unionists who fell on the banks of the Nueces River. As these two events reveal, Texans did not tolerate anti-Confederate views, and they often employed violent means to silence the dissenters.

**Defending the Frontier**

From the outset of the war, the frontier was a major concern for Texans. The first two cavalry regiments organized from Texas, the First and Second Texas Mounted Rifles, were stationed on the frontier in the spring of 1861. However, the growing need for men on eastern battlefronts forced Confederate commanders to transfer soldiers from the frontier, leaving the settlers once again exposed to Indian raids. In response, officials in December 1861 organized a new frontier force, the Frontier Regiment. With approximately 1,000 men in their ranks, they divided their force into 16 camps on the frontier, creating a patrol system scouting for Native Americans' raiding parties. Luckily for the men in the regiment, the frontier was relatively calm in 1862, creating a false sense of success. The following year Comanches and Kiowas launched numerous successful raids from the Indian Territory when they recognized the patterns and vulnerability of the patrol system. In March 1864, Confederate officials pressured Governor Murrah to fulfill the state's quota of servicemen according to the Confederacy's Conscription Act, leaving the governor little choice but to transfer the Frontier Regiment to regular service in the Confederate army.

Once again, Texans on the frontier felt exposed to Indian depredations. As a result, the state created the Frontier Organization. Though this new frontier militia had approximately 4,000 volunteers, the actual number of men on patrol at any one time was much less. According to the state's guidelines, only a quarter of the men enlisted in the Frontier Organization would patrol at a time, while the rest remained at home. Considering that many of the volunteers lived on the frontier, it was assumed that the entire force could be brought together relatively quickly in times of emergencies. Despite the Texans' efforts to defend their western lands, there were only three significant Indian conflicts during the war: Elm Creek (October 13, 1864), Adobe Walls (November 25, 1864), and Dove Creek (January 8, 1865). Elm Creek was the only planned Indian raid on Texan settlements.

Confederates initiated the fight at Dove Creek against a group of peaceful Kickapoo Indians seeking refuge from the Civil War in Mexico and the battle at Adobe Walls took place in the Texas panhandle against Union soldiers from New Mexico. Contrary to the myth that Native Americans successfully pushed the frontier line back 50 miles and killed, wounded, or captured approximately 400 white settlers living on the frontier, the environment had a greater impact on their deaths and displacements. The drought that exacerbated the Texas troubles continued through the years of the war and forced settlers from their dry homesteads. The environmental conditions also drove the buffalo out of Texas for greener pastures and was responsible for the deaths of approximately 4,000 Comanche.

**The End of the War**

After four years of war, the end of the conflict came quickly after news of General Robert E. Lee's surrender at Appomattox Court House, Virginia, in April 1865. Not wanting to surrender, General Edmund Kirby Smith ordered all Texas units to concentrate in Houston on May 27. On that date, Smith arrived in the city to find that there was no army. Realizing that the war would not continue in the Trans-Mississippi, Smith and Magruder boarded a Union ship in Galveston Bay and officially surrendered their nonexistent army. As part of the conditions of surrender, Union officers paroled Texans out of the Confederate army and allowed them to return home. While most initially accepted defeat and returned home, some fled across the Rio Grande into Mexico and other countries in Latin America. With the war over and their society turned upside down by emancipation, the future of Texas remained uncertain.

*Afterward: Searching for Britton "Britt" Johnson*

*Unlike many of the men that fought in the Civil War, Johnson's life ended as storied as he lived it. On January 24, 1871, while leading a wagon train, twenty-five Kiowas attacked him and two other black teamsters four miles east of Salt Creek in Young County. Johnson fought to the last behind a dead horse. Other teamsters later found his mutilated body and those of his party on the roadside. All three men were buried in a common grave along the wagon trail. The teamsters reported that they found 173 rifle and pistol shells where Johnson made his last stand, a tribute to his tenacity. Johnson's life provides a unique insight into the experiences of Texans left behind during the Civil War, especially slaves near the frontier.*

*Johnson' story did not end with his death. His tale was later incorporated into a classic Hollywood film,* **The Searchers** *(1956), starring the most popular movie star of the time, John Wayne. Though the film portrays white settlers and resembles Cynthia Ann Parker's story of being rescued by Sul Ross in 1860, this plot takes place during the waning months of the Civil War. Essentially, the movie synthesizes the two stories, so Johnson's contributions were given to other characters. Fortunately, writers and scholars continue to keep the story of this legendary figure alive in their retelling of this important period of Texas history.*

# Myth & Legend

### Divided Loyalties: Texans and the Confederacy

*According to popular myth, the people of Texas were unwavering in their devotion to the Confederacy. Many residents of the Lone Star State still contend that Texans, with the exception of a handful of Unionists, were willing to leave their homes and to fight on distant battlefields to defend their new nation. Upon further investigation, however, the notion of undying loyalty to the Confederacy is problematic, especially since many of the soldiers, who were demoralized with the war effort, deserted their regiments and returned to their homes. Aside from dissatisfaction with the way the war was proceeding, Confederate Texans were also concerned with potential threats to their homes and families. One of the greatest perceived threats was Confederate military defeats in the Trans-Mississippi and the Western Theater that left Texas vulnerable to invasion. Texans became especially concerned for the safety of the home front after learning of Confederate defeats in the battles of Pea Ridge, New Orleans, Galveston, and Vicksburg. As a result of Union victories in these battles, Federal troops were poised to strike the Lone Star State, or at least isolate it from the rest of the Confederacy by gaining control of the Mississippi River. Thus, it was natural that the thought of Union forces raiding their homes and preying upon their families caused many Texans to abandon their posts.*

*On March 7 and 8, 1862, Union troops won an important victory at the Battle of Pea Ridge (Arkansas), allowing Union forces to secure Missouri as well as most of northern Arkansas. This Federal victory isolated both Kansas and Missouri from the Confederacy and threatened southern positions in Arkansas and in the Indian Territory. Soon after the army's triumph at Pea Ridge, the Union navy captured the port of New Orleans (Louisiana). The loss of New Orleans was a heavy blow to the Confederacy. Not only was the port city one of the largest cities in the South, but, more importantly, it was positioned at the mouth of the Mississippi River. Thus, the Union now was one step closer to severing the Trans-Mississippi from the rest of the Confederacy. Texas soldiers, especially those in units stationed east of the Mississippi River, became concerned for their homes and families.*

*On October 5, 1862, the Union navy established a blockade off Galveston Island that worried all Texans: both civilian and soldier. Four days later, U.S. Marines captured and occupied Galveston for nearly four months. The occupation of the port city was the first time during the war that Union soldiers had set foot on Texas soil, and many Texans believed that soon Federal troops would threaten the interior of the state. Elijah P. Petty, a Confederate Texan, expressed his concern by stating, "My feelings, inclinations and all my yearnings are to be in Texas if she is invaded. My all is there—All that is near and dear to me is there and I want to be there to protect it."*

*The battles at Pea Ridge, New Orleans, and Galveston had a deep impact on the morale of all Texans serving outside of the state, but these battles did not have as big an impact as the fall of Vicksburg on July 4, 1863. Vicksburg was the last stronghold for the Confederacy on the Mississippi River. With Vicksburg, the Union navy now had complete control of the Mississippi River. While strategically important for both sides in the war, the river served as an important psychological barrier for Texans. As long as the Confederacy controlled the river, it was a bulwark between Texas and the bulk of the Union army. One Texan wrote, "Our lines once broken, whether on the Mississippi or the Arkansas, or the Red River, would have thrown open the approach to the invasion of Texas, by an ever alert and powerful foe." When Vicksburg fell, Theophilus V. Ware of the Twenty-seventh Texas Cavalry recognized the importance of the event and expressed the feelings of thousands of Texans when he wrote "this little Confederacy is gone up the spout."*

*Demoralized, isolated from their homes, and fearing the imminent invasion of the Lone Star State, Texas soldiers deserted in waves. Some men simply saw an opportunity to escape the army, but most deserted so they could defend their homes in Texas. Essentially, they believed the Confederacy was less important than their homes and families. By the end of the war, Texans had given up on the Confederacy, and it was difficult to keep them from returning to their beloved Lone Star State.*

## Suggestions for Further Reading

Baum, Dale. *The Shattering of Texas Unionism: Politics in the Lone Star State During the Civil War and Reconstruction.* Baton Rouge: Louisiana State University Press, 1998.

Boswell, Angela. *Her Act and Deed: Women's Lives in a Rural Southern County, 1837-1873.* College Station: Texas A&M University Press, 2001.

Buenger, Walter L. *Secession and the Union in Texas.* Austin: University of Texas Press, 1984.

Campbell, Randolph B. *A Southern Community in Crisis: Harrison County, Texas, 1850-1880.* Austin: Texas State Historical Association, 1983.

Cotham, Edward T., Jr. *Battle on the Bay: The Civil War Struggle for Galveston.* Austin: University of Texas Press, 1998.

Daddysman, James W. *The Matamoros Trade: Confederate Commerce, Diplomacy, and Intrigue.* Newark, Del.: University of Delaware Press, 1984.

Dupree, Stephen A. *Planting the Union Flag in Texas: The Campaign of Major General Nathaniel P. Banks in the West.* College Station: Texas A&M University Press, 2008.

Frazier, Donald S. *Blood and Treasure: Confederate Empire in the Southwest.* College Station: Texas A&M University Press, 1995.

___ . *Tempest over Texas: The Fall and Winter Campaigns of 1863–1864.* Abilene, TX: Statehouse Press, 2020.

Grear, Charles D., ed. *The Fate of Texas: The Civil War and the Lone Star State.* Fayetteville: The University of Arkansas Press, 2008

Joiner, Gary D. *One Damn Blunder from Beginning to End: The Red River Campaign of 1864.* Wilmington, Del.: Scholarly Resources, 2003.

Jordan, Terry. *German Seed in Texas Soil.* Austin: University of Texas Press, 1966.

Marten, James. *Texas Divided: Loyalty and Dissent in the Lone Star State, 1856-1874.* Lexington: The University Press of Kentucky, 1990.

McCaslin, Richard B. *Tainted Breeze: The Great Hanging at Gainesville, Texas, 1862.* Baton Rouge, 1994.

Smith, David Paul. *Frontier Defense in the Civil War: Texas's Rangers and Rebels.* College Station: Texas A&M University Press, 1992.

Thompson, Jerry. *Vaqueros in Blue and Gray.* Reprint, Austin: State House Press, 2000.

Underwood, Rodman L. *Death on the Nueces : German Texans "Treueder Union."* Austin: Eakin Press, 2000.

Wooster, Ralph A. *Texas and Texans in the Civil War.* Austin: Eakin Press, 1995.

**IDENTIFICATION:** Briefly describe each term.

John Bell Hood
Vicksburg
Paul O. Hébert
John B. "Prince John" Magruder
Richard "Dick" Dowling
Battle of Nueces
Great Hanging at Gainesville
Nathaniel P. Banks
Red River Campaign
New Mexico Campaign
Battle of Palmito Ranch
First and Second Texas Cavalry (Union)
Cotton Trade
Refuged Slaves
Frontier Regiment

**MULTIPLE CHOICE:** Choose the correct response.

1. Most Texans served in the _____ during the Civil War:
   A. Eastern Theater
   B. Western Theater
   C. Trans-Mississippi Theater
   D. Navy

2. The most famous Texas unit of the Civil War was:
   A. Hood's Texas Brigade
   B. Gano's Guards
   C. Walker's Texas Division
   D. W. P. Lane Rangers

3. What was the most common motivation for Texans to fight in the Civil War?
   A. States' Rights
   B. Slavery
   C. Economic expansion
   D. Territorial expansion

4. What branch of the army did Texans prefer to serve in during the Civil War?
   A. Infantry
   B. Engineers
   C. Artillery
   D. Cavalry

5. What was the major turning point of the Civil War to Texans?
   A. The Battle of Bull Run
   B. The fall of Vicksburg
   C. The defeat at Gettysburg
   D. The occupation of Galveston

6. What was the greatest impact the Civil War had on the home front?
   A. The death of their husbands, sons, and brothers
   B. It created an economic depression
   C. Wide spread destruction when Union armies marched through their towns
   D. The number of slaves in the state decreased because they fled to the Union army

7. What was the goal of the New Mexico Campaign?
   A. Capture the rich oil deposits in the territory
   B. Capture the silver mines
   C. Capture territory in the American Southwest
   D. Capture El Paso and incorporate the territory into Texas

8. Why is the battle of Sabine Pass called the Thermopylae of the South?
   A. A large number of Confederate soldiers were defeated by a significantly smaller Union force
   B. A large Union fleet defeated a small garrison of Confederate artillerymen
   C. The Union army took Sabine Pass without firing a shot
   D. A small garrison of Texans in a mud fort repulsed a large flotilla of Union gun boats and transports

9. Which event occurred last?
   A. Secession
   B. The Battle of Palmito Ranch
   C. The Red River Campaign
   D. The Battle of Galveston

10. Which of the following is NOT a role played by most Texas women during the war?
    A. Fight alongside their husbands in combat
    B. Influenced men to enlist in the Confederate army
    C. Create societies to provide Texas soldiers with shirts, socks, and blankets during the war
    D. Presided over flag presentation ceremonies

**TRUE/FALSE:** Indicate whether each statement is true or false.

1. Texans fought in both the Confederate and Union armies.

2. Texans fought alongside Native Americans in the Civil War.

3. Texans repulsed the Union army's initial attempt to capture Galveston.

4. Texas was the only Confederate state to have a frontier.

5. Women played a crucial role for Texas in the Civil War.

6. Soldiers from Texas fought in every theater of the war.

7. Through the course of the Civil War, Texans never deserted from the Confederate army.

8. The economic impact of the Civil War devastated the Lone Star State.

9. The last battle of the Civil War took place in Texas.

10. All German immigrants sided with their adopted state.


**MATCHING:** Match the response in column A with the item in column B.

1. Sabine Pass
2. Red River Campaign
3. Cabin Creek
4. Palmito Ranch
5. Vicksburg
6. Richard Dowling
7. John Magruder
8. Albert Sidney Johnston
9. Hood's Texas Brigade
10. Terry's Texas Rangers

A. Most famous regiment of Texas soldiers in the Western Theater
B. Thermopylae of the Civil War
C. Union army's last attempt to capture Texas
D. A raid that captured or destroyed supplies worth 1.5 million dollars
E. Last battle of the Civil War
F. Isolated the Trans-Mississippi from the rest of the Confederacy
G. Irish immigrant that commanded soldiers in the Battle of Sabine Pass
H. Commander of the District of Texas
I. Highest ranking Texan in the Civil War
J. Only Texans to serve in Lee's army in Virginia

**ESSAY QUESTIONS:**

1.  What role did Texas women play in the Civil War?

2.  What motivated Texans to enlist in the Confederate army?

3.  During the Civil War numerous people in the South protested the Confederacy, especially Texas. Explain fully who in Texas dissented against the war, what were their actions, and what was the reaction of Texans loyal to the Confederacy.

4.  In most instances Texas was similar to the rest of the South. Explain fully the few instances that Texas was unique and the impact they had on the state.

# Chapter 8

# Reconstruction in Texas: The Unfinished Civil War, 1865-1874

**Prelude: The Assassination of J. N. Baughman, 1874**

*By 1874, Reconstruction in Texas was over and the Democratic Party reigned supreme in the state. Though Republicans still maintained a presence at the county level in areas with higher concentrations of black voters, conservative Democrats with the aid of terrorist groups, such as the Ku Klux Klan, used violent tactics to silence Republican politicians, especially in statewide races. Isaac Newton Baughman, a leading Republican from Wharton County, reported on the Democratic strategies in his county in 1875. Baughman wrote, "on last Thursday, the 7th of January, I was waited on by an armed mob, composed of the leading democrats of the county, and ordered to leave the county or they would kill me." He continued, "I asked them what their objections were to me staying there; their answer was, 'You are a d__d radical,' and they did not want any of my sort in the county, and they did not intend to let me stay there, me or any other damned radical; and they took the vote on it, and every one [the sheriff and his deputy among the crowd] voted that I should not stay." Without little alternative, Baughman sought the protection of local sheriff. To his dismay, the sheriff bluntly stated that, "he could not give any [protection], as [Baughman] was a damned radical . . . ."*

*Rattled and fearing for his life, Baughman sought refuge by barricading himself in his office. He rightly surmised that if his political foes found him in the open, they would murder him in the streets of his hometown. At one point, six men knocked on his office door with guns drawn, making their intentions clear—they were there to murder him. Fortunately, Baughman evaded the lynch mob and escaped capture, finding safety in the home of a neighbor. His pursuers, however, soon discovered his hideout, threatening to break inside the home and seize him. Before the mob made good on their threat, the neighbor's wife appeared and pleaded with them to leave. Apparently, the women's plea had an effect on the murderous horde, because they abandoned their efforts. Believing that the men might return and that they might harm his neighbors, Baughman left under the cover of darkness, making his way eventually to Austin. In the capital city, he made a formal complaint to Governor Coke and asked him for protection. The governor, a conservative Democrat, refused to become involved in the matter* and offered no protection to the beleaguered Republican. In a report written to the United States Attorney General, Baughman wrote about his troubles in Wharton County, stating, "It seems what started them this particular day, we were having an election for justice of the peace to fill a vacancy, and I was issuing tickets for the republican party at my store, and the first time the crowd waited on me they gave me orders to issue no more tickets." Furthermore, Baughman commented that his service in the Union Army angered many of the ex-Confederates in the county, who refused to accept the results of the Civil War.

Edmund J. Davis, former Republican governor of the state, forwarded Baughman's account to the United States Attorney General, also noted that other regions in the state experienced similar outrages. Concerned about cases of violence against Republic politicians and the freedpeople in Texas and the state government's refusal to provide them adequate protection, Davis asked the simple question: "Where are they to seek help?" Rhetorically, Davis answered his own question that it was the responsibility of the federal government to protect individuals, such as Baughman, especially considering that state authorities were unwilling to aid them in their time of need. Davis sadly proclaimed, "Such persons have no rights that anybody here (who differs with them politically) is bound to respect. Can they, then, get it from the United States authorities? If from neither, it occurs to me that the war for the Union was very much of a farce." Davis's questions and Baughman's circumstances highlighted the frustrations and failures of federal Reconstruction policies in the state.

Traditionally, historians have viewed the American Civil War (1861-1865) and the Reconstruction era (1865-1877) as two distinct and separate periods in United States history. This approach, providing a convenient way to understand two very complex eras, tends to skew the general understanding of the violence that became commonplace in the South during Reconstruction. Additionally, scholarly celebrations of the Union victory in the Civil War tend to ignore the fact that the United States government ultimately failed to reconstruct southern society in the decades following the war. A more constructive way to study this period of American history is to examine the era from 1861 to 1877 as two distinct phases of a continuous conflict between the northern and southern states.

In the first phase of the war (1861-1865), the United States and Confederate governments used conventional military forces to achieve their respective goals. The federal troops fought to preserve the Union and, after the Emancipation Proclamation went into effect in January 1863, to end slavery. The Confederate military fought to win southern independence and to preserve the institution of slavery. The northern states' larger population, greater industrial capabilities, and naval superiority dictated that, almost from the very beginning, the Union would win the first phase of a war of attrition.

During the second phase of the war (1865-1877), also referred to as the War of Reconstruction, white Southerners organized terrorist groups and initiated a prolonged guerilla war against Republican governments in the southern states that sought to guide political and social reform in the South. Given that Radical Republicans supported federal and state legislation that would guarantee African American suffrage rights, white Southerners became concerned about potential changes to their political institutions. They believed that suffrage for former slaves would ultimately lead to complete social and political equality for southern blacks. During this second phase of the Civil War, Texas became a primary battleground for the attempts to keep the newly-freed slaves oppressed and to deter the efforts of the Republican Party in reconstructing the South.

**Presidential Reconstruction**

Following General Robert E. Lee's surrender at Appomattox Courthouse in April 1865, Texans initially seemed willing to accept defeat. However, many ex-Confederates felt a sense of uncertainty as they learned of the political battles emerging in Washington, D.C., between President Abraham Lincoln and Radical Republicans in Congress. The president and members of his party in Congress were divided over how Reconstruction should be accomplished. Lincoln defined secession as an act of rebellion and determined that the Constitution gave the president the authority not only to end the rebellion but also to re-establish loyal governments within the rebellious states. By his definition, the South had not technically left the Union; rather, it was in a state of open rebellion against the federal government. Radical Republicans in Congress disagreed. Radicals stated that the southern states, through the act of secession, had broken away from the Union and had formed a new government. Now, with the war over and the Confederacy defeated, the southern states would have to reapply for readmission to the Union. According to the Radical Republicans, only Congress had the power to admit new states in the Union, and, therefore, only Congress had the power to reconstruct the South.

The tension between the president and Congress increased once Lincoln announced his plan for reconstructing the South. On December 8, 1863, Lincoln set forth his famous Ten Percent Plan, a plan that allowed a southern state to rejoin the Union and to create a new state government once 10 percent of registered voters on the state's 1860 election rolls had taken an oath of allegiance to the United States and officially accepted the end of slavery. In accordance with this plan, the president restored civil government in Tennessee, Arkansas, and Louisiana. Believing that the president's plan failed to secure the loyalty of white Southerners, Congress passed the Wade-Davis Bill on July 2, 1864. The Wade-Davis Bill, also known as the First Congressional Plan of Reconstruction, required that 50 percent of the 1860 registered voters had to pledge their loyalty to the Union and restricted political participation to Southerners who took an "iron-clad" oath that stated they had never willingly taken up arms or aided the Confederacy during the war. Congress then refused to accept the representatives elected from the three states that the president had declared to be reconstructed. In turn, Lincoln refused to sign the bill, killing it with a pocket veto. Within a year after the president's veto of the Wade-Davis Bill, Texans' fears were elevated once again when John Wilkes Booth assassinated President Lincoln just five days after Lee's surrender at Appomattox Courthouse, Virginia.

Following the assassination, many wondered whether the northern states and federal government would hold the South accountable for Lincoln's death. Despite their initial apprehension, optimism returned once Texans understood that President Andrew Johnson planned to continue his predecessor's lenient policy of restoring the Union. Under his plan, Johnson appointed for each state a provisional governor who would oversee the Reconstruction process. The provisional governor was required to call a constitutional convention and to ensure that its delegates created a new governing document that nullified the act of secession, abolished slavery, and repudiated the debts that the state had incurred while part of the Confederacy. In an effort to limit ex-Confederate and pre-war Democrats from participating in the constitutional convention, a state's voters, as well as the delegates elected to the constitutional convention, were required to take a loyalty oath, similar to the "iron-clad" oath. Once the delegates had completed their task, the new constitution had to be ratified by the voters in a statewide referendum. Additionally, voters would elect a new state government under the provisions of the new constitution. At that point the federal government would fully readmit the state to the Union and allow the state to send representatives to the United States Congress.

**The Arrival of Federal Troops**

As political events unfolded in Washington, D.C., the United States Army landed on the Texas coast. The primary concern of the Union commanders was the establishment of a loyal government and the protection of white Unionists and African Americans. On June 2, 1865, following the formal surrender of Confederate General E. Kirby Smith, U.S. General Philip H. Sheridan assumed command of the Military Division of the Southwest, which included Texas. Sheridan established his headquarters in New Orleans and immediately ordered federal troops to occupy the port of Galveston. On June 19, 1865, General Gordon Granger at the command of 1,800 troops landed on Galveston Island and immediately declared that President Lincoln's Emancipation Proclamation was in effect in the state. As such, Granger announced that all slaves in Texas were free, that all legislation passed by the Texas legislature since secession was void, and that remaining Confederate soldiers should lay down their arms and consider themselves paroled. The abolition of slavery in the Lone Star State—the last southern state where military authorities declared Lincoln's Emancipation Proclamation in effect—thereby completely eradicated the peculiar institution from the South. From that day on, people across Texas and around the world celebrate "Juneteenth" on the anniversary of Granger's pronouncement.

As the military occupied various areas of the state, many Texans feared the loss of antebellum political and social institutions. For the most part, their fears were groundless due to a variety of factors that prevented army commanders from effectively carrying out their mission. One of the greatest obstacles confronting the military was the rapid redeployment of troops outside of Texas. Within a year after landing on the gulf coast, troop strength declined from 51,000 soldiers to just over 3,000, and many of the soldiers who remained in the state after 1866 were stationed along the Texas frontier. Reconstructing the former Confederate state was nearly impossible due to the relatively small size of the occupying force. Additionally, turnover among military commanders who attempted to intervene on the behalf of white Unionists and freed slaves prevented the development of sustained Reconstruction policies.

Between May 1865 and March 1870, the command of Union troops in Texas changed eight times. Of these commanders, General Charles Griffin was the most effective in bringing about political change, but his influence was cut short when he died of yellow fever in September 1867. Griffin's successor, General Joseph J. Reynolds, also attempted to enact political change in the state, but changes in command senior to Reynolds, as well as his own incompetence, frustrated these efforts. Even though the army worked diligently in the field to carry out Reconstruction policies, the frequent changes in command and the failure to establish consistent army policies ultimately led ex-Confederates to develop

**General Gordon Granger (left) and General Charles Griffin (right).**
Photo credit: Library of Congress.

strategies to defend prewar political power and to exert control over the black population. Between 1865 and 1874, white Texans engaged federal troops in a continuous guerrilla war, a war that eventually allowed ex-Confederates to regain political control of the state.

## The Bureau of Refugees, Freedmen, and Abandoned Lands

Congress created the Bureau of Refugees, Freedmen, and Abandoned Lands (commonly called the Freedmen's Bureau) in March 1865 as a branch of the United States Army. The Freedmen's Bureau was designed to be a temporary agency, providing relief to refugees who had been displaced from their homes as a result of the war, to help ex-slaves make the transition to freedom, and to administer all lands that the Confederates had abandoned or that were confiscated during the war. Profits from the sale of the lands were supposed to fund the efforts of the bureau. Therefore, Congress did not initially appropriate funds for the agency. However, when President Andrew Johnson ordered that most of the confiscated property be returned to the original landowners, a lack of financial resources forced Congress to reverse course and to fund the bureau. Unfortunately, the bureau never received sufficient money to carry out its daunting tasks.

At its genesis, Congress named General Oliver O. Howard as commissioner of the Freedmen's Bureau, a position that he maintained during the entire existence of the agency. General Howard created an extensive hierarchy of assistant commissioners and subassistants. The assistant commissioners were charged with managing bureau affairs at the state level, with one assistant commissioner for each of the former slaveholding states. The subassistants were stationed at local districts throughout the interior of each state. As local agents, they were responsible for ensuring that the bureau's directives were enforced, and they made monthly reports to the assistant commissioner of their respective state on the conditions within their defined districts.

The Freedmen's Bureau operated in Texas between September 1865 and January 1870. During that time, General Howard appointed five different men to serve as assistant commissioners for the state: Edgar M. Gregory (September 1865—May 1866); Joseph Kiddoo (May 1866—January 1867); Charles Griffin (January 1867—September 1867); Joseph J. Reynolds (September 1867—January 1869); and Edward R.S. Canby (January 1869—April 1869). In early April 1869, Reynolds replaced Canby and briefly remained in office until the end of the month. At its height, the bureau maintained fifty-nine subdistricts in Texas.

The subassistant commissioners were directly responsible for the protection of the freedpeople. As a result, the local agents monitored the courts to ensure that African Americans received justice. They supervised all labor contracts and voided those that were unfair to black laborers and aided in the capture of criminals who committed crimes against the freedpeople. They supervised the partially subsidized schools for African-American children. Finally, bureau agents attempted to help the freedpeople find relatives from whom they had been separated during slavery. While not always successful, the Freedmen's Bureau compiled a remarkable record of success, especially considering the agency's limited financial resources and lack of manpower.

Because the bureau was placed under the direction of the U.S. Army, ex-Confederates viewed the agency as an extension of the army of occupation imposed upon them by the federal government. Additionally, the majority of white Texans rejected the bureau's attempts to give blacks a role in Texas society. Under these conditions, bureau agents were often accused of using extralegal tactics to accomplish their objectives. While the

**The Freedmen's Bureau, 1868, drawn by A.R. Waud.**
**Man representing the Freedman's Bureau stands between armed groups of whites and African Americans. Illus. in *Harper's Weekly*, July 25, 1868.**
**Photo credit: Library of Congress**

vast majority of the agents were competent and dedicated to their mission, the few who proved to be incompetent, or actually guilty of crimes, reinforced what Texans already believed—that the entire agency was corrupt. As a result, the local agents often had to deal with hostile whites who continually tried to obstruct their efforts to protect blacks.

**The Provisional Government**

In accordance with his plan of Reconstruction, President Johnson appointed Andrew Jackson Hamilton as the provisional governor of Texas. Though Hamilton was acceptable to Radical Republicans in Washington, D.C., his appointment proved controversial to many Texans, especially former Confederates and unrepentant Secessionists. Despite having been a noted Texas politician prior to the outbreak of the Civil War, Hamilton was a devoted Unionist and had refused to support the Confederacy. After serving a term in the United States House of Representatives (1859-1861), Hamilton won a seat in the Texas Senate in 1861 where he continued to espouse the Unionist cause. However, plots against his life forced him to flee the state for safe haven first in Mexico, then in various northern states.

Hamilton had become something of a hero in the North and delivered rousing Unionist speeches in such cities as New York and Boston. He joined the Union army in July 1862, taking the rank of brigadier general of volunteers. The same year Hamilton met President Lincoln who appointed him military governor of Texas. In the following year, he accompanied the federal forces that temporarily occupied Brownsville. However, when the forces stationed in the Brownsville region were recalled later that same year, Hamilton moved to New Orleans where he spent the rest of the war. Because of his service to the Union, many Texans considered him a traitor to his state and to the wider South.

Hamilton arrived in Galveston on July 21, 1865, nearly a month after Granger had secured the city. Though he had received little guidance from Johnson, the provisional governor immediately began formulating plans for reconstructing the state. His primary duty was to restore the state to its proper place within the Union. Hamilton began at the local level. Within a month, he had restored civil government in eighty counties by appointing Unionists and a few former Confederates to local offices.

Next, he supervised the voter registration process, supervised the election of delegates to the state constitutional convention, and monitored the convention to ensure that its members properly revised the state's governing document. Critical to these revisions was the adoption of the Thirteenth Amendment to the United States Constitution that abolished slavery, acknowledgment that the act of secession was illegal and therefore null and void from its inception, and recognition that the state's debts that had been incurred during the war were no longer valid. Once the convention completed its task, voters would return to the polls to approve the new governing document and to elect a new slate of local and state officials according to its provisions. Providing that President Johnson and Congress approved of the state's actions, presidential Reconstruction would be complete in Texas, and the state would once again become part of the Union.

Hamilton cautiously moved forward with his plans. He feared that ex-Confederates and former Secessionists would seize control of the polls, assuring that voters only elected men of their own stripe to the convention. Knowing that Radicals in Washington would block the state's readmission to the Union if the new civil government did not reflect a true spirit of reform, Hamilton delayed calling for the election of delegates for more than three months, hoping to appoint a strong contingent of loyal Union men in key political positions throughout the state who would protect the polls from unrepentant rebels. To that end, Hamilton depended on the Union (or Loyal) League for support.

Originally organized as a secret society in the North in 1863, the Union League's purpose was to bolster morale and to give strong support to the policies of President Lincoln. Texans in exile in New Orleans formed a chapter of the Union League in 1865 and moved the organization to Texas when they returned home that summer. After returning home, those exiles worked with other pre-war loyalists to set up local league councils, the first being founded in Galveston as the Loyal Union Association and headed by noted Union man Colbert Caldwell of Navasota. Eventually, the league expanded across Texas with new councils established in many areas. Members vowed to continue their support politically for the Union and to oppose anyone who had voluntarily served or supported the Confederacy during the war. As months passed, the Union League became a force to be reckoned with.

In addition to his worries about politics and his strong support for the Union League, Governor Hamilton was even more concerned that general lawlessness in Texas, especially in the northeastern counties, would become a major barrier to his program of restoring the state to the Union. Events supported his assessment. The bands of brigands forming in Northeast Texas quickly came to the attention of Brevet Major General George A. Custer. After suffering organizational problems and logistical setbacks, Custer's cavalry regiment left Alexandria, Louisiana, on August 8, 1865, crossed the Sabine River, and made its way toward Houston. Before the regiment reached its destination, General Granger, whose headquarters was still in Galveston, ordered Custer's division to bypass Houston and to march to the rural community of Hempstead, where the soldiers would find an abundance of grass and forage for their horses. Custer and his men remained in the small community until the end of October before moving west to Austin.

While stationed in Hempstead, Custer learned from scouting patrols that some of the former rebels had formed bands in the northeastern region of the state and were terrifying white Union men and freedpeople. Without realizing it, Custer's scouts were reporting on the activities of men like Ben Bickerstaff, Cullen Montgomery Baker, and Bob Lee. The rogues had no fear of the military that was trying but failing to re-establish law and order. Later, Custer reported that the renegades attacked army patrols and commissary trains, while various sheriffs and judges loyal to the Old South protected the felons. He also reported that many in the general public helped to protect the raiders because they were deemed as defenders of the "Lost Cause."

In an open letter to President Johnson, Mrs. L. E. Potts of Lamar County confirmed that Custer was correct in his assessment of northeast Texas. A Unionist who went into exile during the war, Mrs. Potts wrote: "In addressing you [Johnson] I do not address you as the Chief Magistrate only, but as the father of our beloved country, one to whom we look more or less for protection, but most especially the <u>poor negro</u> (emphasis in original)." Continuing, she said that "I wish my poor pen could tell you of their persecution here. They are just now out of slavery only a few months, and their masters are so angry to have to lose them that they are trying to persecute them back into slavery." She added that "it is not considered a crime to kill a negro. They are often run down by bloodhounds and shot because they do not do precisely as the white man says . . . there have never been any troops here and everything savors of rebellion."

On a more personal note, Potts said that "the Confederacy has destroyed and ruined mine and my children's property." She added that one reason that she stayed in California during the war was the fear that her young thirteen-year-old son might be forced to fight and to die for the Confederacy. (Indeed, boys that young were killed during the war.) "We left a large estate here which they [Confederate authorities] confiscated and destroyed all that they could. The land is all that is left to us. They stripped it of all the timber and destroyed my houses." Yet, Potts was not begging for herself. She could live with the property losses. Rather, "for humanity's sake I implore you to send protection in some form to these suffering freedmen . . . I have stated only facts. The negroes need protection here. When they work they scarcely get any pay, and what are they to do." Potts closed her letter by asking President Johnson to send troops.

Despite widespread violence in the state, on November 15, 1865, Governor Hamilton issued a proclamation that called on Texas voters to go to the polls on January 8, 1866, and to elect a slate of delegates to a constitutional convention that would convene in Austin on February 7. Political strife soon engulfed the state as election day approached. In Ellis County, one candidate seeking election to the convention stated that "if he had the power he would have swept the last Northerner off the face of God's Earth." It was reported that after these comments, the crowd cheered so loud that the "glass fell out of the windows." In the same county, another prominent citizen stated that "if he now had the power he would sink the entire [national] Republican party forty thousand feet below the Mudsills of Hell."

Such political vitriol was commonplace in January 1866 and that bitterness carried over into the constitutional convention that met in February. Pro-Confederate Southerners in general and pro-Confederate Texans in particular were at first afraid of northern retribution, hoping they would not be punished for treason. However, they became quite haughty when they realized that Lincoln and then Johnson preferred "lenient" Reconstruction policies that forgave Southerners for challenging the Union.

Delegates to the convention met between February 7 and April 2, 1866, and created a new state constitution. In the process, they declared the Secession Ordinance null and void, repudiated the state debt, and recognized the end of slavery. However, they refused to address the secession *ab initio* because that meant that they would have to nullify all laws and transactions made in Texas following secession in 1861. They also avoided official ratification of the Thirteenth Amendment of the United States Constitution, arguing that Congress had already made the amendment part of national law the year before and that, by agreeing to support the Constitution, the members of the convention also supported the amendment. In an effort to thwart Hamilton's plan to provide freedmen limited rights, the delegates denied them the right to vote, to hold political office, to serve on juries, and to give legal testimony against whites in court. However, the delegates did provide the ex-slaves with protection of person and property under the law. Before adjourning, the delegates set June 25, 1866, as the date for the referendum on the newly-created state document and for election of new officials under its provisions.

Following the referendum, ex-Confederates in Texas celebrated the passage of the new state constitution and the subsequent election of James Webb Throckmorton as the governor. In addition, they were satisfied that Texas voters had elected a slate of conservative ex-Confederates to the newly-formed legislature, the members of which would undoubtedly cooperate with the new governor. The election of these men meant that Hamilton's plan for reconstructing the state, in essence, had failed. Throckmorton defeated his opponent, Elisha M. Pease, by a vote of 49,277 to 12,168, thereby signaling that former rebels now controlled the state.

The new governor was not a diehard ex-Confederate who refused to accept the outcome of the war, but his conservative political views prevented him from becoming a supporter of the national Republican Party. Prior to the war, Throckmorton was a Unionist who allied himself with Governor Sam Houston. He became a key advisor to the governor, both men trying to stem the tide of secession that would ultimately drown Texas. At the Secessionist Convention in 1861, Throckmorton became one of the immortal eight who voted against secession. Then, while waiting for the public referendum on the question, he returned home to actively campaign against leaving the Union. His campaigning, coupled with that of Collin McKinney, won the day in Collin County. Its people voted to stay with the Union.

However, statewide results demonstrated that a great majority of its voters had approved secession by a vote of 46,153 to 14,747. Following the firing on Fort Sumter in Charleston, South Carolina harbor and Lincoln's call for 75,000 volunteers to crush the rebellion, Throckmorton became one of the first men in Collin County to join the Confederate army. Although he fought with distinction in several Civil War engagements, recurring health problems forced him to resign in 1863. He served in the Texas Senate in 1864 and apparently recovered his health. In December 1864, Throckmorton became a brigadier general of Texas's First Frontier District. The next year, Confederate General Edmund Kirby Smith appointed him Confederate commissioner to the Indian Nations. As the president of the constitutional convention in 1866, he had expressed his desire to restore Texas to the Union without giving the freedmen full suffrage rights, thereby securing conservative Unionists' and ex-Confederates' support for his gubernatorial candidacy. With the overwhelming majority of the state's voters fitting into these two political factions, his victory in the race was predictable.

The man whom Throckmorton defeated in the governor's race, Elisha M. Pease, was a veteran of the Texas Revolution, and he was a pre-war governor, a Democrat who had served two terms, from 1853 to 1857. A Unionist with no interest in slavery, like Throckmorton, Pease also allied himself with Sam Houston. In 1860 and 1861, he actively campaigned hoping to convince the people that secession would be folly and eventually would damage Texas greatly. Just as a majority of voters rejected his pre-war Unionism, they rejected Pease again in 1866 by choosing Throckmorton for governor.

Once the state government was in place, the public waited to see how a pro-Confederate conservative legislature would deal with the new realities in Texas. Among the legislature's first actions was to create the infamous "Black Codes" in 1866 that returned the newly freed blacks to a status that greatly resembled slavery. Now codified, black Texans could neither vote nor hold political office. They could not serve on juries, testify in cases involving whites, marry whites, claim land under the Texas Homestead Law, or share in public school funds, and they could not escape segregation on common carriers. An apprenticeship law potentially gave whites control of underage blacks, either with parental consent or by order of a county judge. Also heinous was the Contract Labor Code, which forced blacks to sign twelve-month contracts for jobs lasting more than one month. The

(Left) Texas Governor (1853-1857) Elisha M. Pease. (Right) Portrait of Texas Governor (1866-1867) James Webb Throckmorton. Photo credit: UTSA's Institute of Texan Cultures

labor code gave employers certain judicial rights. They could fine workers who failed to perform their work, who damaged tools, who left without permission, and who were generally disobedient.

The Vagrancy Code was also created by which all local authorities could arrest blacks found to be idle, having no apparent livelihood. Those who could not pay the steep fines could be contracted out until they earned enough money to pay the fines. The Convict-Lease Code entrapped blacks, whom judges and juries then sent to county jails or to the state prison. Such unfortunates could be contracted out to private employers and forced to work for little except room and board. Thus a type of semi-slavery was effectively imposed upon the black community.

In addition, the newly-elected Texas legislature chose David G. Burnet, an outspoken critic of Unionists in the state, and Oran M. Roberts, a devoted ex-Confederate, as United States senators. When the senators and the elected members of the House of Representatives arrived in Washington, Congress refused to seat them because they could not take the oath of allegiance affirming that they had never willingly supported the Confederacy in the late war.

Congress became further irritated when Governor Throckmorton recommended that the Texas legislature refuse ratification of the Thirteenth Amendment to the United States Constitution. The legislators were more than willing to follow the governor's advice. They not only refused to ratify the amendment, but they also passed several laws (in addition to the Black Codes) that restricted the freedom of the freedpeople. The legislators took the position that the freedpeople were inferior to whites and, therefore, occupied a subordinate position in society. Essentially, the lawmakers accepted the end of slavery, but they were not willing to recognize the exslaves as their equal. Furthermore, just like other southern legislators, they were not going to provide African Americans or their white allies with equal protection under the law. Soon such crass behavior forced Congress to assume a more active role in the Reconstruction of Texas, as well as in the other southern states.

**Congressional Reconstruction**

Beginning in December 1866, Congressional Republicans declared presidential Reconstruction a failure and took steps to seize control of the Reconstruction process from President Johnson by passing the Civil Rights Act of 1866, by the renewal of the Freedmen's Bureau Act, and by passing the Fourteenth Amendment over the president's objection. To solidify their control of Reconstruction, Congress next passed the Reconstruction Acts. The first of these acts, passed on March 2, 1867, abolished the existing state governments in former Confederate states, except in Tennessee where the state legislature had ratified the Thirteenth Amendment. Subsequent legislation divided the southern states into five military districts, instituted martial law, disenfranchised former Confederate leaders, and established procedures by which the southern states would create new constitutions and ensure the protection of the African Americans' civil rights.

As congressional Republicans seized control of the Reconstruction policy, Governor Throckmorton attempted to establish the supremacy of civil over military authority in his state. To achieve his objective, the governor believed that it was necessary to restore calm to the state by suppressing the lawlessness and terrorism that had been commonplace since the fall of the Confederacy. By curbing violence in the state, the governor hoped to replace military courts with fully-restored local and state courts. Additionally, Throckmorton hoped that he could convince military authorities to transfer troops from the interior of the state to its western frontier, where they could protect frontier settlers from ongoing Indian depredations. Ultimately, the governor failed to accomplish any of his objectives because of his inability to control the widespread violence taking place throughout the state.

At the outset the commanders in charge of the Fifth Military District (Texas and Louisiana) distrusted the Throckmorton administration. General Charles Griffin, who was General Sheridan's handpicked commander in Texas, reported to his superiors that Throckmorton was obstructing the Reconstruction process and requested that Sheridan remove the governor from office. Specifically, General Griffin stated that Throckmorton, as an ex-Confederate, failed to meet the qualifications for holding office under the "military bill" of the Reconstruction Acts, and he argued that the governor refused to cooperate in the punishment of those who had committed violent crimes against the freedpeople and white Unionists. General Sheridan agreed with his Texas commander and removed Throckmorton from office, claiming that the governor was an "impediment to Reconstruction." In the same order that removed the governor from office, General Sheridan named Elisha M. Pease as the provisional governor.

Following the removal of Throckmorton, Griffin and Sheridan received numerous reports that ex-Confederates and former Secessionists were attacking loyal citizens (freedpeople, Unionists, and Freedmen's Bureau agents) and that local officials refused to provide the victims protection under the law. General Griffin immediately began to react by removing questionable officials, but his efforts were cut short when he died during the yellow fever epidemic that swept through eastern Texas in the summer and fall of 1867. General Joseph J. Reynolds, who assumed command in Texas after Griffin's death, continued to receive reports of malicious treatment of freedpeople and their white allies. As a result, Reynolds initiated the systematic removal of ex-Confederates and corrupt conservative Democrats from local offices. In the month of November alone, the general removed more than 400 officeholders, replacing them with individuals who professed their loyalty to the United States and who were willing to swear that they had never willingly aided the Confederacy. The federal government's policy of replacing officeholders continued throughout Congressional Reconstruction.

**Constitutional Convention of 1868-1869**

During Congressional Reconstruction, the federal government required Texans to make additional concessions before rejoining the Union. First, they had to hold county elections for delegates to a new constitutional convention. Voters in the election included all male citizens, regardless of race, who were twenty-one years of age or older. The only individuals barred from voting were convicted felons and ex-Confederates, who remained disenfranchised because of their affiliation with the Confederacy. Once convened, the members of the convention were required by Congress to write a new state constitution in align with federal policies and to recognize adult male suffrage. In addition to writing a new governing document for the state, convention delegates had to ratify the Fourteenth Amendment to the U.S. Constitution. Only then would congressional members consider readmitting the state into the Union. On February 10-14, 1868, Texas voters elected delegates to the convention that was scheduled to convene at the state capital on June 1.

When the constitutional convention delegates arrived in Austin, it was evident that Republicans would dominate the convention, especially considering that they constituted 78 of the 90 members present. Nationalists (southern whites who remained loyal to the United States) made up the bulk of the Republican delegates, while as few as twelve represented northern-born migrants who came to the South after the war. Additionally, voters selected nine African Americans to serve as delegates. The best known was George T. Ruby, a native of New York who earlier had come to Texas as a Freedmen's Bureau teacher in 1866.

Despite the Republican majority, the delegates remained divided. Aside from the small number of Democrats present at the convention, Republican delegates were essentially divided into four different factions, with no single bloc dominating. The most important division was between moderates, led by former provisional governor Andrew Jackson Hamilton, and Radicals, led by Edmund J. Davis. That Davis led the radical faction of the convention seemed natural. A native of Florida, Davis came to Texas before the war and established himself in South Texas. At various times he had lived in Corpus Christi, Laredo, and Brownsville, and he was a state district judge in 1860. During the secession crisis, Davis opposed leaving the Union, and once the Civil War erupted, he helped to form the First Texas Cavalry (Union), which saw action in Texas and Louisiana. Following the war, Davis returned to Corpus Christi, where voters elected him as a delegate to the constitutional conventions of 1866 and 1868-1869. In the latter convention, the delegates selected him as its presiding officer.

Moderate and Radical Republicans argued bitterly over the *ab initio* question once again. With the ordinance of secession declared void by the constitutional convention of 1866, Radicals wanted to push the *ab initio* issue to its ultimate conclusion by having all the legislation passed in the state between 1861 and 1867 declared null and void. Moderates opposed the Radicals' position because such action would have invalidated railroad and educational legislation passed during the war. Another issue of primary concern was the division of Texas into two states, east and west. Radicals from both eastern and western counties favored the creation of a new state in West Texas. In fact, this move would have probably benefited Republicans who were stronger in the western region of the state. However, moderates were opposed to the division, stating that it would increase the tax burden and interfere with efforts to offer education and other public services. Additionally, moderates hoped to garner the support of moderate voters in both sections of the state in future elections. A third issue involved civil rights. Radicals, led by George T. Ruby and other African-American delegates, wanted to include a civil rights provision to outlaw discrimination in public accommodations and to create an integrated system of public education. In this way, Radicals wanted to ensure that blacks would be able to escape the system of sharecropping that emerged after the war and enjoy economic security. Moderates opposed Radicals on the civil rights issue, believing that blacks would continue to serve as a source of agricultural labor for landowners. They saw no reason to extend civil rights beyond what Congress had already enacted—the Civil Rights Act and the Fourteenth Amendment. The delegates eventually compromised on this issue by establishing a desegregated public school system but refusing to specify any additional civil rights beyond the guarantee of equality before the law. Finally, the delegates considered the issue of disenfranchisement of ex-Confederates. Perhaps less controversial, Radicals fully supported the idea of disenfranchising the former Confederates, while moderates, hoping to gain favor with conservative Democrats, questioned the idea.

The only issue that united the Republican delegates was the violence that had plagued the state since the end of the war. The convention's Committee on Lawlessness and Violence reported that 509 whites and 468 blacks had been murdered since the war, suggesting that most of the killings had occurred as a result of the hatred by ex-Confederates and conservative Democrats of the freedpeople and their white allies. The statistics were woefully undercounted because many murders went unreported. Republican leaders, Colbert Caldwell and Morgan Hamilton (A.J. Hamilton's brother), carried a copy of the committee report to Washington, D.C., and asked Congress for further assistance in protecting Unionists and the freedpeople of the state.

After three months of debate, the funds appropriated for convention expenses ran out on August 31, 1868. At the time, the delegates were successful in settling the *ab initio* issue when moderates convinced the convention to reject the Radicals' position. Moderates' success seemed to hinge upon the fact that the state would fall into complete chaos if every contract, court case, and legal action passed since the beginning of the war were voided. In essence, the delegates were forced to adjourn the convention without settling their other issues and without creating a new state constitution, although they did call for the ratification of the Thirteenth and Fourteenth Amendments to the United States Constitution by the first legislature assembled under the new constitution that they hoped to write in the immediate future.

Because the convention had failed to produce a constitution, the delegates agreed to reconvene the convention on the first Monday in December, hoping that this would allow the state enough time to secure additional funding for the continuation of the meeting. It did. In addition, the delegates wanted to wait for the outcome of the 1868 presidential election. When Union General Ulysses S. Grant won the presidency, the Radical Republicans felt a sense of affirmation in their efforts to reconstruct Texas.

When the delegates reconvened in December, Radicals, who were convinced that Washington would support their efforts in Texas, resumed their struggle to divide the state into two or more smaller states. In January 1869, the convention voted to divide the state and sent representatives to Washington to lobby for approval of their actions. Then, while work on the constitution was still ongoing, Radicals unsuccessfully attempted to adjourn the convention. On February 3, a coalition of moderates gained control of the meeting, and five days later they voted to turn over the incomplete constitution to military authorities and adjourn. Rather than extend the convention for a third time, General Joseph J. Reynolds appointed a three-man committee to complete the document, basing its completion on records from the convention. In a referendum vote, the people in November voted to ratify the Constitution of 1869.

Even though its creation had divided the Republican Party in Texas, the Constitution of 1869 contained a number of positive features. The constitution centralized political power in the hands of the governor, who was elected to a four-year term. The governor had the authority to appoint other major executive officers and judges of the state courts. The constitution also guaranteed that no citizen, regardless of "race, color, or former condition" would be denied the right to vote. Only those disenfranchised by the United States Constitution would not be permitted the right to vote. The constitution also provided funding for the education of all children, regardless of race and color.

Because Radicals were unsuccessful in convincing Congress and President Grant to reject the new state constitution and to divide Texas into additional states, they changed strategies, withdrawing their objections to the governing document and endorsing the work of the convention delegates. In addition, they nominated Edmund J. Davis as their candidate for governor in the upcoming state election. Moderates countered their actions by supporting A. J. Hamilton. In the meantime, provisional Governor Pease resigned on September 20. Pease was uncomfortable that General Reynolds had ordered the completion of the state constitution, a duty that Pease felt was the sole responsibility of civil authorities of the state. Worse still, Pease objected to Reynolds's removal of local officials, arguing that most of those removed from office were moderates who favored A. J. Hamilton. According to Pease, Reynolds was replacing Hamilton's supporters with individuals who were favorable to Davis. With elections slated for the end of the year, General Reynolds simply assumed the responsibilities of the governor and ordered the continued registration of voters. With the aid of Reynolds, it appeared to many that Davis had a distinct advantage in the upcoming election, especially considering that Radicals had the support of most African Americans in the state.

In the election held on November 30-December 3, 1869, the new constitution overwhelmingly won approval of the eligible voters by a vote of 72,466 to 4,928. The contest for governor, however, was much closer. Davis received 39,831 votes to Hamilton's 39,060. The close race might have produced political problems for the new administration, but Davis was fortunate in that Republicans carried both houses of the new state legislature (the Twelfth Legislature).

General Reynolds continued to serve as governor until January 8, 1870, when he ordered the newly-elected state officials to take office as a provisional government while the final steps of restoring the state to the Union were completed. The general also called a provisional session of the Twelfth Legislature to elect two new U.S. senators and to ratify the Fourteenth and Fifteenth Amendments to the United States Constitution. Meeting throughout most of February, members of the special session ratified the amendments and elected two Radicals, Morgan Hamilton and James W. Flanagan, to represent the state in the U. S. Senate. On March 30, 1870, President Grant signed a bill from Congress that officially restored Texas to its proper relationship with the Union. On April 16, 1870, General Reynolds turned over all authority to civil officers, officially ending military rule. Radical Republicans had survived factional political divisions in their own party and the wrath of conservative Democrats. Now the question became: How long would they be able to maintain control over the state?

**Violence and Guerilla Warfare**

Throughout Reconstruction, white Southerners claimed that Radical Republicans in Congress were attempting to dominate the southern states through Negro-Carpetbag-Scalawag rule. Carpetbagger and scalawag were derogatory terms. A carpetbagger was a term used to identify northern migrants who came to the South after the war. Scalawags were native Southerners who remained loyal to the United States and supported federal policies, especially the policies of Radical Republicans in Congress. In southern newspapers and posted broadsides, southern politicians outlined how congressional Republicans intended to impose military rule over the South and to force black domination on whites, changing the system of white supremacy that had been in place for more than two centuries. In response to these perceived threats, whites in the South initiated a violent guerilla war (the second phase of the Civil War) that was designed to limit southern support for the Republican Party. The terrorists targeted loyal Unionists throughout the South, especially African Americans who represented the largest block of Republican voters. Texas proved to be one of the more violent battlefronts in what can be considered the second phase of the Civil War.

The violence that ex-Confederates waged against Unionists generally fell into four categories: spontaneous brawls, attacks by one race upon isolated members of the other, full-scale attacks of one race on the other, and random assaults. While there were circumstances in which blacks engaged in violent acts against whites, the majority of racial incidents in Texas between 1865 and 1877 resulted from whites attacking African Americans. In the early phases of Reconstruction, individuals or small gangs were primarily responsible for the violence committed against blacks and their white allies. However, well-organized terrorist groups began to emerge in response to political changes in the southern states, including the infamous Ku Klux Klan.

The Klan's violent intentions were often hidden by southern claims that the terrorist group acted out of self-defense, chivalry, and honor. Often the Klansmen stated that they were merely protecting white Southerners from incipient black uprisings or that they were fighting rampant black crime, a problem that the authorities, especially Republican

**The Union As It Was The Lost Cause, "Worse than Slavery"
by Thomas Nast.
Man "White League" shaking hands with Ku Klux Klan member over shield illustrated with an African-American couple with baby. In background, man is hanging from a tree.
Illus. from *Harper's Weekly*,
October 24, 1874.
Photo credit: Library of Congress**

officials, were accused of ignoring. Klan members also claimed that they disciplined recalcitrant black laborers for the benefit of white employers. Such activities were designed to keep blacks docile and on the job, but these actions often resulted in laborers leaving their jobs and in the disruption of white landowners' economic stability.

As an agent of social control, the Klan enjoyed greater success. To keep African Americans within their defined social bounds, the terrorists prevented them from owning and renting land, lynched black men who cohabited with white women, punished individuals who supported the idea of black social equality, beat or killed African Americans accused of insolence toward whites, and conducted vendettas against the teachers of black schools. After 1867, the Klan developed strong opposition to the Radical Republicans and their agenda, which supported African-American suffrage. In time, the Klan would basically become a paramilitary arm that the Democratic Party used to overwhelm their Republican adversaries and to remove them from political office.

In addition to Klan activities, outlaw gangs initiated a massive crime wave throughout the state, especially in Northeast-East Texas and South Texas. In the northern and eastern counties of the state, outlaws such as Cullen Montgomery Baker, Benjamin F. Bickerstaff, and Bob Lee preyed upon African Americans, federal troops, Freedmen's Bureau agents, and Unionists. In South Texas, the notorious Taylor gang operated a massive cattle rustling operation and enacted a war against lawmen, such as William "Bill" Sutton in the region around De Witt County. These men and their bands of outlaws wrapped themselves in the Confederate flag and pledged loyalty to the South's "Lost Cause." They justified the murdering and robbing of blacks, federal soldiers, bureau agents, and local Unionists as a way to continue the war against "Yankee aggression." Though these outlaw bands often aided the Democratic Party by intimidating blacks and white Unionists, effectively keeping them from the polls during elections, in reality, most of the outlaws were not die-hard southern patriots but, rather, were common criminals who used pro-Confederate claims to insulate themselves from federal and local authorities who attempted to prosecute them for their crimes. By early 1869, Bickerstaff, Baker, and Lee met their violent end, but factions of their gangs continued to operate throughout the region. In South Texas, the Taylor gang continued to operate well into the 1870s.

## Governor Edmund J. Davis and the Republican State Government

Upon taking office, Governor Davis outlined his plan of governing the state. According to the governor, the most immediate issue that had to be addressed was the establishment of law and order. To help curb violence and lawlessness, the legislature passed the state militia bill and created a new state police force in June 1870. The state militia consisted of all able-bodied men between the ages of 18 and 45. As the state's commander-in-chief, the governor could call out the militia to suppress lawlessness in any county in which local law officers could not establish order. The bill creating the state police established an agency of 258 men and was headed by a chief of police, with the adjutant general as the ultimate authority. The legislature charged the state police with the duty of bringing law and order to troubled regions. Both the state police and the state militia were placed under the governor's direct control, even though the adjutant general continued to direct their day-to-day operations. To aid the state police, the legislature also expanded the district court system, increasing the number of judicial districts from 17 to 35. According to the Constitution of 1869, the governor was responsible for making judicial appointments. Therefore, Davis was able to appoint 35 loyal Republicans to key positions in the state's judicial system. This was critical in ensuring law and order because individuals charged with felony crimes were tried in state district courts.

Although controversy surrounded the new law enforcement tactics, Davis's program seemed to achieve its goals. Between 1870 and the end of 1872, the police had arrested over 4,800 criminals and had recovered $200,000 in stolen property. In time, many Texans began to look to the state police for protection. Also, citizens' initial fear that the governor would use the state militia to secure military rule began to subside after Davis had used the militia sparingly. Despite its successes, the state police still produced enemies. Locals complained that the police officers were nothing more than an extension of the Republican Party and that they inappropriately interfered in local matters of law enforcement. Additionally, many white Texans objected to the practice of the state police and the militia using African-American officers and troops. The most serious setback for the reputation of Davis's law enforcement agencies came in 1872 when Adjutant General James Davidson absconded with $32,000 in state funds.

Radical Republicans also sought to address social and economic issues confronting the state. Chief among economic concerns was the development of railroads. The Constitution of 1869 prohibited the legislature from giving land grants to companies for railroad construction, but supporters of railroad development used city or state bonds to subsidize the construction of new lines. Essentially, support for these actions came from conservative Democrats and moderate Republicans, while the majority of Radicals opposed state and local funding. Later in 1873, Texans would amend their constitution to allow the authorization of land grants for railroad construction. Aside from railroad development, Radicals attempted to build a new public road system, to enact a homestead law, and to establish an immigration bureau charged with the duty of attracting new immigrants from Europe. Additionally, Radicals appropriated monies to provide state troops the funding for their inadequate frontier defense currently provided by federal means. The Davis administration also directed attention and funds to establishing a system of free public schools, a development that proved that Radicals were ahead of their time. The legislation not only called for compulsory attendance, but it also levied taxes adequate to maintain the schools.

Despite the success of Davis's administration, Republican programs produced many enemies and offended different interest groups. The centralization of power in the governor's office, the perceived abuses of the state law enforcement agencies, and the cost of new programs that were funded with new taxes provided common ground for opposition amongst a coalition of moderate Republicans and conservative Democrats that emerged during 1870 and 1872. Opposition to Radicals peaked in September 1871 in the Tax-Payers' Convention. Members to this statewide convention wanted to rally opposition to regular Republican candidates in the upcoming fall elections. Conservative businessmen supported the convention because they wanted to avoid paying increases in taxes designed to support radical programs. Landowners, both planters and small farmers, supported the convention because they wanted to avoid disruptions in the black work force and because of their desire to preserve white supremacy. The delegates' charge that Radicals had unnecessarily passed high taxes proved to be the undoing of the Republican Party in Texas. Beginning with the 1871 election, the party experienced one political setback after another. The Republican Party was never able to stem the tide against it, and ultimately it lost power. In 1871, Democratic candidates carried all four congressional seats, and the following year the party elected two new congressmen-at-large as well as gaining control of the House of Representatives in the Thirteenth Legislature. If senatorial terms had not been staggered, the state's Senate seats would have also fallen to Democratic control. Part of the reason that Democratic candidates enjoyed success at the polls was that Congress had passed the Amnesty Act of 1872, once again allowing most of the disenfranchised ex-Confederates to vote and to hold political office.

## The End of Republican Government in Texas

Republican political misfortunes caused the sitting senators to reevaluate their position in the state government. They now became more willing to cooperate with their political opponents in dismantling their party's Reconstruction program. Members of the Thirteenth Legislature abolished the state police and amended the militia law, stripping the governor of his ability to declare martial law. The enabling act that provided the governor with broad powers of appointing officials to vacant offices was limited—now vacant offices would be filled by holding special elections. Additionally, the voting act that stipulated that all voting had to take place at county courthouses was amended to allow precinct voting throughout the counties. Furthermore, the new legislature essentially destroyed the Radicals' public school system, placing the operation of public schools in the hands of local school boards. Although the office of state superintendent continued to exist, its primary function now was recordkeeping. Despite these changes, the conservative factions in the legislature did not make significant changes to the Radicals' economic programs.

In December 1873, the state held its first general election since 1869. Receiving the Republican nomination, Governor Davis ran on the record of his administration. By this time, the coalition between moderate Republicans and Democrats had unraveled, leaving the moderates either to support the Davis administration or to abandon politics altogether. Democrats, in turn, selected their own gubernatorial candidate, Richard Coke. Coke supported the continued dismantling of Republican programs and favored the call for yet another state constitutional convention. Coke easily defeated Governor Davis in the race by a vote of 85,549 to 42,663.

Republican government in Texas was finished, but party members were not willing to leave quietly. A group of Houston Republicans challenged the election results in *Ex parte Rodriguez* (also known as the Semicolon Case). The state supreme court ruled that the election was unconstitutional because it had been carried out improperly according to constitutional mandates, paving the way for confrontation between Davis and governor-elect Coke. Finding cause in the supreme court's decision, Davis refused to transfer power to the newly-elected governor. Upon hearing of Davis's decision, Coke made it clear that he would take office either peacefully or through force. Davis appealed to the federal government to intervene, especially considering that the majority of Texans supported Coke in the controversy. President Grant refused to intervene on Davis's behalf, leaving the beleaguered governor no choice but to step down. In January 1874, Democrats celebrated in the streets of Austin as Coke and his lieutenant governor, Richard Hubbard, were sworn into office. Coke's victory not only brought an end to the Davis administration, but it began a period of Democratic control in the state that lasted for the next century.

## How Should We Remember the Reconstruction Era?

There is no disputing that the Reconstruction era was a tumultuous period in Texas's history. But what are we to make of this period in the state's past? Was it a continuation of the Civil War? Or was it simply a new era—distinct and very different from the years between 1861 and 1865? Because of the violence and the guerilla war waged against federal troops, bureau agents, Unionists, and freedpeople, it seems evident that many white

Texans continued to fight to control the affairs of their state and to maintain as much of their antebellum traditions as possible. Indeed, slavery was a moot issue, but there were other legal labor systems that were almost as oppressive as the South's peculiar institution, namely sharecropping. Ex-Confederates, former Secessionists, and conservative Democrats understood that, if they were to maintain a society based on the principles of white supremacy, they would have to regain control of state politics. Throughout Reconstruction Texas, Democrats and Republicans engaged in a bloody battle for control. Using violence as a primary weapon in this phase of the war, Democrats ultimately wrenched control of the state from the Republicans. Interestingly the statewide violence that persisted during Republican rule of the state subsided once the Democrats took control of the government in 1874. Based on the facts, it seems clear that Reconstruction was indeed a second phase of the Civil War—one in which Texans (as well as their southern counterparts) won.

### *Afterward: The Failures of Reconstruction in Texas*

*Edmund Davis's questions regarding the protection of Republicans and African Americans went unanswered during Reconstruction. Despite the efforts of Radical Republicans to change the social structure of the southern states, including Texas, they failed to bring about lasting reforms. It would take another one hundred years before meaningful change would occur in the South. Unfortunately for Baughman, the federal government failed to answer Davis's call for help. Baughman was murdered in his own home more than a year later. Apparently, thirty men surrounded his house, broke down the door to his home, entered his bedroom, and riddled his body with bullets while he lay in bed too sick to get up. His murderers were never prosecuted, illustrating the type of justice that Republicans and African Americans could expect in Texas during the Reconstruction era. Shamefully, circumstance improved little as the state moved into the twentieth century.*

# Myth & Legend

### Texas Under the Terrible Carpetbaggers

*According to one of the state's most enduring myths, Texas was overrun with carpetbaggers during the Reconstruction era. Carpetbagger was a derogatory term used to describe Northerners who migrated to the South following the Civil War. In Texas, these northern migrants supported the Republican Party, and many of them held public office, especially after 1867. Democratic leaders often complained that these individuals were exploitive, dishonest, and corrupt. According to their detractors, this class of Northerners brought everything they owned in a carpetbag (a soft suitcase made of carpet), seized political power, and pillaged the poor defenseless people of the South. Even though this assessment of the carpetbaggers has maintained an element of credibility well into the twentieth century, it has one fatal flaw—it is a gross exaggeration of the truth.*

*First, carpetbaggers played a very limited role in Texas during Reconstruction. They certainly did not dominate Texas politics as many conservative Democrats claimed. In fact, during the Constitutional Convention of 1868-1869, only 7 of the 93 delegates in attendance could be legitimately considered carpetbaggers. Furthermore, in the Republican administration of Governor Edmund J. Davis, northern Republicans only held the offices of adjutant general and chief justice of the Texas Supreme Court. At the same time, a mere 8 of 60 court judges were from the North, and in the Twelfth Legislature just 12 of 142 of the members came from northern states after the war. Finally, very few carpetbaggers participated in local politics. Texas historian Randolph B. Campbell estimates that Northerners held no more than 12 percent of local offices in the state.*

*According to another noted scholar of Reconstruction Texas, Carl Moneyhon, those carpetbaggers who held public offices in the state typically did not fit the traditional stereotype assigned to them by Southerners. For one thing, most of the "notorious" carpetbaggers came to Texas before the Republicans gained control of the state government in 1868, making it impossible to consider them political opportunists. Additionally, many of the carpetbaggers arrived in Texas as part of either the army* of occupation in 1865, or as employees of the Freedmen's Bureau between 1865 and 1867. For example, Brevt. Maj. Gen. William T. Clark from Connecticut arrived in Texas with the army, resigned his commission that same year, and took a job as a cashier at the First National Bank of Texas at Galveston. Later Clark who was a devoted Republican was elected to the Texas legislature. Similarly, George T. Ruby, a native of Maine, came to Texas by way of Louisiana to work with the Freedmen's Bureau. Later, Ruby played a vital role in Texas politics, serving as a member of the Constitutional Convention of 1868-1869 and as a member of the Texas legislature.

For the most part, the carpetbaggers were well-intentioned politicians, who served with distinction. In part, they were responsible for creating the state's first real public school system and for passing necessary legislation to bring about viable economic recovery in the state. Nevertheless, there were some carpetbaggers who did fit the stereotype applied to them, especially the notorious James Davidson. As adjutant general, Davidson embezzled more than $37,000, fleeing the state before he could be apprehended by the authorities.

Thus, the carpetbaggers, who were few in number, failed to dominate state and local politics. This leaves scholars with the only viable conclusion that can be drawn in relation to the carpetbagger myth—the traditional stereotype of carpetbag rule is unfounded and is no longer suitable for understanding Reconstruction politics in the Lone Star State.

## Suggestions for Further Reading

Barr, Alwyn. *Black Texans: A History of African Americans in Texas, 1528-1971.* Norman: University of Oklahoma Press, 1996.

Baum, Dale, *The Shattering of Texas Unionism.* Baton Rouge: Louisiana State University Press, 1998.

Campbell, Randolph. *Grass Roots Reconstruction in Texas, 1865-1868.* Baton Rouge: Louisiana State University Press, 1997.

Crouch, Barry A. *The Dance of Freedom: Texas African Americans During Reconstruction.* Ed. Larry Madaras. Austin: University of Texas Press, 2007.

___ . *The Freedmen's Bureau and Blacks in Texas.* Austin: University of Texas Press, 1992.

Crouch, Barry A. and Donaly Brice. *Cullen Montgomery Baker: Reconstruction Desperado.* Baton Rouge: Louisiana State University Press, 1997.

Fogelson, Robert M. and Richard E. Rubenstein, eds., *Use of the Army in Certain of the Southern States,* Mass Violence in America series (New York: Arno Press & The New York Times, 1969).

Grear, Charles and Alexander Mendoza, eds. *Texans and War: New Interpretations of the State's Military History.* College Station: Texas A&M University Press, 2012.

Howell, Kenneth W. *Texas Confederate, Reconstruction Governor: James Webb Throckmorton.* College Station: Texas A&M University Press, 2008.

Howell, Kenneth W. ed. *Still the Arena of Civil War: Violence and Turmoil in Reconstruction Texas, 1865-1874.* Denton: University of North Texas Press, 2012.

Moneyhon, Carl H. *Republicanism in Reconstruction Texas.* Austin: University of Texas Press, 1980.

___ . *Texas After the Civil War: The Struggle of Reconstruction.* College Station: Texas A&M University Press, 1004.

Richter, William L. *The Army in Texas During Reconstruction.* College Station: Texas A&M University Press, 1987.

___ . *Overreached on All Sides: The Freedmen's Bureau Administration in Texas, 1865-1868.* College Station: Texas A&M University Press, 1991.

Smallwood, James. *Time of Hope, Time of Despair: Black Texans During Reconstruction.* New York: Kennikat Press, 1981.

Smallwood, James M., Barry A. Crouch, and Larry Peacock. *Murder and Mayhem: The War of Reconstruction in Texas.* College Station: Texas A&M University Press, 2003.

Smallwood, James M., Kenneth W. Howell, and Carol C. Taylor. *The Devil's Triangle: Ben Bickerstaff, Northeast Texans, and the War of Reconstruction in Texas.* Lufkin, Texas: Best of East Texas Publishers, 2007.

**IDENTIFICATION:** Briefly describe each term.

Radical Republicans
"ironclad" oath
Thirteenth Amendment
Gen. Philip H. Sheridan
Gen. Gordon Granger
Gen. Charles Griffin
freedpeople
subassistant commissioners
Gov. Andrew Jackson Hamilton
Gov. James Webb Throckmorton
Oran Roberts
"black codes"
Reconstruction Acts (1867)
Gov. Edmund J. Davis
Ku Klux Klan

**MULTIPLE CHOICE:** Choose the correct response.

1. Who was the first assistant commissioner of the Freedmen's Bureau to serve in Texas?
   A. Gen. Oliver O. Howard
   B. Andrew Jackson Hamilton
   C. George T. Ruby
   D. Edgar M. Gregory

2. Subassistant commissioners of the Freedmen's Bureau were involved in all of the following EXCEPT:
   A. negotiating labor contracts
   B. ensuring that freedpeople received fair trials in criminal courts
   C. supporting ex-Confederates' efforts to regain their voting rights
   D. subsidizing schools for African American children

3. Provisional Governor Hamilton did all of the following, EXCEPT:
   A. called on the state to elect delegates to the constitutional convention of 1866
   B. oversaw voting registration
   C. helped former slaves escape sharecropping by sending them to Mexico
   D. restored civil government to Texas

4. All of the following were Reconstruction desperadoes in Texas, EXCEPT:
   A. Ben Bickerstaff
   B. Elisha Pease
   C. Bob Lee
   D. Cullen Montgomery Baker

5. Mrs. L. E. Potts of Lamar county wrote a letter to President Johnson describing:
   A. The conditions of freedmen in Northeast Texas.
   B. The condition of freedmen in South Texas
   C. The atrocities committed by U.S. soldiers in Texas.
   D. The development of railroads in Texas.

6. Who was the first elected governor of Texas following the Civil War?
   A. Elisha M. Pease
   B. Edmund J. Davis
   C. James Webb Throckmorton
   D. Andrew Jackson Hamilton

7. In their report, members of the Commission on Lawlessness and Violence stated:
   A. Texas was relatively free of serious crimes, such as murder.
   B. Many of the murders in the state were committed by black Texans.
   C. Ex-Confederates were killing blacks and their white allies.
   D. No report was filed.

8. Which statement best describes the activities of the Ku Klux Klan in Texas during Reconstruction?
   A   The KKK did not exist in Texas during Reconstruction.
   B   The KKK functioned as a paramilitary arm of the Democratic party, primarily enacting violent acts against poor whites throughout the state.
   C. The KKK played a pivotal role in bringing Reconstruction to an end in Texas.
   D. The KKK primarily was a social club for politicians who actively supported the Radical Republican agenda.

9. All of the following were arguments that ex-Confederates and Conservative Democrats made against the Davis Administration, EXCEPT:
   A. Davis Administration supported excessive taxation.
   B. Governor Davis used the state militia and state police to ensure dictatorial control of the state.
   C. The Davis Administration was corrupt.
   D. The Davis Administration did little to further public education in the state.

10. The end of Reconstruction in Texas came when:
    A. Richard Coke defeated E. J. Davis in the gubernatorial election in 1873.
    B. The Freedmen's Bureau left the state in January 1869.
    C. Throckmorton was elected governor in 1866.
    D   The Constitutional Convention of 1868-1869 adjourned without completing its task of writing a new state constitution.

**TRUE/FALSE:** Indicate whether each statement is true or false.

1. Presidential Reconstruction began when Congress passed the Reconstruction Acts in 1867.

2. Traditionally, historians have identified 1865 as the end of the Civil War.

3. At the end of the Civil War, Texans felt that they had been overwhelmingly conquered by the Union army.

4. Andrew Johnson became president following the assassination of Abraham Lincoln in 1865.

5. Gen. Gordon Granger led 50,000 U.S. soldiers in Galveston in June 1865.

6. The Freedmen's Bureau primarily helped white landowners in Texas secure title to their lands after the Civil War.

7. Governor E. J. Davis's administration was successful in governing the state, and as a result, the governor gained the respect and admiration of Texas Democrats.

8. The freedpeople in Texas were basically safe from violent crimes, because ex-Confederates primarily targeted Radical Republicans.

9. Reconstruction in Texas was not as violent or complicated as in other southern states because the vast majority of white Texans accepted the results of the Civil War and embraced the idea of equality for African Americans.

10. Provisional Governor E. M. Pease was a staunch Radical Republican, and he supported Congressional Reconstruction policies until he was removed from office by military authorities.

**MATCHING:** Match the response in column A with the item in column B.

1. Ten Percent Plan
2. Fifth Military District
3. *ab initio*
4. Elisha Pease
5. Black Codes
6. freedpeople
7. George T. Ruby
8. State Police
9. Taylor Gang
10. Taxpayers' Convention

A. former slaves
B. Lincoln's plan of Reconstruction
C. included Texas and Louisiana
D. denied blacks many of their basic civil rights
E. nullification of Texas laws passed between 1861-1866
F. black Republican leader
G. moderate Republican
H. Governor Davis's answer to the violence in Texas
I. opposed Governor Davis's tax policy
J. a group of outlaws who operated in the South Texas region

**ESSAY QUESTIONS:**

1. Do you believe Gen. Sheridan was justified in re moving Gov. James W. Throckmorton from office? Provide evidence to support your answer.

2. Compare and Contrast the Constitutional Convention of 1866 with the Constitutional Convention of 1868-1869. Be sure to provide details on the delegates, factional divisions, and the outcomes of both conventions.

3. Some historians contend that the Civil War did not end in 1865, but rather continued into the 1870s. This longer war is often divided into two phases: Phase I (1861-1865) and Phase II (1865-1877). What evidence in Texas supports this historical interpretation?

4. Compare and contrast presidential Reconstruction and congressional Reconstruction in Texas? What were the positive and negative aspects of both periods of Reconstruction?

# Chapter 9

# Economic and Political Reforms, 1874-1890

*Prelude: John Henry Kirby—The Paul Bunyan of East Texas*

*Many people may recall reading about the larger-than-life character Paul Bunyan, the greatest of all lumberjacks. While Bunyan was a fictional figure in American folklore, there was a real-life legendary lumberman in East Texas during the late nineteenth century. His name was John Henry Kirby. On November 16, 1860, he was born in Tyler County, the son of John Thomas and Sarah Payne Kirby. His formal education was limited to a few sessions in the rural schools of Tyler County and less than one semester at Southwestern University in Georgetown, Texas. Despite his lack of formal education, Kirby possessed great ambition. He studied law with the influential state senator Samuel Bronson Cooper, became a calendar clerk for the Texas Senate between 1882 and 1884, passed the bar exam in the fall of 1885, and practiced law in Woodville before moving to Houston with his wife and daughter in 1889. Kirby's rise to prominence came at the same time that the lumber industry began to grow in importance in the woodlands of East Texas.*

*Beginning in 1880 and lasting for the next fifty years, Texas entered what became known as the "bonanza era" in the lumber industry. With railroads spreading throughout the eastern region of the state, entrepreneurs soon followed, establishing lumber plants to supply finished lumber to mainline railroads. Many of the lumber companies built company towns such as Camden, Kirbyville, and Diboll. The mill owners soon dominated the lives of their workers and their families. Companies often paid their employees in company script that could be redeemed for supplies and services at the company commissary or offices. The script was worthless outside of the company town; therefore, dependency of the workers on the company became nearly absolute.*

*While working as a lawyer in Woodville, Kirby was approached by the representatives of Boston businessmen who were having trouble securing a land deal and hired Kirby to settle the matter. Kirby was fortunate enough to secure the land that they sought. As a result of his success, new opportunities opened for him. Little did he know it at the time, but Kirby was about to take his first steps toward becoming one of the largest lumbermen in the state. With* the financial backing of new business associates in Boston, Kirby organized the Texas and Louisiana Land and Lumber Company in 1886. This was the first of numerous such companies that Kirby formed for the purpose of exploiting the rich resources of eastern Texas. The first company, however, was founded for the purpose of manufacturing lumber and purchasing timber lands. This company's success led to the organization of the Texas Pine Lands Association, which Kirby became the general manager. Serving as the head of two of the largest lumber companies in East Texas, Kirby found that he often had to entertain business guests. As such, he decided to move to Houston in 1889, providing his business associates easier access to his home as well as local night life in the city. By this time he had become one of the most successful businessmen in the state and was only thirty years old.

Kirby realized in the early 1890s that much of the rich timberland in East Texas was inaccessible because of limited transportation infrastructure in the region. In 1893, he began to making plans to build the Gulf, Beaumont & Kansas City Railway, which ran into the heart of the East Texas pine district. The road was completed despite the general economic depression the United States experienced between 1893 and 1896. Upon its completion, Kirby sold the railroad to the Atchison, Topeka and Santa Fe Railway, earning himself a significant profit. Also, Kirby used the economic downturn in the 1890s to his advantage, buying up various tracts of timberland from companies that could no longer hold on to depreciating lands. By 1896, Kirby had amassed vast tracts of East Texas timberland, realizing his dream of owning enough land to build a company large enough to sell and deliver lumber to any place in the world—a company that could fill any order, regardless of its size.

In order to fulfill his dream of building a mega company, Kirby brought in his eastern investors. Together they organized what became a ten-million dollar lumber corporation. To meet the needs of the new company, Kirby bought and consolidated the saw mills of fourteen companies. Kirby Lumber Company was the largest of its kind in the South, controlling more than 300,000 acres of timberland. John Henry Kirby, who now earned such whimsical titles as "The Prince of the Pines" and "The Father of Industrial Texas," had truly become as big as the fictional character of Paul Bunyan.

Between 1874 and 1890 Texas experienced growth and prosperity. The state witnessed the emergence of industrialization and new methods of production that would revolutionize its agricultural sector. Contributing significantly to the economic changes was the boom of railroad construction. However, despite rapid changes taking place in the economy, Texas remained an agricultural state, a state heavily dependent on cotton production. As the economy went through evolutionary changes, Texans experienced political transformations as well. Even though the Democratic Party continued to dominate state politics, Republicans and third-party organizations, such as the Grange (National Patrons of Husbandry), the Greenback Party, and the Farmers' Alliance, made their indelible mark on state and local politics. As they rapidly approached the end of the nineteenth century, Texans had to come to grips with a world very different from the one that their fathers and mothers had known.

## Railroad Development and Its Impact on Texans

Numerous economic transformations occurred in the state between 1874 and 1890. Agriculture became more commercialized; the cattle industry emerged in the western regions of the state; and new industries such as lumbering and mining operations began to thrive in the eastern and central counties. The single most important agent leading to change in the state, however, was the railroad industry. In one way or another, railroads touched the lives of all Texans, but not all citizens viewed the railroad with enthusiastic optimism.

At the beginning of the Civil War, Texas had approximately 500 miles of functioning railroad track, most of the lines connecting Houston and Galveston with adjacent communities. By 1900, railroad companies had constructed more than 8,000 miles of track in the state, making railroad construction one of the state's leading nonagricultural industries. Most Texans viewed the railroad as a symbol of progress and prosperity, especially farmers and business owners who needed a cheap and efficient method of shipping their goods to market.

Individual communities also understood the importance of railroads. Community leaders understood that the Iron Horse promised increases in population and economic development. Conversely, local leaders understood that, if the railroad bypassed their communities, it would lead to economic decline and the possible ruin of their settlements. Therefore, it was not uncommon for local communities to offer enticements to railroad companies to bring their lines through or near their towns. While railroad companies might be influenced by local funding, company executives were primarily concerned with state subsidies. Except for the period between 1869 and 1873 when prohibited by the Constitution of 1869, these subsidies were often in the form of land grants. By the mid-1870s, the state offered railroad companies 16 acres of land for every mile of track completed. This arrangement continued until 1882, when the state repealed the land grant act. Collectively, railroad companies received more that 32,000,000 acres of land with the Texas and Pacific line receiving approximately 5,167,000 acres alone.

Railroads were an important factor in the transformation of the state from a rugged frontier society into a modern, progressive state. Eventually every region in Texas enjoyed the economic benefits of rail service. In addition to the Texas and Pacific Railroad and the Southern Pacific, both transcontinental railroads that ran through the state, the Houston and Texas Central, the Gulf, Colorado, and Santa Fe, the Fort Worth and Denver City, and the International and Great Northern were major lines crisscrossing the state. East Texas also had many tap and tram lines (short distance and light rail) that established connections between the major trunk lines and adjacent towns, as well as areas specializing in extractive industries, such as mining and logging.

## Other Leading Industries

Aside from the railroad, Texans witnessed the growth of other industries. Most were what historian John S. Spratt labeled "migratory" industries, meaning that the owners invested limited capital in their businesses and, therefore, could move from one location to another with relative ease. Despite the emergence of industry, scholars estimate that less than 1 percent of the population was employed in manufacturing in the 1870s. During this same decade, the total value of capital invested in Texas manufacturing was just under

$12 million, a figure that represented less than 25 percent of the state's total investment in agricultural industry. By 1890, the value of manufacturing had increased to $92 million, representing approximately 50 percent of the state's agricultural investments.

Most of the industries were involved in processing agricultural products. The most common were flour and grist mills. Nearly every community of any size was home to some kind of a mill. During the 1870s and 1880s, flour milling was the leading manufacturing business, surpassing even the timber industry in East Texas. Meat-packing plants also grew in importance during the late nineteenth century. The first packing house was built in Victoria in 1868, but other plants soon emerged in or near ranching communities, especially in Fort Worth during the late 1880s and early 1890s. Textile industries and cottonseed processors also increased in importance and added to the wealth of Dallas and other North Texas communities.

With the more than 20 million acres of timberland in the East Texas region, it was natural for Texans to engage in the lumber industry. From its humble beginning in the Nacogdoches region during the late 1820s and early 1830s, lumbering became the largest industry in the state by the end of the century. In 1870 Texas sawmills produced about 100 million board feet of lumber annually. Most of this lumber came from mills located in or near the cities of Houston, Orange, and Beaumont. Several factors limited the production of early lumber companies, including the lack of dependable transportation between the mills and their markets, the belief that East Texas yellow pine was inferior to the white pine of the Upper Midwestern states, and the lack of investment capital.

Time and circumstance took care of these early problems. The railroads provided an improved transportation system. A shortage of Midwestern white pine forced consumers to reconsider the value of yellow pine, especially the railroad companies, which purchased large quantities of wood for construction of their line. Finally, the arrival of entrepreneurs, such as Henry J. Lutcher, G. Bedell Moore, John Henry Kirby, and Nathan D. Silsbee, provided the wealth needed to make the industry a success. These lumber tycoons built massive corporations in East Texas. In the case of Kirby and Silsbee,

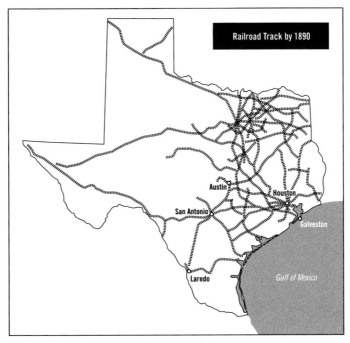

they constructed company towns that often included churches, schools, mercantile stores, and homes. These company towns held mixed blessings for the workers living in them. Even though employees benefitted from the modern conveniences that urban life offered, company owners, who ran the towns as they saw fit, gained almost complete control over the lives of their laborers. In this system, a laborer who lost his job also lost his home.

Although 50 percent of the lumber businesses were still owned by individuals in the 1890s, large corporations dominated the industry, employing three-fourths of the work force and owning about three-fourths of the total value in the business. For example, the Lutcher and Moore mills in Orange engaged in both domestic and international trade and, by the 1890s, were producing approximately 700,000 board feet of lumber per day. These corporate giants continued to prosper well into the next century, with the Kirby Lumber Company becoming Texas's first multimillion-dollar business.

In the 1880s, mining and oil drilling operations contributed to the state's economy. Even though some small companies operated in various locations throughout the state, coal mining companies centered their operations in North Central Texas, including Palo Pinto and Erath Counties. Oil, which became a major industry in the twentieth century, was still in its infant stages of development in the late nineteenth century. As early as 1865, oilman Edward von Harten had unsuccessfully drilled for oil near the small town of Saratoga. The following year, Lyne T. Barret brought in the first Texas oil well at Oil Springs, a small town just east of Nacogdoches. By the 1890s, drillers were beginning to plant wells in the blackland region around Coriscana. However, Texas would not enter its great age of oil exploration until the early twentieth century.

**Labor Unions**

As industries, especially the railroads, began to flourish in Texas, the state witnessed an increase in labor union membership and a growing assertion of workers' rights. Prior to

**This 14-year-old river boy poles the heavy logs into the incline taking them into a mill near Beaumont, Texas, November 1913. The boy worked at this hard and dangerous work for a dollar a day. Photo credit: Library of Congress**

1865, unions were limited to a few skilled trades, such as typographers and carpenters. However, as industry became more concentrated in Texas cities and industrial workers began to suffer under the yoke of large corporations, unions began to make their appearance, just as they had in other industrial regions of the United States. The two most prominent unions in the state were the Galveston Screwmen's Benevolent Association and the Noble Order of the Knights of Labor.

In 1866, longshoremen working on the docks at Galveston organized the Galveston Screwmen's Benevolent Association, a group of specialized workers who used giant screw-jacks to press as much cotton as possible into the holds of large ships. As cotton production increased during the late nineteenth century, the number of screwmen grew as well. The association's membership reached its peak in the early 1890s but rapidly declined after the turn of the century. Typical of most labor unions of the period, the workers sought a shorter work week, higher wages, and more control over the work environment. Unlike other labor unions, however, the screwmen avoided strikes and called for only one work stoppage—and that was to protest the employment of unskilled laborers, primarily African-Americans workers. Because black longshoremen were not represented in the association, Norris Wright Cuney, a noted African-American businessman and politician, helped them to organize their own union in 1883, successfully bringing to an end the monopoly of the white union. One of the most significant reasons for the decline in the association was the implementation of new technology on the docks—the automated cotton compressor. Despite the success of the Galveston Screwmen's Benevolent Association, efforts to create a national labor union remained restricted to regions outside the state prior to the 1880s. However, circumstances changed in 1882 when the Knights of Labor organized their first assembly in Texas.

The Knights of Labor organized nationally in the late 1860s. Between 1878 and 1886, the union enjoyed spectacular growth across the nation. Under the influence of Uriah Stephens, the organization called for the abolition of the wage system and child labor, the regulation of trusts, government ownership of public utilities, the protection of women and African-American laborers, the regulation of alien and contract labor, and the use of boycotts rather than the use of strikes to settle problems between employers and employees. Despite their attempt to avoid strikes, the Knights of Labor participated in national and regional strikes, including the railroad strikes of 1877. In 1879, Terence V. Powderly became the leader of the Knights. Powderly ushered in a period of reorganization and helped to foster a new period of growth. In many respects, the Knights cannot be considered a "true" industrial union, because some of its local chapters covered broad geographical boundaries, and many of its members worked in different occupational fields.

The Knights of Labor was the first national union to enter Texas, as well as the broader southwest region of the United States. The emergence of the organization resulted from its participation against the practices of Jay Gould's southwestern railroads in 1884 and 1885. The struggle against Gould's policies resulted in a dramatic nationwide increase in membership. Unfortunately for the union, the Knights suffered a key loss in the Great Southwest Strike against Gould's Texas and Pacific Railroad in 1886, a circumstance that marked the decline of the organization.

The first local assemblies of the Knights appeared in 1882. Most of the assemblies consisted of members from different occupations, but others were composed of specific laborers, such as longshoremen, telegraph operators, coal miners, railroad laborers, carpenters, bricklayers, lumberjacks, farmers, mechanics, and screwmen. By 1885, Texas newspapers were reporting that the Knights had approximately 30,000 members and more than 300 local assemblies in the state. The largest local assemblies were composed of farmers and those listed as "mixed." As a labor union, the Knights admitted persons of all occupations except bankers, speculators, gamblers, lawyers, and liquor dealers. The organization was unique in that it accepted women as well as African-American members. Black Texans usually founded segregated lodges of the Knights of Labor, but locals in some Texas cities accepted blacks into the main organization. One prominent African American, David Black, served on the union's state executive board.

During the Great Southwest Strike of 1886, the American public, which initially supported the strikers, abandoned the laborers when the strike became violent. The strike resulted when Jay Gould's Texas and Pacific Railway fired a shop foreman supposedly without just cause. The Knights called for a strike of 9,000 workers. This conflict turned into a bloody clash in Fort Worth when the Knights tried to prevent the company from moving a freight train. Governor John Ireland responded to the violence by ordering the state militia and the Texas Rangers into the area with instructions to suppress the disturbance. The public became even more opposed to labor unions following the Haymarket Square bombing and riots in Chicago on May 4, 1886. As a result, the Knights fell into rapid decline, and by 1893 the organization's national membership had dropped from a high of 700,000 members to 75,000. Even though the wounded organization would continue to maintain a national existence until 1917, the last assemblies in Texas disappeared prior to 1900.

With the collapse of the Knights of Labor, Texas workers entered a period of relative inactivity regarding further unionization. Ultimately, labor organization in the state changed dramatically with the emergence of the American Federation of Labor (AFL) in the 1890s. Established in the 1880s, the AFL enlisted only skilled laborers and made no effort to organize the masses of unskilled workers. The demands of the AFL leadership usually centered on the issues of better pay and improved working conditions, especially the development of safer work environments, a shorter work day, and a shorter work week. The AFL in Texas generally avoided intense political partisanship and typically evaded direct confrontations with employers. By 1900, the AFL in Texas boasted a meager 8,500 members, a number that increased significantly during the early decades of the twentieth century following the discovery of oil and the continued development of Texas industries.

**Agriculture: the Mainstay of the Economy**

Overall, despite the expansion of industry in Texas, the state lagged far behind the nation as a whole throughout the latter part of the nineteenth century. The Texas economy almost seemed to run the opposite of the rest of the United States in 1870. While the value of manufactured goods was almost double the value of agricultural products in the United States as a whole, Texas manufacturing was just more than half of the value of farm products. Even though the industrial sector in the state was growing, farming remained the most significant part of the Texas economy.

In Texas, agriculture suffered a dramatic downturn during and immediately following the Civil War. However, between 1870 and 1890, farmers began to witness substantial gains. For example, the number of farms increased from 61,125 in 1870 to 228,126 in 1890. The number of improved acres during the same time period increased from 2,964,836 to 20,746,215 acres. Additionally, the production of corn increased from 20,554,538 to 69,112,150 bushels, and the number of cotton bales produced rose from 350,628 to 1,471,242 in the same twenty-year period. As the statistics suggest, these dramatic increases came from more land being put into production. For example, cotton production in the Blackland Prairie boomed once railways reached the region, providing farmers with a reliable means to ship their crops to distant markets.

As impressive as agricultural growth was in the state, the numbers did not tell the whole story of Texas farmers. Many, perhaps most, farmers suffered serious economic hardships in the latter part of the nineteenth century. Falling prices, increasing debts, and farm tenancy became commonplace in the rural areas of the state. Some tenants paid annual cash rent to the landowners, but most farmed as either share tenants or sharecroppers, paying their rent and other acquired debts at the end of the growing season with portions of the crops they produced. Arrangements between landowners and tenant farmers varied from place to place, but most tenant farmers provided their own seed, work animals, and equipment and paid the landlord one-fourth of their cotton crop and one-third of their corn crop as rent. Conversely, sharecroppers provided only their own labor and received the proceeds of one-half of the cotton crop. As a result, tenant farmers often had more control over their working lives and thereby enjoyed a slightly higher social standing. One fact, however, unified the tenant farmers and the sharecroppers—neither owned their own land, forcing all to live in poverty.

Because of their financial circumstances, most tenant farmers and sharecroppers began each planting season by buying food, clothing, and other necessary items on credit.

As collateral, the farmers would put up all their possessions and potential profits from crops that the farmer hoped to harvest at the end of the season. To protect themselves, store owners often charged higher prices for goods bought on credit. At the end of harvest, the farmers were often lucky if they broke even, prompting them to begin the entire process again in the upcoming growing season.

Following the Civil War, the number of tenant farmers and sharecroppers steadily increased. African Americans had gained their freedom after the war, but that was about all they had. The majority of them had no land, no money, and no economic prospects. As a result, most black farmers became tenant farmers or sharecroppers. Each decade in the late nineteenth century also gave witness to a growing number of white tenant farmers and sharecroppers. Many of these newcomers were previously small farmers who mortgaged their land to buy supplies, only to lose their farms in foreclosures when their crops did not yield enough return to repay their creditors. By 1890, just over 40 percent of all Texas farms were worked by tenants and sharecroppers, a percentage that increased with the passing of each year well into the twentieth century. Any notion that a young man could become a self-made man by working his way up from sharecropping to tenant farming and then to farming his own land was more myth than reality. The best most young men could hope was to make a few dollars each year and to provide a meager existence for their families.

One of the reasons for farmers' economic hardships was the change in the nature of agriculture in Texas. By the 1870s, there was a clear trend toward the commercialization of farming. Most farmers no longer operated subsistence farms but, rather, grew crops for the marketplace and used their profits to purchase necessities for their families. As farmers became more dependent on market production, cotton began to dominate the commercial agricultural economy. Although some scholars have criticized farmers for not diversifying, a closer analysis reveals that farmers had little choice but to stay with cotton. Even though the price of cotton steadily declined between 1870 and 1890, cotton almost always returned more income per acre than any other crop of the period. Essentially, cotton was the most dependable crop grown in the southern states. Cotton more than any other crop grown in the South had well established markets in the northeast and in Europe. According to Texas farmers, it made little sense to grow anything else.

**Texas Ranches and Ranchers—the Cattle Industry**

During the Civil War, Texas ranchers supplied the Confederacy with beef until mid-1863, when federal armies seized control of Vicksburg, Mississippi, effectively ending trade from Texas and Louisiana to the rest of the southern states. With the primary trade routes to the east severed, Texas cattle became worthless, and ranchers allowed their animals to roam the range. Within a short period of time, cattle population increased to a point that contemporaries estimated the animals at eight per capita of the human population in the state. At the conclusion of the war, processed beef in the eastern markets of the United States was selling for 25 to 30 cents per pound. At the same time, a mature, healthy Texas steer brought $6 to $10 per head. Butcher shops in the east were willing to pay $30 to $40 for the same steer. Thus, Texas ranchers began to ship their beef to eastern markets by trailing them to railheads in Missouri and Kansas, where the animals were loaded aboard railcars and shipped first to the stockyards in Chicago and St. Louis and then to butcher shops in other northern cities. Additionally, Texas cattle were driven to Montana gold mines and New Mexico Indian reservations.

Between 1865 and 1885, Texas cowboys trailed more than five million head to markets outside the state. By 1880, once the threat of Indian depredations had subsided in Texas, the cattle industry spread to southern and western regions of the state. Contrary to myths, the cattle industry was not completely founded on "free grass" (public land). Many of the more prosperous ranchers ran their cattle operations on their own lands, including Thomas and Dennis M. O'Connor, Richard King, Mifflin Kenedy, and countless other men who purchased large tracts of land during the antebellum years. Other famous cattlemen bought large tracts of ranch land immediately after the war, including Charles Goodnight, William T. Waggoner, C. C. Slaughter, S. M. Swenson, and William D. and George T. Reynolds. Nevertheless, as the frontier advanced in the 1870s, many stockmen established ranching operations on the open range, without regard for who actually owned the land. In time, when the legitimate property owners appeared, the "squatters" simply moved further west onto a new unsettled domain. In fact, before 1874, when Joseph Glidden invented barbed wire, few stockmen acquired land on which to graze their cattle. If they purchased land at all, they only bought just enough land to establish a headquarters for their operation which served as a central location for working their cattle or land, with rivers or creeks running through the land which gave them control of the limited water sources on the range. To control the water was to control the open range itself.

As the markets became flooded with Texas cattle, ranchers soon looked north to the unpopulated rangeland that extended from the Canadian border and covered the entire Great Plains east of the Rocky Mountains. While they continued to send mature steers to slaughterhouses, Texas ranchers began moving large numbers of their breeding cattle to pasturelands in New Mexico, Montana, Wyoming, Dakota, Colorado, the Indian Territory (present-day Oklahoma), western Kansas, and Nebraska. The intent was to create new herds in these regions of the Great Plains. Thus, the cattle industry that began in Texas spread throughout the western part of the United States. Even though the Panic of 1873 crippled the cattle industry, the men who survived the economic depression profited when the industry experienced an unprecedented boom during the next decade. By the early 1880s, news of the "Beef Bonanza" spread to Great Britain, leading investors there to compete with American capitalists in eastern states for land, cattle, and range rights in the western regions of the United States. As a result, new methods of production transformed the cattle industry. Though the cattle industry originally began as an individual enterprise, corporations began to enter the field, enjoying the benefits of mobilized capital but with the disadvantage of absentee ownership and hired managers.

In the 1880s, the open range became fenced pastures as the larger ranches (especially those owned by European and eastern investment companies) wanted to increase their control over their operations, a move that caused conflict between large and small ranchers, ranchers and farmers, and ranch owner and hired hands. Two events resulted from closed-range ranching—the cutting of fences and the Cowboy Strike of 1883. In the summer and fall of 1883, fence cutting in Texas became commonplace. Landless cattlemen who wanted to retain open-range ranching practices vied with owners who used barbed wire to fence the land to establish permanent ranches. In the same year, a drought settled over Texas, increasing tensions between open-range cattlemen who needed grass and water for their herds and closed-range ranchers who tried to protect the grass and

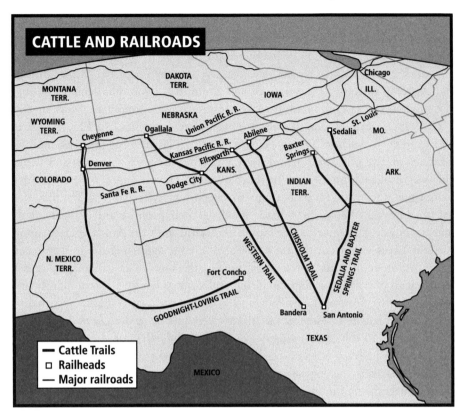

water on their land with fences. Additionally, some ranchers enclosed public lands when they fenced their own property, and others strung wire around farms and small ranches that belonged to other persons. In some cases, these fences blocked public roads, cut off access to schools and churches, and even disrupted the delivery of mail. This wanton fencing led some men whose land was not affected by the fence war to support the side of the open-range ranchers.

As a result, fence cutting became common in Texas cattle country, particularly in a belt extending north and south through the center of the state—the ranchmen's frontier. Primarily operating at night, fence cutters went by various names, such as the Owls, the Javelinas, and the Blue Devils. By the fall of 1883, the damage estimates for cut fences reached $20 million. Many contemporaries claimed that the conflict over fencing had impeded the development of the western counties in the state. Politicians attempted to avoid the issue, but Governor John Ireland called a special session of the legislature on January 8, 1884, and instructed them to pass legislation to end the fence war. After heated debate, the legislators made fence cutting a felony punishable by one to five years in prison. Fencing in public lands or lands belonging to other property owners without their permission was declared a misdemeanor, and builders of such fences were given six months to remove them. Ranchers who built fences across public roads were required to place a gate every three miles and to keep the gates in repair. These laws ended most of the fencing crisis, although sporadic outbreaks of fence cutting continued to occur for another decade.

As investment companies slowly began to take over ranching in Texas, important changes occurred that affected ranch employees. Prior to the 1880s, cowboys often took part of their pay in the form of calves and unbranded mavericks (stray cattle) found on the ranch. The cowboys were sometimes able to build their own small herd and run it on their employer's land. However, new ranch-owner investment companies that were interested in expanding their holdings and increasing their own profits insisted that their hired hands work for wages and claimed mavericks as company property. As a result, a cowboy could expect to earn only an average of $40 a month at a job that demanded long hours and numerous skills. Discontent became commonplace among many working cowboys.

In 1883, a group of men working for five different ranches (the LIT, the LS, the LX, the LE, and the T Anchor ranches) began a strike that lasted more than two months. The cowboys from the LIT, the LS, and the LX ranches drew up an ultimatum demanding higher wages and submitted it to the ranch owners. The men agreed that, if the demands were not met, they would walk out on strike beginning March 31. When their demands went unaddressed, the cowboys made good on their promise and walked off the job. Ranchers, however, found effective means for dealing with the strikers. They simply fired those employees who went out on strike or offered a slight increase in wages and fired workers if they refused the offer. Additionally, the owners and managers were able to continue with planned roundups by hiring replacement workers at temporarily increased wages. After two months, the strike was so weak that the May roundup occurred without incidents of violence. In essence, the strikers were unable to overcome the obstacles that they confronted in the cattle industry. In the months following the strike, some ranchers reported an increase in cattle rustling and suggested that the strikers were to blame. Blaming the strikers was logical considering that some of them went without work and were obviously short of money.

**Democratic Reign in State Politics**

When Democrats regained complete control of the state government from Republicans in 1874, they immediately set out to destroy the Radicals' Constitution of 1869. Specifically, Democrats wanted to reduce the terms and salaries of all officials, abolish voter registration, establish local control of schools, limit the power of the legislature and governor, decrease taxation and state expenditures, institute strict control over corporations, and reestablish state land subsidies for railroad construction. To accomplish these goals, the Democrat-controlled legislature in early 1874 created a joint committee charged with the duty of amending the Constitution of 1869. The committee energetically completed its task, but rather than simply amending the constitution, it wrote a new one and proposed that the legislature approve it. However, some Democratic leaders questioned the legitimacy of establishing a new constitution outside of an elected convention. They also feared that the adoption of a new governing document might bring the renewed wrath of the federal government. Accepting the concerns of their colleagues as legitimate, the legislature rejected the committee's proposal. Governor Richard Coke then suggested that the legislature submit the question of calling forth a new constitutional convention to the people, who then on August 2, 1875, approved the convention and elected three delegates from each of the thirty senatorial districts.

Delegates to the convention assembled in Austin on September 6, 1875. Of the members present, seventy-five were Democrats and fifteen, including six African Americans, were Republicans. None of the members had been present at the Convention of 1868-1869. More importantly, 40 percent of the delegates were members of the Patrons

Richard Coke, Texas Governor, Photo taken between 1870-1880. Photo credit: Library of Congress

of Husbandry, or the "Grange," a cooperative established to protect and improve the lives of farmers who increasingly felt that industrialists threatened their livelihood and that the government had increasingly marginalized their concerns following the financial depression of 1873. In the convention the Grange members consistently supported conservative constitutional measures.

Despite some contentious debate, convention members completed their task. The document represented a complete Democratic triumph. The governor's power was restricted. The chief executive could no longer call out the militia or fill vacancies by appointment with the approval of the state senate. In addition, the governor no longer had constitutional authority over other state executive officers. Government salaries and expenditures were lowered, and the terms of office for state officials were shortened even as the framers made many of the offices elected rather than appointed. Furthermore, the document established that the legislature would meet every other year, its members receiving only a modest sum. Financial support for the legislature would come from established lower tax rates. The new constitution also included a homestead exemption that protected family homes and limited acreage from foreclosure, reflecting the influence of the farmers and the "anti-bank" attitudes prevalent among Texans. Distrust of corporations was reflected in a ban on state-chartered banks and in attempts to regulate railroads by defining them as "common carriers" and by establishing limits on freight and passenger rates. Regarding education, the new constitution followed the suggestions of the Thirteenth Legislature by dismantling the Davis administration's centralized public school system, replacing it with segregated, locally-controlled school systems, and striking compulsory attendance requirements. However, they did allocate some funding through taxation and maintained the idea of a permanent school fund that would receive funding from sales of public lands.

The new constitution was approved by a referendum on February 15, 1876. Despite the addition of numerous amendments, this constitution remains the basis of Texas government. In the end, the document reflected the views of a nineteenth century agrarian society, focusing primarily on the rights of independent farmers. In this regard, the Constitution of 1876 was a poor document for Texas, a state with thousands of tenant farmers and people engaged in non-agricultural pursuits, especially in the emerging industries of the state. Furthermore, the constitution did not reflect the interest of minority groups in the state, a momentous problem considering that African Americans and Tejanos represented a significant percentage of the general population.

With a new constitution complete, the Democrats maintained virtual control of the state until the 1890s. The first "Redeemer" governor of Texas was Richard Coke, a Waco lawyer, ex-Confederate, and district and state judge during Presidential Reconstruction. Governor Coke tried to restore financial order by reducing funding for public printing and for the state asylums. However, the cost of protecting the southern border from Mexican raiders and the western frontier from Comanche and Kiowa Indians offset any fiscal savings for the state. Like his predecessors, Coke's early days in office were spent addressing job applications, pleas for pardons, and requests for various types of state permits. In accordance with the Constitution of 1876, the governor served on a three-member board that supervised the decentralization of the public education system, creating a system of locally operated and supported schools. Additionally, he was involved in establishing and opening the state's first publically supported university—the Texas Agricultural and Mechanical College (present-day Texas A&M University). Though the Radical Republicans under Governor E.J. Davis's administration had founded the school on April 17, 1871, and appropriated $75,000 for its construction and maintenance, delays caused by political and financial irregularities commonplace in Reconstruction prevented the university from opening its doors until October 4, 1876. In the 1876 gubernatorial election, the people of Texas re-elected Coke to a second term by a three-to-one margin over his Republican challenger, William Morton Chambers. Shortly thereafter, Coke was elected to the United States Senate in May 1876, replacing Morgan C. Hamilton. He officially resigned as governor in December of the same year and began his term as senator on March 4, 1877.

Lieutenant Governor Richard B. Hubbard became governor when Coke resigned his office. Hubbard's administration was marred by financial difficulties, by general lawlessness, and by the fact that the legislature did not meet while he was in office. Despite these setbacks, he successfully reduced the public debt, fought land fraud, promoted educational reforms, and restored public control of the state prison system. In the 1878 gubernatorial election, many Texans thought that Hubbard would receive his party's nomination, but he was opposed by James W. Throckmorton, a popular favorite because of his removal from the governorship during Reconstruction. At the Democratic state convention, supporters of the two nominees became deadlocked, prompting the convention to settle on a compromise candidate, Oran M. Roberts, chief justice of the Texas Supreme Court, president of the secession convention in 1861, and an ex-Confederate. Legend has it that Roberts, who was not present at the convention, learned of his nomination while working at his farm, which was located near the prominent East Texas town of Tyler. Upon hearing the news of his selection, Roberts supposedly road into town, where he borrowed a small sum of money from friends, to send a telegraph to the delegates at the convention that he would accept their nomination.

In the summer of 1878, Roberts campaigned throughout northern and central Texas, hoping to neutralize the growing popularity of a new third-party movement in Texas politics, the Greenback Party. The Greenbackers, as the new party members were known, threatened to split the Democratic vote and potentially affect the outcome of the pending

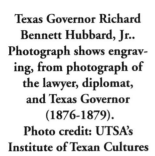
Texas Governor Richard Bennett Hubbard, Jr.. Photograph shows engraving, from photograph of the lawyer, diplomat, and Texas Governor (1876-1879). Photo credit: UTSA's Institute of Texan Cultures

election. Roberts effectively convinced the voters in the state that northern Republicans, African Americans, and dissatisfied Democrats were behind the creation of the Greenback Party, and the election of their members to higher office would end in the ruin of the state. As a result, Roberts won the election by a landslide, receiving 67 percent of all votes cast.

Like his predecessors, Governor Roberts believed in limited government and supported policies that were designed to reduce government expeditures and at the same time to eliminate the state's debt. To accomplish his goals, the governor demanded that the legislature cut state funding for public education. After the governor vetoed an appropriations bill that promised 25 percent of the *ad valorem* tax revenues for public school expenditures, the legislature complied with Roberts's demand in 1879. Later, while in special session, the legislature reduced school funding to 16 percent of the *ad valorem* revenues. Governor Roberts approved of the reduction in school funding and signed the appropriations bill into law. To increase the state's revenues, Governor Roberts called on the legislature to sell the state's remaining public lands, resulting in the passage of the Fifty Cent Law of 1879, which made available public lands to the public for fifty cents per acre. Roberts also worked with the legislature to cut property taxes. In the short-term, Roberts's policies were effective. When the governor left office after his second term, the state treasury had a positive balance of over $300,000. However, in the long-term, his policies proved detrimental to the economic stability of the state. For example, the sale of public land at fifty cents per acre proved disastrous when land prices later rose, costing the state government vast amounts of potential revenue if only the legislature had deferred selling off large tracts of the state's public lands.

In the 1880 gubernatorial election, Governor Roberts was re-nominated by his party for a second term. Roberts easily won the election, carrying 60 percent of the vote, defeating the Greenback Party's candidate William H. Hamman and the Republican challenger, Edmund J. Davis. During his second term, the governor continued to support policies of strict fiscal discipline, however, despite Governor Roberts's position on public school financing, his administration allowed the creation of new institutions in higher learning. During his terms as governor, the legislature created the University of Texas at Austin,

**Agricultural and Mechanical College, Texas. Between 1900 and 1920.
Photo credit: Library of Congress.**

as well as the establishment of two teachers' colleges, Sam Houston Normal Institute in Huntsville and Prairie View Normal Institute..

As early as 1839, Texans had entertained the idea of establishing a state university, but no real measures were taken to build such an institution. Following the Civil War, Texas did take advantage of the federal government's Morrill Land Grant College Act of 1862, creating the Texas Agricultural and Mechanical College, which opened in 1876. However, most of the state's leading political figures viewed the A&M college as a vocational branch of a larger "university of the first class," which by definition meant an institution devoted to a curriculum based on the arts and sciences. In March 1881, voters participating in a special election approved Austin as the home of the University of Texas, which officially opened in September 1883. The voters also elected to open a medical branch of the university in Galveston in 1881, but that campus did not receive students until 1891. Both the University of Texas and Texas A&M College received limited financial assistance from the legislature and the Permanent University Fund, but state funding remained limited until the twentieth century when oil was discovered on the lands that the state had set aside for maintenance of the universities.

The state also witnessed the creation of two new normal schools. In 1876, the "Agricultural and Mechanical College for the Benefit of Colored Youth" was established as part of Texas A&M College. The school, originally named Alta Vista College, opened its doors in 1878. Because Alta Vista's enrollments were limited to only a few students and given the racial views of many whites during the late nineteenth century, Governor Roberts suggested closing the branch campus in 1879. However, before the legislature could act upon Roberts's request, an agent of the George Peabody Fund brokered a deal with the state that offered financial assistance for the conversion of Alta Vista into a normal school, which would meet the needs of black students who were seeking to earn a teaching degree. The legislature accepted the deal, chartering Prairie View Normal Institute as the first public black college in Texas and the second oldest state-supported institution of higher learning in Texas. The legislature in the same year created Sam Houston Normal Institute in Huntsville.

In 1882 Roberts turned down the request to run for a third term, choosing instead to join Robert S. Gould in becoming a law professor at the newly created University of Texas. As such, Democrats selected John Ireland as their candidate. Ireland had served in the House of the Thirteenth Legislature and in the Senate of the Fourteenth Legislature. During his tenure in the legislature, Ireland had expressed his political views on a number of issues confronting the state. For example, he supported the university bill and lower tax rates, but, at the same time, he favored increasing expeditures for the support of public schools. Additionally, he favored reforming the process by which public lands were sold, arguing that state-owned lands should only be sold to homesteaders. Regarding financial issues, Ireland believed in expanding available currency, the abolishment of national banks, and the creation of a revenue tariff. Concerning railroads, Ireland supported the idea of imposing regulation on railway companies operating in the state and ending the practice of providing land grants to subsidize the building of new rail lines. Because of his opposition to the railroads, Ireland earned the moniker, "Oxcart John."

The Greenback Party's candidate, George W. "Wash" Jones, who was sometimes referred to as the "Sage of Bastrop," was a capable challenger, having served two terms in Congress in 1878 and 1880 as an independent candidate. Although Jones was an effective campaigner, Ireland defeated him in convincing fashion by a vote of 150,809 to 102,501.

Even though Ireland favored many of his predecessor's policies, one of his first acts in office was to secure an amendment to the constitution that supported an increase in funding for public schools. In January 1883, he saw his proposed amendment pass, providing an *ad valorem* tax not to exceed twenty per one hundred dollars valuation. Ireland also rescued the lands set aside for public schools from being sold for the low terms that had been fixed by the Roberts's administration. The price of the lands was increased to $2.00 per acre on a thirty-year note. While adding money to the state treasury, the new land policy led to the emergence of large scale cattle ranches, which ultimately created social problems related to the use of barbed wire on what had previously been open range.

John Gates first introduced the use of barbed wire in Texas during the 1870s. Within a decade, the use of barbed wire had become commonplace, especially in the western regions of Texas. Cattle ranchers began to fence off their own land holdings, but they also erected fences on public lands which they did not own. Additionally, ranchers used barbed wire fences to cut off farmers or other ranchers from water on their lands. As such, tensions grew between landowners, especially during times of drought. In 1883, these tensions erupted when ranchers and farmers began to cut the fences and openly trespassed on their neighbor's lands in order to gain access to water. Within a year, the activities of the wirecutters led to numerous violent episodes. Ireland took a special interest in bringing a successful conclusion to the fence-cutting war of 1883. The governor called a special session of the legislature in February 1884, calling on the legislators to authorize the Texas Rangers to bring an end to the violence. Subsequently, the Rangers were able to restore order, but occasional outbreaks of violence still occurred.

Ireland also sought greater state control over the educational process. In 1883, the legislature passed a new education law that provided for the election of a state superintendent, the county school districts to be run by county judges, new requirements for teacher certification, and compulsory education for children between the ages of eight and sixteen. However, independent school districts run by their own officials received an exemption from the law. Ireland's moderate approach proved satisfactory to the voters, and he won re-election in 1884, winning 65 percent of the vote.

Governor Ireland's victory in 1884 basically brought an end to theGreenback Party, but two new movements were emerging in Texas politics—the Farmers' Alliance and a temperance movement demanding the prohibition of alcoholic beverages. Prohibition was not a new idea in Texas, having been a significant reform goal prior to the Civil War, but the arrival of the Women's Christian Temperance Union in 1883 energized the movement. The Constitution of 1876 had addressed the issue of prohibition by establishing a local-option rule that allowed local communities to hold elections to determine whether the manufacturing and sale of alcohol would be legal in their towns. Prohibitionists in the mid-1880s, however, wanted the sale and manufacturing of alcohol outlawed statewide. Facing new challenges from agrarians and prohibitionists, Democrats now found it difficult to dominate state politics simply by promising to limit government and by reminding voters that their party was the one that had "redeemed" the state from Radical Republicans. Fortunately for the party, their gubernatorial candidate in the 1886 and 1888 elections, Lawrence "Sul" Ross, proved to be a charismatic speaker who exhibited enormous popularity with the Texas voters.

A famous Indian fighter and a Confederate veteran, Lawrence Ross was a delegate to the constitutional convention of 1875 and had served as state senator from 1881 to 1885. As a candidate for governor in 1886, he was more moderate than previous Democratic governors. He supported the sale of public lands to actual settlers rather than to land speculators, believed that some railroad regulations were necessary to protect the interest of the people, and favored the local-option rule rather than statewide prohibition. Ross's position on prohibition did not sit well with temperance leaders. Because the Republican candidate, A. M. Cochran, also opposed prohibition, reformers formed a third-party movement and nominated Ebenezer L. Dohoney of Lamar County as their gubernatorial candidate. Nevertheless, Ross's personal popularity and moderate views led him to an overwhelming election victory, receiving 228,776 votes to Cochran's 65,236 and Dohoney's 19,186.

Despite their candidate's poor showing in the election, the Prohibition Party pressed the legislature to pass a constitutional amendment preventing the manufacture and sale of alcohol in Texas. In the spring of 1887, the legislature decided to settle the issue once and for all by calling a referendum vote on the issue. Both "wets" and "drys" organized and campaigned hard. In the end, the "wets" carried the day, casting 220,627 votes to their opponents' 129,270. The overwhelming defeat did not end the prohibition movement in Texas; it merely forced the issue into the background of state politics for the next two decades. Perhaps the most significant long-term consequence of the election was that it weakened party loyalties among Democrats as well as among Republicans and third-party members, meaning that future political divisions over other issues such as economic reform might occur more easily.

During his first term as governor, Ross's most notable accomplishment was the dedication of a new state capitol in Austin. In 1879, the Sixteenth Texas Legislature appropriated three million acres of public land in the Panhandle to finance the construction cost of a new capitol building. The destruction of the old capitol by fire in November 1881 accelerated the process of constructing a new building. In early 1882, Mathis Schnell of Rock Island, Illinois, signed a contract to build the new capitol in return for the land that

The proud state capitol of Austin, Texas. Photo credit: Library of Congress.

had been earlier set aside for that purpose. In turn, Schnell transferred three-fourths of the land to the Taylor, Babcock, and Company in Chicago, which organized the Capitol Syndicate, a group of investors that included Charles B. Farwell, John V. Farwell, Colonel Amos C. Babcock, and Colonel Abner Taylor of Illinois. Several months later Schnell assigned the rest of his contract to the syndicate after rumors surfaced that he had bribed state officials to receive the capitol contract. Since the land was located in the Texas Panhandle, an unsettled area of the state, investors decided to establish the XIT Ranch to utilize the land until it could be sold. The Capitol Syndicate then devoted its time to building the new capitol, which was completed and ready for use in April 1888. Governor Ross easily won re-election in 1888, capturing 72 percent of the vote. He continued to support a moderate position within his party. During his second term, Texas attained more industrial, agricultural, and commercial growth, and the state's educational institutions continued to flourish. Despite some continued political grumblings over prohibition, Ross effectively maintained unity in the Democratic Party during a period of relative calm, devoid of any new political crises.

A number of factors contributed to the election of Democratic governors between 1874 and 1890. One of the most significant factors was the lingering memory of the Civil War and of Reconstruction, which had spawned the Radical Republican government. Simply stated, most white Texans were not willing to vote for Republican candidates because they represented the "party of Reconstruction." A second factor was that the Democratic Party was able to capture the attention of discontent agrarians by supporting moderate agrarian reforms. Additionally, Democrats were able to keep control of the more radical elements in their party by controlling the nominating process. Candidates generally were selected by conventions, where the entrenched political establishment easily controlled the outcome. Primary elections did not become common in Texas until the end of the century. Finally, conservative policies such as promotion of the railroads reduced state expenditures, and lower taxes appealed to most Texas voters, even those who demanded more extensive reforms, such as railroad regulation, expanded state services, and prohibition.

## Agrarian Organizations and Challenges to Democratic Hegemony

The hard times that farmers periodically faced caused many of them to support various political and social reform movements that they hoped would bring economic relief. Texas farmers supported the Grange, the Greenback Party, the Farmers' Alliance, and—later in the 1890s—the People's Party (also known as the Populist Party), and they challenged Democratic politicians whom they believed had aligned themselves with corporate leaders. To varying degrees, these various organizations called for an expanded role for government regarding such issues as currency reform, corporate regulation, and the expansion of democracy. In addition to these agrarian organizations, the Republican Party continued to mount a steady but weakening attack against Democratic rule in the state.

In 1867, Oliver H. Kelley, a clerk in the U.S. Department of Agriculture, founded the Patrons of Husbandry, more commonly referred to as the Grange. Kelley hoped to create a fraternal organization that would bring farmers together and encourage them to act in unison to address their common problems. Originally, the Grange focused more on solving the problems of inadequate education and social isolation than it did on economic matters. However, in the 1870s the organization challenged railroad companies and their political allies in the state legislature as the primary cause of the farmers' economic misfortunes. By 1875, the Grange in Texas boasted over 45,000 members (approximately one-fifth of the state's total electorate) who belonged to more than 1,000 lodges scattered throughout the state.

The Grange's political agenda called for a reduction in the price of farming equipment and supplies, a limit on taxation, and public oversight of the railroads. Regarding the railroad, Grangers also called for legislation that would prohibit discrimination in rates and for the creation of a state agency that would regulate the business practices of railroad companies operating in Texas. Furthermore, the Grange supported the creation of cooperatives, organizing the Texas Grange Manufacturing Association in Marion County to process iron and farm equipment, and the Texas Cooperative Association at Galveston to market farm commodities and to purchase goods at wholesale for their 150 cooperative stores. While the Grange's efforts to create cooperative textile mills that were designed to produce rough cloth and twine ultimately failed, other cooperatives proved more successful, including the Texas State Grange Fair Association and the Texas Grange Mutual Fire Insurance Association. Although the Grange attempted to create cooperatives that would aid farmers, most of their efforts proved beneficial to wealthier farmers who could afford to pay cash for Grange products. Because the Grange was reluctant to issue credit to poorer farmers, the movement failed to provide adequate relief to the vast majority of Texas farmers.

Although the Grange had a substantial following in Texas, some agriculturalists chose to move in different political directions. Farmers who owned their own land typically elected to remain in the Democratic Party. Other farmers suffered financial hardships and wanted immediate relief from their economic woes; they often searched beyond the Grange chapters and the Democratic Party for political assistance. Many of the farmers pinned their hopes on the success of the Texas Greenback Party. Following the lead of national Greenbackers, Texas members opposed federal policies that established specie (hard currency) as the nation's only legal tender, doing away with paper money, also known as greenbacks. The Texas Greenbackers wanted paper money that was printed during and immediately after the Civil War to remain in circulation and urged the federal government to print more paper currency rather than abandoning it. Greenbackers argued that to remove the paper currency from circulation would place an unnecessary and unbearable hardship on small farmers as well as common laborers. They claimed that the debtor class had already suffered from the national economic downturn that had followed the war. Members of the Greenback Party attempted to align themselves with other political factions in the state but experienced only limited success. Early in the 1880s, the party began to decline as other farmer organizations, such as the Grange and the Farmers' Alliance, began to exercise more substantial influence on Texas politics.

At the same time that the Greenback Party entered Texas, farmers in the rural areas of Lampasas, Wise, and Parker Counties established the Farmers' Alliance, an organization designed to help protect agriculturalists from unscrupulous land dealers. In 1879, members reorganized the Alliance as a secret, non-political self-help organization for people living in rural communities, somewhat similar to the structure of the Grange. By the mid-1880s, the Alliance had established approximately 3,000 lodges in the state and was becoming more active in local and state politics. In 1886, Alliance members met in Cleburne, Texas, and restructured the organization once again, making it a viable political machine for farmers and laborers. At the meeting in Cleburne, the Alliance established its political agenda. First, industrial capitalists and powerful corporations were denounced as preying upon the agriculturalists and laborers. Next, in what became known as the "Cleburne Demands," the organization listed its political goals, including the removal of fences from illegally enclosed lands, the restriction of the sale of school lands to settlers only, the passage of higher taxes on land owned by speculators, the regulation of railroads, the free coinage of gold and silver, and the creation of a national bureau of labor. Later, leaders in the Alliance demanded passage of antitrust legislation and reiterated its demands for strict regulation of railroad rates. However, not all members wanted the Alliance to become so blatantly political, and many of those dissatisfied threatened to leave the organization.

Similar to the Grange, the Farmers' Alliance created a network of local cooperatives designed to give Texas farmers greater independence from middlemen, thereby strengthening the agriculturalists' purchasing and selling power. While experiencing initial success, these local cooperatives failed. Most were operated by individuals who did not know how to manage such enterprises. Because the majority of farmers lacked the necessary capital to invest in the cooperatives, the Alliance cooperatives began to extend credit to their members rather than operating on a strict cash-only basis as the Grange cooperatives had done. Meanwhile, they also encountered staunch opposition from the merchants who worked to break the cooperatives by using short-term price-cutting tactics and boycotting distributors who dealt with them.

Given the divisions that developed over the "Cleburne Demands" and the growing failure of the Alliance's local cooperatives, it appeared that the agrarian movement was finished, and it might have failed in 1886 had it not been for the efforts of Charles William Macune. A native of Wisconsin, Macune came to Texas in 1871 and worked several odd jobs before becoming a doctor. He joined the Alliance in 1886 and soon after became chair of the organization's state executive committee. To avoid a split among Alliance members over the Cleburne Demands and to counter the failures of the local cooperatives, Macune proposed the establishment of a statewide cooperative to market members' cotton crops and to act as a central purchasing house. The Farmers' Alliance Exchange of Trade opened later that year in Dallas, but the state cooperative was doomed almost from the beginning. Suffering from poor management decisions and numerous economic setbacks, the Alliance Exchange closed its doors in 1889.

The initial reaction to the exchange plan was positive, and the Alliance witnessed an immediate jump in membership from 75,000 in 1887 to 150,000 the following year. Nevertheless, as the Alliance Exchange fell into disarray, increases in membership slowed, and Macune responded by directing the organization to focus attention on the original issues raised in the Cleburne Demands, especially the limited amount of currency in circulation. However, he went well beyond the Alliance's call for the free coinage of silver and led the charge for developing a new solution to the problem—the subtreasury plan. Essentially, the new plan called on the federal government to create warehouse storage centers for nonperishable agricultural crops such as cotton. At harvest, farmers could store their crops in the government warehouses and receive government loans of up to 80 percent of the current market value of the raw product. The loan would be issued in the form of legal tender paper money—currently without the backing of gold or silver—and would carry a modest annual interest rate of 2 percent. The farmers would later sell their crops when demand and, consequently, prices were higher. In short, the subtreasury plan called on the federal government to aid farmers with two major problems—overproduction and low prices.

By 1890, the Texas Farmers' Alliance moved from being a self-help organization to more of a political action group, endorsing an agenda that called for railroad regulation, expansion of the money supply, and the subtreasury plan. The Alliance's official newspaper, the *Southern Mercury*, regularly printed editorials on these political issues, and members began to use the organization's agenda to judge the worth of Texas politicians. Texas Democrats often failed to measure up to the expectations of Alliance members, but beginning in 1874, Democrats commanded almost total control of the state government and were more accustom to setting agendas rather than bowing to special interest groups in the state.

A final challenge to Democratic hegemony was the Republican Party. Even though their party was weak and declining in importance, Republicans still managed to win office in a few counties in East Texas and along the coast in areas with large black populations. Additionally, Republicans benefitted from patronage when Republican presidents were in office. However, with the percentage of African Americans in the state's population declining from 31 percent in 1870 to 20 percent in 1900, the party witnessed a continuing decline of its influence. Further losses came when white Republicans (known as lily-whites) split from the party. Believing that some whites might join the Republican Party if it became more "white," the lily-whites sought ways to disenfranchise its black members and to move the party away from supporting black rights. With this end in mind, lily-whites organized white men's political clubs, used the court system against African Americans, and resorted to violence and intimidation to keep blacks from the polls. Nevertheless, African Americans continued to support the Republican Party in areas that supported large black populations.

When former Governor E. J. Davis died in 1883, Norris Wright Cuney, an African-American politician from Hempstead, became head of the Republican Party. Cuney proved to be an extraordinary politician, but he could not prevent the state legislature from passing Jim Crow laws, such as the one proposed in 1889 by the state senator from

Marshall, William H. Pope, which required railroads to provide separate passenger cars for blacks and whites. As the party continued to decline in power, Cuney attempted to revive the Republicans' fortunes by allying with disgruntled Democrats and third-party movements. Unfortunately for his party, Cuney's efforts produced few results.

## Conclusions

From 1874 to 1890, Texas politics established a firm foundation of conservatism, including the call for limited government, lower taxes, and fiscal restraint. Even though Republicans and third-party movements emerged during this period, the Democrats remained firmly in control of the state. For the most part, the state's conservative policies tended to benefit railroads, corporations, large ranches, and wealthy merchants rather than rural farmers and urban laborers. Economically, the state embraced the emergence of new industries, such as commercial cattle ranching and farming, railroads, lumbering, and the beginnings of the oil industry. Despite these emerging industries, however, Texas remained an agrarian society, a society trapped in a system of agriculture that ensured the success only of landowners and did little to help the tenant farmers and sharecroppers who struggled to scratch a living from the soil.

*Afterward: Troubled Times for the "Prince of the Pines"*

*John Henry Kirby was the epitome of what it meant to be a successful businessman in Texas during the late nineteenth century. Kirby carried this success with him into the twentieth century. The founder and five-time president of the Southern Pine Association, he served two terms as president of the National Lumber Manufacturers' Association, and served for a brief time as the southern lumber director of the U.S. Shipping Board Emergency Fleet Corporation during World War I.*

*Like many of his wealthy contemporaries, Kirby believed that power naturally followed wealth, and he was suspicious of any social or political movement that threatened the elites' position of power and influence. Except for a brief time during the 1920s, Kirby was a lifelong conservative Democrat. He typically denounced labor movements as socialistic. A man who often viewed himself a generous employer, Kirby believed that labor unions were an abomination because they supposedly inflamed the passions of otherwise contented and hardworking people. He was opposed to Franklin Roosevelt's New Deal, believing that it would destroy traditional American values. In an effort to challenge Roosevelt, Kirby helped to organize the Southern Committee to Uphold the Constitution and contributed large sums of money and time to other anti-New Deal organizations. Unfortunately for Kirby, he went bankrupt in 1933, ending active control of his lumber company and the Kirby Petroleum Company, which he founded in 1920. Still, Kirby continued to sit on the boards of both companies until his death in November 9, 1940. John Henry Kirby's life illustrates well the possibilities open to a few ambitious young men in Texas between 1880s and the 1920s. Unfortunately, not all could take advantage of their circumstances and most poor farm boys did not rise up to be a Paul Bunyan, but instead, remained poor and mostly forgotten in the annals of Texas history.*

# Myth & Legend

## African Americans and Voting in the Late Nineteenth Century

*Were African Americans in Texas legally disenfranchised during the late nineteenth century? The answer to this question is no, but one must also add certain qualifiers. African Americans gained the legal right to vote following Congress's passage and enforcement of the Reconstruction Acts in 1867. As a result, in July 1867, 20 whites and 150 blacks attended the Republican convention in Houston and called on their party to support free public education and free homesteads from public lands. This marked the beginning of black Republicanism in the Lone Star State. Even in the face of violence and intimidation by the Ku Klux Klan and ex-Confederates, many African-American men registered to participate in their first election—the 1868 referendum on holding a new constitutional convention. During the referendum, African-Americans voters and their white allies ensured that a new state constitutional convention would be held. Later, at the Republican-dominated convention, ten black delegates (along with eighty white delegates) helped to forge a constitution that would pave the way for Texas's readmission to the Union in March 1870.*

*African Americans continued to exercise their political voice by participating in statewide elections in 1869, electing a number of African Americans to the Twelfth Legislature. Serving in both the house and senate, black politicians helped pass legislation that led to the development of a new public school system and that led to economic improvements throughout the state. Additionally, the members of the Twelfth Legislature ratified the Fourteenth and Fifteenth Amendments to the U.S. Constitution.*

*The Reconstruction era ended in Texas when Democrat Richard Coke defeated incumbent Edmund J. Davis in the gubernatorial election of 1873. With Democrats regaining control of the state government, the number of blacks serving in the legislature dropped dramatically as did the number of African Americans going to the polls. The decline in participation was directly related to the extralegal activities of ex-Confederates, conservative Democrats, and white supremacists. Nevertheless, African Americans still had a legal right to vote.*

*Throughout the remainder of the nineteenth century, African-Americans voters tried to maintain their political voice increasing their involvement in the Republican Party, creating alliances with factions of the Democratic Party, and collaborating with third parties. None of these proved very effective, and to make matters worse, African Americans were migrating to other states that held greater economic and political promise. During this period, the black population in Texas fell from 31 percent of the total population to 20 percent. Despite their decline in population, African Americans were able to prevent white conservative factions from gaining control of the Republican Party and pushing them* out. Norris Wright Cuney, an astute leader of the black Republicans, was the recognized leader of the party between early 1880s and 1897. Following his death, African Americans began to lose control of the party. The primary reason for their diminishing influence was the struggle among black leaders to replace Cuney and the success of conservative white Republicans to obtain control of the party.

Alliances with factions in the Democratic Party presented less opportunity for African-American voters, especially considering that the majority of Democrats believed in the idea of white supremacy. Nevertheless, blacks sometimes pledged their support for Democrats who were disgruntled with the party's mainstream. For example, in 1892, Cuney urged black Texans to cast their ballots for Democratic George Clark, the conservative gubernatorial candidate who was challenging the incumbent James Hogg. Unfortunately, for Clark only about half the black population voted for him, and Hogg won the election relatively easy. Yet, the larger point remains, African Americans still had the legal right to go to the polls.

Alliances with third party political movements proved even more fruitless. The Greenback Party that focused on the economic conditions of Texas farmers attracted a significant number of rural black voters in 1878. A little over a decade later, the People's Party also enjoyed the support of African Americans. In the gubernatorial election of 1896, approximately 50 percent of black voters in Texas supported the Populist candidate. This swell of support came from the educational efforts of Colored Farmers' Alliance, the organizational efforts of black political leaders, such as John B. Rayner, and the Populist platform that addressed a number of issues important to African Americans.

Unfortunately, African-American's ability to vote was severely limited after the turn of the century. Black Texans' participation at the polls had been stifled slowly during the last decades of the nineteenth century by white's use of violence (lynching some 300 to 500 African Americans), the growth of public segregation, and the push for legislators to pass poll taxes. Additionally, gerrymandering diluted black voting power throughout the state and drastically reduced the number of black legislators. In 1902, the state authorized a poll tax that tended to weigh heaviest on impoverished farmers. As a result, many African Americans found that they were unable to pay the newly imposed poll tax, essentially disenfranchising them. Furthermore, in 1903 and 1905, Democratic political leaders tightened the voter registration laws, and local party leaders adopted the use of the all-white primary. Democratic actions basically led to the disenfranchisement of African Americans, especially considering that the candidates who won the Democratic primary were ensured victory in the general election. Nevertheless, African Americans who were able to pay their poll taxes could still exercise their vote in the general election. Therefore, black voters maintained the right to vote beginning in 1868, but practically speaking, the African-American political voice in Texas elections was stifled throughout much of the nineteenth century and almost completely silenced at the beginning of the twentieth century.

## Suggestions for Further Reading

Allen, Ruth Alice. *Chapters in the History of Organized Labor in Texas.* University of Texas Publication 4143, Austin, 1941.

Barnes, Donna A. *Farmers in Rebellion: The Rise and Fall of the Southern Farmers Alliance and People's Party in Texas.* Austin: University of Texas Press, 1984.

Barr, Alwyn. *Black Texans: A History of African Americans in Texas, 1528-1971.* Norman: University of Oklahoma Press, 1996.

____. *Reconstruction to Reform: Texas Politics, 1876-1906.* Austin: University of Texas Press, 1971.

Cantrell, Gregg. *Feeding the Wolf: John B. Rayner and the Politics of Race, 1850-1918.* Wheeling, Illinois: Harlan Davidson, Inc., 2001.

Green, James R. *Grass Roots Socialism: Radical Movements in the Southwest, 1865-1943.* Baton Rouge: Louisiana State University Press, 1978.

Hare, Maud Cuney. *Norris Wright Cuney: A Tribute of the Black People.* New York: Crisis, 1913.

Martin, Roscoe C. *The People's Party in Texas: A Study in Third Party Politics.* Austin: University of Texas Bulletin No. 3308, 1933.

Maxwell, Robert S, and Robert D. Baker, *Sawdust Empire: The Texas Lumber Industry, 1830-1940.* College Station: Texas A&M University Press, 1983.

McMath, Robert C., Jr. *Populist Vanuguard: A History of the Southern Farmer's Alliance.* Chapel Hill: University of North Carolina Press, 1975.

Reed, S. G. *A History of the Texas Railroads.* Houston: St. Clair, 1941; reprint, New York: Arno, 1981.

Rhinehart, Marilyn D. *A Way of Work and a Way of Life: Coal Mining in Thurber, Texas, 1888-1926.* College Station: Texas A&M University Press, 1992.

Spratt, John S. *The Road to Spindletop: Economic Change in Texas, 1975-1901.* Dallas: Southern Methodist University Press, 1955.

Williams, Patrick G. *Beyond Redemption: Texas Democrats after Reconstruction.* College Station: Texas A&M University Press, 2007.

**IDENTIFICATION:** Briefly describe each term.

"migratory industries"
Galveston Screwmen's Benevolent Association
Knights of Labor
Great Southwest Strike of 1886
American Federation of Labor
Cowboy Strike of 1883
Patrons of Husbandry
Constitution of 1876
Richard B. Hubbard
Texas A&M University
subtreasury plan
Greenback Party
Beef Bonanza
John Ireland
Prohibition Party

**MULTIPLE CHOICE:** Choose the correct response.

1. All the following challenged Democratic authority in the state, EXCEPT:
   A. Greenback Party
   B. Populists
   C. Oran M. Roberts
   D. Farmers' Alliance

2. Between 1870 and 1882, the Texas and Pacific Railroad Company received approximately _____ acres in land grants from the state.
   A. 5,167,000 acres
   B. 1,000,000 acres
   C. 516,700 acres
   D. 10,000,000 acres

3. Which one of the following was the leading non-agricultural industry in Texas between 1874 and 1900?
   A. cotton production
   B. railroads
   C. ship building
   D. oil

4. Between 1865 and 1885, Texas cowboys trailed more than _____ million head to markets outside of the state.
   A. ten
   B. twenty
   C. five
   D. two

5. When the Democrats regained complete control of the state government from Republicans in 1874, they immediately:
   A. set out to destroy the radical's Constitution of 1869.
   B. to find ways to continue Republican policies.
   C. to prosecute Governor E. J. Davis for crimes against the state.
   D. to enact anti-business legislation that hurt the railroad industry.

6. In the decades following the Civil War, _____ increased dramatically.
   A. the number of farmers who owned their own land
   B. the number of tenant farmers and sharecroppers
   C. the number of people receiving government aid
   D. the number of state universities

7. The Grange focused all of the following, EXCEPT:
   A. solving the problems of inadequate education
   B. helping farmers deal with social isolation
   C. challenging railroad companies
   D. prohibition

8. In 1879, members organized the Alliance as a:
   A. Political machine for farmers and laborers.
   B. Official branch of the Greenback Party
   C. secret, non-political, self-help organization for people living in rural communities, somewhat similar to the structure of the Grange.
   D. Official branch of the Democratic Party.

9. The subtreasury plan included all the following, EXCEPT:
   A. The new plan called on the federal government to create warehouse storage centers for nonperishable agricultural crops such as cotton.
   B. The new plan helped farmers increase prices for their crops by calling on farmers to increase production of nonperishable crops such as cotton.
   C. At harvest, farmers could store their crops in the government warehouses and receive government loans of up to 80 percent of the current market value of the raw product.
   D. The loan would be issued in the form of legal tender paper money—currently without the backing of gold or silver—and would carry a modest annual interest rate of two percent.

10. Which statement best describes the Republican Party in Texas between 1874 and 1900?
    A. Republicans managed to win a few local and state offices but were not a powerful force in Texas politics.
    B. African Americans abandoned the party after Governor Davis died.
    C. Even though the Republicans were unable to elect a governor during this period, they maintained enormous influence in the state legislature.
    D. The Republican party was absorbed by the Farmers' Alliance and ceased to exist for a number of decades in Texas.

## Economic and Political Reforms, 1874-1890

**TRUE/FALSE:** Indicate whether each statement is true or false.

1. By 1880, industrial production exceeded agricultural production in Texas.

2. By 1900, railroad companies had constructed more than 8,000 miles of track in the state, making railroad construction one of the state's leading nonagricultural industries.

3. Between 1874 and 1900, the most common industry in Texas was flour and grist mills.

4. When former Governor E. J. Davis died in 1883, John B. Rayner, an African American politician from Hempstead, became the head of the Republican Party.

5. Governor Roberts' administration funded educational and social programs that created large deficits in the state treasury.

6. Texas Agricultural and Mechanical school opened its doors on October 4, 1871.

7. One of the Democrats top priorities in 1874 was to amend the Constitution of 1869.

8. Fence cutting wars was not a major problem in Texas cattle country.

9. Richard B. Hubbard won the gubernatorial election of 1878 because Texans were disappointed with the fiscal policies of Governor Oran Roberts.

10. Prairie View Normal Institute (Prairie View A&M University) became the first public black college in Texas and the second oldest state supported institution of higher learning.


**MATCHING:** Match the response in column A with the item in column B.

1. John Henry Kirby
2. Lyne T. Barret
3. Norris Wright Cuney
4. Blue Devils, Owls, and Javelinas
5. Prairie View Normal School
6. "Wets"
7. Mathis Schnell
8. Charles William Macune
9. "free grass"
10. Richard Coke

A. fence cutters
B. benefitted from the Peabody Fund
C. leader of the Farmers' Alliance
D. lumber tycoon
E. successful African-American businessman and Republican politician
F. drilled first successful oil well in Texas
G. opposed prohibition
H. originally contracted to build new capitol building in Austin
I. first Redeemer governor in Texas
J. open range cattle operation

**ESSAY QUESTIONS:**

1. Discuss the evolution of the Grange movement in Texas. What was its original goals and how did those goals change over time?

2. Discuss the impact of the Greenback Party, the Farmers' Alliance, and the Republican Party on state politics during the late nineteenth century.

3. Explain the economic transformations taking place in Texas between 1874 and 1900.

4. Explain the challenges that the Democratic Party confronted during the final decades of the nineteenth century.

# Chapter 10

# The Populist Movement, 1890-1900

*Prelude: The Southern Mercury—Voice of the Populist Movement in Texas*

*A common refrain one often hears is that the pen is mightier than the sword. In this spirit, E. G. Rust created the* **Southern Mercury**, *a newspaper published in Dallas between 1886 and 1907. The origins of the paper actually dated to 1882, with the publication of the Dallas Mercury. Three years later, the newspaper had aligned with the Texas Farmers' Alliance, and by late 1886, Rust had changed the name to the* **Southern Mercury.** *During that same year, at the Farmers' Alliance state convention in Cleburne, the Dallas-based newspaper replaced the* **Jacksboro Rural Citizen** *as the official journal of the organization. The paper's circulation increased as a result of its new affiliation with the Farmers' Alliance. In 1887, the paper, which was published weekly, reportedly had a circulation of 5,460; in 1889 that number had grown to 30,000. Also, the* **Southern Mercury** *went through a number of editors between 1886 and 1891, including J. P. Burnett, L. S. Thayer, and Samuel H. Dixon. Like the alliance that it represented, the* **Southern Mercury** *officially was nonpartisan, though it generally was noted that the editors favored the policies of the reform wing of the Democratic Party. In the early 1890s, however, the newspaper was affected by a political split in the Texas Farmers' Alliance. The main source of contention between the members was whether or not to support the re-election of Governor James S. Hogg or to turn to third-party political leaders who might bring greater political reform to Texas. As a result of the split, Milton Park became the new editor of the paper, replacing Dixon who was an opponent of Governor Hogg. In 1891, the newspaper also became a member of the National Reform Press Association, an organization of newspaper men advocating reform movements and the creation of new political party. A year later, the* **Southern Mercury** *fully supported the newly created People's party, although the paper continued to be the voice of the Texas Farmers' Alliance.*

*As the official newspaper of the Texas Farmers' Alliance, the* **Southern Mercury** *generally published at least one page of news that organizational members would find useful, including a list of local political leaders, the place and times of Alliance speaking engagements, reports and proceedings of county meetings, and any changes in state policies that the Alliance deemed important. The remainder of the paper consisted of editorials, articles, letters, relating to vari-*

ous political issues. Dominating the pages of the **Southern Mercury** were articles related to the subtreasury plan, a greenback monetary system, land reform, and public ownership of the railroads and communication systems. Furthermore, the newspaper printed articles that interpreted state and national economic, social and political activities, usually from the perspectives of the Alliance's antimonopoly, fiat monetary policies. Occasionally, the editors carried articles related to women and children, general information on farming, coverage of events taking place in Washington, D. C., and fictional literature. Between 20 and 25 percent of the paper was dedicated to advertisements.

The peak of the **Southern Mercury's** influence was between 1891 and 1896, when it became one of the most important reform publications in the United States. By 1896, the paper's circulation swelled to over 40,000 subscribers. In 1894, the **Southern Mercury** became the official voice of the Texas People's Party, though, at the same time, it also maintained it distinction as the official paper of the Texas Farmers' Alliance. The **Southern Mercury** emerged in the midst of political turmoil and hitched its future prosperity with the Texas Farmers' Alliance and Texas People's Party. As long as these institutions commanded the public's attention, the newspaper seemingly would continue to grow. Unfortunately, the People's Party and Alliance proved to be short-lived.

The conservative policies of the Democratic Party in the years following Reconstruction were not acceptable to many Texans. Downtrodden and convinced that their impoverished conditions were unfair and unjust, these individuals believed that government intervention was the only way to improve their economic condition. Even as the economy improved during the 1880s, growing dissatisfaction among agrarians and poor laborers increased. By 1890, the increasing demand for political and economic reform could no longer be ignored. During the last decade of the nineteenth century and the first decade of the twentieth century, the legislature passed laws that regulated business, expanded education, altered the electoral process, and aided the state's transition into a modern society. At the forefront of these changes were agrarian protesters. Calling for the expansion of democracy and economic equality, radicals among the agrarians organized the People's Party (Populist Party) and challenged the Democrats for control of the state government, while those who were more conservative in their views attempted to enact reform measures within the Democratic Party itself.

**Foundations of the People's Party**

During the Civil War and continuing throughout the last quarter of the nineteenth century, Texas suffered economic alienation from the rest of the country. Approximately 80 percent of Americans still lived in rural areas, and the percentage of Texans living on farms was even greater. However, between 1865 and 1900, the United States continued to experience the effects of the Industrial Revolution, which made towns and cities the center of economic development. As the northeastern states experienced a boom in their economies, agrarian Southerners failed to keep pace with their northern brethren, especially in terms of urbanization and industrialization.

"Renters." Many Texas farmers rented a farm for a year before moving, living almost nomadic lifestyles. Children from five years of age picked cotton and helped with the farm work. Location: Corsicana, Texas, October 1913. Photo credit: Library of Congress

In many ways, Texans continued to depend on an early nineteenth century economy, which was property based and void of any real signs of capitalist development. The merchants and bankers operating in the state after the Civil War were neither industrial-minded nor productive. Even though they were able to gain control of the state's land, Texas capitalists failed to produce any real measure of growth concerning the development of new industries. This essential fact alienated Texans from citizens living in the Northeast.

To complicate the scenario, beginning in 1873, a number of economic and financial factors tended to overwhelm small farmers throughout the country. The increasing mechanization of farming and the rising trend of mass production made it nearly impossible for subsistence farmers to survive—the farmers needed cash to keep their land out of foreclosure and to purchase the needed manufactured goods that would make their farms more productive. Government policy at both the national and state level centered on reestablishing and maintaining the gold standard, while recurring economic depression tightened credit. Furthermore, in foreign agricultural markets countries such as India and Egypt began producing large quantities of cotton, leading to overproduction in the global market and a dramatic decrease in cotton prices. Under such circumstances, southern cotton farmers, including those in Texas, were devastated financially. Other commodities produced in the state experienced similar declines. In fact, prices for commodities produced in Texas, when adjusted for inflation, were generally lower in the late nineteenth century than they were 100 years earlier. Even though there was enough capital to finance industrial growth, there was not enough to finance industrial development as well as agricultural pursuits. In a world growing increasingly dependent on industry, agriculture generally suffered.

In Texas, farmers were economically tied to one crop—cotton. More than any other crop, cotton connected Texans with the industrialized world, with half the crop going to European markets and the other half departing for the northern textile industries. In both markets, raw cotton prices continuously fell during the late nineteenth century, bringing thirty-one cents per pound in 1865, eleven cents between 1875 and 1884, and just five cents in 1898. Texas farmers would have been better served by diversifying their crop production, but they found themselves bound to cotton because it was the only marketable commodity they knew. Adding to the farmers' plight was the fact that the more cotton they produced, the lower prices fell. Taxes on their lands remained constant and had to be paid in specie currency, and the cost of the farmers' requisite manufactured goods increased substantially. Unfortunately, farmers became trapped, virtual prisoners on their own farms. Unlike agrarians in the northern states, most small farmers in Texas could not escape to nearby large cities where emerging industries promised new types of employment. Moreover, they possessed little money with which to leave the state. Thus, in late nineteenth century Texas, hundreds of thousands of impoverished whites and blacks attempted to scratch a living from the exhausted soil.

While the availability of cheap land in Texas attracted migrant farmers from areas outside the state, the low land cost did little to help suffering agriculturalists. With aspirations to acquire their own land, many farmers migrated to Texas from other southern and midwestern states. However, most arrived to the state too poor to purchase land, and many of them soon found themselves trapped in the same economic nightmare that they thought they had left behind. During their first year in Texas, these migrant farmers generally had to borrow money to put their first crop in the ground. To this end, some agrarians mortgaged their land (if they owned any), or, as was more common, some put up their next crop as collateral. As time passed, credit became more difficult for agrarians to acquire, especially considering that poor farmers represented a high risk to creditors.

African Americans at work in a cotton field with the overseer on horseback in the background. near Dallas, Texas, c. 1900-1910
Photo credit:
Library of Congress

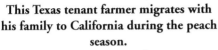
This Texas tenant farmer migrates with his family to California during the peach season.
Photo credit: Library of Congress

Eventually, farmers found themselves trapped in a form of debt peonage. The impact was devastating. Whereas most white farmers in 1860 had owned their own land, the majority had become tenants and sharecroppers by 1880. Those who were able to avoid tenancy worked most of the year with little or no return. As Texans were being forced into something resembling serfdom, a large group of people who traditionally thought of themselves as free and equal was increasingly becoming a new American peasantry.

While white agrarians suffered in this oppressive system, blacks endured even greater hardships. African Americans were not only trapped in the same tenancy and sharecropping system, but they also had to tolerate racial prejudices that often limited their economic opportunities. Nevertheless, throughout the state many black Texans thrived during this era, creating island communities known as "freedom colonies." Some scholars estimate that perhaps as many as 25 percent of the black population in Texas were landowners. Inside the freedom colonies, blacks tended to prosper more economically than their counterparts who lived in isolation among whites.

Despite Texas's ties to agriculture, the state government was not hostile to commerce or business. The idea that industry and farming were mutually hostile, or that the railroads represented an obstacle to progress, was an idea that developed over time. Texans, like most Americans, possessed an antipathy towards corporations, not because of what corporations did but because they believed that business enterprises should not be granted full protection under the laws. Many people claimed that the government had placed the rights of big business before those of citizens. When farmers became increasingly impoverished, they often blamed land companies, railroads, and banks for their misery.

The People's Party was nothing less than the continued manifestation of the agrarian protest movements that preceded it—the Grange in the 1860s, the Greenback Party in the 1870s, and the Farmers' Alliance in the 1880s. These earlier movements primarily functioned as quasi-political parties, dividing their time between political activism and serving the needs of the farmers directly by organizing cooperatives and social events.

Unlike the earlier movements, however, the People's Party (also known as the Populist Party) was a full-fledged political party that sought to bring about reform by winning public office and by enacting legislation that would prove beneficial to the majority of Texas farmers. In addition to receiving support from disgruntled members of the Democratic Party (who called themselves the Jeffersonian Democrats), the People's Party also drew strength from Republicans and Prohibitionists, but the Populist electorate primarily consisted of small farmers, sheep ranchers, and laborers. The party's major demands were fairly straightforward, calling for the protection of land from speculators and foreign owners, for regulation of the railroads and other corporations, and for an increase in the amount of money in circulation. No less important were the party's minor demands that included tax reform and trust regulation, popular election of officials, lower salaries for public officials, direct legislation through referendums, the popular recall of ineffective politicians, and proportional representation.

Support for the People' Party in the South, especially in Texas, was tied to the activities of the Southern Farmers' Alliance, an organization that could trace its birth to South-Central Texas. In his presidential address at the Alliance's national convention in 1889, Charles W. Macune stated that the impoverished conditions of the farmer and the depressed state of the American economy had resulted from an insufficient supply of currency in circulation. His remedy was the subtreasury plan, which called on the government to issue loans directly to agrarians. In essence, Macune's plan called on the government to build warehouses, known as subtreasuries, in counties that produced $500,000 or more in commercial crops, especially focusing on cotton producing areas. When farmers harvested their crops, they could deposit them in the subtreasuries and receive a federal loan in the amount of 80 percent of the total value of the crops. Afterwards, the farmer had a one-year window of time to sell his deposited crops and pay off his government loan. To cover the cost of storing the farmers' crops, the government charged the farmers who participated in the program a 1 percent per annum fee on their loans, plus a small storage fee. If the farmer was unsuccessful in selling his crops, the government confiscated his crops and sold them at a special auction. The subtreasury plan would basically create a fiat currency system based on the annual demands for farmers' crops, rather than leaving them at the mercy of a credit system that fluctuated based on gold and silver reserves. After endorsing Macune's subtreasury plan, the Alliance members discussed the best approach for enacting it. The majority felt that it was best to work through the Democratic Party, but a strong minority believed that it might be necessary to create a new political party. To appease both sides of the debate, Macune suggested that the Alliance send delegates to St. Louis in February 1892 to discuss the viability of creating a third-party movement with other reform organizations. Prior to the meeting, reformers could attempt to secure economic reform legislation through the Democratic Party.

While the Alliance was reluctant to embark on the creation of a new political party, other reform organizations in the South were not. In May 1891, a national convention in Cincinnati, Ohio, of approximately 400 delegates from different reform organizations established the People's Party. To gain the support of Southerners, the delegates adopted a platform that was identical to the Alliance platform of 1889. In addition, they postponed the nominations for the forthcoming elections until after the Alliance's St. Louis convention, hoping that the southern states that were poorly represented at the Cincinnati convention would support the People's Party. The plan worked, especially considering that the Democratic Party continued to shun the Alliance members, who they considered radical troublemakers. Shortly after the convention in Cincinnati, Newton W. Finley, chairman of the Texas Democratic executive committee, issued an ultimatum to the members of the Texas Alliance, stating that they must abandon the support of the subtreasury plan or forfeit their right to vote in the upcoming Democratic primaries. Rather than abandon their principles, the Texas Alliance endorsed the newly-formed People's Party.

The success of the People's Party was closely linked to the emergence and growth of the Farmers' Alliance, a grass-roots agrarian movement that originated in Texas. Beginning in the late 1880s, the Alliance steadily became more politically active, believing that the Democratic Party no longer championed issues important to small farmers in the state. On August 18, 1891, leaders in the Farmers' Alliance organized the Texas People's Party. The Populists, as party members were known, proved effective organizers. In accord with the organizational activities associated with the Alliance, Populists created support clubs, held conventions, formed committees, and provided extensive educational campaign designed to inform their constituents on issues and causes associated with their new party. Through such strategies, the party leaders quickly attracted new followers to their cause. It became commonplace during political campaigns to see Populist speakers waging an oratorical and literary war against Democratic candidates in the state. Weekly newspapers, such as the *Texas Advocate* and the *Southern Mercury*, became the voice of the party. By 1895, Texans in 70 counties had access to approximately 100 newspapers that favored the People's Party.

**Governor Hogg and the Democratic Response to Populism**

Beginning in 1886, James Stephen Hogg was instrumental in setting the tone of Texas politics. In that year, Hogg had become the attorney general in Governor Lawrence Ross's administration. He seemed an unlikely choice, as Hogg stood in direct contrast to other leaders in the Democratic Party. Born to Joseph Lewis Hogg and Lucanda McMath Hogg in 1851 near the small East Texas town of Rusk, young James suffered great personal losses during the Civil War. His father, a brigadier general in the Confederate army, was killed in 1862, and his mother died the following year. Hogg and his two brothers were left with two older sisters to run the family plantation. Only through grit and determination were they able to maintain the family's property. The years following the war proved equally difficult. Throughout most of 1866, Hogg attended school at Tuscaloosa, Alabama. After returning to Texas, he worked as a typesetter in Andrew Jackson's newspaper office in Rusk. While working for the newspaper, Hogg perfected his spelling and improved his vocabulary. Eventually, the Hogg family estate had to be liquidated so the family could pay back taxes on their land and buy food, clothes, and books for his brothers who were studying law.

During the late 1860s, Hogg became a marked man while helping the sheriff at Quitman bring law and order to the town. During one episode, outlaws lured Hogg to the county line between Van Zandt and Smith Counties, shot him in the back, and left him for dead. Hogg, however, recovered from his wounds and returned again to newspaper work in Tyler. Between 1871 and 1873, he operated two newspaper offices—one in Longview and the other in Quitman. His papers often ran editorials that argued against subsidies for the railroads, condemned the corruption of President Grant's administra-

254   *Beyond Myths and Legends*

**Photograph shows bust portrait of James S. Hogg, Governor of Texas, 1891-1895. Photo credit: UTSA's Institute of Texan Cultures**

tion, and bemoaned local lawlessness. Hogg's newspaper experience provided him with the background for a sympathetic understanding of the problems of common people.

In 1873, Hogg became the justice of the peace in Quitman, a position that he held until 1875. Also in 1875, he studied law and was admitted to the bar. Hogg's political career began in earnest with a disappointing defeat in 1876, when John S. Griffith defeated him for a position in the Texas Senate. This proved to be Hogg's only defeat in a contest for public office. Two years later, he was elected county attorney for Wood County, a post he held until 1880, when he was elected as the district attorney for the old Seventh District. In 1884, prominent Democrats courted Hogg to run for Congress, but he declined, choosing instead to return to private life, practicing law in Tyler.

In 1886, Hogg's friends convinced him to run for Texas attorney general. After receiving the Democratic nomination, he easily won the election. As attorney general, Hogg encouraged new legislation to protect the lands set aside for public schools and institutional funds, enforced laws that stipulated railroad and land corporations must sell their holdings to settlers within a certain period of time, and succeeded in breaking up the illegal Texas Traffic Association. Railroad companies had formed this organization to affect collectively rail traffic by fixing rates and controlling competition. In addition, Hogg forced unscrupulous insurance companies either to leave the state or to engage only in legitimate business practices. Furthermore, he was one of the authors of the second state antitrust law in the nation, and he forced railroad companies to comply with Texas statutes. Finally, realizing that state government alone could not fulfill its obligations and protect the interests of the people from the railroad corporations, Hogg advocated the establishment of a railroad commission designated with the sole task of monitoring the railroad companies. In accordance with the attorney general's recommendation, in 1889 the Texas legislature approved a constitutional amendment that created the commission with its ratification resting with the voters in the November election the following year. In general, agrarians and laborers hailed Hogg as their champion, a Democrat committed to protecting the common man's economic interests against corrupt politicians and powerful corporations.

In 1890, Hogg sought the Democratic nomination for governor on a platform that called for the passage of the railroad commission amendment. Because he favored the passage of the amendment, Hogg received valuable support from a group of businessmen called the State Freight Rate Convention, as well as from the Farmers' Alliance, both groups wanting the regulation of rail rates. Despite opposition from the railroads and their political allies, Hogg won the nomination. In November, voters overwhelmingly elected James Hogg governor, and they ratified the amendment creating the railroad commission. With the passage of the amendment, the legislature in April 1891 established the Texas Railroad Commission and gave it the power to set railroad rates and fares. Originally, the commission consisted of three members who were appointed by the governor. The new body generated so much interest that John H. Reagan resigned his seat in the U.S. Senate to become the first chairman of the commission. In 1894, the legislature proposed and the voters ratified a second constitutional amendment that made the commissioners elected officials.

The Texas Railroad Commission had an immediate impact on the railroad industry. The commissioners were able to secure reductions in freight rates, and they claimed credit for increases in milling and manufacturing in the state. In an effort to restrain the commission from enforcing its orders, railroad companies filed suit against the railroad commission in 1892, which prevented the commissioners from performing their duties while the cases were brought to trial. The state finally won its legal battles with the railroads in July 1894, and the commission once again assumed its role in regulating rates. While the railroads and the state battled in court, the commission acquired additional authority. The legislature passed a law that limited the amount of stock that a railroad company might issue to an amount approximately equal to the value of the railroad.

The question of railroad politics divided the Democratic Party during the months leading up to the 1892 gubernatorial election. Railroad men and leading newspapers supported George Clark, a railroad attorney from Waco. Clark had adamantly opposed the railroad commission amendment in 1890. In 1891, the commission began monitoring the rates and operations of railroads, terminals, wharves, and express companies. Governor Hogg's first appointed railroad commissioners were John H. Reagan (chairman), William Pinckney McLean, and Lafayette L. Foster. Despite its initial success, however, Clark wanted to modify the structure of the agency, especially in the way the railroad commissioners were chosen, preferring that the commissioners be elected officials rather than appointed. If the commissioners were elected, the railroad companies would have an opportunity to place their men in office and to gain control of the agency. Clark also wanted the railroads to have the right to appeal the commission's decision in court. As might be assumed, Governor Hogg disagreed with Clark's assessment of the commission, using every opportunity to praise the agency. In August 1892 at the Democratic convention in Houston (known as the Street Car Barn Convention), Democrats divided into two factions—one group nominated Hogg, the other Clark. For the next two months the factions engaged in a bitter battle for the governorship. Although Clark received support of wealthy railroad men, a significant number of newspapers editors, and a limited number of Republicans, Hogg won re-election by a substantial majority. Clark could take some satisfaction in that his call to make the commission more democratic was answered. In 1894, the legislature made the agency's commissioners elected officials.

Governor Hogg supported other reform measures during his tenure as governor. At Hogg's suggestion, the legislature passed several laws—commonly referred to as "Hogg's laws"—that limited the rights of foreign and corporate land companies to own land in Texas, promoted prison reform, established a board of pardon advisors, extended the terms of public schools from four to six months, and provided additional funding to the University of Texas and Texas A&M College. He also devoted attention to the normal schools and supported teacher training scholarships. Furthermore, Hogg's own interest in Texas history prompted him to give the Texas State Library an annual appropriation of $500 to collect Texas historical data. He appointed his longtime friend Cadwell W. Raines as librarian of the State Library. Raines worked diligently to procure new historical materials and to preserve those already in the library's possession. In regards to race relations, Governor Hogg had a mixed record. For example, he signed a bill that made it legal for railroads to segregate facilities for blacks and whites. Yet, he also organized "Negro Hogg Clubs" to attract African-American voters to his campaign. Furthermore, he campaigned against racial violence and urged the legislature to pass an anti-lynching law. Governor Hogg retired from public office in 1895. In many ways, Hogg had embraced reform as a significant part of his administration, making him a symbol of the Texas reform movement.

## The Elections of 1892: A Promising Start

Even though Governor Hogg initiated many reforms, the Democrats did not go far enough to please the more radical agrarian in the Farmers' Alliance, especially those who supported public ownership of the railroads. Hogg's failure to name a member of the Alliance to the railroad commission enraged many radical agrarians. Hogg and the Democrats had refused to embrace the Alliance's subtreasury plan, and in 1891, Democratic leaders purged from the party those Alliance men who supported that economic proposal. The Farmers' Alliance, thus disenchanted with Governor Hogg's reforms and snubbed by the Democratic Party, joined the People's Party and set out to gain control of the state government. To accomplish their political objectives, the Populists nominated candidates for public office in 1892 who posed real threats to the dominance of the Democrats.

To divert the attention away from the Alliance's subtreasury plan, Democrats sponsored a more conservative economic reform, primarily the coinage of silver to expand the money supply. In 1873, the federal government returned to the gold standard, a monetary system in which the standard economic unit is based on a specific quantity of gold. In the same year, Congress passed the Coinage Act, which demonetized silver. Both actions were designed to correct financial problems that resulted from the Civil War. During that conflict, inflation peaked, making it difficult for the federal government to pay for the war in specie (gold and silver). As a result, paper money, known as greenbacks, was declared legal tender in 1862. This temporarily solved the nation's financial problems because the government could print sufficient amounts of paper money to finance the war effort. Following the Civil War, however, Congress desired to restore the metallic (gold and silver) standard and to set rates of exchange between greenbacks and specie at pre-war prices. When the gold standard was restored, the government severely contracted the supply of greenbacks and ushered in a major economic crisis, a financial panic. While many Democrats favored the federal government's action, some expressed opposition. Throughout the nation, including Texas, a political war emerged between bimetallists, goldbugs (sound-money men who supported the gold standard), and a third group who criticized all forms of fiat monetary systems. In Texas during the early 1890s, Governor James Hogg led the bimetallists faction, while George W. Clark, a prominent Democratic politician in the state, led the gold standard advocates. During the gubernatorial campaign of 1892, Clark, who ran as a candidate with the support of railroad men, accused the incumbent governor of bowing before third-party interests that supported the bimetallism. Once Clark realized that he could not win the Democratic nomination for governor, he and his supporters broke ranks with the party and ran on an independent ticket. Third-party activists, including Harry Tracy and H.S.P. "Stump" Ashby, both leaders in the Farmers' Alliance, criticized both goldbugs and bimetallists. These fringe political groups generally supported the development of an irredeemable fiat currency system, such as the Populists' subtreasury plan. By 1892, calls for a flexible monetary system led many members of the Farmers' Alliance to join the People's Party.

Despite growing support, the People's Party experienced limited success in the 1892 elections. The Populists nominated Thomas Nugent as their gubernatorial candidate. Nugent, a native of Louisiana, had moved to Texas in 1861. He joined the Confederate army in 1862 and served with distinction, especially during the fighting at the Battle of Shiloh. Returning to Texas after the war, Nugent entertained the idea of becoming a Methodist minister. However, he soon became disillusioned with preaching and found his calling as a lawyer. He was admitted to the State Bar of Texas in 1870, and after briefly spending time in Austin and Meridian, Nugent settled in Stephenville, where he opened a successful law practice. In 1879, Governor Roberts appointed Nugent to the 29th District Court, to which he was reelected twice. He served on the central committee of prohibition forces, which lost the statewide referendum in 1887. Democrats considered nominating Nugent for the Texas Court of Appeals, but he failed to win the party's nomination. In 1888, a nonpartisan convention of the Alliance nominated him for the state Supreme Court, and the fragile Union Labor Party endorsed their choice. After losing the election, Nugent retired from the bench in July 1888 and moved to El Paso for health reasons. He returned to Stephenville in 1890, and in 1891 moved to Fort Worth where he practiced law until his death in 1895.

Although he was unanimously selected as the Populists' choice for governor, Nugent personally believed the 1892 canvass was hopelessly lost; yet, he still campaigned vigorously for office. Results of the 1892 gubernatorial election proved Nugent correct. Nugent placed third in a field of five candidates, winning approximately 25 percent of the vote. In the presidential election, Populist James B. Weaver won 24 percent of the Texas vote, while Democrat Grover Cleveland won 57 percent. The party's poor showing in the statewide election can partly be explained by its failure to build a coalition of white and black voters, as well as the popularity of James Hogg who favored some Populist goals. In 1892 Populist leaders convinced John B. Rayner, a noted black politician from the small town of Calvert, to organize the black vote behind the People's Party. Despite making numerous stump speeches, Rayner experienced only limited success in attracting black voters to the new party. Most African Americans were unwilling to abandon the Republican Party, which they had supported since emancipation. The rank and file members of the People's Party also proved to be another obstacle to biracial politics. Whites could not set aside their racial prejudices, and when confronted with the choice of a white supremacy or a Populist governor, they chose the former.

The Populists also failed to meet two critical challenges. First, they were unsuccessful in convincing the majority of voters that the party's reforms were necessary and justifiable. Second, they were not able to convince the voters that they could win the election. Many voters who might have otherwise voted for the Populists simply cast ballots for the less objectionable of the old-party candidates. In the 1892 gubernatorial election, these voters believed that if they voted for Populist candidate Nugent, they would split the reform vote which in turn might lead to Clark's victory, an outcome that many potential third-party voters were unwilling to chance. In the national election, most voters realized that the People's Party stood little chance for victory. There was also very little difference between the Republican and the Democratic presidential candidates. Texans generally voted for the same political party as they did in the gubernatorial election.

## The Elections of 1894: Sustained Hopes

Under President Grover Cleveland's administration, the economy of the country continued to decline. As a result, agrarian discontent and protest in Texas gained strength. Democrats in the state realized that its party might not survive another split ticket in the forthcoming gubernatorial election. At the 1894 Democratic convention, party leaders agreed that factions would settle their differences within the party, instead of dividing the party by running an independent candidate. To ease tensions within the party, the convention adopted a platform that did not contain any monetary reform demands. However, in a strange twist of fate, the convention nominated the free-silver reformer Charles Culberson for governor. In fact, a majority of the nominations for state office went to reform candidates, creating an interesting situation wherein the candidates essentially opposed the platform of the party that had nominated them.

Populists campaigned on the idea that voters could not expect the Democratic Party to pass reform measures, especially considering that it was running on a platform that ignored the critical issue of monetary reform. Many Texans agreed with the Populists. They elected 22 Populists candidates to the State House of Representatives and two Populists to the State Senate. Additionally, in the gubernatorial election, Culberson won the race with 49 percent of the vote, but Thomas Nugent had polled well, receiving 36 percent of the vote, an eleven-point increase from 1892. The increase might have actually been more, but Democrats engaged in dirty politics and illegal electoral practices. For example, penitentiary employees in Huntsville who refused to pledge support for the Democratic Party were fired from their jobs. As news of this and similar events became known, state employees fell into the Democratic ranks. Similar types of intimidation were also witnessed in the private sector, where employers forced their employees to support Democratic candidates. The African-American population was particularly vulnerable to the Democrats' fraud and intimidation tactics. In fact, Culberson's margin of victory was supported by an unusually large Democratic vote in heavily black-populated counties. In contrast to the results in

Texas, the People's Party at the national level did poorly in the 1894 mid-term elections. The party was only able to win 40 percent of the vote in 33 of the 350 congressional seats up for reelection. This was a serious blow to the party, especially considering that reform of the currency system would have to originate in Congress.

**The Elections of 1896: The Final Curtain Call**

While the 1896 campaign between bimetallist reformers and gold-standard Democrats continued in Texas, the national party chairman for the People's Party, Herman E. Taubeneck, became convinced that the only means by which his party could achieve monetary reform was through compromise with one of the established national parties. Therefore, he suggested that the Populists embrace the bimetallists' position on free coinage of silver, abandoning the Populists' subtreasury plan. James H. "Cyclone" Davis, a noted Texas Populist, agreed with Taubeneck, even though many party members opposed his compromise plan. Despite strong opposition, Taubeneck gained increasing support at the national convention of the People's Party in 1896. It seemed that Taubebeck was on the threshold of victory when an unanticipated political disaster foiled his efforts. Democrats changed their position, endorsing bimetallism and nominating William Jennings Bryan, a noted free-silverite, for president. Because Taubeneck did not have time to develop a new strategy and because many Populists supported Bryan and the Democratic Party's new platform, convention delegates endorsed Bryan as the People's Party presidential candidate, creating a "fusion ticket" with the Democrats, meaning that both political parties would support the same presidential candidate. Many in the party disagreed with the idea of a fusion ticket, fearing that the Democratic Party might eclipse their own party in the immediate future. The Texas delegation at the People's Party convention were especially adamant in their opposition to the fusion ticket. In fact, all 103 Texas delegates cast their votes for Colonel Seymour F. Norton, an old-time member of the Greenback Party from Chicago, Illinois, and a fierce opponent to Bryan. While the Texas delegation failed to prevent their party from endorsing Bryan, the Anti-fusionists were able to avoid a complete fusion ticket between the Populists and Democrats when they moved their party to nominate Tom Watson, a noted member of the People's Party from Georgia, as their vice-presidential candidate.

A week after the national convention, the Texas People's Party held its convention. The assembly applauded the efforts of Ashby and the "Immortal 103" anti-fusionists. To ensure that Watson was added to the Populist ticket in other states, members of the convention suggested sending a telegram to the other conventions, stating "No Watson, No Bryan." The state party treasurer and chairman of the platform and resolutions committees, Charles H. Jenkins, warned that sending such a telegram might fracture the party completely. Jenkins argued that the national convention had nominated Bryan and, like it or not, the nomination was binding. To his credit, Jenkins was able to delay the Texas convention's actions long enough that the issue became a moot point, since most of the other state conventions had already adjourned. Believing that the Democrats were threatening to destroy their party, some Texas Populists vowed to stay away from the polls rather than cast a ballot for a Democratic candidate.

Complicating matters further was the fact that many Texas newspaper editors began to spread rumors that Populists and Republicans in Texas were working together. According to these editors, the Populists' were trading their support for the Republican presidential candidate in exchange for Republican support of Populist candidates in state races. Essentially, the rumors claimed that a faction of the Populists had created a fusion party with the Republicans, a charge that leadership in the Texas People's Party denied. Ultimately, the Bryan-Watson ticket in the 1896 election capture a meager 15 percent of the statewide vote. Texas Populists blamed their national leaders and Taubeneck's fusion strategy for the party's poor performance. To prove its point, Texas Populists pointed out that its gubernatorial candidate, Jerome Kearby, received approximately 44 percent of the vote. However, Kearby's success was likely more attributable to the fact that the Republicans did not field a candidate; but instead, the Republican ballots listed the names of Populist candidates running for office, leaving the impression that the earlier news stories were more than just rumor.

**Populist Women**

As it evolved, the Populist Party drew strength from Texas women. In rural states, such as Texas, agrarian women often labored alongside their husbands and sons, shouldering part of the responsibility of family survival. Leaders of the Farmers' Alliance recognized the burdens that women endured on the farm, and they opened their membership to white rural women who were over sixteen years of age. By the end of the Alliance movement, approximately 25 percent of its members were women. Many of these women would later join the Populist Party.

Women's roles in the party varied. A number of them, such as Fannie Moss of Cleburne; Fannie Leak, an Austin physician; and Mary Clardy of Sulpher Springs, held offices in the Alliance. Others, including Bettie Gay of Columbus and Ellen Dabbs, a physician also from Sulpher Springs, were representatives at the organization's state and national conventions. More common, however, were the numerous women in small rural communities who supported the movement. Their families represented the heart and soul of the grass-roots movement, and they came from marginal families—tenants, poor landowners, teachers, preachers, and doctors operating farms in economically oppressed sections of the country. Collectively, this population supported the Alliance's (and later the Populists') desire to bring economic relief to the rural South. They also supported issues that were more of a concern to women than to men, such as women's suffrage and prohibition. In the early twentieth century, Populist women continued their struggle for economic, social, and political reform by helping to establish the foundations of the Progressive movement.

**The End of the Movement**

By the end of the century, division within the People's Party between the anti-fusion and fusion factions led to the Populists' demise. Voters slowly left the party, and many returned to the Democratic camp. In the 1898 elections, the Populist gubernatorial candidate, Barney Gibbs, received a mere 28 percent of the vote. In 1900, anti-fusionists left the national party and called for their own convention to be held in Cincinnati, Ohio. At the Texas convention, the majority of the Populists voted to send delegates to Cincinnati, but a minority, including key leaders in the party's national and state executive committees, bolted. The delegates of the regular People's Party convention in 1900 nominated Bryan as their presidential candidate and Charles Towne, a free-silver Republican, as vice president. Prior to the general election, Towne withdrew from the race, and the national executive committee simply accepted as their candidate Adlai Stevenson, the Democratic nominee for vice president. In supporting Stevenson, regular party members embraced a complete fusion ticket. Anti-fusionists, on the other hand, selected a straight Populist ticket, with Wharton Barker as president and Ignatius Donnelly as vice president. The move proved disastrous for the anti-fusionists, their candidates receiving only 5 percent of the vote in Texas. The Populists' gubernatorial candidate did not fair well either, receiving only 6 percent of the vote. Despite nominating candidates for governor in 1904 and 1908, support for the party continued to wane after 1900.

### *Afterward: The Southern Mercury's Fall from Stardom*

*In 1896, the* **Southern Mercury** *began a downward spiral that continued until the paper completely collapsed in 1907. During the 1896 elections, Populist candidates in Texas failed to gain control of the state government and William Jennings Bryan, the Democratic presidential candidate who had received Populists' support, was defeated by the Republican candidate, William McKinley. As the future political prospects for the People's Party crumbled, so too did the future of their Texas newspaper. Between 1895 and 1902, the* **Southern Mercury's** *circulation dropped from its height of 40,000 subscribers to just over 20,000. In 1899, the newspaper ceased being the official paper of the People's Party, though the editors of the paper continued to support Populist candidates. By 1908, the paper had ceased to exist. Like the People's Party, the* **Southern Mercury's** *time had come and gone. Texas was now entering a new century, one that seemingly no longer had room for third-party politics, or newspaper men who supported nineteenth-century agrarian reforms.*

# *Myth & Legend*

### Women's Political Participation in the Late Nineteenth Century

*A common perception among Texans today is that women did not begin participating in state and national politics until 1920 when Congress passed the Nineteenth Amendment that gave women the right to vote. If voting was the only form of political participation, then this assessment would be correct. However, voting only represents the most direct, formal method of participation in electoral politics. Women have been actively influencing the political process in Texas since the beginning of the state's history, but their political participation was particularly evident in the late nineteenth century. Scholars usually label women outsiders when discussing politics in the latter decades of the 1800s, especially considering that they did not have suffrage rights until after the turn of the century. Nevertheless, women in Texas were politically active. In a modern sense, women involved in Texas politics between 1870 and 1900 would have been identified as lobbyists, but in their own day they were often simply called reformers.*

*For the most part, Texas women promoted causes that related to family and community welfare. Representing the interests of the middle class, these women used voluntary associations and women's clubs to address a variety of issues, including prohibition, women's suffrage, and public education. To promote their cause, women activists pioneered many of the strategies that professional lobbyists use today. For example, they created greater awareness of their issues through educational campaigns that targeted the general public; they mounted extensive letter writing and petition campaigns to state legislators advocating policy changes; and they urged their male counterparts to vote out incumbents who were unsympathetic to their cause.*

*Texas women embraced many causes in the late nineteenth century, but prohibition was one of the first major issues that they united behind. In the 1880s, the Women's Christian Temperance Union (WCTU) united woman on the issue. Members of the WCTU argued that alcohol was the root of many social problems that directly affected women and children, including poverty and domestic violence that often occurred when husbands drank to excess. Women who began as temperance crusaders soon began to lobby the state legislature over other issues. For example, in 1887, Christian women lobbied to keep juveniles from being incarcerated with adult criminals. Later, in 1893, they asked lawmakers to require alcohol education in the public schools, and six years later they pushed legislators to pass a law forbidding the sale of cigarettes to minors. Additionally, they lobbied the legislature to increase the age of consent for minor girls from age ten to twelve in 1891, to age fifteen in 1895, and to eighteen in 1918.*

*Aside from their lobbying activities, Texas women actively participated in third party politics in the 1880s and 1890s. At the conventions of the Texas Prohibition Party in*

1886, and again in 1890, both Jenny B. Beauchamp and Mary M. Clardy were official members of the party's platform committee. Beauchamp even had the distinction of serving as a delegate to the party's national convention in 1887. Women were even more active in the Texas Farmers' Alliance. Some local chapters reported female membership in excess of 40 percent, a staggering figure considering that women were shunned from participation in the Republican and Democratic Parties. Furthermore, Texas was the only state where Alliance membership elected women to high office. Mary Clardy served as the association's assistant state lecturer and Fannie Moss served as its secretary-treasurer in 1892. Two years later, Frances Leak succeeded Moss. Ellen L. Dabbs and Bettie M. Gay also attended the National Farmers' Alliance convention in 1892, a historic meeting because it served as the genesis of the People's Party.

Naturally, Texas women also were involved in the crusade for women's suffrage rights. Suffragettes first organized in Texas when Rebecca Henry Hayes of Galveston, along with ten other women, most who were members of the WCTU, issued a call for a convention of like-minded women in April 1893. The following month, approximately fifty people, including both women and men, met in Dallas and created the first statewide female suffrage organization, the Texas Equal Rights Association (TERA). Hayes was elected as the organization's first president. TERA very quickly established branch offices in Denison, Dallas, Fort Worth, Taylor, Granger, San Antonio, Belton, and Beaumont. Because of the organization's efforts, Texans became more aware of women's rights arguments, and TERA began to gain support throughout the state, especially when prominent newspapers in the state began to cover suffrage news. In 1895, the Texas House of Representatives introduced a bill designed to give women the right to vote. Unfortunately, the bill was referred to the committee on constitutional amendments, where it died. Shortly afterwards, TERA's influence began to decline. In 1896, the association ceased to function, primarily due to dissention among the organization's members. At TERA's third state convention in Dallas in 1895, members elected Elizabeth Goode Houston instead of Hayes to the presidency. During the convention, members also decided not to side with any particular political party, preferring instead to organize at the county level. Following the convention adjournment, Houston appointed ten members to organize local and county suffrage clubs, but despite their efforts, the association was in rapid decline. By 1894, a lack of funding forced TERA's office of state organizer to close. Less than a year later, the superintendent of press work announced that she could no longer fulfill her duties because of insufficient funds—the treasurer reported in the same year that the once thriving organization only had $105 in the bank. As a result, local offices closed, and by the end of 1896, TERA ceased all operations.

While some organizations were more successful than others, the point remains the same—Texas women were actively engaged in political activities of their state. In some cases, they exhibited enormous influence over government officials. In other instances, they simply laid the foundation for reforms that would be realized early in the twentieth century during the Progressive era.

## Suggestions for Further Reading

Barnes, Donna A. *Farmers in Rebellion: The Rise and Fall of the Southern Farmers Alliance and People's Party in Texas.* Austin: University of Texas Press, 1984.

Barr, Alwyn. *Black Texans: A History of African Americans in Texas, 1528-1971.* Norman: University of Oklahoma Press, 1996.

____. *Reconstruction to Reform: Texas Politics, 1876-1906.* Austin: University of Texas Press, 1971.

Barthelme, Marion K., ed. *Women in the Texas Populist Movement: Letters to the Southern Mercury.* College Station: Texas A&M University Press, 1997.

Cantrell, Gregg. *Feeding the Wolf: John B. Rayner and the Politics of Race, 1850-1918.* Wheeling, Illinois: Harlan Davidson, Inc., 2001.

Cotner, Robert C. *James Stephen Hogg, A Biography.* Austin: University of TX Press, 1959.

Goodwyn, Lawrence. *Democratic Promise: The Populist Moment in America.* New York: Oxford University Press, 1976.

____. *The Populist Moment: A Short History of the Agrarian Revolt in America.* New York: Oxford University Press, 1978.

Martin, Roscoe C. *The People's Party in Texas: A Study in Third Party Politics.* Austin: University of Texas Bulletin No. 3308, 1933.

McMath, Robert C., Jr. *Populist Vanguard: A History of the Southern Farmer's Alliance.* Chapel Hill: University of North Carolina Press, 1975.

Palmer, Bruce. *Man over Money: The Southern Populist Critique of American Capitalism.* Chapel Hill: University of North Carolina Press, 1980.

Williams, Patrick G. *Beyond Redemption: Texas Democrats after Reconstruction.* College Station: Texas A&M University Press, 2007.

**IDENTIFICATION:** Briefly describe each term.

freedom colonies
Charles W. Macune
Cincinnati Convention (May 1891)
Southern Mercury
James Stephen Hogg
Texas Railroad Commission
George Clark
"Hogg's laws"
bimetallic monetary system
Thomas Nugent
John B. Rayner
Charles Culberson
Herman E. Taubeneck
William Jennings Bryan
"Immortal 103"

**MULTIPLE CHOICE:** Choose the correct response.

1. Which of the following economic factors contributed to the hardships of Texas agrarians?
   A. increased mechanization of farming and mass production associated with commercial farming
   B. The federal government's decision to abandon the gold standard
   C. easy access to credit during times of economic depression
   D. the general trend to diversify farming, moving away from cotton production

2. Which of the following is not a true statement about James Stephen Hogg?
   A. He favored some Populist reforms such as regulation of the railroads.
   B. In the 1860s, outlaws shot him in the back and left him for dead.
   C. Hogg was admitted to the state bar in 1885.
   D. Hogg served as the state attorney general before being elected to the governorship.

3. All of these men were appointed to the first Texas Railroad Commission, EXCEPT:
   A. John H. Reagan
   B. William Pinckney McLean
   C. James Webb Throckmorton
   D. Lafayette L. Foster

4. "Hogg's laws" addressed all of the following issues, EXCEPT:
   A. the rights of foreign and corporate land companies
   B. prison reform
   C. public education
   D. financing a new capitol building

5. Who did Governor Hogg appoint as the librarian of the State Library?
   A. Oran Roberts
   B. Cadwell W. Raines
   C. John H. Reagan
   D. The governor does not appoint a state librarian.

6. In the 1892 election, Democrats, known as "gold-standard" men, opposed Governor Hogg's bimetallist position. Who led this faction of politicians against Governor Hogg?
   A. George Clark
   B. Thomas Nugent
   C. John B. Rayner
   D. Cadwell W. Raines

7. Thomas Nugent is correctly represented by all the following statements, EXCEPT:
   A. Nugent was the Populist candidate for governor in 1892.
   B. Nugent was an ex-Confederate.
   C. Nugent entertained the idea of becoming a Methodist minister.
   D. Nugent attempted to become a lawyer, but failed the state bar exam.

8. What was one of the primary reasons that the Populists failed in Texas?
   A. They were unable to convince a majority of the voters that the party's reforms were necessary and justifiable.
   B. Very few people in the state could identify with agrarian problems because most Texas laborers worked in some type of industry or factory by the 1890s.
   C. They chose religious zealots as their political candidates, isolating many of the Protestant and Catholic voters in the state.
   D. They tended to be opportunists who attempted to further their own political ambitions by supporting minor reforms that were of little consequence or substance.

9. What national politician did the People's Party support in the 1896 presidential election?
   A. William Jennings Bryan
   B. James H. "Cyclone" Davis
   C. Herman E. Taubeneck
   D. William McKinley

10. The "Immortal 103":
    A. were antifusionists who opposed nominating William J. Bryan in the 1896 presidential election.
    B. cast votes at the 1896 national convention of the People's Party for Col. Seymour F. Norton.
    C. supported Tom Watson of Georgia as the People's Party candidate for vice president.
    D. are correctly represented by all of the above.

**TRUE/FALSE:** Indicate whether each statement is true or false.

1. During the late nineteenth century, the Texas economy generally remained property based and was void of any real signs of capitalist development.

2. Texas farmers were economically tied to one commercial crop—cotton.

3. Similar to farmers in the northeastern states, Texas agrarians found it easy to move to urban areas and find employment in emerging industries.

4. Almost no migrant farmers came to Texas during the last decades of the nineteenth century.

5. To gain the support of Southerners, the People's Party adopted a political platform that was almost identical to the Farmers' Alliance platform of 1889.

6. Texas Democrats generally favored the idea of the subtreasury plan.

7. Of the nearly 600 newspapers printed in Texas in 1895, seventy-five were considered favorable to the Populist cause.

8. In 1894, Populist candidates won twenty-four seats in the Texas legislature.

9. In the 1894 gubernatorial election, Thomas Nugent defeated Charles Culberson by winning 49 percent of the vote.

10. Approximately 25 percent of the members in the Farmers' Alliance were women, an important fact considering that many of these women later joined the Populist Party.

**MATCHING:** Match the response in column A with the item in column B.

1. People's Party
2. subtreasury plan
3. Southern Mercury
4. Texas Railroad Commission
5. John H. Reagan
6. Street Car Barn Convention
7. "Negro Hogg Clubs"
8. Silverites
9. John B. Rayner
10. James H. "Cyclone" Davis

A. tried to organize black voters behind the People's Party
B. gained support of disgruntled members of the Democratic Party
C. Populist newspaper in Dallas
D. based on a fiat currency system
E. Democratic convention in Houston (1892)
F. regulated rates and fairs of railroads operating in Texas
G. first chairman of the Texas Railroad Commission
H. Governor Hogg's attempt to reach across racial lines
I. supporters of bimetal monetary system
J. Texas Populist who supported fusion ticket with Democrats in 1896 elections

**ESSAY QUESTIONS:**

1. Explain the role that women played in the People's Party.

2. Discuss the founding of the People's Party, including the various agrarian reform organizations that supported the creation of the Populist movement.

3. Discuss the accomplishments of Governor James Stephen Hogg administration. Was Governor Hogg acceptable to members of the People's Party. If so, why? If not, why?

4. Discuss the success and failures of the People's Party in the elections of 1892, 1894, and 1896, explaining why the party ultimately failed in Texas.

# Chapter 11

# Society and Culture, 1874-1900

*Prelude: The Making of a Texas Baptist Legend—Benajah Harvey Carroll*

It is often said that the best preachers are those who have experienced life. This was certainly true of Benajah Harvey Carroll. Born on December 27, 1843, Carroll was the seventh child of Benajah and Mary Mallard Carroll. His father was a country preacher who made a living for his family by farming a small plot of land near Carrollton, Mississippi. The family moved to Arkansas in 1850, before relocating eight years later to Burleson County, Texas. Shortly after his family's arrival to Texas, young Benajah studied philosophy at Baylor University, which was then located in the small town of Independence, but he would not remain there long enough to earn his degree. In 1861, Carroll volunteered for military service in the Civil War, joining Benjamin McCulloch's Texas Rangers and later transferring to the Seventeenth Texas Infantry of the Confederate Army. He served in the Seventeenth Texas Infantry until he was wounded at the Battle of Mansfield. Though he left Baylor before receiving his degree, Carroll had completed enough courses to merit special considerations so the university granted him a B.A. degree when he returned home from the war. Carroll also obtained honorary degrees from the University of Tennessee and Keatchie College in Louisiana.

Though his parents had provided him sound spiritual guidance, Carroll was troubled over his personal faith and privately skeptical about the origins of Christianity. Life after service in the war proved difficult for Benajah, especially considering that the wounds he received in the war left him crippled. His fortunes, however, soon improved. In 1865, Carroll renewed his commitment to God at a Methodist revival near Caldwell, Texas. The following year, Carroll became an ordained Baptist minister, preaching in rural churches in Burleson and McLennan counties between 1866 and 1869. To help his family meet financial obligations, the young preacher taught school and farmed. In 1871, Carroll became the pastor of the First Baptist Church in Waco, Texas, a position that he retained for the next 28 years. Under his leadership, the church became the flagship institution of Texas Baptists. Carroll's prominence rose in the 1870s. Securing numerous influential positions in the General Association (forerunner of the Baptist General Convention of Texas), he became one of the leading figures who negotiated and supported efforts aimed at centralizing Texas Baptist educational institutions. During the

1880s, the Waco preacher supported the consolidation of regional associations and conventions into a single unified body, creating the Baptist General Convention of Texas. Because of his active role, Carroll was elected to serve on several Southern Baptist Convention committees and addressed the convention on numerous occasions.

Carroll was active in numerous moral crusades. During the 1880s, he led statewide prohibition efforts. At one event before a crowd of more than 7,000 onlookers, the preacher debated Roger Q. Mills for over three hours regarding the merits of prohibition. The debate was so heated that a brawl nearly broke out several times during the course of the event. Such political sorties served Carroll well as he developed an ability to ignore his opponents' criticism and to push forward when he thought that he was right about an issue.

At the turn of the century, Carroll left the First Baptist Church in Waco and became the secretary to the Baptist Educational Commission, an agency dedicated to securing financial support for Baptist schools operating in the state. It was natural for him to take up the cause of Christian education. He taught theological courses at Baylor between 1872 and 1905, served as a trustee of the Southern Baptist Theological Seminary in Louisville, Kentucky, in the 1880s, and organized the Baylor Theological Seminary in 1905, which led to the founding of the Southwest Baptist Theological Seminary in 1908. Before Southwest Baptist moved to Fort Worth in 1910, Carroll served as one of its instructors. Once the new school was relocated, the central Texas preacher would become its president, an office he held until his death. By this time, Carroll's reputation was legendary among Texas Baptists.

The signs of modernity in Texas during the late nineteenth century included an increase in the number of towns, the rapid development of railroads, the emergence of labor unions, and a struggling but permanent system of public education. But in many ways, Texas culture and society in the late nineteenth century still maintained many of its pre-Civil War attributes. Most people still lived in rural areas and made their living by farming. Towns remained small isolated communities that serviced the agrarians living nearby. Urban areas in Texas paled in comparison to the major cities of the northeast such as Chicago, New York, Boston, and Washington, D.C. The transportation network in Texas remained inadequate with the railroads servicing only a limited number of regions. Still, the end of the nineteenth century showed signs of change. The population was increasing due to migration from southern and midwestern states. Industry was beginning to grow in the state's urban areas, and farming and ranching were becoming more commercialized. These changes, however limited, altered the social and cultural fabric of Texas.

**Population Demographics**

The population of Texas increased substantially during the last three decades of the nineteenth century. In 1860, the population was 604,215, but by 1900, it had increased to more than three million people. The migrants were primarily white Southerners who came to Texas seeking new opportunities. Texas had managed to retain control of its public lands and generously had made vast tracts of the public domain open to settlers.

Farmers and merchants made their way from Arkansas, Alabama, Mississippi, Tennessee, Missouri, Louisiana, and Georgia with the hopes of gaining a fresh start in life.

Texas attempted to attract migrants from other southern states by establishing the Texas Bureau of Immigration in 1871. Unfortunately, the bureau had limited success, primarily because the legislature never adequately funded its operations and because it was identified as a Radical Republican program. As soon as the Democrats (also referred to as Redeemers during this period) regained control of the state, members of the legislature prohibited state funding for recruitment of immigrants, effectively abolishing the Texas Bureau of Immigration. Private companies, however, continued to recruit new settlers. These companies, including railroads, agricultural organizations such as the Grange, and local societies, sent brochures to other southern states and to Europe to recruit white settlers.

Most of the newcomers followed pre-war migration patterns of settlement. North-Northeast Texas was primarily the home of migrants from the Upper South (Arkansas, Tennessee, Kentucky, Virginia, North Carolina). East-Southeast Texas harbored people from the Lower South (Louisiana, Mississippi, Alabama, Georgia, South Carolina, and Florida). Because migrants came from the same general locations outside of the state, they did little to change the cultural and social climate of the state. In fact, new arrivals simply assimilated into existing regional cultures. As land became available in West Texas, migrants from these regions moved westward.

TABLE 11.1: **The Texas Population, 1860-1900**

| YEAR | POPULATION |
|---|---|
| 1860 | 604,215 |
| 1870 | 818,579 |
| 1880 | 1,591,749 |
| 1890 | 2,235,521 |
| 1900 | 3,048,710 |

A variety of factors brought people to Texas. The end of the Civil War permitted expansionist-minded people to resume their quest to populate the West. The federal government's successful efforts to subdue the Native American population and force them onto reservations (mostly outside of Texas) removed a significant obstacle for settlers pushing into the western regions of the state. The discovery that West Texas could sustain the cattle industry also contributed to the development of small communities in the region. Following close behind the ranchers were farming families who attempted to scratch a living from the dry lands of the Texas plains. Finally, the expansion of railroads to the far reaches of the state helped push a small number of settlers further westward and southward.

**Living and Working Conditions**

During the last two decades of the nineteenth century, approximately 80 percent of the population continued to live in rural communities, and an estimated 6 out of every 10 workers were employed in the agricultural sector. Though some farmers experimented with steam tractors, threshing machines, reapers, and other new innovations, the majority still toiled behind horses and mules. Regardless of the methods used to make a living from the soil, the farmers followed many of the pioneer practices that their fathers had known. The farm family remained a tight, cohesive unit, and all shared in the work. Members of the family rose at daybreak and worked until dark, some plowing, planting, and cultivating crops in the field, while others took care of vegetable gardens and tended to livestock. Harvest time was the busiest time of the year for agrarians. Time was of the essence, especially considering that most farmers were engaged in cotton production. Once matured, cotton had to be harvested as quickly as possible. Often children living on the farm remained in the fields instead of going to school until the cotton crop was at the local gin.

The work schedule in Texas towns was usually less demanding. Urban family income generally was provided by business ownership or by the father's employment. However, some women were beginning to find employment outside of the home, especially African-American women. In smaller towns when the opportunity presented itself, urban youth often found summer employment as laborers on nearby farms.

Living conditions of Texas laborers retained many aspects of the mid-nineteenth century. Farm houses were warmed by fireplaces, iron heaters with coal, or wood-burning stoves. At night, kerosene lamps provided light. City homes varied in size and design, but most occupants lived in conditions similar to neighboring farmers. Though gas and electricity were available in larger cities such as Galveston, few homes in Texas enjoyed

**Scene in the cotton field of the Baptist Orphanage, near Waxahachie. These boys, from seven-years-old and upward, picked cotton and helped this man outside of school hours. There were 20 children, mostly girls, in the orphanage that was supported by the Baptists of Texas. Waxahachie [vicinity], Texas. October 1913. Photo credit: Library of Congress**

this modern convenience before the 1920s. Nevertheless, larger cities did benefit from modernization. By 1900, all cities had telephone exchanges, and telegraph exchanges connected most of the smaller towns.

Despite improvements in the state's transportation system, travel remained crude and difficult in both rural and urban areas. Long-distance travelers often made use of the railroads, which tended to be relatively safe, fast, and comfortable. For shorter trips, Texans continued to use wagons, buggies, horses, and mules. Paved roads and bridges were few in number, and the existing dirt roads were usually poorly maintained and vulnerable to weather conditions—dusty in dry weather and muddy in wet. A journey of twenty miles might take a traveler all day to complete. In the cities, street construction and maintenance presented special problems for city dwellers. Large cities such as Houston, Galveston, and Dallas began to pave the main thoroughfares, but side streets often continued to be packed dirt. Electric streetcars and trolleys were increasingly commonplace by the end of the century and helped to improve travel in the inner cities.

## Urban Growth

While most Texans still lived in rural areas, urban life became more common. In 1870, only 6.7 percent of the population lived in incorporated urban areas with a population of 2,500 or more residents; however, by 1900, that number had risen to 17.1 percent. Perhaps more impressive was the increase in the number of urban centers. In 1870, only two towns—Galveston with 13,818 and San Antonio with 12,256—maintained populations greater than 10,000 people. The next largest cities included Houston (9,000 residents), Dallas (3,000), and Fort Worth (500). By 1900, the number of cities possessing 10,000 or more people had grown to eleven. San Antonio was the largest city with 53,321, followed by Houston, Dallas, Galveston, and Fort Worth. By the end of the decade, more than 350,000 people lived in cities and towns.

One explanation for the rapid urbanization was directly related to the development of new railroads. In nearly every case, any boom in a town's population can be traced to the arrival of the railroads. For example, Dallas doubled its population from 1872-1873 when the Houston & Texas Central and the Texas & Pacific lines arrived. The city witnessed a growth from 3,000 inhabitants in 1870 to more than 38,000 in 1890. The East Texas town of Marshall increased its population from 1,960 to 5,624 during the decade in which the Texas & Pacific Railroad located its headquarters there. Laredo's population was 3,521 in 1880 but grew to more than 11,000 people in 1890 after the arrival of the Texas Mexican Railroad from Corpus Christi and the International and Great Northern Railroads from Austin. By contrast, Brownsville had approximately 1000 more people than Laredo in 1880 but did not have a rail connection until 1904. Consequently, its population only increased to 6,134 during the same decade. Perhaps the greatest growth was experienced in Fort Worth. The city's population grew from 500 in 1870 to more than 23,000 people in 1890 after the Fort Worth & Denver City line was completed.

## Health

For most Texans, disease was a part of everyday life. Just as in the days prior to the Civil War, cholera, typhoid, diphtheria, and smallpox epidemics swept through the state affecting thousands of people. Malaria and yellow fever epidemics along the Gulf Coast region became less frequent during the latter decades of the nineteenth century, but many families throughout the state were still impacted by childhood diseases such as measles, whooping cough, mumps, and chicken pox. These diseases often claimed the lives of young and old alike.

Because of the continued prevalence of disease, Texans improved their health-care system. In Galveston in 1875, residents built a new city hospital and enlarged St. Mary's Infirmary the next year. Other cities with substantial populations followed Galveston's example by building and expanding their own medical facilities. Despite the new medical centers, most rural Texans did not receive attention from trained physicians. At best, rural inhabitants might receive treatment from partially trained healers traveling through their area. Such was the case when Henry F. Hoyt arrived in the Llano Estacado region in November 1877 and wandered throughout the Panhandle treating patients. In Tascosa, the only town of any size west of Fort Elliott, Hoyt treated the fifteen-year-old daughter of Casimero Romero—the wealthiest of the ranchers in that town—for smallpox. As part of his treatment, Hoyt made a paste of water and gunpowder and smeared it over the girl's body. Remarkably, the patient recovered, and Hoyt became a well-known healer in the area, but he did not remain in the region for long. Like many frontier doctors, he simply moved to the next community of ailing patients. Sherman Goodwin, suffering from tuberculosis, relocated his family in 1849 from Burton, Ohio, to Victoria, Texas, where he recovered and then practiced medicine until his death in 1884. Like Goodwin, many people suffering from tuberculosis came to Central and West Texas, where the dryer climate seemed to alleviate the symptoms of their incurable malady. These infirmed travelers often settled near Boerne, Fredericksburg, Luling Springs, and San Antonio. So many people came to the popular South Texas city of San Antonio that it earned the moniker "Sanitarium of the West." As the railroads reached other western towns, an increased number of "lungers" made Texas their new home. Some communities, such as Mineral Wells and Wooten Wells, became popular health resorts. Even wealthy railroad tycoon Jay Gould, who suffered from consumption, rode a Pullman car to El Paso in 1892 hoping to improve his health.

Due to the limited number of trained doctors throughout the state, most people relied on more traditional forms of health care. Mothers used home remedies. *Curanderos* (Hispanic folk healers) advised loyal clients and provided herbal remedies. Chuckwagon cooks provided care to drovers. Army surgeons attended to soldiers' wounds. Midwives delivered babies. General stores and pharmacies sold numerous remedies for various ailments, most of which had very little medicinal effect. General practitioners traveled from one small community to the next by horse, buggy, boat, and train to attend to patients who suffered from mysterious infections, injuries, and chronic diseases. Even though Texans were accustomed to making do when it came to health care, new features in services also developed, including improved custodial care of those with chronic conditions, improved sanitation and public health, improved and more successful surgical operations, an increase in the number of public hospitals, increased organizations of doctors and other health-care professionals, and the establishment of medical schools.

During the last decades of the nineteenth century, institutional care became more commonplace in Texas. The number of patients admitted to asylums for the blind, deaf, and mentally ill increased. Between 1856 and 1873, the legislature recognized the importance of these asylums, appropriating more than $600,000 for the maintenance and construction of new institutions. In 1885, the state opened the Terrell State Hospital to care for the mentally ill and in 1892, the San Antonio State Hospital for the same purpose. While the number of patients increased in these specialized asylums, the number of institutions treating tubercular could not keep pace with migrants afflicted with the disease. Between 1892 and 1925, twelve private sanatoria for these patients opened in El Paso alone, while fifty beds at the Hotel Dieu were set aside for consumptives between 1894 and 1914.

Beginning in 1870, the state witnessed the emergence of stable local agencies to supervise sanitation, quarantine, water resources, and food inspection. For example, the citizens of Galveston created a Board of Health in 1877 and appointed Cary Wilkinson as its health physician. At the end of the decade, the state assumed responsibility for organizing quarantines and authorized quarantine locations in five different coastal cities, including Galveston. Cities such as Dallas, Houston, and Galveston began to use artesian wells to supply their citizens with purer drinking water. Despite the safer water, many infants and children still died from drinking impure milk. As a result, public officials adopted ordinances that improved the quality of milk and food supplies, which significantly reduced the number of deaths among infants and children. Additionally, mortality from surgical procedures decreased during the last two decades of the nineteenth century as doctors learned more about antiseptic and aseptic techniques. Beginning in 1880, doctors performed pain-free procedures, such as hernia surgery, the setting of broken bones, and hysterectomies on their patients without fear of losing them in post-surgery recovery from blood poisoning and gangrene.

With the development of x-rays in 1895, surgeons now needed permanent locations to house the equipment used to treat their patients. As a result, private and public hospitals sprang up throughout the state. Many of these early hospitals were built by industries as a way of providing health care to their employees. For example, the Gulf, Colorado, and Santa Fe Railroad established a hospital in Temple in 1891. Arthur Carroll Scott moved from Gainesville to Temple in 1892 to become the new hospital's chief surgeon. Later in 1904, Scott and Raleigh R. White opened and operated the Temple Sanitarium, which eventually became the Scott and White Memorial Hospital.

To improve health care, doctors also continued to organize their fellows. Professional societies began to emerge as early as 1865 when the doctors in Galveston organized the Galveston Medical Society. The next year, ten doctors created the Waco Medical Society. Later, in 1869, twenty-eight physicians met in Houston and reorganized the Texas State Medical Association, an antebellum institution. Likewise, the Travis County Medical Society was reconstituted in 1870, and San Antonio doctors created the Western Texas Medical Association in 1876. In the early 1900s, these independent associations joined the American Medical Association, increasing the state organizations' prestige and power.

During the last decades of the nineteenth century, some hospitals became centers for training doctors and other health professionals. On January 10, 1890, the John Sealy Hospital in Galveston opened its doors and two months later initiated a training program for nurses. Originally built with private funds, the Sealy family gave the hospital to the city, which in turn gave it to the state. The legislature appropriated funds to operate the institution. It eventually became the first university medical school in Texas, the University of Texas Medical Branch (UTMB). The medical school began training physicians and nurses in October 1891. A pharmacy school was added to UTMB in 1893. Because standards were high and many students were poorly prepared for the medical profession, only 12 of the starting 22 medical students graduated. However, by 1900 these schools graduated 182 men and 4 women as doctors, 44 men and 6 women as pharmacists, and 33 women as nurses.

**Entertainment**

During the last decades of the nineteenth century, Texans engaged in a variety of leisure activities. The most common form of entertainment was simply visiting with nearby friends and neighbors, especially after church services on Sunday afternoons. Church-sponsored functions, the local general store, sewing clubs, and community dances provided numerous occasions for people to gather and discuss the major issues affecting their lives. Dances were perhaps one of the most important social events of the nineteenth century, especially considering that many young people attended these events with the hope of meeting a future husband or wife. However, during the last decades of the nineteenth century, some areas witnessed a decline in the number of organized dances, in part because some Protestant church groups, particularly the Baptists, frowned upon close contact between women and men who were unmarried. Church groups often pressured their communities to abandon the practice of holding dances.

Holidays were an important time in the lives of Texans, especially the Fourth of July and Christmas. Citizens often celebrated Independence Day with community picnics and parties, but Christmas was a more family-oriented occasion. African Americans celebrated Juneteenth (June 19), a day set aside to remember their emancipation, and Tejanos celebrated Cinco de Mayo and Diez y Seis de Septiembre. Communities generally did not have elaborate celebrations for Thanksgiving and Easter holidays, although families held intimate gatherings.

While not as important as they would become in the twentieth century, spectator sports increasingly became popular. Horse racing continued to draw large crowds throughout the state. In 1887, the Texas League of Professional Baseball Clubs was organized, and during the next decade, a few Texas schools began to field football teams. Boxing also increasingly became popular during the close of the nineteenth century. In 1908, Texas was home to the famous Jack Johnson, the first African-American heavyweight champion of the world.

Music, theater, and vaudeville shows provided diversions for some people, particularly those who lived in urban areas. Local talent sometimes entertained their peers, but professional groups also traveled throughout the state. At one time or another, Texas billboards displayed the names of almost every distinguished actor who played in the United States during the late nineteenth century. Among the most famous were Joseph Jefferson, noted for his role as Rip Van Winkle; Edwin Booth, a famous Shakespearean actor; and Sarah Bernhardt, one of the greatest female actors of her day. Many towns, both large and small, built their own theaters for the performing arts. Some communities organized bands, others had singing groups, and Tejanos enjoyed the music of traveling musicians who played conjunto music, a mix of traditional Mexican instruments of the flute, guitar, and drum with the accordion, a favorite instrument of the German, Poles, and Czechs.

Jack Johnson, the first African-American heavyweight champion of the world. Photo credit: Library of Congress

The circus was popular with Texas audiences. Throughout the nineteenth century, the Mollie Bailey Circus carried its show throughout the state, entertaining crowds with its tigers, elephants, acrobats, and clowns. The circus company opened its tent flaps in 1879 when Mollie Bailey traded the showboat that she owned for a small circus. She named the new business venture the Bailey Circus, "A Texas Show for Texas People." After her husband's health failed and he retired to Blum, Texas, she changed the name of the show to the Mollie A. Bailey Show. Mollie, also known as "Aunt Mollie," distinguished her troupe by flying the United States, Lone Star, and Confederate flags over the big top, and she made it common practice to give war veterans, Union or Confederate, free tickets. At its height, the one-ring tent circus had 31 wagons and about 200 animals. Elephant and camel acts were added in 1902.

After her husband died in 1896, Mollie continued to operate the business. In an effort to escape paying "occupation" taxes levied on traveling shows, she cleverly bought lots in many of the towns where the circus performed. When the circus moved on, Mollie donated these lots to locals who used the land to build parks. Later, many of these lots reverted back to the towns. Mollie Bailey was also noted for her generosity to various churches and for allowing indigent children to attend the circus free.

### Religion

By the end of the nineteenth century, churches had experienced a transformation from their mid-century origins. At the end of the Civil War, the Methodist Church was the largest denomination in Texas, maintaining more than 400 churches and 30,000 members. The Baptists were second, claiming more congregations than the Methodists but enjoying fewer members. Presbyterians, Disciples of Christ, Episcopalians, and Catholics were present in Texas, but all were considerably smaller in number. By the end of the century, however, the Baptist membership had exceeded the Methodists, representing approximately 33 percent of the state's faithful. The Methodists in contrast represented approximately 27 percent of churchgoers. Catholic membership had also grown, making it the third largest church in Texas. Catholic growth primarily resulted from a growing number of immigrants entering the state from Germany, Poland, Czechoslovakia, and Mexico. Other denominations, including Presbyterians, Lutherans, and Episcopalians, continued to maintain a presence in the state. By 1900, the Texas Jewish population, which had origins that extended back to the Spanish era, had increased to more than 15,000.

Regardless of their denomination, Texas churches became actively involved with many of the social and political issues of the era. For Protestant faiths, prohibition became a special issue of concern. Many preachers taught their congregations that alcohol was the root of all the evils that confronted the nation. Prohibitionists' success during the early decades of the twentieth century was directly related to the foundations earlier laid by Baptists, Methodists, and members of other Protestant faiths. Also, Protestant churches attacked other vices and perceived "social ills," including gambling, prostitution, and dancing.

Not all Texas denominations supported the Protestants' attacks on Prohibition, gambling, and dancing. In areas with large populations of Germans, Czechs, Poles, and Mexicans, the zeal for prohibition was almost nonexistent. Often these segments of the population were Catholic, but other denominations, especially those located in the state's cities, supported views similar to the immigrants' beliefs.

**Education**

As Texans approached the twentieth century, they began to focus on improving public education. To this end, they organized the state's first public school system. The legislature set land aside for support of the new school system during the early Republic and again during early statehood. However, no viable school system had yet been created. During Reconstruction, Governor Edmund J. Davis's administration created a system of public schools and provided viable funding for it. However, the Redeemer government and the Constitution of 1876 basically destroyed this effort. In place of the Republican's system, in 1876 the Redeemers adopted an ill-defined "community school system." The new plan did not define school boundaries; it provided no means for communities to acquire and maintain school properties, and it gave no assurances that the school system would be continued from one year to the next. When Governor Oran Milo Roberts vetoed the school appropriation bill in 1879, it seemed like the Democrats' system of education might fail completely.

African-American children suffered even more under the Democrats' school plan. Even though black legislators were among the most vociferous supporters of public schools, the Democrats' Constitution of 1876 ensured that the new system would be segregated. Although black schools were supposed to receive the same resources as white schools, they rarely did. By the early 1900s, black schools were receiving less than one-third of the funding that white schools received, and black teachers were paid substantially less than white teachers.

While white Texans generally supported the segregated school system, many whites demanded that the state's schools receive an adequate share of the education funds. However, the support of education through the sale of public lands failed to provide schools with a secure financial base. As the fiscal crisis of public education grew, a number of prosperous Texans championed the cause of public education. The most outspoken proponents of the state's educational system included: Orlando N. Hollingsworth, secretary of the state board of education; Dr. Ashbel Smith, a supporter of education since the days of the Republic; Rufus C. Burleson, president of Waco University; and William C. Crane, president of Baylor University. Through the efforts of these men, the people approved an 1883 constitutional amendment that provided for a 20 percent state ad valorem school tax and allowed district voters to supplement these funds with local taxes.

In 1884, the legislature completely rewrote the state school laws and took a significant step toward the development of a meaningful system of public education. The new law called for an elective state superintendent of instruction and placed the schools under the supervision of county judges. Counties were required to create new school districts and gave the districts the authority to assess and collect local taxes. The law stipulated compulsory attendance for children between the ages of 8 to 16 years of age, and it required teachers to obtain certification. Additionally, it called on local districts to file regular reports with the state about its day-to-day operations.

Even though Texas now had a new school system, development and progress remained slow. One of the major problems facing educators was that immigrant populations and a high birth rate caused the school-age population to rapidly outpace available resources. The law of 1884 placed responsibility of maintaining and supporting the public schools on local taxpayers, but voters often were reluctant to approve increases in school taxes. In some cases, they voted down the collection of the school taxes entirely. Some progress was realized during Governor James Hogg's administration in the 1890s. One measure that the governor signed into law was a bill extending the school term from four to six months.

Unfortunately, education in the late nineteenth century remained woefully inadequate. Counties organized common school districts under county control, but county school systems lagged behind urban schools. Because of the nature of rural education, Texas ranked near the bottom when compared with other states. At the turn of the century, larger towns and cities spent an average of $8.35 per student for education, while schools in small rural communities spent about half as much. Students in urban areas generally attended school for 162 days per year, while their rural counterparts only spent 98 days on average in the classroom. One of the primary problems confronting rural communities was a restriction in the Constitution of 1876 that attempted to force small rural schools to consolidate into larger districts by limiting the taxing authority of the smaller districts to less than one-half that of the larger independent school districts. Adding to the hardship of rural schools was the fact that they serviced more than 75 percent of the school-age children in the state.

## Women

Although women in Texas enjoyed more rights than their counterparts in other states, they still did not have legal equality with men. Women could not vote and only had limited rights to conduct their own business affairs. Because of its heritage of Spanish civil law, Texas granted women the right to own and convey property, to make contracts, and to seek legal recourse in the courts. However, once a woman married, she forfeited many of her legal rights. For example, her husband was granted the right to manage her property even if she owned the property prior to their marriage. Additionally, a married woman could not sell her property without the consent of her husband. In this social structure, single women in Texas clearly enjoyed more rights than married women, considering that unmarried females were responsible for their own acts and could legally manage their own property.

Educational opportunities for women during the last decades of the nineteenth century existed but were more limited than men's opportunities. By 1890, more female students than male students attended public schools, but few women went to college. While some women enrolled in business colleges and trade schools that prepared women for careers in the business world, most who were fortunate enough to attend college enrolled in more "traditional" forms of women's education. Often the women attending institutions, such as Baylor University and the University of Texas, took courses that were less academically demanding than their male counterparts. Many of the courses in which women enrolled concerned social graces and the arts.

Most women in Texas during this time did not attend school beyond the primary grades, instead devoting their lives to the role of wife, mother, and caregiver. Women generally married at an earlier age than men, and because their spouses tended to be older, a significant number became widows when they were relatively young. Divorce was uncommon—only about 12 percent of the adult female population was divorced.

Beginning in 1890, about 8 percent of the women in the state were involved in occupations outside the home, and approximately half of those were in agricultural jobs such as laborers or farmers. Most who worked outside the agricultural sector held jobs as domestic servants. A smaller group of women became school teachers, journalists, ministers, lawyers, physicians, merchants, clerks, seamstresses, and other various odd jobs. Two women even worked as locomotive engineers.

Toward the end of the century, women's organizations emerged and attempted to improve their condition in society. Suffrage and temperance were the most common objectives of these organizations. Men often dismissed women's clubs as insignificant social organizations, but in reality, the clubs served as vehicles for Texas women to express their political views, particularly considering that women could not vote. Activism took numerous forms. In 1898 at the first statewide convention of the Texas Federation of Women's Clubs, leaders passed a resolution endorsing the creation of public libraries, launching a statewide campaign that resulted in the establishment of libraries in many Texas communities. This activism laid the foundation for future reform movements and created a formidable lobbyist group that expressed the concerns of women throughout the state.

African-American women shared many similar circumstances. Their lives centered around their families, forming complex relationships with men and their children. While impossible to know the exact number of African-American marriages in Texas, scholars estimate that approximately 95 percent of black women married before 45 years of age. Just as among white women, African-American women found marriage a fragile institution during the late nineteenth century. With the average life expectancy of black males at 40 years of age, many black women became grieving widows. Others saw their marriage end in divorce, though the divorce rate for African Americans remained low, comparable to that of whites.

Most African-American women lived in rural Texas and helped their families to survive life on the farm. Like white women, they engaged in a variety of agrarian tasks, including planting and harvesting crops, milking cows, and raising chickens and hogs. In addition, they prepared meals and took care of their young children. Some black women found employment in urban areas, especially as the African-American population rapidly increased in the state's cities. The move from the farm to urban areas created significant changes in the lives of black women. Even though their economic opportunities remained limited, African-American women found more diverse employment in the cities than were available in rural communities. Nevertheless, one circumstance that remained the same was that women often had to work outside of the home. For example, in Dallas, approximately 14 percent of white women were forced to take jobs outside the home to ensure their families' survival, a small percentage in comparison to 75 percent of African-American women. Statewide, figures suggest that African-American women constituted 68 percent of the total female labor force but only represented 23 percent of the total female population in the state. These women did a variety of jobs, such as laundresses, and domestic servants—cooks, maids, nurses, and seamstresses. Only a select few found employment in professional occupations such as school teachers and physicians.

Like white women, black females had to deal with gender discrimination, but unlike white women, they also had to contend with life in Jim Crow Texas (legal segregation in public facilities). To cope with the pressures of segregation and gender discrimination, black women created women's clubs similar to the ones that white women had formed. Most of the organized clubs emerged during the early twentieth century, but some (including the Grand Order, Court of Calanthe, founded in 1897 by Mrs. S. H. Norris of Dallas) were founded in the last decades of the nineteenth century. The most prominent club of the era was the Colored Division of the Women's Christian Temperance Union founded in Dallas in 1897.

**Lawlessness and the Texas Rangers**

As a frontier state, Texas developed a culture of violence from its very inception. Texans' penchant towards violence continued through the end of the nineteenth century. This is not to say that all citizens were prone to violent acts; most did not directly engage in violent acts and behaviors. However, a significant number of them did believe in extralegal means of administering justice, seeing nothing wrong when vigilante groups sought justice against accused criminals through means such as lynching. During the last three decades of the nineteenth century, scholars estimate that approximately 75 to 100 incidents involving vigilantes occurred throughout the state.

Outlaws were abundant in the state during the late nineteenth century. Some men traveled the countryside alone, but most rode in gangs. For example, in South Texas, no less than 197 men at different times were members of the infamous Taylor crime ring. These men had one thing in common: between the 1850s and 1880, they all rode with Creed Taylor or members of his extended family and engaged in an assortment of crimes, including theft of personal property, cattle rustling, murder, and other vile acts against humanity. William "Bill" Sutton, Deputy Sheriff of De Witt County and arch nemesis of the Taylor ring, would not live to see the gang members brought to justice—they killed him in 1874. The end of violence in the region came only after the Texas Rangers were sent to De Witt County in the same year.

Some individuals gained reputations as notorious gunfighters. One of the most famous Texas gunmen was John Wesley Hardin, who reportedly killed more men than the infamous Billy the Kid and Jesse James. Between 1868 and 1878, Hardin supposedly killed more than twenty men, many in one-on-one confrontations with the professional killer. As a professed supporter of the Confederate cause, he often terrorized blacks and their white allies. In 1878, the legal system caught up with Hardin, sending him to the state penitentiary for murdering a deputy sheriff. In 1895, a year after his release from prison, Hardin moved to El Paso, where he worked as a lawyer. Ironically, while in prison, he studied law and passed the state bar shortly after leaving the penal system. While in El Paso, another Texas gunfighter, John Selman, killed Hardin, bringing a violent end to one of Texas's most noted outlaws.

Numerous other outlaws populated the state, some achieving reputations and notoriety comparable to that of Hardin. This select group included Ben Thompson, Cullen Montgomery Baker, Ben Bickerstaff, and Bill Longley. Longley, who gained the moniker "the nigger killer," indiscriminately killed African Americans with little or no provocation. However, Longley murdered men of every color, and by the time he was executed in 1878, he reportedly had killed 32 men. It seems likely that this was a conservative estimate.

All racial and ethnic groups experienced some form of violence during this era. White men persecuted black people for a variety of reasons, but often they used violence as a means of social and political control. Lynching, or the threat of it, was a common means by which whites kept black voters from polling places and forced them to conform to social norms forged by the false ideals of white supremacy. Between 1870 and 1900, approximately 500 blacks were lynched in Texas. In some cases, the victims of white oppression were tortured before hundreds of onlookers. During a couple of these heinous episodes, the black victims were burned alive before being hanged. Events were so out of control that the legislature passed an anti-lynching law in 1897. Unfortunately, the law was never rigorously enforced.

Equally disturbing were the attacks made against the Tejano community, especially in areas of South and West Texas. Just as with African Americans, whites lynched Hispanics with little or no provocation. Many whites believed that Mexican Americans along the border were in collusion with border raiders who crossed the Rio Grande into the United States and then attacked white settlements. After Mexican banditos raided Corpus Christi in 1875, vigilantes moved through the surrounding countryside, persecuting Mexican farmers and ranchers. Unfortunately, this was not an isolated circumstance—whites regularly harassed, maimed, and murdered Mexican Americans.

To cope with the continuing threats of violence, the legislature revived the Texas Rangers in 1874, replacing Governor Davis's disbanded state police. The legislature actually created two Ranger units: The Special Force was placed under the command of Captain L. H. McNelly; the Frontier Battalion was placed under the command of Major John B. Jones. The Rangers engaged in all types of law enforcement activities including tax collection, protecting prisoners from vigilante mobs and transporting them to safe holding facilities, monitoring elections, enforcing quarantines against deadly diseases such as smallpox, and a variety of other public services. The most noted activities of the Rangers were the protection of frontier settlers from Indians and the tracking down of infamous outlaws.

Sometimes, the Rangers' efforts to maintain the peace led them to break the very laws that they were sworn to protect. On several occasions, the Rangers violated international law by chasing outlaws across the Rio Grande into Mexico. Additionally, many of the Rangers' prisoners, especially Mexican nationals and Tejanos, were killed while trying to escape custody. This happened so frequently that it seems probable that the lawmen were murdering their prisoners. As a whole, many white Texans condoned the Rangers' use of excessive force (including justifiable homicide) as necessary to thwart heinous crimes and apprehend ardent criminals.

Aside from their reputation for taking the law into their own hands, the Rangers became a powerful force in state law enforcement. On several occasions, citizens called on the Rangers to suppress riots, including the El Paso Salt War of 1877, the Laredo Election Riot in 1886, and the Rio Grande City Riot of 1888. As they did many times, the Rangers often used extralegal tactics to bring an end to the riots, such as beating and shooting civilian protesters, especially when the protestors were foreign-born ethnics, African Americans, and Indians. The Rangers also patrolled the sparsely-settled ranching areas of West and South Texas, arresting cattle rustlers and other miscreants. In 1877, three Ranger companies in the Frontier Battalion under Major Jones rode into Kimble County, a well-known haunt for West Texas cattle rustlers, and began to sweep the area of criminals. When the lawmen finished their task, they had arrested more than 30 outlaws and chased those fortunate enough to escape from the region. Other Rangers, including the famous Captain Leander H. McNelly, were credited with breaking up crime rings throughout the state.

Despite their mythical reputation, the Texas Rangers have probably received more credit than rightly due for clearing the state of criminal elements. Just as important were the untold hundreds of local peace officers who restored law and order in their towns and counties without the aid of the more famous Rangers. These local lawmen administered justice just as bravely as did the Rangers and probably more in alignment with the state's statutes.

## The Final Destruction of the Plains Indians

Following the Civil War, Native Americans were well aware that the Texas frontier remained virtually unprotected. Consequently, various Indian tribes increased their raids in late 1865. Federal officials tried to bring stability to the region by traditional means, primarily with a land treaty. In October 1865, the Kiowas and a few Comanche bands signed the Treaty of the Little Arkansas, which promised the Native Americans a large reservation that included lands in the Panhandle and a large segment of West Texas. However, Texans were not pleased with the treaty. The state still controlled its public lands, and its leaders were not willing to cede any lands to the Indians. In 1867, the Kiowas and Comanches negotiated the Medicine Lodge Creek Treaty, which set aside land for them in Indian Territory (present-day Oklahoma). The pact accomplished what President Ulysses S. Grant hoped would be a peaceful resolution of the "Indian problem." However, the chiefs did not speak for all the Comanche and Kiowa bands operating in Texas. Therefore, even with the establishment of a reservation, the federal government still had to deal with hostile warriors on the frontier.

During the early 1870s as the government issued rations and provisions at Fort Sill Reservation in Indian Territory, Kiowa and Comanche bands continued to raid the Texas frontier. President Grant's peace policy afforded Texans little relief because it barred federal troops from pursuing Indian raiders onto the reservations. Following the Salt Creek Massacre of 1871, which resulted in the death of seven federal teamsters, the army obtained permission to operate against hostile bands even in Indian Territory. The conflict reached a climax in June 1874 when Comanche, Kiowa, and Cheyenne warriors attacked a camp of buffalo hunters at Adobe Walls, northeast of present-day Borger. Indians of all three tribes fled their reservations and took refuge on the Staked Plains of the Texas Panhandle. The U.S. Army quickly pursued the hostile Indians but had limited success in confronting them. The only battle of any significance occurred when Ranald S. Mackenzie surprised a group of Comanches camped at Palo Duro Canyon. Because the Native Americans eluded the army and would only fight under favorable conditions, the army resorted to desperate tactics to defeat the Plains tribes, including slaughtering captured horses, ravaging villages, and confiscating food, weapons, and anything that the Indians needed for their continued survival. During what became known as the Red River War,

Aerial 1923 view of the officers' quarters, parade ground, barracks, and stable area at Fort Davis, Texas. The 9th and 10th Cavalry Regiments (African American soldiers) were stationed there. Photo credit: UTSA Institute of Texan Cultures

the army effectively used their new tactics and forced most of the Indians to surrender and to return to the reservations in Indian Territory in the winter of 1874-1875. The Red River War ended hostilities on the southern Plains and brought to a close more than fifty years of race wars between the Plains Indians and their white adversaries.

The final defeat of the Indians in Texas came in the summer of 1880, when units of the famed "Buffalo Soldiers" of the Tenth Cavalry stationed at Fort Davis confronted the infamous Apache war chief Victorio and his band of followers. The Indians called the black troops of the Ninth and Tenth Cavalry and the Twenty-fourth and Twenty-fifth Infantry buffalo soldiers, probably because the texture of their hair reminded the Native Americans of the buffalo, an animal that they revered. Having rejected reservation life, Victorio and his warriors survived on the Plains by raiding ranches in both Texas and in Mexico. Victorio also attacked stagecoaches and travelers on the San Antonio-El Paso Road. For several years, the raiders successfully eluded army personnel, leading them on wild chases across New Mexico, Mexico, and Texas. To bring an end to the violence, Colonel Benjamin H. Grierson devised a plan in August 1880 to ambush Victorio's band at Tinaja de las Palmas, located fifteen miles southeast of Sierra Blanca and Rattlesnake Springs, forty miles north of present-day Van Horn, Texas. The location was a well-known haunt of Victorio's band, especially considering that the springs in the region were the only source of water in the dry desert environment. Reaching the springs in advance of the Apaches, the soldiers secured the high grounds surrounding the watering holes. When Victorio arrived at the location, a battle ensued, and the soldiers forced the Indians

Photograph shows oil painting of Victorio, Apache Chief. Courtesy of Fort Davis Museum Fort Davis, Tex. Photo credit: UTSA's Institute of Texan Cultures

to flee toward Mexico. After crossing the Rio Grande in October, Mexican troops assaulted Victorio's band on the rocky slopes of Tres Castillos, killing the charismatic chief and most of his followers. Victorio's death represented the end of the Native American's ancestral way of life in Texas. A proud people had been swept from Texas forever as a result of Anglo expansion.

**The Trials and Tribulations of African Americans**

During the nineteenth century, African Americans in Texas continued to experience the same hardships that had plagued their race during the eras of slavery and Reconstruction. Violence, Jim Crow segregation, discrimination, and political oppression remained common aspects of black Texans' everyday life. Despite such conditions, African Americans strove to build racial solidarity and to achieve economic stability. Several social and cultural institutions aided them in their efforts, including benevolent associations and mutual aid societies. These local organizations provided charitable and humanitarian aid, such as insurance and death benefits, to black members during times of crisis. Between 1870 and 1900, African-American editors printed more than sixty newspapers for the benefit of the black community. Most of these newspapers suffered from a lack of paying advertisers and low subscription rates, but these newspapers also kept black Texans informed about current events both in the state and in the nation.

Perhaps the most influential social institution in the African-American community was the church. Aside from providing blacks religious independence from whites, the church also became a central headquarters for black activities in local communities. Within the walls of the church building, African Americans developed leadership abilities and established political agendas. Many of their more prominent leaders came out of the churches, among them Meshack Roberts, who during the 1870s served three terms in the state legislature from Harrison County. Even though Methodists, Presbyterians, and Episcopalians maintained churches in some black settlements, the Baptist church was the most prominent probably due to black parishioners being drawn to the theology and autonomy of the Baptist church. By 1890, black Baptists totaled more than 111,000.

African Americans during this period enjoyed various forms of entertainment, including community gatherings, barbecues, card games, horse races, and political rallies. One of the most meaningful celebrations remained "Juneteenth," the anniversary of June 19, 1865, when General Gordon Granger declared President Lincoln's Emancipation Proclamation was in effect in Texas, thereby freeing all slaves in the state. Every black community celebrated the day with parades, inspiring speeches, picnics, and dances.

While social forces brought the black communities together in the eastern part of the state, the military brought cohesion to blacks on the western frontier. Stationed in fortifications in South and West Texas, African Americans served in segregated units in the U.S. Army. These units were responsible for scouting, patrolling, and protecting Texas settlers on the frontier from hostile Indian bands and Mexican border raiders. On many occasions, the black troops proved themselves in combat. For example, Emanuel Stance received the Medal of Honor in 1870 for bravery against the Apaches in a series of battles near Fort McKavett. At the Battle of Rattlesnake Springs on August 6, 1880, the buffalo soldiers forced the Apache chief Victorio to abandon Texas for Mexico. When black troops left the state in the mid-1880s, they left behind a legacy of bravery and te-

Henry Flipper, first African American to graduate from West Point, in army uniform. Courtesy of the United States National Archives. Credit: UTSA's Institute of Texan Cultures

nacity in battle. Black soldiers took great pride in the knowledge that they had brought peace and security to West Texas settlers. Among those who served in Texas during the post Civil War era was Lieutenant Henry O. Flipper, the first black to graduate from the United States Military Academy at West Point and the first black officer in the U.S. Army. Unfortunately, Lieutenant Flipper became a victim of racial prejudice in the military. He was accused of stealing military funds while serving at Fort Davis. The commander of the post immediately brought charges against the young officer. Although a divided court-martial acquitted Flipper of the charges of embezzling funds, he was dismissed from the army on the charges that he had exhibited conduct unbecoming an officer and a gentleman, a charge seemingly based more on his race than on his actual behavior.

## Mexican Americans and European Immigrants

Unlike African Americans, many members of the other ethnic groups in Texas were born outside of the United States. The foreign-born population of the state in 1890 numbered more than 152,000, about 7 percent of the total population. In 1890 the census listed 710 Chinese, 3 Japanese, and 704 "civilized" Indians. The remaining immigrants were either Mexican or European.

In 1890, there were 105,000 Hispanics living in Texas of which 49 percent had been born in Mexico. By 1900, their numbers increased to more than 164,000 with 43 percent being foreign-born. Although Tejanos were dispersed throughout the state, the largest population of Mexican Americans lived in South Texas, where they greatly outnumbered

Anglos. In West Texas, the population was more ethnically balanced; the Tejano population roughly equaled that of Anglo Americans. In contrast, Central Texas was primarily the home of Anglos and European immigrants, and Mexican Americans were outnumbered by more than 2 to 1 by 1900.

As a community, Tejanos created a bicultural world that borrowed certain features from white society, yet retained many attributes of their traditional Hispanic culture. They preserved their heritage by continuing to speak their native language, by observing secular and religious holidays, by cooking and consuming traditional Hispanic foods, by practicing folk medicine, and by maintaining family values consistent with the Mexican culture. As a way of preserving their traditions, Mexican Americans established mutual aid societies, such as the Sociedad Benito Juárez. To keep their communities abreast of current events in the United States and Mexico (as well as their local region), Tejanos published several Spanish-language newspapers in the latter decades of the nineteenth century.

While maintaining their cultural heritage, Mexican Americans also attempted to fit into mainstream public life in Texas by adapting to Anglo institutions. For example, some successful Tejanos operated ranches in South Texas, including Don Macedonio Vela who owned the Laguna Seca and Dionisio Guerra who owned the Los Ojuelos. Additionally, Tejanos owned and operated various small businesses, such as mercantile stores and specialty shops inside urban areas. Politics also allowed them to enter the mainstream culture. In areas where Tejanos were predominant, such as Laredo, Brownsville, and El Paso, their political participation secured the election of Tejano mayors and other local officials. Though few in number, some served in the state legislature, including Gregorio N. Garcia of El Paso, Santos Benavides of Laredo, and Thomas A. Rodríguez of Pleasanton.

In addition to Tejanos, a large contingent of European immigrants made Texas their new home. Aside from the immigrants who lived in urban areas, many of the Europeans settled in Central Texas in a region known as the "German Belt." Approximately 35,000 Germans lived in Texas in 1860 (65 percent of whom were foreign-born). In the post-Civil War era, the German population increased substantially. Most of the later arrivals moved to the eastern end of the "German Belt," where they purchased land from railroad companies, former plantation owners, and settlers who decided to seek their fortunes further west. This wave of newcomers strengthened the existing German communities and established a number of new settlements. By 1887, the number of Texas Germans had increased to more than 130,000, a number that represented more than half of the European immigrants living in the state.

A diverse group of European immigrants composed the rest of the state's foreign-born population. Slavic settlers began to arrive in the mid-1850s and continued to trickle in throughout the remainder of the nineteenth century. Czech immigrants primarily settled the area around Fayetteville, Fayette County. Serbians originally migrated to Lee County, a community that became home to the Wends. From there, the Serbs moved to South Texas, particularly to Corpus Christi, and to the region around Vernon in Wilbarger County. In Karnes County, Polish settlers established the settlement of Panna Maria in 1854 and from there branched out along the San Antonio River to establish other colonies. During the latter part of the nineteenth century, new Polish immigrants built settlements along the Brazos River, including Bremond in Robertson County.

Other groups eventually made Texas their new home. Italians founded a colony in Montague County and in mining towns such as Thurber, Erath County. Dutch immigrants settled in southeastern Texas, founding the town of Nederland, Jefferson County. Greeks moved into coastal towns where they engaged in commercial fishing. Asian immigrants, though few in number, arrived in Texas during the 1870s and settled in isolated communities in El Paso and Robertson Counties. Asians primarily worked as railroad laborers, and many of them left the region once the railroads were completed. In Robertson County, a few of the Chinese laborers remained, marrying into black families and helping to establish the "Black Chinese" population that inhabited the present-day town of Calvert.

These ethnic Texans helped to establish a diverse society, and each made unique contributions to the state's language, folkways, and behaviors. Distinctive features of each ethnic group, such as food, dances, and music, blended into the existing Texas culture. For the most part, these immigrants became loyal citizens, contributing to the common good of the state through civic participation, military service, and hard-working laborers. Presently, the Institute of Texan Cultures in San Antonio preserves the histories of all cultures who have made Texas their home.

**Literature and the Arts**

During the final decades of the nineteenth century, Texans witnessed the emergence of a distinct literary culture. Authors of the period tended to retell stories from the state's past, focusing especially on the Texas Revolution and early statehood. One of the more famous works was *The Adventure of Big Foot Wallace,* a biography of a noted Texas Ranger who moved to the state to avenge the death of his brother, one of the individuals massacred at Goliad. Some of the authors wrote about their own experiences in Texas. For example, Charles A. Siringo, a West Texas cowboy, entertained readers with his *Texas Cowboy; or Fifteen Years on the Hurricane Deck of a Spanish Pony.* Published in 1885, Siringo's book told of his exploits as a working cowboy. Also popular during this period were stories about notorious outlaws such as Sam Bass and John Wesley Hardin. Many of the myths about Texas's early history were constructed in the writings of this period.

Poetry during this period seemed to lack the same appeal as the adventure stories. Only two Texas poets gained notoriety—William Lawrence Chittenden and John P. Sjolander. Chittenden began writing poetry in the 1880s. His first poem, supposedly inspired by a young San Angelo man, was "The Odd Fellow's Ball" (1885). His most famous work was "The Cowboys' Christmas Ball," which was first published in 1890 in the Anson *Texas Western.* Since its first appearance, the poem has been reprinted and anthologized numerous times. In 1893, G.P. Putnam's sons published a collection of Chittenden's Texas poems entitled *Ranch Verses.* The book went through sixteen editions and earned the author the moniker of "poet-ranchman." Sjolander (pronounced Sholander), who was also known as the "Sage of Cedar Bayou," began publishing poems in *Peterson's Magazine,* the *New York Weekly,* and the *New Orleans Times-Democrat* during the late 1870s and early 1880s. Unlike most writers of his day, Sjolander refused to accept regular writing assignments, claiming that his expression came from "an inward urge," which could not be forced onto the page. In 1928, Hilton R. Greer published *Salt of the Earth and Sea,* a compilation of Sjolander's poems written between 1876 and 1910.

Several noted works of fiction appeared in the final decades of the nineteenth century. Mollie E. Moore Davis wrote *Under the Man-Fig*, a novel that dealt with the destructive nature of gossip in a small town. William Sidney Porter, who wrote under the pen name O. Henry, produced a collection of short stories entitled *Heart of the West*. Published in the early twentieth century, Porter's volume of short stories reflected his own experiences in Texas. He moved to the state in 1882 and worked on a ranch in La Salle County before relocating to Austin and then later Houston.

The preservation of Texas history took a major step forward in 1897 when a group of prominent Texans and scholars formed the Texas State Historical Association. The association began publishing a journal, *Quarterly of the Texas State Historical Association*, which in 1912 became the *Southwestern Historical Quarterly*. During the early twentieth century, both the association and the journal prospered under the direction of noted historians such as George Pierce Garrison, Herbert E. Bolton, and Eugene C. Barker.

One of the state's most prominent artists was Henry Arthur McArdle, a native of Ireland. At fourteen, McArdle's parents died, and he moved to the United States with an aunt, settling first in Baltimore, Maryland. There he studied with David A. Woodward at the Maryland Institute for the Promotion of Mechanic Arts. During the Civil War, he served in the Confederate Navy as a draftsman and later as a topographer for General Robert E. Lee. After the war, McArdle moved to Independence, Texas, where he taught at the Baylor Female College for several years. In Texas, McArdle became interested in Texas history. After Baylor University and Baylor Female College relocated in Waco, McArdle set up a studio in San Antonio. With the support of patron James T. DeShields, he devoted most of his time to painting portraits of Sam Houston, other historical figures of Texas, and battle scenes from the Texas Revolution. Among his most noted works were the twin pieces, *Dawn at the Alamo* (painted between 1876-1905) and *The Battle of San Jacinto* (completed in 1898). Both historical canvases hang in the Senate Chamber in the Texas Capitol. Additionally, McArdle painted *The Settlement of Austin's Colony* (1875), which hangs in the hall of the House of Representatives in the state capitol. Other famous artists of the period included William H. Huddle, whose *Surrender of Santa Anna* (1886) commemorated the fiftieth anniversary of the famous battle and which now hangs in the capitol, and Robert Jenkins Onderdonk who painted various portraits and landscapes of the Dallas and San Antonio areas.

In sculpture, one artist stood above the rest—Elisabet Ney. In 1870, Ney came to Texas with her husband, Dr. Edmund Montgomery, from Bavaria. For Texans, Ney's most famous pieces are her marble statues of Stephen F. Austin, Sam Houston, and Albert Sidney Johnston. For the rest of the country, Elisabet Ney gained fame for her *Sursum*, now at the Chicago Art Institute, and her statue of Lady Macbeth on display at the National Gallery in Washington, D.C.

## Conclusion

Texas during the late nineteenth century experienced numerous changes. The state population was growing and becoming more diverse. While remaining heavily agricultural and rural, signs of industrialization and urbanization were beginning to leave their mark on social and cultural institutions. Even though facilities were unevenly dispersed throughout the state, health care increasingly was available to more Texans than it had been in earlier decades. Women and some ethnic groups made minor gains toward equality, but African Americans still endured many obstacles to complete citizenship. Native Americans perhaps were the biggest losers during this period, as they were forcibly removed from their ancestral lands and placed on reservations in the Indian Territory. A distinct literary and artistic culture emerged in the state but still lagged behind other areas in the country. Nevertheless, Texans had laid the foundations for the tremendous changes that their state would undergo during the next century.

*Afterward: The Legacy of a Baptist Legend*

*Benajah Harvey Carroll died on November 11, 1914. His life had been dedicated to serving the Baptist Church, helping to make the Baptist Church the largest religious denomination in Texas during the late nineteenth century. With the aid of other prominent Baptists, Caroll furthered the church's position on key social issues, such as prohibition, gambling, prostitution, and dancing. Finally, the preacher worked diligently to further education, especially in Baptist-sponsored schools. Viewed collectively, the efforts of the Baptists and other Christian denominations guided Texas into the twentieth century, contributing to the conservative mindset that still prevails in the modern era.*

# Myth & Legend

### African-Americans Landownership in Texas During the Decades Following the Civil War

*One of the enduring myths in Texas history is that less than 10 percent of the African-American population in Texas during the final decades of the nineteenth century owned land. As such, in the decades following the Civil War, the vast majority of black Texans found themselves trapped in a system of debt peonage—sharecropping. Scholars have well documented the plight of southern black sharecroppers, and their assessments have served as the basis for the historical community's understanding of rural Texas life between 1875 and 1900. Recent scholarship, however, has illustrated that African Americans in the Lone Star State were able to break free from the slave-like bonds of sharecropping. In their book* **Freedom Colonies: Independent Black Texans in the Time of Jim Crow** *(University of Texas Press, 2005), Thad Sitton and James Conard, both noted Texas historians, have correctly suggested that this group of African Americans were able to maintain their independence by securing title to their own lands. According to their research, black Texans achieved landownership by a variety of methods: some simply became squatters on unclaimed lands that white Texans deemed unsuitable for farming, while others purchased land from benevolent whites. In a few rare cases, former slaveholders gave plots of land to their former slaves once emancipation was enforced in the state. From these humble landholdings emerged self-sufficient rural communities, known as "freedom colonies." In time, these "colonies" offered African Americans a refuge from a white-dominated world that often treated them with disdain and contempt.*

*Between 1870 and 1890, as the majority of African Americans in the South became trapped in sharecropping, approximately 25 percent of black farmers in Texas acquired their own land. Landownership among the black population grew more rapidly in Texas than in any other southern state. In 1870 only 1.8 percent of the state's black farmers owned land, but by 1890 that number had grown to 26 percent. After the turn of the century, black Texas landownership rose to 31 percent.*

*In many ways, African Americans in Texas became modern-day pioneers. They hunted wild animals on their lands, fished in nearby rivers and streams, built log homes by cutting down trees in surrounding woods, used nineteenth-century farming methods to scratch a living from the ground, and practiced various forms of folk medicine to take care of their injured and sick. As the "freedom colonies" matured into full-fledged communities, African Americans engaged in skilled trades, becoming blacksmiths, carpenters, wagon mak-*

ers, harness makers, basket weavers, millers, and midwives. Through their resourcefulness, blacks living in these communities successfully maintained their independence and limited their need for contact with whites living in the areas surrounding their lands.

Additionally, landownership meant that black social institutions could flourish, including churches and schools. In most communities, the church was the center of life. Often congregations listened to laymen preach the gospel, but occasionally they gathered to hear circuit preachers. The topics of their sermons often resonated with circumstances familiar to African-American audiences, including the fragility of life, the need for love and compassion, the necessity for Christian redemption for sins, and the coming glories of heaven. Though planting and harvesting seasons sometimes disrupted African-American children's education, most communities also maintained a one-room schoolhouse.

African-American landownership in Texas declined fairly rapidly after the 1920s. One of the most important factors contributing to this decline was the division of original land holdings among immediate family members. As decades passed, patriarchs left their land holdings to their children. After a few generations, individual land titles became too small to support commercial farming, prompting the residents to seek financial security in urban areas where economic opportunities were more prevalent. Additionally, whites in the late 1920s and early 1930s began to find legal and extralegal means of taking property away from black landowners. Regardless, some of the communities that blacks forged out of the wilderness continued to thrive and prosper into the twenty-first century.

Thus the myth that only a few (less than 10 percent) of African Americans owned land in Texas in the decades after the Civil War is incorrect. Instead, approximately one-fourth of the African-American population in Texas owned their own land during this period. These landholdings proved extremely beneficial to the development of African—American communities that provided blacks a significant measure of independence.

## Suggestions for Further Reading

Barr, Alwyn. *Black Texans: A History of African Americans in Texas, 1528-1971.* Norman: University of Oklahoma Press, 1996.

Carrigan, William D. *The Making of a Lynching Culture: Violence and Vigilantism in Central Texas, 1836-1916.* Urbana: University of Illinois Press, 2004.

De León, Arnoldo. *The Tejano Community, 1836-1900.* Albuquerque: University of New Mexico Press, 1982.

____. *They Called Them Greasers: Anglo Attitudes toward Mexicans in Texas, 1821-1900.* Austin: University of Texas Press, 1983.

Fairchild, Louis. *The Lonesome Plains: Death and Revival on an American Frontier.* College Station: Texas A&M University Press, 2002.

Glasrud, Bruce and Merline Pitre, eds. *Black Women in Texas History.* College Station: Texas A&M University, 2008.

Glasrud, Bruce and Michael Searles, eds. *Buffalo Soldiers in the West: A Black Soldiers Anthology.* College Station: Texas A&M University Press, 2007.

Jones, Billy M. *Health Seekers in the Southwest, 1817-1900.* Norman, Oklahoma: University of Oklahoma Press, 1967.

Malone, Ann Patton. *Women in the Texas Frontier.* El Paso: Texas Western Press, 1985.

Martin, Robert L. *The City Moves West: Economic and Industrial Growth in Central West Texas.* Austin: University of Texas Press, 1969.

Nixon, Pat Ireland. *A History of the Texas Medical Association, 1853-1953.* Austin: University of Texas Press, 1953.

Price, Johanna E. "Tuberculosis in West Texas, 1870-1940." Ph.D. diss., University of Texas Medical Branch, 1982.

Sitton, Thad and James H. Conrad. *Freedom Colonies: Independent Black Texans in the Time of Jim Crow.* Austin: University of Texas Press, 2005.

Sitton, Thad and Utley, Dan K. Utley. *From Can See to Can't See: Texas Cotton Farmers on the Southern Prairie.* Austin: University of Texas Press, 1997.

Smallwood, James M. *The Feud That Wasn't: The Taylor Ring, Bill Sutton, John Wesley Hardin, and Violence in Texas.* College Station: Texas A&M University Press, 2008.

Rozek, Barbara J. *Come to Texas: Attracting Immigrants, 1865-1915.* College Station: Texas A&M University Press, 2003.

Utley, Robert. *The Indian Frontier of the American West, 1846-1890.* Albuquerque: University of New Mexico Press, 1984.

____. *Lone Star Justice: The First Century of the Texas Rangers.* New York: Oxford University Press, 2002.

**IDENTIFICATION:** Briefly describe each term.

Texas Bureau of Immigration
"Sanitarium of the West"
Temple Sanitarium
Texas State Medical Association
University of Texas Medical Branch
"Aunt Mollie"
Chief Victorio
Buffalo Soldiers
"Juneteenth"
Lt. Henry O. Flipper
Charles A. Siringo
Terrell State Hospital
Taylor Crime Ring
Red River War
Battle of Rattlesnake Springs


**MULTIPLE CHOICE:** Choose the correct response.

1. Living conditions of Texas laborers retained many aspects of the mid-nineteenth century, including:
   A. the heating of homes with fireplaces, iron heaters with coal, and electric stoves.
   B. the heating of homes with fireplaces and wood burning stoves.
   C. the heating of homes with gas and electric furnaces.
   D. traveling from one city to another by electric train.

2. In 1870, all the following cities had populations of more than 3,000, EXCEPT:
   A. Fort Worth
   B. Dallas
   C. Galveston
   D. San Antonio

3. Which diseases became less frequent along the Texas Gulf Coast?
   A. Chicken Pox
   B. Malaria and Yellow Fever
   C. Whooping Cough
   D. Measles

4. By 1900, what was the largest religious denomination practicing in Texas?
   A. Catholics
   B. Methodists
   C. Baptists
   D. Disciples of Christ

5. In 1884, the legislature revised the state school laws. The new school law required all of the following, EXCEPT:
   A. an elected state superintendent of instruction
   B. counties to create new school districts
   C. compulsory attendance for children between 8 and 16 years of age
   D. "hot lunch program" for all students attending Texas schools

6. Who killed the infamous Texas outlaw John Wesley Hardin?
   A. John Selman
   B. Hardin committed suicide
   C. Cullen Montgomery Baker
   D. Bill Longley

7. All of the following were Mexican Americans who served in the state legislature, EXCEPT:
   A. Gregorio N. Garcia
   B. Thomas A. Rodríguez
   C. Don Macedonio Vela
   D. Santos Benavides

8. All the following Texans were noted authors in the nineteenth century, EXCEPT:
   A. Charles A. Siringo
   B. William Lawrence Chittenden
   C. Henry Arthur McArdle
   D. Molley E. Moore Davis

9. Who was the most famous Texas sculptor in Texas during the late 1800s?
   A. Elisabet Ney
   B. Henry Arthur McArdle
   C. William Sidney Porter
   D. John P. Sjolander

10. Who was the Texas Ranger originally placed in command of the Frontier Battalion?
    A. Captain L. H. McNelly
    B. Major John B. Jones
    C. Ben Bickerstaff
    D. John Wesley Hardin

**TRUE/FALSE:** Indicate whether each statement is true or false.

1. By 1900, more than three million people lived in Texas.

2. Railroad development helped to aid the settlement of West Texas.

3. During the last decades of the nineteenth century, more people lived in urban areas than in rural communities.

4. In rural areas of Texas during the late nineteenth century, a journey of 20 miles might take a traveler all day to complete.

5. The two largest Texas cities in 1870 was Galveston and Dallas.

6. Railroads were deemed vital to community development in the late 1800s.

7. In 1887, the Texas League of Professional Baseball Clubs was organized.

8. At the end of the Civil War, the Baptist Church was the largest religious denomination in Texas.

9. All religious groups in Texas during the late 1800s supported prohibition.

10. The Texas educational system was the best in the nation in the late nineteenth century.

**MATCHING:** Match the response in column A with the item in column B.

1. Henry F. Hoyt
2. "lungers"
3. Curanderos
4. Mollie Bailey
5. Texas Federation of Women's Clubs
6. Texas Rangers
7. John Wesley Hardin
8. Bill Longley
9. Captain L. H. McNelly
10. "Buffalo Soldiers"

A. Hispanic folk healers
B. replaced Gov. Davis's state police force
C. led a campaign to create public libraries in the state
D. doctor in the Llano Estacado region
E. noted Texas outlaw who went to prison in 1878
F. owner of a traveling circus
G. desperado noted for indiscriminately killing African Americans
H. African-American troops serving along the frontier
I. a famous Texas Ranger
J. people suffering from tuberculosis

**ESSAY QUESTIONS:**

1. Briefly explain the role that the Texas Rangers played in suppressing lawlessness in Texas during the late nineteenth century.

2. Explain the role women played in society during the late 1800s. Were their lives very different from the lives that their mothers had lived a generation before?

3. Explain how society and culture was changing in Texas between 1875 and 1900. In what ways was Texas society the same? Did urbanization and industrialization change Texas? If so, how? If not, why?

4. Discuss the experiences of African Americans and other ethnic groups in Texas during this era. What hardships did they face? What gains, if any, did they achieve? How did these groups cope with white discrimination?

# The Progressive Era and WWI, 1900-1919

*Prelude: Spindletop—The Beginning of King Oil*

On January 10, 1901, the modern petroleum industry was born near Beaumont, Texas. On that day a group of determined oilmen struck what became the first oil geyser in the history of the United States oil industry. Success, however, had come only after numerous failures. In 1893, the Gladys City Oil, Gas, and Manufacturing Company, founded by George W. O'Brien, George W. Carroll, Pattillo Higgins, Emma E. John, and J. F. Lanier, was the first company to drill on the salt dome formation at Spindletop Hill located on the southern outskirts of town. The company drilled three shallow wells between 1893 and 1895, but discovered no oil.

After Lanier and Higgins left the company, Anthony F. Lucas, a leading expert on salt dome formations, entered into a lease with the Gladys City Company in 1899. Lucas made a separate lease with Higgins a short time later. The lease agreement gave Lucas control of all drilling operations on the salt dome. He set up new oil derricks on land that the Gladys City Company owned. Lucas drilled down to a depth of 575 feet before running out of money. Finances were not the only problem; the drillers were having difficulty with oil sand clogging up their equipment.

Despite these setbacks and negative reports from other geologists who claimed there was no oil at the location, Lucas was able to secure additional financial support from John H. Galey and James M. Guffey. The new investors insisted that Lucas add Al and Curt Hamill, who were experienced drillers from the Corsicana fields in East Texas, to his drilling team. Lucas agreed and turned over drilling operation to the two brothers. Lucas started drilling a new well on October 27, 1900, making use of new advanced drilling equipment that was better suited for drilling in the oil sand that had frustrated Lucas's earlier efforts. On January 10, the well, reaching a depth of 1,139 feet, began to shake and rumble as mud bubbled to the surface. Increasingly, pressure in the well built up, eventually forcing sections of drill pipe out of the hole and through the top of the oil derrick, sending the drilling crew scrambling for safety. After a few minutes, mud, then gas, then oil uncontrollably shot out of the well. It took nearly two weeks for the crew to cap off the well, bringing it under control. Spindletop was the largest gusher in the history of the American oil industry.

*Before the end of the year, oilmen drilled six more wells near Spindletop. Beaumont real estate reached unprecedented heights as speculators moved to the region, hoping to make a fortune in land and oil. For example, one land owner who tried to sell his property for less than $200 in the years prior to 1901, sold his land for $20,000 after news of Spindletop made the newspapers. Within the next fifteen minutes of closing the deal, the property was resold to another investor for $50,000. One well that sold for $1,250,000 made its investors an unprecedented profit, considering that their initial investment was only $10,000. In 1901, $235 million was invested in Texas oil with much of the investments concentrated in the Beaumont area. The city of Beaumont became a boom town with its population increasing from 10,000 to over 50,000 in less than a year after oil was discovered at Spindletop Hill.*

During the Progressive Era (circa 1900 to 1920), optimism and confidence about the state of the nation permeated American society, and Texans shared such sentiments with their counterparts in other states. Spawned by rapid economic and social change, Progressivism appealed to the urban middle class professionals who championed efficiency in government, abhorred corrupt politics, and wanted strict regulation of the economy. Reform movements flourished with different groups of people championing women's suffrage, prohibition, and laws strictly regulating the business community, including railroad companies. Essentially, these reformers promoted ideals that would create a more orderly and equitable society.

Nationally, the Progressive Era spanned the presidencies of Theodore Roosevelt (1901-1909), William Howard Taft (1909-1913), and Woodrow Wilson (1913-1921). At the federal level, all three administrations were responsible for initiating numerous political reforms. Aside from the pursuit of large corporations that violated the nation's antitrust laws, Roosevelt's administration also supported reform legislation designed to improve society, such as the Meat Inspection Act (1906), the Pure Food and Drug Act (1906) and the Hepburn Act (1906). The Meat Inspection Act protected consumers by implementing federal inspections of meat packing companies, while the Pure Food and Drug Act forbade the manufacture and sale of contaminated food products and ineffective patent medicines. The Hepburn Act strengthened the Interstate Commerce Commission's authority to set maximum railroad rates and eventually led to the discontinuation of the rebate system. Furthermore, the act gave the Interstate Commerce Commission authorization to examine the financial records of railroad companies. Finally, the act placed bridges, terminals, ferries, sleeping cars, express companies, and oil pipelines under the control of the commission. President Roosevelt also proved friendly toward labor unions that had emerged during the late nineteenth century to protect workers from the tremendous economic power of corporations. Roosevelt mediated a major conflict between the United Mine Workers and the corporate owners of the eastern coal mines and produced a result that labor leaders believed was fair. At Roosevelt's urging, Congress passed the Federal Employers' Liability Act of 1906 that increased railroad safety regulations, making the companies responsible to employees (and their families) who were injured or killed on the job due to unsafe working conditions. In addition, Roosevelt was a conservationist. He supported the National Reclamation Act of 1902, which, among other things, dealt with water management and irrigation in the arid Southwest. He also set aside 200 million acres of public land as national forests and withstood lobbyists of the timber interests who advocated cutting public timber in six Western states.

William H. Taft won the presidential election of 1908 and, though a conservative by nature, supported numerous Progressive causes. He campaigned in favor of both the Sixteenth and Seventeenth Amendments to the United States Constitution, the former establishing an income tax to relieve the tax burden of farmers and other landholders, the latter calling for the direct election of United States senators. President Taft also supported the development of postal savings banks, allowing rural people without a local depository the opportunity to deposit money in a bank instead of their homes or their persons. He supported the Mann-Elkins Act of 1910, which increased the power of the Interstate Commerce Commission and extended its authority to include regulation of telephone and telegraph companies. Additionally he continued Roosevelt's trust-busting by actually filing more antitrust suits than his predecessor.

After taking office in 1913, Democrat Woodrow Wilson continued the Progressive thrust of the federal government. Like Taft, he championed the Sixteenth and Seventeenth Amendments. Additionally, he supported the creation of the Federal Reserve Act of 1913, which provided currency and banking reform by establishing a strong, publicly-controlled Federal Reserve System. The Federal Reserve Board that oversaw the newly created system allowed the federal government a direct means of influencing the nation's currency supply. In 1913, Wilson championed the Underwood Tariff, which lowered import taxes by an average of 15 percent in an effort to allow foreign goods to compete with America's large companies that had established monopolies over consumer goods and had artificially inflated the price of their products. Other reforms that Wilson championed included passage of the Federal Trade Commission Act of 1914, which established a commission to investigate unfair trade practices, as well as the Clayton Antitrust Act of 1914, which specifically enumerated various illegal practices of monopoly corporations, such as selling at a loss to drive competitors out of business. Overall, the Wilson administration brought almost one hundred lawsuits against capitalists engaged in various illegal activities, especially violations of antitrust legislation.

Furthermore, Wilson and his supporters favored action to help farmers and laborers. In 1916, the Federal Farm Loan Act and the Federal Warehouse Act allowed agrarians to secure long-term, low-interest loans using their land or crops as collateral. The Adamson Act of 1916 established an eight-hour workday for interstate railway workers, and the Workmen's Compensation Act gave federal workers accident and injury protection. Finally, the Keating-Owen Act outlawed the use of child labor to make products traveling in interstate commerce.

In the midst of the reforms taking place at the national level, the Progressives began to enact various reforms throughout the southern states, but the South's reform movement differed dramatically from the movement in the North and West. For example, Texas remained a strong one-party state with Democrats holding supreme power. Unlike Populists, Progressives in the state did not attempt to create a third-party movement. Instead, most of them chose to use the Democratic Party as their vehicle for social and political change. Like the rest of the South, the Progressive movement was primarily concerned with reforms that benefitted whites only. Most Texas politicians firmly supported the idea of white supremacy as well as the segregation of blacks and whites. At best, they were willing to tolerate Tejanos. Restrictions on the right to vote virtually eliminated black and Mexican-American influence in the state government, while Texas politicians argued the legitimacy of "states' rights" every time national politicians commented on the state's refusal to extend the right to vote to all adults and on the state's laws that elevated whites and demoted minority groups.

**Texas: Population and Economic Demographics**

According to the 1900 census, the Texas population was 3,048,710 inhabitants, a number that rose to 3,896,542 ten years later and increased to 4,663,228 by 1920. Among the whites, most were native Texans, but those who did migrate to the state tended to come from other southern states, a development that meant Texans identified strongly with the culture and customs of the South. Most scholars recognize that Texas in the early twentieth century was predominately southern in political ideology, as well as in thought and feeling. Although the state was on the threshold of rapid urbanization, two-thirds of the population lived in rural areas in 1900. Only 20 percent of the people lived in towns of more than 10,000 residents. Likewise, agriculture still dominated the Texas economy at the turn of the century, with at least 800,000 men identifying their occupation as "farmer." As late as 1912, the value of farm and ranch products totaled more than $660 million, a number five times the value of what Texas factories produced. By 1920, Texas led the country in total crop value with the state scoring number one in a number of sub-categories, including cotton production and cattle ranching.

Actually, cotton production was the principle cash crop in Texas, as in most southern states. With cotton prices hovering around 14 cents a pound in 1909 and 1910, farmers produced about 2.5 million bales of cotton in both of those years, suggesting that overall

**Group of Mill Girls. Dallas Cotton Mill, Dallas, Texas. October 1913.**
Photo credit: Library of Congress

agrarians were prosperous. During World War I, prices reached a record high of 35 cents a pound, which suggests that cotton farmers throughout the state also prospered during the war years. However, all farmers did not share equally in the bounty from cotton production. Landowners received the lion's share of the wealth. While some tenants paid landowners cash rent, most gave one-fourth of their crops. Meanwhile, sharecroppers typically received as wages only one-half of the cotton they raised and still had to pay landowners or local merchants high rates of interest for items advanced on credit during the growing season. Both poor whites and poor blacks were caught up in "the system," working and living from season to season, often falling even further in debt. Such farm families lived in squalor but could not escape the land because of the state's overall economic attachment to agriculture. By 1910, 52 percent of all farmers were non-landowner tenants or sharecroppers who remained mired in poverty.

Compared to the wealth that agriculture gave the privileged few, industry was relatively underdeveloped before 1920. The most important exceptions included the lumber, oil, and railroad industries. Centered in East Texas, the lumber industry produced approximately 2.25 billion feet of board lumber in 1907, the area being the nation's third largest producer. However, owners received most of the wealth, while workers endured long hours, low pay, and hazardous working conditions. The national census listed loggers and sawmill workers as among those who were employed in the most dangerous jobs in the nation. In 1900, workers in the lumber industry averaged an eleven-hour workday, a figure that improved to a nine-hour day by World War I. Child labor was rampant in the industry. Between 1900 and 1920, adult workers' average daily pay ranged between $1.50 and $2.50, and children earned even less. Such were the wages of capitalism. Workers tried to improve their conditions by forming labor unions, but their efforts were mostly unsuccessful. For example, in 1910-1911, the Brotherhood of Timber Workers challenged the Southern Lumber Operators' Association, seeking improved wages and working conditions. Their efforts were in vain, producing few measurable results.

The health of the lumber industry was further undermined by owners who had a cut-and-run philosophy. Having little thought about conservation, they cut and logged as quickly as they could and then moved on to new areas, leaving behind barren land where once had stood teeming forests. Production declined during the 1920s, reaching a new low in 1932, as owners produced only 350 million board feet of lumber, a number significantly below the billions of feet produced earlier. The cut-and-run strategy worked well for logging companies during the industry's earlier years of operation, but poor management of the environment spelled disaster for the industry as well as for the conservation movement that would come later.

A second industry emerged after the turn of the century—oil. The oil industry became significant to the state's economy in 1901 when oilmen discovered the Spindletop field near Beaumont. For a time, Spindletop was the most productive field in the United States, but by 1905, the industry had shifted its attention to Oklahoma where new fields promised to be more productive. Nevertheless, in 1909, Texas ranked sixth among all oil-producing states in the country. Just two years later, the state became one of the top five oil producers after drillers discovered the Electra (Wichita County) oil field. During the war years, oil producers successfully drilled wells near the Ranger (Eastland County) and Burkburnett (Wichita County) areas. Additionally, new wells were drilled in areas near

304  *Beyond Myths and Legends*

Oil Gusher,
Port Arthur, Texas,
c. 1901
Photo credit:
Library of Congress

Wichita Falls (Wichita County). By 1920, Texas wells gushed forth 85,000,000 barrels with yet more production coming in the rest of the decade.

While oilmen were discovering new deposits of black gold, railroad companies continued to expand across the state. By 1904, Texas had 11,000 miles of track that were used by seventy-one companies, all regulated by the new Texas Railroad Commission. Slowly, trains were beginning to be supplanted by the new automobile, which was making its way to Texas during the second decade of the twentieth century. Still, railroads were vital to the state's transportation structure and its economy, especially the agricultural sector that used the rail system to ship goods to distant markets. The Railroad Commission worked relentlessly to make sure that freight rates were fair to producers. The commissioners' success in lowering rates was particularly beneficial to small farmers and manufacturers who struggled to survive in a world that had become dominated by large corporations.

During the early twentieth century, Texans began to turn to the use of automobiles and trucks to meet their diverse needs. With cars and trucks came a need for improved roads in both rural and urban areas. By 1910, Texas had 3,591 miles of paved roads. Their efforts to construct new roads was augmented by the Federal Highway Act of 1916, which provided partial federal subsidies for states that aggressively supported road construction.

**Urban Growth and the Galveston Plan**

Although there were 132 urban areas in 1910, only four had populations of more than 50,000 people: San Antonio, Dallas, Fort Worth, and Houston. Cities with a population between 25,000 and 50,000 included Austin, El Paso, Galveston, and Waco. Of all the urban areas, more than 90 had less than 5,000 people, and most were small isolated communities surrounded by wide spans of agricultural lands.

Despite having relatively small populations, many cities in Texas contributed significantly to the national progressive movement by becoming proving grounds for the city commission form of governance. In 1900, Galveston was completely destroyed by a violent hurricane that claimed 6,000 lives. In an effort to deal efficiently and effectively with the aftermath of the disaster, local officials adopted a new system of city government—the commission system—that emphasized efficiency and problem-solving rather than politics. In the city commission government, also known as the Galveston Plan, voters elect members to a governing body known simply as a commission. City commissions typically consist of five to seven members who are responsible for the governance of the city, including taxation, appropriations, ordinances, and other municipal functions. Individual commissioners are assigned specific municipal tasks such as public works, finance, public safety, and waste management. In some cases, one of the commissioners is designated as a chairman, or mayor, but this is usually a formality and the designee does not exercise greater authority than the other commissioners. This form of government body blends the executive and legislative branches. The city commission system worked well after the hurricane destroyed Galveston because each commissioner was responsible for a specific task of rebuilding the city, including the disposal of the dead (both animals and humans), the removal of wrecked buildings, the rebuilding of docks and buildings, the construction of a seawall to prevent a similar event from occurring during future hurricanes, and other governmental responsibilities.

By 1910, the commission model had spread to Dallas, Fort Worth, and Houston, as well as numerous small cities and towns in Texas, and the concept caught on in other

**Rows of tents are set up to house survivors of the 1900 Galveston hurricane.
Photo credit: Library of Congress**

states as well. In many areas nationwide, businessmen and professionals lobbied for the new system of municipal government because it was efficient, and it also weakened local aldermen and replaced the old ward system that many reformers believed was hopelessly corrupt. Progressives continued to support the city commission plan until the end of World War I, when the council-manager form of government (a system closely aligned to familiar corporate business structures) became more popular among urbanites.

**Texas Politics: Early Progressive Era**

Beginning with the twentieth century, Texas voters once again found favor with the more conservative politics of the Democratic Party, particularly since the Populist threat had subsided and the Republican Party was hopelessly divided along racial lines. The Democrats were fortunate in that party infighting had been kept to a minimum, primarily due to the efforts of one man—Colonel Edward M. House, a successful Houston businessman who enjoyed the campaign battles associated with partisan politics. He first became involved in campaign politics when he helped Governor James Hogg win reelection in 1892. Thereafter, he was involved in the campaigns of Governor Charles Culberson in 1894 and 1896, of Joseph Sayers in 1898 and 1900, and of Samuel Willis Tucker Lanham in 1902 and 1904. House's success resulted from his tactics. He relied on careful, calculated organization and a few powerful friends to influence the outcomes of elections. In 1912, Colonel House served as campaign advisor to President Woodrow Wilson and helped him win the election, securing a place for himself in the Wilson administration as his closest advisor.

Further bolstering conservative politics in Texas were the gubernatorial victories of Sayers and Lanham. Both were Confederate veterans, and both favored pro-business legislation that tended to favor the emerging oil industry and the surging lumber interests. Neither individual served as a force for political, social, or economic change.

Despite the conservative nature of politics, the last vestiges of Populism contributed to the movement to disenfranchise black and poor white voters in Texas. After 1900, individuals who supported limiting voting rights were divided by their motives. A majority of whites, especially conservative Democrats, reform-minded Hogg Democrats, and Populists, were disturbed that political parties during the 1890s had attempted to appeal to and use black voters to win state elections. They agreed that disenfranchisement of blacks would mean less violent political battles between whites. The more reform-minded Democrats viewed disenfranchisement of black voters as a means for bringing Populists back to their party so that they could join ranks against conservatives. Disenfranchisement of black voters, however, was an elusive and complicated task, especially considering that the Fifteenth Amendment to the United States Constitution prevented the legislature from singling out one particular group of voters. Thus, if they disenfranchised blacks, they would likely disenfranchise a large segment of poor whites at the same time. Nevertheless, Texas politicians of all stripes initiated a movement for political reform (disenfranchisement) that carried over into the twentieth century, primarily in the renewed call for a poll tax as a requirement for voting. While only one dollar, the tax was large enough to prevent many of the poorer citizens of the state, regardless of color, from voting. In 1902, the legislature proposed a constitutional amendment that permitted the use of a poll tax as a requirement for voting. Despite opposition from North Texas Populists, South Texas political bosses, labor organizations, and the State Brewers Association (all of which depended in one way or another on the votes of the poor and the minorities), with the aid of reform Democrats, East Texas Populists, and prohibitionists, conservative Democrats were able to see the amendment pass with a 2 to 1 vote.

Following the referendum on the poll tax amendment, Alexander Watkins Terrell sponsored two additional election-reform bills that passed in 1903 and 1905. The earlier legislation law provided stricter enforcement of the poll tax and established a specific day for primary elections. Furthermore, the Democratic county committees could create standards for participation in a primary, which meant that they could prevent black voters from participating in the party's nomination process. The "white primary" became a common feature of nominating Democratic candidates for more than three decades. The Terrell Law of 1903 also identified procedures for conducting elections, such as the Australian ballot (secret ballot), and for removing responsibility of working the elections from the hands of the parties. While these reforms promised to help clean up corrupt election practices, Terrell was still unsatisfied that the law made it difficult for independents to get on the ballot, that it did not provide for election poll watchers, and that it failed to state that election judges in the general elections must be from different parties. More importantly, Terrell was disappointed that the law left it up to the discretion of the parties whether to hold primaries or to rely on conventions in selecting their candidates.

The Terrell Election Law of 1905 strengthened the earlier law by giving independent parties a place on the ballot and by requesting that parties that polled more than 100,000 votes in the general election hold primaries in July. In Section 120, legislators stipulated that, in county conventions where no single candidate won a clear majority of the primary vote, delegates would be divided equally among the candidates. Furthermore, candidates would be listed on the ballot according to the office sought rather than being grouped together according to party affiliation. Finally, the law required that poll watchers would come from all parties, and it banned newspaper articles for or against candidates that had not been written by the editor, except for paid advertisements.

Refinements of the new laws came in 1907, 1913, and 1918, the result of which gave Texas a modern, orderly, democratic system of choosing a slate of political candidates. Despite such progress, most African Americans and poor whites still found it difficult to vote, because they often could not pay the poll tax. In addition, the Terrell Election Laws established the basis for primaries where only whites could participate in the primary elections. Because Texas was a one-party state, whites were able to basically disenfranchise black voters by not allowing them to participate in the primary elections, where the "real" race for office was decided, especially considering that whichever candidate won the Democratic primary was assured victory in the general election. Texas would make white primaries legal throughout the state in 1923, but many counties had already effectively barred blacks from participating in the primary process prior to the passage of the statute.

Between 1900 and 1920, reform-minded politicians aided organized labor by passing pro-labor legislation, including laws that limited railroad workers (especially porters) to sixteen hour days, that made it illegal to blacklist employees, and that made it illegal for companies to force their employees to trade at the company stores or to force their employees to use company scrip. These laws were specifically designed to prevent corporations from exploiting their employees to maximize their profits. Additionally, new laws were passed to ban child labor in the workplace. However, because the child labor laws were loosely enforced, businessmen simply ignored the new ban and continued to exploit children for higher profits.

During this same period, state lawmakers passed several laws designed to reform the state's economy. They raised taxes on corporations, including the railroad and insurance industries. Urged on by Thomas B. Love, a Progressive from Dallas, the legislature established a commission of banking and insurance to monitor the activities of companies operating in those specific fields. To prevent banking abuses and to spur local investments, the legislature also initiated a constitutional amendment in 1903, ratified in 1904, that allowed the government to charter state banks, a practice previously outlawed by the Constitution of 1876. Directed by Love, the new commission chartered 500 new state banks by 1910.

Despite the passage of various Progressive measures, conservative legislators effectively blocked many of the reformers' proposals. For example, the legislature failed to pass laws to regulate usurious interest rates, to regulate the operations of private banks, to raise fees on liquor licenses, and to create a comprehensive pure food and drug policy. Progressives, however, did enjoy some limited success in regulating monopoly trusts. Having witnessed increased industrialization in Texas during the late nineteenth and early twentieth centuries, the legislature passed antitrust laws in 1889 and 1903 to protect consumers and local business interests. By 1917, the state had prosecuted more than one hundred companies for violating the state's antitrust laws. The most notable case involved Waters-Pierce Oil Company, a Missouri-based business that had extensive drilling operations in Texas. Because Waters-Pierce was a member of the Standard Oil of New Jersey trust agreement, Texas Attorney General Martin M. Crane initiated an antitrust suit against the company in 1897. In the case, the court ruled against Waters-Pierce and revoked its state charter, which had allowed the company to conduct business in Texas. After the court decision, Henry Clay Pierce appealed to his friend Joseph Weldon Bailey, a Texas congressman and later senator. After examining the matter, Bailey asked Pierce to reorganize his company to comply with the state's antitrust statutes, a suggestion that Pierce followed. Once the company had been reorganized to comply with state regulations, Congressman Bailey asked Governor Sayers to push a new grant through the legislature providing the company a new charter. Again operating in Texas, the Waters-Pierce Oil Company experienced a rocky time. In 1906, Missouri officials investigated Waters-Pierce's activities in Missouri and found that the company's connection with Standard Oil (which held 3,000 shares in Waters-Pierce) violated the Missouri antitrust laws. The actions against Waters-Pierce in Missouri led to further legal actions taken against the company in Texas.

Some critics had always held that Bailey had a conflict of interest in representing his friend, Henry Clay Pierce, because Bailey, now a United States Senator, had received fees for representing Pierce and also secured a $13,300 loan from him. As well, information turned up showing that Bailey had also accepted money from both the Kirby lumber interests and Standard Oil. Prosecuted again in 1906, Waters-Pierce again lost its Texas charter and paid a fine of just over $1.8 million for violation of state laws. Although Bailey received much negative notice for his ties to both Standard Oil and Waters-Pierce, Texas's Democratic voters returned him to the U.S. Senate in the 1906 primary election. Nevertheless, Bailey found himself out of step with Progressive politicians who constituted a strong force in Washington, D.C. The Texas senator opposed many Progressive issues, including prohibition, women's suffrage, and the selection of national Democratic presidential candidate Woodrow Wilson who received the Texas delegation's votes in the Democratic Convention of 1912. Given trends against him, Bailey retired in 1913 only to return to politics for a final hurrah by campaigning for governor in 1920. He was soundly defeated by Pat Neff in the Democratic primary, after which he spent his later years in political obscurity.

Meanwhile, Progressives continued to dominate the governorship. Thomas A. Campbell held the office from 1907-1911. From Palestine, Texas, Campbell led the most reform-oriented legislature in state history. Perhaps the most important law passed during Campbell's term was the Robertson Insurance Law of 1907, which forced insurance companies to invest at least 75 percent of money drawn from Texans in real estate or in securities, and which limited premiums and regulated other aspects of the insurance business. During Campbell's administration, the legislature passed laws prohibiting insolvent corporations from entering Texas, strengthening existing antitrust legislation (especially against the railroad monopoly), stopping the wholesale granting of railroad passes designed to controlling nepotism in hiring state employees, and raising fees on liquor dealers. Campbell also wanted a state income tax but failed to secure it. However, the legislators did pass an inheritance tax, which the governor strongly supported. In 1909, the state passed the Bank Deposit Guaranty Law, which protected deposits in the newly-chartered state banks. The plan worked well until circa 1927 when a downturn in the state's economy strained the system and forced lawmakers to repeal the law.

Following Campbell, Oscar B. Colquitt became the next governor of Texas even though he won only a plurality in both the Democratic primary and the general election of 1910. Governor from 1911 to 1915, he opposed prohibition and generally represented himself as a conservative. Yet, when the legislature acted, Colquitt did not always stand in the way of reform. During his term, lawmakers passed statutes regulating child labor, the hours of women workers, and factory safety provisions. The legislators also passed a law providing state employees with workmen's compensation, and they passed legislation that called for major prison reforms. They provided money to build a state tuberculosis hospital, allowed counties to set up poor farms for the impoverished, and provided resources to build a training school for delinquent children.

Beyond the support of selected reforms, Colquitt's administration faced two major issues: problems along the Rio Grande border with Mexico and problems with the state's finances. The Mexican Revolution of 1910 had a significant impact on the regions along the Texas-Mexico border. The revolutionaries bought arms and other military items from Texas merchants and recruited north of the border, targeting Tejanos who sympathized with the insurgents. They also led raids into South Texas to secure needed supplies in which they sabotaged trains that were taking materials to the established government of Mexican dictator Porfirio Díaz. Generally speaking, South Texas became part of the battleground in the 1910 Mexican Revolution. As the revolution was developing, President Taft (and later President Wilson) had to remain cautious even though both sent troops to the border at different times. Colquitt eventually acted forcefully by sending Texas Rangers to border areas where he feared for the lives of Texans and the safety of their property. After the United States military occupied Vera Cruz in 1914, the governor sent National Guard units to Brownsville to alleviate the fears of South Texans who were concerned that Mexican troops might invade their towns. Critical of President Wilson, Colquitt wanted him to react more strongly and to intervene directly in the Mexican Revolution. The president's refusal strained relations between the governor and many other Progressives who tentatively supported Wilson's policies. Aside from foreign problems, Colquitt inherited a low tax base for running the state government and implementing its programs. He entered office with Texas having a $1 million deficit. He raised tax rates but the expanding expenditures for a modern state seeking reforms continued to worry him throughout his term.

When Colquitt retired after his second term, James E. Ferguson emerged as the next front-runner for the governorship in 1914. A banker from Temple, Texas and a self-taught lawyer, Ferguson won two terms as governor, serving from 1915 to 1917. While his supporters hailed him as a friend of sharecroppers and tenants, Ferguson's political career was marred by what his critics said about his demagoguery and corruption. Unlike the majority of Progressives, he stood against prohibition and tried to rise above the issue by ignoring it. He campaigned hard in the agricultural areas of the state, while promising to limit the amount of rent that landlords could charge tenants. Many scholars claim that he rode the backs of poor farmers to the governor's mansion; however, their assessment of the election is unlikely, primarily because poor farmers were the least able to pay the required poll tax for voting. It seems certain that Ferguson rode into office on the coattails of Oscar Colquitt, particularly in light of the fact that they differed little in many political stances, especially in relation to prohibition. Regardless of the actual turnout, Ferguson received enough votes to defeat Thomas H. Ball of Houston (who was a prohibitionist) in the Democratic primary, a clear indication that prohibitionists did not have majority support in the state. With Texas still a one-party state, Ferguson easily carried the general election.

In his first term, Ferguson fulfilled his promise to tenant farmers by signing a bill into law that limited tenant rent. But the state attorney general did not rigorously enforce the law, and the United States Supreme Court eventually ruled that the law was unconstitutional, thereby handing Ferguson a stinging defeat. On other issues, the governor and the legislature were more successful. Together they appropriated more funding for state colleges and for the University of Texas, and they founded the State Department of Forestry. After winning a second term, Ferguson again increased money for education, supported the founding of new colleges, and supported the creation of the Texas Highway Department.

Nevertheless, Ferguson's second term was wracked with continual problems, especially on the Mexico-Texas border where Mexican revolutionaries engaged in cross-border raids of Texas towns in the Rio Grande Valley. In addition, the *Plan de San Diego* (1915), supposedly written in 1915 in San Diego in Duval County, called on Tejanos to rise up and support the revolution. Furthermore, the plan called for other minority groups to fight Texas and to create a republic out of the land that the United States had taken from Mexico in 1848 (see Mexican-American War, 1846-1848). Ferguson responded to the threat by sending all available Texas Rangers into the fray until the trouble abated, only to have violence flare up again in 1916, whereupon the governor sent in units of the National Guard. The South Texas region quieted somewhat in late 1916 when Mexico and the United States entered negotiations to reach a diplomatic solution to the difficulties occurring on the border. Still, sporadic raids continued to occur between 1917 and 1918.

Because the local and state lawmen believed that many Mexican Texans cooperated with leaders of the raids, local law enforcement, Texas Rangers, and vigilante groups indiscriminately murdered many innocent Tejanos. The attacks were so frequent and severe that lawmakers eventually abolished several companies of Texas Rangers.

Aside from the border issue, Ferguson also had trouble brewing in his own backyard in Austin. Because he demanded control over the University of Texas budget, he suffered a deteriorating relationship with the school's administrators, starting with acting president William J. Battle. Opponents suggested that Ferguson's early rhetoric disguised what he really wanted—to remove faculty and administrators who opposed his political positions. Additional complications added to the muddle, and the governor vetoed the university's appropriations as he had threatened to do if university administrators did not meet his demands. University personnel then called for the governor's impeachment. The university quickly gained support from outside organizations. The first such organization was the Texas Equal Suffrage Association, which supported university officials primarily because its members were dissatisfied with Governor Ferguson's stance against women's suffrage. Many Progressives who favored prohibition also lined up as opponents of the governor. Ferguson's deteriorating political fortune continued to decline after questions surfaced concerning his mingling state revenues with his own private funds, as well as about questionable loans from lobbyist groups. For example, it became known that Ferguson had taken a $156,000 loan from brewing interests in the state, but he had not made any effort to pay the loan off.

The political storm intensified when the speaker of the house called for a special session on July 23, 1917. The speaker's action was unconstitutional (only the governor can call the legislature into special session), but Ferguson concurred with the decision and approved the special session, perhaps believing that he could win any fight that the legislators threw his way. As events proved, the Texas House of Representatives impeached the governor on twenty-one separate charges. The Texas Senate confirmed ten of the charges and was preparing to convict Ferguson on seven of them when the governor resigned on September 2, hoping to avoid what seemed to be an assured conviction. The legislators acted anyway, removed him, and barred him forever from holding another state office. Despite his defeat, Ferguson refused to retire from politics. Instead, when Lieutenant Governor William P. Hobby announced his campaign to run for governor in 1918, Ferguson ran against him, arguing that his resignation trumped the senate's conviction and its ban on him. The ex-governor lost the race but started another political circus later by running unsuccessfully for a United States Senate seat. Governor Ferguson would later surface again as the power behind his wife, Miriam, who was elected to two terms as governor (1925-1927 and 1933-1935).

## Texas and World War I

Texans were keenly interested in European events that eventually led to the beginning of World War I in August 1914. Shortly after the sinking of the British luxury liner, the *Lusitania*, in May 1915, a group of legislators introduced a resolution into the Texas senate asking for the United States to break diplomatic relations with Germany. Not only were they upset that the Germans were engaged in unrestricted submarine warfare, but the Texans were also concerned because Germany had attempted to cause trouble along the Mexican border. Germany wanted to provoke a war between Mexico and the United States in an effort to keep the American military out of the war in Europe. To achieve their goal, Germany encouraged internal divisions in the Mexican government, primarily between President Venustiano Carranza, General Victoriano Huerta, and Pancho Villa. The United States closely monitored the revolutionary activities taking place in Mexico. In March 1916, the United States was forced to send military personnel to the border when Pancho Villa's men raided the small town of Columbus, New Mexico. President Woodrow Wilson sent General John J. Pershing in charge of what became known as the "Punitive Expedition" into northern Mexico to capture Villa, but the American forces were unsuccessful. In Texas, the National Guard was placed on call.

Despite the problems on the border, President Wilson remained hesitant to enter the war in Europe until British agents intercepted and decoded an important message from the German foreign secretary, Arthur Zimmermann, to his minister in Mexico. The telegram instructed the German minister to offer an alliance and financial assistance to Mexico in the event that the United States entered the European war against Germany. In return for their loyalty, Germany promised to return to Mexico all the lost territory in Texas, New Mexico, and Arizona. The Texas media quickly spread word of the intrigue. The *San Antonio Light* stated that Texans would fight to the death to protect their state from a German-Mexican invasion. Newspapers across the state expressed the same sentiments. Due to growing public pressure and his outrage over the Zimmermann telegram, President Wilson asked Congress for a declaration of war against Germany on April 2, 1917. Four days later, Congress officially authorized the declaration.

Texans overwhelmingly supported Congress's decision to go to war, including the federal draft, in which more than 989,000 men registered. By the war's end, 197,789 Texas volunteers and draftees saw service in the armed forces. Two noted units from Texas were the Thirty-Sixth Infantry Division and the Nineteenth Division. Added to the count were 449 Texas women who served as nurses or hospital staff. A total of 5,171 (including one nurse) died in the armed services (4,748 in the army), but slightly more than one-third of the armed forces perished while still in the United States as a result of the Spanish influenza outbreak that swept the globe in 1918, killing millions of people. Four Texans were awarded the Medal of Honor: David Hayden, Samuel Sampler, David Barkley, and Daniel Edwards.

Texas experienced positive economic growth during the war, primarily from the military training camps established in the state, including Camp MacArthur (Waco), Camp Logan (Houston), Camp Travis (San Antonio), and Camp Bowie (Fort Worth). Additionally, Leon Springs Military Reservation, an officer's training school, was built at Leon Springs, and several aviator schools were established throughout the state, including Hicks Field (near Fort Worth), Call Field (near Wichita Falls), and Kelly Field (San Antonio). While some of these camps were closed at the end of the war (November 11, 1918), others remained open and continued to help support the economies of the nearby communities.

Blacks comprised about 25 percent of the Texans who served during World War I, and their wartime experience strained race relations in the state. For example, in Huntsville, a black man stood accused of draft-dodging, and a white lynch-mob murdered him and six members of his family. Because of white racial discrimination, a major riot erupted in Houston, resulting in several deaths and courtmartials of black soldiers who were severely punished. In the imbroglio, blacks killed sixteen whites, while wounding eleven more. Of the African Americans involved, four died in the fight. While ugly racial episodes occurred, no one could deny the otherwise valiant effort that black Texans gave their country.

To coordinate the war effort, Congress created the National Council of Defense. In parallel moves, each state created its own council, as did most local areas. Texans created 240 county councils and 15,000 local ones. The work of the councils included many tasks. They organized liberty bond drives, solicited donations for the Red Cross, set up dining halls and rest areas for traveling soldiers, and helped direct scrap metal drives and the collection of other material including used rubber tires. Additionally, council members organized children's brigades, which collected anything of use for the war effort; enforced the occasional rationing of commodities needed by the military men, including meat, wheat, and oils; encouraged patriotism; and publicized the war effort. On the negative side, councilmen were ever on the alert for "disloyal slackers" who did not contribute to the effort. After Congress passed the national Sedition and Espionage Acts, they acted as snoops, ready to give names to the authorities of anyone whom they suspected of interfering with the cause.

In Texas, as in the rest of the nation, the war caused economic dislocations and changes in traditional gender roles. Inflation increased, and wages failed to match it. People found that their money bought less. The cost of state and local government went up as officials coped with the costs of the war effort and the cost of various social programs and institutions associated with Progressive reformers. Women experienced temporary gains in the workforce. Middle and working class women began to find employment in factories where they replaced the men who had joined the military. Many took jobs that had previously been labeled as "men's jobs." They also joined volunteer efforts, including the defense councils and the Red Cross. They staffed most of the soldiers' canteens, working often without pay. Additionally, women sold liberty bonds and war saving stamps; made kits for soldiers that included cigarettes, candy, and other non-perishable goods; made ready-to-use bandages; collected books and magazines to send to the fighting men; and helped with rationing by giving lessons on successful vegetable gardening to increase yield and teaching others to can their vegetable output. Some women took a more active role in overseas operations by joining the nursing corps and tending to injured service men in military hospitals.

**Women and the Vote**

Women in Texas had long yearned to participate in politics on an equal footing with men. As a result, they petitioned the constitutional conventions of 1868 and 1875 for the franchise without success. Later, in May 1893, Rebecca Henry Hayes of Galveston helped to organize the Texas Equal Rights Association in Dallas. The association soon had numerous branches throughout Texas, and its members were successful in pushing state legislators to consider a bill enfranchising women in 1895. Unfortunately, the organization was short-lived. In June 1895, divisions emerged between Hayes and the executive members at the organization's state convention in Dallas, and the membership chose not to reelect Hayes as its president. Without her leadership, the organization fell into decline, eventually ceasing to exist in 1896.

Following the turn of the century, interest in women's suffrage was revived when Annette Finnigan and her sisters, Elizabeth and Katherine, founded the Equal Suffrage League of Houston in early 1903. A similar organization was soon founded in Galveston, and together the two groups established the Texas Woman Suffrage Association, electing Annette Finnigan as the new organization's president. However, the suffrage movement experienced another setback when the Finnigan sisters moved out of state just two years after the founding of the organization. Without the Finnigan's leadership, the Texas Woman Suffrage Association eventually became defunct. Still, the issue of women's suffrage continued to attract the attention of Texans. In 1907, Representative Jess A. Baker of Granbury introduced a resolution before the Texas House of Representative to enfranchise women. During legislative hearings, the famous artist, Elisabet Ney, and the president of the Women's Christian Temperance Union, Helen M. Stoddard, along with several other prominent Texas women, spoke in full support of the bill. Despite their efforts, however, the legislators remained unmoved, and the committee on constitutional amendments recommended that the resolution be dropped from consideration.

In April 1913 members of several smaller suffrage clubs banded together and reactivated the Texas Woman Suffrage Association. They selected Mary Eleanor Brackenridge as their president, a position she held until April 1914, when she was replaced by Annette Finnigan, who had returned to the state. The following year Finnigan was replaced by Minnie Fisher Cunningham of Galveston. In 1916, the organization voted to change its name to the Texas Equal Suffrage Association. Cunningham remained the president of the organization until it was replaced by the League of Women Voters in Texas in October of 1919.

In Texas, women's suffrage gained rapid acceptance after World War I, especially following the impeachment and removal from office of Governor Ferguson, who was replaced by Lieutenant Governor William P. Hobby, a supporter of suffrage rights for women. With the aid of the new governor and other like-minded politicians, in 1918 the Texas legislature passed a bill that gave women the right to vote in primaries. Considering that Texas was almost a single-party state, women's ability to vote in the Democratic primary was almost equivalent to full enfranchisement. As a result of that development, women soon emerged as a solid voting bloc and helped get many of their favorite candidates elected to office, including some women officeholders. In 1919, Texas became the first southern state to ratify the Nineteenth Amendment and the ninth among all the states. In 1920, the amendment was ratified, officially granting women full access to the polls.

**Minorities and the Progressive Movement**

Although Texas women had numerical parity with the male population, they still had minority status during the early Progressive Era. Women certainly had a restricted place in society, and they were expected to marry, have children, and remain homemakers for all their days.

They could not vote, and laws gave males control of communal property within a marriage. Those who worked outside the home suffered from wage discrimination and from strict limits on the types of jobs available to women. Poor and lower middle class women saw little improvement of their caste status before 1920, but reform was stirring within the women's movement of the middle and upper classes. Under Anna Pennybacker, the Texas Federation of Women's Clubs pursued moderate reform—including suffrage—for improving the status of women. More forceful in their demands, Minnie Cunningham, Jessie Ames, and other leaders of the Texas Woman Suffrage Association explained that a country that deprived half its population from voting was not a true democracy, a most valid point. More negative was the association's propaganda that argued that white men needed their wives' and daughters' votes to counter the votes of blacks, Hispanics, and ethnic groups such as the German-Americans. Gaining political strength from the national women's movement and from participation in the impeachment of Governor James E. Ferguson in 1917, suffragists won the approval of female voting in the Democratic primary, but in 1919 voters refused to support an amendment to the state constitution that would have given women the right to vote in general elections. Despite that setback, Texas suffragettes celebrated victory when the state legislature ratified the Nineteenth Amendment to the U.S. Constitution that gave women the vote. Many of the state's women and women's groups also participated in the drive for prohibition.

During the Progressive Era, blacks remained the state's biggest minority. The census of 1910 reported that 18 percent of all Texans were African Americans, the great majority of whom lived in the eastern one-third of the state, their home since the days of slavery. They had a majority of the population in only ten counties, but earlier disfranchisement guaranteed that they would have little political input even there. Thus, politically powerless, the state's black community lived with all the humiliations and limitations of social segregation in almost all aspects of life.

Texas had segregated schools by law and had complete social and housing segregation by custom. In most cities and towns, residential areas were racially defined. Blacks lived in the poorer section of the community, while whites tended to live in the more modern areas. Segregated public transportation was also the rule, as were cemeteries, grocery stores, physicians' offices, movie theaters, and other public places where whites and blacks might come into contact with one another. The state even had segregated commercial telephone booths. Although the new National Association for the Advancement of Colored People (NAACP) and the new Negro Business League tried to secure some improvements for the black community, such efforts usually failed due to white hostility to any proposed changes in race relations. White race riots in Houston in 1917 and in Longview in 1919 underscored white determination to keep blacks in a subservient position relative to the Anglo population.

The Tejano population did not suffer the complete social segregation that blacks endured, but they still suffered repression and second-class citizenship. Some 250,000 lived in South Texas where they were mired in poverty—able to enjoy very few of life's modern conveniences. By 1901, many Hispanics worked for fifty cents a day. Politically, many remained subordinate to political machines managed by whites, like James B. Wells of Cameron County and Archer Parr of Duval County, who ruled in their respective counties with iron fists. Such political bosses provided Hispanics with a few social services, but the political price was high. Tejanos generally voted for the interests of the machines and generally had little choice but to accept their fate. Uplift of the Hispanic population would not occur for several more decades.

Indian Texans also suffered at the hands of the white power structure. So much oppression of Native Americans in Texas had occurred that, according to the United States

Census, only 470 people identified themselves as "Indian." They were no doubt trying to avoid the stigma of the word. Native Americans generally lived a life of poverty, a life with little hope for improvement. During the early part of the new century, most Indians lived on land earlier allotted by the government or in small, isolated rural settlements that could scarcely be called towns. They lived well apart from the economic activity and the job opportunities that urban areas offered other Texans.

**The Drive for Prohibition**

Before the Progressive Era, reformers made halting efforts to ban alcohol in Texas, but in 1887, voters failed to approve a prohibition amendment to the Texas Constitution. For years thereafter, people seemed to accept the local-option rule wherein municipalities, precincts, and counties had the option to ban alcohol. In subsequent years, most of North Texas, with the exception of Dallas and Fort Worth, went "dry" (supported prohibition) with some areas in East and Central Texas moving in the same direction. Areas in South-Central Texas, which supported large populations of Hispanic Catholics and ethnic Germans, tended to remain "wet" (opposed prohibition). Liquor interests noted the dry trends in areas other than South Texas and finally became alarmed. In 1901, they organized the Texas Brewers Association. In 1903, the new group supported a legislative initiative that provided a two-year mandatory waiting period between local-option elections to prevent temperance groups from forever having the prohibition issue in front of the public. A majority in the legislature voted down the mandatory limit, but the brewers' strong stand convinced prohibitionists to launch a stronger campaign against the "wets."

In 1903, the Texas Local Option Association emerged and began to dispense propaganda and speakers to wet areas, trying to convince the communities to ban alcohol and its evils. The Local Option Association fight against alcohol was strengthened in 1907 when the Anti-Saloon League entered Texas. The league stressed tight organization at the local level and lobbied to convince members of the legislature to take action, while simultaneously working through evangelical churches and their pastors to alert the public about the dangers of alcohol. Members also advocated and helped to plan popular protests against demon rum. With Baptists and Methodists advancing in the front ranks of the movement, their newspapers (the *Baptist Standard* and the *Texas Christian Advocate*, a Methodist publication) carried propaganda messages labeling alcohol as the tool of Satan himself.

The anti-alcohol movement maintained the support of most Texas Progressives. Although anti-prohibition forces labeled the prohibitionists as religious cranks and condemned their activities, the temperance movement would ultimately be triumphant on January 1, 1920, when the Eighteenth Amendment to the Constitution went into effect. Under the amendment's provisions, Americans were forbidden by law from selling, manufacturing, and transporting intoxicating liquors. Actually, in Texas, prohibitionists had enjoyed even earlier success, because voters narrowly passed an amendment to the state constitution that banned alcohol in May 1919 prior to the Eighteenth Amendment going into effect but after the state had already approved the national amendment in February of 1918.

### *Afterward: The Bequests of Spindletop—The Oil Industry in Texas*

*Overproduction in the Spindletop oil fields led to a rapid decline in production. Having yielded 17,500,000 barrels of oil by 1902, production dropped during the next two years to 10,000 barrels a day. Even so, the Spindletop fields had not dried out. A second boom would come as companies began to drill deeper wells. The wells at and near the Spindletop fields continued to be productive throughout the 1920s and subsequent decades. In fact, by 1985, the Spindletop fields had produced over 153,000,000 barrels of oil.*

*The discovery of oil at Spindletop had a profound effect on the oil industry. Companies quickly began to search for similar deposits, and investors spent billions of dollars in oil and gas exploration throughout Texas. The fossil fuels that they found revitalized and revolutionized the American transportation systems and created new industries in the United States. In Texas alone, more than 500 corporations were doing business in the Beaumont area. Many of the major oil companies were founded during the era or grew in size, including the Texas Company (later became Texaco), Gulf Oil Corporation, Sun Oil Company, Magnolia Petroleum Company, and Humble (which later became the Exxon Company). The Texas economy benefited immensely from the oil boom that started at Spindletop. Texans would use the money generated by oil production to build one of the strongest state economies in the Union.*

# Myth & Legend

### A Strange Tale from the Galveston Hurricane of 1900

*On the morning of September 8, 1900, crowds bustled through the streets of Galveston. Aside from the wind and rain, their day began the same as any other workday in the port city. But in the Gulf of Mexico, a murderous storm was slowly making its way to the Texas coast. Throughout the morning, the tide continued to rise, and the wind gradually increased. Slightly alarmed, Isaac M. Cline, the local Weather Bureau official, began warning people living in low areas to evacuate the city. However, few people had followed his advice before the bridge connecting Galveston Island to the mainland collapsed. Like the bridge, houses near the Gulf began to disappear when the storm lifted debris from one row of homes and buildings and hurled it against the next row until the majority of the city had been destroyed. As the storm grew more intense, people who were trying to make their way to safe shelters were bombarded with flying debris, and according to some reports, a few individuals were decapitated by flying slate from roofs of homes. As the storm reached its peak (at approximately 5:15 PM), the winds reportedly reached a sustained speed of 84 miles per hour, but gusts of more than 100 miles per hour were recorded. At approximately 6:30 PM, the island was hit with a tidal surge that caused a sudden rise of four feet in water depth, and shortly afterwards, fifteen feet of water inundated the entire island, completely devastating the port city. Sometime around 10:00 PM the tide began to slowly subside.*

*The next morning the destruction of Galveston became evident to survivors. More than 6,000 Galvestonians died with reports of casualties for the entire island reaching more than 10,000 people. Property damage was said to have been between $20 and $30 million with 2,636 homes destroyed and 300 feet of shoreline washed out to sea. Additionally, sixteen ships anchored in the harbor suffered extensive damage. While costlier and more violent hurricanes have ravaged the United States coastal areas since 1900, the enormous loss of life in the Galveston Hurricane of 1900 remains the worst recorded natural disaster ever to hit the North American continent.*

*As is the case with such traumatic events in history, the hurricane that hit Galveston spawned numerous stories of odd events, such as ships passing by windows of buildings and washing ashore, people trapped beneath buildings, and the exhibition of superhuman heroics. Having been retold by one generation to the next, many of these stories have been exaggerated to the point that they have become more myth than reality. One story, perhaps more than any other, clearly demonstrates this point—the account of Charles Coghlan's eight year journey from Galveston to his rented home on Prince Edward Island, Canada.*

*According to Texas lore, Coghlan, who was an actor of notable fame in the late nineteenth century, was performing in Galveston when he suddenly died on November 27, 1899. His body apparently was buried in the city's local cemetery. Almost a year later, the 1900*

Galveston Hurricane blew across the island, and in the process, the flood waters and strong current unearthed coffins from their burial places. Coghlan's coffin was one of the many that were ripped from their final resting place and washed out to sea. Supposedly, eight years later fisherman found Coghlan's casket floating in waters near Prince Edward Island, Canada. The fishermen were able to identify the remains by the inscribed name plate on the actor's coffin.

Although numerous people had retold this story, Coghlan's 2000-mile journey was made famous when his story was published in "Ripley's Believe It or Not" syndicated column, and republished in Ripley's first published book in 1929. But the question remains was this story true, partially true, or completely false?

As is the case with all myths, this story has certain elements of truth to it. First, there was a noted actor named Charles Coghlan who died in Galveston in 1899. The storm obviously happened in 1900, and numerous caskets were unearthed and washed out to sea. However, beyond these few facts, the story becomes somewhat confused. For example, some sources report that Coghlan was born on Prince Edward Island, while others, including the **Galveston Daily News,** reported that he was born in Ireland. Additionally, some sources claimed that Coghlan died on the stage, while others reported that Coghlan had been staying at the Tremont Hotel in Galveston for approximately a month before his death. Supposedly he was scheduled to appear in a play that he wrote ("The Royal Box"), but another actor had to take Coghlan's place because he was stricken with gastritis soon after arriving in Galveston. When the acting company finished their stay in the port city, they moved to their next appearance somewhere in the Midwest, leaving behind the ailing Coghlan and his wife who was traveling with him. He died a short time later.

Further evidence, however, brings into question the validity of this story. Primarily, it is doubtful that the dead actor was buried in the Galveston cemetery. The **Galveston Daily News** reported on November 28, 1899, that Coghlan's body was going to be sent immediately back to Prince Edward Island for burial. The next day, the newspaper reported that the actor's widow planned to have her husband's remains cremated, according to his wishes. Mrs. Coghlan was planning to take the body to New York, where other family members would join her and the cremation would take place. The only other mention in the **Daily News** of Coghlan was that he was at the Levy Brothers funeral home, awaiting transport to the eastern seaboard.

It is highly unlikely that Charles Coghlan's story as reported in Ripley's column, and later in his book, is true. However, this unusual story is an excellent example of how myths and legends often emerge from catastrophic events, such as the 1900 hurricane. A few facts, a little misinformation, added to a pound of over exaggeration, are the perfect recipe for an enduring myth. Only with these ingredients can we have a dead actor embarking on an eight year, 2000-mile journey from the Texas coast to a Canadian island.

## Suggestions for Further Reading

Anders, Evan. *Boss Rule in South Texas: The Progressive Era.* Austin: University of Texas Press, 1982.

Barr, Alwyn. *From Reconstruction to Reform: Texas Politics, 1876-1906.* Austin: University of Texas Press, 1971.

Brown, Norman D. *Hood, Bonnet and Little Brown Jug: Texas Politics, 1921-1928.* College Station: Texas A&M University Press, 1984.

Buenger, Walter L. *The Path to a Modern South: Northeast Texas Between Reconstruction and the Great Depression.* Austin: University of Texas Press, 2001.

Casdorph, Paul D. *Republicans, Negroes, and Progressives in the South, 1912-1916.* University of Alabama Press, 1981.

Davis, Ronald L. *Twentieth Century Cultural Life in Texas.* Boston: American Press, 1981.

De Leon, Arnoldo. *Mexican Americans in Texas: A Brief History.* 2d ed. Wheeling, IL: Harlan Davidson, 1999.

Foley, Neil. *The White Scourge: Mexicans, Blacks, and Poor Whites in Texas Cotton Culture.* Berkeley: University of California Press, 1997.

Gould, Lewis L. *Progressives and Prohibitionists: Texas Democrats in the Wilson Era.* Austin: University of Texas Press, 1973.

Green, James R. *Grass-Roots Socialism: Radical Movements in the Southwest, 1895-1943.* Baton Rouge: Louisiana State University Press, 1978.

Maxwell, Robert S. *Texas Economic Growth, 1890 to World War II: From Frontier to Industrial Giant.* Boston: American Press, 1986.

Rice, Robert. *Progressive Cities: The Commission Government Movement in America, 1901-1920.* Austin: University of Texas Press, 1977.

Sharpless, Rebecca. *Fertile Ground, Narrow Choices: Women on the Texas Cotton Farms, 1900-1940.* Chapel Hill: University of North Carolina Press, 1999.

Smallwood, James M. *The Indian Texans.* College Station: Texas A&M Press, 2004.

_____. *The Struggle for Equality: Blacks in Texas.* Boston: American Press, 1983.

Tindall, George B. *The Emergence of the New South, 1913-1945.* Baton Rouge: Louisiana State University Press, 1967.

**IDENTIFICATION:** Briefly describe each term.

Progressives
commission system of municipal government
Terrell Election Laws
poll tax
"all white" primaries
Waters-Pierce Oil Company case
Robertson Insurance Law (1907)
Zimmermann Telegram
National Council of Defense
Texas Equal Rights Association
Equal Suffrage League of Houston
Texas Women Suffrage Association
Texas Federation of Women's Clubs
National Association for the Advancement of Colored People
Texas Local Option Association


**MULTIPLE CHOICE:** Choose the correct response.

1. According to the U.S. Census, the population of Texas in 1900 was:
    A. between 3 and 4 million people
    B. less than 3 million people
    C. between 5 and 8 million people
    D. more than 10 million people

2. During World War I, the price of cotton rose from .14 cents/pound to:
    A. .75 cents/pound
    B. $1.00/pound
    C. .35 cents/pound
    D. Cotton prices actually fell during the war.

3. In 1900, which of the following coastal cities was destroyed by a hurricane?
    A. Corpus Christi
    B. Brownsville
    C. Indianola
    D. Galveston

4. Between 1900 and 1907, the Texas governorship could best be described as:
    A. liberal
    B. conservative
    C. Populist
    D. Socialist

5. Section 120 of the Terrell Election Law of 1905 stipulated that:
   A. in county conventions where no single candidate won a majority in the primary vote, delegates would be divided equally among the candidates.
   B. in county conventions where no single candidate won a clear majority in the primary vote, all the delegates would go to the candidate with the most votes.
   C. the poll tax was optional in each county.
   D. primaries would allow all voters to participate, regardless of race, creed, color, gender, or age.

6. Why did the Texas courts revoke the Waters-Pierce Oil Company state charter, which allowed the company to do business in the state?
   A. The company violated the states' labor laws.
   B. The company offered Joseph Bailey an improper bribe.
   C. The company was in violation of the state's antitrust laws.
   D. The company was in violation of the state's environmental protection laws.

7. Governor Thomas Campbell supported all of the following, EXCEPT:
   A. reform legislation related to insurance companies.
   B. legislation preventing insolvent companies from moving into Texas
   C. antitrust legislation
   D. lowering fees on liquor dealers operating in the state.

8. What was one of the most pressing problems confronting Governor Colquitt's administration?
   A. Mexican revolutionary activity on the Texas-Mexico border
   B. antiprohibitionists campaigns against the governor
   C. failure to pass child-labor laws
   D. Governor Colquitt and his administration were found to be corrupt because the governor had received large sums of money in the form of loans from the Waters-Pierce Oil Company.

9. What did James E. Ferguson promise farmers during his first campaign for governor?
   A. He would lower taxes on farm equipment.
   B. He would redistribute public lands making sure all farmers had enough land to support their families.
   C. He would give more financial support to Texas A&M University than the University of Texas.
   D. He would limit the amount landowners could charge tenant farmers in rent.

10. Approximately one-third of all the Texas servicemen that died during World War I lost their life as a result of:
    A. combat in Europe
    B. training accidents in the United States
    C. from the Spanish Influenza outbreak in 1918
    D. self-inflicted wounds

**TRUE/FALSE:** Indicate whether each statement is true or false.

1. The most important Texas industries prior to 1920 included lumber, oil, and railroads.

2. Oil became significant to the Texas economy with the discovery of the Spindletop field, near Beaumont.

3. By 1910, Texas had fewer than 2,000 miles of paved roads.

4. Of the 132 urban areas in Texas in 1910, fourteen had populations greater than 50,000 people.

5. In 1900, Galveston was destroyed by a devastating tsunami.

6. Texas's all-white Democratic primaries ultimately led to the disenfranchisement of African-American voters.

7. During the early twentieth century, Texas became known as a "one-party" state because voters overwhelmingly supported the Republican Party.

8. Gov. James E. Ferguson's administration was marred by corruption.

9. Thomas H. Ball defeated James Ferguson in the gubernatorial election of 1914.

10. Minnie Fisher Cunningham served as the president of the Texas Woman Suffrage Association in 1915.

**MATCHING:** Match the response in column A with the item in column B.

1. Galveston Plan
2. Col. Edward M. House
3. Samuel W. L. Lanham
4. Election Law of 1905
5. Thomas B. Love
6. Joseph W. Bailey
7. Thomas A. Campbell
8. Oscar B. Colquitt
9. James E. Ferguson
10. Plan de San Diego

A. Strong antiprohibitionist
B. supported bank and insurance reforms
C. governor between 1902 and 1907
D. pro-business congressman who was involved in questionable activities with the Waters-Pierce Oil Company
E. the most reform-minded governor serving between 1900 and 1911.
F. Gave independent party candidates a place on the ballot
G. impeached and removed from office in 1917
H. Successful businessman who became a political advisor to President Wilson
I. Called on Tejanos to support the Mexican Revolution
J. original commission form of government

**ESSAY QUESTIONS:**

1. Discuss in detail the women's suffrage movement in Texas between 1900 and 1920.

2. Analyze and discuss the various reasons leading Texans to support President Wilson's call for a declaration of war against Germany in 1917.

3. What were the most significant political developments in Texas during the first two decades of the twentieth century? Explain in detail.

4. Define the term Progressive. Explain how Progressives shaped political, social, and economic developments in Texas.

# Chapter 13

# The Rise of Urbanization, Expanding Opportunities, and the Invisible Empire, 1920-1929

### Prelude: The All-Woman Supreme Court

*For five months in 1925, three Texas women made history as the first females to serve on a state supreme court anywhere in the country when Governor Pat Neff chose them to fill in for the High Court's regular male members who recused themselves from a case. Though a one-time event, Governor Neff's appointments, coming just five years after ratification of the Nineteenth Amendment barring states from denying women the right to vote based on their gender and three years after the election of the first females to the Texas state legislature, marked another step forward for full female participation in society at a time when no women served as state district judges nor were women yet allowed to serve on Texas juries.*

The particulars of the case that led to the creation of the "All-Woman Supreme Court" are fairly straight-forward. J.M. Darr and other trustees of the Woodmen of the World (a fraternal organization whose membership consisted of many of the state's most powerful political and business elite) deeded two tracts of land in El Paso to F.P. Jones, who then signed an unrecorded agreement to deed the land back if ever requested by the Woodmen. When Jones eventually had creditors seeking the land as payment for debts, the Woodmen filed suit to prevent the land's transfer, arguing that even though they did not publicly record their agreement with Jones, the land should revert to the Woodmen's control. In the case of **W.T. Johnson et al. vs. J.M. Darr et al.**, a state district court ruled that the creditors should be awarded one of the land tracts in question while the Woodmen could retain possession of the other. The Woodmen appealed the decision to the El Paso Court of Appeals, which decided that the Woodmen should be allowed to keep both tracts. When W.T. Johnson and other creditors appealed this ruling to the state Supreme Court, the three male justices, all members of the Woodmen of the World, disqualified themselves from hearing the case. Texas state law allowed the governor to name temporary special justices, setting the stage for Neff's historic appointments.

The common telling of the story relates how the governor supposedly became so frustrated trying to find three men qualified to serve on the tribunal who were not members of the Woodmen that he decided to solve his dilemma by appointing three women—because the Woodmen had no female members, there would be guaranteed no conflict of interest. Upon further analysis, however, there are numerous problems with such a description. To begin, prior to 1925, three other cases came before the Texas Supreme Court leading to justices removing themselves due to their connections to the Woodmen. Yet, in each case, Governor Neff did not seem to encounter particular difficulty finding three male attorneys to serve as special justices. Further, after he initially chose three women to hear the **Johnson** case, two of the female appointees could not serve because they each fell just short of the state constitutional requirement stating that they must have practiced law in Texas for seven years. Thus, Neff could have appointed one woman and then probably found one or two male replacements, but the governor seems to have deliberately sought to have women hold all three positions on the temporary court.

The most prestigious of the three female appointees proved to be "Chief Justice" Hortense Ward—the first woman to pass the Texas bar exam (1910) and the primary author of the state law allowing women to vote in primary elections in Texas. Governor Neff also appointed Hattie Lenenberg, a practicing attorney in Dallas, and Ruth Brazzil, a Galveston insurance company executive, to serve as associate justices. On January 8, 1925, the women held a hearing during which they decided there was enough merit to take on the case, with oral arguments scheduled to occur three weeks later. In the intervening months before the special court's decision, the three male members of the regular Supreme Court continued to function, hearing arguments and deciding numerous cases. In May, the three female justices ruled unanimously in favor of the Woodmen, upholding the El Paso Appeals Court's ruling that the fraternity was entitled to maintain ownership of both tracts of land in question. With its work done, the All-Woman Supreme Court promptly disbanded.

An enduring myth about 1920s life is the notion that most Americans broke away from their traditional values and beliefs after World War I. They supposedly celebrated the end of the war and postwar economic prosperity by partaking in a binge of hedonistic excess characterized by attending wild parties, taking part in silly "ballyhoo" behavior, gyrating to the latest wild dance crazes, consuming copious amounts of alcohol, and allegedly discarding the old-time religion for the latest findings of science. A majority of women presumably basked in the achievement of woman suffrage and the liberation provided by new modern household appliances by getting out more and having fun while dressing in the new provocative styles touted by New York City fashion designers. This image of the decade as the "Roaring Twenties," however, is a caricature based on the activities of some Americans that have been popularized by the contemporary and current media.

While some Texans indulged in the new behavior and lifestyle associated with the Roaring Twenties, most did not. Nevertheless, many important modernizing influences crept into Texas life during the 1920s, foreshadowing what would later become commonplace. Though many Texans embraced certain aspects of this social and economic change, others were rabidly determined to contain and reverse these trends, lest the traditional way of life that they understood and provided them with comfort be lost to an age of uncertainty and moral confusion.

## Economic Developments: Industry and Agriculture

During the 1920s Texas remained primarily an agricultural state, but signs of the emergent post-World War II industrial economy were already appearing on the horizon. While small when compared to the northeastern region of the country, Texas continued to experience sustained manufacturing growth during the decade. Meatpacking plants, along with lumber, cottonseed, and grain mills, did not grow in number during the 1920s, but 26 percent more workers were employed in these businesses, while the value added to their products via manufacturing increased by 56 percent.

The rapidly expanding oil industry made the largest contribution to the state's postwar economic boom. By mid-decade, drilling operations in two regions of West Texas—the Panhandle and the Permian Basin—produced fantastic results. Centered in the Borger area of Hutchinson County, the Panhandle fields became a major oil-producing region, yielding 30-40 million barrels annually. Nearby Amarillo in Potter County more than tripled in population during the 1920s (from 16,000 to 52,000) as a result of the associated economic activity. In the Permian Basin, Midland and Odessa likewise grew after major oil finds. Odessa swelled from a population of 750 in 1925 to 5,000 by 1929; Midland expanded from 1,800 residents in 1920 to 5,500 by 1930. Drillers made a significant discovery in Reagan County on lands owned by the state's Permanent University Fund (PUF)—a public endowment of two million acres authorized by the Texas Legislature in the nineteenth century to provide financial support for the University of Texas and Texas A&M University. Prior to 1923, most income accrued to the fund had come from grazing leases (amounting to only $40,000 in 1900). This all changed when the Santa Rita well inaugurated a massive windfall for the fund. Other oil strikes on PUF lands soon followed. In 1931 the legislature arranged a formal division of the enlarged fund, with the University of Texas receiving two-thirds of the proceeds and Texas A&M receiving the remainder. Though the principal of the fund (valued at $9.4 billion in 2005) cannot be spent, the two universities (and now other schools within the UT and A&M systems) benefit greatly from surface leasing PUF lands plus the use of interest income and dividends from PUF investments (the "Available University Fund," valued at $450 million in 2005).

Texas emerged as the leading oil-producing state in 1928. In that year, the Lone Star State produced over 250 million barrels, or almost 20 percent of the world's supply. Jobs in the oil industry were plentiful as companies hired laborers to work at the wells, to lay down thousands of miles of pipelines, and to process petroleum at the growing number of refineries. The oil industry also produced a windfall for the state's treasury, rising from $1 million in 1919 to almost $6 million by 1929.

Though industry was gaining a foothold, agriculture remained the predominant base for the Texas economy. The value of Texas agricultural products was three times the value of oil and other manufactured goods, and far more Texans earned a living though agricultural pursuits than industry. Though ample amounts of corn, wheat, sorghum, oats, and rice continued to be produced, and the commercial raising of citrus fruits in the Lower Rio Grande Valley commenced, cotton remained king. Over two-thirds of the population of Texas earned a living from raising, picking, ginning, shipping, or financing the annual crop.

Though East Texas remained the core cotton-growing area, the 1920s witnessed the growth of cotton production into the southern High Plains around Lubbock. Farmers freed from boll weevil infestation because of the cold winters and relatively arid growing season used irrigation water from the Ogallala Aquifer to initiate a tremendous expansion of cotton acreage. Chronic labor shortages in the region led to unique harvesting methods. One picking method was known as "snapping," whereby laborers simply pulled the entire boll off the stalk and threw it into their sacks. Other growers used a specially designed harvester known as "stripper," which was a wooden box with protruding prongs that, when pulled over the stalks by work stock, would act like a mechanical snapping device and rip the bolls off the stalk. Though the snapping and stripping produced a lower grade of cotton due to the presence of trash mixed with the lint, the methods resulted in quicker harvesting and reduced labor costs. Cotton production in the southern High Plains jumped from 50,000 bales in 1918 to over one million by 1926.

As cotton farmers over much of the South increased production during the 1920s, prices began to decline accordingly. In 1920, the fiber was fetching prices as high as 40 cents per pound. As late as 1925, growers received an average of 20 cents per pound. A large carryover of unconsumed cotton coupled with a record-breaking crop in 1926, however, drove southern growers into a panic as prices plummeted below 10 cents per pound, threatening many with financial ruin. A group of Dallas bankers led an effort by financiers in some other southern states to underwrite private pools to purchase cotton at higher-than-market prices to keep the fiber off the market in return for pledges by farmers to reduce their planted acreage the next year by 25 percent. Major newspapers across Texas and the South endorsed the movement. Despite much expended energy, efforts to persuade farmers to sell to a private pool and reduce plantings ultimately failed. For the rest of the decade, producers tried to survive on cotton receiving from 9 to 20 cents per pound. Often, they increased the amount of cotton they raised so they could make up the difference with increased volume. As farmers across the South began to implement the same formula, they actually set the stage for the southern cotton market's collapse in the early 1930s.

As cotton prices fell and the cost of living rose in the first decades of the twentieth century, many Texas growers found themselves destitute. The number of farmers who became tenants (those who paid rent for use of the land with either cash or a portion of the crop) or sharecroppers continued to increase. In 1910, 51.7 percent of Texas producers did not own the land that they worked for a living. By 1930 that figure reached 61 percent, including over half of the state's white farmers and over 70 percent of black farmers.

**Farm Women**

A majority of farm families lacked many of the modern amenities of home life enjoyed by many wealthy and middle-class urban dwellers. Less than 5 percent of Texas farms, for example, had electricity, while less than 8 percent enjoyed indoor plumbing. The result of this technology lag was a perpetual burden for most farm women whether white, black, or Hispanic. They continued to cook on wood-burning stoves. Laundry cleaning involved dousing clothes in tubs filled with hot water followed by intense scrubbing on washboards. These time-consuming duties were just a portion of farm women's overall obligations. In addition to cooking and cleaning, farm women preserved food, sewed, tended gardens, raised poultry and livestock, and held primary responsibility for raising the children.

Many farm women also helped their families by performing agricultural labor when needed, despite the social stigma often attached to it. Most commonly, husbands and fathers employed female family members when it was time to chop weeds around cotton stalks or pick the cotton crop. Some women even plowed the fields and planted crops, albeit rarely. Contemporary studies show that tenure status and race were key variables in determining the frequency of farm women labor in the fields. About a third of white females in farm-owning families performed some work in the fields, but half to two-thirds of females in black farm-owning families worked outside the home. Meanwhile, half of the females in white tenant farming families and 90 percent of women in black tenant farming families worked in the fields.

## Tejanos

The 1920s witnessed the arrival of a large number of Mexican immigrants into Texas. Pushed by the tumult of the Mexican Revolution and pulled by the demand for cheap agricultural labor, perhaps as many as a half million crossed the border, soon overwhelming the native-born Tejano population. By the end of the decade, over 700,000 Hispanic Texans resided in the state.

Prior to 1920, most Tejanos engaged in Texas agriculture were sharecroppers, South Texas ranch hands, or small South Texas farm owners. The tremendous increase in the Tejano population, however, led to an explosion in the use of migrant labor during the 1920s. Though some Tejanos had been traveling from their San Antonio homes to pick cotton in central and eastern Texas fields as early as the 1880s, the practice greatly increased after the post-Revolution influx. Numerous private companies and individual contractors emerged to work with landowners to provide needed cotton and fruit pickers. Starting in the 1920s, women, children, and extended family members began to accompany laborers in the fields. Landowners preferred larger families over single workers, not only because they could provide additional labor, but also because they viewed them as less likely to break their contracts and flee if disagreements arose.

The cotton picking circuit, nicknamed the "Big Swing," began in South Texas fields in June and followed a northward trajectory into central and northern Texas as the cotton bolls matured from south-to-north, culminating with the harvest in the Panhandle fields by early winter. Migrant laborers provided needed manual resources for farm families who needed help bringing in the crop, often supplementing hired day laborers from the surrounding countryside and nearby urban areas. At the end of the circuit, most migrants returned to their homes in San Antonio, El Paso, or towns in South Texas, though some eventually remained in the Panhandle.

Tejanos living in San Antonio and El Paso dwelled in *barrios* that, however viable from a social and cultural standpoint, were characterized by horrendous living conditions. In San Antonio, for example, many of the city's 82,000 Hispanic and Mexican Americans lived in a neighborhood west of downtown with a core area containing over 12,000 people per square mile. It had the reputation of being one of the worst slums in the nation. Rather than displaying a continual series of five-story tenements crammed close together as in New York, Boston, Philadelphia, or Chicago, San Antonio's slum dwellers lived in dilapidated wooden hovels. Though some were long, narrow subdivided buildings built by landlords for multiple families, others were smaller shacks for single families converted from former horse stalls by the occupants. Both types of structures had flimsy metal roofs, wooden or stucco walls, and dirt floors. Most of them lacked electricity, and virtually all of them lacked indoor running water.

Native-born Tejanos and recent Mexican arrivals to Texas faced continuous discrimination by most non-Hispanic Texans. Segregation by custom, rather than by law, was the tradition. Most Anglo Texans, consumed by contemporary racist theories that portrayed Hispanics as a "dirty" people, chose to keep their distance from the "greasers." Except for certain South Texas counties where political bosses provided social services in exchange for votes, local Democratic Party officials usually enforced the state's "white primary" against Tejanos as a means of denying them any political influence.

By the end of the 1920s, some middle-class Tejanos began to organize in order to challenge this treatment. Founded in Corpus Christi in 1929 was the League of United Latin American Citizens (LULAC). Activists sought better schooling, an end to segregation, voting rights, and the elimination of racial prejudice. LULAC adopted an accommodationist style by limiting membership to native-born or naturalized U.S. citizens, stressing their Americanism, and promoting their desire to enter into the national mainstream by insisting on the use of the English language. Like the National Association for the Advancement of Colored People (NAACP), LULAC chose to challenge the status quo primarily through legal challenges and publicity campaigns. Also similar to the NAACP, the rewards for their efforts largely did not come until after the Second World War.

**African Americans**

The number of blacks living in Texas from 1920 to 1930 grew from 741,694 to 854,964, with most still living in rural areas. Though some (like James E. Youngblood of Limestone County) were small farm owners, the vast majority were tenant farmers, sharecroppers, and general farm laborers.

A sizeable number of blacks attempted to escape rural poverty by leaving the countryside. Though many joined the movement out of the South entirely as blacks in other southern states, many more moved to Texas cities. By 1930, one-third of the population of Texas cities was African American. Segregation and discrimination forced black urbanites to reside in slum districts where two-thirds worked as unskilled laborers, janitors, porters, or domestic servants. Limited employment opportunities and low pay for black males contributed to the necessity for many African-American women to remain in the urban workforce after marriage. Almost half of black married women were laboring in the state's five largest cities during the 1920s, whereas only one in six married white women in those cities needed to work.

Despite the persistence of black urban poverty, it was primarily in the cities where a small African-American middle-class emerged. By 1930 Texas had 205 black doctors, 99 dentists, and 20 lawyers. These individuals (such as Dr. George Conner of Waco, educated at Flint Medical College in New Orleans, Louisiana) were able to take advantage of educational opportunities out of the state, allowing them to earn degrees, and then return to Texas and provide valuable services while establishing themselves as leaders in their communities. In addition to a growing number of African-American urban professionals

**Youngsters like this 9-year-old boy could be found in many Texas cities, selling newspapers early in the morning and late at night. San Antonio, Texas.
Photo credit: Library of Congress**

by 1930, Texas had 1,736 black store owners (half of them were in the grocery business, but many others were drug store owners, restaurateurs, and funeral home directors).

As with Tejanos, local Democratic Party officials consistently employed the white primary (and poll taxes) to deny African Americans from having any influence on the voting process. In 1923 the state legislature attempted to legalize the Democratic Party custom begun in the early 1900s of barring blacks from voting in their primary elections. Dr. Lawrence Nixon of El Paso (a Meharry graduate) and the NAACP challenged the law, however, arguing that the state could not pass a law restricting blacks from voting in a primary since that would violate the equal protection clause of the Fourteenth Amendment to the United States Constitution. In 1927 the U.S. Supreme Court unanimously agreed with the plaintiff in the *Nixon v. Herndon* case on the grounds that states were forbidden by the equal protection clause of the Fourteenth Amendment from denying a person from voting in this manner. The victory, however, was short lived. After attempting to legislate the white primary by giving the executive committee of each state party the power to decide who could vote in its primary (struck down by the Supreme Court in the 1932 *Nixon v. Condon* case), the legislature simply allowed the Democratic Party's state convention to adopt a resolution excluding blacks from voting in their primaries. In 1935, the U.S. Supreme Court finally heard the *Grovey v. Townsend* case, which challenged this tactic, and ruled unanimously that the Democratic Party was a private organization whose state convention could determine membership qualifications, and, therefore, its members could vote in its primary elections. Thereafter, if they were required to pay poll taxes, black voter participation was limited to voting for candidates only in the general elections (when it no longer mattered) and in small nonpartisan municipal and school board elections. Until 1944, when a new Supreme Court finally overturned the *Grovey* decision, most black Texans did not participate in the electoral process.

## The Growing Cities and Urbanization

Though the 1920 U.S. Census recorded for the first time that a majority of Americans lived in urban areas, this often-cited national statistic does not relay accurately the situation in numerous states, including Texas. An urbanization trend, however, was clearly underway—urban areas witnessed a 58 percent population growth during the 1920s, while rural areas gained only 9 percent more inhabitants. In 1920, 68 percent of the state's 4.7 million people lived in rural areas or small towns of less than 2,500 residents; by 1930, that number decreased to 59 percent of the state's 5.8 million people.

Texas cities grew at tremendous rates (see Table 13.1) as rural Texans of all races and backgrounds joined the urban migration movement. In addition to such "push" factors from the countryside as low crop prices and the drudgery of farm work, the cities enticed many with "pull" factors such as plentiful jobs, modern conveniences, and a faster pace of life.

TABLE 13.1
### Population of Ten Largest Texas Cities: 1920 & 1930

| City | 1920 | 1930 | Percent Increase, 1920-30 |
|---|---|---|---|
| Houston | 138,276 | 292,352 | 111.4% |
| Dallas | 158,976 | 260,475 | 63.8% |
| San Antonio | 161,379 | 231,542 | 43.5% |
| Fort Worth | 106,482 | 163,447 | 53.5% |
| El Paso | 77,560 | 102,421 | 32.0% |
| Beaumont | 40,422 | 57,732 | 42.8% |
| Austin | 34,876 | 53,120 | 52.3% |
| Galveston | 44,255 | 52,938 | 19.6% |
| Waco | 38,500 | 52,848 | 37.3% |
| Port Arthur | 22,251 | 50,902 | 128.8% |

SOURCE: *1931 Texas Almanac and State Industrial Guide*, pp. 151-152

Economic opportunity was the biggest attraction for rural Texans to the burgeoning cities. Urban jobs were bountiful and paid, on average, one-third more than rural work. Annual earnings of Texas urban workers averaged $1,129, or about 80 percent of the national average. Salaried corporate employees earned twice the state average. Skilled workers in heavy industries such as petroleum plants, machine shops, and foundries earned 25 percent more than the state average, while laborers in the meatpacking and cotton processing industries made 30 percent less.

Increased economic activity also affected Texas city women in significant ways. Urban women first started working outside the home during World War I. This trend continued after the war as more people accepted the notion of working women, and employers became impressed with their abilities. Many city women found jobs as telephone operators, clerical workers, and salespeople, while dominating such professional fields as teaching, nursing, and library work (though less than 2 percent found employment as a doctor or lawyer). Large numbers of women continued to labor as domestic servants, two-thirds of which were black or Hispanic.

The availability of modern amenities was another draw to Texas cities. Electricity and natural gas increasingly powered the cities. If affordable, urban residents could take advantage of indoor plumbing, the telephone, the radio, a myriad of new electric appliances, and electric lighting. Public facilities abounded in the form of public parks, swimming pools, gymnasiums, and sports stadiums. Movie theaters became packed with audiences who viewed a per capita average of twenty Hollywood films per year.

A faster pace of life existed in the cities to draw newcomers and retain those pledging never to go back to the farm. Electric-powered streetcars whisked residents about the major cities. Electric lighting created a vibrant night life. As in other American metropolitan areas, Texas cities experienced an onrush of social change as new ideas concerning what constituted acceptable behavior appeared. Taking their cues from the new Hollywood movies, national magazines, and popular novels, some Texans began to imitate the dress and behavior of their urban counterparts in other parts of the country. Some younger women began to follow the latest fashion trends by cutting their hair short and raising hemlines. Others flouted adherence to the Prohibition laws and patronized hidden speakeasies. Many began to listen to jazz music for the first time. Wild (for the day) new dances such as the Charleston and the Fox Trot became popular, as did the seductive Tango. Some unmarried youths, no doubt, engaged in sexual experimentation. In portions of some cities, such as Dallas's African-American Deep Ellum district, this adoption of new social behaviors converged with racial mixing in social clubs to produce what some today might view as "cultural vitality." Many contemporaries, however, interpreted such behavior as rampant immorality and licentiousness run amok.

Though only a minority of Texans had the time, money, and desire to indulge in the new lifestyles developing primarily in the cities, numerous preachers, newspaper editors, and other social leaders condemned the flight from traditional dress, behavior, modes of entertainment, and taste that they believed were engulfing their communities. Many citizens, freshly migrated from the rural areas, were bewildered and appalled by what they witnessed. Some citizens tried to deal with the situation by passing laws regulating public bathing attire, censoring Hollywood movies, banning film showings on Sundays, and demanding strict enforcement of the state's Prohibition statutes. But as the realization grew that these efforts were not changing behavior, the groundwork was laid for the arrival of the Second Ku Klux Klan, which emerged during World War I as both a fraternal organization and a vigilante force to use extralegal means of enforcing the social and moral traditions of an increasingly disappearing era.

## J. Frank Norris and the Rise of Fundamentalism

The rise of religious fundamentalism became a strong cultural reaction to the modernizing influences within American society at the turn of the twentieth century. Over the previous decades, many scientists and intellectuals had begun to build upon recent scientific developments and new theories to present secular challenges to many aspects of organized religion. In response, some liberal theologians began to examine the Bible with a more critical eye. Countless religious conservatives, however, responded negatively to any updating of orthodox Christianity. Many evangelicals began to label themselves "Fundamentalists," with the name derived from the title of a noted series of essays—*The Fundamentals*—published from 1910 to 1915 and written by an assortment of conservative theologians who stated their beliefs in the fundamentals of Christian faith (including the virgin birth, the resurrection of Jesus, and the Bible as the inspired word of God to be read literally) while attacking liberal theology, atheism, Catholicism, and an assortment of new scientific theories. Financed by wealthy California oil men, millions of copies of the essays were sent free to ministers and other active Christians, helping to spread the views presented in *The Fundamentals* in an effort to unify the faithful.

In addition to being fueled by resentment toward secular challengers and liberal theologians, not to mention the influx of millions of Catholic and Jewish immigrants into the United States from 1880-1910, fundamentalism also spread rapidly across the country because of the dynamic efforts of many energetic and charismatic preachers who attracted multitudes to their messages. Among the myriad of evangelical leaders to emerge, the most famous nationally was Billy Sunday. An ex-major league baseball player from Iowa, he became a convert after his playing days ended and began his career as an electrifying religious campaigner. Preaching with a classic revivalist style, he delivered powerful orations to large crowds across the country in a loud booming voice, often filling his sermons with animation as he contorted his face, flailed his arms, ran across the stage and dove as a ballplayer, and even smashed chairs to assert his points as the Spirit moved him. His messages reflected all the doctrinal tenets of fundamentalism, including the existence of the Devil, attacks on modernism, and an affirmation of a literal interpretation of the Bible.

From the Pentecostal strand of fundamentalism, Aimee Semple McPherson presented a fresh face during the 1920s. Beginning her career as an itinerant minister, she traveled the countryside in her "Gospel Car," a Packard touring vehicle adorned with religious slogans written along the chassis. Though some were uncomfortable with a woman preaching the Gospel, McPherson attracted large crowds as she hosted revivals across the eastern United States. As she honed her oratorical skills, McPherson delivered deeply conservative messages that resonated with her audiences—constantly railing against numerous aspects of modernity and demanding that people remain true to the fundamental- ist faith of the old time religion. In 1923, after moving to Los Angeles, California, she raised enough money to dedicate the new 5,300-seat Angelus Temple, which often filled to capacity. Besides the sense of community provided by the large crowds attending the Temple, devotees also flocked to the church because of McPherson's personal charisma and her sense of dramatic flair. Arriving in grand fashion (often in a deluge of bright light surrounded by bouquets of roses), she produced elaborate stage presentations with orchestral accompaniment to drive home her messages and keep the audiences entertained. Unlike Billy Sunday and many other fundamentalist evangelists, McPherson preached optimism rather than fire and brimstone. In addition to showing a gift for oratory and theatrics, she also displayed a keen awareness of the potential of new media outlets to reach new potential converts. In 1924, McPherson purchased a radio station and began preaching over the airwaves to the entire city.

Not only did a growing number of Texans during this time adhere to the tenets of fundamentalism, the Lone Star State also produced one of the movement's most noteworthy and controversial leaders—J. Frank Norris. Until the 1920s, fundamentalism had been largely a northern phenomenon, but the fiery Texas preacher would soon change that. After graduating from Baylor and receiving a master's degree in theology from the Baptist seminary in Louisville, Kentucky, Norris pastored at a Dallas church for two years. He edited the influential *Baptist Standard* newspaper for two years before resigning over a disagreement with Baptist leaders over his tendency for sensationalism. In 1909, he became the pastor of Fort Worth's First Baptist Church, a position he would hold for the next 45 years. During the Progressive Era, Norris became known locally for his passionate battles against Fort Worth's liquor, gambling, and prostitution establishments. During the 1920s, he not only tapped into the growing popularity of fundamentalist doctrine but also the resonance among the masses of the flamboyant style of preaching and other trappings often associated with the movement. In 1920, Norris created the nation's first "megachurch" when the First Baptist Church christened a 5,000-seat auditorium (complete with a revolving electric sign and bright spotlight on the roof to attract attention) where his powerful oratory and frenetic hand gestures while speaking energized parishioners. Three years later, at the same time that Aimee McPherson began capitalizing on the idea of utilizing the new invention of radio, he became one of the first ministers in the United States to begin broadcasting the Gospel via his own radio station—KFQB (for "Keep Folks Quoting the Bible").

Riding the success of a growing movement, fundamentalists during the 1920s sought to put their ideas into action to shape the direction of society. The largest *bête noir* for them was the spreading of Charles Darwin's theory of evolution. For those who unquestioningly believed the story of creation of mankind as literally presented in the Book of Genesis, Darwin's proposition that humans ascended from primates was a blasphemous doctrine that had to be crushed. To them, if the story of creation were to be disregarded, the entire Bible would then become disputed ground. The issue became a divisive one during the 1920s. Besides secularists, many Baptists, Methodists, and other Christians also received Darwin's findings positively, believing it was possible to reconcile their faith with the theory by accepting so-called "theistic evolution," or the notion that the hand of God was behind the gradual development of mankind over the eons.

To counter evolution's growing acceptance, three-time former Democratic presidential nominee William Jennings Bryan, himself a devout fundamentalist, led an effort in numerous states during the decade to pass laws removing the teaching of Darwinian theories from public education. A politician with strong reform credentials, Bryan believed that evolution enhanced political conservatism by justifying a "survival of the fittest" mentality. He also thought that acceptance of Darwin's views removed the consciousness of God's presence in people's daily lives, leading one to conclude that "no spiritual force has touched the life of man and shaped the destiny of nations." The anti-Darwin movement achieved its only successes in the South, where several states banned textbooks with any mention of Darwin and made it a crime to teach evolution in public schools. In 1925, Tennessee fundamentalists, whipped into a frenzy by a recent Billy Sunday crusade, pressured members of their legislature to pass a law making it a misdemeanor "to teach any theory that denies the story of the Divine Creation of man as taught in the Bible, and to teach instead that man had descended from a lower order of animal." When some in the state decided to challenge the constitutionality of the new law, with the help and encouragement of the newly formed American Civil Liberties Union (ACLU), the stage was set for the biggest clash of the decade between evolutionists and fundamentalists—the famous Scopes "Monkey Trial," in which Bryan joined the team of local prosecutors against John Scopes, a high school teacher in Dayton, Tennessee, who deliberately taught evolution to his biology class in order to be arrested and set up a test case that would hopefully end with the courts throwing out the new law.

In Texas, Frank Norris had already established himself as a frenetic leader in the effort to stymie the spread of Darwinism within the state. Throughout the decade he waged a highly publicized campaign to keep the teaching of evolution out of his alma mater, Baylor, as well as the public schools. After the Scopes Trial, Norris held a revival in Arlington where he once again attacked Darwin's theories, moving about the platform with a Bible in one hand and a newspaper with stories about the trial in another (though this time without the accompaniment of live monkeys on the stage, a customary prop that he previously deployed when slamming evolution). Though nothing came of it, he challenged John Scopes's defense attorney, the celebrated agnostic Clarence Darrow, to a series of debates, vowing to "skin the skunk's hide from one end of the country to the other." Norris stepped up his efforts on the legislature to pass a bill banning Darwin's theories from state public schools. Though the Texas legislature never approved such a law, Norris and other fundamentalists did manage to have discussions of evolution removed from state-adopted textbooks by the Texas State Textbook Commission, chaired by Governor Miriam Ferguson, who stated: "I'm a Christian woman . . . and I am not going to let that kind of rot go into Texas textbooks."

Norris remained a controversial, yet influential, voice in the state's social, cultural, and political affairs for decades to come. Egotistical, thriving on controversy, and uncompromising to the core, the firebrand pastor divided Baptists and inflamed secularists with his rhetoric, but he retained a devout multitude of passionate supporters who agreed with his words, if not always his actions. Unfortunately, the power of Norris's beliefs and his growing media empire also spread fear and intolerance within the state during the 1920s as he became an outspoken supporter of the Second Ku Klux Klan. His anti-Catholic views also led him to play an important role in loosening the Democratic Party's grip on Texas politics when he vigorously supported Herbert Hoover in the 1928 presidential campaign against the Catholic governor of New York, Al Smith.

**The "Invisible Empire" Appears In Texas**

In 1915 an unsuccessful former Methodist minister named William J. Simmons founded the Second Ku Klux Klan as a fraternal organization with membership limited to white, Protestant, native-born adults. Taking advantage of the popularity of the recently released film *Birth Of A Nation,* which glorified the original Klan of Reconstruction days, Simmons borrowed the dress and many rituals from the hooded order to create a living memorial to the old group while focusing on new issues that were supposedly destroying American society.

The Klan grew at a glacial pace over the next five years, largely reflecting Simmons's lack of organizational and promotional ability. By 1920 the group had only 5,000 members in Georgia and Alabama when Simmons entered into a business deal with Edward Clarke and Elizabeth Tyler—two Atlanta-area publicists with promotional and fundraising experience. Using corporate publicity techniques and a trained staff of one thousand recruiters (or "kleagles," as they were called by the Klan), Clarke and Tyler added greatly to Klan membership rolls by exploiting fear and prejudice against blacks, Mexicans, Catholics, Jews, and immigrants while championing support for Prohibition, patriotism, and traditional moral standards. They also got rich in the process. For every $10 "klectoken" (initiation fee) collected, Clarke and Tyler pocketed $4, the kleagle received $4, and the remainder went to Klan national headquarters in Atlanta. Kleagles received instructions to take a top-down approach when recruiting in a locality; that is, to contact local business, religious, and political leaders first in order to gain prestige, work down to the middle-class, then finish by convincing those at society's bottom to join. These techniques proved to be very successful. By the end of 1922, the Ku Klux Klan boasted 700,000 members nationally.

In September 1920, the "Invisible Empire" (as the Klan often referred to themselves because of their vows of secrecy concerning their activities) made its dramatic arrival into Texas when a kleagle came to Houston during an annual Confederate veteran celebration. After contacting prominent bankers, business owners, and professionals, the kleagle offered them free membership and a visit by William Simmons and Edward Clarke at a private initiation ceremony. They received many takers. A few days later, Klansmen joined a parade of Confederate veterans in downtown Houston followed by a large initiation ceremony in a suburban Bellaire field complete with burning crosses. Thus culminated the formation of the Klan's first "klavern" (chapter) in Texas, dubbed "Sam Houston Klan No. 1."

After this successful beginning, the Klan spread rapidly in Texas over the next two years, with membership ultimately estimated at 150,000. The Klan established klaverns in every major Texas city, with its largest membership in Dallas, Fort Worth, and Austin. Many female Texans agreed with the Klan's efforts so strongly that they organized a "Women of the Klan" auxiliary. (In June 1923, 1,500 masked and robed women of this parallel group paraded through downtown Fort Worth to show their support.) No doubt some joined the Klan for simple business reasons, as Klan leaders preached a message of "vocational Klanishness" whereby members were expected to trade with each other at the expense of nonmembers. Others who disliked the Klan's many hate-filled statements and acts of violence nevertheless supported the order because they sympathized with its concerns, if not all of its deeds. The vast majority joined the Klan, however, because the groups seemed capable of providing a strong counterforce to all the negative aspects of life appearing in 1920s America. While providing a link to the glorified and mythologized past, the 1920s Klan attracted bewildered people many of whom were bored or otherwise disgruntled with their mediocre lives and promised to make them part of a cause greater than themselves.

A couple of misconceptions about the 1920s Ku Klux Klan should be addressed. One popular myth is that this second manifestation of the Klan was primarily dominated by the "lower orders" of society. While the Klan did have lower-class members, research has shown that not only did the klaverns have modest numbers of upper-class individuals, the Klan's base in Texas, as in other states, consisted of middle-class membership. While many middle-class Texans would have nothing to do with the Klan, the fact remains that many middle-class men with such varied occupations as store owner, dentist, druggist, realtor, salesman, bookkeeper, clerk, skilled tradesman, and farm owner joined the group in large numbers.

A second misconception about the 1920s Klan in Texas is that the order was primarily an anti-black and anti-Mexican organization. While Texas Klansmen held strong white supremacist views, and some performed acts of violence against African Americans and Hispanics, the relatively low proportion of blacks and Tejanos in the state tempered any idea that these groups could ever constitute a plausible statewide threat to whites.

Other motivations accounted for the Klan's rise in Texas. Far beyond fears of blacks crossing the color barrier, or even Mexican immigrants flooding the state, the majority of Klan members tended to view those issues as lesser aspects of the overall goal of controlling the rapidly modernizing world. Even more important to them were signs of moral decay and the breakdown of traditional societal norms represented by new "scandalous" forms of entertainment and dress, rampant lawlessness exhibited by evasion of the Prohibition laws, challenges to traditional Christianity, and decrepit moral behavior displayed by gamblers, prostitutes, and individuals who engaged in premarital and extramarital sex. Klansmen wanted to use their organization as a device to take the country back to an alleged time when these behaviors were rare. Many did not mind using violence and other extralegal means to enforce their models of social conformity.

**Klan Violence And Reaction**

While the Klan provided a sense of community for its members through grand parades, dramatic initiation ceremonies, casual social events, and even occasional charity work, the hooded order became an outlet for others who wished to impose their desires through vigilantism. They spied on neighbors, issued threats to suspected wrongdoers, and took part in brutal acts of violence against their adversaries. Texas newspapers abound with stories of Klan violence during the early 1920s (over eighty floggings in 1921 alone). Though only a minor portion of Klan attacks in Texas were directed against African Americans, violent incidents did occur. Among Klan victims were a Dallas bellhop attacked and branded on his forehead with "KKK" in acid for allegedly associating with white women; a Houston dentist was castrated for dating a white woman; nine blacks were killed by Texas Klansmen in May 1922 alone for various offenses. The majority of Klan victims in Texas, however, were white: a Houston lawyer tarred and feathered for defending blacks, bootleggers, and gamblers; a Bay City banker flogged for adultery; a Beaumont doctor whipped for performing two abortions; a Brenham man beaten for supposed disloyalty during World War I and speaking German in public; and a woman kidnapped from a Tenaha hotel who was stripped, beaten with a wet rope, and tarred and feathered because there was some question whether her second marriage had been preceded by a divorce.

Klansmen escaped prosecution for these and other offenses because eyewitnesses were too afraid to testify, grand juries refused to indict offenders, and law enforcement officials (many of whom were Klansmen themselves) often looked the other way. Opposition to the Klan, however, eventually emerged. Some judges tried to press grand juries for indictments. Major newspapers including the *Dallas Morning News* and the *Houston Chronicle* began to issue anti-Klan editorials and carry reports of Klan violence on its front pages. Many local chambers of commerce and professional organizations, such as the Texas State Bar Association, began to speak out against the Klan's lawlessness and damage to the state's image.

Though acts of violence continued, the hooded order experienced its first legal setback in 1923 with the first convictions of its members for a violent crime. In Taylor (a small town northeast of Austin), local Klansmen had threatened a white traveling salesman named Ralph Burleson who was known to frequently visit a local widow who was a friend of his family. Rumors of an affair (apparently untrue) flew after Burleson stayed two weeks at the widow's home while selling his products around the county. After Burleson spurned the threats, Klansmen ran his car off the road, kidnapped him, tied him to a tree, whipped him senseless, dumped hot tar on his head, and deposited him in the Taylor town square. Dan Moody, a young ambitious district attorney in Williamson County, not only succeeded in receiving grand jury indictments, he ended up destroying the local klavern by obtaining numerous convictions against many of those responsible for the attack and subsequent efforts to cover up involvement. The Klan's aura of invincibility with respect to the law had been broken, but at the time it remained to be seen if the Invisible Empire's efforts to gain political control of the state would succeed.

**Governor Pat Neff**

Pat Neff, a Waco attorney, governed the Lone Star State during the early 1920s. After defeating former senator Joseph Bailey in the 1920 Democratic primary runoff, Neff trounced his Republican challenger in the 1920 general election. Though he had served in the state House of Representatives at the turn of the century (including four years as Speaker), Neff had a rocky relationship with the legislature during his two terms in office. Much like U.S. President Woodrow Wilson, the governor adopted a highly idealistic and moral tone that endeared him to many supporters but often made others view him as someone who arrogantly assumed an aura of patronizing superiority. Neff had a penchant for alienating many legislators by relaying his desires through special messages and then berating them for inaction if they rejected his requests.

Despite the antagonistic rapport, some achievements took place during Neff's tenure. Responding to the appearance of the mass-produced automobile (by 1930 there were close to 1.5 million cars in Texas) and motivated by a desire to promote tourism, the governor and the legislature teamed up to appropriate state funds for highway construction. By the end of the decade, Texas had almost 20,000 miles of highways, half of

**Governor Thomas G. McLeod of South Carolina and Pat Neff of Texas, October 23, 1923.**
**Photo credit: Library of Congress**

which were hard-surfaced roads. Funds were also allocated with the governor's approval for important water conservation surveys and the creation of Texas Technological College in Lubbock. Neff reversed the trend of liberal pardoning policies by abolishing the Board of Pardon Advisors. Personally reviewing all pardon applications, the governor issued less than 200 in four years (by contrast, James Ferguson issued 2,253 pardons during his two and a half years in office, and William Hobby pardoned 1,518 criminals in his three and a half years). Finally, Neff deserves credit for the creation of the State Parks System. The governor managed to get the legislature to approve a non-salaried Parks Board to oversee potential park lands received from communities (the state had long since sold or given up all available land for recreation purposes). Neff actively solicited donations and gradually began to acquire lands, but the parks system did not develop into a real tourist draw until federal aid arrived during the Great Depression.

These achievements represented a small portion of Neff's overall agenda. The legislature denied most of his other calls for consolidation of government agencies, proposed prison and education reforms, and a constitutional convention to replace the Constitution of 1876. (The document was so outdated, Neff once commented, that "all of our good laws are unconstitutional" under its terms.)

The state legislature's inability to deliver on Neff's proposed law enforcement reforms, especially efforts to combat evasion of the Prohibition laws, deeply disappointed Neff. A devout Baptist who cancelled the traditional governor's inaugural ball due to his strong dislike of public dancing, Neff was also a devout "dry" who demanded that the legislature aid him in enforcing Prohibition. Though he called for such changes as the removal of law enforcement officials found not to be enforcing Prohibition, allowing alcohol buyers to testify in cases against bootleggers, and the elimination of suspended sentences for criminals, the governor sulked when the legislature rejected each request. Though not a Klan sympathizer, Neff's apparent belief that the Invisible Empire might be a bulwark against lawlessness (at least on Prohibition matters) and certainly his respect for the Klan's growing electoral clout in the state explain his much-criticized reluctance to denounce the Ku Klux Klan publicly by name during his governorship.

**The Klan Enters Politics**

In 1921 Klansmen focused their first full year in Texas on recruitment, hosting social events and regulating the behavior of residents in their communities. There were only a few municipal elections in that year, plus "Imperial Wizard" William Simmons was not very interested in getting the group involved in politics. The Klan's move into politics in Texas and other states started in 1922 after a faction led by Hiram Wesley Evans, a Dallas dentist who had served as cyclops of the Dallas klavern, gained control of the national organization. Unhappy with Simmons's leadership, Evans and his supporters supplanted the Klan's founders, eventually buying out Simmons and banishing Edward Clarke. Afterwards, Evans pushed for Klan entry into Democratic Party politics across the nation. He also sought to change the Klan's image as a violent organization (somewhat ironic since he led the group of Klansmen who brutally attacked and branded the Dallas bellhop during the previous year).

In 1922 Evans sought to elect a slate of candidates in numerous local campaigns and state legislature races. The great prize was a U.S. Senate seat currently held by Charles

Culberson. The sixty-seven-year old senator announced that he would be seeking a fifth term, despite the fact that he did not plan to return for the campaign due to ill health. (Indeed, he had not traveled back home to Texas in the past ten years!) Klansmen disliked Culberson because he was strongly against their organization, plus he was an outspoken opponent of Prohibition. Of the five candidates who entered the race to unseat the senator, three were Klansmen. The leading choice was Earle Mayfield, a former state senator serving on the Railroad Commission. Hiram Evans and his influential Dallas klavern solidly backed Mayfield in its "elimination primary"—a straw poll used to decide who would get the group's endorsement in an effort to unify the strength of the organization behind one candidate. Other klaverns soon fell into line behind Mayfield.

The major candidate emerging to challenge Culberson and Mayfield was none other than James Ferguson. Though banned by the legislature from holding state office, this restriction did not apply to federal posts such as a U.S. Senate seat. The former governor could always count on support from tenant farmers, low-wage workers, and strong wets. During the Democratic primary, Ferguson focused his attention more on the aging Culberson than the Klan. In one instance, he accused the senator of not possessing enough of his mental faculties to carry out his job. In another speech, Ferguson pledged to quit the race and support Culberson if he would return to Texas and deliver a twenty-minute speech. Results of the primary vote showed Culberson finishing a distant third to the leader Mayfield and the runner-up Ferguson. Klansmen were ecstatic at Mayfield's success and the fine performance of other local and statewide Klan-endorsed candidates. However, because Mayfield and the other Klan candidates for Lieutenant Governor, State Treasurer, and State Superintendent of Public Instruction did not garner at least 50 percent of the vote, runoff elections had to take place.

Democratic voters had an interesting choice in the 1922 Senate race: a Klansman or an impeached and removed former governor! Ever the opportunist, Ferguson tried to make the election all about the Klan, knowing the group's unpopularity with many Texas voters. Lambasting Hiram Wesley Evans as the "Imperial Gizzard," Ferguson used his oratorical talents to picture Earle Mayfield as his minion, doing the bidding of the Invisible Empire's leader rather than following the wishes of most Texans. The choice was either "Prince Earle or Farmer Jim," he exclaimed. Mayfield's common response to the ex-governor's venom was simply to dismiss such words because "they come from the mouth of James E. Ferguson." Despite Ferguson's best mudslinging efforts, Mayfield carried the day in the runoff election 317,591 to 265,233. Mayfield benefited from solid Klan support, endorsements from prominent non-Klansmen such as Senator Morris Sheppard and former governor William Hobby, vital backing from most of the state's drys who despised James Ferguson, and other voters who disliked the ex-governor for countless other reasons. Despite the defeat, this was not the last Texas would see of James Ferguson.

The notion that a strong non-Ferguson, anti-Klan opponent would have defeated Mayfield is evident from the returns in the other statewide runoffs—all Klan-supported candidates went down to defeat by healthy margins to their rivals. Nevertheless, the Senate nomination was a huge achievement for Klansmen who also celebrated victories in a majority of the Texas House of Representatives races along with local triumphs in Dallas, Fort Worth, Houston, Austin, Beaumont, Waco, and Wichita Falls. (Klan candidates also won statewide and local races in Oklahoma, Arkansas, Louisiana, Georgia, Indiana, and Oregon.)

**Senator Morris Sheppard seated at his desk. September 1938.**
**Photo credit: Library of Congress**

A group of disgruntled anti-Klan Democrats and opportunistic Republicans attempted to thwart Mayfield in the general election by throwing their support to George Peddy, a thirty-year-old assistant district attorney from Houston whose prior claim to fame was leading a highly-publicized protest against Governor Ferguson while student body president at the University of Texas. The attorney general, however, ruled that Peddy could not appear on the ballot as a Republican or as an independent candidate because he had voted in the 1922 Democratic primary. Peddy challenged Mayfield anyway with a valiant write-in effort, but Mayfield won the general election by a two-to-one margin of 264,260 to 130,744. Peddy and his backers continued the fight in the U.S. Senate where they filed a petition contesting the election results, citing questionable financial support and various Klan activities during the election. A prolonged investigation that Republicans used to embarrass the Democrats by publicizing the Klan's power in Texas and other states eventually concluded, and Mayfield was finally seated in February 1925, over two years after his election. Nevertheless, coupled with state legislature and local government victories, Mayfield's victory allowed Texas Klansmen to boast that they were the leading state in the entire realm of the Invisible Empire. They looked forward to the 1924 governor's race and securing political control over the Lone Star State.

**The Klan Seeks The Governorship**

In 1924 Texas Klansmen were confident about their chances of winning the governorship. After holding local elimination primaries, they unified behind the candidacy of Felix D. Robertson. A district judge whose father and grandfather served as Confederate generals, Robertson was a charter member of the Dallas Klan and a zealous Prohibitionist who preached strict economy in state government and tough enforcement of the laws, especially the Prohibition statutes. He pledged to use his gubernatorial powers to combat lynchings, whippings, and other forms of mob violence while working to end foreign immigration, to suppress foreign-language newspapers, and to promote white supremacy. Calling for a return to traditional Christianity, Robertson stated that if Texans would simply follow the Ten Commandments and the Golden Rule, all of the state's problems would take care of themselves.

Four other major anti-Klan candidates announced their run, but none was more controversial than James Ferguson, who argued in vain that his ban from public office was null and void because he had resigned as governor in 1917 before the Senate removed him. When the State Democratic Executive Committee refused to place Ferguson's name on the ballot and the state supreme court upheld the decision, the former governor simply asked his wife Miriam to run in his place, and she obliged.

A housewife, mother of two daughters, and grandmother, Miriam Amanda "Ma" Ferguson was 49-years-old when she sought the Democratic nomination for governor on her husband's behalf. Though completely lacking in political experience, Ma Ferguson stated that she was in the race to vindicate the family name. After endorsing her husband's platform, she addressed the issue of her qualifications by stating: "I know I can't talk about the Constitution and the making of laws and the science of government like some other candidates, and I believe they have talked too much, but I have a trusting and abiding faith 'that my Redeemer liveth,' and I am trusting in him to guide my footsteps in the path of righteousness for the good of our people and the good of our State."

On the campaign trail Miriam Ferguson did very little speaking, preferring to thank audiences for attending and then to introduce her quick-tongued husband to handle the oratorical duties. As in the 1922 Senate race, Jim Ferguson tried to make the race all about the Klan. "If a man is so narrow and so intolerant that he wants to believe in the principles of the Ku Klux, that is his right and his business," he often stated. "But when he covers up his face and goes out in disguise to whip and assault some woman or murder and maim some man, then that is mine and every other good citizen's business." A top priority for the Ferguson administration, he promised, would be passage of an anti-disguise law plus a measure requiring the listing of membership rolls of all secret societies and fraternal organizations in the state.

Felix Robertson rode Klan support to emerge from the Democratic primary with a 50,000-vote lead over runner-up Miriam Ferguson, who finished 5,000 votes ahead

**Governor Miriam Ferguson**
**Photo credit: Library of Congress**

of her nearest competitor. Robertson's tally of 193,508, however, was far short from the majority of the record 703,123 votes cast in order to stave off a runoff. The appearance of many anti-Klan contestants in the field (including two able candidates who unfortunately had the same last name of Davidson) diluted the first vote. Yet, it remained to be seen if Miriam Ferguson could rally enough anti-Klan voters to succeed where her husband had failed in the Senate race two years earlier.

Once again Texas Democratic voters had to choose between a Klansman and a Ferguson. Most of the eliminated candidates threw their reluctant support behind Ma Ferguson, as did many of the state's leading newspapers. After a lively one-month campaign, Texas voters finally decided for Miriam Ferguson's bonnet over the Klan's hood by a 413,751 to 316,019 margin. Such was the Klan's unpopularity among a majority of Texans by mid-1924 that an inexperienced wife of an impeached governor was able to win the Democratic nomination. Further, Dan Moody was able to ride his reputation as a hard-nosed, Klan-busting district attorney all the way to the Democratic nomination for attorney general over his Klan-backed opponent.

Texas Republicans hoped to capitalize on lingering anti-Ferguson feelings by nominating George C. Butte, the respected Dean of the University of Texas Law School. Despite getting the support of many anti-Ferguson Democrats, most of them disgruntled Klansmen, Miriam Ferguson became the first woman elected governor in American history when she soundly defeated Butte ("a little mutton-headed professor with a Dutch diploma," Jim Ferguson callously called him) by a 422,528 to 294,970 margin. The Klan also lost its control of the state House of Representatives and its political dominance in most Texas counties.

With the reins of government denied them, the hooded order began a rapid descent. Tremendous disillusionment with its stunning electoral defeat, continuous negative press delivered by the state's major dailies, the departure of prominent men from the organization, ongoing citizen disgust with continuing acts of violence by renegade Klansmen, and highly-publicized scandals involving the group's leaders outside of the Lone Star State—all contributed to the Klan's demise. Anti-Klan sentiment reached a fever pitch in Texas by the end of 1924, reflected in some instances of violent acts against the group. In a sign of the changing times, just a few days after the November election, unknown assailants detonated two bombs at the 4,000-seat klavern hall of Fort Worth Klan No. 101, completely destroying the building. By the end of the 1920s, the Invisible Empire had largely vanished from Texas.

**Governor Miriam Ferguson**

The hopes of staunch Ferguson opponents that Miriam Ferguson's administration would be quieter than her husband's tenure were dashed early when James Ferguson soon dominated his wife's administration. Her dependence was symbolized profoundly by the placement of James's office next door to the governor's office in the Capitol building. The contemporary belief that "Jim's the governor, Ma just signs the papers" was largely true. Miriam Ferguson was governor in name only—James Ferguson ran his wife's administration. Indeed, most Ferguson supporters realized that this would be the case. If they did not think that James Ferguson would act as governor himself, they would have never voted for Ma. He became a constant presence in the chambers of government by attending state board meetings, receiving his wife's political callers, and generally "advising"

Miriam on policy matters. Ma's decisions reflected her husband's desires and policies, among them reduced appropriations (especially for the University of Texas) and support for an anti-disguise law targeting the Ku Klux Klan that the legislature eventually passed, though a state appeals court later ruled it to be unconstitutional.

Controversy eventually engulfed Miriam Ferguson's administration. One area of contention was her liberal pardoning policies. The governor issued 239 pardons in her first 70 days in office, eventually announcing 3,595 clemency proclamations of all types by the end of 1926. Political opponents, ministers, and newspaper editors decried the policy (the *Fort Worth Star-Telegram* even kept a running total of Ferguson pardons on its front pages), accusing the governor and her husband of extracting payments in return for the releases. No evidence was produced to prove that the Fergusons ever profited financially from the pardons. They believed that Texas courts sent too many poor people to prison, especially for minor Prohibition offenses. Generous use of the pardoning power would lessen this practice and save the state prison system money while simultaneously helping the Fergusons gain political points among their core constituency.

Accusations of favoritism within Miriam Ferguson's administration abounded. Questions arose over textbooks adopted by the State Textbook Commission, which consisted of Ferguson appointees. The commission often granted contracts to companies submitting the highest bid. Not coincidentally, the owners or field agents of the winning companies were known Ferguson associates. A storm of debate also arose over the *Ferguson Forum*—a Ferguson-owned newspaper that James Ferguson used to profit from his wife's administration. Ferguson compelled companies to buy expensive advertising space in the journal if they wished to do any business with the state government. The *Forum* proved to be valuable for the Fergusons over the next two years as a steady source of income and as an administration mouthpiece.

A scandal involving the Ferguson-appointed State Highway Commission, however, proved to be the major embarrassment of Miriam Ferguson's governorship. At its meetings, which James Ferguson always attended, the board made important decisions regarding the issuing of construction and maintenance contracts for state-funded roads. In all instances, the commission granted contracts to loyal Ferguson supporters and *Ferguson Forum* advertisers, whether the winning company's bid was the lowest, or if it even had road-building experience. The result was huge sums of state money wasted on unnecessary roads, poorly constructed and maintained highways, and other thoroughfares never being built. Attorney General Dan Moody investigated the rumors of malfeasance and filed lawsuits against two companies for overcharging the state, eventually receiving refunds and cancellation of the contracts.

Many ramifications resulted from the attorney general's investigation: taxpayers saved millions of dollars, two members of the Highway Commission resigned, the Ferguson administration looked increasingly corrupt, and Dan Moody became frequently mentioned as a possible gubernatorial candidate in 1926. Calls for Miriam Ferguson's impeachment and removal from office were tempered not only by the realization that Ma was not directly involved in the Highway Commission's transgressions but also by the strong hope that Moody might run against her in the next election. James Ferguson certainly realized that the young attorney general ("the Boy Wonder," as he derisively called Moody) was his wife's main rival, often claiming that Moody fabricated the highway contract charges because he wanted to be governor.

Moody announced in March 1926 that he would seek the Democratic nomination for governor. Citing the controversies over the road contracts, textbook adoptions, and other instances of questionable ethics, he lambasted the current administration as totally corrupt and promised to restore honest government in Texas. James Ferguson had big reason to worry because Moody was the dream candidate for many Texans: a reputable anti-Ferguson politician with impeccable anti-Klan credentials. All of the state's leading newspapers and most major Democratic Party leaders supported Moody. Nevertheless, the Fergusons retained the loyal support of many rural voters. ("Jim Ferguson," humorist Will Rogers once observed, "has 150,000 voters in Texas that would be with him if he blew up the Capitol building in Washington." They would say, "Well, Jim was right. The thing ought to have been blowed up years ago.") James used his best demagogic tactics on Moody, not only labeling him an inexperienced upstart but also trying to characterize him as the Klan's choice because he supported Prohibition. Miriam (a former opponent of woman's suffrage) even played the gender card when she told a gathering during a rare public speech that her election loss would set back the cause of women's rights one hundred years. Despite such desperate efforts, Moody led Miriam Ferguson and other minor candidates in the Democratic primary by 409,732 to 283,482, just 1,771 votes shy of a majority. In the runoff, Moody trounced Ferguson with a decisive 495,723 to 270,595 rout. The 33-year-old Moody proceeded to swamp the Republican candidate in the general election to become the state's youngest governor. The Fergusons quietly left the governor's mansion, but unknown to many elated Texans at the time, Ma and Pa Ferguson would return.

**Governor Dan Moody**

Dan Moody served two terms as Texas governor, providing competent, scandal-free leadership for the remainder of the decade. He made good appointments, pardoned far fewer criminals than the Fergusons, and worked with the legislature to create a state auditor's office to oversee spending by government agencies. Like Governor Neff, however, the legislature refused to adopt most of Moody's reform proposals designed to bring more efficient government services. Legislators who were hesitant to change the status quo, especially by concentrating more power in the governor's hands, rejected Moody's desire for a civil service law, relocation of state prisons to a single central Texas location, changes in the textbook adoption process, creation of a board of higher education, and proposed judicial reforms.

Despite his limited success with the legislature, Moody was extremely popular with the Texas electorate and had no serious opposition for re-election in 1928. The Fergusons respected the governor's stature and wisely stayed out of the race. Moody easily secured the Democratic nomination without the need of a runoff by defeating Fort Worth lawyer and stock raiser Louis Wardlaw (a friend of James Ferguson) 442,080 votes to 245,508. He proceeded to beat the Republican nominee in the general election by a five-to-one margin.

Other political contests that year caught the interest of Texas voters. In the Senate race, five candidates (including Minnie Fisher Cunningham) emerged to challenge Earle Mayfield's re-election bid. Though Mayfield received more votes in the Democratic primary (Cunningham finished a distant fifth), he lost the runoff election to six-term congressman Tom Connally of Marlin by a vote of 320,071 to 257,747. Mayfield's defeat marked the last vestiges of Klan influence in statewide Texas politics. In the presidential race, Herbert Hoover made history by becoming the first Republican to receive Texas's electoral votes on his way to winning the presidency over Democrat Al Smith. Though Governor Moody eventually endorsed the Democratic Party nominee, Smith, a second-generation Irish Catholic governor from New York City who strongly opposed Prohibition, simply had too many negatives to receive the support of a majority of Texas voters. Hoover won Texas with 52 percent of the vote.

The new president enjoyed a six-month "honeymoon" before the bottom fell out of the American economy. The October 1929 stock market crash, when coupled with glaring structural problems in the national economy, produced an unprecedented disaster that most Texans could not escape. By early 1930 the Great Depression had arrived full force, making the major issues of the 1920s fade as the main concerns turned to matters of unemployment and record-low crop prices. At this tumultuous time, Texans had no idea how long the Depression would last or how it would change their lives forever.

## *Afterward: The Beginning of a Slow Ascent*

*More than just an anomaly, the appointment of Hortense Ward, Hattie Lenenberg, and Ruth Brazzil to the "All-Woman Supreme Court" reflected the rise of women in Texas and American society during the 1920s. While garnering public attention (the episode made headlines in state and national newspapers), Governor Pat Neff's appointments promoted the women's movement just as he was leaving office—soon to be succeeded by the state's first female governor, Miriam Ferguson. Referring to his appointments of the three women in a letter to Nellie Metcalfe of the Texas Woman's Chamber of Commerce, Neff wrote: "I am in hopes that this recognition of the womanhood of the State as attorneys will be helpful in many ways to those women, wherever they may be, who are fighting single-handed the battles of life." Through prior actions, the governor had already recognized the increased political clout of women's groups by naming at least one female to every state government board and commission. He also became the first Texas governor to appoint a woman to be his private secretary, the modern-day equivalent of chief-of-staff. During the remainder of the 1920s, women across the state began serving in numerous public positions as county treasurers, school superintendents, county clerks, and tax assessors. In 1926, Margie Neal became the first woman elected to the Texas State Senate. Meanwhile, four additional women won election to the Texas House of Representatives.*

*Despite these advances for women in public life during the 1920s, several decades passed before Texas women served once again on the state Supreme Court. In 1958, Sarah Hughes, the first woman appointed to serve as a Texas District Court judge, tried and failed to win election to a seat on the Texas Supreme Court. Not until 1982 would a woman serve on the High Court in a full-time capacity, when Governor William Clements appointed Ruby Sondock to fill the remainder of an interim seat. Finally, in 1992, Rose Spector became the first woman to win election to the Texas Supreme Court. She served a full term then lost her reelection bid in 1998 to another woman, Harriet O'Neill.*

## *Myth & Legend*

**The 1920s as the "Roaring Twenties"**

*An enduring myth still held by many is the idea that the 1920s was a wild and crazy decade characterized by revelry and hedonism. These so-called "Roaring Twenties" were defined by a majority of citizens supposedly dressing and behaving in provocative new ways that openly challenged accepted social norms while drinking alcohol extensively at rowdy parties and discarding the old time religion.*

*This stereotype has two main origins. First, there were, in fact, some individuals during the 1920s who did partake in rowdy behavior deemed unacceptable by traditional standards. After the First World War, they adopted a more care-free lifestyle in an effort to put the negativity of the war behind them, to take advantage of new freedoms provided by technological advances such as the widespread availability of the automobile, and to follow the lead of mainstream magazines and movies. Second, during the 1920s and since, popularizers of the myth in books and films have crafted and promoted this depiction of the era. Writing in the 1930s, journalist Frederick Lewis Allen produced a best-selling reflection of the just-concluded decade entitled* **Only Yesterday**, *in which he focused solely on the new modes of dress, the fads and crazes that made the news, and examples of individuals who discarded old thoughts and beliefs to further the notion that these activities were the norm for most people living during these times. Allen's book, F. Scott Fitzgerald's novels such as* **The Great Gatsby**, *and many films during the decade did much to solidify the view that wildness and excitement dominated the years between World War I and the Great Depression.*

*Serious historians now discard such depictions of the 1920s. They point out that only certain middle- and upper-class urban youth who had the time, money, and inclination to pursue the new behaviors, modes of dress, and popular fads were largely the individuals involved in such activities that the media at the time, and since, have blown out of proportion. Incorrectly, popularizers have taken new thoughts and acts performed by a minority of the population and applied them to explain the mentality and lifestyle of the majority.*

*In fact, a majority of Texans rejected most of these new ideas and deeds. As evidence, historians note that while millions have read F. Scott Fitzgerald's novels, very few actually did so during the 1920s. Instead, one of the most popular authors of the decade was an Ohio dentist named Zane Grey who wrote westerns containing simple good-versus-evil plots promoting traditional values of duty, sobriety, fidelity, and rugged individualism. Texas politics during the 1920s, as elsewhere in the country, also maintained a conservative bent. Neither Socialists nor radical experimentalists were elected to public office. Other aspects that do not fit the Roaring Twenties image include the rise of religious fundamentalism, the rise of the second Ku Klux Klan, and the fact that Prohibition of alcohol was the law of the land throughout the decade. These elements fly in the face of the idea that a majority of Texans believed it was socially acceptable to discard their traditional beliefs, values, and behavior.*

## Suggestions for Further Reading

Alexander, Charles C. *Crusade for Conformity, 1920-1930.* Houston: Texas Gulf Coast Historical Association, 1962.

___. *The Ku Klux Klan in the Southwest.* Norman: University of Oklahoma Press, 1995.

Bernstein, Patricia, *Ten Dollars to Hate: The Texas Man Who Fought the Klan* College Station: Texas A&M University Press, 2017.

Blodgett, Dorothy, Terrell Blodgett, and David L. Scott. *The Land, the Law and the Lord: The Life of Pat Neff.* Austin: Home Place Publishers, 2007.

Brown, Norman D., *Biscuits, the Dole, and Nodding Donkeys: Texas Politics, 1929-1932* Austin: University of Texas Press, 2019.

___. *Hood, Bonnet, and Little Brown Jug: Texas Politics, 1921-1928.* College Station: Texas A&M University Press, 1984.

Fass, Paula. *The Damned and the Beautiful: American Youth in the 1920s.* New York: Oxford University Press, 1979.

Foley, Neil. *The White Scourge: Mexicans, Blacks, and Poor Whites in Texas Cotton Culture, 1900-1940.* Berkeley: University of California Press, 1999.

Guzman, Will, *Civil Rights in the Texas Borderlands: Dr. Lawrence A. Nixon and Black Activism* Urbana: University of Illinois Press, 2015.

Hankins, Barry, *God's Rascal: J. Frank Norris and the Beginnings of Southern Fundamentalism* Lexington: University Press of Kentucky, 1996.

Hine, Darlene Clark. *Black Victory: The Rise and Fall of the White Primary in Texas.* Columbia: University of Missouri Press, 2003.

Jackson, Kenneth. *The Ku Klux Klan in the City, 1915-1930.* Chicago: Ivan R. Dee,1992.

McAfee, Alice G. "The All-Woman Texas Supreme Court: The History Behind a Brief Moment on the Bench," Vol. 39 *St. Mary's Law Journal* 2008, pp. 468-500.

Nash, Roderick. *The Nervous Generation: American Thought, 1917-1930.* Chicago: Ivan Dee, 1990.

Orozco, Cynthia E., *No Mexican, Women, or Dogs Allowed: The Rise of the Mexican American Civil Rights Movement* Austin: University of Texas Press, 2009.

Phillips, Michael. *White Metropolis: Race, Ethnicity, and Religion in Dallas, 1841-2001.* Austin: University of Texas Press, 2006.

Sharpless, Rebecca. *Fertile Ground, Narrow Choices: Women on Texas Cotton Farms, 1900-1940.* Chapel Hill: University of North Carolina Press, 1999.

Zelden, Charles L., *The Battle for the Ballot: Smith v. Allwright and the Defeat of the Texas All-White Primary* Lawrence: University of Kansas Press, 1994.

# Rise of Urbanization, Expanding Opportunities, & Invisible Empire, 1920-1929

**IDENTIFICATION:** Briefly describe each term.

All-Woman Supreme Courr
Permanent University Fund (PUF)
"Big Swing"
LULAC
white primary
1920s urbanization
J. Frank Norris
Ku Klux Klan
Pat Neff
Hiram Wesley Evans
Earle Mayfield
James Ferguson
Felix Robertson
Miriam Ferguson
Dan Moody

**MULTIPLE CHOICE:** Choose the correct response.

1. A majority of farm women lacked which of the following during the 1920s?
    A. indoor plumbing
    B. electric stoves
    C. radios
    D. washing machines
    E. all of the above

2. Founded in the late-1920s, LULAC promotes civil rights for _____.
    A. women
    B. blacks
    C. Hispanics
    D. gays
    E. none of the above

3. By the end of the 1920s, _____ had the largest population of any Texas city.
    A. Houston
    B. Dallas
    C. Austin
    D. El Paso
    E. Fort Worth

4. A "kleagle" was a Ku Klux Klan
    A. local chapter
    B. statewide leader
    C. recruiter
    D. initiation fee

5. Of the following, who was not a candidate for the U.S. Senate in 1922?
   A. Hiram Wesley Evans
   B. Charles Culberson
   C. Earle Mayfield
   D. James Ferguson

6. The Ku Klux Klan
   A. led a strong third-party movement to challenge the Democrats and Republicans during the 1920s.
   B. was not strong in any Texas city.
   C. elected a U.S. Senator in Texas during the 1920s.
   D. elected one of their own governor during the 1920s.
   E. focused mainly on denying rights to blacks but ignored other groups and activities by whites.

7. The election of Miriam Ferguson as governor in 1924
   A. was just one of a series of elections won by Texas women in the 1920s.
   B. demonstrated Miriam Ferguson's widespread personal popularity as a reform leader.
   C. probably reflected the general conclusion of many Texans that a vote for Ferguson was preferable to a vote for a Klansman.
   D. reflected the widespread Texas support for Prohibition at the time.

8. After Miriam Ferguson's election as governor in 1924, the Ku Klux Klan _____.
   A. gained even more supporters
   B. went into sharp decline
   C. tried to assassinate the newly-elected governor
   D. supported her governorship

9. _____ was the young attorney general who ran an anti-corruption campaign against Miriam Ferguson and ended up defeating her in the 1926 Democratic Party primary.
   A. Dan Moody
   B. Oscar Colquitt
   C. Pat Neff
   D. Joseph Sayers
   E. Hiram Wesley Evans

10. Dan Moody _____.
    A. was a former Klansman
    B. was the youngest person ever elected Texas governor
    C. was the oldest person ever elected Texas governor
    D. resigned as U.S. Senator to run against Miriam Ferguson
    E. eventually appointed James Ferguson to be his chief of staff

**TRUE/FALSE:** Indicate whether each statement is true or false.

1. The primary source of revenue for the Permanent University Fund derives from West Texas oil fields, first discovered during the 1920s.

2. "Snapping" was a popular social fad in Texas cities during the 1920s.

3. The "Big Swing" was a popular dance of the "Roaring 20s."

4. Tenant farmers were strong supports of the Fergusons.

5. The Ku Klux Klan was not strong in any Texas city during the 1920s.

6. The Ku Klux Klan focused mainly on denying rights to blacks but ignored other groups and activities by whites.

7. Unlike other parts of the country, the 1920s Klan in Texas largely avoided undertaking acts of violence against their opponents.

8. Pat Neff was a strong opponent of the Ku Klux Klan throughout his two terms as governor.

9. Dan Moody was defeated when he ran for re-election in 1928.

10. Though his administration was noted for its efficiency and lack of scandals, the Texas Legislature passed few of Dan Moody's proposals during his two terms as governor.


**MATCHING:** Match the response in column A with the item in column B.

1. Hiram Wesley Evans
2. Felix Robertson
3. William Simmons
4. Earle Mayfield
5. Edward Clarke
6. Miriam Ferguson
7. James Ferguson
8. Dan Moody
9. Pat Neff
10. Charles Culberson

A. Klan publicist
B. 1924 Klan candidate for governor
C. 1922 Klan candidate for U.S. Senate
D. 1920s Klan founder
E. Imperial Wizard who pushed Klan entry into politics
F. youngest governor in Texas history
G. defeated Klan candidate in 1924 governor's race
H. ex-governor barred from holding state office
I. two-term governor from 1921 to 1925
J. denied 5th term in 1922 U.S. Senate race

**ESSAY QUESTIONS:**

1.  Describe the rise of urbanization in Texas during the 1920s including identification of the factors that attracted people to Texas cities during the decade.

2.  Describe the political career of Dan Moody during the 1920s. How did he position himself to be a "dream candidate" for many Texas voters in the 1926 governor's race?

3.  Identify the major economic and social changes taking place in Texas during the 1920s and explain how these changes impacted the state.

4.  Describe the rise and fall of the Ku Klux Klan in Texas during the 1920s.

# Chapter 14

# The Great Depression and the New Deal, 1929-1940

*Prelude: The New London School Explosion*

As the strangling grip of the Great Depression began to reach the Lone Star State, the discovery of a massive deposit of oil underneath the Piney Woods of Northeast Texas in early September 1930 proved to be a godsend to one of the state's poorest regions. Producing a much-needed economic boom, the find led to skyrocketing population growth in Rusk and surrounding counties as oil workers and entrepreneurs alike flooded into the area. The people of London, Texas, a farming community located in northwestern Rusk County in the heart of the new oil field, saw rapid changes in a relatively short period of time. They first had to change their town's name to "New London" when they formally applied for a U.S. Post Office and learned that another London, Texas already existed. The immediate need for public services and the county's sudden accumulation of oil wealth allowed for the construction of new roads and, by the mid-1930s, a state-of-the-art educational campus consisting of a prominent 30,000-square foot main building for high school students, an elementary school building, a two-story auditorium, gymnasium, cafeteria, and even an athletic field with bleachers and stadium lighting. By 1937, over 1,200 students attended classes at the New London School.

Despite the prosperity generated by the oil boom that led many to refer to the New London School as the "Richest School in America," the school board tried to save money on heating bills by discontinuing the purchase of natural gas from a commercial gas company and, instead, authorizing the facility to tap into a free gas line that ran adjacent to the school. Oil companies in the area often allowed homes, churches, and businesses to use these "residual gas" lines because they contained unsellable byproducts that cost the companies to burn off anyway. A faulty connection to the residual gas line, however, doomed the school, as leaking odorless natural gas began to slowly accumulate into an open cavity underneath the west wing of the main building.

On the late-Thursday afternoon of March 18, 1937, as the elementary-school parents finished picking up their children and high school students awaited their dismissal for the beginning of a three-day weekend, a cataclysmic explosion felt up to eight miles away erupted with enough force to lift the main building several feet off its foundation before crashing back to the earth, destroying the school and trapping hundreds of students and staff members, both *dead and alive. Oil field workers who initially believed that a distant well blew frantically raced to the school when they received word about the true source of the blast. Parents arriving on the scene found mangled corpses in the school yard as they began to search for their loved ones. Volunteers started working to remove debris and try to save those trapped inside before it was too late while pulling out the bodies of those already lost. A horrific scene met the young journalist Walter Cronkite, then working for the United Press, as he arrived from Dallas to cover the story. Only twenty years old and on his first major news story, the future legendary newsman arrived at dusk to witness hundreds of residents working under floodlights, many with their bloodied bare hands and tears in their eyes, frantically digging through the rubble, in many cases looking for their own children. Into the night, even while a thunderstorm raged, over a thousand workers continued their grim task. Cheers of elation went up whenever rescuers found a survivor, but more often wails of grief were heard when workers pulled a dead child's body identified by a family member. By the next morning, with the wreckage cleared, the work was complete. In all, 298 students and school staff members were killed and hundreds more injured in the worst school disaster in American history.*

Beginning in late 1929 and lasting until the early 1940s, the Great Depression was the worst economic calamity in the history of Texas and the United States. Caused by structural defects in the national economy and precipitated by the stock market crash in far-away New York City, the ripple effects of the economic collapse greatly impacted Texas. Soon, large numbers of urban Texans found themselves unemployed, while the state's farmers and cattlemen began to receive record-low prices for their commodities, threatening them with financial ruin.

After four years of ineffective leadership by President Herbert Hoover, in late 1932 Texas and the nation turned to the Democratic governor of New York, Franklin D. Roosevelt (FDR) and his promise of a "new deal" for the American people. The Roosevelt administration intervened on an unprecedented scale as it experimented with new ways to stabilize the economy, promote recovery, and establish permanent reforms to prevent the return of a similar calamity in the future. After the Depression, Texans' relationship with the federal government would never be the same.

**Arrival of the Great Depression**

Though stock market prices soared and corporations earned high profits during much of the 1920s, serious structural problems existed in the national economy. Because companies continued to charge high prices for goods while keeping wages stagnant, a chronic maldistribution of wealth developed, making it difficult for consumers to maintain spending at a level adequate to keep the economy growing. Several months before the infamous stock market crash of October 1929, the country had actually slipped into a recession. The bottom fell out of the economy soon after investors began to pull their money out of the New York Stock Exchange. The rapid decline in stock prices ruined many investors who could not sell their shares before the collapse devastated their holdings. Many banks and brokerages that loaned to broken investors suffered major hits. Those banks that did not go out of business lost confidence and began to curtail their lending operations. This retrenchment hurt businesses, forcing many companies to curtail production or to end it completely, leading to layoffs and a worsening of the downward economic spiral.

At first, Texans seemed dismissive about these events. The media initially propagated beliefs that the economic downturn would be short-lived, with its effects largely bypassing Texas. The state, however, could not possibly isolate itself from the national economy. The economic depression led to reduced demand for Texas agricultural products, driving prices down to record-low levels. Budding Texas industries experienced a similar decline in demand for their goods, leading to reduced production and rising urban unemployment.

As the Depression worsened, many civic leaders and newspaper editors focused on ways that people could aid their neighbors. Taking a cue from Herbert Hoover, the new president, who strongly encouraged volunteerism, urged citizens to donate to their local charities and to help friends and family members in need. Discontent began to grow, however, as matters failed to improve. The number of soup kitchens and bread lines only increased during each subsequent year of Hoover's term. Farm prices plummeted. The number of crimes committed by desperate people and gangsters alike rose. By the end of Hoover's term, national morale reached an all-time low. Nobody knew how or when the country would recover.

**Governor Ross Sterling**

When Dan Moody announced in 1930 that he was following the two-term tradition and not seeking a third term as governor, eleven candidates entered the race for the Democratic nomination. Two leading candidates emerged: Houston businessman Ross Sterling (founder of Humble Oil and Refining Company and owner of the *Houston Post-Dispatch*) and Miriam Ferguson, making yet another run at the governor's mansion. After the primary, Ma Ferguson was in the lead by 70,000 votes over Sterling, but she fell far short of the votes necessary to avoid a runoff. The Fergusons's enemies joined up with the other eliminated candidates to throw their support behind Sterling, who won the runoff by a 90,000 vote margin. Sterling easily won the general election to become the next governor and the inheritor of rough times for the state. But if anyone thought that this result marked the end of the Fergusons, they were sadly mistaken.

The state's economic troubles dominated Governor Sterling's two years in office. He clashed with the legislature over expenditures, vetoing numerous appropriation bills that were without sufficient revenue to finance them. Like President Hoover, Sterling refused to support proposals for direct government aid to the unemployed. Eventually, people believed that both men either did not know or simply did not care about the plight of average people. Sterling's reactions to two events in particular—the East Texas oil boom and the proposed "Cotton Holiday" Plan—did him irreparable political harm and greatly limited his re-election chances.

**The East Texas Oil Boom**

In one of Texas history's most interesting coincidences, the first name of the man most responsible for the East Texas oil boom of the 1930s was identical to the surname of another explorer who also achieved fame after stumbling upon an important discovery based largely on faulty information. Just as Christopher Columbus centered his belief of a smaller Earth to justify his westward explorations on a combination of mythology, astrology, and pseudo-science, Columbus Marion "Dad" Joiner also relied on the misguided preaching of a self-educated, self-proclaimed "geologist" going by the name A. D. "Doc" Lloyd (his real name was Joseph Idelbert Durham) during his search for oil in the northeast Texas Piney Woods. By 1930, Joiner was a seventy-year-old "wildcatter" (someone searching for oil where no one believed any existed) who, like thousands of others, roamed the southwestern U.S. looking for a big strike. He made his living through constant promotion: hyping up a potential drilling area to donors and selling shares of the proceeds from any oil deposits his crew might discover. In the meantime, he used the money that he raised to pay his bills and to drill for oil with his outdated equipment. Desperate people in the Piney Woods, among the poorest regions in the state, bought shares in Joiner's gambles. Others allowed his crew to drill on their land in the hope of hitting it big. Joiner benefited from men willing to work on his crew for free on the promise of a big paycheck if they ever made a lucky strike.

On September 5, 1930, at a depth of about 3,500 feet, Joiner's crew hit pay dirt on a third attempt to drill for oil in Rusk County. His "Daisy Bradford No. 3" Well (named after the landowner of the drilling site) punctured the largest reservoir of oil in the contiguous United States, dwarfing the earlier Spindletop and Borger strikes. Initially, large oil companies had stayed out of the region, being told by geologists that large deposits were not to be found there. A slew of small independent drillers, however, flocked to the region to tap into the field which, unbeknownst to them at the time, spanned underneath several counties in east-central Texas (primarily central Gregg and western Rusk, but also included southern Upshur, southeastern Smith, and northeastern Cherokee counties). Located in the center of the field, Kilgore (in Gregg County, about 125 miles east of Dallas) became a boomtown, serving as the focal point of production, processing, service, and supplies. Within weeks, thousands poured into the town, erecting tents and shacks in every available space. The population surged from about 500 in 1929 to 12,000 by 1936. At the height of the boom, there were over a thousand producing wells within the city limits of Kilgore itself.

Truly astonished at the vast discovery, Dad Joiner had a looming problem. In order to increase his income in the months before the strike, he had completely oversold his shares. Now he had people expecting to get paid. One of the independent-drillers arriving in the area, H. L. Hunt, eventually relieved Joiner of his legal burdens. Hunt took advantage of Joiner's potential troubles by buying him out for $1.3 million ($30,000 up front and the remainder via production royalties over time). Along with other independents, Hunt continued to develop the field with a vast number of wells in the area (900 wells by 1932) and made an incredible fortune. By 1948, a national business journal cited H. L. Hunt as the richest man in America with the value of his oil properties at $263 million.

The huge oil boom led, however, to a sharp decline in oil prices—from one dollar a barrel to 10 cents (sometimes even lower). As prices slid, small producers increased their production to make up the difference. These actions forced prices to drop even more. The Texas Railroad Commission tried to intervene in April 1931 by ordering production restrictions, but drillers disregarded the agency's authority. They continued to produce and ship tremendous amounts of petroleum above assigned quotas—"hot oil," as it began to be called. Many producers sued the commission because state law only allowed production limits for conservation reasons, not for particular market conditions. After a federal court in July 1931 agreed with the plaintiffs, Governor Sterling declared martial law in the East Texas oil field. On August 17, he ordered over 1,000 National Guardsmen and Texas Rangers into the fields to establish order and temporarily shut down production.

In addition to filing renewed protests and legal challenges, many operators continued to disregard Sterling's efforts. Because he used to head the Humble Oil Company, opponents charged the governor with supporting the interests of big oil companies. (It did not help that Sterling sent National Guard General Jacob Wolters to enforce martial law. Though experienced in maintaining order, Wolters also happened to serve as general counsel for Texaco.) Despite many East Texan pleas for government intervention to arrest the price decline, other locals resented the imposition because they feared it would dampen prosperity in the region. The oil boom offered jobs for drilling crews as well as those who provided various services to the workers. Hot oil producers and moonshiners alike showed their anger by occasionally firing upon patrolling National Guard planes.

On February 2, 1932, the Texas Supreme Court ended martial law in the East Texas oil field by ruling that the governor's action was illegal. Finally, in January 1933 the legislature gave the Railroad Commission clear authority to limit oil production based on market conditions and to enforce individual production levels. Despite the new law, hot oil continued to flow in violation of Railroad Commission quotas. (It would take federal intervention during the New Deal to seriously stymie this traffic.) By this time, Sterling was a man with limited time in office. Resentment in East Texas against many of his actions, coupled with the anger he produced in farmers over the "Cotton Holiday" Plan, contributed to his defeat.

## The "Cotton Holiday" Plan

While dealing with the chaos in the East Texas oil field, Governor Sterling also had to manage a growing protest among the state's cotton farmers. Southern cotton farmers were plagued with the same problem affecting the oil markets: overproduction. In 1931, Huey Long, the bombastic governor of Louisiana, assumed leadership of a radical plan to deal with the deteriorating cotton market. His proposal was the "Cotton Holiday" Plan—an

**Louisiana politician Huey Long**

effort to eliminate large cotton surpluses and raise low prices by ceasing all planting in 1932. This scheme promised to create a tremendous spike in 1931 cotton prices, leading to more than enough income to carry farmers into 1932. Though critics labeled the plan everything from unworkable to communistic, the cotton holiday movement had a growing number of supporters.

At an August 1931 conference of cotton state representatives held in New Orleans, Long called for state laws banning cotton production in 1932. If cotton states pledged to remove 75 percent of the South's acreage out of production, the plan would go into effect. He promised that Louisiana would lead the way by passing appropriate legislation first. By agreeing with Long, the conferees clearly placed the ball in Texas's court. Because Texas produced one-third of the South's cotton crop, the plan could not go into operation if the Texas legislature declined to participate.

Governor Sterling never supported the cotton holiday idea, believing that farmers were getting "unduly excited" over the drop in cotton prices. Though he spoke publicly against the plan, Sterling succumbed to the demands and called for a special session to meet in September 1931 to consider the proposal. After a ten-day special session, the legislature killed the cotton holiday bill proposal by a wide margin. To appease the agitated farmers, however, the legislature passed a bill limiting cotton acreage in 1932 and 1933 to no more than 30 percent of the acreage cultivated during the previous year. This Texas Cotton Acreage Control Law never had an opportunity to demonstrate whether it could be a sufficient alternative to Long's plan. Arguing that the law violated the state and federal constitutions on various grounds, in February 1932 a state judge voided the legislation. No further attempt was made to limit cotton production until the New Deal. Meanwhile, Sterling's opposition to the cotton holiday movement only earned him additional political enemies among many of the state's disgruntled farmers.

**The Return of the Fergusons**

The enduring depression and Sterling's growing unpopularity with certain elements of the electorate provided a ripe opportunity for a pair of career opportunists: the Fergusons. In February 1932, Miriam Ferguson announced once again that she was a candidate for governor. On the campaign trail, James Ferguson portrayed Sterling as a rich uncaring millionaire, while representing the Fergusons as the champions of the common man. He attacked Sterling for declaring martial law in East Texas and constantly repeated a false charge that the governor had wasted $100 million in state highway funds. Ferguson offered no specific formula for fighting the Depression other than promising to lower taxes. As in 1930, Ma Ferguson led all candidates after the Democratic primary, but Sterling finished second with enough votes to force a runoff. Once again, other candidates, ex-Governor Moody, other prominent Democrats, and the state press threw their support behind Sterling. This time, however, Miriam Ferguson came out ahead by a slim margin of just under 3,800 votes. Sterling's campaign cried fraud, citing the fact that in many pro-Ferguson East Texas counties the number of votes exceeded the number of poll tax receipts, but the Texas Supreme Court allowed the result to stand. In the November general election, Mrs. Ferguson defeated the Republican candidate with 62 percent of the vote. Meanwhile, in the presidential race, Texans repudiated Herbert Hoover by giving Franklin D. Roosevelt 89 percent of their vote.

Franklin D. Roosevelt and John Nance Garner in Peekskill, New York. 08/14/1932
Photo credits: FDR Presidential Library

**Texas Influence on the New Deal**

Texans would play a prominent role in Washington, D.C. during Franklin Roosevelt's presidency beginning, in fact, before FDR's election. During the 1932 campaign for the Democratic presidential nomination, Uvalde congressman and Speaker of the House John Nance Garner became Roosevelt's major challenger. Among others, Roosevelt had Garner's mentor, Congressman Sam Rayburn of Bonham, to thank for securing Garner's eventual support (in exchange for Garner becoming Roosevelt's running mate). After the election, Garner played a pivotal role for Roosevelt in the early years of his administration by acting as a liaison between the White House and Congress, using the relationships that he had nurtured during the past thirty years to help assure passage of the president's agenda.

The vice president played only one part of the large Texas influence on the New Deal. Houston banker Jesse Jones also wielded considerable power as the head of the Reconstruction Finance Corporation (RFC), a government agency initially created under Hoover to aid banks and large businesses in financial constraints. Roosevelt transformed the RFC into the primary funding agency for many New Deal programs. Additionally, the RFC loaned over $10 billion to American businesses during the 1930s. Along with Garner, Jones was instrumental in convincing President Roosevelt to drop his resistance to what would become a cornerstone New Deal reform—the guarantee of bank deposits through the creation of the Federal Deposit Insurance Corporation (FDIC).

**Tom Connally**
Photo credit: Library of Congress

Texans flexed substantial political muscle in Congress throughout the 1930s. Not only did U.S. Senators Morris Sheppard and Tom Connally exert influence on the basis of their seniority, reputations, and committee assignments, nine Texans also chaired committees in the House of Representatives, thus assuring influential roles in passing New Deal legislation. Among them was Sam Rayburn, chairman of the Interstate and Foreign Commerce Committee (who became House Majority Leader in 1937 and Speaker of the House in 1940). Rayburn steered passage of the Truth In Securities Act, bills establishing the Securities And Exchange Commission, the Federal Communications Commission, and the Rural Electrification Act. Agriculture Chairman Marvin Jones of Amarillo worked with the Roosevelt administration on its farm bills, sponsoring the Soil Conservation Act and co-authoring the Second Agricultural Adjustment Act. While not always agreeing with FDR's agricultural proposals, Jones respected the president's popularity and wisely refused to block measures that the president questioned. Finally, James P. Buchanan of Brenham, chairman of the powerful Committee on Appropriations, also played an important role handling huge sums of money earmarked for relief and economic recovery.

**Immediate Relief Efforts**

In early 1933, a growing bank panic hit Texas and most other states. Because many questioned whether their financial institutions would close their doors and take away their life savings, numerous bank "runs" occurred as nervous depositors raced to withdraw their funds quickly. On questionable legal grounds, Governor Ferguson ordered the state's banks to be closed for business on March 2, 1933. No one challenged this move, however, because soon after his inauguration on March 6, President Roosevelt declared a "bank holiday," closing all of the nation's banks. The order allowed time for the bank runs to cease while government officials assessed the banking situation and crafted appropriate relief measures. The resulting Emergency Banking Act of 1933, a rather conservative piece of legislation, continued the banking holiday until government inspectors could evaluate each individual bank's financial situation. The government gave its approval to banks found to be in good financial shape and allowed them to reopen immediately. Those banks determined to be on the verge of collapse (about 5 percent nationally) were closed permanently. The government classified a large number of banks as capable of being saved if they received government help. Jesse Jones's RFC provided this aid, often by buying a bank's preferred stock. With this infusion of government relief, the banking system stabilized, and a sense of calm returned to the public. The New Deal's first order of business had been accomplished.

In early 1933, Congress authorized the creation of two agencies designed to save Americans' homes and farms from foreclosure: the Home Owners Loan Corporation (HOLC) and the Farm Credit Administration (FCA). The HOLC provided interest-bearing government bonds to creditors in exchange for defaulted home mortgages. The agency then offered homeowners lower monthly payments with longer payout periods. The HOLC eventually advanced over $100 million to cover over 44,000 Texas home mortgages. Although the agency eventually foreclosed on over 200,000 homes nationally, including almost 8,000 in Texas, the HOLC actually returned a slight profit to Congress when it ceased its operations in the early 1950s. Meanwhile, starting in June 1933, the FCA began pumping $2 billion into the federal land banks for the purposes of refinancing farm mortgages. By the end of 1938, Texans had received more than 100,000 loans worth $250 million to protect their farm properties from foreclosure.

Unlike the Hoover administration, Roosevelt had plans to directly aid the nation's unemployed through partnerships with the state governments. The Fergusons supported the New Deal's unemployment relief efforts partly because the programs would help those greatly affected by the Depression but also because distribution of federal relief dollars provided a tremendous opportunity to establish a patronage system to reward their political supporters.

In May 1933, Congress created the Federal Emergency Relief Administration (FERA) to provide funds for the needy on the basis of one federal dollar for every three provided by the states. To determine level of need and to distribute the funds, the legislature created the Texas State Rehabilitation and Relief Commission. Without legal authority, James Ferguson chaired the commission's initial session and arranged for the commission to appoint Ferguson supporters to the various county boards empowered to oversee local relief operations. By the end of 1933, rumors abounded that wide-scale corruption involving the Relief Commission was taking place. The Texas Senate began an extensive investigation and provided much evidence of malfeasance, including favoritism in the selection of clients, use of relief funds to pay the poll taxes of recipients, diversion of relief money to make improvements on private property, and gross expenditures on local relief board salaries. The revelations led to a new chair of the Relief Commission, tougher oversight rules, and closer observation by the FERA director. In mid-1935, over one million Texas clients (17.5 percent of the 1930 population) were receiving FERA aid.

## Work Relief

Though the Roosevelt administration did not hesitate to provide direct payments to the unemployed, FDR and his key advisers preferred sponsoring "workfare" projects over continuous welfare payments. Congress responded by creating numerous work programs, all of which would have a lasting impact on the Lone Star State.

**Poster for the WPA encouraging laborers to work for America.**

The Public Works Administration (PWA) specialized in large-scale work projects, such as construction of public buildings, highways, bridges, ports, dams, naval vessels, municipal sewers, and water treatment plants. The PWA typically employed large work crews for substantial periods of time. PWA officials approved projects and then provided 45 percent of the funding with the remainder being matched by states and localities. During the 1930s, the PWA approved over $100 million to fund 922 projects in Texas, including Mansfield Dam (and other dams directed by the newly-created Lower Colorado River Authority), the Port of Brownsville, slum clearance and public housing projects in San Antonio, Dallas, and Houston, the University of Texas Main Building (along with its famous tower), John Peter Smith City-County Hospital in Fort Worth, the Fort Worth Public Library, and a hangar and terminal at Houston Municipal (Hobby) Airport (now the 1940 Air Terminal Museum).

Though the agency eventually proved to be a solid relief agency producing projects of lasting importance, PWA Administrator Harold Ickes had a well-deserved reputation for meticulousness. His obsession with avoiding waste and corruption led to approval of projects at a snail's pace, hardly conducive to the administration's desire to get money quickly circulating into the national economy. In response to Ickes's continued scrutiny of PWA projects and with the winter months approaching, Roosevelt issued an executive order in November 1933 empowering FERA Director Harry Hopkins to oversee the creation of the Civil Works Administration (CWA). This agency bypassed state authorities and channeled federal jobs and salaries directly to needy individuals hired by the CWA. Almost a quarter-million Texans worked for the CWA during the six months that it existed, primarily performing road construction and repair work.

Under criticism for its alleged waste and the types of projects undertaken, Roosevelt terminated the CWA in May 1934. The idea of work relief that emphasized placing dollars in unemployed hands lived on, however, with the creation of the Works Progress Administration (WPA) in May 1935. This massive work relief endeavor, under the directorship of Harry Hopkins, gave jobs to over 8 million unemployed Americans, including more than 600,000 Texans. Three-quarters of the WPA's employees worked on construction jobs (though on smaller-scale projects than the PWA). Examples of the WPA's work in Texas include the Houston City Hall, the Will Rogers Memorial Center in Fort Worth, the Fort Worth Botanic Gardens, exhibits and other improvements to the Dallas and San

Antonio Zoos, Dealey Plaza in Dallas, San Antonio's Riverwalk, the Art Deco-style buildings and the lagoon in Dallas's Fair Park, the San Jacinto Battlefield Monument outside of Houston, the Corps of Cadets Dormitories on the Texas A&M University campus, Mt. Pleasant Country Club (Titus County), and the University of Houston's Robertson Stadium.

Creativity marked the WPA's programs for the 25 percent of its workers who did not perform construction work. Many arts projects stand out. For example, the WPA created the Federal Theater Project that was active in Dallas, Houston, and San Antonio to provide jobs for unemployed actors, directors, and stage hands. These men and women produced plays for paying customers in their cities and other communities. The WPA Music Project paid unemployed musicians to perform concerts and teach music classes in schools who had laid off their music teachers. The WPA Art Project paid approved artists to display their work and also to teach art classes in school districts. (A famous New Deal project that paid artists to produce murals to be displayed in post offices and other public buildings across the country has often been associated with the WPA Arts Project, but the project was actually managed by the U.S. Treasury Department). The WPA Writers' Project hired out-of-work writers to produce, among other items, state travel guides and books promoting tourism. The WPA also paid archeologists and their assistants to excavate and catalog findings, maintained day care facilities, surveyed historical records, preserved and catalogued books in libraries, operated bookmobiles, and even produced audio books for the blind.

In screening job applicants, WPA administrators in Texas, as elsewhere in the country, often discriminated against women. The WPA gave preferences for jobs to unemployed male family heads at the expense of unemployed single females or married women. The agency barred women from performing any work considered to be heavy outdoor labor. The WPA often channeled women into jobs involving "traditional work," such as sewing, food processing, child care, health care, and (especially for black and Hispanic women) domestic service.

**A New Deal For Youth**

Two popular New Deal agencies, the Civilian Conservation Corps (CCC) and the National Youth Administration (NYA), provided work relief specifically for unemployed youth coming from families receiving FERA aid. Both programs enjoyed wide popularity with the public throughout their existence.

In March 1933, Congress followed FDR's suggestion and created the CCC to conserve the nation's natural and human resources. Fifty thousand young Texans aged 18 to 25 served in the CCC over its ten-year existence. After recruitment by the U.S. Department of Labor, enrollees worked in rural camps operated by the U.S. Army on projects usually supervised by the Interior and Agriculture Departments. Most of the projects involved building or maintaining state and national parks and forests. CCC boys built roads, erected small dams, developed campsites, constructed lodging facilities, created swimming pools and recreation halls, planted millions of trees, and fought forest fires. The Corps built up the bodies and the morale of the young men. Though some got homesick and either asked to be released or deserted, most enjoyed the experience to work at a challenging job some distance from home for the opportunity to provide their

NYA Project: Men working on metal bridge project in Texas, 1936
Photo credit: FDR Presidential Library

dollar-a-day salary to their families. The CCC also provided educational opportunities for off-duty enrollees. Enrollees could take on-site classes or correspondence courses from the remedial stage up to college level.

Communities across the state petitioned the CCC for placement of a camp nearby, though they usually balked if the agency offered to place an African-American camp in the area (the CCC segregated camps in Texas by 1935). Today, the work of the CCC can be seen in any Texas state park or forest dating back to the 1930s, including the swimming pool and recreation hall at Abilene State Park, the trees surrounding White Rock Lake Park in Dallas, the refectories at Garner State Park and Huntsville State Park, the access roads to Big Bend National Park, the Indian Lodge at the Davis Mountains State Park, the entrance way and interior pathways at Longhorn Caverns State Park outside of Austin, and the restored mission at Goliad State Park.

In May 1935, Congress created the NYA as a youth program under the Works Progress Administration. The agency provided jobs for eligible youth who either could not or would not enlist in the CCC. Some joined the NYA instead of the CCC because they were reluctant to distance themselves from home. Other NYA enrollees were female and, therefore, were ineligible to join the CCC. In Texas, future president Lyndon Johnson directed the NYA for its first three years until giving up his post to run successfully for James P. Buchanan's House seat after the congressman's death in 1937. Johnson has been credited with being an able administrator who worked hard to provide for the state's youth, including African Americans. Johnson did not discriminate against blacks during his tenure, and he gave regular inspections of black projects and channeled additional monies to help fund black projects when available.

The NYA had two main programs to offer Texas youth. The most well-known NYA program provided part-time jobs for high school and college students on their campuses. The NYA employed about 175,000 Texas youths to perform such jobs as landscape maintenance, library work, office work, and teacher assistance. The other lesser-known NYA program aided out-of-school youth through work programs that later served as the inspiration for the Job Corps. In Texas, about 75,000 NYA youths worked for wages and to gain marketable skills. Though the NYA did much of its training at established work centers, the agency also provided many opportunities for on-the-job training. Some examples of lasting NYA projects in Texas include the La Villita arts and tourist section of San Antonio, a replica log cabin at the Witte Museum in San Antonio, the San Benito (Cameron County) Public Library, the Little Chapel-in-the-Woods at Texas Woman's University in Denton, and numerous roadside parks for highway travelers.

**Agricultural Recovery**

Overproduction difficulties plagued American farmers, especially southern cotton producers, for a decade prior to the Depression. During the 1932 campaign, Roosevelt made aid to the nation's farmers an important part of his platform. He endorsed a plan calling for voluntary crop reduction in exchange for government payments (subsidized by an excise tax on processors—mills, in the case of cotton). Aid for agriculture further promised to stimulate industrial recovery because farmers also bought industrial products. On May 12, 1933, after a two-month debate in Congress over the administration's proposal, the president finally signed the Agricultural Adjustment Act into law. Cooperating producers of seven major commodities, including cotton, wheat, and rice, would receive payments. Congress charged a new agency placed within the Department of Agriculture—the Agricultural Adjustment Administration (AAA)—to oversee the programs.

Though Texas wheat and rice producers had no difficulty preparing for the AAA's first program, late passage of the farm bill created a special problem for cotton farmers because they had already planted their crops. Government officials decided to pay growers in exchange for destruction of up to a third of their crops. The "plow-up campaign," as the AAA called it, was a massive effort needing quick implementation before harvest time. The AAA used Agricultural Extension Service agents and appointed farmer committees to educate farmers about the campaign, sign them up, oversee crop destruction, and deliver benefit payments. The government's representatives encountered problems due to the haste involved and reluctance by many growers. Some producers cited religious reasons for not destroying a growing crop. Others simply did not trust the government to pay them. Even when farmer cooperation could be attained, balking mules sometimes refused to pull their plows over the growing crops due to fear that they would be whipped for doing something that they had been trained over the years specifically not to do! Ultimately, a quarter million Texas producers pledged 4.35 million acres for destruction—27 percent of the state's total cotton acreage. Farmers benefited psychologically and financially from the boost received by $43 million in government payments plus the doubling of cotton prices (up to ten cents per pound by the end of 1933). It should be noted, however, that many tenants and sharecroppers complained that they failed to receive their rightful share of the government money because their landlords kept most or all of the payments despite AAA rules against such practices.

**Dust Storm Approaching Spearman, Texas. April 14, 1935**
Photo credit: FDR Presidential Library

Important changes occurred to the AAA's cotton program in 1934, as many southern cooperating producers demanded that crop reduction become mandatory. This plea resulted from the fact that during the previous year non-cooperators often benefited more than cooperators, because the income that non-cooperators received for producing a full crop at doubled prices outweighed the income that cooperators received from their reduced crops plus the government checks. The Bankhead Cotton Control Act fulfilled the desire of growers wishing to have compulsory production control (tobacco farmers succeeded in getting a similar law passed for their crop). The law specified that, if two-thirds of southern growers agreed in an annual referendum, the AAA would assign production quotas for the next season. A producer could theoretically raise more crops than his assigned quota, but he would not profit from the excess amount due to heavy taxation. By the end of 1935, New Deal policies resulted in raising cotton prices to 12 cents per pound.

A severe drought in 1934 greatly affected Texas cattle producers. Though initially too proud and independent to receive any form of federal government aid, ranchers eventually supported the Jones-Connally Act making cattle an AAA commodity subject to reductions in exchange for payments. To carry out an immediate drought purchase program in 1934 for the purposes of compensating cattle owners for removing diseased cattle from stockpiles and healthy cattle from the marketplace, the AAA worked through local committees and inspectors with the USDA Bureau of Animal Industries. These AAA representatives visited individual ranches and farms and purchased livestock. Diseased and emaciated animals found to be unfit for human consumption were shot and buried on the spot. The agents turned over healthy stock to the Federal Surplus Relief Corporation

**Dust Storm in Amarillo, Texas, 1936.
Photo credit:
FDR Presidential Library**

(FSRC) for slaughter and canning. In Texas, FSRC canneries employed 30,000 Texans to handle 420,000 cattle and distributed about 50 million cans of beef to the needy.

West Texas grain farmers also received drought relief funds in 1934, but for those residing in the Panhandle, the worst had yet to come. Removal of the native grass by grazing and plowing, combined with an extended spell of dry weather, led to the creation of the infamous "Dust Bowl" of the 1930s, spanning portions of several Southern Plains states and centered in the Texas-Oklahoma Panhandles. Huge dust storms, often shooting hundreds of feet into the air and encompassing several square miles, blackened the skies for hours at a time, making life unhealthy for local residents and lethal for many animals and crops. Unable to make a living, about a third of the area's farmers fled the region. This ecological disaster led to renewed government efforts to counter wasteful soil practices. In 1935, Congress passed a bill authored by U.S. Congressman Marvin Jones of Texas creating the Soil Conservation Service, charged with promotion of efficient soil conservation methods throughout the country.

Soil conservation gained a larger role in New Deal farm relief after the Supreme Court ruled against the constitutionality of the AAA's production control contracts and its processor taxes. Along with a repeal of the Bankhead Act to avoid useless litigation (since it appeared that the Supreme Court would also rule against that law), this ruling forced the Roosevelt administration to work with Congress to find a quick replacement. Congress soon passed the Soil Conservation and Domestic Allotment Act (SCDAA), signed by FDR on February 29, 1936, under which the government would continue to make payments to farmers (from the Federal Treasury rather than from processor taxes) ostensibly for soil conservation practices rather than solely for production control. Growers would receive checks for diverting acreage formerly used to raise "soil-depleting crops" (such as cotton) to "soil-building crops" (such as grasses and legumes), and for implementing approved soil conservation practices.

The SCDAA proved to be an inadequate production control measure. Drought conditions kept agricultural production low in 1936. However, the return of good weather in 1937, coupled with the absence of planting restrictions, led to a record southern cotton crop. (Texas growers produced over 5 million bales—the third largest yield ever.) Cotton prices plummeted to 8.4 cents per pound until Roosevelt agreed to offer price-support measures guaranteeing growers 12 cents per pound if they pledged to participate in a new production control program being devised by the government.

On February 16, 1938, Congress passed the Agricultural Adjustment Act of 1938. This law was the culmination of efforts undertaken to create a long-term price-support scheme for American farmers based on a combination of the administration's previous efforts: acreage restrictions, production quotas, conservation payments, and price-support loans. This system provided the basis for the federal government's agricultural programs for decades after World War II. By this time, Roosevelt did not have to worry about potential legal challenges—a much friendlier Supreme Court now presided than during his first term.

By 1940, as a result of the New Deal's agricultural policies, the federal government sent almost $3 billion to Texas farmers, but farm owners were the primary beneficiaries. Not only did tenants and sharecroppers often fail to see their fair share of government payments, but by the mid-1930s, it became increasingly difficult for tenants and croppers to find land to work. With the government paying farmers to grow fewer crops, the need for agricultural labor declined. Large numbers of non-land owning farmers found themselves displaced as many planters evicted sharecroppers, because farm owners often declined to contract with tenants for another growing season. From 1930 to 1940, the number of Texas tenants and sharecroppers significantly decreased (32 percent in 1930 and 62 percent in 1940 respectively). Meanwhile, the percentage of Texas farmers who owned the land they operated increased from 39 percent to 51 percent.

**Agricultural Aid and Reform**

The New Deal made sporadic efforts to provide relief to displaced croppers and tenants as well as other impoverished Americans in the South's rural areas. The first New Deal agency to address southern rural poverty was the FERA, which improvised a series of programs designed to promote self-support among destitute farm families. The main FERA programs involved "rural rehabilitation" efforts (providing supervised credit for farmers working good land) and resettlement projects, whereby the government purchased submarginal land in order to relocate farmers to more productive land. Although providing assistance for a fortunate few, overall these programs did very little to alleviate the problem of rural poverty in the South due to inadequate federal funding.

On April 30, 1935, FDR issued an executive order that consolidated the FERA programs and other rural poverty-based projects from other agencies under the new Resettlement Administration (RA). The new agency struggled to help clients despite low appropriations and strong conservative criticism. Over the next two years, the RA retired submarginal land and relocated its owners. The agency also constructed and maintained sanitary camps for migratory workers. Farmers in Texas and other southern states made up over half of the RA's half-million rehabilitation clients who received loans and other assistance to increase their chances of remaining on the land. The RA also maintained resettlement communities. Nevertheless, like the FERA's programs, these efforts were only able to aid a fraction of those in need.

Following Roosevelt's signing of the Bankhead-Jones Act on July 22, 1937, the Farm Security Administration (FSA) continued the RA's work while appearing to address the specific concerns of southern tenant farmers and sharecroppers, which were highlighted in a report issued by a presidential commission investigating these issues. However, FSA funds provided by Congress for its most publicized function—making loans to tenants wishing to purchase farms—were paltry. During its first two years of operation, only 542 Texans out of over 15,000 applicants (a miniscule 4 percent) received FSA financing. Only those deemed to be the least risk received any aid; the most desperate who applied were simply passed over.

One rural reform effort stands out as a significant achievement of the New Deal. Created by executive order in 1935 and made permanent the next year by the Norris-Rayburn Bill co-sponsored by Texas Congressman Sam Rayburn, the Rural Electrification Administration (REA) helped to usher in a new age in the American countryside. Before the REA's creation, only 10 percent of the nation's rural areas had electric power. In Texas, private power companies serviced only 2 percent of the state's rural residents. By the mid-1960s, 2 percent of rural Texans did not have access to electrical power. The REA accounted for much of this change by providing low-interest loans to communities that established cooperatives consisting of rural residents. The loans paid for laying down power lines in localities that private electric companies had previously ignored. The cooperatives' customers retired the loans over a 30-year span. With the rural markets shown to be profitable, private power companies eventually stepped in and began providing additional service to rural America.

The lifestyle changes brought about by rural electrification were revolutionary. Radio and television use broke down cultural isolation. Electric pumps provided indoor plumbing, resulting in immediate access to hot water for cooking and cleaning. Indoor toilets and hot water tubs led to improved sanitation. Electric kitchen appliances eased the burden of cooking, while refrigeration improved diet and overall health for farm families. Reduced time from chores freed up more time for relaxation, recreation, and entertainment, thus increasing the quality of rural life. Simply put, electrification provided rural Americans with an escape from the pre-industrial age.

**Industry and Labor**

During the first two years of the New Deal, the National Recovery Administration (NRA) served as the center of the federal government's efforts to revive the American industrial economy. Created in June 1933 by the National Industrial Recovery Act (NIRA), the NRA was a bold experiment in cooperation between government, business, and labor. In return for suspending federal antitrust laws, the government allowed the nation's industries to work with labor and government representatives to write codes, which established minimum prices and production levels. The idea was to eliminate cutthroat competition in the midst of the Depression. If businessmen could charge higher prices for their goods without worrying about their competitor undercutting them, profits would return, and the overall economy would see a revival. Participation was voluntary, but cooperators who agreed to abide by their industry's code would be in violation of the law if they failed to comply. The government undertook a massive publicity campaign promising economic prosperity and pushing the patriotism angle in order to get businesses on board.

The NIRA also contained important provisions for labor. Section 7(a) of the legislation guaranteed the right of collective bargaining. Section 7(b) guaranteed minimum wages, which theoretically should have been higher than pre-NIRA levels to offset the rise in industrial prices. Individual industrial codes established further guidelines for improved working conditions.

The NIRA proved to be a very difficult law to administer. With over 500 codes to enforce nationally, the effort turned into a bureaucratic nightmare. Businesses raised their prices but often did not follow other rules regarding forbidden trade practices. Many companies refused to adhere to the labor provisions of their industry's code. In Texas, workers for the Hughes Tool Company of Houston and the Trinity Portland Cement Company of Dallas, for example, endured repeated confrontations with management over their right to unionize under section 7(a).

Another portion of the NIRA difficult to enforce involved a section prohibiting the transport of petroleum exceeding state production quotas. In an effort to aid Texas in stopping the flow of hot oil traffic, the law authorized the use of federal agents to assist state authorities. Though often ineffective in reducing hot oil shipments, federal enforcement efforts improved markedly with passage of the Connally Hot Oil Act in February 1935. Intended to protect interstate commerce against "contraband oil" and to encourage the conservation of United States crude-oil deposits, the legislation made it a federal crime to ship hot oil across state lines.

The NRA existed for two years until struck down by the U.S. Supreme Court in May 1935. The Supreme Court ruled that the industrial codes represented an unconstitutional delegation of legislative authority to the executive branch. By this time, the decision relieved many in the Roosevelt Administration. Though New Dealers objected to the Court's intervention, the NRA had proved to be an administrative quagmire and, most importantly, failed to generate industrial recovery.

With the NIRA invalidated, Congress passed the Wagner National Labor Relations Act in July 1935 to preserve the labor provisions from the previous law. The Wagner Act outlawed unfair labor practices (such as employing spies), guaranteed the right of workers to organize, and created the National Labor Relations Board (NLRB) to investigate charges of unfair labor practices and to oversee elections to decide if a majority of workers wished to form a union. Union strength in Texas remained small after passage of the Wagner Act, but growth did occur as workers organized in many Texas industries. By 1940, the American Federation of Labor reached an agreement with the Trinity Company that recognized the cement workers' union, established grievance procedures, and granted numerous benefits. The new Congress of Industrial Organizations began to organize workers in the state's oil refineries and won victories with the NLRB on behalf of Hughes Tool Company workers.

The Fair Labor Standards Act of 1938 constituted another important New Deal labor reform that impacted Texans. The law established a national minimum wage, initially set at 25 cents per hour. Though the legislation failed to include agricultural and domestic workers, Congress later removed that exemption. Another section of the law required overtime pay at a rate of 1.5 times the regular hourly wage for work performed over a weekly maximum. (Originally 44 hours per week, the weekly rate currently is 40 hours.) Finally, the Fair Labor Standards Act outlawed child labor in the United States.

**Group of Texas Rangers presenting pistols to Governor James V. Allred. c. 1935**
Photo credit: UTSA's Institute of Texan Cultures

Many Texas laborers did not rely solely on the federal government to improve their situations. Throughout the 1930s, workers fought for better pay and improved working conditions at the local level. In San Antonio, for example, cigar company employees, garment workers, and pecan shellers went on strike on several occasions to press their demands, though with mixed results. Elsewhere in the state, rural and urban workers tried to overcome official and vigilante harassment as they sought to organize and appeal for better treatment.

## State and National Politics

Though Miriam Ferguson cooperated with federal officials in implementing New Deal initiatives, strained relations with the legislature and more controversial actions caused difficulties for the governor during her second tenure in office. Ferguson proposed new sales taxes and income taxes to address the state government's $14 million debt, but the legislature responded by enacting only a two-cent per barrel oil tax and legalizing horse race gambling to increase revenue.

One statewide political issue that began to be resolved during Ferguson's term involved the repeal of Prohibition. By 1933, a majority (but certainly not all) of Americans believed that the national experiment to legislate sobriety had failed. The law reduced alcohol use and closed public drinking establishments but wholly failed to eliminate alcohol from American life. Though often fetching higher prices than before Prohibition, people could still gain access to liquor smuggled from foreign countries or made domestically in private stills and vats. The media carried numerous stories publicizing the huge profits that gangsters and other outlaws made from the production and distribution of illegal alcohol. Enforcement of Prohibition became a cumbersome drain on state and federal law enforcement resources. Supporters of repeal also pointed out that renewed legal alcohol production would provide numerous jobs for the unemployed during the Depression, in addition to the alcohol taxes that promised to add much-needed revenue for state and federal governments.

In February 1933, Congress sent to the states for ratification a proposed Twenty-first Amendment to the U.S. Constitution that would repeal the Eighteenth Amendment. Supporters of the amendment succeeded in bypassing the state legislatures by authorizing state conventions to consider ratification—a process expressly provided by Article V of the U.S. Constitution. In an August 1933 referendum, voters elected pro-repeal delegates to the state convention, which unanimously approved the Twenty-first Amendment in November. On December 5, 1933, the required three-quarters of the states ratified the amendment, and national Prohibition immediately ended. Two years later, through the referendum process, voters lifted the statewide ban on alcohol with the exception of a number of counties and municipalities that exercised the local option to remain "dry." The Texas state legislature did, however, set certain limits on consumption by banning the sale of hard liquor by the drink.

Though other actions further embarrassed the Fergusons, such as a return to liberal pardoning and the wholesale dismissal of all Texas Rangers with their replacement by men of questionable qualifications, the backlash over unemployment relief distribution caused the Fergusons the most political damage, ensuring that the governor would not seek another term. With the issues of Prohibition and "Fergusonism" removed, the 1934 gubernatorial election focused squarely on the Depression. Seven Democrats vied for their party's nomination, led by James V Allred (like Harry S Truman, "V" was his middle name, not an initial), the 35-year-old attorney general from Wichita Falls. Allred's vibrant personality and his reputation as an opponent of monopoly propelled him to the lead in the primary. After dispensing with his opponent in a runoff, Allred easily won the general election to become the state's next governor.

Cooperation with the New Deal characterized Allred's tenure as governor. Implementation of the national Social Security Act of 1935 presented challenges for Allred as he worked with the state legislature and the state's citizens to fund the mandates prescribed by the legislation. In addition to setting up the current mandatory retirement pension system for workers through a combination of employer and employee payroll taxes, the law also required states to provide matching funds for assistance to the elderly, dependent children, the blind, the disabled, and to establish an unemployment compensation system.

Of all the aspects of the Social Security Act, determination of eligibility and funding of payments to current elderly Texans (separate from the retirement pensions funded by payroll taxes) produced the most debate. In August 1935, voters approved a state constitutional amendment allowing for state funds to be paid to the elderly, but the amendment did not establish eligibility requirements or benefit levels. As applications for aid overwhelmed state offices, Allred advocated providing pensions only for elderly who were truly in need. The governor called three special sessions of the legislature to deal with this and other pressing issues. The legislature eventually followed Allred's wishes and funded payments for the elderly, which were then offset by higher oil, gas, and liquor taxes. Although eligibility was now more difficult, by June 1937 over 125,000 aged Texans were receiving payments under the Social Security Act.

Governor Allred enjoyed a good position going into the 1936 election. Not only was he identified with supporting New Deal efforts, he also benefited from his efforts with the legislature to clean up the Fergusons's damage to the law enforcement credibility by reorganizing the Texas Rangers and the Highway Department into the new Department of Public Safety. These successes allowed the governor to win the Democratic nomination without need of a runoff. Allred won easily in the general election, as did President Roosevelt. Though Texans realized that the nation was not yet out of the Depression, they showed their appreciation for the New Deal by giving Roosevelt 87 percent of their vote.

Budget issues expended much of Governor Allred's time during his second term. The demands of new Social Security obligations, a voter-approved teacher retirement fund, public education, and state government agencies provided much of the strain. A $3 million expenditure (though matched by federal government funds) to carry out the voters' wishes to sponsor a Texas centennial celebration in 1936 caused an additional burden, as did the loss of gambling taxes after the legislature repealed legalized horse race gambling. Despite these considerations, the legislature failed to raise additional revenue through new taxes, and Allred left the gubernatorial office in 1939 with the state government $3 million in debt.

President Roosevelt had problems of his own during his second term despite being re-elected by a huge margin. The president faced growing conservative (both Democratic and Republican) opposition to his policies and proposals. Many businessmen were already on record as opposing such aspects of the New Deal as the NRA, the AAA, the Bankhead Act, the Wagner Act, and banking regulations. Ignoring the psychological and economic value of the work relief projects, other conservatives opposed their expense and attacked social security as being contrary to "traditional self-reliance."

Roosevelt's proposal to have Congress reform the Supreme Court by allowing for additional members if sitting justices refused to retire at the age of seventy created new antagonisms. The Supreme Court had upset many Americans (including probably a majority of Texans) by brazenly ruling against the constitutionality of the NRA and the AAA. Many worried that the Court might rule against the new Social Security Act, the Wagner Act, and other New Deal laws, and yet still, only a minority of congressmen agreed with the president's solution. Though legal, some Democrats feared FDR's proposed reform would open the door for a future Republican-dominated Congress and president to alter the makeup of the Supreme Court to suit their policies. Others argued that the reform would upset the Constitution's checks and balances and separation of powers principles by gutting the supposed independence of the judicial branch. Roosevelt's "court packing plan," as opponents labeled it, caused irreparable harm to his relationship with Vice President Garner and many others within the Democratic Party, including Senator Tom Connally. From his chairmanship of the House Committee on the Judiciary, Hatton W. Sumners of Dallas stalled the measure, which never passed Congress.

Thirteen candidates entered the 1938 Democratic primary race for governor. Though Attorney General William McCraw and Railroad Commission Chairman Ernest Thompson initially seemed to be the favorites, popular flour salesman and radio personality Wilbert Lee "Pappy" O'Daniel soon emerged as a major contender. A life-long Republican born in Ohio and reared in Kansas, O'Daniel moved to Fort Worth in 1925 to work as a sales manager with a local flour company. For advertising purposes, he began to host a daily noontime radio show heard across most of Texas (featuring for a while fiddler Bob Wills) with an orchestra known as the "Light Crust Doughboys." By 1935, O'Daniel started his own company and began to tout his "Hillbilly Flour" on a new radio program with a new band, the Hillbilly Boys. The salesman filled his shows with a mixture of traditional hillbilly and religious music, self-composed tunes and poetry, humorous anecdotes, moral stories, and business advice. Asked previously by his fans to run for governor, O'Daniel announced in 1938 that he would finally make a run for the office, a process that at the very least would provide the office of the governor free publicity for Hillbilly Flour, a benefit that O'Daniel did not deny.

On the campaign trail, O'Daniel announced a simple platform: the Ten Commandments. When pressed for something a little more specific, he called for state assistance to all elderly Texans and expounded on his opposition to a sales tax to generate revenue. The state government could get all the money it needed, he claimed, from rigid enforcement of existing tax laws. Large crowds turned out to see O'Daniel and his band. During his short musings posing as stump speeches, the candidate constantly railed against professional politicians and promised the return of a businesslike administration in Austin. The hillbilly country-boy image that O'Daniel cultivated, however, was purely a performance he managed with the assistance of a public relations firm. (Far from being the common man trying to make ends meet in the midst of the Depression, O'Daniel was a business college graduate worth a half-million dollars during the 1930s.) Nevertheless, his image and his message resonated with the populace, which responded by turning out *en masse* for O'Daniel to the extent that he received 97 percent of the vote in the November general election.

Pappy O'Daniel proved to be a most ineffective governor. Combat between the governor and the "professional politicians" in the legislature led to frequent stalemates. Faced with the state government's budget shortfall, the governor modified his campaign promises on old-age assistance and sales taxes. He changed his desire of generous pensions for all elderly Texans to a proposal for all needy Texans over the age of 65 to receive payments of a dollar a day, though not exerting much effort on behalf of the idea. When O'Daniel switched his position and supported a proposal for a sales tax to produce revenue, the legislature rejected the measure. Meanwhile, the governor vetoed numerous acts of the legislature. He refused to support higher taxes on natural resources and utilities, vetoed appropriations for new orphanages and mental health facilities, and slashed the budget of the Department of Public Safety.

Six challengers emerged in the 1940 Democratic primary to take on Governor O'Daniel: Ernest Thompson, four minor challengers, and Miriam Ferguson. Making one last grasp for glory, 69-year-old James Ferguson proclaimed that the "Fergusons won't deny milk to insane patients" and referred to O'Daniel as a "slick-haired banjo picker" who "attempted to ward off pertinent questions by grinning like a jackass in a thistle patch." The Ferguson magic, however, was gone. Though he received no major newspaper endorsements, O'Daniel easily received the Democratic nomination, again without the need of a runoff. Thompson, who did receive most of the media endorsements, finished a distant second, while Ma Ferguson came in a dismal fourth place and finally retired from politics.

**Evaluation of the New Deal**

Two enduring myths concerning FDR and his presidency involve the notion that Roosevelt was a radical reformer and that his New Deal programs marked the beginning of government dictation to the states. Both ideas are preposterous. Roosevelt never advocated government ownership of banks, top-down national economic planning directed from Washington D.C., or any similar type of radical initiatives. Further, when the federal government intervened, cooperation with the states typically dominated the arrangement.

For eight years, Roosevelt's administration intervened on an unprecedented scale with federal government resources to combat the Depression. Though economic indicators improved during the 1930s, complete economic recovery did not emerge until World War II. Still, life improved for Texans when compared to the Hoover years. The New Deal provided jobs, kept farm and home owners on their property, and encouraged hope that prosperity would eventually return.

In the final analysis, the New Deal acted as a great holding operation. Except for many displaced tenant and sharecroppers, New Deal programs did not considerably alter the structure of Texas life during the 1930s. In contrast, the Second World War would set the stage for revolutionary social, political, and economic changes that would alter the Lone Star State forever.

*Afterward: A Town Recovers—A Memory Endures*

*After investigations into the New London explosion determined that a faulty connection led to the accumulation of natural gas ultimately leading to the blast, the Texas legislature passed a law requiring gas companies to add a malodorant to commercial and industrial natural gas in order to help detect dangerous leaks. Upon building a new school on the site of the old building, the community tried to move on from the tragedy. A tall granite cenotaph with the names of most victims stands across the street from the school in memory of those who were lost. Though news of the explosion led to an outpouring of grief from across the country and overseas, the tragic event soon faded from the minds of those outside the Piney Woods as the world soon became immersed in the Second World War.*

# Myth & Legend

## The Real Bonnie and Clyde

*Even before they died in a hail of bullets at the hands of a Texas Ranger and his posse along a country road in northwest Louisiana, the image of Depression Era-outlaws Bonnie Parker and Clyde Barrow as renegade nonconformists thumbing their noses at authority by robbing banks and outwitting hapless law enforcement officials began to take hold in much of the country's mainstream media. In reality, both were bored criminals who only cared about excitement, were frequently careless and inept, and often lacked mercy as they murdered anyone who got in their way. This depiction was certainly not unique. At a time when public opinion for bankers was at an all- time low due to the role of financial institutions in bringing on the Great Depression, many crooks who robbed banks like John Dillinger, Pretty Boy Floyd, and Baby Face Nelson not only gained notoriety but even some fans who read with interest about their exploits in the newspapers or heard about their acts from movie theater news- reels. Soon, Bonnie and Clyde would join this notorious but legendary pantheon.*

*Bonnie Parker was born in Rowena, Texas, in 1910. After her father, a bricklay- er, died when she was four years old, her mother moved the family to West Dallas, an industrial section of the growing city where she found work as a seamstress. Though not yet 16, Parker married Roy Thornton who she knew from their high school. Thornton was frequently absent from their home, often womanizing or committing petty crimes, and she never saw him again after 1929. She moved back in with her mother and began waiting tables at a café when she met Clyde Barrow, a recent migrant to West Dallas from a poor Ellis County sharecropping family. Twenty-one years old in early 1930, Barrow was already involved in various criminal activities, mostly robbing stores and stealing cars, when he was arrested and sent to an East Texas prison farm where he endured grueling work assignments and eventually killed his first person—a fellow inmate who had repeatedly sexually assaulted him. Paroled in 1932, Barrow emerged from prison a bitter young man, hardly reha- bilitated, with an abiding hatred for law enforcement officials. He soon assembled a gang, which soon began their famous two-year crime spree ranging from Texas to as far north as Minnesota and Indiana. The group included Bonnie Parker—the bored waitress who was smitten with the troubled bad boy—Clyde's older brother Buck, and Buck's wife Blanche.*

*Before their increasingly violent string of bank robberies, gas station holdups, car- jack- ings ended, they had killed at least thirteen people, most of them law enforce- ment person- nel but some ordinary citizens who interfered with them as well. In their attempt to escape justice, the gang hid out for a time at a garage apartment in Joplin, Missouri, but their raucous, alcohol-fueled card games soon drew suspicion in* the quiet residential neighborhood. When local police expecting to arrest bootleggers arrived on April 13, 1933, the Barrow gang shot their way out, killing two officers in the process. As a result of their hasty escape, the criminals left behind a trove of weapons and ammunition, some poetry written by Bonnie Parker, and a camera. When developed, the film in the camera revealed images of the gang members ham- ming it up, most famously of Bonnie cockily leaning against a car packing a pistol at her side while clenching a cigar between her teeth. The publication of the photos and Bonnie's poetry greatly elevated the story of the criminals from one about a small group of Dallas thugs into an over-glamorized drama that made national headlines.

Over the next three months, their crime spree continued across the Plains states, but as the death toll rose accordingly, public opinion began to turn against them. Their growing fame, which they apparently had initially coveted, began to hinder their operations as they could no longer risk eating at restaurants or staying at motels without garnering attention. Nevertheless, they were forced to check into a motor court to tend to injuries that Bonnie Parker received after Clyde accidentally drove their automobile into a ditch and acid from the car's battery badly burned her right leg. When authorities were alerted, the gang once again had to shoot their way out, but this time Buck Barrow was killed while Blanche was wounded and captured.

The end finally came to Bonnie and Clyde when retired Texas Ranger Frank Hamer was recruited to assemble a posse and track down them down. Hamer's big break occurred after Barrow helped a gang member escape from the same prison farm where he was formerly an inmate. Other convicts also escaped and befriended the Barrow gang, leading the father of one of them to arrange a deal that would commute his son's sentence in exchange for revealing the couple's whereabouts. Wait- ing in ambush along State Highway 154 near Gibsland, Louisiana, Hamer and his cohorts emptied 130 rounds fired from their small automatic machine guns into Bonnie and Clyde's car. After displaying the bullet-ridden bodies and vehicle to lo- cal citizens and members of the news media, the criminals were buried in separate Dallas cemeteries and largely forgotten for the next 35 years until Hollywood revived their legend with a version of their lives that did exceptionally well at the box office and won two Academy Awards. Starring Warren Beatty and Faye Dunaway, Bon- nie and Clyde romanticized the couple as good-looking, impeccably-dressed counter- culture figures seeking action as a means of escaping a conformist lifestyle. Though groundbreaking for its graphic portrayal of violence, the movie takes great leaps with the truth, not only with its depiction of real-life events but especially in its portrayal of the two outlaws who seem to have had few redeeming qualities. While one should always be leery of seeking role models among habitual lawbreakers, they should be even more reluctant about getting their historical information from Hollywood.

## Suggestions for Further Reading

Adams, John A. Jr. *Damming the Colorado: The Rise of the Lower Colorado River Authority, 1933-1939* College Station: Texas A & M University Press, 1990.

Andrews, Gregg. "Unionizing the Trinity Portland Cement Company in Dallas, Texas, 1934-1939," *Southwestern Historical Quarterly* 111, no.1, pp. 31-49.

Blackwelder, Julia Kirk. *Women of the Depression: Caste and Culture in San Antonio, 1929-1939* College Station: Texas A & M University Press, 1984.

Brown, D. Clayton. "Rural Electrification in the South, 1920-1955," Ph.D. diss, UCLA, 1970.

Brown, Norman D., *Biscuits, the Dole, and Nodding Donkeys: Texas Politics, 1929-1932* Austin: University of Texas Press, 2019.

Clark, James A. and Michael T. Halbouty. *The Last Boom* New York: Random House, 1972.

Cotner, Robert C. ed. *Texas Cities and the Great Depression* Austin: Texas Memorial Museum, 1973.

Egan, Timothy, *The Worst Hard Time: The Untold Story of Those Who Survived the Great American Dust Bowl* Boston: Houghton Mifflin, 2006.

Fenberg, Steven, *Unprecedented Power: Jesse Jones, Capitalism, and the Common Good* College Station: Texas A&M University Press, 2011.

Green, George N. *The Establishment in Texas Politics* Westport, Conn.: Greenwood, 1979.

Milton S. Jordan and George Cooper, eds., *Conflict and Cooperation: Reflections on the New Deal in Texas* Nacogdoches: Stephen F. Austin University Press, 2019.

Olson, Lori, *New London School: In Memoriam, March 18, 1937, 3:17 P.M.* Austin, Texas: Eakin Press, 2001.

Parisi, Philip. *Texas Post Office Murals: Art for the People* College Station: Texas A & M University Press, 2005.

Patenaude, Lionel V. *Texans, Politics, and the New Deal* New York: Garland Publishing, 1983.

Rozelle, Ron, *My Boys and Girls Are in There: The 1937 New London School Explosion* College Station: Texas A&M Press, 2012.

Steely, James. *Parks for Texas: Enduring Landscapes of the New Deal* Austin: University of Texas Press, 1998.

Smallwood, James M. *The Great Recovery: Texas and the New Deal* Boston: America Press, 1983.

Volanto, Keith J. *Texas, Cotton, and the New Deal* College Station: Texas A & M University Press, 2005.

Weisenberger, Carol A. *Dollars and Dreams: The National Youth Administration in Texas* New York: Peter Lang Publishing, 1994.

Whisenhunt, Donald W. *The Depression in Texas: The Hoover Years* New York: Garland Publishing, 1983.

Whisenhunt, Donald W. ed. *The Depression in the Southwest* Port Washington, N.Y.: Kennikat Press, 1980.

**IDENTIFICATION:** Briefly describe each term.

Ross Sterling
East Texas Oil Boom
"Cotton Holiday" Plan
Miriam Ferguson
Federal Emergency Relief Administration (FERA)
Public Works Administration (PWA)
Works Progress Administration (WPA)
Civilian Conservation Corps (CCC)
National Youth Administration (NYA)
Agricultural Adjustment Administration (AAA)
Dust Bowl
Farm Security Administration (FSA)
National Recovery Administration (NRA)
James V. Allred
W. Lee "Pappy" O'Daniel

**MULTIPLE CHOICE:** Choose the correct response.

1. _____ succeeded Dan Moody as Texas governor in 1930.
   A. Miriam Ferguson
   B. James Allred
   C. Ross Sterling
   D. Pappy O' Daniel

2. A major conflict developed in the East Texas oil fields in the 1930s over:
   A. the efforts of the state government to regulate oil production;
   B. the efforts of labor unions to organize oil field workers;
   C. competition between railroad companies and truck drivers over who would transport the oil to market;
   D. competition between oil and lumber companies over title to land where oil was discovered.

3. In 1932, _____ took advantage of discontent with Ross Sterling's administration to narrowly defeat him in the Democratic primary for governor.
   A. John Nance Garner
   B. James Ferguson
   C. Dad Joiner
   D. Miriam Ferguson

4. Franklin Roosevelt's first action as president was to
   A. authorize loans for big businesses;
   B. deal with the bank panic hitting the country;
   C. create the Civilian Conservation Corps;
   D. authorize aid to farmers.

5. The Dust Bowl was centered near _____.
   A. the East Texas Oil Field;
   B. El Paso in West Texas;
   C. the Lower Rio Grande Valley in South Texas;
   D. the Texas Panhandle in northwest Texas.

6. Which of the following is true about the Civilian Conservation Corps?
   A. they hired unemployed female workers;
   B. they hired elderly unemployed men;
   C. they hired unemployed youth from families receiving government relief;
   D. none of the above are true.

7. Among other responsibilities, the National Youth Administration:
   A. provided on-campus work for high school and college students;
   B. ran training camps before sending youth off to the armed forces;
   C. operated kindergartens and grammar schools for poor children;
   D. none of the above.

8. The National Recovery Administration attempted to establish minimum wages and prices through a series of _____.
   A. elections;
   B. court decisions;
   C. laws passed by state legislatures;
   D. codes established by representatives of industry, labor, and government.

9. Though it remained largely ineffective as a means of helping large numbers of poor farmers, Congress transformed the Resettlement Administration into the _____ in 1937.
   A. Agricultural Adjustment Administration;
   B. Rural Electrification Administration;
   C. Soil Conservation Service;
   D. Farm Security Administration.

10. Before running for governor, Pappy O'Daniel was a _____
    A. state legislator;
    B. judge;
    C. flour company salesman and radio personality;
    D. labor union leader;
    E. farmer.

**TRUE/FALSE:** Indicate whether each statement is true or false.

1. Huey Long's Cotton Holiday Plan called for the cotton-growing states to cease all cotton production for one year.

2. Columbus "Dad" Joiner led a vocal group of East Texas cotton farmers who supported Huey Long's Cotton Holiday Plan.

3. "Hot oil" refers to oil stolen by desperate people to fuel their homes during the Great Depression.

4. Franklin Roosevelt strongly opposed the creation of the Agricultural Adjustment Administration but bowed to public opinion.

5. Miriam Ferguson succeeded Ross Sterling as governor.

6. During the New Deal period, the federal government's program to aid Texas farmers changed quite often due to politics and Supreme Court decisions.

7. The Wagner Act guarantees the right of collective bargaining for workers.

8. The Rural Electrification Administration was an ineffective bureaucratic nightmare eventually ruled unconstitutional by the Supreme Court.

9. Among other features of the legislation, the Fair Labor Standards Act established a national minimum wage.

10. By most measures, Pappy O'Daniel was an effective governor with numerous accomplishments by the end of his terms.

**MATCHING:** Match the response in column A with the item in column B.

1. National Recovery Administration (NRA)
2. Public Works Administration (PWA)
3. Miriam Ferguson
4. Works Progress Administration (WPA)
5. Civilian Conservation Corps (CCC)
6. National Youth Administration (NYA)
7. Ross Sterling
8. James Allred
9. Dad Joiner
10. Pappy O'Daniel

A. built large-scale construction works
B. employed young men who worked in rural camps
C. paid students for on-campus work
D. hired unemployed artists and musicians
E. set up codes for companies to abide
F. succeeded Miriam Ferguson as governor
G. declared martial law in East Texas oil fields
H. endured scandal involving distribution of relief funds
I. flour salesman turned governor
J. discovered oil in East Texas

**ESSAY QUESTIONS:**

1. What major problems did Ross Sterling face as governor? How did he respond and what impact did that response have on his re-election bid in 1932?

2. Describe the major New Deal agricultural policies affecting Texas farmers. Who was helped and who was hurt by New Deal agricultural policies?

3. Describe three major New Deal work programs and how they impacted Texas.

4. Compare and contrast the records of Texas's governors during the Great Depression, from Ross Sterling through Pappy O'Daniel.

# Chapter 15

# World War II and Texas, 1941-1945

*Prelude: Frank Fujita, Jr.—A Japanese Texan Prisoner of the Empire of the Rising Sun*

*Due to his unique situation of being the only Japanese-American combat soldier captured by Japanese forces during World War II, Frank Fujita's wartime experiences differed from those of any other Texan. Fujita's father, Frank Fujita, Sr., arrived in America from Nagasaki, Japan in 1914, ostensibly to study American methods of agriculture. Shunning such an education, however, he chose instead to work as a travelling private chef for railroad company officials. While on a layover in Illinois, he met Fujita's future mother, a white woman from Oklahoma working as a waitress in a local hotel, and they eventually married. Born in 1921, Frank Fujita, Jr. became the second-oldest of the couple's five children. Though the family often moved around Oklahoma and North Texas during his youth, the family finally settled in Abilene, Texas in 1937. Young Frank Fujita attended Abilene High School where he stood out because of his ethnicity and his incredible drawing ability, which led to his cartoons being showcased in school and local newspapers.*

*Following the lead of one of his friends who served in the Texas National Guard and painted a picture of excitement and adventure, Fujita received permission from his parents to join an artillery battalion of the 36th Infantry Division in 1938. In late 1941, as hostilities with Japan seemed more imminent, the U.S. Army separated Fujita's battalion from the already-activated 36th Division and shipped the unit to the Pacific Theater to form a new artillery brigade to bolster American defenses in the Philippines. Eight days after embarking from California, Fujita's convoy received word of the Japanese attack on Pearl Harbor. Diverted initially to Australia, Fujita's unit was ordered to the Dutch East Indies in January 1942 to help defend Java. Japanese forces invaded the island on March 1, 1942, and overwhelmed the Allied defenders within a week, resulting in Fujita's capture.*

*The first half of Fujita's 42-month long incarceration mirrored the experiences of other Allied POWs, largely because the enemy guards had not yet discovered his Japanese ancestry. On Java, Japanese guards brutally mistreated Fujita and his comrades while demanding immediate compliance to their orders and expecting the POWs to constantly bow to them. Failure to do so resulted in severe beatings. The Japanese forced the prisoners to labor on the island while being crowded in squalid camps with horrendous sanitation issues. Latrines in the camps consisted of open pits infested with disease-carrying flies. The prisoners' quarters were constantly infested with bedbugs, fleas, and lice while the food provided was meager and of poor quality, often consisting of small quantities of rice, bread, and soup infested with worms. Eventually, Fujita developed pellagra—a condition that led to cracked skin all about his body. The coating came off his tongue and the skin around his scrotum peeled off leading to unbearably painful chafing while walking.*

*After six months on Java, the Japanese crammed Fujita and other chosen prisoners into the holds of cargo ships and transported them to Changi prison camp in Singapore, a larger facility containing over 15,000 British and Australian prisoners. Living conditions there proved to be no better than on Java. Fujita and the other POWs ate whatever they could find—large snails, stray birds, and, in one instance, they killed and ate a small dog that turned out to be the British officers' mascot. In December 1942, Fujita and a contingent of men from his unit were again loaded into cargo ships, this time to be transported to Nagasaki, Japan—his father's former home—for hard labor at local shipyards. There the climate was much chillier than in Indonesia, with Siberian winds blowing through the cramped quarters which had no doors or windows. Thin straw mats and a few cotton blankets provided the only protection from the extreme cold. The food provided was usually a small allotment of rice and barley plus a soup consisting of discarded vegetables and fish parts. At the work site, the Japanese formed the prisoners into groups by task, with Fujita's crew used to build and maintain scaffolding for other work crews.*

*Fujita toiled in the shipyards for four months until a Japanese guard who could read English discovered his heritage while skimming over the prison roster. This was the moment Fujita had long feared, convinced that the Japanese would single him out and kill him for being a racial traitor even though he was a proud American. Instead, enemy officers tried in vain to teach him the Japanese language and indoctrinate him to their cause. For many months, Fujita was given lighter workloads and protected from harassment by guards. One day in August 1943, however, hateful guards took out their anger on Fujita. When their officers left the base to attend important meetings, the guards took him into a room where they took turns bending him over and smacking him full force in the back and buttocks with clubs the size of baseball bats while kicking and punching him in the face. Despite the thrashing he received, Fujita refused to fall to the ground, partly out of spite, but also because he had seen beaten prisoners who fell down receive even worse treatment, sometimes resulting in death. When the guards finally tired, they marched him back to his fellow prisoners where he promptly passed out.*

*In October 1943, the Japanese ordered Fujita to Tokyo and informed him that he would deliver propaganda messages over the radio or "his life would not be guaranteed." A dozen other coerced POWs joined Fujita in the broadcasts, mostly individuals with previous radio or entertainment experience, but there were also a couple of Americans who willingly collaborated with the enemy and were greatly despised by Fujita and the other prisoners. For the remainder of the war, Fujita passed the time delivering lackluster radio messages, observing the Allied bombings of Tokyo, and making entries into a secret diary he had kept since being captured on Java despite the Japanese military's threat to shoot any POWs caught possessing a journal.*

In December 1941, Texas joined the nation in rallying for war after the Japanese attack on Pearl Harbor, Hawaii. As hundreds of thousands of Texans volunteered (and were drafted) to fight overseas, dramatic changes began to occur as the Lone Star State mobilized for the conflict. In fact, World War II served as a catalyst for unprecedented social and economic change. By placing an incredible amount of orders for food, military equipment, and war supplies (funded by increased taxes and unprecedented levels of deficit spending), the federal government generated massive employment opportunities, thus ending the Great Depression. By the end of the conflict, Texas had become a more industrialized and urbanized state. Additionally, the war encouraged minorities in Texas to clamor for more rights in the postwar years as just recognition of their contributions to victory.

**The Roots of War**

Though the incident that drove the nation into the Second World War surprised everyone, American entry into the conflict was not unexpected. The United States government took preparatory steps for the possibility of entering the war as early as 1940 when President Franklin Delano Roosevelt (FDR) signed the Burke-Wadsworth Act into law, establishing the first peacetime draft in American history (only two Texas congressmen, Martin Dies and Hatton Sumners, voted against it). Despite declaring neutrality, the United States government also began to funnel aid to the enemies of Germany, Italy, and Japan. American involvement in the war inched closer in early 1941 when Roosevelt asked Congress to authorize "Lend-Lease" aid to England, allowing the British access to American arms and war supplies without expecting repayment. Guided successfully through the legislative process by Texas Senator Tom Connally, who served as chair of the Senate Foreign Relations Committee, and unanimously supported by all Texas congressmen, Congress later extended this aid to the Russians after the June 1941 Nazi invasion of the Soviet Union. Though American aid to their enemies greatly upset the leaders of Germany and Italy, Adolf Hitler and Benito Mussolini, both wanted to keep the United States from direct involvement in the hostilities for a much longer period of time.

Even before these events unfolded in Europe, the Japanese had been expanding in Asia. In 1931, Japan seized Manchuria. Six years later, Japanese forces attacked China. After Japan's July 1941 takeover of French Indochina, FDR tried to apply economic pressure by suspending most trade with Japan, including the most important resource that country needed—oil. Not wishing to reverse their expansionist policies as the American government desired, Japanese leaders planned to seize the Dutch East Indies (Indonesia) to gain control of its vital oil resources. Because they could not surmise how President Roosevelt would react to such a provocative act, the leaders assumed the worst—that the United States would declare war on Japan. Given that supposition, they decided that the best opportunity to get the upper hand in the western Pacific region would be to inflict maximum damage upon the United States with a surprise attack on the American Pacific fleet based at Pearl Harbor. The raid crippled the fleet, destroyed over 150 aircraft, and killed almost 2,400 Americans. Though the attack achieved many Japanese goals, it failed to eliminate any aircraft carriers (which were away on maneuvers at the time), did not destroy oil storage facilities or repair docks, and unified the United States against Japan like nothing else could have done.

President Roosevelt promptly asked Congress for a formal declaration of war against Japan. Senator Connally introduced the resolution, which soon passed by near-unanimous consent. Two days later, Germany and Italy declared war on the United States. Hitler and Mussolini made this decision in retaliation for American aid to England and the Soviet Union, plus the added benefit of bogging down the United States in a two-front war with theaters of operation in Europe and Asia separated by thousands of miles.

**Synopsis of the War**

The European situation looked grim when the United States entered World War II. Germany and Italy had conquered France and controlled most of Europe, northern Africa, and western Russia. The infusion of American material and manpower, however, gave the enemies of Hitler and Mussolini vast new resources and a large morale boost.

American troops first engaged the enemy in November 1942 with attacks in northwest Africa. Eventually, the Allies captured all of North Africa before invading Sicily and southern Italy in 1943. The 36th Division, originally a Texas National Guard unit, joined other U.S. and British troops in driving Italy out of the conflict (though Germans continued the fight on the Italian peninsula throughout the war). Also in 1943, the western Allies initiated a strategic bombing campaign to pummel the Nazis into submission with long-range, high-altitude bombers. The effort eventually failed. The bombing proved to be highly inaccurate, and the cost in planes and crew members was astonishing. The U.S. lost over 50,000 men on these missions, including Lieutenant Clyde Cosper of Dodd City, Texas, who heroically gave his life as he maintained control of his crippled B-17 long enough to allow his crew to eject over England, then steer clear of residential areas as the plane crashed in a field near an English town.

The end of German control of France began on D-Day, June 6, 1944, when a multinational force spearheaded by units such as Texan James Earl Rudder's Second Ranger Battalion came ashore at Normandy. After a hard fight to establish a beachhead, U.S. and British forces pressed on to liberate Paris and then turned toward the German border. As Russian armies drove from the east, British and American soldiers, including 20-year old José Angel López of Jourdantown, Texas (honored by war's end with two Bronze Stars), endured the harsh winter and Germany's last desperate attempt to halt the advance of the Allied forces at the Battle of the Bulge. Fighting to the finish, the Germans finally capitulated in May 1945 after the Russians captured the capital city of Berlin.

Meanwhile, the United States had the equally daunting task of trying to subdue the Japanese in the Pacific. After the Pearl Harbor raid, the Japanese undertook a series of attacks in the western Pacific, eventually gaining control over Guam, Wake Island, the Philippines, Malaysia, French Indochina, the Dutch East Indies, and most of Polynesia. Japan's fortunes began to change in June 1942, however, as a result of the American victory at the Battle of Midway. American pilots, such as George Gay from Waco, Texas, destroyed four prime Japanese carriers, turning the tide of the Pacific War. From that point, the Japanese were on the defensive, entrenching to maintain control of the territory already seized.

The U.S. Army and Navy in the Pacific, under the command of General Douglas MacArthur (who had attended West Texas Military Academy in San Antonio before entering West Point in 1898) and Admiral Chester Nimitz (a native-born son of Fredericksburg, Texas), respectively, began their "island hopping" campaign in late 1943. Rather than attempting to capture all Japanese-held possessions, the leaders chose instead to fight on selected islands of strategic value and bypass the remainder on the way to Japan. The U.S. won fierce battles for control of such islands as Guadalcanal, Tarawa, Saipan, Iwo Jima, and Okinawa, but the high casualty rates verified the logic of bypassing islands of lesser importance.

From late-1944 through mid-1945, U.S. bombers delivered devastating attacks on Japanese military and civilian targets, flattening entire Japanese cities with conventional explosives and fire bombing tactics. Despite the damage, the Japanese government still refused to surrender unconditionally as FDR's successor (Roosevelt had died from a cerebral hemorrhage in April 1945) Harry Truman demanded, holding out hope for more favorable terms and protection for their emperor. The new president then ordered the dropping of two atomic bombs. (Joseph Stiborik from Taylor, Texas, served as radio operator aboard the *Enola Gay*, the B-29 that dropped the first bomb on Hiroshima, Japan.) Five days after the United States dropped the second bomb on Nagasaki, the Japanese government formally requested peace.

Historians still engage in heated debates about which factor most played into Japan's decision to surrender. Many hold the position that the atomic bombs sped up the Japanese desire for peace and precluded the need for a deadly invasion of their country. Other historians challenge this notion. While some oppose the decision on strictly moral grounds, others believe that the atomic attacks simply were not necessary to force surrender. They argue that Japan already neared total destruction and the Soviet Union's late entry into the war against Japan probably played a more important role in their deci-

**General MacArthur, FDR, and Admiral Nimitz in Pearl Harbor, Hawaii. July 26, 1944.
Photo credit: FDR Presidential Library**

sion to surrender. One must also consider the opinions of such respected military men as Chester Nimitz, Dwight Eisenhower, and Douglas MacArthur, who believed that the demand for unconditional surrender hampered peace efforts that could have ended the war sooner. (Truman eventually deviated from unconditional surrender by agreeing to the preservation of the institution of the emperor.) Regardless of the circumstances, the war finally ended with Japan's capitulation in early September 1945.

**Texas Military Installations**

During World War II, Texas became America's largest military training ground. Vast terrain, relatively favorable year-round weather, and an effective congressional delegation all contributed to the military's decision to place a large number of training installations in Texas, not to mention numerous camps to incarcerate enemy prisoners and civilian detainees.

Fifteen army training camps were located in Texas during the war. Some posts existed before the conflict, such as Fort Sam Houston in San Antonio and Fort Bliss outside of El Paso. Others arose during the war, such as Fort Hood, created as a massive armor training facility near Killeen. Twenty army combat divisions totaling 1.2 million men eventually trained in Texas, with many serving in the 3rd and 4th Armies headquartered in San Antonio. Over 200,000 army and navy pilots, bombardiers, navigators, gunners, and aerial photographers trained at 40 Texas military airfields, including at the Naval Air Station at Corpus Christi, which was the only primary, basic, and advanced pilot training facility in existence in the United States at that time.

During World War II, the United States for the first time in its history held large numbers of foreign prisoners of war. Texas hosted twice as many prisoner-of-war (POW) camps than any other state. In part, this resulted from the large amount of available land (over 250,000 square miles; the only state larger is Alaska), but a Geneva Convention requirement stating that nations must hold prisoners of war in a climate similar to the place of capture provided another reason. The U.S. military eventually interpreted this provision by sending to Texas close to 50,000 German and 2,500 Italian prisoners captured in North Africa and 1,000 Japanese captured on various Pacific islands. In addition to seven camps set up especially for POWs in Brady (McCulloch County), Hearne (Robertson County), Hereford (Deaf Smith County), Huntsville (Walker County), McLean (Gray

**Fort Sam Houston, Texas. c. 1941**
**Photo credit: Library of Congress**

County), Mexia (Limestone County), and at Camp Wallace (Galveston County), the military held enemy prisoners at fourteen army posts scattered across the state.

Due to the chronic labor shortages produced by the war, the War Department authorized the use of POW labor, often with prisoners based at "branch camps" located some distance away from the permanent camp facilities. Texas had twenty-two of these smaller sites, typically housing up to forty prisoners in tents, barracks, and old buildings. Farmers and construction companies paid the prevailing wage of $1.50 per day to secure the POWs' services, 80 cents of which went to the prisoner in the form of canteen coupons while the rest went to the U.S. Treasury to help pay for prisoner upkeep. The main contribution of POW labor in Texas involved agricultural work such as picking cotton, harvesting rice, baling hay, threshing grain, and picking fruit for farmers. The state also used German prisoners to help build roads and for construction projects such as the Denison Dam.

Twenty-one POWs in Texas escaped from their camps, only to be recaptured within a few days or weeks. The desperate attempts to break the bonds of confinement often ended comically. One farmer captured an escaped prisoner from Mexia when the POW called for help after being chased up a tree by the man's bull. Three other escapees from Hearne were captured in a makeshift raft floating down the Brazos River apparently trying to make it back to Germany via the Gulf of Mexico.

In addition to POW camps, the United States contained twenty lesser-known internment camps operated by the Immigration and Naturalization Service (INS) to hold Japanese Americans in FBI custody, enemy sailors captured in American ports at the start of the war, and enemy nationals deported by Latin American nations to the United States. (In a majority of cases, Peruvian Japanese were removed mainly because of racism and the elimination of economic competition, rather than for national security concerns.) Texas contained three INS internment facilities. The Seagoville camp (southeast of Dallas) housed 650 prisoners at a minimum security women's reformatory. In Kenedy (located halfway between San Antonio and Victoria), the INS oversaw 3,500 aliens at the site of an abandoned CCC camp. The INS held another 3,500 in Crystal City (south of Uvalde) at a large Farm Security Administration migratory workers' camp. None of these camps reported any escapes. After the war, the U.S. government repatriated most German and Italian nationals to their home counties. Some returned to their Latin American homes. Very few Japanese, however, returned to Latin America. The U.S. government sent over 600 Peruvian Japanese held in Texas camps to Japan because the government of Peru denied their ability to return. Those unwilling to be sent to Japan were eventually allowed to remain in America.

**Texans in Uniform**

When the United States entered World War II, Texas volunteers inundated recruiting centers. Throughout the war they would be joined by additional volunteers and draftees. While Texans made up 5 percent of the nation's population in 1940, 7 percent of Texans (approximately 750,000) served in the armed forces during the war. Of this total, three-quarters served in the army and air forces while one-quarter served in the navy, marines, or coast guard. By the end of the conflict, 22,022 Texans died in combat. While countless Texans distinguished themselves, a few noteworthy examples must suffice.

**Admiral Chester W. Nimitz, Commander-in-Chief, Pacific Fleet, pins the Navy Cross on Doris Miller, at a ceremony on board a U.S. Navy warship in Pearl Harbor.
May 27, 1942**

As a result of his actions during the Pearl Harbor attack, Doris Miller from Waco, Texas, became one of the first American heroes of World War II. A strong man who played football and boxed (he was named "Doris" by a midwife who was positive before his birth that the baby would be a girl, and his mother chose to keep the name), Miller joined the U.S. Navy in 1939 to help his family in the midst of the Depression. Because he was an African American, his opportunities were quite limited. The Navy confined blacks who served on ships to support roles, such as stewards, cooks, and mess attendants. After basic training, the Navy assigned Mess Attendant Third Class Doris Miller to the *USS West Virginia*, a battleship stationed at Pearl Harbor. When the Japanese attacked, Miller threw down the soiled laundry he had collected, helped move his mortally-wounded captain, and raced to an unattended anti-aircraft gun on the main deck. Though denied formal gunnery training, Miller fired back as best he could at the enemy torpedo and dive bombers. Afterwards, he told Navy officials that he thought he had hit only one plane, but a country in need of ultra-heroes decided to credit Miller with hitting several more. This discrepancy cannot diminish from the courage that Miller exhibited under fire that morning. For his actions, the Navy awarded Miller the Navy Cross, promoted him to Mess Attendant First Class, and allowed him a lengthy furlough. Two years later, while serving as an officer's cook aboard an aircraft carrier, he was killed in action when a submarine torpedoed his ship during a battle in the Gilbert Islands.

Eventually, over 80,000 black Texans served in the U.S. armed forces during World War II. In addition to Doris Miller, three other blacks received the Navy Cross, including Texan Leonard Roy Harmon from Cuero. Like Miller, Harmon enlisted in 1939 and became a mess attendant. In November 1942, Harmon served aboard the heavy cruiser *USS San Francisco,* supporting the assault upon Guadalcanal in the Solomon Islands. During a devastating aerial attack, Harmon disregarded his own personal safety by helping other crew members evacuate wounded personnel and was killed while shielding a wounded shipmate during an enemy strafing run. For his extraordinary heroism under fire, the Navy posthumously awarded Harmon the Navy Cross and announced that a new destroyer escort would be called the *USS Harmon*—the first U.S. Navy ship to be named after an African American.

Samuel Dealey of Dallas (nephew of long-time *Dallas Morning News* publisher George B. Dealey) became the most-decorated American sailor of the war. During 1943 and 1944, Dealey served as commander of the *USS Harder,* an attack submarine that made five highly successful missions deep into enemy waters, sinking the most total tonnage of any U.S. submarine up to that time, a total of eighteen ships. He won the Navy Cross with three gold stars, the Distinguished Service Cross, and two presidential unit citations for these attacks, but Dealey and his crew failed to return from their sixth sortie in August 1944 after being depth-charged off Luzon in the Philippines. Near the end of the war, Dealey posthumously received a Silver Star and the Congressional Medal of Honor for his heroism.

Many Texans like to claim native sons Dwight Eisenhower (born in Denison, Texas), who became the Supreme Allied Commander in Europe, and Claire Chennault (born in Commerce, Texas), who led the famous American volunteer pilots in China known as the Flying Tigers. However, both future generals' families left Texas while they were infants. U.S. Pacific Naval Commander Chester Nimitz of Fredericksburg, however, actually grew up in the Lone Star State. A descendent of German immigrants arriving in the Hill Country in the 1840s, Nimitz originally desired to attend the U.S. Military Academy at West Point to obtain a free college education, but he failed to receive an appointment. The Naval Academy, however, accepted him. After rising through the ranks, he became commander of the U.S. Pacific Fleet after the Pearl Harbor attack. From his headquarters in Hawaii, Nimitz conducted the naval counterattack against the over-extended Japanese forces across the Pacific leading to their ultimate defeat.

In the European theater, many Texans distinguished themselves, including James Earl Rudder from Eden. After graduating from Texas A&M, Rudder served in the Army Reserves as a second lieutenant while working as a teacher and football coach at Brady High School. He was called into active duty in 1941, promoted to lieutenant colonel, and ultimately commanded the Second Ranger Battalion, which played a major role in the Normandy invasion. On D-Day, Rudder and his men hit the beaches and endured withering enemy fire as they scaled hundred-foot cliffs to take out embedded German gunnery crews. Rudder's Rangers succeeded in clearing the heights to allow the establishment of an Allied beachhead, but they suffered a casualty rate over 50 percent. Rudder himself suffered two wounds during the attack. He later fought in the Battle of the Bulge and continued to receive numerous citations and decorations, ending the war as a full colonel. In postwar years, Rudder became a major general in the Reserves and served as president of Texas A&M University.

Close to a half-million Mexican Americans volunteered or served in the armed forces as draftees. The military generally integrated Mexican-American servicemen into regular units during the war, but some served in segregated Mexican-American units, such as Company C of the 141st Regiment, 36th Division. Five Tejanos distinguished themselves by receiving the Congressional Medal of Honor, including Staff Sergeant Macario García. Born into a farm worker family from Villa de Castaño, Mexico, García's parents immigrated to Texas during the early 1920s. While raising crops with his family near Sugar

Land, the U.S. Army drafted him in 1942. After recovering from wounds received during the Normandy invasion, García rejoined his unit and earned the nation's highest military honor for his actions near Grosshau, Germany, in late November, 1944. While an acting squad leader, he single-handedly assaulted an enemy machine gun emplacement that had pinned down his men. Although gravely wounded, García crawled forward on his own initiative, reached the enemy position, and destroyed it with grenades. After rejoining his company, a second machine gun crew opened fire, and again García disregarded his own safety by storming the position, destroying the gun, and capturing prisoners. On August 23, 1945, García received his Medal of Honor from President Harry Truman at a White House ceremony.

Of all American foot soldiers during World War II, none has been more celebrated than Audie Murphy from Hunt County, Texas. Born into a poor sharecropper family, Murphy enlisted in June 1942. He fought in eight campaigns in Sicily, Italy, France, and Germany, rising from a private to the rank of second lieutenant as a result of his leadership and battlefield heroics. He became one of Texas's 36 Medal of Honor recipients for his actions in January 1945 while defending a position in France against 200 attacking German infantrymen supported by six tanks. After ordering his men to take cover in nearby woods, Murphy mounted a disabled tank destroyer recently set ablaze. Using its .50 caliber machine gun to hold off the advancing Germans, killing about fifty of them, he was able to call in supporting artillery fire to chase off the remaining attackers. By the end of his war career, Murphy had become the U.S. military's most decorated combat soldier. He received thirty-three awards, citations, and every medal that the nation gives for valor, including two of them twice. He also received three Purple Hearts for his combat wounds. After the war, Murphy became a Hollywood actor, playing himself in the film version of his autobiography, *To Hell and Back*. He died in a 1971 plane crash and is buried in Arlington National Cemetery in Washington, D.C.

Not all Texans serving in the military had an opportunity to distinguish themselves on the battlefield, including the women in uniform who provided valuable support services. About 200,000 American women, including 12,000 Texans, served in the Women's Army Corps (WACs) under the command of Colonel Oveta Culp Hobby (the wife of former governor William Hobby) from Killeen, Texas. WACs performed 239 important support roles, ranging from secretarial duties to motor vehicle maintenance, freeing up men for other assignments including combat duty. One hundred thousand American women performed similar duty in the Navy as "Women Accepted for Volunteer Emergency Service" (WAVES).

**Wartime Voluntarism**

While Texans fought overseas, citizens on the home front patriotically endured the inconvenience of scarce resources to support the war effort. Unlike World War I, rationing soon became a reality. Beginning with sugar, the federal government's Office of Price Administration (OPA) eventually rationed meat, coffee, shoes, rubber, and even gasoline. (Although the U.S. had plenty of oil, government leaders ordered gasoline to be rationed primarily to reduce wear on rubber tires.) Through rationing, food could be equally distributed while better ensuring the availability of enough items for a majority of the population. Even if someone had enough OPA coupons, however, there was no guarantee that

Oveta (Culp) Hobby, February 1953. Photo credit: Library of Congress

desired items would remain in stock. Many other consumer items were perpetually unavailable because manufacturers did not make them during the war. Texas civilians could no longer purchase such items as new automobiles, lawn mowers, musical instruments, radios and other electrical appliances, safety pins, silk stockings, and rifle ammunition. As the vast majority of Americans sacrificed, most Texans also accepted these privations for the duration of the war. They generally accepted the 35 miles per hour speed limit (often fined in rationing coupons when they did not) and began to travel more often by bus and train. Housewives used meat substitutes, replaced butter with the less-appealing margarine, and experimented with vegetables with which they were previously unfamiliar. Hoarding, black market operations, and other means of evading the law occurred but at a much smaller rate than might be expected.

In addition to taking part in "meatless Tuesdays" and giving up their favorite desserts, growing "victory gardens" provided another way for Texans to cope with wartime shortages. Similar to their experiences during World War I, many Texans converted their flower beds, backyards, and empty city lots into small agricultural plots. Collectively, these gardens yielded several hundred thousand tons of produce to help meet civilian needs while ensuring that the largest inventory possible went directly toward the war effort.

Texans supported the war effort at home through participation in numerous organized drives for scarce resources, blood donations, and war bonds. Learning the value of recycling while simultaneously boosting their sense of patriotism, Texans contributed old tin cans and pots to metal drives, old newspapers and magazines for paper drives, and broken bottles and windows for glass drives. They even organized drives to collect animal fats, old bones, and grease (to be used in the manufacture of explosives). Thousands of Texans also helped the war effort by serving as volunteer nurses and blood donors for the Red Cross. Patriotism and the inability to purchase many consumer items drove Texans to invest in the war effort by loaning millions of dollars to the government during bond drives. After the war, their efforts contributed to the postwar economic expansion when they cashed in those bonds to make vast consumer purchases.

Texas citizens donated their time in ways that directly aided the war effort. Civilian pilots for the Civil Air Patrol, for example, aided the military by reporting sightings of German U-boats in the Gulf of Mexico (sometimes even attacking them with depth charges), reporting ships in distress, and helping to rescue survivors of submarine attacks. The organization also involved itself in border patrols, towing targets for military gunnery practice, moving mail, and transporting military passengers.

The Women's Airforce Service Pilots (WASPs), created to overcome the shortage of pilots and to free up more male pilots for combat duty, provided another valuable volunteer service. Commanded by aviator Jacqueline Cochran, the WASPs trained at Avenger Field in Sweetwater, Texas, before its graduates transferred to flying assignments across the country. Though the federal government refused to grant the civilian WASPs any recognized military status (let alone use the women in combat), they played vital support roles throughout the war by ferrying all types of military aircraft (including heavy bombers), providing instrument instruction and towing targets for male trainee pilots, testing damaged planes, and transporting cargo. Ultimately, over 25,000 women applied to be WASPs, 1,830 were accepted, 1,074 graduated, and 38 died while performing their duties.

**The Texas Wartime Economy**

World War II stimulated the Texas economy and set in motion the state's future postwar industrial and urban base. The value of Texas manufactured products quadrupled during the war, from $453,105,423 in 1939 to $1,900,000,000 in 1944. New war factories created fresh job opportunities in the cities, leading to an influx of a half-million intrastate rural migrants coupled with the arrival of over 400,000 out-of-state workers. Before the war, 45 percent of the state's population resided in urban areas containing at least 2,500 people. By 1950, the number of Texan urbanites rose to 60 percent.

Though no aircraft manufacturing existed in the state before 1940, Texas definitely made up for lost time. Enormous aircraft plants located in North Texas provided considerable employment. A Consolidated Vultee Aircraft Corporation plant outside Fort Worth, one of the world's largest factories, doubled the number of industrial wage earners in the city (close to 40,000 at one point). The factory's main building, used to build B-24 bombers and C-87 transports, measured 14 city blocks long and more than a block wide covering a total of 30 acres. Other North Texas aircraft manufacturing examples include the military training aircraft built at a large Southern Aircraft Corporation plant in Garland and North Atlantic Aviation's massive Grand Prairie facility, which produced long-range P-51 Mustang fighters.

Shipbuilding also emerged as an important Texas wartime industry. For the first time since World War I, shipyards along the Gulf Coast bustled with activity filling orders for cargo ships, amphibious landing boats, destroyers, and minesweepers. In addition to construction facilities, ports in Orange, Port Arthur, Houston, Galveston, Corpus Christi, and Brownsville also provided valuable repair and refitting services for military and commercial vessels.

The state's most important industry—petroleum—contributed greatly to the war effort. By 1943, Texas fields operated at maximum capacity. Wartime demand stimulated the search for new fields, leading to modest discoveries that made significant additions to Texas reserves. German U-boat activity threatened American tankers, however, as evidenced by sinkings in the Gulf of Mexico early in the war. Realizing this threat as early as 1940, Interior Secretary Harold Ickes lobbied strongly for the construction of pipelines to carry Texas petroleum to the northeastern states. In 1942, the government started building the first conduit, measuring twenty-four inches in diameter and nicknamed the "Big Inch" to transport crude oil. Completed in August 1943, the line carried Texas oil as far east as Philadelphia, 1,254 miles away. Meanwhile, workers on another twenty-inch diameter pipeline called the "Little Big Inch" began construction in 1943 and completed their task by March 1944. This line transported refined oil from Houston and Port Arthur to Linden, New Jersey. By the war's end, both pipelines carried over 350 million barrels of petroleum to the East Coast.

Petrochemical plants also opened for business across the state. The war led directly to the establishment of the synthetic rubber industry in Texas. By 1950, Texas produced half of the country's synthetic rubber products. Other manufacturing that benefited from the

**Answering the nation's need for womanpower, Mrs. Virginia Davis made arrangements for the care of her two children during the day and joined her husband at work in the Naval Air Base in Corpus Christi, Texas. Both were employed under Civil Service in the assembly and repair department. Mrs. Davis's training enabled her to take the place of her husband if he was called by the armed services. August 1942. Photo credit: Library of Congress**

war boom included a revived East Texas paper and wood-pulp industry, new steel mills in Houston and Daingerfield, munitions plants in Amarillo and Texarkana, and the erection of the Western Hemisphere's only tin smelter in Texas City.

The labor shortages caused by the exodus of workers into military service produced new labor opportunities for Texas women. Because the country needed working women to help win the war, the United States War Manpower Commission recruited women across the country to work in vital industries. Before the war, single females comprised most of the nation's 12 million women in the workforce. By 1945, married housewives made up a majority of the nation's 18 million working women (over one-third of the civilian labor force). Besides good pay and patriotic fervor, personal reasons also motivated many married women to do their part—over half of the women had husbands or brothers in the military. Leaving home to work in a factory could be threatening and intimidating, but many Texas women overcame their fears to start performing work traditionally done by men, such as ship welding, working on aircraft assembly lines, and manufacturing radio equipment. While they received high wages, the work was challenging, the hours were long, and after completing their workday, the women often had to undertake regular household duties. Nevertheless, most stayed at their jobs and contributed greatly to victory.

The wartime demand for labor benefited many African-American Texans and some Tejanos. The number of African-American manufacturing workers in Texas doubled during the war, from 150,000 to almost 300,000. Discrimination in different forms continued, however, from segregated assembly lines at war plants to relegation to lower-paying unskilled jobs. Few Tejanos found industrial jobs during the war, but the military hired over 10,000 Mexican Americans living in San Antonio to work at Kelly Field, which had been recently converted into an aircraft maintenance, modification, and repair facility.

World War II had a profound effect on Texas agriculture, instigating changes that would continue to reshape the countryside in the postwar years. The exodus of a half-million rural Texans to the military or urban industrial jobs (most of them never to return) produced a tremendous strain on the rural labor force. In order to sustain themselves, many farm women added to their normal responsibilities by working in the fields to maintain and harvest crops. As previously mentioned, some Texas farmers used German POW labor to perform needed work. In 1942, the federal government tried to help by negotiating the Mexican Farm Labor Program Agreement (also known as the *bracero* program) to provide Mexican laborers to work legally for American farmers and ranchers. The agreement's terms called for workers to be guaranteed a minimum wage of 30 cents an hour and humane treatment in the form of adequate shelter, food, and sanitation. Though many farmers balked at these terms, the program failed to provide sufficient Mexican wartime labor for the state because restrictive actions by the Mexican government postponed participation with Texas until after the war. In 1943, responding to political pressure from Tejano activists (including members of LULAC) and sympathetic supporters within Mexico who sought the passage of state laws in Texas banning discrimination against Hispanics, the Mexican government refused to allow temporary work visas for migrant farm workers to enter Texas. Though the state legislature in 1943 passed a resolution stating that "all members of the Caucasian Race" (Hispanics included) should be entitled to full and equal accommodations plus all privileges in public places of business and amusement, this symbolic action fell far short of what Tejano activists and Mexican government officials were seeking. Nevertheless, farmers in South Texas benefited during the war from access to undocumented Mexican labor.

Texas cotton contributed to the war effort, converted to such uses as material for uniforms and tents, insulation, packing, and even explosives. Texas growers received prices for the white fiber that they had not seen since the pre-World War I years. In 1940, farmers received 10 cents per pound, but by 1945, prices had doubled to over 21 cents per pound. However, Texas producers began to raise less cotton during the war than in the past (from 3.2 million bales on 9 million acres in 1940 to just 1.8 million bales on 6 million acres in 1945). The labor shortage partially explains this decline, but many farmers also shifted to cattle and other crops, especially in East Texas. Whereas cotton represented 75 percent of all Texas farm crops in 1941, by 1945 that figure dropped to less than 50 percent as farmers increasingly dedicated land to food crops (especially grains, vegetables, sugar, and citrus fruits) to satisfy wartime demand.

The war accelerated other changes in Texas agriculture that had been underway since the 1930s. Texas farms began to convert to larger units utilizing more machinery (a 33 percent increase from 1940 to 1945). The number of tenants and sharecroppers continued to decline from 244,000 in 1940 to 169,000 by 1946. Favorable soil, climate, topography, and especially new irrigation techniques prompted a shift in the geography of the state's cotton production. After 1945, the southern high plains and lower Rio Grande valley replaced northern and eastern Texas as the state's core cotton-producing regions. Meanwhile, by 1945 East Texas began to produce more cattle than West Texas ranchers.

**Wartime Politics**

While the war tended to reduce the degree of political infighting in Texas, factionalism and personality differences among Democratic Party politicians continued to thwart total unity. Even before the war, President Roosevelt upset many Texas supporters of John Nance Garner. Not only did FDR's decision to seek an unprecedented third term in 1940 deny Garner a chance at the presidency, but Roosevelt also replaced his vice president on the ticket with Secretary of Agriculture Henry A. Wallace. Governor Wilbert Lee "Pappy" O'Daniel refused to endorse Roosevelt, but the president still received 81 percent of the Texas vote on his way to winning reelection.

In 1940 Texans reelected Governor O'Daniel, who served another unproductive term as he squabbled frequently with the legislature, especially over taxation. The governor continued to demand passage of a sales tax while a majority of legislators sought increased taxes on the oil industry, insurance and utilities companies, and automobile sales. Partially to divert attention away from the stalemate, O'Daniel created a false impression that corrupt labor union "racketeers" had infiltrated the state. Despite the weakness of Texas labor unions and the rarity of strikes, the legislature responded by passing an anti-labor law with O'Daniel's approval making it a crime to threaten violence to prevent anyone from working or to picket in the vicinity of a labor dispute.

The governor decided to leave office in April 1941 when longstanding Texas Senator Morris Sheppard died, leaving the U.S. Senate seat vacant. As a safe interim appointment while he prepared for his own bid for the seat, O'Daniel chose Andrew Jackson Houston, the 87-year-old son of Sam Houston. The replacement senator received the honor of becoming the oldest person to date to serve in the U.S. Senate before dying less than

**Lyndon B. Johnson campaigning for the U.S. Senate in Johnson City, Texas. June 28, 1941.**
June 28, 1941. Credit: LBJ Library photo by Austin Statesman

three weeks later. In the special election held to decide who would fill out the remainder of Sheppard's term, the governor received a strong challenge from Congressman Lyndon Baines Johnson. While O'Daniel ran his typical anti-establishment campaign, Johnson ran as a solid New Dealer and almost pulled off an upset, losing by a mere 1,300 votes. Though the congressman believed fraud had cost him the election, Johnson did not formally contest the results. He intended to learn from the experience, however, to make certain that a similar occurrence would not happen in the future.

In 1942, O'Daniel ran for reelection to a full Senate term. He encountered vibrant opposition in the Democratic primaries from ex-governors Dan Moody and James Allred. Moody suffered his only political defeat when he finished a dismal third to O'Daniel and Allred, who then faced each other in a runoff. Allred received encouragement from the Roosevelt administration, running his campaign as a firm supporter of Roosevelt's domestic and foreign agenda while trying not to appear as a "yes" man. To appease voters who still admired Roosevelt, O'Daniel publicly praised the president, though many knew he disliked FDR and his policies. He also continued to deliver baseless accusations that "communistic labor leader racketeers" were active in Texas supporting the candidacies of politicians such as Allred through a massive slush fund. Though Allred gained the support of most major Texas newspapers, Democratic politicians, South Texas party bosses, and a cadre of wealthy Dallas businessmen, O'Daniel received substantial rural support to eke

**Rally of women at Austin Hotel during Lyndon B. Johnson's U.S. Senate campaign. Lady Bird Johnson is 3rd from left. June 6, 1941.
Credit: LBJ Library photo by Austin Statesman**

out a 451,359 to 433,203 victory. For the fourth consecutive election, the flour salesman-turned-politician emerged victorious by virtue of his false image as a humble and sincere bumpkin, coupled with his deft use of finely crafted anti-establishment rhetoric.

When Pappy O'Daniel left for the Senate, Lieutenant Governor Coke Stevenson moved into the governor's mansion. Raised on a Kimble County ranch, Stevenson became a prominent businessman, rancher, banker, and lawyer in Junction, Texas, before his election to the state legislature in 1928. After becoming the first person to serve two consecutive terms as Speaker of the Texas House, he won the lieutenant governor's race in 1938. A reserved and unpretentious conservative politician, Stevenson held strong anti-central planning beliefs that led him to oppose most of the New Deal in addition to opposing the wartime national speed limit and gasoline rationing.

Stevenson enjoyed great popularity as Texas's wartime governor, winning reelection in 1942 and again in 1944. The return of economic prosperity proved to be the major factor driving his popular support. Beginning his governorship with a $34 million debt, he left office in 1947 with a $35 million surplus. While increased wartime business activity largely explains the reversal, Stevenson contributed by refusing to raise taxes and supporting deep funding cuts for state government services. Though he supported increased funding for the state highway system, a building program for the University of Texas, and elevated teachers' salaries, most colleges and government agencies (especially mental health facilities, orphanages, and hospitals) received greatly reduced appropriations. The governor also endorsed a state constitutional amendment, passed by voters in 1942, requiring a balanced state government budget.

The governor had a mixed record with organized labor. Though he negotiated a no-strike agreement with unions for the war's duration, Stevenson bowed to political pressure and allowed the Manford Act to become law without his signature. The legislation placed many burdens on unions. Labor organizers had to register with the state and carry identification cards; unions had to file comprehensive annual reports containing financial and organizational records with the state; and unions could no longer contribute to political campaigns.

On racial matters, Stevenson's views mirrored the feelings of a majority of Anglo Texans. Although he occasionally supported overtures against Mexican American discrimination, such as approving the legislature's "Caucasian Race Resolution," which proclaimed that "all persons of the Caucasian Race" (including presumably persons of Hispanic descent) were entitled to equal access to all public places of business and amusement, plus the establishment of a "Good Neighbor Commission" designed to combat discrimination, the motivation behind these gestures lay more in trying to convince the Mexican government to send braceros to Texas than a genuine concern to combat injustice.

With regard to blacks, the governor showed even less concern. After a Texarkana mob kidnapped Willie Vinson from his hospital bed, dragged him by automobile, and lynched him on July 13, 1942, for allegedly assaulting a white woman, Stevenson replied to a letter sent by U.S. Attorney General Francis Biddle with a rather callous tone, adding that "certain members of the Negro race from time to time furnish the setting for mob violence by the outrageous crimes which they commit." He also added another outrageous assertion that even a white person would have been lynched for committing the same offense.

Stevenson displayed further indifference when Beaumont erupted in racial violence. Since 1940, the city had experienced rapid, unplanned growth as it filled with white and black workers arriving to labor in the city's shipyards and refineries. Housing and transportation shortages contributed to a situation that challenged the ability of local authorities to maintain segregated facilities. Incidents of racial discord culminated on June 15, 1943 with an allegation by a white woman (later proven to be false) that she had been raped by a black man. Upon hearing the news, two thousand white shipyard workers walked off the job, entered black neighborhoods, and began randomly assaulting its residents. Ultimately, three African Americans died and more than fifty were injured before the mob's fury subsided. As Beaumont joined other American cities experiencing race riots during the summer of 1943 (along with Baltimore, Detroit, Indianapolis, Los Angeles, Mobile, New York, Philadelphia, St. Louis, and Washington, D.C.), the governor received word of the violence while traveling to the nation's capital; yet, he chose not to return to Texas.

During the 1944 presidential election, disfavor with Roosevelt among many wealthy Texas business interests led them to create a movement to challenge the president's bid for an unprecedented fourth term. While much of their discontent revolved around the government's wartime restrictions on gas and oil prices and the New Deal's pro-labor stance, another source of resentment originated with outrage over the Supreme Court's ruling in the *Smith v. Allwright* case against the constitutionality of Texas's law permitting white-only primary elections. Unable to control the Texas Democratic Party's presidential electors, this conservative faction began to call itself the "Texas Regulars" and evolved into a third-party effort to divert enough votes away from Roosevelt to allow his Republican challenger, Thomas Dewey, to receive Texas's electoral votes. The Regulars received financial support from Texas oil men and political assistance from anti-New Deal politicians such as Pappy O'Daniel and Congressman Martin Dies. With rhetoric harkening back to another effort by wealthy anti-New Deal Democrats—the "Jeffersonian Democrats" of the 1936 election—the Regulars ran a well-financed anti-union, anti-New Deal, white supremacist campaign but ultimately failed to defeat Roosevelt, who received 72 percent of the vote in Texas. Although having no official candidate, the Regulars received 12 percent of the vote in Texas. Nevertheless, the emergence of the Regulars foretold the future divisions for Texas Democrats in the postwar years.

**The "Greatest Generation" Returns Home**

When World War II veterans returned home to Texas, they could not help but notice that the Lone Star State had begun to change. A majority of Texans now lived and worked in cities. Industries launched during the war remained and were thriving. Agriculture continued to be important to the state, but Texas was increasingly becoming progressively mechanized and diversified. Attitudes toward women were slowly changing due to their wartime contributions. Blacks and Tejanos started to assert their rights, claiming that their patriotism and support for the war effort warranted the granting of basic civil rights. The dominance of the Democratic Party in Texas looked more tentative as conservative elements began to challenge the national organization's policies. Many conservatives began to display a willingness to leave the party over key differences on economic and racial issues. While some years would transpire before these changes were completely realized, the Second World War contributed greatly to the transformations leading to the creation of modern Texas.

*Afterward: Liberation*

*As the war drew to a close, Frank Fujita greatly feared that he and the other prisoners would be executed and began making preliminary plans to escape. A lack of opportunity to flee and the war's abrupt end negated such thoughts. Instead, Fujita and the other prisoners' morale soared as American planes identified their camp and dropped packages of food and medical supplies. The next day, U.S. Navy ships were spotted in Tokyo Bay with small boats heading for the prison camp located along the coast. Though physically weakened from years of mistreatment and malnourishment (his pre-war frame of 145 pounds had been reduced to 90 pounds), Fujita was so elated at the sight of American ships that he joined other POWs who foolishly jumped into the bay to swim out to the incoming boats, almost drowning in the process before being plucked out of the water by the shocked sailors.*

*After the war, Fujita's secret war diary served as evidence in various war crimes trials before being returned. Though partially disabled due to his wartime treatment, Fujita eventually used his artistic talents to work as an illustrator for the Air Force. Before his death in 1996, Fujita published his memoirs based on his diary, which include many drawings and intricate maps he created to powerfully relay to his readers many important aspects of his brutal incarceration.*

# Myth & Legend

### Texan Doris Miller Shot Down Numerous Japanese Planes During the Pearl Harbor Raid

*Mess Attendant Third Class Doris Miller inadvertently joined the pantheon of legendary Texas military figures when, despite lacking formal gunnery training because he was an African American, he manned a deck gun aboard the battleship **West Virginia** during the Japanese attack on Pearl Harbor and began firing away. Soon, lore replaced reality, and many believed the story that Miller shot down a large number of enemy planes that morning.*

*The actual number of planes that Miller destroyed is a matter of conjecture. The confusion surrounding the facts of the incident began ten days after the government ended a news blackout in Hawaii. During an inspection tour of the crippled base, Secretary of the Navy Frank Knox attempted to lift national morale by making a vague reference to a report he received stating that a seaman aboard one of the battleships docked at Pearl Harbor single-handedly blasted a Japanese torpedo plane out of the sky. Another anonymous source later disclosed that an unidentified black mess attendant courageously tried to fight off the attacking planes with a deck gun despite lacking any previous experience with the weapon.*

*Lobbying by the National Association for the Advancement of Colored People, the black press, and some members of Congress eventually led the Navy to reveal Miller's identity. An intense campaign commenced to secure him the Congressional Medal of Honor for his heroics. During this time, Miller's legendary status grew as some newspapers and magazines began reporting for the first time that he had shot down multiple Japanese planes, perhaps as many as six. (The political pressure ultimately resulted in Miller becoming the first black recipient of the Navy Cross followed by a promotion to Mess Attendant First Class). Over the years, misinformed people have inadvertently kept the story alive that Miller downed multiple aircraft during the raid. In fact, even some authors of high school and college textbooks perpetuated the version that elevated the number of planes Miller may have actually hit with the deck gun.*

*The consensus opinion of most historians based on evaluation of the available evidence is that Doris Miller could have contributed to the destruction of as many as four enemy aircraft, probably hit no more than one plane, and quite possibly did not hit a single plane at all. Miller himself believed that he might have hit one of the planes. "It wasn't hard," he later declared. "I just pulled the trigger and she worked fine. I had watched the others with these guns. I guess I fired her for about fifteen minutes. I think I got one of those Jap planes. They were diving pretty close to us." Eyewitness testimony ranges from those who thought that Miller's gun hit many enemy aircraft to those who claim that he did not hit anything. Miller's Navy Cross citation states that he was receiving the medal for his brave actions under enemy fire (including helping to move his mortally wounded captain to a position of greater safety) but does not mention a confirmed "kill."*

*Ultimately, most historians concur that it does not really matter how many enemy planes, if any, Miller may have struck down. The seaman acted above and beyond the call of duty during the attack, not only with his efforts to aid his mortally wounded captain and other injured personnel, but especially with his truly heroic mounting of the deck gun under enemy fire despite being denied gunnery training. There is simply no question that Miller earned his medal for his brave actions that morning—whether he shot down one enemy plane or one hundred.*

## Suggestions for Further Reading

Alexander, Thomas E. *The Wings of Change: The Army Air Experience during World War II* Abilene: McWhiney Foundation Press, 2003.

Burran, James A. "Violence in an `Arsenal of Democracy'," *East Texas Historical Journal* 14 Spring 1976.

Cutrer, Thomas W. and T. Michael Parrish, *Doris Miller, Pearl Harbor, and the Birth of the Civil Rights Movement* College Station: Texas A&M University Press, 2017.

Fujita, Frank, Foo: *A Japanese-American Prisoner of the Rising Sun: The Secret Prison Diary of Frank "Foo" Fujita* Denton: University of North Texas, 1993.

Graham, Don. *No Name on the Bullet: A Biography of Audie Murphy* New York: Viking Penguin, 1989.

Green, George N. *The Establishment in Texas Politics: The Primitive Years, 1938-1957* Westport, Conn.: Greenwood, 1979.

Hatfield, Thomas M., *Rudder: From Leader to Legend* College Station: Texas A&M University Press, 2014.

Hine, Darlene Clark. *Black Victory: The Rise and Fall of the White Primary in Texas* Columbia: University of Missouri Press, 2003.

Krammer, Arnold P. "When the Afrika Korps Came to Texas," *Southwestern Historical Quarterly* 80 January 1977.

Lee, James Ward, ed. *1941: Texas Goes to War* Denton: University of North Texas Press, 1991.

Noggle, Anne. *For God, Country, and the Thrill of It: Women Airforce Service Pilots in World War II* College Station: Texas A&M University Press, 1990.

Olson, James S. and Sharon Phair. "Anatomy of a Race Riot: Beaumont, Texas, 1943," *Texana* 11 1973.

Pollard, Clarice. "WAACs in Texas during World War II," *Southwestern Historical Quarterly* 93 July 1989.

Thonhoff, Robert H. *Camp Kenedy, Texas* Waco: Eakin Press, 2003.

Wagner, Robert L. *The Texas Army: A History of the 36th Division in the Italian Campaign* Austin: State House Press, 1972.

Waters, Michael R. *Lone Star Stalag: German Prisoners of War at Camp Hearne* College Station: Texas A&M University Press, 2006.

Wiggins, Melanie. *Torpedoes in the Gulf: Galveston and the U-Boats, 1942-1943* College Station: Texas A&M University Press, 1995.

**IDENTIFICATION:** Briefly describe each term.

Texas training installations
Doris Miller
Samuel Dealey
Chester Nimitz
James Earl Rudder
Macario García
Audie Murphy
Oveta Culp Hobby
Civil Air Patrol
Women Airforce Service Pilots (WASPs)
wartime industries
Big Inch and Little Big Inch
female workers
Coke Stevenson
*Smith v. Allwright*


**MULTIPLE CHOICE:** Choose the correct response.

1. Soon after the Pearl Harbor attack, _____.
   A. the U.S. provided Lend-Lease aid to England;
   B. Germany and Italy declared war on the United States;
   C. Russia declared war on Japan;
   D. none of the above.

2. Women Airforce Service Pilots, or WASPs,_____
   A. proved to be the most capable American combat pilots of the war;
   B. were led by Oveta Culp Hobby;
   C. served as bomber pilots but were not allowed to provide fighter escort during the war;
   D. served as support pilots training male pilots, towing military targets, and ferrying aircraft.

3. Besides Doris Miller, _____ was the other African American from Texas who earned the Navy Cross during World War II.
   A. Samuel Dealey;
   B. James Brock;
   C. Leonard Roy Harmon;
   D. Franklin Jones;
   E. none of the above.

4. _____ commanded the U.S. Pacific fleet after the Pearl Harbor attack.
   A. Chester Nimitz;
   B. Dwight Eisenhower;
   C. Douglas MacArthur;
   D. Samuel Dealey;
   E. none of the above.

5. Though also on border patrol duty, the Civil Air Patrol monitored _____ during the war.
   A. Dust Bowl;
   B. the Gulf Coast;
   C. state parks;
   D. none of the above.

6. German prisoners of war held in Texas _____.
   A. never tried to escape;
   B. were outnumbered by Japanese and Italian prisoners held in Texas;
   C. sometimes were put to work in Texas agricultural fields;
   D. often rioted, leading to frequent scenes of violence in the POW camps.

7. Which of the following industries did not thrive in Texas during World War II?
   A. aircraft;
   B. synthetic rubber;
   C. shipbuilding;
   D. petroleum;
   E. automobile.

8. _____ was the scene of a violent race riot in 1943.
   A. Waco;
   B. Beaumont;
   C. Houston;
   D. Corpus Christi;
   E. Arlington.

9. Which best describes Governor Coke Stevenson's attitude toward blacks?
   A. much sympathy and compassion;
   B. extreme hatred bordering on fanaticism;
   C. indifference;
   D. passing interest.

10. The _____ challenged Franklin Roosevelt during the 1944 presidential election.
    A. Dixiecrats;
    B. Libertarians;
    C. Federalists;
    D. Texas Regulars;
    E. none of the above.

**TRUE/FALSE:** Indicate whether each statement is true or false.

1. The Japanese attacked Pearl Harbor because their leaders believed an American attack on Japan was imminent.

2. The WASPs were the most decorated American combat pilots of World War II.

3. Most Texans evaded the nation's rationing laws during World War II.

4. Most Texans refused to take part in war bond drives, arguing that taxpayer money should have been enough to finance the war effort.

5. The Supreme Court's decision in the *Smith v. Allwright* case resulted in the end of the white primary in Texas.

6. Black Texans were denied the opportunity to work in Texas factories during WW II.

7. Though cotton prices rose greatly, Texas agriculture became more diversified during the war as many farmers diverted land to raising cattle and other crops.

8. Coke Stevenson served as governor of Texas during World War II.

9. The Mexican government did not allow braceros to enter Texas during WW II.

10. Pappy O'Daniel defeated ex-governor James Allred in his 1942 bid to serve a full term in the U.S. Senate.


**MATCHING:** Match the response in column A with the item in column B.

1. aircraft
2. Bracero program
3. victory gardens
4. The Big Inch
5. INS internment camps
6. Oveta Culp Hobby
7. Doris Miller
8. James Earl Rudder
9. Macario García
10. Samuel Dealey

A. built in large numbers in North Texas during the war
B. transported a tremendous amount of oil to the East Coast
C. held citizens of Germany, Italy, and Japan during the war
D. many Texans produced these at home during the war
E. not utilized in Texas during the war
F. decorated submarine commander
G. won the Navy Cross for his actions at Pearl Harbor
H. commanded Rangers during D-Day
I. awarded Medal of Honor
J. led the WACS

**ESSAY QUESTIONS:**

1. Describe the main types of military installations that existed in Texas and how they served the war effort.

2. How did Texas civilians who remained at home support the war effort?

3. Elaborate on the record of several noteworthy Texans in uniform during World War II.

4. Describe the transforming effects of World War II upon Texas.

# Chapter 16

# *On the Threshold of Modernization, 1945-1959*

**Prelude: The Texas City Disaster**

*In the years following World War II, the Lone Star State continued the trend toward a more urban industrial economy, connected like never before to global markets. With the rapid rise of industry and foreign commerce, however, came the increased danger of deadly and expensive industrial accidents. On April 16, 1947, explosions aboard two docked cargo ships completely destroyed the waterfront of Texas City, the state's most important port, located on the west side of Galveston Bay about 10 miles north of Galveston Island. The blasts decimated adjacent warehouses, oil storage tanks, a Monsanto chemical plant, and significantly damaged nine in ten homes in the nearby town. Killing close to 600 people and injuring thousands more, the Texas City Disaster became the worst industrial disaster in American history.*

*The immediate cause of the disaster proved to be a small fire (probably caused by a carelessly discarded cigarette) that broke out aboard the* **Grandcamp**, *a former American cargo ship given to the French after the war. The variety of agricultural and manufactured items on board the vessel bound for war-ravaged Europe included peanuts, cotton, twine, tobacco, small arms ammunition, and, most hazardous of all, 2,300 tons of ammonium nitrate fertilizer deposited in 100-pound bags. Longshoremen noticed the fire just before 8 a.m. and firefighters combated the blaze for over an hour as a crowd of several hundred onlookers, attracted by the smoke and the sound of the alarms, appeared to watch the event unfold from the nearby wharf. Nobody seemed to understand the extreme combustibility of the fertilizer—some dock workers who survived the disaster testified they believed the bags of fertilizer to be no more dangerous than bags of cement or flour.*

*At 9:12 a.m., the* **Grandcamp** *erupted in a cataclysmic explosion. Over a hundred bystanders, firefighters, and crew members still on board were instantly vaporized. (One man standing 100 feet from the stern of the vessel, however, miraculously survived. Upon regaining consciousness, he found himself nearly naked in a hole filled with four feet of oily water — one mile away from the explosion.) The force of the blast was so powerful that it completely destroyed a nearby Monsanto chemical plant (killing 150 of the 450 workers present that morning) and contained enough force to knock down some people walking on the streets of downtown Galveston and shatter windows in Houston forty miles away. Two sightseeing* airplanes flying over the gulf had their wings clipped by the ship's debris, forcing both to crash. Pieces of the **Grandcamp** as heavy as two tons fell like meteors on the adjacent oil refineries and residential areas of Texas City (the vessel's 1.5-ton anchor landed over two miles away). Lighter shrapnel from the ship and the burning cargo continued to rain down upon the town for several minutes, killing and maiming residents, setting buildings ablaze, and igniting numerous oil storage tanks.

As locals frantically scampered to deal with the immediate impact of the **Grandcamp** detonation, the **High Flyer**—another cargo ship with a large cache of fertilizer in its cargo holds—escaped immediate notice. The vessel had come loose from its mooring, became tangled with another vessel at the docks, and soon experienced fires onboard. About ten minutes after 1 a.m. on April 17, the **High Flyer** exploded with an intensity eyewitnesses to both blasts said was even more powerful than that of the **Grandkamp**. Casualties were lighter than the first eruption because the docks had been evacuated, but the explosion greatly added to the area's property damage and recovery efforts. Several days transpired before the thick clouds of dark acrid smoke subsided as weary firefighters finally extinguished the blazes, or they burned themselves out. While the exact number of casualties will never be known, the Red Cross finally counted 405 identified bodies, 63 unidentified dead, and another 113 residents who simply disappeared, bringing the minimum death toll to 581, with over 3,500 individuals physically injured.

Efforts to aid the survivors took many forms. Without the equivalent of today's Federal Emergency Management Agency (FEMA) to rush needed supplies and economic assistance to the devastated area, Texas City residents relied on a decentralized network of charities, company sponsorships, churches, volunteer agencies, and local and state government grants to slowly rebuild. A class-action lawsuit in federal court brought on behalf of over 8,000 plaintiffs won a decision in district court against the federal government, finding fault on 80 different points including negligent oversight, but a federal appeals court and later the U.S. Supreme Court dismissed the case in 1953. Eventually, the U.S. Congress appropriated $17 million to partially compensate 1,400 victims' claims.

During the first two decades after World War II, Texas experienced profound economic, social, and political changes. In becoming more urban and industrial, the state continued the wartime trend away from its traditional rural and agricultural base. Although resisted by a majority of the state's white citizens, life became more inclusive as Tejanos and blacks began to assert their rights. The Democratic Party's dominance of the state's political system began to show the early signs of evolution into a two-party system. These changes were not fully in place by the start of the 1960s, but signs of how Texas would be during the early twenty-first century were clearly underway. Texas life in 1960 already looked very different from the world of 1940.

**Postwar Manufacturing**

The Texas economy avoided a drift back into depression after World War II. In fact, the Lone Star State joined much of the nation in the enjoyment of a prolonged economic boom during the immediate postwar decades. Increased manufacturing from traditional Texas industries as well as new arrivals helped to fuel this unprecedented economic expansion. By 1955, more than a half million Texans labored for manufacturing companies, ranking the state twelfth nationally in industrial employment.

Oil refining and the petrochemical industry continued to lead the state. Texas producers benefited immensely from the country's skyrocketing need for oil after the war (the U.S. became a net importer of oil by 1948). The industry expanded to meet this increased demand, in part by drilling new wells in the coastal waters of the Gulf of Mexico. Meanwhile, by the mid-1960s, more than 200 Texas plants (largely concentrated along the Gulf Coast) supplied a majority of the nation's major petrochemicals such as ethylene, propylene, butadiene, and benzene for American plastic, rubber, and synthetic fiber companies. From 1950 to the early 1970s, production of petroleum-derived synthetic rubber at Texas Gulf Coast plants (plus a Phillips Petroleum plant at Borger in the Panhandle) increased from half of the nation's total to 80 percent. The expansion not only provided oil, natural gas, and petrochemical corporations with immense profits but also employed over 125,000 Texans by the end of the 1960s.

Despite an inevitable temporary decline soon after the war as factories converted to peacetime demand levels, the aeronautics industry established a permanent presence in North Texas by the 1950s. In 1949, Chance Vought Aircraft took over Grand Prairie's North American plant to produce jet aircraft, specializing in U.S. Navy fighters. The Bell Aircraft Corporation in 1950 established the world's first plant dedicated solely to helicopter production on a site in Hurst and Euless, outside of Fort Worth. In 1954, General Dynamics Corporation purchased Fort Worth's massive Consolidated Vultee plant whose 20,000 workers continued to produce aircraft for the U.S. military. By the 1960s, Texas aircraft companies employed 60,000 workers at 60 plants, ranking the state second in aircraft production behind only California.

The aerospace industry, which had arrived in Texas during World War II when the U.S. Army established an Air Defense Center at Fort Bliss near El Paso to test and develop military rockets, expanded greatly during the 1950s. Because of the Cold War, the federal government provided millions of dollars in defense contracts to companies such as General Dynamics and Boeing to undertake ballistics research at many Texas facilities. In 1961, Texas became a major player in space exploration when the National Aeronautics and Space Administration (NASA) located its Manned Spacecraft Center (now Lyndon B. Johnson Space Center) in Houston. This decision not only made Texas's largest city home to NASA's command post for the effort to send men to the moon by the end of 1960, it also solidified the public's connection of the Lone Star State with the national space program.

The electronics industry witnessed tremendous growth in Texas during the 1950s. Small firms and large corporations began to produce a startling array of items from consumer products, such as phonographs, radios, and televisions, to electronic navigation, guidance, radar, and communication equipment for the military. During the mid-1950s, Houston headquartered most of Texas's electronics firms, but the Dallas-Fort Worth area also became a major player, led by Texas Instruments (TI). TI began in 1930 as Geophysical Service, Incorporated (GSI) by John Karcher and Eugene McDermott, two physicists who had previously applied electronic seismology techniques to aid in oil exploration. (GSI modified this technology to produce submarine-detection equipment for the Navy during the war.) The company changed its name to Texas Instruments in 1951 and became the first company to develop a means to mass-produce the recently invented transistor. While the company dominated transistor sales, a TI development team in 1954 produced the first portable transistor radio. In 1958, TI engineer Jack Kilby invented the world's first integrated circuit, a device which soon revolutionized the new computer industry. TI continued to lead the electronics industry into the 1960s, developing the first computer microprocessor and the first portable hand-held calculator by the end of the decade.

Food processing, the third-largest industry, rose to greater importance in the postwar years, as did the wholesale and retail trade and financial services, which employed a third of the work force. Two industries that did not exist in Texas before 1945—automobile assembly and leisure boat manufacturing—ranked third statewide in number of employees.

Begun during the war years, rapid industrialization led to increased recruitment efforts in Texas by national labor unions. By 1946, 350,000 Texans held union membership, about three-quarters in unions affiliated with the American Federation of Labor (AFL) and the Congress of Industrial Organizations (CIO), which eventually merged in 1957. Union membership increased over the next decade, largely the result of rapid economic expansion and population growth. Total union membership, however, peaked at 400,000 workers by the end of the 1950s, or only about 17 percent of the state's nonagricultural work force. Despite this low statewide percentage, a majority of large industrial workplaces in Texas contained high union membership. More than 60 percent of manufacturing plants employing more than 250 workers had organized laborers, compared to less than 10 percent of plants with fewer than 250 workers. Union membership tended to be higher in the newer industries such as oil refining and petrochemicals, automobile manufacturing, and communications. The growth of labor unions resulted in massive resistance by management and many Texas politicians alike, with the latter's attempt to make unions and their supposed dominance by corrupt, radical leaders an important political issue during the decade.

## Changes in Agriculture

A new Texas emerged in the countryside after World War II as the trend toward large mechanized units that had begun during the 1930s continued unabated. By 1960, only 10 percent of the state's population farmed the land. The cost to perform farming operations, the continuation of federal government crop-reduction policies, and sweeping technological changes led to a great reduction in the number of Texas farmers, especially those engaged in eastern and central Texas cotton growing. The invention of the mechanical cotton picker during the war years greatly altered cotton farming forever. Not only did this device perform the labor of countless human pickers, it also encouraged the planting of crops on vast stretches of flat terrain. Effective chemical herbicides further replaced the need for human "choppers" who previously used hoes to remove unwanted vegetation throughout the growing season. These developments, coupled with advances in irrigation techniques, encouraged the migration of cotton culture to the Southern High Plains and the Lower Rio Grande Valley. Cotton farming endured there but as large-scale mechanized agribusinesses. With the demise of traditional cotton culture, sharecropping also ended. Already declining since the 1930s, the number of sharecroppers became so insignificant by 1959 that the U.S. Census Bureau did not even bother counting those remaining.

Though the number of Texans involved in agriculture dwindled after the war, the state retained its national importance if one looks at aggregate production figures. In 1960, Texas farmers turned out $2 billion in agricultural revenue, second nationally only to California, while the state led the country in the production of cotton, grain sorghums, rice, cattle, and sheep.

**Postwar Urbanization and Suburbanization**

The population of Texas rose greatly in the decades following World War II. From a total of 6.4 million in 1940, the number of Texans climbed to 7.7 million in 1950, to 9.6 million in 1960, and to 11.2 million by 1970. By the 1960s, Texas became the fourth largest state in the country behind only California, New York, and Pennsylvania. Most of the population increase since 1945 occurred in the cities, a result of increased industrialization and the reduced need for agricultural labor in the countryside. The 1950 census showed that Texans did not return to the farm after the war—for the first time, more Texans lived in urban areas with greater than 2,500 people than resided in rural areas. By 1970, the ten largest Texas cities all contained over 100,000 residents, while over 80 percent of the state's population lived in urban areas.

**TABLE 16.1—Population of Ten Largest Texas Cities: 1940 - 1970**

| City | 1940 | 1950 | 1960 | 1970 |
|---|---|---|---|---|
| Houston | 384,514 | 596,163 | 938,219 | 1,232,802 |
| Dallas | 294,734 | 434,462 | 679,684 | 844,401 |
| San Antonio | 253,854 | 408,442 | 587,718 | 654,153 |
| Fort Worth | 177,662 | 278,778 | 356,268 | 393,476 |
| El Paso | 96,810 | 130,485 | 276,687 | 322,261 |
| Austin | 87,930 | 132,459 | 186,545 | 251,808 |
| Corpus Christi | 57,301 | 108,287 | 167,690 | 204,525 |
| Lubbock | 31,853 | 71,747 | 128,691 | 149,101 |
| Amarillo | 51,686 | 74,443 | 137,969 | 127,010 |
| Beaumont | 59,061 | 94,014 | 119,175 | 115,919 |

SOURCE: U.S. Bureau of the Census

Though more jobs could be found in Texas cities during the 1950s, clear economic disparities existed based on race. In 1960, the median income for white urban families in Texas was $5,693 while the amount for black and Hispanic urban families totaled $2,915 and $1,134, respectively. A majority of blacks and Tejanos continued to perform a disproportionate number of low-paying, unskilled jobs. Compared to African Americans, the situation was slightly better for Hispanics. By 1960, over 30 percent of urban Tejanos performed jobs that could be classified as middle-class occupations, such as professional work, store owners or managers, and skilled craftsmen.

The immediate postwar decades also witnessed continued involvement of women in the workforce despite the mainstream media's campaign to celebrate traditional women's roles as wives and mothers who stayed at home. The percentage of females in the workforce rose from 23 percent in 1940 to 33 percent by 1960. Though Texas women worked more than before the Second World War, most job opportunities during the 1950s involved laboring at familiar tasks. A third of employed Texas women performed clerical work, while women continued to greatly outnumber men as elementary school teachers, librarians, and nurses. Hispanic and black women remained largely relegated to domestic housework and food service jobs. Overall, women still constituted less than 5 percent of the state's doctors, lawyers, and engineers.

In addition to urban growth, suburbs surrounding major Texas metropolitan areas also grew tremendously during the 1950s, largely occupied by white residents. Inexpensive land, availability of federal government loans, increased highway construction, and the strong desire by many whites to offset the effects of federal court rulings on school integration all contributed to middle- and upper-class "white flight" from the core population centers of Texas cities to the suburbs.

Many Texans experienced the well-known aspects of 1950s suburban life that existed elsewhere in the nation. The combination of pent-up demand for new consumer goods plus the desire to spend wartime savings led to the development of a mass postwar consumer culture. Purchases from this generation of Americans who were forced to "do without" during the Great Depression and World War II fueled the economy. Televisions began to be mass-purchased for the first time (by 1960, 81 percent of Texas households owned one). A host of new electronic devices, such as TI's portable radios, flew off merchants' shelves. As elsewhere in the nation, new models of automobiles sold briskly and greatly impacted Texas culture including the arrival of drive-in restaurants, drive-in theaters, shopping centers, and other novel ways designed to cater to patrons seeking goods and services without leaving the comfort of their cars.

The postwar "Baby Boom" greatly aided state and national economic expansion. After the war, Texas joined the rest of the United States in making children like never before. Though more babies were born into non-marital relationships during the 1940s and 1950s than commonly assumed, a majority of the record number of children entered the world as products of the unprecedented number of marriages during the 1940s and 1950s. (The divorce rate in Texas, however, was also high at 16 percent.) The Baby Boom stimulated the economy by creating a large demand for many goods and services. The huge need for more family-sized homes, for example, aided home builders and lawnmower salesmen alike. The great demand for health-care facilities and medical services provided jobs for hospital staff, pediatricians, and nurses. The arrival of large numbers of babies and toddlers led to extensive employment opportunities in education, providing a vast amount of jobs for school builders, teachers, administrative personnel, librarians, and janitors.

By the late-1950s, as American children of the Baby Boom generation began entering their teenage years, rock and roll music splashed on the social scene. Rock and roll artists and producers catered the new sound to the large numbers of youth. Energetic and danceable with relatable lyrics for teenagers, rock and roll became a multi-million dollar business as well as a cultural phenomenon. Texas not only experienced the new music revolution; it took an active part in its promotion and development. Rock and roll music was not technically "new"—it was actually a fresh combination of older musical styles, especially western swing and African-American rhythm and blues. Among the pioneers of western swing music, Bob Wills (an original member of Pappy O'Daniel's Light Crust Doughboys) and his Texas Playboys were hugely popular during the 1930s and 1940s and influenced many future rock and roll musicians. From the blues genre, Texan Aaron Thibeaux "T-Bone" Walker (a protégé of Blind Lemon Jefferson and Huddie "Leadbelly" Ledbetter) had a strong influence on the first generation of rock artists, from his playing style to his much-copied wild performances. The music community has acknowledged the contribution of these two Texas legends by enshrining them as members of the Rock and Roll Hall of Fame.

Roy Orbison was an early Texas rock legend who contributed directly to the rising popularity of rock and roll during the 1950s. Orbison grew up in Wink, a small West Texas oil town, where he sang and played guitar in a high school western band. He formed his first rock band during a brief stint at North Texas State College in Denton. After dropping out of school, Orbison toured West Texas where he came to the attention of the Sun Record label in Memphis, Tennessee. In 1956, he recorded his first chart hit, "Ooby Dooby." From that point, much of his future success came as a songwriter rather than a performer (despite all his talent, he simply did not have the attraction of Elvis Presley's looks and swagger), including such rock classics as "Only the Lonely," "Blue Bayou," and "Oh, Pretty Woman." In 1988, Orbison enjoyed renewed popularity when he released the album "The Traveling Wilburys, Volume One," a collaboration featuring Orbison and his friends Bob Dylan, George Harrison of the Beatles, Tom Petty, and Jeff Lynne of the Electric Light Orchestra. Many of the album's songs became hits, and Orbison became briefly known to a new generation of listeners. The album was on Billboard Magazine's Top Ten list in December 1988 when he died from a heart attack. Just the year before, he had been inducted into the Rock and Roll Hall of Fame.

Texas's greatest contribution to early rock and roll was Charles Hardin Holley (Buddy Holly) from Lubbock. Like Orbison, Holly was strongly influenced by the western swing sound of Bob Wills and began playing country music at a young age. Holly also listened to T-Bone Walker and other African-American blues artists, who had a strong impact on his own original music. (When many of Holly's first songs received radio play, many actually assumed that he and his band, "The Crickets," were black.) In 1957, Holly began a meteoric rise to fame as he (with or without The Crickets) produced a stream of hits, such as "That'll Be the Day," "Peggy Sue," "Oh Boy!," "Maybe Baby," "It's So Easy," and "Rave On." We will never know the full extent of Holly's potential. On the morning of February 3, 1959, while on a Midwestern tour, Holly's charter plane crashed in an Iowa cornfield killing all on board, including rising stars J. P. (the Big Bopper) Richardson and Richie Valenzuela (Valens). Though he was only 22 at the time of his death, his music and influence on future musicians have lived on. In 1986, Holly became a charter member of the Rock and Roll Hall of Fame, along with such legends as Elvis Presley and Chuck Berry.

**Tejano Civil Rights Activism during the 1950s**

In addition to economic and cultural changes, the civil rights movement proved to be one of the most important social developments to occur in America and in Texas during

**LULAC meeting at Aztec No. 3 club on Main Street, Victoria, Texas 1940s.
Source: Tensy Quinbar, San Antonio, Texas Credit: Institute of Texan Cultures**

the postwar decades. Through legal action and grass-roots protest, Tejanos and Texas blacks (aided by many sympathetic white Texans) demanded an end to segregation and disfranchisement.

Two well-publicized events involving Hispanic veterans fueled Tejano activism in the immediate postwar years. First, in September 1945, authorities in Richmond (located a few miles southwest of Houston) arrested Congressional Medal of Honor recipient Macario García for fighting with a restaurant owner who denied the ex-soldier service because he was Hispanic. The League of United Latin American Citizens (LULAC) and other groups raised money for his defense and did much to publicize the trial. (A jury eventually acquitted García.) The second incident involved the January 1949 decision by a funeral home director in Three Rivers (located half-way between San Antonio and Corpus Christi) to refuse use of his chapel for a wake in honor of Felix Longoria, a local Tejano killed in the Philippines during the war whose body had been returned home for reburial in the local cemetery. Longoria's widow, Beatrice, discussed the matter with Hector García, founder of a newly-formed Mexican American civil rights organization—the American G.I. Forum. García and the Forum organized a protest to publicize this dishonor—the denial of the use of a chapel—to the memory of a Bronze Star recipient, which soon generated outrage and caught the attention of Texas Senator Lyndon B. Johnson. The senator offered his support and arranged for Longoria to be interred with full honors at Arlington National Cemetery. Both incidents galvanized the Tejano community and led many to agitate for an end to discrimination.

LULAC and the G.I. Forum emerged as important civil rights groups leading the fight for equal treatment, beginning with efforts to end de facto segregation for Hispanics in Texas public schools. By custom, rather than by legal means, school districts either

Dr. Hector P. García founder of the American G.I. Forum.
Credit: Institute of Texan Cultures

placed Tejanos in separate, inferior "Mexican schools" or (in cases where the Hispanic population was low) into separate classes within predominately white schools. In 1948, LULAC challenged this arrangement in federal district court on behalf of Minerva Delgado and other Hispanic parents in Bastrop. In *Delgado v. Bastrop ISD*, LULAC attorney Gus García successfully argued that segregation of Tejanos (who were commonly considered a distinct class of white people in Texas) was unconstitutional because no specific law

Leaders of the Latino civil rights struggle gather outside the Casa Blanca restaurant in San Antonio, Texas, during a celebration of victory in the landmark 1948 *Delgado v. Bastrop ISD* decision that outlawed segregation against Latino students. Pictured, from left to right: Dr. Arthur Campa, a University of Denver professor; Dr. George I. Sanchez, a professor at the University of Texas at Austin; Joe Castanuela, president of a local LULAC chapter; and Ramon Galindo, president of local Mexican-American Chamber of Commerce.
Credit: Institute of Texan Cultures

existed to justify the separation. During the fifties, LULAC and G.I. Forum lawyers filed fifteen desegregation cases to thwart efforts of local districts to hinder and delay enforcement of the *Delgado* decision.

Another legal challenge in the 1950s directly confronted the injustice of jury discrimination in Texas. In 1950, Gus García agreed to defend migrant cotton picker Pete Hernández, who was accused of murdering another Tejano in Edna, a small Jackson County town near Victoria. If the jury convicted Hernandez, García planned to appeal the case to the U.S. Supreme Court on the grounds of jury discrimination. (No Tejanos served on the jury, nor had any person of Hispanic ethnicity served on a Jackson County jury for at least twenty-five years—a practice common in many other Texas counties.) After the jury convicted Hernandez and the Texas Court of Criminal Appeals upheld the conviction, García filed his grievance. In 1954, García and other prominent Tejano attorneys for the American G.I. Forum and LULAC argued before the United States Supreme Court in the case of *Hernandez v. State of Texas* that Texas denied Hernandez his constitutional rights under the Fourteenth Amendment, claiming that the amendment guaranteed protection not only on the basis of race, but also of class. The Court unanimously agreed and overturned Hernandez's conviction, stating that he had "the right to be indicted and tried by juries from which all members of his class are not systematically excluded." The ruling meant that Mexican-American citizens could not be excluded as jurors simply because of their Hispanic heritage. For Tejano activists, once again the legal strategy of challenging Mexican-American discrimination on the basis of the improper treatment of a group within the white population and the absence of statutory foundation proved fruitful.

Tejano political involvement increased dramatically during the 1950s. Prior to the 1950s, levels of Mexican-American participation in politics varied. Tejanos voted in predominately Hispanic rural counties of South Texas but usually for candidates approved by the local political machines (reminiscent of the manner in which similar organizations functioned in northern industrial cities). In return, the machine paid the impoverished voters' poll taxes and provided sorely needed social services. Outside of South Texas, however, Hispanics often had been excluded from voting by poll taxes and the white primary. Tejano political activism greatly increased after the Supreme Court's 1944 *Smith v. Allwright* decision ended the white primary. LULAC, the G.I. Forum, and other reform groups began to pressure for change through such tactics as poll tax drives, voter education, and registration projects. During the 1950s, these efforts, especially in cities with large numbers of Hispanic residents, produced much success. Wishing to promote the image of their cities as inclusive and to create a favorable climate for business expansion, white leaders in San Antonio and El Paso began to include Tejanos in local governance. In 1953, Henry B. Gonzalez became the first Hispanic elected to the San Antonio City Council. Three years later, he became the first Tejano elected to the Texas State Senate in over 100 years. In 1961, Gonzalez made history again when he became the first Mexican American from Texas to be elected to the U.S. House of Representatives, representing a district including San Antonio. Meanwhile, in 1957, voters elected Raymond L. Telles to his first of two terms as El Paso's first Mexican-American mayor.

Representative Henry B. Gonzalez, Austin, Texas, 1850s

## African American Civil Rights Activism during the 1950s

The 1940s and 1950s witnessed parallel efforts to promote civil rights by black Texans who experienced even harsher discrimination than Tejanos. Led by the national NAACP and their local chapters, African-American Texans mobilized for an end to segregation, unequal economic opportunities, and disfranchisement. Though much still needed to be accomplished by the end of the 1950s, some important achievements were made in the efforts to end segregated public schools and to provide access to higher education.

Soon after World War II concluded, the Texas NAACP launched efforts to chip away at segregation in higher education. In 1946, at the urging of Lulu White (the head of the Houston Branch of the NAACP—the South's largest chapter) Heman Sweatt volunteered to be the plaintiff in a NAACP lawsuit seeking his admission to the segregated University of Texas Law School. Though he had received a biology degree from Wiley College in Marshall, Sweatt had been forced by limited opportunities to take a job at a U.S. Post Office in Houston. While attending Wiley, however, he had become inspired by one of his teachers, acclaimed poet Melvin B. Tolson (known to many Americans today by Denzel Washington's portrayal of the professor in the 2007 movie *The Great Debaters*), and his orations against racial discrimination. After college, Sweatt became an active member of the Houston NAACP, aiding the group in voter registration drives and fundraising efforts. He was also acquainted with Richard Grovey (his barber) and Lonnie Smith (his dentist), both of whom were plaintiffs in NAACP cases against the white primary.

The entrance to the "Negro Waiting Room" at the Katy Depot in San Antonio, Texas, in 1956.

While helping to prepare documentation in a legal case involving discrimination against blacks in the post office, Sweatt became interested in the law as a means of challenging discrimination. His new desire to seek a law degree in Texas coincided perfectly with the Texas NAACP's desire to challenge the University of Texas's segregated law school. Sweatt met all eligibility requirements for admission except for his race. Upon his being denied admission, the NAACP sued UT President Theophilus S. Painter, citing the fact that Texas did not comply with the section of the state constitution that addressed educational facilities for blacks: "Separate schools shall be provided for the white and colored children, and impartial provision shall be made for both."

After a state district court ruled that Texas had six months to implement a law education program for black Texans equal to the University of Texas, the state hurriedly attempted to create "separate but equal" all-black law schools. The legislature passed bills that established Texas State University for Negroes (later Texas Southern University) in Houston and changed Prairie View's A&M's name to Prairie View University, and both schools were authorized to teach law and other subjects taught at the University of Texas. The state also hastily set up a temporary law school in Austin in the basement of a building in a low-income black neighborhood with access to the UT library and classes taught by some UT faculty.

Though these moves satisfied the state courts, Sweatt refused to attend any of the new inferior schools. Thurgood Marshall and other state and national NAACP lawyers decided to appeal to the United States Supreme Court to challenge the entire system of segregation in higher education. As he sought a favorable verdict, Sweatt endured threats against himself and his wife, the vandalization of his home, and painful ulcer attacks but was also heartened by the support that he received from many students who founded the nation's largest all-white chapter of the NAACP on the University of Texas campus. In the 1950 *Sweatt v. Painter* case, the Supreme Court unanimously ruled that Texas's late attempts at accommodation failed to provide Sweatt with a legal education comparable in quality to that received by white students at the University of Texas and, therefore, ordered him to be admitted. The decision not only opened the door for blacks to attend the University of Texas Law School but also UT's medical and dental schools, and all graduate programs not existing at other black colleges in Texas. Sweatt registered for classes at UT Law School in September 1950, but the whole affair took its toll as he suffered from emotional and physical problems that contributed to poor academic performance and eventual divorce from his wife. By the summer of 1952, Sweatt gave up law school and returned to Houston, though he later attended Atlanta University Graduate School of Social Work, earned a master's degree, remarried, and enjoyed a successful career over the next 25 years working for the NAACP and the National Urban League.

Though segregation in Texas education took a hit with the *Sweatt v. Painter* decision, the ruling only affected postgraduate education in the state's public colleges and universities. More transformative would be the Supreme Court's unanimous determination in favor of the NAACP's arguments in the landmark 1954 *Brown v. Board of Education of Topeka, Kansas* case that segregation at all levels of public education was inherently unequal and, therefore, unconstitutional under the Fourteenth Amendment's equal protection guarantee. However, the end of the state's separate school systems—superior, better-funded schools for whites and inferior schools with lower financial resources for blacks—did not occur instantaneously. First, the Court clarified in a follow-up ruling that desegregation could take place gradually: "with all deliberate speed," as the justices noted. Second, many school district officials in Texas and across the South, often in league with local and state government leaders, began systematic efforts to delay and to stymie the enforcement of the *Brown* decision.

Desegregation in Texas moved quickly in the western and southern portions of the state where the number of black students was low. Close to a hundred local school districts began desegregation procedures soon after the Court's ruling. In the fall of 1954, the small Panhandle town of Friona became the first to comply with the Court's decision by adding five black children to its local elementary school. Larger towns and cities in West and South Texas followed in 1955, including San Angelo, El Paso, and San Antonio.

Desegregation in Central and East Texas where the black population was much larger than the state's western and southern regions occurred at a snail's pace. A contentious showdown over desegregation took place during the fall of 1956 in Mansfield, a small town located less than 20 miles southeast of Fort Worth. At the time, Mansfield ISD had been placing its younger African-American children into an inferior separate elementary school while busing its teenage students to a black high school in Fort Worth. In August, the Texas NAACP successfully received a desegregation order from a federal appeals court (the first involving a Texas school district) allowing three black students to attend Mansfield High School. Angry locals and outsiders protested the ruling by burning crosses in the town's black section and hanging effigies on the campus and in the downtown area.

A mob of several hundred people secured the perimeter of the school to deny entry to the students when they appeared to register for classes. Though Governor Allan Shivers labeled these brazen actions to be an "orderly protest," a desire to remove the appearance of disorder led him to send Texas Rangers to maintain control in the town. While the governor gave orders for the Rangers to disperse disorderly crowds, Shivers also directed them to arrest any black students trying to attend the high school under the pretense of disturbing the peace. This deliberate attempt at "interposition," or intervening with the state government to negate an order of the federal government, succeeded because President Dwight Eisenhower, then running for re-election and unwilling to upset white Texas and southern voters, allowed Shivers's actions to stand. With presidential inaction, the parents of the black teenagers ended their attempt to integrate the high school, wishing to protect their children from further threats and potential violence. Shivers's move also encouraged residents in Little Rock, Arkansas, during the next year, to resist their local school board's efforts to desegregate the city's Central High School. By that time, however, with the election out of the way, President Eisenhower baffled many in Arkansas and much of the South when he decided to do what he had deliberately avoided in Mansfield—sending in hundreds of federal troops to enforce desegregation rulings of the federal courts.

Due to open resistance by Texas politicians and citizens, the pace of desegregation in Texas public schools dragged on for more than two decades after the *Brown* decision. Voters in 1956 approved three pro-segregation referendums, including one that opposed compulsory attendance at integrated public schools. In 1957, the Texas legislature passed a law denying state funding for school districts that integrated without local voter approval and another that allowed school districts to cite transportation problems, lack of adequate space, and other reasons to avoid compliance with federal desegregation orders. Texas's new governor, Price Daniel, reluctantly signed these bills into law but did nothing to enforce them. (All were later thrown out by the federal courts.) Still, by the middle of the next decade, desegregation in Texas, as elsewhere in the South, had moved glacially. By 1964, only 18,000 of Texas's 325,000 African-American students attended integrated schools. The rate of rapid public school desegregation only began to occur in the late-1960s when the provisions of the Civil Rights Act of 1964, which allowed the denial of federal funds to segregated schools, began to be enforced. By 1970, over three-quarters of black students in Texas attended a school that had begun to undertake the desegregation process.

Though the rate of progress proved slow for public schools, desegregation in Texas higher education took place more smoothly. In fact, a couple of Texas two-year institutions, Amarillo College and Del Mar Junior College in Corpus Christi, both voluntarily desegregated even before the *Brown* decision. Though threatening crowds turned away black students at Texarkana Junior College (1955) and attempted to do the same at Lamar State College in Beaumont (1956) while some education officials (such as those at North Texas State College in Denton) refused to integrate until ordered by a federal court, many community colleges, four-year colleges, and universities nevertheless began to desegregate during the mid-1950s. In 1955, Texas Western (now the University of Texas at El Paso) became the first four-year school in Texas to integrate, followed by the University of Texas and Southern Methodist University in 1956. By 1958, close to two-thirds of Texas colleges and universities had integrated their undergraduate classes (though Texas A&M

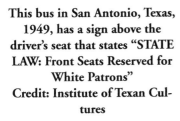
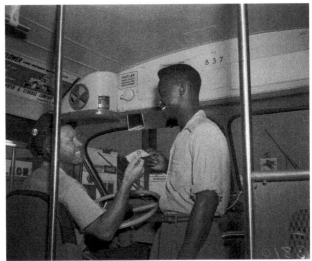

This bus in San Antonio, Texas, 1949, has a sign above the driver's seat that states "STATE LAW: Front Seats Reserved for White Patrons"
Credit: Institute of Texan Cultures

University did not begin the process until 1963 and three East Texas colleges—Sam Houston State College, Stephen F. Austin State College, and East Texas State College—held out until the following year). The acceptance of some black students, however, did not mean that they enjoyed immediate access to dormitories and cafeterias and equality in scholarship opportunities, or that the colleges would hire African-American professors. Additional efforts in subsequent years would be needed to bring about these important changes.

By the end of the 1950s, Texas blacks achieved much progress, but more still needed to be done to secure their basic civil rights. Despite signs of a new tomorrow for African Americans as seen by the steady demise of the Jim Crow system in public education, segregated public facilities and voting barriers continued to exist. Though some organizational efforts by young Texas activists to overturn these injustices occurred during the fifties, the phase of the civil rights movement seeking equal access to all public facilities (especially swimming pools, lunch counters, theaters) and voting rights through grassroots protesting did not begin to receive strong support in many segments of the black community in Texas until the early 1960s.

**Texas Politics during the Beauford Jester Years**

The 1940s and 1950s witnessed an escalation of the ideological divisiveness within the Democratic Party that had started in the 1930s. Competing factions of liberals and conservatives continued to fight for control of their party during the postwar decades, opening the door for Republicans to attract enough disaffected conservative Democrats to begin winning statewide offices and threaten Democratic Party hegemony by the 1970s.

The first signs of the growing rift within the Democratic Party in the immediate postwar years occurred during the 1946 gubernatorial campaign to pick Coke Stevenson's successor. The race drew five candidates for the Democratic Party nomination. Homer Rainey, a former University of Texas president, proved to be the most liberal candidate. He entered the race partially to seek vindication for his removal following a clash with UT's board of regents (who were dominated by right-wing conservatives appointed by Governors O'Daniel and Stevenson) over tenure and academic freedom issues. The professor campaigned on a progressive program based on additional aid for education, health services, and the elderly funded by increased oil and gas industry taxes. Rainey garnered the support of liberals, labor unions, and black voters able to pay their poll taxes (the 1946 election was the first statewide contest since the *Smith v. Allwright* case ended the white primary). He ran against four conservative candidates who concentrated their fire upon him. Rainey's most bombastic opponent, Lieutenant Governor John Lee Smith, had been the early favorite, but Smith's extreme statements against Rainey, blacks, and labor unions alienated too many voters. Conservatives eventually rallied behind Railroad Commissioner Beauford Jester, a former oil company attorney who adopted a much milder campaign approach, making pledges of no additional taxes and firm opposition to labor unions. After the first primary, Jester led with 443,804 votes, but Rainey's 291,282 votes (coupled with votes for the lesser candidates) forced a runoff. Despite Rainey's appeal to voters for a New Deal approach to the state's problems, Jester emerged victorious by a two-to-one margin (701,018 to 355,654) and easily defeated his Republican opponent in the November general election.

Similar to previous governors, Jester opposed new taxes. The expanding postwar economy produced additional tax revenues, allowing him to recommend more government expenditures, including sorely-needed increases in funding for hospitals and orphanages. Among the many issues that the new governor confronted during his first term was the predominant issue of labor unions. During the first two years following World War II, conservatives led a growing national backlash against rising union membership and a wave of strikes by workers desiring additional compensation to help deal with the rising cost of living. Conservatives characterized these actions by organized labor as misguided efforts directed by corrupt, communist-inspired union leaders. At the national level, this feeling was reflected in the passage of the Taft-Hartley Act over President Harry Truman's veto. The law significantly amended the Wagner National Labor Relations Act, which Congress had passed during the Great Depression to empower labor unions and to recognize the right of workers to bargain collectively. The Taft-Hartley Act added a list of prohibited "unfair labor practices," including political strikes and monetary donations by unions to federal political campaigns. The act also required union leaders to sign affidavits stating that they were not Communist Party members, and it further allowed states to pass so-called "right to work" laws forbidding the denial of employment to a worker who refused to join a union.

During Jester's first term, the state legislature deluged him with legislation designed to contain labor unions within the state. The governor obliged by signing a right-to-work statute, another bill placing strong limits on picketing, a prohibition against strikes by public employees, and other restrictive laws. To show his frustration with the radical, anti-union mindset within the legislature, a pro-labor member of the House cynically proposed an amendment to a bill calling for the abolition of all labor unions, the confiscation of union member property, and the execution of all union members in the state by firing squad. (The bill was rejected 63:8.)

Governor Jester was so popular with the voters in 1948 that he sailed through his reelection bid. The presidential race that year proved more interesting because many conservative Texas Democrats opposed Truman's reelection, viewing him as soft on communism, soft on labor unions, and soft on racial issues. Still, only a relatively small number of Texans joined the "Dixiecrat" movement of disgruntled southern segregationists who walked out of the Democratic National Convention to protest the party's acceptance of a civil rights platform and threw their support behind South Carolina Governor J. Strom Thurmond. Truman won Texas with 750,700 votes (65.4 percent) compared to Republican Thomas Dewey's 282,240 and Thurmond's 106,909 (only 9.3 percent).

The real political drama of 1948 played out in the United States Senate race for Pappy O'Daniel's successor. Though George Peddy joined the field, former governor Coke Stevenson and Congressman Lyndon Johnson enjoyed higher levels of support. When Stevenson and Johnson faced each other in a runoff, the stage was set for a battle that further symbolized the growing split within the Texas Democratic Party. While the conservative Stevenson despised the New Deal and strongly supported the maintenance of segregation, the moderate Johnson embraced the New Deal (though he supported the Taft-Hartley Act and pragmatically distanced himself from civil rights issues). Stevenson appeared to be the favorite (he won the primary 477,077 to Johnson's 405,617), but the youthful and energetic Johnson outcampaigned him. While the congressman traveled across the state in a helicopter to draw frequent big crowds, the former governor toured the state in an old Plymouth to meet smaller groups of voters and often took weekends off at his ranch. After voters went to the polls, they were left in a lurch for days, unaware of who would be declared the winner. Four days after the election, Stevenson held a slight advantage of only a few hundred votes (out of a million votes cast), but that lead disappeared when "revised results" began to arrive from a few South Texas counties (whose political bosses had endorsed Johnson). Finally, after a precinct in Jim Wells County reported that a clerical error had been corrected and that Johnson should receive 202 additional votes (with Stevenson receiving two more), the end result, if it stood, would be an 87-vote statewide margin of victory for Johnson. Though there is no doubt that pro-Johnson poll workers jiggled the books in favor of their preferred candidate, there is sufficient evidence to surmise that Stevenson's supporters undertook similar actions in other counties to give their favored candidate an edge. Stevenson's campaign, nevertheless, cried foul and appealed first unsuccessfully to the Democratic Party state convention, and then to the federal courts. Ultimately, the Supreme Court received Stevenson's petition and chose not to intervene in the contest, citing the tradition that such matters were state concerns (a tradition broken with the Court's *Bush v. Gore* decision involving disputed results in Florida during the 2000 presidential election). Thus, Texas election officials placed Johnson's name on the ballot for the general election against his Republican opponent whom he defeated handily.

During Governor Jester's second term, the legislature met for the longest session in its history as it acted on many measures to move Texas toward the modern age. Upon the governor's suggestion, lawmakers passed an anti-lynching bill and a proposed state constitutional amendment to abolish the poll tax, which voters failed to approve. The legislature also secured appropriate funds to modernize prison facilities with new fences, guard towers, and flood lights plus new cell-block construction to alleviate overcrowding. Lawmakers also appropriated funds for the maintenance and expansion of the state highway system, improved supervision of state mental hospitals and schools for handicapped children, and the establishment of Lamar College and the Texas State University for Negroes (now Texas Southern University).

The passage of the Gilmer-Aikin Laws marked the most lasting achievement of the 51st legislature and Governor Jester's second term. This important legislation overhauled the administration and financing of the Texas public school system and remains the basis for the state's public school system today. One law changed the State Board of Education from an appointed to an elected body. Two other laws immediately doubled the state government's appropriations for public schools, mandated that Texas children receive nine months of schooling (for at least twelve years with at least 175 days of instruction), consolidated hundreds of smaller school districts into more efficient units, allocated state money (with amounts dependent upon attendance levels) to supplement local taxes, and provided for teacher certification with increased teacher pay to attract more qualified instructors. Critics have noted inadequacies with the new laws, such as the fact that ordinary Texans disproportionately bore the brunt of the necessary additional funding because increased consumer taxes financed these reforms, plus teachers' salaries remained low compared to the rest of the country. Nevertheless, the Gilmer-Aikin Laws were an important improvement in the movement to modernize Texas public school education.

**Governor Allan Shivers**

On July 11, 1949, Beauford Jester became the only Texas governor to die in office when he succumbed to a heart attack. As a result, forty-one-year-old two-term Lieutenant Governor Allan Shivers succeeded him. Rising from a modest background in East Texas, Shivers attended the University of Texas, intent on eventually becoming a lawyer. Upon graduation and passing the state bar exam, Shivers established a private practice in Port Arthur before deciding to run for the state senate as a Democrat in 1934. Upon his victory, the twenty-seven-year-old attorney became the youngest member ever of the state senate. Marriage to the daughter of a wealthy Rio Grande River family (the Sharys) brought him further prestige and financial security. After serving as a military lawyer during World War II, Shivers sought and won the post of lieutenant governor vacated by John Lee Smith in 1946, when the latter sought the Democratic Party nomination for governor.

Upon Governor Jester's death, Shivers called the legislature into special session to appropriate funds for the increased expenditures required by the programs that the lawmakers had recently approved. Like Jester, the new governor did not oppose new taxes to fund public services as long as additional consumer taxes financed them rather than supplemental taxes on oil and gas companies. The legislature eventually obliged, with much of the new revenue coming from increased cigarette taxes.

After completing Jester's term in 1950, Shivers won a full term in his own right without serious competition. He continued to press the legislature to provide additional funds for roads, eleemosynary institutions, aid to the elderly, and higher teacher salaries, all of which were to be paid by increased consumer taxes. Once again, the legislature acquiesced. Reflecting the growing importance of automobiles in Texas, Shivers signed another act requiring cars to receive safety inspections and their owners to possess liability insurance. Also important, the legislature acknowledged the state's demographic realities by redrawing legislative district boundaries for the first time in thirty years, giving the rapidly growing urban and suburban areas more clout at the expense of the legislature's traditional rural power base.

In 1952, Shivers received tougher competition in the Democratic primary from a rival soon to become the leading Texas liberal of the 1950s and 1960s—Ralph Yarborough.

**Chinese American boys from the Chinese Optimist Club with Texas Governor Allan Shivers, Austin, Texas. c. 1949-1957. Photo credit: UTSA Institute of Texan Cultures**

Hailing from an established East Texas family, Yarborough received a law degree in 1927 from the University of Texas before working in the attorney general's office during the 1930s. He served in the U.S. Army during World War II and saw significant combat action, eventually earning a Bronze Star and Combat Medal in addition to promotion to the rank of lieutenant colonel. In 1946 he returned home to resume practicing law in Austin before seeking the governorship, espousing President Truman's efforts to extend the New Deal in the postwar era. Yarborough received close to a half-million votes in the 1952 race, but the more conservative Shivers avoided a runoff with over 880,000 votes and ran unopposed in the general election. The liberal-conservative split within the Democratic Party was also evident in the 1952 Senate race to replace the retiring Tom Connally when conservative Attorney General Price Daniel, an open critic of the Truman administration, challenged and defeated pro-Truman congressman Lindley Beckworth.

During the 1952 campaign, Governor Shivers made headlines when he openly broke with his national party by refusing to support the Democratic presidential ticket headed by liberal Illinois governor Adlai Stevenson. The reason for the rift was Stevenson's refusal to support Texas's position (argued vociferously in the federal courts by Attorney General Daniel) regarding ownership of the oil-rich coastal lands often incorrectly labeled by many Texans as "the Tidelands" (none of the undersea area was ever exposed by the tide). Daniel asserted that the Republic of Texas had received a guarantee to retain control of coastal waters out to 10.5 miles from shore by the 1845 annexation treaty. Nevertheless, the federal courts agreed with the Truman administration's assertion, as did Adlai Stevenson, that the national government had the paramount right to control offshore lands.

Shivers initially agreed with House Speaker Sam Rayburn's proposed compromise that Texas would not assert claims to the coastal area but the proposal would nevertheless allow the state and the federal government to split royalties (27.5 percent each) from oil leases. Pressure from powerful oil interests (who desired to retain the smaller state royalty of 12.5 percent on oil production) and Attorney General Daniel (who threatened to run against Shivers), however, convinced the governor to oppose anything short of full state retention of the Tidelands. More than simply refusing to support the Democratic presidential nominee, Shivers endorsed Stevenson's rival, Dwight D. Eisenhower, after the popular World War II general promised to sign a bill vacating federal government control over the Tidelands (President Truman by that time had vetoed two similar bills). Though many Texas Democrats remained loyal to the party, Stevenson's position in the Tidelands controversy, Governor Shivers's endorsement of Eisenhower, and the general's overall popularity combined to make Eisenhower the second Republican presidential candidate to collect Texas's electoral votes (the first was Herbert Hoover in 1928), receiving 1,102,878 votes to Stevenson's 969,228. (Eisenhower defeated Stevenson in Texas a second time by 1,080,619 to 859,958 during his successful 1956 reelection bid.) The new president delighted Shivers and most Texans when he fulfilled his campaign promise by signing legislation giving Texas control of the Tidelands.

The 1952 election provided further signs that statewide Texas politics was slowly changing from traditional patterns. Though Eisenhower's victory did not translate into huge gains for the Texas Republican Party in other races, that day was approaching. The ideological split in the Texas Democratic Party on many issues would only widen in the coming years, exacerbated by inherent tensions created when blacks and Tejanos began to assert their rights and sought enhanced political power. Most conservative Democrats did not consider abandoning their party to join the Republicans (except for certain presidential contests) until the 1960s. Nevertheless, the Republican Party began to benefit from a sizeable migration of residents from northern and midwestern states, making more local races competitive during the 1950s than ever before. The days of one-party rule in Texas were numbered.

In 1954, Allan Shivers faced a rematch with Ralph Yarborough in the Democratic primary as the governor sought an unprecedented third full term. In an effort to deny Yarborough an opening line of attack for not maintaining public services, Shivers met with some of the state's leading corporate leaders and informed them that higher corporate franchise, gas gathering, and beer taxes were needed to fund his plans for increased appropriations to raise teacher salaries and to provide additional aid to schools and charitable institutions. Preferring Shivers to the liberal Yarborough, these leaders influenced their contacts in the legislature to ensure that the governor's desires were met. Fortunately for Yarborough, he had further political ammunition, including the wave of insurance company collapses (seventeen businesses in the previous seventeen months) in Texas. On Shivers's watch, the state began to gain the reputation of having the worst insurance laws in the country. Yarborough demanded an investigation, blaming the governor for allowing a lax regulatory system to flourish.

Shivers countered by capitalizing on voter discontent with two major issues making headlines during the mid-1950s: communism and civil rights. By the 1950s, the postwar rivalry between the United States and the Soviet Union known as the Cold War was in full swing, provoking fears over the global and domestic spread of communism. This trepidation, escalated by the Soviet Union's successful test of an atomic bomb in 1949 and the outbreak of the Korean War in 1950, created an anxiety sometimes bordering on hysteria among many American citizens, including quite a few Texans. Shivers tapped into this nervousness when he brazenly responded to a strike by several hundred CIO retail workers against twenty Port Arthur stores. Accusing the workers of being led by radical agitators, the governor created a highly publicized commission to investigate communist influence in Gulf Coast labor unions. Meanwhile, he called a special session of the legislature to deal with the "communist threat to Texas." Shivers even proposed a bill for consideration that would make membership in the Communist Party of America punishable by death. The legislature balked at the governor's request, but it still dealt a blow to civil liberties by voting overwhelmingly to make Communist Party membership a felony punishable by a $20,000 fine and twenty years in prison. Shivers claimed that he had protected Texans from the best-laid plans of domestic communists who had allegedly hoped to spread their influence into the heart of the Lone Star State. The governor also lambasted Yarborough for receiving the support of many of the state's "radical" union elements.

Likewise, Shivers grandstanded on the civil rights issue in an effort to portray himself as the only choice for segregationists. Shivers made the most of the 1954 *Brown v. Board of Education* ruling by playing on voters' racism. Pledging to uphold segregated schools and segregated communities as a whole, Shivers regularly attacked the Supreme Court's decision and demanded that his opponent do the same. Yarborough understood that most white Texas voters disagreed with the *Brown* decision and attempted to evade the issue as long as possible. His eventual response did his campaign no good. Reporters noted that the challenger stated that he opposed "forced commingling" and favored separate but truly equal schools. Nevertheless, he refused to condemn the Supreme Court's judgment or fight to preserve school segregation. Yarborough's answers pleased few voters as he fell into the classic political trap of antagonizing both sides. Liberals and black voters became agitated over his refusal to openly support school desegregation, while devout segregationists believed he was not firm enough on the issue.

Yarborough nevertheless performed well enough in the primary (receiving 645,994 to Shivers's 668,913) to force a runoff. He came surprisingly close to beating Shivers despite being greatly outspent, receiving few newspaper endorsements and suffering blistering attacks from the governor and his surrogates. In the end, Shivers scored the Democratic nomination with a 775,088 to 683,132 victory and made history by being elected to a third full term when he handily defeated his Republican opponent in the November general election.

Shivers's last term as governor was a disappointing one dominated by scandals, with the most damaging one involving the Veterans' Land Board. Created after World War II to enable military veterans to buy land more easily, the legislature appropriated $100 million for the board to purchase land and to make loans for acquisition of the land to veterans at 3 percent interest with up to 40 years for repayment. The Land Board members who bought the land and approved the veterans' applications consisted of the state land commissioner (serving as chairman), the governor, and the attorney general. In November 1954, Roland Kenneth Towery, managing editor for the *Cuero Record*, broke a story revealing irregularities in the veterans' land program. The South Texas small town newsman's report (for which he received a Pulitzer Prize in 1955 for distinguished reporting of local affairs) sparked state government investigations that revealed, among other findings, that land speculators made small fortunes selling inaccurately appraised land to the state at artificially inflated prices. In addition, investigators discovered that the state land commissioner, Land Board Chairman Bascom Giles, had accepted bribes to approve the purchases. Because Governor Shivers and Attorney General John Ben Sheppard were also on the Land Board, many assumed that they were involved in the nefarious undertakings. Both men claimed that they rarely attended board meetings due to other public service obligations. The legislature ultimately found no evidence to prove malfeasance, but it chose to reprimand them for not keeping a closer eye on Commissioner Giles and the board's affairs.

Shivers's popularity also suffered when additional insurance company collapses occurred in Texas. Though the public could have accepted these failures as part of the normal cycle of business, subsequent legislative investigations revealed that the Shivers-appointed state insurance commissioners performed extremely lax oversight and often engaged in obvious conflicts of interest by accepting loans, retainers, and other gifts from the same insurance companies they were supposed to regulate. By the end of 1955, the governor's approval rating had plummeted from 64 percent in January to 22 percent. Shivers had remained in office too long.

**Politics during the Late-1950s**

During the 1956 Democratic gubernatorial race, the party's liberal-conservative split resurfaced. Once again, liberal Ralph Yarborough ran for the party's nomination, now facing Senator Price Daniel and several reactionaries, including West Texas rancher J. Evetts Haley and ex-governor Pappy O'Daniel. Haley's and O'Daniel's campaigns were classic race-baiting affairs, excoriating the Supreme Court for its "communist-inspired" *Brown* decision. For his part, Daniel was less brazen, though he still tried to link labor union activity with the NAACP. Meanwhile, Yarborough continued to espouse an anti-lobbying law plus increased funding for schools, public health, and old-age pensions. Daniel led after the primary with 628,914 votes but could not avoid a runoff. Yarborough finished in second place with 463,416, followed by O'Daniel with 347,757. Though Daniel received Governor Shivers's endorsement, Yarborough managed to get O'Daniel's blessing, apparently believing that the liberal would make an easier opponent if the former governor chose to run against him as an independent in the general election. The tactic almost worked. Yarborough lost by less than 5,000 votes (698,001 to 694,830). Daniel easily won in November against his Republican opponent.

All was not lost for the defeated Yarborough, who soon decided to seek Daniel's recently-vacated senate seat. With no runoff required in the special election, he won with 38 percent of the vote, as conservatives divided their support between Democrat Martin Dies, who received 29 percent, and Republican Thad Hutcheson, who picked up 23 percent. Two years later, Yarborough defeated a conservative in the Democratic primary and another Republican in the general election to win a full six-year term. In the U.S. Senate, Yarborough and Lyndon Johnson (who had become Senate Majority Leader) both favored national Democratic goals of increased funding for health care, education, and the environment. They also attracted attention for their support of the Civil Rights Act of 1957 and their refusal to sign the segregationists' so-called "Southern Manifesto" pledging to oppose integration.

During his three terms as governor from 1957 to 1963, Price Daniel proved to be more moderate when compared to his previous years as attorney general and U.S. Senator. As previously mentioned, although Daniel signed three anti-integration measures into law in 1957, he did not enforce them prior to the courts' ruling them unconstitutional. He also worked with the legislature to fund state highways, to require the registration of lobbyists, to encourage water conservation, to elevate teachers' salaries, and to establish the current Texas State Library and Archives Building, which houses many important papers and Texas government documents. On the important issue of taxes, the governor and the legislature often clashed. In 1961, despite his fervent objections, the legislature rejected his desire for increased tobacco, alcohol, and business taxes in favor of approval for a 2 percent state sales tax (with exemptions for food, drugs, clothing, and other minor items), which became law without his signature. Though sales taxes disproportionately affect lower- and middle-class residents who pay a higher percentage of their income on purchases than the wealthy, the sales tax (broadened in coverage and with an increased rate over the years) became an important revenue-collecting device for the state, bringing in 62 percent of the state's total revenue by 1970. Consequently, the proportion of revenue generated from business taxes declined during the late 1950s and throughout the 1960s.

**Into the 1960s**

Like other Americans, Texans entered the 1960s optimistic about their future and unaware of the extraordinary events that would soon unfold. A nuclear showdown with the Soviet Union (the Cuban Missile Crisis) and the Vietnam War reminded Texans of their connection to the outside world. At home, a major push for civil rights, the open challenging of societal norms by disgruntled youth, and a presidential assassination in Dallas would all leave their impression on the Lone Star State. The forces of modernization and change that were forged out of the Great Depression and World War II and nurtured during the 1950s began to show their full impact on Texas during the tumultuous 1960s.

*Afterward: Learning from Tragedy*

*Subsequent investigations of the Texas City Disaster revealed the extent of the ignorance regarding the potential dangers of transporting large amounts of industrial fertilizer without close supervision. The close concentration of petrochemical production and storage facilities near the docks also added to the extent of the devastation—in a relatively tight-knit area near the wharves, Texas City housed a total of four oil refineries, two chemical companies, two aviation gasoline units, and large numbers of oil storage tanks, many of which were destroyed after the ships exploded. The Texas City Disaster eventually led to government regulations regarding fertilizer shipment and storage, improved safety awareness and redesign of Texas port facilities, and contributed to the movement for better disaster preparedness and response procedures nationwide.*

# Myth & Legend

**Lyndon Johnson Stole the 1948 Democratic Party Nomination for a U.S. Senate Seat from Coke Stevenson**

*Much controversy has surrounded the 1948 Democratic race for a U.S. Senate seat between ex-governor Coke Stevenson and Congressman Lyndon Baines Johnson. A common contemporary belief, promoted by some ever since, asserts that Johnson's campaign stole the election from Stevenson, who was unfairly denied the Democratic Party's nomination.*

*Accusations of electoral fraud levied against the Johnson campaign began soon after the final results trickled in. Many county election boards reported local results late while some updated their initial returns to correct errors. On election night, Stevenson held a slim lead, but his margin slowly dwindled as counties submitted more returns and revisions. Stevenson's early lead of less than 100 votes (out of over a million cast) finally vanished when the election board of Jim Wells County in South Texas tendered a revised result for one of its precincts, supposedly due to a "clerical error," that increased Johnson's vote total by 200 and Stevenson's by 2. At this point, Johnson stood to win the election by a grand total of 87 votes, leading to Stevenson's protests to the state party convention and the federal courts, which did not succeed.*

*Despite Stevenson's failure to win his appeals, the common perception endures among many that Johnson won his party's Senate nomination through shenanigans. One reason for this notion is that the political machine in Jim Wells County certainly engaged in fraud to help their favored candidate receive a higher vote count. Many biographers of Johnson's early years have cited the details of the election in their efforts to portray Johnson as an ambitious politician bent on winning at all costs. Journalist Robert Caro's negative description of Johnson in his popular biography* **The Years of Lyndon Johnson: The Means of Ascent** *carries this theme to the fullest, developing the false impression that Coke Stevenson was a heroic victim of Johnson's campaign tactics. The ex-governor's campaign was supposedly innocent of employing similar maneuvers elsewhere in the state.*

While Johnson's campaign certainly received help of a dubious nature from some South Texas political bosses and supporters in other parts of the state, one can only obtain an accurate understanding of the election by looking at the big picture. In fact, both campaigns' supporters engaged in various degrees of unethical, immoral, and illegal activity to put their candidates over the top. In large part, Stevenson's campaign focused on the returns from the single ballot box in Jim Wells County, not only because it could swing the runoff election results in their favor by revealing an obvious example of fraud that they thought could be proven but also because they knew that any effort to appeal the statewide results through a recount or other recourse would expose efforts by their supporters in other counties to tinker with the local results. Indeed, Johnson had always believed, and there is evidence to support the notion, that he had been denied victory in the 1941 special election for a U.S. Senate seat when supporters of Pappy O'Daniel's campaign had undertaken blatant examples of voter fraud in many localities. Holding a rather cynical view of the state electoral process from that point on, Johnson vowed not to lose another election due to passively allowing his opponents to undercut his campaign, even if it meant employing similar tactics to ensure victory.

In an extensive quantitative analysis of the election returns, historian Dale Baum concludes that too much emphasis has been placed on the revised results from Jim Wells County. He believes that due to many instances of fraud perpetrated by both sides, we will never know the "true results" of the election. The race was basically a tie, and the details concerning the official winner then, as in some of our current contested elections, had as much to do with the legal system as the political system. Nevertheless, Baum has shown through his analysis that lower turnout by Stevenson supporters when compared to the initial primary explains why the runoff was close in the first place. In many ways, Johnson outhustled Stevenson with his unbridled campaigning. As a result, most of his supporters from the primary turned out again for the runoff a month later. Had Johnson's supporters not maintained their enthusiasm for their candidate, or had Stevenson's supporters not become complacent and had come out to vote again, then the mischief undertaken by "Landslide Lyndon" Johnson's supporters (and Stevenson's) would not have mattered.

## Suggestions for Further Reading

Allsup, Carl, *The American G.I. Forum: Origins and Evolution* University of Texas Center for Mexican American Studies Monograph 6, Austin, 1982.

Carroll, Patrick. *Felix Longoria's Wake: Bereavement, Racism, and the Rise of Mexican American Activism* Austin: University of Texas Press, 2003.

Cox, Patrick L. *Ralph W. Yarborough: The People's Senator* Austin: University of Texas Press, 2002.

Dobbs, Ricky F. *Yellow Dogs and Republicans: Allan Shivers and Texas Two-Party Politics* College Station: Texas A&M University Press, 2005.

Gillette, Michael L. "Blacks Challenge the White University," *Southwestern Historical Quarterly* 86 Oct. 1982, 321-44.

____, "The Rise of the NAACP in Texas," *Southwestern Historical Quarterly* 81 April 1978, 393-416.

Goldstone, Dwonna. *Integrating the 40 Acres: The 50-Year Struggle for Racial Equality at the University of Texas.* Athens: The University of Georgia Press, 2006.

Green, George N. *The Establishment in Texas Politics: The Primitive Years, 1938-1957* Westport, Conn.: Greenwood, 1979.

Kuhlman, Martin. "The Civil Rights Movement in Texas: Desegregation of Public Accommodations, 1950-1964," Ph.D. Texas Tech University, 1994.

____, "Direct Action at the University of Texas during the Civil Rights Movement, 1960-1965." *Southwestern Historical Quarterly* 98 1995: 550-566.

Ladino, Robyn Duff. *Desegregating Texas Schools: Eisenhower, Shivers, and the Crisis at Mansfield High* Austin: University of Texas Press, 1996.

San Miguel, Jr., Guadalupe, *"Let All of Them Take Heed": Mexican Americans and the Campaign for Educational Equality in Texas* Austin: University of Texas Press, 1987.

Shabazz, Amilcar. *Advancing Democracy: African Americans and the Struggle for Access and Equity in Higher Education in Texas* Chapel Hill: University of North Carolina Press, 2004.

Stephens, Hugh W., *The Texas City Disaster, 1947* Austin: University of Texas Press, 1997.

**IDENTIFICATION:** Briefly describe each term.

postwar industrialization
agricultural changes
postwar urbanization
LULAC
American G.I. Forum
Henry B. Gonzalez
NAACP
*Sweatt v. Painter*
Mansfield High School Crisis
Beauford Jester
Gilmer-Aikin Laws
Allan Shivers
Tidelands Controversy
Ralph Yarborough
Price Daniel

**MULTIPLE CHOICE:** Choose the correct response.

1. Which of the following was not an important industry in Texas during the 1950s?
   A. oil refining;
   B. petrochemicals;
   C. aircraft manufacturing;
   D. electronics;
   E. shoe manufacturing.

2. _____ developed the first portable transistor radio.
   A. General Dynamics;
   B. IBM;
   C. Texas Instruments;
   D. none of the above.

3. Changes in postwar Texas agriculture led to the movement of traditional cotton culture to the:
   A. Southern High Plains and Lower Rio Grande Valley;
   B. eastern and central portions of the state;
   C. Gulf Coast region;
   D. Hill Country region.

4. _____was the first Hispanic from Texas to be elected to the U.S. Congress.
   A. Felix Longoria;
   B. Gus García;
   C. Macario García;
   D. Henry Gonzalez.

5. Texan _____ was among the first class of inductees into the Rock and Roll Hall of Fame.
   A. Roy Orbison;
   B. Buddy Holly;
   C. Janis Joplin;
   D. Stevie Ray Vaughan;
   E. Hank Williams, Sr.

6. Of the following, who was never a governor of Texas?
   A. Coke Stevenson;
   B. Allan Shivers;
   C. Ralph Yarborough;
   D. Beauford Jester.

7. As a result of *Hernandez v. Texas*, Tejanos could not be excluded from _____ just for being Hispanic.
   A. white public schools;
   B. juries;
   C. the military;
   D. all of the above.

8. As a result of *Sweatt v. Painter*, blacks:
   A. could use public beaches;
   B. could not be refused service at lunch counters;
   C. could not be denied admission to the University of Texas Law School solely for racial reasons;
   D. did not have to pay poll taxes in order to vote.

9. Beauford Jester and Allan Shivers both favored:
   A. desegregation of public schools;
   B. massive cuts in state spending and public services;
   C. increased spending for public services funded by increased consumer taxes;
   D. decreased spending on public services and great increases in oil and gas company taxes.

10. _____ served as governor of Texas as the state entered the 1960s.
    A. John Connally;
    B. Ralph Yarborough;
    C. Allan Shivers ;
    D. Price Daniel.

**TRUE/FALSE:** Indicate whether each statement is true or false.

1. Jack Kilby invented the mechanical cotton picker.

2. Texas cotton farming continued in Texas after World War II, but it became an insignificant crop hardly produced within the state by 1960.

3. Dallas passed Houston in number of residents in 1950 and ever since has been the most populous city in Texas.

4. Unlike many other American states during the 1950s, the so-called "Baby Boom" largely bypassed Texas.

5. Felix Longoria was the first Hispanic from Texas to be elected to the U.S. Congress.

6. In the *Delgado v. Bastrop ISD* case, LULAC attorney Gus García successfully argued that segregation of Tejanos in public schools was unconstitutional because majority sentiment in the state considered Hispanics to be a distinct class of white people.

7. Lyndon Johnson was declared the winner of the controversial Senate race for the Democratic Party nomination in 1948.

8. During the late-1940s, Governor Beauford Jester vetoed most of the Texas Legislature's efforts to pass anti-labor laws in the spirit of the national Taft-Hartley Act.

9. The Gilmer-Aikin Laws revamped Texas public school education.

10. Texas gave its electoral votes in the 1948 presidential race to "Dixiecrat" Strom Thurmond.


**MATCHING:** Match the response in column A with the item in column B.

1. Jack Kilby             A. sent Texas Rangers to Mansfield High School
2. Roy Orbison            B. early rock and roll pioneer
3. Allan Shivers          C. only Texas governor to die in office
4. Beauford Jester        D. invented the integrated circuit
5. Felix Longoria         E. furor over his wake led to his burial at Arlington Nat'l Cemetery
6. LULAC                  F. allowed blacks to enter UT Law School
7. NAACP                  G. Hispanic civil rights organization
8. Gilmer-Aikin Laws      H. revamped Texas public school education
9. Baby Boom              I. black civil rights organization
10. *Sweatt v. Painter*   J. provided a boost to the postwar Texas economy

**ESSAY QUESTIONS:**

1. Identify and describe the major industries that developed in Texas during the 1950s.

2. Identify and describe the major changes taking place in Texas agriculture from 1940 to 1960.

3. Identify some key civil rights achievements of blacks and Tejanos during the 1950s. What had yet to be accomplished by 1960?

4. Describe the major positions taken by Governors Jester, Shivers, and Daniel on many important postwar political issues in Texas. How were they similar? How did they differ?

# Chapter 17

# *The Turbulent Decade: Reform and Reaction, 1960-1972*

**Prelude: The Marshall Sit-In Movement**

*The famous Greensboro, North Carolina sit-in begun by four black college students at a segregated B.F. Woolworth's lunch counter on February 1, 1960, initiated a protest movement spreading across the South that soon reached the Lone Star State. Within weeks, college students undertook highly-publicized sit-ins in Houston, Austin, Galveston, and San Antonio. The movement also reached the small East Texas town of Marshall, whose population of 25,000 was 43 percent African American. Marshall was home to two black colleges—Wiley and Bishop—containing many enthusiastic students eager to show sympathy to the larger movement and willing to protest for the cause of civil rights.*

*Organizers associated with Martin Luther King's Southern Christian Leadership Conference worked with students from both colleges to create a plan of action and train volunteers in tactics of non-violent protest. The segregated businesses of downtown Marshall became the chosen targets, with an initial demonstration to take place at the local Woolworth's lunch counter. On Saturday of March 26 at 10 a.m., after ten protesters arrived, the store manager responded by ending all food service and soon shutting down the entire store for the day. The students then went to Wiley to hold a rally and to plan an afternoon demonstration at the Union bus terminal café. When the protesters arrived, all but two white patrons walked out. The manager soon closed the counter while local police escorted the activists out of the building. After regrouping on Sunday, activists planned to target the same two establishments in addition to a lunch counter at a Rexall drugstore the following day. Though the protesters found the bus terminal café to be closed, they began sitting-in at the other two eateries open for business. After repeated requests to leave by police and management, the students were arrested and shipped to a holding facility where the local district attorney proclaimed that order would be maintained and he would press formal charges if they continued to protest in this manner. Meanwhile, the city council met and announced their support for the right of the merchants to serve or not serve whoever they wished.*

*On Wednesday, March 30, the Marshall protests began to make national news. When students arrived at the same three previous protest targets, they were promptly arrested and escorted to the local courthouse as they were jeered and occasionally spat upon by white onlookers. Though the prosecutor stood on shaky legal ground, the demonstrators were charged with engaging in an "unlawful assembly" based on a state statute originally designed to limit the power of unions to undertake strikes by making it unlawful for a group of three or more individuals to deprive a person from pursuing any labor, occupation, or employment. Later in the afternoon, another wave of thirty-seven student protestors arrived at the lunch counters, only to be promptly arrested and shipped to the courthouse. Awaiting arraignment in the courtroom, many of the students began reading Bible verses aloud and sang patriotic songs such as "America the beautiful" and "God Bless America." Joining them in song on the courthouse lawn was a group of close to 600 Bishop and Wiley students (out of the schools' combined enrollment of 900). When the district attorney asked to speak to student leaders inside, most of the throng of students entered the building, continuing to sing. Soon, a protest leader told everyone that the arrested students would be set free on their own recognizance if the protests stopped. The students agreed to leave the building but would not vacate the town square until the arrested students were released. In an effort to disperse the protestors, fire department personnel were deployed to spray the demonstrators with water from high-pressure hoses. Moved by the deluge but not removed, the protestors did not leave the area until they triumphantly marched back to their campuses after the arrested students were let go. A race riot was potentially thwarted when Marshall police officers intercepted a group of fifty white men planning to attack the demonstrators.*

*Word of the protests spread rapidly across the country. By dawn the next day, national reporters converged on Marshall as the demonstrations continued, this time by activists working in pairs in order to avoid charges under terms of the state anti-labor statute used to justify the original protesters' arrests. Officers made arrests nevertheless, with prosecutors charging activists under a local ordinance which made it illegal for a person to remain on the premises of another person after being directed to leave. The fifty-seven protesters who had been released on Wednesday were also rounded up on their campuses and detained.*

*Under pressure from local government and business leaders, the presidents of Wiley and Bishop both called for an end to the protests. Within a couple of days, the sit-ins ceased, but civil rights protesting continued as students began planning boycotts of local businesses, demanding equal treatment and increased employment opportunities. The boycotts failed to sway local proprietors. Because students had relatively light spending power compared to local African-American adults, the protestors needed large involvement from the local black community to exact enough economic pressure on local businessmen to force them to reconsider their discriminatory policies. While some local black adults supported the students, the required level of participation failed to materialize. Though formal agitation soon dissipated, the students of Wiley and Bishop remained energized, vowing that conditions would never go back to "normal."*

Texas experienced tremendous social and political changes during the 1960s. Among the many social developments of the decade, the most important proved to be the demise of segregation and voter discrimination. Some continue to cling to a lingering myth that nothing happened in Texas during the Civil Rights Movement because the violent clashes between defenders of segregation and peaceful protestors that consumed the Deep South largely bypassed the Lone Star State. In fact, Texas had dynamic African-American and Tejano activists whose inspired efforts contributed greatly to the successful promotion of civil rights resulting in the end of the unjust Jim Crow regime and the election of minorities to political office. These social and political transformations, however, produced a strong reaction by supporters of the old system, helping to bolster the rise of the Republican Party in Texas to challenge the Democrats for control of the state government.

**Early 1960s Texas Politics**

At the beginning of the 1960s, Texas became a major player in national politics when native son Lyndon B. Johnson sought the 1960 Democratic Party presidential nomination. First elected to the U.S. Senate in 1948 after the controversial race against Coke Stevenson, Johnson became minority leader in 1952, then majority leader in 1954 after the Democrats reclaimed control of the Senate. He proved to be an effective congressional leader for the remainder of the decade, working with House Speaker Sam Rayburn (a fellow Texan) and President Dwight Eisenhower to pass important legislation. Because the Texas legislature altered state law during its 1959 session to allow Johnson to run simultaneously for the presidency and re-election to the Senate, both races promised to raise voter interest.

Though Johnson and his supporters vigorously pursued the Democratic Party presidential nomination, their efforts succumbed to the popularity of another senator—John F. Kennedy of Massachusetts. Delegates to the Democratic National Convention in Los Angeles nominated Kennedy on the first ballot. The Massachusetts senator then proceeded to surprise many, including Johnson himself, when he offered the Texan a slot on the ticket as his running mate. Many Kennedy supporters protested the decision (including his brother and campaign manager Robert Kennedy), but Kennedy felt he needed an experienced southern politician on the ballot for balance.

Kennedy's choice proved to be a strong one politically—Johnson's popularity in Texas provided solid dividends in the fall. With 24 electoral votes available in a tight race, the campaign in Texas promised to be very influential in determining the overall victor in the November general election. Further, Johnson could hold some other southern states for Kennedy. Though President Eisenhower had won Texas for the Republicans during the two previous elections, there was no guarantee that the current Republican nominee, Vice President Richard Nixon, could replicate those results. Nixon received the endorsement of former governor Allan Shivers and other prominent conservative Democrats, but ultimately, the galvanization of the Tejano and African-American communities helped to tip the scale in favor of the Democrats. Mexican Americans leaders, most notably Hector P. García of the American G.I. Forum, organized "Viva Kennedy" clubs to promote Hispanic voter registration and the Kennedy-Johnson candidacy. Tejanos overwhelmingly supported Kennedy because the Democratic national convention had endorsed civil rights, school desegregation, equal opportunity, fair housing, migrant worker legislation, and voting rights. Black Texans also came out in large numbers for Kennedy in appreciation for the Democratic Party's pro-civil rights platform and the senator's personal efforts to obtain the release of Martin Luther King from a Georgia prison after his conviction for a parole violation following participation in a sit-in against segregated public accommodations in Atlanta. The impact of these two minority groups proved essential for victory in Texas. Kennedy defeated Nixon by less than 50,000 votes out of 2.3 million—1,167,567 or 50.5 percent to 1,121,310 or 48.5 percent. (Nationally, Kennedy won by 118,000 votes out of 68 million cast.)

Despite the presidential election loss, Texas Republicans had reason to be optimistic about their party's future chances. First, Nixon received the largest vote tally of any previous Republican candidate during a presidential contest in Texas. Second, Johnson's Republican opponent in the Senate race, Midwestern University political science professor John Tower, campaigned well despite being unknown to most voters before the election. He received 900,000 votes to Johnson's 1.3 million. Third, when Lyndon Johnson became vice president in 1961, Tower entered the special election to fill Johnson's vacant Senate post in an advantageous position. Democrats were divided among three liberal candidates including Henry B. Gonzalez and conservative Dallas businessman Bill Blakley. Tower and Blakley faced each other in a runoff. (The legislature had changed the law since Yarborough's 1957 win to require a runoff if no special election candidate received 50 percent of the vote.) When many liberal Democrats refused to support Blakley, Tower achieved a narrow victory with 448,217 votes (50.6 percent) to Blakley's 437,872 (49.4 percent) and, therefore, became the first Republican to win a statewide office in Texas since Reconstruction.

Texas Republicans hoped to build on the momentum produced by Tower's victory by winning the 1962 gubernatorial race. Jack Cox, a former conservative Democratic state legislator, won the Republican nomination. On the Democratic side, six candidates vied for their party's nomination, including Governor Price Daniel who was seeking an unprecedented fourth term. Houston attorney Don Yarborough (no relation to Senator Ralph Yarborough) received solid support from liberal Democrats. Many moderates and conservatives supported the candidacy of the tall and personable Secretary of the Navy John Connally who had initially made a name for himself in Texas politics by serving as Lyndon Johnson's legislative aide and campaign manager. Many extreme right-wing conservative Democrats supported retired U.S. Army Major General Edwin Walker, a rabid anti-communist and pro-segregationist who publicly protested the federal government's recent efforts favoring integration by flying an American flag upside down in front of his Dallas residence. Governor Daniel finished third, failing to be re-nominated due to a backlash against his seeking a fourth term plus his refusal to veto an unpopular state sales tax bill even though he strongly opposed it. Yarborough and Connally faced each other in the runoff, with Connally narrowly winning by 26,000 votes. In the general election, Cox performed better than any previous Republican candidate for governor in the twentieth century. Though Connally defeated him, Cox received 46 percent of the vote. Two Republicans, Bruce Alger of Dallas and Ed Foreman of Odessa, won their respective congressional races. Thus, in the early 1960s, the fortunes of Texas Republicans seemed to be on the rise.

**Early 1960s Civil Rights Activism**

Following the lead of demonstrators elsewhere in the South, Texas civil rights activists began to utilize direct action techniques to press for an end to segregated public facilities during the early 1960s. Though the struggle was lengthy and bitter due to hesitation and resistance by most white political leaders and citizens, the civil rights movement in Texas largely escaped the widespread violence experienced in the Deep South. Drawing inspiration (though little leadership) from the broader movement, Texas protestors successfully pressed for change by threatening to publicize statewide injustices and to taint the positive image that many urban business, civic, and political leaders were trying to cultivate for their growing cities.

The efforts of civil rights activists in Houston and Austin provide good examples for the approach often employed in Texas. In March 1960, African-American students at Texas Southern University organized the first Texas sit-in (refusing to leave when denied service) at a Houston lunch counter near their campus to challenge segregation and to show solidarity with students in Greensboro, North Carolina, who recently pioneered the tactic. Impatient with the slow pace of reform through NAACP legal challenges, the students soon widened their protests to boycott segregated downtown department stores. Leaders in the black community began simultaneous negotiations with Houston's white business elite to shepherd desegregation quietly without producing a violent white backlash. Houston's business leaders sought accommodation in order to avoid becoming embroiled in a highly-publicized racial conflict (as would soon occur in many Deep South cities such as Birmingham, Alabama) that could smear the city's image and repel the outside business investors that they desired to attract. When the deal involving gradual desegregation of lunch counters and department stores was struck, local television, radio, and newspaper outlets quashed the story for over a week to ease the transition and to stymie possible organized protests by white residents. Over the next three years the pattern continued: as students picketed against segregated bus terminals, theaters, restaurants, and hotels, older black community leaders negotiated with the city's elite to broker desegregation deals. In 1962, mounting pressure resulted ending local segregated hotels and the opening of the new Astrodome stadium on a desegregated basis as a condition for Houston to receive an expansion major league baseball team. In May 1963, planned protests during a parade to celebrate astronaut Gordon Cooper's return from space resulted in a quiet arrangement (again with help from local media outlets who ignored the story for a while) to end segregated theaters and restaurants in the city.

In Austin, civil rights activism was centered on the University of Texas campus. Though the university began to gradually desegregate its admissions in the 1950s, the campus itself continued its Jim Crow ways, as did the surrounding community. In March 1960, as the Houston lunch counter protests were underway, a group of twenty-five black and seven white students began a three-day demonstration outside the campus to alert the student body to the school's continued segregation policies, such as the inability of African Americans to participate in intercollegiate athletics, dormitory segregation, and exclusion from university-sponsored theatrical productions. The students also began to picket nearby off-campus lunch counters and soon challenged segregated theaters (with help from students at nearby Huston-Tillotson College, Concordia Lutheran College, and St. Edwards University) by standing in line, asking if all Americans would be given a ticket, and returning to the back of the line when told that only whites could receive tickets. Though occasional episodes of harassment took place by local passersby and the students' actions were condemned by university president Harry Ransom and the Board of Regents, the protests continued. Backdoor negotiations ultimately led to many instances of desegregation in exchange for an end to the agitation.

Activists replicated these tactics in Dallas and other major Texas cities, producing a gradual breakdown in the system of segregation in many urban areas within the state before the federal Civil Rights Act of 1964 outlawed the practice nationally. These efforts on behalf of civil rights did, however, lead to a growing rift among Democrats that threatened to split the party. While most white liberals and many moderates generally supported these social changes, conservatives and many other moderates demurred. Understanding the necessity of unity among Texas Democrats for his 1964 re-election chances, President Kennedy planned a two-day trip to the Lone Star State in late November 1963 designed to rally the party faithful, culminating in an important speech before the Texas State Party Convention in Austin.

**The Kennedy Assassination**

Kennedy's Texas sojourn began well on November 21, 1963, with stops in San Antonio and Houston—huge crowds appeared to glimpse the president during downtown motorcades, which experienced no incidents. The president then flew to Fort Worth where he stayed the night before attending a morning breakfast and delivering remarks to a local gathering. There was concern among some in the president's traveling party about the next stop, Dallas, because of growing right-wing extremism that led boisterous demonstrations and shoving incidents involving vice presidential candidate Johnson in 1960 and, just the previous month, United Nations Ambassador Adlai Stevenson. The president brushed aside such worries, favoring yet another motorcade so he could be seen by as many Dallas residents as possible.

It is ironic, given the worries about right-wing extremists in Dallas, that it turned out to be an extreme left-wing resident who killed President Kennedy. The parade through downtown went perfectly as huge crowds came out to welcome the president. Near the end of the motorcade, however, as the limousines and police motorcycle escorts entered Dealey Plaza at the west end of downtown Dallas, shots rang out. One bullet, probably the second fired, hit President Kennedy in the back, exited through his neck, and entered the body of Governor Connally (who was seated ahead of Kennedy in the presidential car). The last shot tore into the president's head, mortally wounding him. Though Connally survived, doctors pronounced President Kennedy dead thirty minutes after his arrival to nearby Parkland Hospital.

A few hours after the assassination, the Dallas Police Department arrested Lee Harvey Oswald, an employee of the Dallas School Book Depository Building (located in Dealey Plaza). Initially charged with killing a Dallas police officer in his Oak Cliff neighborhood an hour after the assassination, Oswald was later charged with Kennedy's murder. Two days later, as much of the nation tried to cope with its shock and grief, the inadequately-protected Oswald was killed by Dallas nightclub owner Jack Ruby as police attempted to transfer the alleged assassin to a more secure facility.

Why did Oswald and Ruby commit their murders? Regarding a possible motive for Oswald, one must understand certain facts about his early life. Born in New Orleans to a mother who recently lost her husband, Oswald grew up experiencing constant flux as his mother remarried and his family moved constantly, finally settling in the Dallas-Fort Worth area. During his teen years, Oswald became drawn to communist literature that he read constantly, imbedding into the troubled teen a fiery critique of the American system. Oswald's choice of reading material did not prevent him at age seventeen from joining the Marine Corps (where he proved to be an accomplished marksman), but before his twenty-first birthday, he left the Marines and traveled to the Soviet Union, brashly renouncing his American citizenship. After the Russian government allowed him to stay, he married a local woman and worked in a radio factory until the American government approved his request to return to the United States in June 1962.

During the next eighteen months, Oswald displayed increasingly erratic behavior. After ordering an Italian army surplus rifle (a Mannlicher-Carcano) through the mail, he attempted to murder the controversial retired right-wing General Edwin Walker by firing a shot through the front window of his Dallas residence, narrowly missing his head by inches. Though the identity of the general's assailant was unknown for months, FBI ballistics analysis performed after the Kennedy assassination confirmed that Oswald's Mannlicher-Carcano was not only the same rifle used to kill the president but also the gun that fired the bullet intended for General Walker. That crucial evidence has sometimes been referred to as the "Rosetta Stone" of the Kennedy assassination because, in linking Oswald's weapon to both crimes, it provides a credible display of the former marine's propensity for violence against famous individuals holding different political viewpoints.

A few weeks after the attempt on Walker, Oswald arrived in New Orleans possibly not only to evade authorities but also to organize a local chapter of the "Fair Play for Cuba Committee"—an activist group seeking grassroots support in the United States for the Cuban Revolution of Fidel Castro. After going to Mexico City in an unsuccessful effort to receive a visa to Cuba, he returned to Dallas in October 1963 and happened to land a job stacking books at the Texas School Book Depository Building in Dealey Plaza.

Oswald's employment at the depository building provided the opportunity for the assassination. Dallas newspapers published the motorcade route to the public three days before the president's arrival, giving Oswald sufficient time to become aware that the president's entourage would enter Dealey Plaza and to plan an assassination attempt. On the day of the killing, Oswald was seen bringing to work a long package that he described as curtain rods for his boarding house. From a self-made sniper's nest of textbook boxes in a corner of the sixth floor of the depository building, Oswald fired three shots at Kennedy's motorcade within ten seconds. It was not a difficult act to perform. Oswald then took advantage of the ensuing chaos and fled the building.

When a head count of employees showed that Oswald was the only worker unaccounted for, police were alerted to look for a man with his description. Meanwhile, Oswald had taken a taxi to his Oak Cliff neighborhood, retrieved a pistol from his boarding house, and left the premises. When Dallas police officer J.D. Tippit spotted Oswald and noticed that he fit the profile of the person wanted for questioning in the president's murder, he stopped his patrol car alongside Oswald. As the officer emerged from the vehicle, Oswald panicked and shot him several times with his pistol, killing the officer and fleeing the scene past numerous eyewitnesses. He was later arrested in a local theater after someone alerted the police that a man who ducked away from a passing police car had suspiciously entered the movie house without paying.

Despite repeated denials of his guilt to the police and to the general public when given an opportunity to address a huge gathering of reporters, the Dallas Police Department believed that they had the murderer of President Kennedy and Officer Tippit in custody. They did a poor job, however, of protecting him. Two days after the Kennedy

**Lyndon B. Johnson takes the presidential oath aboard Air Force One, Love Field, Dallas, Texas. November 22, 1963**
**Photo credit: LBJ Library Photo**

murder, police planned to transfer Oswald from Dallas City Jail to the Dallas County Jail. Reporters and others were allowed to witness the transfer. One of them happened to be Dallas strip club owner Jack Ruby, who had just sent a money order nearby and stopped by the jailhouse simply to see the action. (Ruby had also shown up at the jailhouse two days earlier out of curiosity to hear Oswald address the reporters.) When police brought out Oswald, Ruby became enraged at the man for his crime and his perceived smugness. In that instant, Ruby whipped out a pistol that he carried with him for protection and shot Oswald once in the abdomen, killing him. (Ruby was later convicted of murder. He won an appeal but died of cancer while awaiting a new trial.)

Occurring so close to each other, the twin killings generated much fear and anxiety across the country and led many to question whether something sinister was happening at a higher level. Who had really killed Kennedy? If Oswald did it, did he act alone? How was Ruby able to kill Oswald? Why did Ruby kill Oswald? Was Oswald's killing part of a cover-up? The new president, Lyndon Johnson, created the Warren Commission (chaired by Supreme Court Chief Justice Earl Warren) to investigate the killings. Though the Warren Commission concluded that both Oswald and Ruby acted alone, many have made a career out of questioning the commission's findings. Some honestly wish to alert readers that the commission did not have access to evidentiary material or to point out inconsistencies in the commission's approach and conclusions. Others have simply used the assassination and the commission's report to publicize a separate agenda or to make a quick buck off the large numbers of people fascinated by the whole affair. Though some critics of the Warren Report have demonstrated that the commission's members did not receive complete access to relevant government documents held by the CIA and the FBI (due to efforts by these agencies to avoid the taint of incompetence plus the desire to conceal ongoing nefarious activities), reliable evidence pointing to any conspiracy to kill President Kennedy is lacking. All credible signs point to Oswald as the sole perpetrator of the crime for which he had both motive and opportunity to execute.

**Johnson's Great Society and the Vietnam War**

As the nation tried to deal with the shocking events of November 1963, Texan Lyndon Johnson became the new president. Driven by manic energy, a strong desire to help others, and an incredible ego and ambition to acquire and wield power, Johnson's five years as president produced both proud domestic accomplishments and the deepening quagmire of U.S. involvement in the Vietnam War.

After completing the last year of Kennedy's term, Johnson easily defeated the Republican Party nominee, Arizona Senator Barry Goldwater, to earn a full term in his own right. (Johnson received 63 percent of the vote in Texas.) He then embarked on an ambitious domestic agenda that he labeled the "Great Society," a bold effort to extend the New Deal to address persistent national problems in a time of relative prosperity. Though federal aid to education, promotion of the arts, environmental advocacy, consumer protection, and establishment of the Medicare program (national health insurance for retired Americans) became important lasting domestic achievements of Johnson's presidency, the two boldest goals of Johnson's Great Society involved tackling racial injustice and eliminating poverty in America. The monumental Civil Rights Act of 1964, initially introduced by Kennedy and pushed aggressively in Congress by Johnson after the president's death, directly attacked decades of injustice by outlawing segregated public facilities across the country while also prohibiting race and gender discrimination in employment. Ralph Yarborough and Al Gore, Sr., of Tennessee were the only southern senators to support the measure. (John Tower voted against it.) Meanwhile, Johnson worked with Congress to establish numerous programs to fight a "war on poverty." Many of these programs continue to exist today, including the Job Corps (to teach marketable job skills to low-income Americans who cannot afford college), the Food Stamps program (to offer monthly stipends to supplement the diets of the poor), Medicaid (the national health insurance program for the poorest Americans), Medicare (as mentioned earlier), and Head Start (to make available preschool education for the children of low-income Americans). Though many complained (and still complain) about the cost of such programs, supporters of the initiatives countered that the economic and social costs of doing nothing were worse and that, if America invested in the poor and worked with them to improve their economic situation, the programs would pay for themselves. By producing more law-abiding, tax-paying citizens, these programs over the years would contribute to the federal treasury

**Signing of the Civil Rights Act of 1964. July 2, 1964.
Photo credit: LBJ Library Photo**

while reducing costs for prisons and law enforcement. Nationally, the Great Society programs produced some noteworthy successes. Though certainly not achieving the lofty goal of completely ending poverty in America, statistics demonstrate that Great Society programs contributed greatly to an almost 50 percent decline in the national poverty rate by the end of the 1960s, from 22 percent in 1963 to 12.5 percent in 1970. (The national poverty rate for blacks also fell dramatically, from 55 percent in 1960 to 27 percent in 1968.)

Though Johnson made a great impact on the country with his Great Society programs, America's commitment of combat troops to Vietnam eventually engrossed his presidency. Citing the growing chaos in South Vietnam from internal strife and an active communist guerilla movement (the Viet Cong), Johnson agreed in July 1965 to send 50,000 troops to Indochina, soon surging to 200,000 by the end of the year. The president believed that U.S. troops could accomplish their mission of aiding the South Vietnamese military and then pull out within a couple of years. For the remainder of his term, Johnson became overwhelmed by the effort. Eventually, over a half million soldiers served in Vietnam, casualties continued to mount, and no end appeared in sight. Though the presence of such a large contingency of American troops prevented the government of South Vietnam from collapsing, the insurgency continued unabated. Antiwar protests in Texas (as elsewhere in the country) gravitated around many of the state's college campuses as some students and professors publicized their growing dissent. Johnson's popularity with a majority of the American people declined precipitously after the Viet Cong's January 1968 Tet Offensive. While the attacks eventually petered out and resulted in an estimated 50,000 Viet Cong casualties, a growing number of Americans who had been constantly told that the war was nearing completion began to believe that their govern-

**Protest vigil for peace taken outside the Alamo, San Antonio, Texas.
February 4, 1967. Photo credit: Institute of Texas Cultures**

ment was not being truthful about the conflict. How could a nearly-defeated enemy, they asked, even be capable of launching an attack while the U.S. could lose 50,000 men? After Johnson underperformed in the Democratic Party's first presidential primaries, he shocked the nation in early March 1968 by announcing that he would not seek, nor accept, the nomination of his party for another term as president.

**Black Political Gains and Late-1960s Activism**

During Johnson's presidency, important voting rights breakthroughs led to great increases in black voter participation and office holding. In 1964, the Twenty-fourth Amendment to the U.S. Constitution outlawed the collection of poll taxes in federal elections. Two years later, the U.S. Supreme Court ruled that the poll-tax ban also applied to state and local elections. The Court also decided in two separate cases that state legislators had to be elected from districts consisting of approximately the same number of citizens. These so-called "one-man, one-vote" rulings ended the practice of allocating "at-large" seats that diluted local black voting strength by permitting all voters in a county to vote for state representatives regardless of where they resided in a county. With Johnson's strong support, Congress passed the Voting Rights Act of 1965, eliminating local voting restrictions and allowing federal marshals to monitor election proceedings. Each of these developments contributed to a tremendous increase in black voter registration in Texas (from approximately 227,000 in 1960 to 400,000 in 1966, or 76 percent).

**Martin Luther King, Jr. talks with President Lyndon B. Johnson in the Oval Office, White House. December 3, 1963
by Yoichi R. Okamoto. Photo credit: LBJ Library**

Beginning in the mid-1960s, increased African-American voter participation translated into black electoral victories in Texas for the first time in the twentieth century. African Americans began to serve municipalities as city councilmen, mayors, sheriffs, constables, and local school board members. Barbara Jordan, who failed in two previous attempts to win a state House of Representatives seat, benefited from the end of at-large voting in Harris County to win her 1966 race for a state senate seat representing a section of Houston. When Curtis Graves, a student civil rights protester and graduate of Texas Southern University, and Joseph Lockridge, a Dallas attorney, also won House seats in 1966, they joined Jordan to become the first blacks to serve in the state legislature since 1898. In 1972, Jordan became the first Texas African American (and first southern black woman) ever to serve in the United States House of Representatives. She subsequently gained national attention for an eloquent speech supporting the impeachment of President Richard Nixon during the Watergate scandal and later gained notoriety for delivering a memorable keynote address at the 1976 Democratic National Convention.

The Civil Rights Movement for African Americans did not end with the demise of segregation or the achievement of voting rights. After 1965, many activists began to concern themselves with new issues, such as economic equality, housing discrimination, aid for poor black neighborhoods, and police brutality. A growing number of young African Americans supported the call of some national civil rights leaders for "Black Power," though the phrase tended to have different connotations with various people. For many, it simply meant proclaiming racial pride. For others, the term implied eschewing Martin Luther King's and other civil rights leaders' strict reliance on nonviolent tactics to combat injustice. Some radicals even believed it called for complete black separatism from whites.

Though Texas escaped the ghetto fires and race riots that plagued Los Angeles, Detroit, Newark, and other cities during the mid-and late-1960s, occasional outbreaks of violence occurred in the state. On the campus of Texas Southern University in May 1967, a clash occurred between local police and a group of students who were meeting to discuss local public school problems and police misconduct in black neighborhoods. Some of the students greeted the police with stones and bottles. The police then fired their weapons, resulting in one policeman being killed by a ricocheting bullet. Five students were arrested for inciting a riot, but none were tried due to a lack of evidence. In 1970, members of a radical separatist group with ties to the famous Black Panthers known as the People's Party II engaged in a shootout with Houston police, resulting in the death of the group's leader, Carl Hampton. Most African Americans rejected such extremist groups and welcomed the promising new social opportunities made possible by desegregation, though it should be noted that desegregation did hurt some black middle-class professionals when many former customers began to patronize white establishments for legal, medical, and dental aid, believing white practitioners could provide superior services. As Black Power rhetoric began to replace the peaceful demonstrations of the early civil rights years, the attitudes of a growing number of whites began to harden against further efforts to promote black equality and the belief that the Civil Rights Movement had gone far enough. By the early 1970s, this reaction had already begun to manifest itself in a growing flight of many conservative and moderate Democrats towards the Republican Party.

**Tejano Activism during the 1960s**

Mexican Americans also took part in civil rights agitation while engaging in increased political activism during the 1960s. Inspired by a growing national Chicano movement, impatient with the slow pace of change, and increasingly annoyed with the opposition of LULAC and the G.I. Forum to engage in grassroots protests, many Tejano youths answered the call for "Brown Power" by promoting racial pride and seeking to produce change through such direct action tactics as labor strikes, school boycotts, and protest marches.

During the late-1950s, the election of Henry B. Gonzalez to a state senate seat representing San Antonio and Raymond Telles's election as mayor of El Paso portended future change. In 1963, Mexican Americans for the first time gained control of the local government of a South Texas Hispanic-majority town when residents of Crystal City in Zavala County elected Tejanos to all five city council positions. This victory resulted from the efforts of the newly-formed Political Association of Spanish-Speaking Organizations (PASO) and the local Teamsters union chapter who recruited the candidates and organized voters. Though internal divisions among the councilmen allowed a coalition of middle-class white and Hispanic residents to defeat them two years later, the Chicano movement for self-determination and an end to discrimination and injustice—the "*movimiento*," as activists called it—received a large boost from the 1963 victory, providing a vision for how things could be if unity could be maintained.

During the summer of 1966, Tejano farm workers in South Texas's Starr County organized into an affiliate of the United Farm Workers and went on strike against local melon growers, demanding a minimum wage of $1.25 an hour. The strike lasted less than a month after scab Mexican laborers arrived to harvest the crops and local law enforcement officials (aided by Texas Rangers) made mass arrests of the picketers on grounds of violating various local laws later to be declared unconstitutional. Following the conclusion of the strike, the workers organized a two-month long "minimum wage march" to the state capital to publicize their cause beginning on July 4. Accompanied by House Speaker Ben Barnes and Attorney General Waggoner Carr, Governor Connally agreed to meet the protestors halfway at New Braunfels, but he refused to call a special session of the legislature to deal with their grievances or to speak at a planned post-march rally on Labor Day. Nevertheless, the march generated much publicity, and the workers were eventually joined by thousands of sympathetic LULAC, G.I. Forum, and PASO members for the final stretch of the protest march and subsequent rally in Austin.

The Starr County strike and the minimum wage march succeeded in galvanizing Mexican-American youth to continue using direct action tactics to promote their cause. In 1967, José Ángel Gutierrez and four other co-founders organized the Mexican American Youth Organization (MAYO) in San Antonio to seek social justice through direct political confrontation and mass demonstrations. Over thirty MAYO chapters soon appeared in such cities as Austin, Kingsville, Uvalde, and across the Rio Grande Valley as the group rallied many disaffected Tejano teenagers and university students to become the most important political organization for Mexican-American youth in Texas.

MAYO sought to promote economic opportunity, political strength through unity among Mexican Americans, and local control of education. The group's most publicized effort involved a series of organized student strikes in the late 1960s, beginning with a famous walkout at Crystal City High School in December 1969. The protest marked a culmination of discontent over discrimination against Tejanos and the generally low opinion that Anglo teachers and administrators displayed toward their Hispanic students. Though the school offered college preparatory classes to the Anglo students (who made up 15 percent of the school's population), none were offered to Mexican-American students. The curriculum had no Mexican-centered elements, nor did the school teach any courses in a bilingual language. In fact, teachers and administrators so discouraged the speaking of Spanish that they often hit students with rulers if they uttered any Spanish words. The precipitating event that brought this swelling dissatisfaction to the breaking point turned out to be a dispute over the school's established policy of setting a quota of one Mexican-American cheerleader out of 4 total slots. When many students and their supportive parents, galvanized by MAYO activists (especially José Ángel Gutierrez)

**Attorney and Professor José Ángel Gutierrez holds up a T-shirt reading "Superman was an illegal alien," at an event for Texas U.S. Senate candidates.**

**Source: Library of Congress**

decided that this type of treatment had gone on long enough, they mimicked a form of direct action already being utilized by Mexican-American youth in other states by simply walking out of their classes (soon joined by many students at the local middle and elementary schools). While picketing, the students continued to demand access to college preparatory courses, bicultural and bilingual educational opportunities, more Hispanic counselors and teachers, and open student body elections for all cheerleader slots and student government positions. The students received occasional harassment, ranging from water balloon attacks by Anglo students to termination from their part-time off-campus jobs. The walkout proved to be effective when the local school board, suffering from reduced state appropriations caused by low student attendance, reached a settlement and conceded most of the students' demands. MAYO also organized walkouts with differing degrees of success in over thirty other South Texas towns.

Soon after the Crystal City strike's successful conclusion in early 1970, José Ángel Gutiérrez, Mario Compean, and other MAYO leaders formed La Raza Unida Party (RUP) to press for change through the political process. The RUP's first success came in Crystal City when the new party captured control of the local school board and city council, thus beginning its determined effort during the 1970s for greater Tejano economic, social, and political self-determination independent from the Democratic and Republican Parties.

## Governor Connally and Late-1960s State Politics

The Kennedy assassination affected the country and the world in many profound ways. Among the many ramifications of the murder was a delay in the ascendancy of the Republican Party to political supremacy in Texas. With the 1964 general election ballot including native son Lyndon Johnson running for president and the nearly-martyred John

Governor John B. Connally and President Lyndon B. Johnson at the Institute of Texan Cultures taken in 1968, in San Antonio, Texas.
Photo credit: UTSA Institute of Texan Cultures

Connally seeking another term for governor, Democrats scored huge electoral victories. After trouncing Don Yarborough in the Democratic primary, Connally received almost 75 percent of the vote against his Republican opponent to win reelection. Johnson's and Connally's coattails helped Senator Ralph Yarborough defeat his Republican challenger, oil company executive and future U.S. President George H.W. Bush. Yarborough received 56 percent of the vote by skillfully parrying Bush's attacks on his liberal voting record and support for the Civil Rights Act of 1964 while successfully portraying Bush, the Connecticut-born son of U.S. Senator Prescott Bush, as a wealthy "carpetbagger" who could not adequately represent the average Texan. If these victories were not enough for the Texas Republican Party, Bruce Alger of Dallas and Ed Foreman of Odessa—the party's only congressmen—both lost to Democratic challengers.

Connally enjoyed incredible popularity over the next four years (he easily won reelection in 1966) and translated that good favor with the public into many notable achievements in the promotion of higher education and statewide economic expansion. With Connally's strong support, the legislature expanded the community college and state university systems, increased college and university faculty pay, funded campus construction projects, and created the Texas College and University Coordinating Board (now Texas Higher Education Coordinating Board) in 1965 to oversee the entire structure. Connally also spent much of his energy promoting tourism to the Lone Star State and creating a favorable business climate to attract out-of-state industry, generally succeeding in both initiatives.

Connally proved to be more cautious about social issues and failed to be a strong advocate for minorities or the poor. He opposed the desegregation portion of the proposed Civil Rights Act of 1964 (though he went along with the legislation after it became law). While his pro-business policies aided many middle- and upper-class Texans, liberals noted that the regressive state sales tax that funded the governor's economic expansion agenda disproportionately hurt the poor. Connally also renounced many of his friend Lyndon Johnson's Great Society programs. After serving as governor, Connally joined many conservative Democrats with similar thinking and left the Democratic Party in the early 1970s to become a Republican.

Though Connally's tenure as governor succeeded in stymieing the advance of both liberalism and the Republican Party in Texas for the remainder of the decade, liberal Democrats and conservative Republicans each had a representative in the U.S. Senate to promote their ideals. Texas's liberal senior senator, Ralph Yarborough, voted for the Civil Rights Act of 1964 and the Voting Rights Act of 1965 while strongly supporting many other key Great Society bills. During his 12-year stay in Washington, he sponsored or co-sponsored the Elementary and Secondary Education Act, the Higher Education Act, the Bilingual Education Act, and a revised G.I. Bill (1966) that extended benefits to veterans who served during times of peace as well as times of war. Yarborough also supported numerous environmental efforts, co-writing the Endangered Species Act of 1969 and sponsoring laws establishing three national wildlife sanctuaries (Texas-Padre Island National Seashore, Guadalupe Mountains National Park, and Big Thicket National Preserve). Texas's Republican senator during these years, John Tower, opposed Yarborough on numerous matters including federal civil rights legislation. In 1965 he was named to the important Armed Services Committee, serving as an influential member and later chairman (from 1981 to 1984), earning a reputation as a forceful promoter of a modernized military. During his 24-year senate career, Tower provided a visible symbol of Republican Party success in Texas.

The discontent of many Texas Democrats with their national party's policies of promoting civil rights and social welfare programs encouraged Republicans during the late-1960s. In 1966 they won two congressional seats (including Bush in the Houston area), and re-elected John Tower to the Senate over Attorney General Waggoner Carr. During the 1968 election, Republican presidential nominee Richard Nixon would have carried the state if segregationist Alabama Governor George Wallace's third-party movement had not intervened. Though Wallace drew many votes away from the Democratic Party nominee Vice President Hubert Humphrey of Minnesota (Wallace received 584,269, or 19 percent of the vote), a majority of the governor's supporters would probably have preferred Nixon over Humphrey. The result was a narrow 41-40 percent victory for Humphrey. Conservative Democrat Preston Smith defeated Republican Paul Eggers by a 57:43 margin in the general election, but three Republicans won U.S. House seats. In 1970, Republicans retained these three congressional seats, and after conservative Democrat Lloyd Bentsen, Jr. defeated Ralph Yarborough's re-nomination bid, George H.W. Bush narrowly lost to Bentsen in the general election by a 53:47 margin. The anticipated political breakthrough that would allow the Republicans to wrest control of the state government failed to materialize by the end of the 1960s due to the Kennedy assassination, the elevation of Lyndon Johnson to the presidency, and the continued dominance of the conservative faction in the Texas Democratic Party. Nevertheless, the Republican Party's fortunes were rising, and the Democrats could not take many races for granted as they had in the past. For the first time since Reconstruction, two-party politics existed in the Lone Star State.

## Afterward: Vindication

*After the Marshall civil rights protests ceased, the local district attorney sought to prosecute the Bishop and Wiley student demonstrators. Eighty in all faced stiff fines for unlawful assembly and picketing or failure to leave a business when requested by the owner. Judges promptly found all the defendants guilty. To help with their appeals, the students held fund raisers at local black churches and acquired help from the National Association for the Advancement of Colored People (NAACP) Legal Fund. In December 1960, the Texas Court of Criminal Appeals ruled in favor of the students, throwing out the city ordinance as unconstitutional and the state statute too vague to justify prosecution of the protestors. In crafting his opinion, Judge K.K. Woodley conspicuously avoided any ruling on the constitutionality of segregation in public accommodations. Though Marshall's businesses continued to discriminate over the next three years, Bishop and Wiley College students' dissatisfaction with the status quo was duly noted and the practice of segregation would eventually end, as elsewhere, with passage of the historic Civil Rights Act of 1964.*

## *Myth & Legend*

**Members of a Vast Conspiracy Killed President John Kennedy in Dallas**

*The nation's most commonly held conspiracy theory asserts that Lee Harvey Oswald did not act alone in killing President John F. Kennedy in Dallas. Further, many believe that Jack Ruby killed Oswald to silence him so that he would not reveal the extent of a vast conspiracy to assassinate the president.*

*The myth of a grand conspiracy being responsible for the death of President Kennedy began almost immediately following Kennedy's and Oswald's deaths. Not only could large numbers of Americans not believe that someone as inconsequential as Lee Harvey Oswald could be responsible for affecting American and world history in such a dramatic way, Oswald's murder left many questions unanswered and instantly led the more critical to suspect that Ruby had killed the assassin solely to silence him.*

*In the ensuing decades, a slew of writers and filmmakers challenged the Warren Report's conclusions that Oswald and Ruby acted alone when they committed their murderous acts. Many simply did not believe the Commission's findings and honestly pored over the available evidence to question many inconsistencies in the commission's approach and findings. Others simply sought to capitalize on the public's interest in the story to make money from publishing books and producing documentaries that fanned the flames of doubt concerning the Warren Commission, often basing their hypotheses on dubious evidence. Still others, most notably film director Oliver Stone, have used the Kennedy assassination as a platform to criticize the American government for various policies pursued after the Kennedy years. Stone's "JFK" postulates that Kennedy was killed by hardened Cold Warriors afraid that the president would end U.S. aid to the South Vietnamese government, allowing it to fall to communists. The film implicates Lyndon Johnson as a co-conspirator in a* **coup d' état,** *which led to the disastrous U.S. military intervention in South Vietnam just two years later.*

*Despite popular acceptance of such notions, the historical consensus among most reputable historians is that both Oswald and Ruby acted alone when they committed their violent deeds. Certainly there is much to criticize the Warren Commission for: first, the board undertook its deliberations relatively quickly. President Johnson sought a swift resolution so that the controversy would not interfere with his 1964 re-election efforts. The speedy pace of the committee's work meant that some avenues of inquiry would not receive careful consideration; second, we now know that much information was kept from the Commission. Many government agencies, most notably the FBI and the CIA, failed to provide materials that would have certainly raised eyebrows. The FBI, for example, did not provide the Commission with all the files it had on Oswald—not because of a government cover-up, but, rather, because officials did not want to reveal just how incompetent they were in monitoring Oswald's movements after he returned to America from his stint in the Soviet Union. Further, the CIA chose not to release much information concerning the agency's operations against Cuban leader Fidel Castro. To have done so would have divulged, among other revelations, the CIA's efforts to kill the dictator. This information would have led to a much more detailed investigation into the agency's secret operations since it would have provided a possible motivation for Castro to retaliate against the American president. Nevertheless, these disclosures alone do not prove the allegations made by countless conspiracy theorists.*

*Ultimately, the main accusations of the Kennedy assassination conspiracy theorists are baseless. Theorists have yet to provide any conclusive evidence that events occurred in a way fundamentally different from that posited by the Warren Commission. Mere supposition cannot replace solid evidence. To date, there is no indisputable proof in the form of credible witnesses, verified documents, or scientific evidence that can substantiate any theory contrary to the Warren Report's general conclusions. Theorists often fall victim to nitpicking discrepancies while ignoring the bulk of the available evidence pointing in another direction. In the end, the evidence against Oswald acting alone in killing Kennedy, while not 100 percent conclusive, is rather overwhelming. Similarly, Jack Ruby had no proven association with Oswald before murdering him and seems to have acted through a hero complex when he spontaneously decided to avenge Kennedy. Sometimes, the simplest explanations are the correct ones.*

## Suggestions for Further Reading

Behnken, Brian D. "The 'Dallas Way': Protest, Response, and the Civil Rights Experience in Big D and Beyond," *Southwestern Historical Quarterly* 111 2007: 1-29.

Cox, Patrick L. *Ralph W. Yarborough: The People's Senator* Austin: University of Texas Press, 2002.

Dallek, Robert. *Flawed Giant: Lyndon Johnson and His Times, 1961-1973* New York: Oxford University Press, 1999.

____, *Lone Star Rising: Lyndon Johnson and His Times, 1908-1960* New York: Oxford University Press, 1991.

Davidson, Chandler. *Race and Class in Texas Politics* Princeton: Princeton University Press, 1990.

Green, George N. *The Establishment in Texas Politics: The Primitive Years, 1938-1957* Westport, Conn.: Greenwood, 1979.

Knaggs, John R. *Two-Party Texas: The John Tower Era, 1961-1984* Austin: Eakin Press, 1986.

Krochmal, Max, *Blue Texas: The Making of a Multiracial Democratic Coalition in the Civil Rights Era* Chapel Hill: University of North Carolina University Press, 2016.

Kuhlman, Martin. "The Civil Rights Movement in Texas: Desegregation of Public Accommodations, 1950-1964," Ph.D. Texas Tech University, 1994.

____, "Direct Action at the University of Texas during the Civil Rights Movement, 1960-1965." *Southwestern Historical Quarterly* 98 1995: 550-566.

Montejano, David. *Anglos and Mexicans in the Making of Texas, 1836-1986* Austin: University of Texas Press, 1987.

Navarro, Armando. *Mexican American Youth Organization: Avant-Garde of the Chicano Movement in Texas* Austin: University of Texas Press, 1995.

Olien, Roger M. *From Token to Triumph: The Texas Republicans since 1920* Dallas: Southern Methodist University Press, 1982.

Phillips, Michael. *White Metropolis: Race, Ethnicity, and Religion in Dallas, 1841-2001* Austin: University of Texas Press, 2006.

Posner, Gerald. *Case Closed: Lee Harvey Oswald and the Assassination of JFK* New York: Random House, 1993.

Reston, James, Jr. *Lone Star: The Life of John Connally* New York: Harper and Row, 1989.

Seals, Jr., Donald, "The Wiley-Bishop Student Movement: A Case Study in the 1960 Civil Rights Sit-Ins," *Southwestern Historical Quarterly*, Vol. 106, No. 3, Jan. 2003: 418-440.

Shockley, John Staples. *Chicano Revolt in a Texas Town* Notre Dame, Indiana: University of Notre Dame Press, 1974.

**IDENTIFICATION:** Briefly describe each term.

"Viva Kennedy" clubs
John Tower
Lee Harvey Oswald
Lyndon Johnson
Great Society
Civil Rights Act of 1964
"War on Poverty"
Barbara Jordan
Minimum Wage March
José Ángel Gutierrez
Crystal City Walkout
MAYO
George H.W. Bush
John Connally
Ralph Yarborough

**MULTIPLE CHOICE:** Choose the correct response.

1. Before running for president in 1960, Lyndon Johnson served as:
   A. a Supreme Court Justice;
   B. Senate Majority Leader;
   C. Director of the Food Stamps Program;
   D. Director of the Head Start Program.

2. John Kennedy was able to carry Texas in the 1960 presidential election because he won the support of:
   A. most conservative Democrats;
   B. most African Americans and Tejanos;
   C. about half of the state's Republicans;
   D. John Tower.

3. Before killing John Kennedy, Lee Harvey Oswald tried to shoot _____ in Dallas several months earlier.
   A. Lyndon Johnson;
   B. Jack Cox;
   C. Jack Ruby;
   D. Edwin Walker;
   E. none of the above.

4. Of the following, which was not a part of Lyndon Johnson's "Great Society"?
   A. a "war on poverty";
   B. civil rights;
   C. Medicare;
   D. the Federal Reserve.

5. Lyndon Johnson chose not to run for another term as president primarily because:
   A. He had already served two terms.
   B. His Great Society agenda failed to pass through Congress.
   C. His popularity with a majority of Americans plummeted as the Vietnam War dragged on.
   D. none of the above.

6. _____ took part in the so-called "Minimum Wage March" in the summer of 1966.
   A. Mexican American maids and other domestic workers;
   B. Mexican American agricultural workers;
   C. black school janitors;
   D. none of the above.

7. Of the following, which was an important Chicano organization during the 1960s?
   A. LULAC;
   B. NAACP;
   C. MAYO;
   D. TOTO;
   E. G.I. Forum.

8. _____ served longer than any other governor of Texas during the 1960s.
   A. John Connally;
   B. Ralph Yarborough;
   C. Allan Shivers;
   D. Price Daniel.

9. _____ served for twelve years as a liberal leader in the U.S. Senate representing Texas.
   A. John Tower;
   B. George H.W. Bush;
   C. Preston Smith;
   D. Ralph Yarborough.

10. All of the following constituted a major part of John Connally's agenda as governor except:
    A. promotion of civil rights;
    B. increased funding for higher education;
    C. promotion of tourism;
    D. attraction of out-of-state business and industry.

**TRUE/FALSE:** Indicate whether each statement is true or false.

1. Desegregation took place in most major Texas cities with significantly less violence than occurred in the Deep South.

2. The Civil Rights Act of 1964 legally ended segregation in all public facilities.

3. John Connally chose not to run for another term as governor after the Kennedy assassination.

4. José Ángel Gutierrez disagreed with direct action techniques such as strikes and protest marches to bring about social change.

5. The students involved in the Crystal City Student Walkout never got agreement for any of their demands by the local school board.

6. La Raza Unida was a solid supporter of the Democratic Party in Texas elections held during the late-1960s.

7. Lyndon Johnson's "War on Poverty" programs not only failed to reduce poverty in America but also led to a slight increase in national poverty rates.

8. The unpopularity of continued U.S. involvement in the Vietnam War directly led to Lyndon Johnson's decision not to seek another term as president.

9. John Connally proved to be a weak advocate for minority rights and policies designed to help the poor of all races.

10. George H.W. Bush joined John Tower as a Republican member of the U.S. Senate after he defeated Ralph Yarborough in a highly contested race.

**MATCHING:** Match the response in column A with the item in column B.

1. John Tower
2. John Connally
3. Jack Ruby
4. La Raza Unida
5. Barbara Jordan
6. MAYO
7. Ralph Yarborough
8. Great Society
9. Civil Rights Act of 1964
10. Vietnam War

A. killer of Lee Harvey Oswald
B. Texas governor injured during the Kennedy assassination
C. first African American from Texas ever elected to the U.S. Congress
D. liberal Texas senator who voted for the Civil Rights Act of 1964
E. first Republican to win statewide office since Reconstruction
F. label for LBJ's domestic agenda
G. Mexican-American youth civil rights organization
H. one of LBJ's most important domestic achievements
I. Tejano political party
J. did much to damage LBJ's credibility with the American people

**ESSAY QUESTIONS:**

1. Compare and contrast black and Tejano efforts for civil rights during the 1960s. In what ways were these efforts similar in terms of the goals they sought, the approaches taken, and the results? In what ways were they different?

2. Describe the process by which racial desegregation was achieved in many major Texas cities before passage of the Civil Rights Act of 1964.

3. Describe the motive and opportunity Lee Harvey Oswald had for killing President John Kennedy in Dallas.

4. Evaluate the major achievements and setbacks of Lyndon Johnson's presidency.

# Chapter 18

# *A Transitional Decade 1972-1979*

*Prelude: Tom Landry—Texas Sports Icon*

On January 16, 1972, Tom Landry, head coach of the National Football League (NFL) Dallas Cowboys, calmly walked out onto the Tulane Stadium football field in New Orleans as his team prepared to play the Miami Dolphins in Super Bowl VI. Having lost the Super Bowl to the Baltimore Colts, not to mention the 1966 and 1967 NFL Championship Games prior to the 1970 merger of the NFL with the American Football League, Landry and his squad had to overcome the psychological pressure of "not being able to win the big games" if they were to emerge victorious.

Landry had come a long way from his humble beginnings in Mission, Texas, where he was born on September 11, 1924. A star quarterback for his South Texas town's high school football team, he moved on to the University of Texas where he planned to study industrial engineering. With the outbreak of World War II, his older brother Robert enlisted in the Army Air Corps but died when the B-17 he was ferrying to England crashed. Inspired by his brother's sacrifice, Tom Landry followed his brother's footsteps and enlisted in the Air Corps. After training in Texas and Iowa, in 1944 he was assigned to the Eighth Air Force based in England and began taking part in offensive operations as a co-pilot on a B-17 bomber. From November 1944 through April 1945, Landry survived 30 combat missions, including one that resulted in a crash-landing in Belgium after his plane ran out of fuel.

Returning to the University of Texas after the war, he starred as a fullback and defensive back for the Longhorns football team, graduating with a bachelor's degree in 1949 followed by a Master's degree in industrial engineering from the University of Houston in 1952. During the first half of the 1950s, Landry served as a player-coach for the New York Giants. In the latter half of the decade, he became the team's defensive coordinator and became a highly sought-after head coaching prospect.

In 1960, Landry accepted the head coaching position for the NFL expansion franchise, the Dallas Cowboys, allowing him to come home to the Lone Star State. He was rewarded with a mediocre team that produced a zero-win first season. Despite three more lackluster campaigns, the team's owner, Clint Murchison, Jr., believed in Landry and granted him a ten-year extension on his contract in 1964. The team soon rebounded, reaching two championship games in the 1960s, but had yet to "win the big one." Nevertheless, Landry believed by the 1970s that his team was poised to achieve greatness.

The last quarter century of the 1900s witnessed one of the most surprising political twists in Texas history—the success and growing dominance of the Republican Party. Like other southern states, Texas had been a one-party state since the failure of Reconstruction. What occurred politically in the Lone Star State beginning in the late 1960s and early 1970s mirrored developments taking place in other southern states, with social and business conservatives joining the Republican ranks in reaction to policies of the national Democratic Party, especially support for the Civil Rights Movement and increased federal government involvement in the economy.

The 1970s also produced important economic and cultural changes. Oil industry profits exploded built upon previous decades of oil exploration. Overseas events rendered Texas oil in high demand, boosting the state's economy. When policies of the international oil cartel known as the Organization of Petroleum Exporting Countries (OPEC) squeezed international markets, many Texans actually benefitted, despite higher gasoline prices that hurt everyday consumers. Bolstered by the growth of new industries and the increasing expansion of the airline industry, Texas enjoyed a decade of economic success while the country suffered the grips of a national recession. Meanwhile, a slew of Texas entertainers and the arrival of new sports franchises to the Lone Star State further contributed to the surprising economic and cultural dynamism of the decade.

**The Sharpstown Scandal**

During the 1970s, a major political scandal shook the faith of Texas voters. Known as the Sharpstown Scandal, the issue involved Houston banker Frank Sharp, who hoped the legislature would approve new laws amenable to his business holdings such as the Sharpstown State Bank and the National Bankers Life Insurance Corporation. Sharp offered legislators and other state officials hundreds of thousands of dollars in loans to buy stock in his company and reap profits. The scandal broke with the filing of a lawsuit by the Securities and Exchange Commission alleging that Governor Preston Smith and Speaker of the House Gus Mutscher received some of Sharp's bribes. Thirty Democratic and Republican legislators, known by the press as the "Dirty Thirty," pressured the governor to investigate the scandal. Indictments followed a 1972 grand jury investigation while prosecutors named Governor Smith an unindicted co-conspirator. Speaker Mutscher, one of the Speaker's aides, and Texas state legislator Tommy Shannon were all convicted of conspiracy and bribery charges and sentenced to five years probation. Sharp was found guilty of violating federal banking and securities laws and sentenced to probation for three years and issued a $5,000 fine.

In the wake of the Sharpstown Scandal, Texans felt that they needed a fresh start. Though Texas voters were increasingly choosing Republican presidential candidates, most had not yet made the decision to vote for Republicans in statewide races. Though leading

Democrats in the state were tainted by the Sharpstown incident (including Lieutenant Governor Ben Barnes, who denied involvement and was never charged but had received a loan from Sharp's bank), partisan voting patterns did not change significantly in the wake of the scandal. However, citizens demanded legislation to remedy the transgressions illustrated by Sharpstown. New election laws soon passed requiring candidates to make full financial disclosures, to list their campaign contributors, and to be subject to new ethics legislation. It was hoped that these rules would prevent such episodes of lawbreaking in the future. In retrospect, the value of these changes was greatly heightened when, soon thereafter, the Watergate scandal erupted in national politics.

**Texans and Watergate**

The Watergate Affair became one of the most serious political scandals in American history. The country first heard of Watergate on June 17, 1972, after authorities arrested five men for breaking into the Democratic National Committee Headquarters, which was located in the Watergate Complex along the Potomac River in Washington, D.C. The burglars had actually broken into the headquarters days earlier and had copied files and "tapped" the phones important to the Democratic Party's campaign operations. Though successful in their first illegal entry, the "bunglers" (as the media soon dubbed them) were caught during their second attempt to break into the building in order to copy more documents and adjust their bugging devices. While the investigation (by the police and by the press) became a long one, people eventually learned that the orders to break into the Watergate Building went to the highest level of the Republican Party and that eventually the press identified members of President Richard Nixon's staff as those who ordered the "bunglers" to do their work. (At the very least, President Nixon was involved in an extensive effort to cover up White House connections to the burglary.) Investigative reporters Bob Woodward and Carl Bernstein of the *Washington Post* continued to break news questioning the facts of the case for months using anonymous sources—including one they called "Deep Throat" (revealed thirty years later to be Mark Felt, the Deputy Director of the Federal Bureau of Investigation). One small story followed another until a larger tale emerged. Eventually, the Federal Bureau of Investigation learned that the Republican Committee to Re-elect the President had created a slush fund to pay the burglars and others engaged in what were called "dirty tricks" to tar the Democrats and to soil their candidate for president, South Dakota Senator George McGovern.

When authorities had amassed enough evidence that Republicans were implicated in the Watergate break-ins, the Senate formed a Watergate Investigation Committee while the House organized a parallel effort through the Judiciary Committee. Several Texans became involved in the subsequent investigations. Bombastic Congressman Wright Patman, an icon to Democrats, was among the first to call for investigations. Credited with helping expose Republican dirty tricks, Congresswoman Barbara Jordan of Houston gave what many observers called the most effective speeches during the hearings. "My faith in the Constitution," she said, "is complete, it is total. I am not going to sit here and be an idle spectator to the diminution, the subversion, and the destruction of the Constitution." Attorney Leon Jaworski of Houston headed the Watergate special prosecution team, which made him indispensable as new facts about Watergate surfaced. Before the United States Supreme Court, he argued in *United States v. Nixon* that the president must turn over White House tapes that had relevance to the crime. The tapes proved that the president and some members of his staff had engaged in a conspiracy to obstruct justice. In 1976, he wrote his book, *The Right and the Power*, on his efforts to bring the guilty men in the Republican Party to justice.

As a result of the Watergate hearings, the House, led by Jordan, was eventually poised to impeach Richard Nixon—and observers believed that the Senate would convict the president. However, before he was officially charged with obstructing justice, Nixon resigned as president on August 9, 1974, vindicating the work of those Texans who had worked diligently to see justice carried out and the Constitution defended. One of the more dire consequences of the Watergate scandal was that Americans became more and more jaded about politics, some believing that the word "politician" and "crook" were synonymous.

**Post-Sharpstown Politics**

The 1972 elections took place just before the Watergate scandal surfaced. At the state level, the main action took place in the Democratic Party primaries. Conservative rancher and former state legislator Dolph Briscoe squared up against incumbent Governor Preston Smith, who was seeking a third two-year term, Lieutenant Governor Ben Barnes, and liberal state legislator Frances "Sissy" Farenthold of Corpus Christi, who had gained prominence as one of the "Dirty Thirty." With voters giving limited support to the Sharpstown-tainted Smith and Barnes, Briscoe and Farenthold found themselves in a run-off election. While Farenthold's supporters were ardent in promoting her candidacy, her campaign lacked funding. Meanwhile, Briscoe was more attractive to corporate interests who donated millions to his campaign. In the run-off Briscoe defeated Farenthold by more than 200,000 votes but narrowly won the general election with 48 percent of the vote over Republican Henry Grover (45 percent) and third-party La Raza Unida candidate Ramsey Muñiz (6 percent). Texans also returned Republican John Tower to the U.S. Senate by re-electing him over Democratic Judge Harold Barefoot Sanders. In the Democratic primary, Ralph Yarborough had won a plurality of votes in his final attempt to return to national political office, but Sanders bested him in a run-off. Meanwhile, at twenty-nine years of age, Republican Alan Steelman of Dallas became the youngest candidate ever elected to the U.S. Congress when he won a seat in the House of Representatives.

Dolph Briscoe became Texas's first governor to be elected by less than 50 percent voter support in the general election. Briscoe hailed from Uvalde, where he ran his family's extensive ranch holdings and worked as a local businessman. Estimates were that Briscoe either owned or controlled a million acres in Texas, making him the largest landowner in the state. He served as governor in a time of prosperity, when high oil prices boosted oil and gas industries and helped grow the economy. With prosperous times generating higher tax revenues, Briscoe did not have to worry about shortfalls in the state budget and no new taxes were enacted during his years in office. The budget surplus allowed Briscoe to focus on internal improvements, such as highway projects, and restoring public faith in the state government after the Sharpstown scandal. His emphasis on road construction was not a surprise since during his earlier legislative career he helped lead the effort to build the farm-to-market transportation road system for rural areas. Briscoe also approved the first Texas Open Records Act (now called the Texas Public Information Act) and other new reform laws following the Sharpstown scandal.

In 1972, Texas voters gave their approval to the extension of the governor's term to four years, set to take effect during the next gubernatorial term. In addition, the lieutenant governor, attorney general, treasurer, comptroller of public accounts, commissioner of the General Land Office, and the secretary of state also saw their terms lengthened to four years. In 1974, Briscoe became the first Texas governor elected to a four-year term, earning 1,016,334 (61 percent) to 514,725 (31 percent) for his Republican opponent Jim Granberry, with Ramsey Muñiz running a distant third with 93,295 votes (6 percent).

During the mid-1970s, Texas voters alternated between Republican and Democratic presidential candidates as national party politics continued to be contentious in the state. Richard Nixon easily won his re-election bid in 1972 before the Watergate scandal broke. Texans supported the Republican incumbent with 66 percent of the vote while the Democratic candidate, South Dakota Senator George McGovern, pulled in just 33 percent. Rural voters—long the bastion of the Democratic Party—had begun voting for Nixon and the Republicans in 1972. This result, replicated elsewhere in the South, displayed the fruits of the Republican Party's "southern strategy" developed during the 1970s, which sought to boost growing support for the party among whites at the expense of African American voters by taking firm stands on states' rights issues at the expense of federal government responsibilities, especially in the realm of civil rights. Nevertheless, despite Republican gains, the Democrats continued to dominate the 1974 mid-term elections for U.S. Congress and carried all the statewide offices. Further, in the wake of Watergate, Democrat Jimmy Carter defeated Republican President Gerald Ford in the 1976 election by a 51-48 percent margin. Still, though Texas returned to the Democrats in 1976, Texans would make political history just two years later by electing the state's first Republican governor since Reconstruction. It was no longer a given that certain Texas voters would remain "Yellow Dog Democrats" forever.

In 1978 Briscoe hoped for a third term but suffered a surprising defeat in the Democratic primary at the hands of Attorney General John Hill who won 51.4 percent of the vote. Hill had cultivated the support of the education community and charged that Briscoe had done little to improve public education while in office. Though Democrats had been torn over whom to support in the primary (with Democratic leader and state comptroller Bob Bullock supporting Briscoe and calling Hill a "turkey"), the primary outcome came as a shock. The prevailing wisdom held that Hill as a Democrat would win the governor's office easily, and, consequently, he ran a lackluster campaign against the Republican candidate, William P. "Bill" Clements.

Clements had lived the proverbial rags-to-riches story. Born in Dallas, he came of age during the Great Depression while working as a teenager in the oil fields as a roughneck to help support his family after losing their farm. He attended Southern Methodist University for a few years before seeking a successful career in oil drilling. After World War II, Clements and two associates borrowed money to buy two oil drilling rigs, which became the basis of SEDCO, the world's largest offshore drilling company by the 1970s. Clements had been a long-time contributor to the Republican Party and had been approached often to run for governor but had always turned down the party's offer. By 1977 he believed a Republican had a chance to win the governorship. After unsuccessfully trying to persuade several prominent politicians to run for the office, he finally decided to enter the race himself. Clements spent millions of his own fortune on his campaign and toured relentlessly through rural areas of the state hoping to lure conservative voters into the Republican Party. Brash and blunt in his personal appearances, Clements came across as quite a contrast to his more sophisticated Democratic opponent, Attorney General Hill. The election was close, so close that it took some local recounts and weeks to determine the actual winner. Clements seized the governor's office by less than one percent of the vote in the most expensive election in state history.

One cannot underestimate the importance of Clements' victory as he became the first Republican to occupy the Texas Governor's Mansion in 105 years. His victory was a harbinger of things to come. Conservative Texas Democrats increasingly shifted their loyalty to the Republican Party, influenced by the party's southern strategy and helped by the influx of many recent northern and western transplants into the state. In 1978, Republican John Tower also received just enough support to win re-election to the U.S. Senate as he edged Democratic Congressman Robert Krueger by less than 1 percent of the vote.

Despite these notable Republican successes in the state, some Democratic politicians remained popular with the voters. Senator Lloyd Bentsen continued to win elections throughout the 1970s and 1980s. Other Democrats, such as Bob Bullock who served as both Secretary of State and State Comptroller in the 1970s, were also still able to appeal to voters, entrenching themselves in the halls of power. Bullock made a point of making a "splash" and earning positive public opinion by going after businesses that were delinquent in paying their taxes.

Though having limited powers, the governor of Texas has the power to appoint a number of officials. Not surprisingly, more Republicans entered into state government during the Clements administration even while the governor sought to downsize state government by having all state offices justify the number of people in their employ as part of his efforts to bring "corporate business practices" to state government. In the end, no positions were eliminated, but due to the fact that the state population had increased substantially and no new employees were hired, the state bureaucracy actually retrenched. Clements also championed an anti-crime package from the day of his inauguration but was unable to follow up on it until the last half of his second administration.

Another trend that was developing in the 1970s would carry through the subsequent decades—the growing relationship between Protestant religions and conservative politics. Many Protestant faiths began to focus increasingly on evangelism in the 1970s. In June of 1972, 75,000 mostly college and high school students convened in Dallas to discuss ways to incorporate evangelism more in their daily life. One manifestation of such evan- gelism became tied into vocal support of political candidates that shared common values with Protestant church members. This phenomenon would slowly result in a "shifting of loyalties from the Democratic Party to the Republican Party." The conservative religious values of groups such as the Southern Baptist Convention would lead to Texas voters exhibiting more support for a political party—the Republican Party—that cast itself as the conservative choice. It also introduced issues of morality into the ballot box in a new way in the last part of the twentieth century. This move was paralleled in national life, for example, with the creation of the Moral Majority organization by Jerry Falwell in the 1980s which specifically tied together political action and religious morality.

## Constitutional Convention

Problems had long existed with the Texas State Constitution of 1876. The constitution embodied a fundamental distrust of government, a product of the Democratic response to the Republican E.J. Davis administration during the Reconstruction Era. The governor had limited power; the legislature did not meet annually; and, the document needed amendments to remain relevant to modern Texas. In 1971 the process of revising the constitution began. This process gained momentum as the Sharpstown scandal came to light, after which people wanted to ensure that Texas had a more effective and ethical government. Over the next three years, commissions studied various reforms and public meetings were held to solicit input from citizens before a constitutional convention finally took place. Among the suggested changes were proposals to have the state legislature meet annually instead of every other year, grant more power to the governor, and to reorganize the judicial branch.

One of the main problems encountered at the convention proved to be the inclusion of state legislators as delegates. This fact created a hyper-political situation. The delegates not only had a troubled history of working with one another, but they also faced the distracting election of 1974 during the convention. The Speaker of the House of Representatives, Price Daniel, Jr., served as the president of the convention. In the summer of 1974, the delegates finally voted on the eleven-article constitution over which they had been laboring for several months. The vote was three shy of approval for the constitution to be sent to Texas voters. Many problems existed with the proposed constitution. People disagreed over a "right-to-work" provision ("right-to-work" was generally favored by businessmen since employees do not have to join a union when they begin their jobs; unions generally were against these provisions because it weakened employees' bargaining power). About the constitution generally, some people wanted more reform, some wanted less, and some believed there was no need for a new constitution. Furthermore, Governor Briscoe opposed the document.

During the following year, the state legislature tried to revive support for the new constitution by adding a set of eight new proposed amendments to the old 1876 document. The legislature approved the measure, but the voters did not, leaving constitutional revision dead in the water. Thus ended the last major attempt to revise and streamline the Texas Constitution after the taxpayers spent millions of dollars on the effort. Consequently, the constitution under which the Lone Star State still operates remains one that is unwieldy and reflects more of the fears of Texas Democrats after Reconstruction than one established to create an efficient government to address today's modern problems.

Since 1876, more than 690 amendments to the Texas Constitution have been proposed, and by 2020, 507 have been enacted. At times it has become necessary to pass new amendments to deal with the limitations of older amendments. For the legislature to write new amendments on a regular basis can be daunting to the point of causing inaction by legislators. Further, as required by the constitution, all amendments must be approved by a majority of Texas voters. As it currently stands, Texas voters are asked to approve or reject amendments that often deal with the minutiae of the legislative process—a difficult task if one wishes to ensure that all voters are properly educated about the issues reflected in the proposed amendments. The entire process tends to put a damper on legislative activity and demoralizes legislators and citizens alike.

## La Raza Unida Party

During the 1960s, Mexican Americans in Texas experienced a political awakening with increased voter participation and the founding of the state's newest third party. La Raza Unida Party (RUP), named for *la raza*, meaning "the race" in Spanish, sought to galvanize Hispanics into a political force for change by achieving greater economic, social, and political self-determination, especially in South Texas where they held little or no power despite being a majority of the population. Founded by José Ángel Gutiérrez and Mario Compean, the height of the party's impact occurred during the 1970s. In the 1972 governor's race, the RUP selected Ramsey Muñiz as the party's candidate. An attorney, Muñiz had previously worked with the Great Society's Model Cities Program in Waco, Texas. Young, accomplished, and confident, he projected the image that the party wished to display to Texas voters. For lieutenant governor, the RUP chose Alma Canales, a twenty-four-year-old student originally from Edinburg. Though she did not meet the age requirement stipulated by the Texas Constitution for holding the lieutenant governor's office, RUP leaders enthusiastically endorsed her candidacy believing her background as a migrant worker was central to the party's agenda and her candidacy would also signal the importance of women to the party.

The RUP effort to win the governor's office began without a campaign committee or state funds, but party activists visited numerous Texas cities to spread the party's positions on public issues. The RUP platform focused on education, demanding multi-lingual and multi-cultural programs in public schools, school boards that represented the makeup of Hispanic communities, and free pre-school for all citizens. Other sections of the platform concentrated on lowering the voting age to eighteen, abolishing the death penalty, and breaking up business monopolies. Some of the platform had a more radical tone, such as provisions allowing foreigners to vote and ending the embargo on Cuba. In addition to the gubernatorial race, the RUP ran candidates for nine state offices and numerous local offices. On election day in 1972 turnout was substantial, and Muñiz received 214,000 votes (6 percent), a good showing for a new party that had limited financial backing. This showing, however, could not be duplicated in future election cycles. In 1974 the RUP experienced reduced turnout although Muñiz ran for the governorship once again. The party won many local races in South Texas but failed to win any seats in the state legislature. Furthermore, La Raza Unida suffered a major setback in 1976 when authorities arrested Muñiz on drug smuggling charges. Though proclaiming his innocence and that he was only guilty of "being Latino and an activist in America," a jury convicted Muñiz and sentenced him to fifteen years in prison.

With no proven candidate for the 1978 election, La Raza Unida turned to Mario Compean, one of La Raza's founders, to run for the governor's office. After Compean only received 15,000 votes, the party was denied state political funding for subsequent elections. As the RUP continued to have problems connecting with voters in urban areas, La Raza's influence on statewide elections waned. The organization that had spawned La Raza, the Mexican American Youth Organization (MAYO), similarly saw a downturn in support.

Democratic Party leaders realized that they had lost significant Tejano support with the rise of La Raza. A newly formed organization, Mexican-American Democrats, worked to reestablish good relations and to recruit more Hispanic voters into the Democratic

Jordan delivering the Keynote Address at the Democratic National Convention in New York City, July 12, 1976.
Photo credit: Library of Congress

Party. This attempt included the luring of one of La Raza's founders, Willie Velasquez, back to the Democratic Party. Velasquez had been interested in voter registration while working with La Raza. He founded the Southwest Voter Registration Education Project (SVREP) in 1974 to bring more Mexican American voters into the political process. In 1975, changes in the Voting Rights Act of 1965 effectively applied the act to the Hispanic populations of the Southwest. By the end of the 1970s, these efforts bore fruit with an increase in Mexican American political participation helped by the drawing of legislative and congressional districts with Hispanic majorities.

**Women's Rights and Political Representation**

Texas women achieved enormous gains in the twentieth century. The suffrage movement had worked tirelessly to get women the vote. Females received recognition for their participation in both world wars. After World War II, married women received control over their own property. During the 1970s, progress on women's issues continued. In 1972, Texas voters approved the state's Equal Rights Amendment by a large margin. Designed to extend the same legal rights to women that were enjoyed by men, this reform effort had begun as the Equal Legal Rights Amendment in the late 1950s. The amendment ended many practices, such as discrimination in loan applications and the sale of real estate. Also in 1972, the Texas legislature became one of the first southern states to ratify the national Equal Rights Amendment. The first chapter of the National Organization for Women (NOW) in Texas organized the following year, as did other groups such as the National Women's Political Caucus (NWPC) and the Texas Women's Political Caucus (TWPC). The TWPC, dedicated to the election of more women to political positions in the state, began its work in 1971. Two years later it welcomed representatives of the NWPC at a convention in Houston attended by more than one thousand Texas delegates.

The activism of female politicians during the 1970s resulted in numerous election wins. Voters put six women in the state legislature in 1972, including Kay Bailey Hutchison, a future United States Senator. Two victors were the first Republican women elected to the Texas House and the Texas Senate. In 1976, Irma Rangel became the first Hispanic woman elected to the state legislature. Barbara Jordan's career continued to be impressive when she became a national figure in 1974. Jordan sat on the House Judiciary Committee as it debated charges of impeachment against President Richard Nixon for his involvement in the Watergate scandal. Jordan emerged as an eloquent and passionate defender of the U.S. Constitution, fought for the civil rights of all minority groups, and gave the Keynote Address to the 1976 Democratic Party National Convention.

In 1977, the National Women's Conference was held in Houston, the first national conference of its kind since the Seneca Falls Convention of 1848, which was a touchstone in the women's rights movement. Delegates attended from all fifty states. The conference in Houston submitted several recommendations to President Jimmy Carter's administration. In the aftermath of the conference, the U.S. Senate extended the ratification period for the Equal Rights Amendment (ERA) for an additional three years. After the three-year extension, thirty-five states had ratified the amendment—three short of the thirty-eight needed for passage. Since 1982, Congress has reintroduced the Equal Rights Amendment in every session. In the 110th Congress (2007-2008), the Equal Rights Amendment bills were introduced by Massachusetts Senator Edward Kennedy and New York Representative Carolyn Maloney. These bills contained no clauses imposing a deadline on the ratification process. Despite no clarity about a deadline and no explicit extension, some states have continued to approve the ERA, including the state of Illinois in 2018.

In 1973, the U.S. Supreme Court's decision in the *Roe v. Wade* case involving abortion rights made national headlines. The legal case grew out of events that occurred in Dallas beginning in 1970. The plaintiff, a pregnant woman referred to as Jane Roe to protect her identity, filed suit against Dallas District Attorney Henry Wade through her lawyer, state legislator Sarah Weddington. Roe's attorney argued that state laws prohibiting abortion during the first trimester were unconstitutional. Lower courts agreed, but Wade refused to stop prosecuting physicians who performed abortions. The case finally reached the Supreme Court, which ruled that such laws were indeed unconstitutional, though the justices left the door open regarding possible restrictions according to length of pregnancy.

Another important development affecting Texas women during the 1970s was passage in 1972 of Title IX of the Educational Amendments to the Civil Rights Act, which stated: "No person in the United States shall, on the basis of sex, be excluded from participation in, be denied the benefits of, or be subjected to discrimination under any education program or activity receiving Federal financial assistance." Over the years, one of the most visible impacts of this important federal law is the requirement that highs schools, colleges, and universities receiving federal funding must provide equal funding for men's and women's athletic programs. Since the enactment of Title IX, female participation in sports has soared in Texas, as elsewhere in the United States.

Despite the achievements made during the decade, the women's movement appeared to be losing steam by the end of the 1970s. The ERA failed to be ratified by the requisite number of states. Critics such as Phyllis Schlafly's Eagle Forum and Jerry Falwell's Moral Majority helped to stymie the movement by questioning the amendment's supposed repercussions, citing a potential negative impact on traditional family roles and possibly reducing the morale and effectiveness of the armed forces.

**Long lines of cars at a gas station waiting for fuel. June 15, 1979.**
Photo credit: Library of Congress

Female politicians nevertheless continued to make strides in both the Democratic and Republican Parties during the decade, a trend that would continue unabated into the early twenty-first century. During the 1970s, Texas women first began to achieve political success by winning election to prominent local-level positions in urban areas. In 1976, Ann Richards, a future governor, ran for a county commissioner seat in Travis County (Austin), easily defeating the incumbent. Lila Cockrell first won election as mayor of San Antonio in 1975 before triumphing again fourteen years later. In 1977, Carole Keeton McClellan (later, Rylander Strayhorn) became Austin's first female mayor.

## Oil Growth in the 1970s

In the twentieth century, the money earned from oil was the single most important factor shaping the fate of the Texas economy. Beginning with the Spindletop gusher in 1901, Texas became synonymous with oil. Some of the biggest oil companies in the world had their start in the Texas oil fields. During World War II, hundreds of millions of dollars went into the state's petrochemical industry. By the early 1970s, Texas oil and natural gas production hit its peak. In 1972, Texas companies refined more than 1.3 billion barrels of oil, for an average daily production level of 3.5 million.

But the 1970s saw major changes in energy prices, mostly centering on oil. The federal government carefully regulated oil prices, establishing price caps that kept the price of crude low, selling for only a few dollars per barrel. In 1972 the Texas Railroad Commission stopped restricting production as it had since the East Texas oil wars over wildcatting in the early 1930s. During the 1970s, events overseas began to change the price of this valuable commodity. In 1973, Saudi Arabia, the United Arab Emirates, Kuwait, and

Ross Perot, May 2, 1980
Photo credit: UTSA's Institute of Texan Cultures

other Arab members of OPEC issued an oil embargo because the United States had been supportive of Israel in the Yom Kippur War. Within weeks, the price of oil tripled, federal price ceilings were removed, and more money was invested in oil exploration. During the crisis, the United States became more reliant on Texas oil producers who benefitted greatly from the growing demand for domestic petroleum. Despite the dramatic increase in the number of drilling rigs, oil prices remained high, hitting American consumers particularly hard. Gas stations frequently ran out of gas often while customers waited in line to fill their tanks.

During this time, Humble Oil, which had been operating jointly with Standard Oil of New Jersey, changed its name to Exxon. The company soon established gas stations across Texas and the rest of the country. Exxon capitalized on the old Humble Oil discovery of oil in Prudhoe Bay, Alaska, by spearheading the building of a pipeline across Alaska to insure the delivery of oil to market.

Oil prices eventually stabilized in the mid-1970s. More exploration resulted in new discoveries of oil deposits in areas not previously probed, including Galveston Bay. These new discoveries, coupled with the oil available through the Alaska Pipeline, worked to keep prices in check. During the late 1970s, however, events in the Middle East again affected oil prices. In Iran, Muslim fundamentalist critics of the Shah emerged to challenge their leader's secular rule and autocratic regime, eventually leading a revolt that ousted the Shah in 1978. In the furor of the revolution some students with the tacit approval of the government stormed the U.S. Embassy in the capital of Tehran and seized hostages, which they held for over a year, provoking a land standoff with the United States. In 1980, war began after Iraq's leader, Saddam Hussein, attacked Iran over border differences. The outbreak of hostilities in the Middle East caused the price of oil to triple between 1979 and

1980s. As the flow of Middle East oil decreased, ordinary citizens in the United States experienced many unpleasant changes in their way of life. Once again, there were long lines at gas stations and some gas stations ran out of fuel. Foreign automobile companies began marketing smaller cars to consumers, placing increased pressure on American automobile manufacturers that were still producing large gas-guzzling vehicles. In addition, home heating fuel prices escalated. These occurrences became commonplace throughout the country, including Texas. However, the increase in oil-industry revenue helped to offset the ill-effects of statewide gas shortages and inflation in Texas. People continued to migrate to Texas for jobs in the oil industry and producers contributed to a sustained boom in the state's economy.

**Growth of New Industries**

While the Texas economy owed much to the oil industry, several other industries emerged in the 1970s to contribute positively to the state. Texas became the home of several of the nation's leading high-tech companies. Dallas-headquartered Texas Instruments launched several new consumer products during the 1970s that revolutionized the electronics market, including the first hand-held calculators and speech synthesizers that electronically replicated the human voice in various games and educational products. The company also developed the first microprocessors, which soon made personal computers possible.

As businesses became more automated by the early 1970s, the data processing services provided by Ross Perot's Electronic Data Systems (EDS) were in high demand. Federal government agencies helped EDS grow by giving the company lucrative contracts for such services as processing Social Security and Medicare payments. Though this extreme growth wasn't continued throughout the decade, EDS diversified and grew by working with smaller clients, such as small businesses, and providing hardware and software systems for its users. Holding various positions with the company, Perot stayed involved with EDS until 1986 following its 1984 purchase by General Motors.

By the late twentieth century, the airline industry became a significant contributor to Texas's economy, producing both jobs and profits. Much of this growth began in the 1970s. In 1972, the industry provided 22,604 aviation-related jobs throughout the state. This level of employment remained fairly consistent through the mid-1970s and reached 36,646 by 1980. (By 2000, this number reached an estimated 119,000 jobs. According to the Texas Department of Transportation's Aviation Division, general and commercial aviation added over $48 billion to the state's economy.)

American Airlines, the largest airline in the United States, moved its headquarters to Fort Worth from New York City in 1979, and Dallas-Fort Worth International Airport (completed in 1973) remains one of its main hubs. More expansion occurred when Continental Airlines established its headquarters in Houston where Bush-Intercontinental Airport serves as one of the company's major hubs. In 2010 following a merger between Continental and United Airlines, the company announced it would move its headquarters to Chicago. Even so, Houston will remain the company's largest hub.

For many years Dallas served as the company headquarters of Braniff Airways, once one of the largest airlines in the world, with its major hub at Love Field. The 1970s, however, proved disastrous for Braniff. Due to rising fuel prices, overly aggressive expansion efforts, and fierce competition following passage of the Airline Deregulation Act of 1978 (which removed government control of fares, routes, and market entry of new airlines), the company rapidly lost money. After attempting to survive by cutting routes and personnel, Braniff finally collapsed in the early 1980s.

While Braniff declined during the 1970s, a new airline headquartered in Texas started its ascent. Founded in 1971, Southwest Airlines started as the original "no frills" airline. The company often advertised that its tickets cost peanuts, which was the primary food served on its flights. The company turned a profit within two years of operation, with Dallas' Love Field serving as its major hub. Southwest continued to fly out of Love Field even after the new Dallas-Fort Worth International Airport opened. Other airlines fought to limit their upstart competitor. In 1979, Congress passed the Wright Amendment, which limited Southwest's non-stop flights from Love Field to only Texas and adjoining states. Southwest campaigned for years to have the restrictions removed, allowing the company to fly non-stop to more destinations around the country. For many years, American Airlines and the Dallas-Fort Worth Airport opposed, arguing that this would be detrimental to their airport's financial operations. A compromise was finally reached in late 2006. In exchange for a reduction in the number of gates at Love Field, Southwest Airlines would be allowed to phase in over a number of years non-stop service to new locations. Despite the heavy competition and political restrictions, Southwest became a billion dollar company by the 1990s.

**Ranching and Farming**

The traditional industries of ranching and farming have taken a backseat to the dynamic and growing industries of the late twentieth century. However, both ranching and farming continue to contribute to the state's overall economic health and provide jobs for Texans though, as a percentage, fewer Texans (about 5 percent) engage in such work when compared to previous decades.

The number of Texas farms has decreased substantially since World War II. Yet, Texas has the largest amount of farmland of any state in the union, and the value of the farmland has increased greatly over the years. Reasons for the drop in the number of farms are varied, but the 1970s were a particularly difficult period for Texas farmers. They faced a two-fold problem of increased overseas competition and reduced federal government subsidies. At the same time, the general economic trouble of the nation drove interest rates higher causing a credit crunch for farmers. Many small farmers were left with no choice but to file for bankruptcy protection. One trend of the 1970s that continued into the new century was the increase in the number of "part-time" farmers and cattlemen. Many landowners have various kinds of regular employment, and they grow crops and handle livestock in their evenings and weekends.

Despite the clear problems farmers and ranchers faced, they had better access to manufacturers for some products. Cotton, mohair, and wool were readily absorbed by the textile mills strewn throughout the state, turning out everything from curtains to neckties to bed sheets. New irrigated farmland meant expanded farming in the Panhandle region for corn, cotton, and wheat. Over half of Texas's wheat crop was grown on the High Plains during the 1970s. In addition, cotton farmers on the Plains grew more of the white fiber than the traditional Texas home of cotton—East Texas.

## Texas in Literature, Television, and Film

Texas often considers itself a region unto itself. People refer to "Texas Literature" as a separate entity from "Southwestern Literature" or other types of regional writing. Yet, overall, not a large body of work constitutes Texas literature. As Tom Pilkington has noted in *State of Mind*, "intellectual activity" and cultural and literary accomplishments have never been Texas's priority. The myths of Texas celebrate the individual, a person of action. The undramatic art of writing has not always been appreciated. Writings regarding Texas go back centuries to Cabeza de Vaca's account of his travels through the region. The exploration of themes and personalities, rather than purely historical accounts, has only more recently been practiced; therefore, most Texas literature is largely a twentieth-century phenomenon. While the "frontier mythology" exerted a strong influence on Texas literature (as evidenced by the continued popularity of Elmer Kelton's traditional cowboy novels), as well as television and film, a growing number of works dealing with modern and urban themes also began to emerge by the 1970s.

Writer Larry L. King has secured a place among the most popular of authors from Texas. Originally from Midland, King spent several years working for a Texas congressman during the 1950s and 1960s in Washington, D.C. In 1964, he decided to become a full-time writer of articles, essays, novels, and plays. One of his chief successes was the musical *The Best Little Whorehouse in Texas,* which started playing on Broadway in 1978. Based on a house of ill-repute known as the Chicken Ranch in La Grange, Texas, the musical was developed into a Hollywood movie adaptation starring Dolly Parton and Burt Reynolds. Another of King's plays, *The Dead President's Club*, draws on his political interests as it depicts four former presidents waiting to find out if they are admitted to heaven.

Larry McMurtry became one of the best known novelists in Texas with a number of popular and prize-winning works. In the 1970s, he penned his urban trilogy—*Moving On* (1970), *All My Friends Are Going to Be Strangers* (1972), and *Terms of Endearment* (1975), the last of which became a movie in 1983 starring Shirley MacLaine. McMurtry also wrote a trilogy of novels set in the fictional town of Thalia, which was modeled on his own home town of Archer City in North Texas. *The Last Picture Show* (1966), *Texasville* (1987), and *Duane's Depressed* (1999) all explored small town life, ranching, and the future of such places. In the 1980s, McMurtry came out with his first work about a traditional theme—the Old West. In 1985 he published *Lonesome Dove,* which centered on two former Texas Rangers, Gus McCrae and Woodrow Call, working on a cattle drive during the late 1800s. The book won the Pulitzer Prize and served as the basis of a television mini-series starring Robert Duvall and Tommy Lee Jones as the main characters. McMurtry continued to explore western themes with *Lonesome Dove* sequels *Streets of Laredo* (1993), *Dead Man's Walk* (1995) and *Comanche Moon* (1997), and later won an Academy Award in 2006 for co-writing the adapted screenplay for the nontraditional cowboy film, *Brokeback Mountain,* that examined issues of race, gender roles, and homosexuality.

On the small screen, the television series "Dallas" became an American and global phenomenon during the 1970s, focusing on the lives of a fictitious modern oil tycoon, J.R. Ewing, and his family, as they ruthlessly held on to their empire from their luxurious Southfork Ranch. To Americans living outside the Lone Star State and to foreigners view-

**First Lady Rosalynn Carter with Waylon Jennings, smoking a cigarette, and Jesse Colter at a reception preceding a concert to benefit the Carter-Mondale campaign. April 23, 1980. Photo credit: Library of Congress**

ing re-runs of the show in syndication abroad, the drama reinforced many stereotypes about Texas, from the assumed widespread distribution of wealth to the way most Texans supposedly looked (like glamorous supermodels) and dressed (in large western hats and cowboy boots). A testament to the show's impact remains the large number of domestic and foreign tourists who continue to venture to the real Southfork Ranch located in Plano (a north Dallas suburb), even though only an aerial shot during the show's opening credits and sporadic outdoor scenes were ever filmed there.

Other elements of modern Texas culture were put on display in film during the 1970s, though none proved to be as popular as the John Travolta movie *Urban Cowboy*. Set in Pasadena, Texas (an eastern suburb of Houston), the romantic drama focused on the working-class lifestyle of urban oil laborers. While certain elements of that culture represented in the film, from "Texas chic" cowboy attire, honky-tonk music, country dancing, and even mechanical bull riding became wildly popular outside of Texas by the early 1980s, less positive aspects of the culture depicted in the film, such as domestic violence, alcoholism, poor housing, and dangerous working conditions, tended to be forgotten.

**The Influence of Texas Musicians**

After World War II, Texas produced musicians from multiple genres enjoyed mainstream success while influencing artists across the country. Texas country and western music stars going as far back as "Bob Wills and His Texas Playboys" during the 1930s have done much to make that style of music synonymous with Texas, but their popularity often tends to obscure the impact of Texans who perform other varieties of music, ranging from blues and rock and roll to jazz and modern Tejano.

While traditional country stars from Texas such as the ubiquitous George Jones continued their stellar careers, other Texans began to redefine country music during the 1970s. Willie Nelson, a native of Abbott, Texas, emerged as one of the nation's most recognizable musical artists. Nelson moved to Nashville in 1960 to write and record music. Though selling many of his songs (most famously Patsy Cline's hit "Crazy"), music company executives told him that he could not sing well enough to have the recording career that he desired. Frustrated, Nelson returned to Texas in the 1970s to develop a bolder version of country music that did not conform to the tamer formulaic style produced in Nashville. Among others joining Nelson in this effort was Waylon Jennings, a native of Littlefield, Texas, who lived for a time in Lubbock where he befriended Buddy Holly and became a member of his band. Jennings recorded standard country music during the 1960s, but with Nelson during the 1970s he began to personify the new "outlaw country" that rebelled against the top-down creative management of Nashville producers by creating livelier music often with individualistic, working-class themes. In 1979, Jennings recorded the popular theme song for the hit television show "The Dukes of Hazzard," which reinforced outlaw country's celebration of the non-conformist bad boy.

Texas artists of genres besides country music also became influential during the 1970s. Among the top jazz artists was Ornette Coleman. Born in Fort Worth in 1930, he traveled widely, playing saxophone and trumpet with numerous touring groups before releasing albums in the 1950s that pioneered what has since become known as "free jazz," which has an emphasis on improvisation. In 2007 he was awarded the Pulitzer Prize in music and has won a Grammy Lifetime Achievement Award.

Tejano country musicians first achieved mainstream success during the 1970s. Freddy Fender (Baldemar Huerta) from San Benito and Johnny Rodríguez of Sabinal gained widespread popularity, often infusing their country music with Latin sounds and interchanging verses in both English and Spanish, such as in Fender's "Before the Next Teardrop Falls" and "Vaya Con Dios." Most Tejano musicians during the 1970s, however, continued to cater to the local Mexican American community rather than seeking mainstream success. Conjunto (or *norteño*) music continued to grow in popularity in South Texas and northern Mexico, popularized by such renowned artists as accordionist Flaco Jimenez. Played primarily with the button accordion, bajo sexto, electric bass, and drums, the style evolved throughout the twentieth century but still resembled the German and Eastern European polka music on which it is based.

Dallas' Aaron Thibeaux "T-Bone" Walker had hits over several decades and set the standard for blues (and later rock) guitarists. Playing an electric guitar with a lively style as early as World War II, Walker had hits with "They Call It Stormy Monday (But Tuesday's Just as Bad)" and "T-Bone Shuffle." In 1971 Walker won his first and only Grammy award for his hit song "Good Feelin'." He continued to perform live shows until his death in 1975. Many have credited Walker's influence in not only developing the rock and roll sound but also aspects of its more flamboyant style of presentation. (Among other innovations, he was the first to play the electric guitar with his teeth or behind his back.). As an acknowledgement of his lasting influence, Walker was inducted into the Rock and Roll Hall of Fame in 1987.

On the rock music scene, Port Arthur's Janis Joplin rose quickly to prominence in the mid-1960s. Dubbed by *Time Magazine* as "probably the most powerful singer to emerge from the white rock movement," Joplin attended Lamar State College of Technology in

Beaumont, Texas, and later the University of Texas at Austin before embarking on her meteoric rise as a passionate blues-inspired rock singer. After five years singing in front of other bands, she embarked on a solo career at the height of her popularity in 1969. The next year, at the age of twenty-seven, the hard-drinking, drug-using woman died of a heroin overdose possibly combined with the effects of alcohol. Her final album *Pearl*, released posthumously in 1971, included her biggest hit—a cover of Kris Kristofferson's "Me and Bobby McGee." Joplin's style and persona influenced future generations of female rock artists. The music community certified her legacy with Joplin's induction into the Rock and Roll Hall of Fame in 1995.

Beginning in the mid-1970s, Austin gained a reputation for its live music venues. In 1976, the Public Broadcasting System (PBS) began airing its long-running popular live music show "Austin City Limits," which did much to promote the city as a place where musicians of rock, folk, blues, country, bluegrass, and other music genres would be welcomed. The epicenter of this movement became a collection of clubs located on 6th Street near the University of Texas campus where performers from all across Texas and beyond came to showcase their talents. Since the late 1980s, Austin has hosted the South by Southwest Music Festival each March during which over a thousand different shows are conducted on stages in the downtown area.

**The Rise of Major League Sports in Texas**

During the 1970s, the sports arena became a major outlet for entertainment in Texas urban areas. No discussion of Texas culture is complete without addressing the role that athletics play in the Texas psyche. Of all sports in Texas, the adage "football is king" began to ring true during the 1970s with the success of its two professional franchises. By the 1970s, Texas had two National Football League (NFL) teams—the Dallas Cowboys and the Houston Oilers. The Cowboys came to Dallas as part of the NFL's expansion in 1960. At the same time, the Dallas Texans, a team affiliated with the American Football League (AFL)—a newly created rival league begun by a group of Texas and Oklahoma oil men—started playing in the city. The Cowboys shared the Cotton Bowl with the Texans until 1963 when the Texans relocated and became known as the Kansas City Chiefs (later joining other AFL teams in a merger with the NFL in 1970). After a lackluster start, the Cowboys finally began to achieve success in the late 1960s, reaching the Super Bowl after the 1970 season (a 16-13 loss to the Baltimore Colts). In 1971, Texas Stadium opened in Irving to house the team. Built with a center opening in the otherwise covered stadium, Texas Stadium's unique architecture was explained by fans who claimed the hole existed "so God can watch his team." Coupled with NFL Films touting of the team as "America's Team" in promotional videos, the Cowboys became a "love them or hate them" enterprise. Following the 1971 regular season, the Cowboys rewarded their fans with another trip to the Super Bowl, this time emerging with a 24-3 victory over the Miami Dolphins. The Cowboys would play in three more Super Bowls during the 1970s, defeating the Denver Broncos after the 1977 regular season but losing twice to the Pittsburgh Steelers.

Houston had its own former AFL team, the Houston Oilers, which started operations in 1960 and achieved success and popularity during the 1970s. One of the AFL's creators, Oklahoma oil man Bud Adams, owned the team throughout its residency in Houston. The team started out well, winning the first two AFL championships before

**Houston Astrodome**

sliding into mediocrity. After playing at a couple of different locations, the team moved into the Astrodome in 1968. Two years later, the Oilers joined the NFL. Largely languishing after the NFL-AFL merger, the heyday of the Oilers took place soon after the team drafted University of Texas running back Earl Campbell. A 1977 Heisman Trophy winner, Campbell became one of the best running backs in NFL history during his professional career with the Oilers. Despite playing against teams utilizing stacked defensive lines, Campbell's combination of speed and power enabled him to run over defenders with a bruising running style. He led the league in rushing three consecutive years from 1978-1980 before the combination of overuse by coaches plus the effects of playing on Astroturf began to slow him down and led to his early retirement.

Professional basketball also developed a large fan base in Texas during the 1970s. All three current professional teams in the state—the San Antonio Spurs, the Houston Rockets, and the Dallas Mavericks—began playing during the decade. The Spurs first came to San Antonio as one of the teams of the American Basketball Association (ABA) in 1973. Its previous incarnation had been as the Dallas Chaparrals. In 1976, the Spurs joined the National Basketball Association (NBA) after a merger with the ABA. The Houston Rockets originally played in San Diego, California before relocating to Houston in 1971. After the NBA awarded Dallas an expansion franchise in the late 1970s, the new Dallas Mavericks began their first year of play during the 1980 season.

Baseball made its entry into Texas over a hundred years ago as a popular pastime. Since 1888, the Texas League has fielded professional ball clubs, mainly serving as minor league "farm teams" for major league organizations during the twentieth century. For many years after World War II, the Houston Eagles played in the Negro Leagues. The integration of major league baseball led to the demise of the Negro Leagues. Meanwhile, the arrival of major league teams to Texas contributed to the decline of the Texas League,

**Texas Rangers Ballpark, Arlington, Texas**

though it continues to exist as a lower-cost alternative for avid baseball fans. In 1960, Houston became the first southern city to be awarded a major league franchise. The expansion Houston Colt .45s began playing in 1962. In 1965, the team was renamed the Houston Astros and began playing in the Houston Astrodome—the nation's first domed stadium. The Astrodome also hosted football games and other entertainment events. (In 1973, female tennis legend Billie Jean King accepted former pro player Bobby Riggs' challenge and defeated him before a huge Astrodome crowd, and national television audience, in the much-publicized "Battle of the Sexes" match.) When the stadium's glass roof panels caused issues for players trying to follow fly balls, the organization first tried to solve the problem by painting two panel sections white. Though this effort minimized the sight problem, the grass died from the subsequent lack of sunlight. The team then turned to a new synthetic substance that quickly was dubbed "Astroturf" as the new playing surface for the Astrodome. The Astros did not produce winning seasons until the 1970s, aided by legendary pitcher, and native Texan, Nolan Ryan.

The other major league baseball club in Texas, the Rangers, began playing in the state during the 1972 season. The team had begun as an expansion team in 1961 named the Washington Senators to replace the original Washington Senators franchise that had recently moved to Minnesota and became known as the Twins. In 1971, after Dallas had failed for years to get an expansion team, the new owner of the Senators (purchased in December 1968) moved the Senators to the Dallas-Fort Worth area to play at a stadium in nearby Arlington. Turnpike Stadium was renamed Arlington Stadium, and the Rangers settled in for the next twenty years, though failing to produce a club that reached the playoffs before the mid-1990s.

## A Decade of Transitions

Though antecedents can be traced to earlier decades, many forces shaping Texas as it would exist in the early twenty-first century were well underway during the 1970s. Politics had become a lot less predictable as support for the Republican Party, though not yet predominant, had taken hold. Sizeable numbers of Texas voters consistently supported Republican presidential candidates, and the Lone Star State chose its first Republican governor since Reconstruction. Concurrently, Texas became a more politically inclusive state, with minority groups having a voice in Texas politics and female politicians finding a greater degree of voter support, particularly within the Democratic Party.

Meanwhile, events in the Middle East began to exert a direct impact on the Texas economy. Yet, as Texas witnessed both the positive and negative effects of those circumstances, a more diversified economy, less dependent on oil and cotton, continued to emerge. Though wealth remained far from distributed equally, unemployment rates remained below the national average contributing to greater prosperity for a growing number of residents.

Culturally, Texas became more like the rest of the United States while continuing to influence the nation. In the arts and entertainment world, Texans reflected on more modern themes than in the past while more frequently becoming the subject of social and cultural exploration from outside the state. Like much of the country during the Cold War years, many Texans for the first time found entertainment in the form of wild devotion for new major league athletic teams. In many ways, indeed, the 1970s proved to be a truly transitional decade for Texas from its traditional moorings to its modern manifestation.

### *Afterward: Tom Landry Finally Wins the "Big One"—and Many More*

*In Super Bowl VI, the Dallas Cowboys dominated the Miami Dolphins, winning 24-3. After the victory, team owner Clint Murchison congratulated Landry and referred humorously to their "twelve-year plan" to winning the NFL Championship.*

*Landry became the image of the Cowboys. His silhouette alone was recognizable with the outlines of a suit and his trademark fedora. Landry required his assistant coaches and players to wear suits while traveling. He expected everyone to show up on time for meetings and practices and did not tolerate any behavior that reflected negatively on the team.*

*As the people of Texas responded to the Cowboys' winning seasons with enthusiasm, Tom Landry became a beloved figure, winning a total of 250 games by the end of his career in 1989. Along with the existence of the NFL's Houston Oilers and Major League Baseball's Houston Astros and Texas Rangers, the Cowboys' success helped make professional sports become a major entertainment attraction in the Lone Star State during the 1970s. The Cowboys played in five Super Bowls during the decade (winning twice), which was a testament to the solid "system" that Landry employed. In a highlight film of the 1978 season, NFL Films dubbed the Cowboys "America's Team." Much to the modest Landry's chagrin, the name stuck.*

# Myth & Legend

### Myth of the Citizen-Legislator

*Many people in Texas believe in the myth that their legislators are more representative of ordinary citizens than the legislators of other states in the Union. These Texans support their claim by arguing that members of the Texas legislature are not career politicians. Texans claim that the state constitution prevents a professional political class from governing the state. In part, this myth can be traced to the constitutional convention in the mid-1870s.*

*When delegates gathered in 1875 to write a new constitution for the state of Texas, they wanted to limit the state government by placing certain limits on the legislative branch. For example, the legislature would only meet every other year, and its regular sessions would only last for 187 days. Because of these limitations, some of the delegates argued that the legislators could not become career politicians; instead, they would be ordinary citizens except when the legislature was in session in Austin. The myth of the citizen-legislator has persisted since that time. Reinforcing this myth is the fact that today's state legislators are not paid well—both Texas senators and representatives receive an annual salary of $7,200. Even when one factors in the state per diem allowances, legislators still make less than $17,000 a year. Thus, it is impossible for a Texas legislator to make a living as a public servant. Therefore, many Texans believe in the myth that their legislators are "ordinary citizens" who hold office because they truly wish to serve the public.*

*The reality is far different than the myth. While it is true that no one can make a living by serving in the Texas legislature, it is also true that many obstacles prevent ordinary people from being able to serve. For example, even though the legislature only meets every other year, this is still too long of a time commitment to accommodate most people who work 40 hours a week. Aside from the regular biennial session, legislators might have to attend special sessions of the legislature, which can last several weeks at a time; they are required to attend hearings and meetings held throughout the state in relation to committee assignments; and they are required to consult with their constituents. It is rare that the common working man or woman can leave work for extended periods of time and still retain employment. Therefore, the only people who can afford to serve as a legislator are those who are independently wealthy. Their wealth might come from owning a successful business, from earning a substantial amount of money in various high profile service industries, such as the medical or legal profession, or from personal inheritance. Typically, the ordinary Texan that works a shift in a factory or a 40-hour a week job is not going to also serve in the state legislature. Thus, just as other states in the Union, legislators represent the elite in society and not the common people.*

*This is a myth that still clouds people's understanding of legislative members. A legislator is not a modern-day Cincinnatus—the Roman general who left his farm to lead the Roman legions only to return to his farm happily when he was no longer needed. While some boast that Texas is not tainted by corrupt politics, the limited salaries of politicians often lead to greater corruption in the government rather than less. The Sharpstown scandal discussed in this chapter is one example of corruption. Because legislators are so poorly compensated, they often find themselves more susceptible to bribes and other corrupt schemes. Even honest legislators can find themselves in situations that test their ethics. For instance, some legislators have been known to take jobs as lobbyists while still holding public office because lobbying offers the flexible time and lucrative pay.*

*In the final analysis, Texas politics is no different than other states in the Union. Legislators in the Lone Star State come from, and typically identify with, the upper class in society. Still, the common man and woman of Texas can take some comfort in the fact that legislative members cannot hold office without the consent of the voters. Therefore, the smart legislator will continue to listen to his/her constituents and address issues important to the common people.*

**Suggestions for Further Reading**

Barta, Carolyn. *Bill Clements: Texian to His Toenails,* Austin, Texas: Eakin Press, 1996.

Bridges, Kenneth. *Twilight of the Texas Democrats: The 1978 Governor's Race.* College Station: Texas A&M University Press, 2008.

Briscoe, Jr., Dolph. *Dolph Briscoe: My Life in Texas Ranching and Politics.* Austin: University of Texas Press, 2008

Clifford, Craig Edward. *In the Deep Heart's Core: Reflections on Life, Letters, and Texas.* College Station: Texas A&M University Press, 1985.

Elliott, Charles P., Kay Hofer, and Robert E. Biles, *The World of Texas Politics,* New York: St. Martin's Press, 1998.

García, Ignacio M. *United We Win: The Rise and Fall of La Raza Unida Party,* Tucson: The University of Arizona Press, 1989.

Golenbock, Peter. *Cowboys Have Always Been My Heroes: The Definitive Oral History of America's Team.* New York: Warner Books, 1997.

Jones, Nancy Baker and Ruthie Winegarten, *Capitol Women: Texas Female Legislators, 1923-1999,* Austin: University of Texas Press, 2000.

Knaggs, John R. *Two-Party Texas: The John Tower Era 1961-1984,* Austin, Texas: Eakin Press, 1986.

Milner, Jay Dunston. *Confessions of a Maddog: A Romp through the High-flying Texas Music and Literary Era of the Fifties to the Seventies.* Denton, Texas: University of North Texas Press, 1998.

Olien, Roger M. *From Token to Triumph: The Texas Republicans since 1920.* Dallas: Southern Methodist University Press, 1982.

Pilkington, Tom. *State of Mind: Texas Literature and Culture.* College Station: Texas A&M University Press, 1998.

# A Transitional Decade, 1972-1979

**IDENTIFICATION:** Briefly describe each term.

Sharpstown
Dolph Briscoe
William Clements
"Dirty Thirty"
*Roe v. Wade*
Constitutional Convention
Southwest Airlines
Title IX
Equal Rights Amendment
La Raza Unida
Dallas Cowboys
Ramsey Muñiz
Larry McMurtry
Willie Nelson
OPEC Crisis

**MULTIPLE CHOICE:** Choose the correct response.

1. Which of the following did NOT take place as a result of the Sharpstown Scandal?
   A. A Republican won the next election for governor.
   B. The legislature passed a series of political reform laws.
   C. Some members of the legislature were convicted of various offenses.
   D. Though not convicted of any crime, Governor Preston Smith did not win re-election.

2. A member of the group of state legislators nicknamed the "Dirty Thirty," _____ sought the governorship in 1972 but lost to Dolph Briscoe in the Democratic Party primary.
   A. Ann Richards
   B. Frances "Sissy" Farenthold
   C. Kay Bailey Hutchison
   D. None of the above

3. Which of the following occurred as a result of the effort to revise the state constitution during the 1970s?
   A. a new progressive constitution that gave more power to the people
   B. a much more conservative constitution that greatly weakened the state government's powers
   C. a new constitution that was so similar to the Constitution of 1876 that there were no notable differences
   D. no new constitution was approved by Texas voters.

4. The landmark case *Roe v. Wade* addressed
   A. abortion rights
   B. married women retaining ownership of property
   C. water rights
   D. desegregation

5. John Tower was a long-time _____ U.S. Senator from Texas.
   A. Democrat
   B. Republican
   C. Libertarian
   D. Green

6. Which of the following is true about Braniff Airlines?
   A. Its long-time company president was George W. Bush.
   B. It was the only major airline not operating in Texas by the 1970s.
   C. The Airline Deregulation Act of 1978 contributed to its eventual demise in the early 1980s.
   D. None of the above.

7. H. Ross Perot's company, Electronic Data Systems (EDS), grew dramatically because of its work:
   A. managing campaign contributions for William Clements
   B. data processing for private companies and the federal government
   C. processing ticketing reservations for the airline industry
   D. manufacturing parts for oil drilling equipment

8. Which of the following is NOT an airline headquartered in Texas?
   A. Southwest Airlines
   B. Delta Airlines
   C. American Airlines
   D. Continental Airlines

9. _____ returned to Texas after being frustrated as a musician and songwriter in Nashville and helped found the "Outlaw Country" style.
   A. Willie Nelson
   B. Billy Lee Brammer
   C. George Jones
   D. George Strait

10. This *Lonesome Dove* author also wrote *Terms of Endearment* during the 1970s and later co-wrote the screenplay for "Brokeback Mountain."
    A. Larry McMurtry
    B. John Tower
    C. Larry L. King
    D. Cormac McCarthy

# A Transitional Decade, 1972-1979

**TRUE/FALSE:** Indicate whether each statement is true or false.

1. During the Sharpstown scandal the governor of Texas, Preston Smith, was named an un-indicted co-conspirator.

2. Several prominent Texans played a role in the Watergate investigation.

3. The Texas Legislature approved the Equal Rights Amendment to the U.S. Constitution.

4. The La Raza Unida candidate, Ramsey Muñiz, barely missed being elected to the U.S. Senate in 1972 and 1976.

5. One of the most visible impacts of Title IX of the Educational Amendments to the Civil Rights Act is the requirement that high schools, colleges, and universities receiving federal funding must provide equal funding for men's and women's athletic programs.

6. Texas was hit hard by the oil production limits that OPEC instituted in the 1970s.

7. Since the 1970s, the Wright Amendment exempts airlines in Texas from having to pay any taxes.

8. Founded in 1971, Southwest Airlines started as the original "no frills" airline and became a billion-dollar company by the 1990s.

9. The Dallas Cowboys was among the worst NFL teams of the 1970s.

10. By the beginning of the 1980s, Texas had major league professional franchises in baseball, basketball, and football.

**MATCHING:** Match the response in column A with the item in column B.

1. H. Ross Perot
2. OPEC
3. Janis Joplin
4. Dolph Briscoe
5. Frances "Sissy" Farenthold
6. Sarah Weddington
7. Earl Campbell
8. Gus Mutscher
9. Barbara Jordan
10. William Clements

A. lawyer for Jane Roe in the *Roe v. Wade* case
B. governor elected following the Sharpstown scandal
C. founder of Electronic Data Systems (EDS)
D. member of the "Dirty Thirty" who later ran for governor
E. cartel of Middle Eastern oil-producing countries
F. Speaker of the House involved in the Sharpstown scandal
G. congresswoman who played a prominent role in the Watergate investigations
H. Texas rock and soul singer who died of a drug overdose during her prime.
I. businessman turned politician who was elected as the first Republican governor since Reconstruction
J. Heisman Trophy winner who excelled for many years with the Houston Oilers

**ESSAY QUESTIONS:**

1. The rise of the Republican Party in Texas was one of the more surprising political twists in the state's history. How and why did the Republicans begin to win more elections in the 1970s?

2. Explain the rise of women in Texas politics during the 1970s.

3. How was Texas affected, both positively and negatively, by events taking place in the Middle East during the 1970s?

4. Describe the impact of Texas musicians on the American music scene during the 1970s

# Chapter 19

# Complex Times, 1980-1994

### Prelude: The Waco Siege

*By the late twentieth century, organized religion maintained a strong influence on the lives of a majority of Texans. The particular denomination of Christianity (or Judaism, Buddhism, Hinduism, or Islam) claimed by an individual Texan, however, varied widely. Whereas large numbers of Christian Texans considered themselves Baptists (25 percent of the state's population in 1990), Catholics (21 percent), or Methodists (7 percent), the Lone Star State had become home to followers of numerous religions, some containing a myriad of factions.*

*The members of the religious sect calling themselves the Branch Davidians traced their origins back to a schism within the Seventh-day Adventist Church taking place during the 1930s when a Bulgarian immigrant named Victor Houteff and his followers were banished from the group. Houteff published a book titled* **The Shepherd's Rod** *in which he promoted the standard Adventist teachings of Christ's imminent return, Saturday worship, dietary regulations and pacifism, but also criticized the Church's leaders for increasingly compromising with modern standards of personal behavior. Following his personal interpretation of a chapter in the Book of Revelation, Houteff taught that an elect group of 144,000 followers would form a reformed church as a prerequisite for Christ's return.*

*In 1935, when the Seventh-day Adventist Conference excommunicated him, Houteff and thirty-seven followers (now referring to themselves as "Davidians" to reflect their belief in the restoration of King David's reign over Israel as a prerequisite for the second coming of Jesus to take place) moved to a site a few miles west of Waco, Texas, where they established a utopian commune they called "Mount Carmel." After Houteff's death in 1955, the Davidians split over who should succeed their leader as president—a position in which they believed required the claimant must be blessed with the gift of prophecy. The group with the largest faction eventually followed Benjamin Roden, began calling themselves "Branch Davidians" to distinguish themselves from other Davidians, and moved to a new site nine miles east of Waco that they dubbed "New Mount Carmel." Differing from practices established under Houteff's leadership, they began undertaking outreach operations with the outside world in the U.S. and abroad.*

*When Benjamin Roden died in 1978, Lois Roden, his widow announced that she had received visions from God, thus allowing her to claim that she was also a prophet, and, therefore, eligible for leadership of the Branch Davidians. In 1981, a 22-year-old man named Vernon*

Wayne Howell joined the group after meeting Lois Roden believing her to be a true prophet. Howell arrived after being expelled from his Seventh-day Adventist church in Tyler, Texas, and a failed trip to California to become a rock star. Howell had memorized whole sections of the Bible and impressed many members of the Davidians with his recall. His handy-man skills were also welcomed by the group. Howell gained influence within the Davidians because of his close personal relationship with the elderly Lois Roden (she was 76 years old in 1981), which eventually became sexual. When Lois started allowing Howell to lead Bible study sessions, his energy began to breathe new life into the group. He also began assuming a messiah complex, soon demanding that a member follow "God's wishes" by allowing him to marry the man's 14-year-old daughter (he consented).

A power struggle eventually emerged between Howell and Lois' son, George Roden, which briefly ended when Roden forced Howell off the Mt. Carmel property at gunpoint. For a short time, Howell retreated with his followers to Palestine, Texas, but in late 1987, after Lois Roden's death, he returned with seven heavily-armed followers and a gunfight ensued. Howell and his accomplices went on trial for attempted murder but were acquitted. In 1989, Roden was convicted of murder after killing a man who claimed to be the true Messiah. With Mt. Carmel in disarray, Howell and his followers raised thousands of dollars to pay back taxes and assumed title to the property.

By 1990, Howell had become the undisputed leader of the Branch Davidians, legally changing his name to "David Koresh," claiming the move reflected his belief that he was the new leader of the biblical House of David ("Koresh" referred to the Hebrew transliteration of Cyrus, the king of Persia who allowed captive Jews in Babylon to return to Israel). He preached that a forthcoming violent apocalypse was about to descend upon the Earth. In anticipation of the end of times, the Branch Davidians began collecting weapons and placing orders for ammunition, grenades, and rifle parts. Outsiders soon became concerned about the group's stockpile of weapons, as well as rumors of other non-traditional religious practices that the sect practiced. In 1992, local authorities investigated charges of child abuse against Howell, but the investigation closed with no official charges filed. It later became known that Howell had indeed committed statutory rape of many girls at the compound and also had started demanding that most adult female Davidians have sexual relations with him in order to procreate the group with special children of the prophet. (In all, Howell fathered at least fourteen children with numerous female members at Mt. Carmel).

The large deliveries of weapons and ammunition eventually drew the attention of authorities, who began to suspect that the Davidians were illegally manufacturing assault rifles. The federal Bureau of Alcohol, Tobacco and Firearms (ATF) soon obtained search warrants for a raid on Mt. Carmel, expecting to secure the compound and arrest Koresh. The raid on February 28, 1993, however, proved to be a disaster. Forewarned by locals, the Davidians made extensive preparations. With Koresh at the lead, they defended their compound with gunfire, killing four ATF agents. Six Davidians were also killed. With the deaths of federal agents, the Federal Bureau of Investigation (FBI) assumed jurisdiction and established contact with Koresh as federal personnel moved to secure a wide perimeter around the compound and prepare for a prolonged siege. For the next 51 days, FBI negotiators sparred with Koresh in an effort to get the Davidians to surrender, all under the watchful eye of the national news media, which became fixated on an event that fascinated some and disgusted others.

As Texans entered the late twentieth century, they found themselves living in increasingly complex times when compared to the past. Politics had become a lot less predictable. The arrival of a competitive two-party system proved to be the most significant development, characterized by the fact that no party controlled the governor's office for two consecutive terms from 1974 to 1995. The state also witnessed substantial economic upheaval with the collapse of the oil market in the mid-1980s. As a result, many Texans suffered, though by the early 1990s the state's economy emerged more stable and diverse than before, with less reliance on resource extraction. Increasingly, economic prosperity would come from service industries within specific sectors of the economy such as retail trade, hospitality, tourism, entertainment, health, and education. New social issues also emerged as the continued influx of out-of-state and international migrants produced a more diverse population and, sometimes, a challenge to traditional views. Overall, the bustle of the modern era made it harder for Texas to maintain its unique identity in a rapidly changing and interconnected world.

**Texas and National Politics**

During the 1980 Republican presidential primary season, Texan George H. W. Bush emerged as a major challenger to the party's frontrunner, conservative Ronald Reagan, a former Hollywood movie actor who served as Governor of California from 1967 to 1975. Bush gained some traction by delivering strong attacks against Reagan's policy proposals, most famously when he described Reagan's belief that huge tax cuts for the rich would promote general prosperity as "voodoo economics." Reagan eventually scored his party's nomination and greatly aided his campaign in Texas when he chose Bush to be his running mate. Texas voters responded favorably by supporting Reagan over the incumbent Democratic president, Jimmy Carter, by a 55-41 percent margin. A lingering recession plus Carter's inability to end the Iranian hostage crisis took its toll on his presidency. In Texas, voters also cast their ballots for Reagan because they identified strongly with his brand of politics which merged economic and social conservative views—a blueprint for future Republican success in the South.

Though initially popular in Texas, Reagan's support for banking deregulation ultimately impacted the state negatively. During the campaign, Reagan, conservative Republicans, and some Democrats strongly supported the relaxation or removal of many government regulations affecting banks and other industries, believing that reduced responsibilities for the federal government promoted more freedom for citizens. They also argued that businesses would liberate capital for expansion projects and be able to hire more workers if they did not have to concern themselves with meeting federal regulations dating back to the New Deal era, which they felt were no longer necessary to ensure stability.

Deregulation significantly changed the savings and loan industry in Texas. Savings and loan associations (S&Ls), or thrifts as they were also known, were designed to serve local needs by offering savings accounts, mortgages, and auto loans. The federal government closely regulated S&Ls until the late 1970s when some rules were relaxed. In 1982, Congress followed Reagan's lead by allowing S&Ls to buy real estate and other holdings for the first time. The S&Ls were also permitted to extend new types of loans and to borrow more from the Federal Reserve System. These changes resulted in many S&Ls over-

**Vice President George H.W. Bush and President Reagan met with Soviet General Secretary Mikhail Gorbachev on Governor's Island, New York.
December 7, 1988
Photo credit: Reagan Presidential Library**

extending themselves, especially into the petroleum industry. Commercial real estate speculation was at a high during the oil boom in the early 1980s, and the S&Ls moved to extend loans to these speculators. When the oil industry went bust in the early 1980s, numerous borrowers defaulted, putting not only the real estate market but also the S&Ls in a bad financial position.

One by one, Texas S&Ls began to fail. Savings and loan companies had invested heavily in commercial real estate, anticipating increased growth in urban centers in the state. The anticipated growth failed to meet expectations. Thus, the bank managers were saddled with real estate that they could not quickly dump on the market. Of the ten largest commercial banks in the state, seven of them failed by 1990. From 1985 through 1990, 455 banks failed in Texas. Over 200 thrifts went bankrupt. The federal government through the Federal Deposit Insurance Corporation (FDIC) was beholden to repay depositors up to $100,000 of the money they lost in a bank's or thrift's closing. The cost of the thrift bailout in Texas alone exceeded $44 billion.

Ross Perot, January 24, 1990.
Photo credit: UTSA's Institute of Texas Cultures

The trend toward federal business deregulation impacted other Texas industries, though not so negatively. The Airline Deregulation Act of 1978, for example, opened up routes that previously had been closed to competition. This move significantly aided Southwest Airlines as it expanded service to twenty new cities. The deregulation of interstate trucking allowed certain companies to grow, such as Central Freight Lines, which now operates one of the largest trucking operations in the state. Railroad deregulation, however, tended to benefit larger companies and contributed to the demise of smaller lines that could not remain competitive.

This focus on ending government intervention was shared not only by business leaders but by an increasing number of conservative Protestant religious groups. Beginning in the 1970s, pastors such as W. A. Criswell of First Baptist Church in Dallas began interjecting more political commentary into their ministries. Issues such as the Equal Rights Amendment and *Roe v. Wade* galvanized churches to make more pro-family statements. Supporters of these religious positions began to see the federal government as interfering with their choices and religious traditions. It was not a stretch to similarly oppose all types of government intervention and regulation. The number of voters that could be affected by these new perceptions was immense. Criswell's church alone had over 20,000 members in the early 1980s, and he cultivated relationships with powerful oilmen and businessmen insuring that a steady financial backing would underlay his social and fiscally conservative message.

Religious conservatism and fundamentalism was becoming more respectable and more evident amongst the middle-class in Texas. They saw their own lives as evidence that one did not need "government hand-outs." As Robert Wuthnow has pointed out in his work on religion in Texas, Texans saw religion often as a means to exercise their conservative nature. And, as the national realignment of political parties occurred with the Democrats becoming more liberal on social and spending issues, the Republican Party became the home for these voters.

Throughout the 1980s, the Republican Party enjoyed great success in the statewide races for U.S. Senator and president. In 1984, when John Tower declined to seek re-election to the Senate, Congressman Phil Gramm emerged as his likely successor. Previously a professor of economics at Texas A&M University, Gramm first won election to the U.S. House in 1978 as a conservative Democrat. Soon after being reelected in 1982, however, Democratic congressional leaders removed him from the House Budget Committee due to Gramm's support for President Reagan's tax cuts. Gramm responded by resigning his House seat, switching allegiance to the Republican Party, and running for the vacancy in a 1983 special election, which he won. In the 1984 general election for Tower's seat, Gramm easily defeated liberal Democratic State Senator Lloyd Doggett by a 59-41 percent margin. (Voters subsequently reelected Gramm in 1990 and 1996.) Meanwhile, a majority of Texas voters viewed Democratic presidential nominees during the 1980s as too liberal. In 1984, Texans supported Reagan in his re-election bid with 63.6 percent of their votes to former Vice President Walter Mondale's 36.1 percent. In 1988, Texans voted strongly for George H.W. Bush over Massachusetts governor Michael Dukakis (56-43 percent) despite the inclusion of Texas Senator Lloyd Bentsen as Dukakis's running mate. Many conservative Democrats began realigning themselves with the Republican Party by formally changing their party affiliation as future governor Rick Perry did in 1989.

In 1992, voters experienced an interesting presidential race involving two Texans. While the Republican Party re-nominated President Bush and the Democrats supported Arkansas governor Bill Clinton, Dallas billionaire H. Ross Perot, entered the contest as a well-financed independent. With the country experiencing another recession in 1992, Perot leaned heavily on his success in business to argue that he had the best economic ideas to solve the nation's economic woes. Appearing on numerous talk shows and purchasing his own half-hour time blocs on network television, Perot aggressively sought to explain his program by using charts and graphs to illustrate economic problems and possible solutions. In the general election, Texans cast 22 percent of their votes for Perot, while Clinton earned 37 percent and Bush carried the state with 40 percent, though nationally Clinton emerged as the winner.

During Clinton's first term, Senator Lloyd Bentsen decided against running for re-election. Instead, he joined the new Democratic White House as Secretary of the Treasury for two years before retiring from politics. In Bentsen's place, Republican Kay Bailey Hutchison won a special election in 1993 to become the first female U.S. senator from Texas. Former San Antonio mayor Henry Cisneros also joined the Clinton administration. Very popular among Hispanic voters, Cisneros served as Secretary of Housing and Urban Development during Clinton's first term in office. Cisneros's chances for advancing his political career, however, ended when the public became aware of his involvement in an extra-marital affair and subsequent payoffs to his mistress while he served as mayor.

The growing success that the Republican Party enjoyed in Texas mirrored regional and national developments. In 1994, congressional Republicans touted their "Contract with America" as a way to nationalize state and local races, and undoubtedly Texas Republicans benefited from the success of the strategy. Helping Georgia congressman Newt Gingrich to push the Contract with America was Texas Republican Representative Dick Armey. Upon gaining control of the House, Gingrich became Speaker while Armey became the new Majority Leader. Another factor aiding Texas Republicans was the growing relationship between the Republican Party and the members of the Religious Right. This new "Christian Coalition," coupled with the "Get Out the Vote" efforts of socially conservative churches, ensured that more Republican votes would be cast than in previous elections. By the mid-1990s, an unmistakable trend was underway—the Republican Party benefited greatly from socially conservative Democrats leaving their party to join traditional pro-business conservative Republicans. This new joint effort helped the Republicans achieve great success at the national level while also exerting great influence at the state level.

**1980s State Politics: White, Clements, and Education Reform**

Republican governor William Clements decided to run for a second term in 1982, but met a particularly strong challenge from Attorney General Mark White, the Democratic nominee. White emerged victorious over Clements in part because of a lingering recession but also from the national Democratic Party's efforts to aid the election of other high-priority candidates in Texas. The Democrats ran what they called a "unified campaign," involving the coordination of all statewide candidates' campaigns. Democratic voter turnout subsequently surged. White won a majority of African-American and Mexican-American votes. He also made a concerted effort to win the votes of Texas teachers. Though no major changes had been made to the educational system since Governor Beauford Jester's administration during the 1940s, White promised to support educational reform if elected. In addition to White's victory over Clements (by a 53 percent to 46 percent margin), all other statewide Democratic candidates for office succeeded in their election bids. Aside from conservative Democratic Senator Lloyd Bentsen, these victors included four liberals, namely, Jim Mattox (attorney general), Jim Hightower (agriculture commissioner), Gary Mauro (land commissioner), and Ann Richards (state treasurer).

Often described as ordinary, White did not seem destined for the governor's mansion. Born in Henderson, a small town in East Texas, White's family moved to Houston where he attended public schools before graduating from Lamar High School in 1958. White then attended Baylor University, earning a business degree in 1962 and a law degree in 1965. He became involved in politics during the 1970s, serving as Secretary of State during Dolph Briscoe's administration before his election as the state's attorney general in 1978. Overall, the public tended to view him as a conservative Democrat similar in many ways to his political ally, Dolph Briscoe.

As governor, White surprised many by targeting issues championed by liberals, such as increased health care for the poor, and workman's compensation and unemployment insurance for farm workers. His most notable effort, however, involved comprehensive educational reform, which he initially addressed by creating a select committee headed by

Ross Perot to study the existing state of education in Texas. Perot later described his task as "the meanest, bloodiest and most difficult thing I have ever been into." There were many complex problems with the state's educational system as it stood. The state had been plagued for over a decade with declining standardized test scores and low literacy rates among students. Texas ranked in the lower tier in comparisons of student performance nationwide. Recommendations for educational reform became House Bill 72 and were introduced by the legislature in 1984. Enacted as the Educational Reform Act, the law established standards not only for student proficiency but also for teacher competency. Standardized testing for both groups began. Though teachers objected to the requirement that they prove basic competency in their field, they did enjoy the benefits of broad salary increases. The legislation also included a highly controversial "no pass, no play" provision that stated any student falling below a passing grade in any class during a six-week grading period was not eligible to participate in any extracurricular activities. While this prohibition applied to all activities (including membership in school clubs, cheerleading, and bands), the primary controversy centered on high school athletes. In a state where sports are king, many feared that "no pass, no play" would interfere with their school's ability to field winning teams.

The Education Reform Act had many problems. The standardized testing for teachers was an affront to educators and would cost White many future votes. Teacher pay and future raises were tied to student achievement on standardized tests, and the Texas State Teachers Association was unsure how the state would enact the new pay scale and how proficiency would be measured. Many also criticized the "no pass, no play" rule, arguing that many students stayed in school solely to participate in extracurricular activities and that preventing them from engaging in these activities would result in rising high school dropout rates. In spite of these complaints, school administrators still enforced the new law, making Texas the first state to implement such educational reforms.

Governor White ran for a second term in 1986. Once again, he faced William Clements, who led in the polls from the beginning of the campaign. While Clements ran an organized and well-funded campaign, the election hinged on the public's general dissatisfaction with the governor's policies. White's acceptance of the possibility of tax increases during hard economic times upset many citizens, including minority voters who had come out in sizeable numbers to elect the governor four years before. Unsatisfied with White's education reforms, teachers who had supported White strongly in 1982 abandoned him in 1986. Also, die-hard sports fans turned against White over "no-pass, no-play." (Ten years later, these sports enthusiasts would eventually be successful in prompting changes to the "no pass, no play" rule by shortening the sit-out time from six weeks to three.) Ultimately, Clements secured a 52-46 percent margin of victory over White.

Education reform continued to be a hot topic throughout the 1980s, especially regarding funding issues. Though the legislature passed a new tax bill to fund educational expenses, legislators from both parties wanted public school financing. Under Texas law, property taxes served as the primary source of funds for public education. Therefore, more affluent areas tended to build better schools than those located in districts with lower property rates. In an attempt to deal with this problem, the legislature enacted a new system of financing that provided additional state aid for bilingual programs, special education classes, and teacher recruitment for lower-income school districts.

By that time, the financing problems of Texas schools had already entered the court system. The Mexican American Legal Defense Fund (MALDEF) filed a lawsuit in 1984 against William Kirby, the commissioner of education. MALDEF represented San Antonio's Edgewood Independent School District, one of the poorest districts in the state. The plaintiffs claimed that the state funding scheme violated four basic principles of the state constitution that called on the legislators to provide a free public education to their citizens. Joined by eight other school districts and more than twenty individual parents, the Edgewood plaintiffs continued the legal struggle over school financing that had begun with the 1971 *Rodriguez v. San Antonio ISD* case, which had ended in defeat in the United States Supreme Court two years later.

Though the legislators and governor had approved a new state finance bill one month after the MALDEF filed its suit, the plaintiffs continued their suit, claiming that the new finance law did not address all the inequities in the public school system. Eventually, nearly seventy districts joined in the *Edgewood ISD v. Kirby* lawsuit to argue that reliance on property taxes created inherent inequity among wealthy and poor districts, a circumstance that contradicted the government's mandate to provide a free public school system. Furthermore, the lawsuit contended that current state funding of education discriminated against poorer school districts where the majority population was Hispanic, adding the charge of racial inequality to the legal case. In 1987, state district judge Harley Clark ruled in favor of the plaintiffs, finding that the current system of financing was unconstitutional and ordered the state legislature to formulate a more equitable system by September 1989. The state appealed the judge's decision, successfully pleading their case before the Third Court of Appeals. On December 14, 1988, the appellate court justices reversed the lower court's ruling by a two-to-one decision on the grounds that education was not deemed a "basic right." The justices also decided that the new funding law was constitutional. In turn, the plaintiffs appealed the appellate court's decision to the Texas Supreme Court, where the justices ruled unanimously in favor of the Edgewood school district and ordered the state to enact a new, equitable system of funding public education by the 1990-1991 school year.

In accordance with the Supreme Court's decision, the legislature devised a financing scheme that the press soon dubbed the "Robin Hood Plan." State money designated for wealthier districts would be transferred to poorer districts to create an equal amount of state spending per student across the state. Still unsatisfied, the Edgewood plaintiffs won a decision in state court necessitating yet another finance plan after convincing a district judge that the Robin Hood Plan still did not deal with the disparity of property taxes between the wealthy and impoverished districts. After Governor Clements appealed to the State Supreme Court, the justices determined that the state's reliance on property taxes to fund public education still created inequality among districts across the state and, therefore, was unconstitutional.

Legislators continued to address the problem of school funding. After another financing method was rejected by the courts in 1993, the legislature finally approved a multi-option funding plan for reforming school financing. Under this plan, school districts would seek to equalize funding through one of five options: The districts could (1) merge its tax base with a poorer district; (2) send money to the state to help pay for students in poorer districts; (3) contract to educate students in other districts; (4) consolidate voluntarily with one or more other districts; or (5) transfer some of its commercial taxable

Inauguration of Ann Richards, January 15, 1991.
Photo credit: UTSA's Institute of Texas Cultures

property to another district's tax rolls. If a district did not select one of these options, the state would order the transfer of its taxable property to poorer districts. If a district's budget still exceeded the spending cap per student, the state would force the district to consolidate with others in its region. Though a more complex solution, the state courts ruled that the new scheme was constitutional in 1995. However, the state made no efforts to increase the amount of funding available through the new distribution scheme, and therefore, the state contribution to education actually declined during the first decade of the twenty-first century. While school funding issues mostly center on funding for K-12 grades, decreases in funding have also hit the state's public colleges and universities. In 2003 the state legislature deregulated tuition which meant that universities could set tuition rates without legislative oversight. This change occurred at the same time that the legislature lowered its contributions to these universities, creating a rapid increase in tuition and a rise in student-loan debt.

During his second term, Governor Clements often butted heads with the Democratic-controlled legislature on a variety of issues, resulting in few victories for the governor.

Meanwhile, he continued to block much of the agenda of Democratic legislators by issuing a record number of vetoes (a total of 55 for his two terms). Overall, Clements did not enjoy the same success as he experienced during his first term. His administration was plagued by budget fights as the Texas economy suffered from lower oil prices. He ultimately signed off on an increase in taxes to deal with the state's floundering budget. The governor, a member of the Board of Regents for Southern Methodist University, also became embroiled in a scandal surrounding the SMU's football program. Beginning in the fall of 1987, reports began to surface that SMU football players were receiving cash payments and gifts from wealthy supporters of the athletic program, a violation of National Collegiate Athletic Association (NCAA) rules. These new charges were troubling, especially considering that NCAA officials had already placed SMU on probation for similar violations. Clements initially insisted that he knew nothing about any improper payments, but early in his second term the governor admitted that he had always known about the misconduct. The NCAA punished SMU by shutting down the university's football program for one year and allowing only a limited number of scholarships when the program resumed.

**Ann Richards and Early 1990s State Politics**

During the 1990s, the Democrats were losing ground to the Republicans but were not willing to give up control of the state government without a fight. In 1990, when Bill Clements decided not to run for re-election, the Democrats believed that they had an opportunity to retake the governor's mansion. The Democratic primary proved to be a heated race between Attorney General Jim Mattox, Ann Richards, and former governor Mark White. Richards gained national popularity after serving as the keynote speaker at the 1988 Democratic National Convention. She lambasted the Republican candidate, George H. W. Bush, by saying "Poor George, he can't help it. He was born with a silver foot in his mouth." Despite her popularity among Democrats on both the national and state levels, it was by no means clear that she would become the party's nominee. Richards had to contend with unfavorable press coverage of her personal life, which included a battle against alcoholism and an acrimonious divorce. Richards won the primary but not by enough votes to avoid a run-off election. She described the upcoming battle against Mattox in the run-off as a "mud-wrestling contest" as Mattox repeatedly implied that Richards had used illegal drugs in the past, including cocaine. Nevertheless, Richards bested Mattox in the run-off, garnering 54 percent of the vote.

The Republicans rallied around Clayton Williams, a West Texas rancher and businessman who vowed to spend some of his own money on the campaign, an approach that had worked well for Clements over a decade earlier. Williams ultimately spent $8 million of his personal fortune, enabling him to develop a major advertising strategy centered on television ads. His tough talk and no-nonsense approach paid off as he won an overwhelming victory in the Republican primary, earning more than 60 percent of the vote.

In the general election, Williams created quite a stir with several comments he made during the campaign. On one occasion while speaking with reporters, he likened a day of bad weather to a woman being raped. Williams continued, "As long as it's inevitable, you might as well lie back and enjoy it." He also admitted going to a prostitute while a student at Texas A&M and paying no federal income tax in the wake of the oil bust of 1986 (though he found a way to donate thousands of dollars to Governor Clements' campaign). Richards' victory in the general election in November was as much a result of Williams's missteps as her popularity with voters.

As Richards took office in 1991, Texas faced continued budget difficulties. Lieutenant Governor Bob Bullock went on record proposing a state income tax for Texas, a position unpopular with the majority of Texans. State legislators had another solution in mind. In the summer of 1991, the state legislature approved the establishment of a state lottery, which required a constitutional amendment since the Constitution of 1876 prohibited gambling. Voters approved the amendment by a vote of 2:1. With the state government looking at a multi-billion dollar deficit, the lottery was designed to add hundreds of millions of dollars to state coffers. The revenue from the state lottery goes into the state's general fund, and while part of this money does aid education in Texas, lottery revenue is not specifically reserved for educational purposes.

Ann Richards had a mixed record as governor. An outspoken liberal on many subjects, her policies often drew the ire of conservatives. Capital punishment, however, was not one of the divisive issues of her tenure. Bowing to the reality of the pro-death penalty Texas legislature, she refused to be a vocal critic of the state's death penalty law. During her first race for governor, a reporter asked her if she supported or opposed the death penalty. Richards judiciously answered, "I will uphold the laws of the State of Texas." When asked what she would you do if the legislature passed a bill repealing the death penalty, she quickly replied, "I would faint." Also arousing less controversy, Richards led an effort to reform the Texas prison system by establishing a substance abuse program for inmates, reducing the number of violent offenders released, and increasing prison space. She also

**President Bush with son, George W. Bush, and baseball broadcaster, Joe Morgan, in the locker room in Dallas, Texas, April 8, 1991.**
**Photo credit: George H.W. Bush Presidential Library**

oversaw the beginning of the Texas Lottery and the "Robin Hood" educational funding plan and strongly supported passage of the North American Free Trade Agreement as a boost for the Texas economy.

During her four years in office, Richards championed more diversity in government. Promoting what she called the "New Texas," she appointed more women and minorities, including the first black University of Texas regent and the first black and female Texas Rangers, to state posts than any of her predecessors.

Though Governor Richards enjoyed some notable achievements as governor, Lieutenant Governor Bob Bullock in many ways was actually the most powerful Democrat in the state government during the 1990s. Bullock had served as a state legislator, Secretary of State, and Comptroller of Public Accounts before becoming Lieutenant Governor in 1991. Though critics believed him to be a temperamental bully, Bullock's no-nonsense, nonpartisan management style while serving as the presiding officer of the Texas Senate allowed him to use his influence to get many measures that he wanted approved. If Governor Richards (and future Governor George W. Bush) wanted to get anything involving the legislature accomplished, they would first have to secure Bullock's support.

When Governor Richards ran for re-election in 1994, she faced a tough campaign against her Republican challenger George W. Bush, the son of former President George H. W. Bush. The younger Bush had run unsuccessfully for Congress in 1978. Politically, he worked with his father's presidential campaign in 1988, but he had never been elected to any political office when he became a gubernatorial candidate in 1994. Instead, Bush spent his time working in the oil industry and later, with a group of investors, bought and ran the Texas Rangers baseball team.

Ultimately, Bush defeated Richards by a 53-47 percent margin. Richards enjoyed great support from minority groups, receiving 75 percent and 90 percent of the vote from Tejanos and African Americans, respectively, but a combination of state and national factors combined to defeat Richards. Texas conservatives rallied behind Bush because of his notoriety, his stand on many current issues, and their contempt for many of Richards's actions as governor, such as her support for proposals to reduce the sale of semi-automatic weapons and her veto of a concealed handgun bill. Another factor was general disdain in Texas for President Bill Clinton and many of the national Democratic Party's policies. In 1994, the Republican Party successfully "nationalized" state elections to win back control of Congress while scoring victories in key governors' races across the country. In many ways, Richards was simply swept up in the rising conservative tide of that mid-term year, but no Democrat has served as governor since Richards.

By the mid-1990s, Texas had become a legitimate two-party state. What began in 1961 with John Tower's Senate win and continued sporadically for the next few decades had come full circle. The 100-year dominance of the Democratic Party gave way to a more competitive and soon-to-be dominant Republican Party. Yet, a majority of Texans had not discarded their dominant ideology. They had always shown a strong conservative bent. What changed was the agenda of the political parties. Whereas once the Democrats claimed to be the true conservatives, now the Republican Party seized that mantle and Texas voters veered accordingly. Republicans had always embraced at least the idea of small government, low tax rates, and a *laissez-faire* approach to the business world. Now they sought to appeal to social conservatives, especially in the South. Many socially conservative Texans resented the national Democratic Party's embrace of the civil rights movement and later welfare policies, along with other positions on such social issues as abortion, gun rights, and religion. As the parties recast themselves, the Republican Party developed policies built around these issues and pitched them to voters both on the national and state levels. By the end of the twentieth century, Republicans found success with this approach not only in Texas but throughout the South.

## Decline in the Oil Industry

During the early 1980s, great changes began to occur in the Texas economy as a result of a major decline in global oil prices. Elevated price levels began to drop in 1983 as the result of conservation efforts and increased domestic production. The major plummet in prices starting in 1986, however, resulted from the decision of the Organization of Petroleum Exporting Countries (OPEC) to lift all production controls in 1986, a development which devastated the Texas economy for many years. The severe drop in oil prices (from $50 per barrel in 1980 to $7 per barrel by 1986) led to the closure of over 20 refineries. From 1985 to 1993, the number of functioning oil rigs fell by over 80 percent. Over a quarter million Texas workers for oil-related companies lost their jobs. While some oil companies weathered the storm through corporate mergers, others simply went out of business.

Many other Texas businesses suffered greatly. The banking industry, which provided much financing for the growing oil industry during the 1970s, experienced a series of collapses. By the end of 1983, the largest independent bank in the state, the First National Bank of Midland, went bankrupt. Between 1987 and 1990, seven of the largest commercial banks in the state failed. As oil refineries closed, subsequent demand for fabricated metals and new machinery declined. Manufacturing along the Gulf Coast was hardest hit. Hundreds of thousands of jobs disappeared from that region in the early 1980s and never reappeared. The real estate industry, which had grown reliant on new offices and commercial property for oil companies, also witnessed a rapid decline.

As employees in the oil companies and related industries lost their jobs, the state government lost revenue generated from the oil industry, dropping from 26.5 percent of total taxes in 1983 to less than 7 percent in 1993. As a result, the state government cut back on government services. Meanwhile, because of the vast open spaces travelled in Texas, demand for oil and gasoline remained high, forcing the "oil-rich" state to import oil to meet its own residents' needs.

By the early 1990s, the price of oil stabilized between $16 and $22 per barrel, but due to the contraction of the Texas oil industry, the price increases resulted only in modest growth for the Texas economy—a trend that would continue into the early twenty-first century. When oil prices rapidly increased to over $145 per barrel in 2008, Texas did not experience a repeat of the 1970s boom years.

## The North American Free Trade Agreement

By the early 1990s, the United States and other nations around the world had become more integrated into international markets than ever before. The end of the Cold War, technological advances in communication, and increased foreign investment opportunities all contributed to American competition with other countries for goods and services in a truly global marketplace. As globalization began to take hold, many American business leaders and government officials advocated the reduction of tariff barriers as a means for the country to better compete with other nations in an increasingly complex economic environment.

One of the most controversial economic programs of the 1990s was the North American Free Trade Agreement (NAFTA), which removed trade barriers between the United States, Canada, and Mexico. Designed to increase trade across the borders of the three nations, outgoing President George H.W. Bush signed the deal in December 1992. Incoming president Bill Clinton introduced sections to the agreement in order to protect American workers and the environment before sending it to Congress. In June 1993, Clinton signed NAFTA's implementation legislation into law and the agreement went into effect on January 1, 1994. From the beginning, the focus in Texas centered on trade across the U.S.-Mexico border. The concerns surrounding NAFTA were many, such as how U.S. highways (in particular, Texas highways) would accommodate the increased truck traffic, how trucks from Mexico with lower emission standards would affect air pollution, and whether factories in Mexico (*maquiladoras*) with new American customers would harm the environment through their operating and disposal practices.

The Federal Reserve has studied the impact of NAFTA on Texas, finding that the state experienced increased exports of goods to both Mexico and Canada, and, interestingly, increased exports to Europe, Asia, and other parts of Latin America since its adoption. According to U.S. government figures from 1999 to 2005, the U.S. exported more farm and food items to Mexico than previously, approximately $9.4 billion annually (up from $3.7 billion). The trade of similar products with Canada has increased 80 percent.

By the year 2000, certain Texas industries benefited more from NAFTA than others. Controlling for exchange rates and other trade alternatives, the rubber and plastics industry enjoyed an 80 percent increase in exports to Mexico. Also profiting from NAFTA were the printing industry, the textile industry, and the petroleum and coal industries. Some industries, such as the timber industry, however, experienced marked declines during the same period. Overall exports from Texas to Canada increased 47 percent by 2000, a rate far ahead of the rest of the nation. Many critics continue to maintain that NAFTA overall has been mainly beneficial to business owners and elites in all three countries, while having a negative impact on Mexican farmers competing with American agricultural imports, and American factory workers who lost jobs as many companies moved their operations to Mexico in order to take advantage of the ample supply of low-wage labor.

**Post-Cold War Base Closures**

Defense-related industries boomed during the 1970s and 1980s, but the end of the Cold War in the early 1990s sent a shudder through the military-industrial complex. Despite subsequent military downsizing (though by not as large a margin as many advocates who expected a "peace dividend" had anticipated), many defense corporations operating in Texas, such as Bell Helicopter located in Fort Worth, Lockheed Martin also located in Fort Worth, and Raytheon located throughout the state, retained a significant presence. Nevertheless, the defense economy in Texas suffered losses in the 1990s with several military base closings and realignments. The Department of Defense decided to close and restructure numerous bases across the country to better serve the needs of the post-Cold

War era. Among the closures in Texas were Carswell Air Force Base near Fort Worth (which reopened as the Fort Worth Naval Air Station) and Kelly Air Force Base in San Antonio. Redeveloping the areas for the private sector and performing environmental cleanup has been costly, but the closures and restructuring continue to the present day. In some cases, areas received an economic boost from such realignment. The development of the San Antonio Regional Medical Center at Fort Sam Houston in San Antonio is one such example. By 2010, the military spent close to a billion dollars to close antiquated medical facilities, to hire additional personnel, and to create the new center, which will consolidate combat medical training for multiple branches of the military.

**The Growing Tech Industry**

While the oil industry and traditional manufacturing declined in importance in the late-twentieth century, the Lone Star State became a major home for several leading high-tech companies. When computers were initially built and took up entire rooms, the idea of a personal home computer seemed more science fiction than reality. By the 1980s, however, Texas Instruments (TI) developed a small personal computer (PC) to compete in the new market of home computing. Although TI ceased its production after a few years, three former senior managers of the company, Rod Canion, Jim Harris and Bill Murto, later started the Compaq (Compatibility and Quality) Computer line. By the mid-1990s, TI divested itself from its computer software line in order to concentrate on producing semiconductors, which today accounts for most of its sales. (TI later developed Digital Light Processing (DLP) technology, which is used to create sharper images in HDTV televisions and video projectors.)

Numerous other corporations retained headquarters or production facilities in Texas, such as Advanced Micro Devices (AMD), Motorola, Intel, IBM, and Sun Microsystems, and many joint ventures were formed between technology companies and Texas universities, such as the Balcones Research Center at the University of Texas at Austin and the Texas Center for Superconductivity located at the University of Houston, which examines high temperature superconductors. Hundreds of computer software companies located in Houston and the Dallas/Fort Worth area began to produce programs for a variety of tasks from managing inventory supplies to software created to aid construction firms.

The federal government also continued to promote scientific research in Texas. One controversial effort, however, ended before even being completed. After an extensive review by the Department of Energy, and with the support of U.S. House Speaker Jim Wright of Fort Worth, Congress selected the town of Waxahachie (south of Dallas/Fort Worth) to be the home of the Superconducting Super Collider—a scientific venture designed to study the collision of atoms. Beginning in 1991, the construction project employed over 2,000 people and brought a large amount of money into the area. Concerns over costs, however, doomed completion of the facility. Originally slated to cost $4.4 billion, revised projections in 1993 placing the actual costs in excess of $12 billion led Congress to cut funding in response to intense criticism of the endeavor as a wasteful "pork-barrel" project.

Certainly any discussion of technology in Texas would be remiss if it failed to include the National Aeronautics and Space Administration (NASA). In the mid-1990s, the headquarters in Houston employed more than 3,000 civilian workers plus more than

View of one of NASA's space shuttles sitting on top of a 747 jet aircraft used to move it from its landing point back to the launching site in Florida. Photo taken at Ellington Air Force Base, Houston, Texas.
Photo credit: Library of Congress

13,000 contractors. In addition, many high-tech companies located their offices at NASA's Houston facilities. Total NASA spending in Texas exceeded $3.5 billion, including millions for educational grants and support for non-profit organizations in the state. The Johnson Space Center is home to NASA's astronauts and functions as NASA's lead center for the International Space Station. There are numerous opportunities to tour the Johnson Space Center and participate in its educational outreach programs.

## Environmental Issues

Numerous new environmental issues began to impact Texas during the 1980s and early 1990s as the economy evolved and the state became more urbanized. The extensive use of trucks and automobiles, especially in the bustling cities and suburbs, contributed to growing air pollution problems. Houston regularly ranked among the smoggiest American cities with the rapidly growing Dallas/Fort Worth area rising higher on the list every year.

Another complex environmental issue heating up was the fight over water rights. Some areas of Texas rely on groundwater supplies such as lakes, while others depend on underground aquifers. Periods of drought affect all areas, leading many growing communities to examine future water resources. In particular, a contentious fight between city dwellers and farmers emerged. Historically, the state did not restrict landowners from pumping water from the ground. Under the right of capture, owners could access any water located beneath their land. New questions now emerged: Should landowners continue to be allowed to pump water freely to irrigate from underground sources? Could nearby cities relying upon the same water resources be able to regulate rural pumping?

In San Antonio, the question of water usage came to a head in 1991 when Ron Pucek, a large catfish farm owner, drilled the world's largest water well to pump an estimated 40,000 gallons of water per minute from the Edwards Underground Aquifer, or enough to fulfill the water needs of approximately 250,000 people living in San Antonio. State water officials and many in the general public viewed the owner as an unconcerned "water hog" who was wasting a valuable resource. Others, however, believed Pucek's rights were being violated. Legal challenges began almost immediately. Ultimately, the catfish farm operated for only one year before it was forced to shut down because Pucek could not secure a permit to discharge waste water into the nearby Medina River. The city of San Antonio eventually bought Pucek's farm and water rights, so the key issue of water usage remained unresolved.

**The Death of the SWC and the Ongoing Allure of Texas Football**

Texans have found numerous ways to keep themselves entertained, and, for many, football stands near the top. Those who have studied the phenomenon of Texas football point out that there is more to this particular aspect of Texas culture than simply the game. For small towns, high school football provides an important socializing mechanism to foster community cohesion. Loyalty provides the appeal for many college graduates who root for the teams of their alma maters, though schools continue to have many fans who never attended the institutions. Professional teams have rabid support among fans, in part, because they bring friends and families together to cheer for the team representing their city or state. In large metropolitan areas, football teams also provide a sense of community for people living in huge impersonal urban areas by unifying the residents behind a common cause.

For much of the twentieth century, college football in Texas meant the Southwest Conference (SWC). Founded in 1914, eight Texas schools and the University of Arkansas comprised the conference for most of its existence. From the late-1930s until 1995, the SWC champion hosted the annual Cotton Bowl in Dallas on New Year's Day. Eight SWC teams won national championships. Five SWC players from Texas schools have won the Heisman Trophy for being the best player in college football—Davey O'Brien from TCU in 1938; SMU's Doak Walker in 1948; John David Crow of Texas A&M in 1957; University of Texas' running back Earl Campbell in 1977; and the University of Houston's quarterback Andre Ware in 1989.

Despite the history behind the SWC, the conference began to decline after the 1970s. The popularity of professional teams in Texas diluted some interest. More importantly, other conferences began to consistently outcompete the SWC, plus many SWC programs were dogged by National Collegiate Athletic Association (NCAA) rules violations. A series of scandals rocked the University of Houston, Texas Christian University, Texas A&M, while Southern Methodist University became the first college to receive the NCAA's "death penalty" because of repeated recruiting and other violations, resulting in its football program being shut down by the NCAA for one full season, the forfeiture of all home games the following year (leading the school to decide not to field a team at all that season), and a large reduction of scholarships.

By the 1990s, in a reflection of the growing complexity of college athletics, discussions began to take place concerning the creation of a larger football conference with more competitive teams that could garner more money in contracts with television networks. The original proposal would merge part of the Southwest Conference (U.T. and A&M)

with the Big 8 Conference (which included the perennial powerhouses Oklahoma and Nebraska), leaving the rest of the Texas teams in an unattractive remnant of the SWC. However, politics soon came into play. Several prominent political leaders who were graduates of Baylor University and Texas Tech University did not want to see their alma maters' football programs lose their prominence by residing in an inferior conference. Lieutenant Governor Bob Bullock spoke with representatives of both U.T. and A&M and explained that Baylor and Texas Tech needed to be included in the new conference or he would reduce appropriations to U.T. and A&M. A new conference then emerged and became known as the Big 12. The Southwest Conference officially disbanded in 1996.

To understand the zeal which many Texans hold for their football teams, bordering on religion in some parts of the state, one could gain much insight from reading the journalist H.G. Bissinger's 1990 book *Friday Night Lights: A Town, A Team, and A Dream*. In 1988, Bissinger moved to Odessa to research and write a book on Texas high school football. The picture that emerged was shattering to the people of Odessa and other Texas communities. In his account of a year in the life of the Odessa Permian Panthers football team as it sought the Texas state football championship, Bissinger exposed both the highs and lows of high school football, questioning the practice of placing so many hopes and dreams on the shoulders of teenage boys. In the case of Odessa, replicated many times elsewhere in the state, Bissinger explains that more than a simple love of the game was involved in the town's obsession with football—the economic decline of the West Texas city (a large oil town) during the oil bust years of the late-1980s contributed greatly to the need of the townspeople to rally behind a common symbol with which they could identify.

**Two Texas Tragedies—Stevie Ray Vaughan and Selena**

As the twenty-first century approached, Texans continued to contribute to the American music scene. Among its feature artists, Stevie Ray Vaughan and Selena Quintanilla Perez were two performers from very different backgrounds in Texas who achieved fame as they brought their style of music to the American mainstream. They both also died at the height of their careers under different circumstances before their full potential could be realized.

Born in the Oak Cliff section of Dallas in 1954, blues guitarist Stevie Ray Vaughan stayed up all night as a teenager playing in various clubs before moving to Austin at age seventeen to become a player on the city's music scene. Though achieving some local notoriety, his career did not take off until the late 1970s when he formed the band Triple Threat, which later evolved into his most famous band, Double Trouble. By the early 1980s the group gathered a large Texas following and cut their first album, *Texas Flood*, in 1983. Vaughan's fame rose dramatically as he helped to popularize the blues style to a new generation of listeners. His follow-up albums were commercially successful and received positive reviews from music critics, receiving multiple Grammy nominations in the blues and rock categories.

In addition to his rapid fame, Vaughan's life became overwhelmed by an ongoing battle with alcoholism and drug abuse. After collapsing during a European tour, he checked himself into a rehabilitation center. Leaving the clinic a sober man, he resumed his career and continued to prosper. However, at the height of his resurgence, Vaughan died in a helicopter crash on August 27, 1990, while en route to Chicago after a concert in Wisconsin. Over 1,500 people attended Vaughan's memorial service in Dallas. In 1994, the city of Austin dedicated the Stevie Ray Vaughan Memorial Statue at Auditorium Shores on Lady Bird Lake, the site of many Vaughan concerts. It soon became one of Austin's most popular tourist attractions. A model of a proposed statue of Vaughan to be placed in Dallas was unveiled at a 2010 community festival in his native Oak Cliff.

Singer and entertainer Selena Quintanilla Perez was born in 1971 in Lake Jackson, Texas. While attending public schools through the eighth grade in Lake Jackson and Corpus Christi, she began performing in the family group "Selena y Los Dinos" formed by her father who had played for several years with a Tejano band. Selena's father taught all of his children to sing and play music, teaching young Selena to sing in Spanish. They started performing at their family's restaurant and at weddings in the Lake Jackson area. In 1982 the group moved to Corpus Christi and played Tejano music at such venues as dance halls, nightclubs, weddings, and quinceañeras. Selena recorded her first album in 1985, with her father selling the copies at their concerts. Within two years she became a star in the Tejano music world, winning the Tejano Music Award for Female Entertainer of the Year in 1987. In 1994 her album *Selena Live* won a Grammy for Best Mexican-American Album. She signed with SBK Records to produce an all-English album, but the bilingual *Dreaming of You* (released posthumously) would eventually appear instead.

Though her success remained largely within the Spanish-language market, by the early 1990s Selena's manager-father sought to expose her to a wider audience. Her image showed up in corporate advertisements, she appeared occasionally on a Mexican soap opera, and she performed a cameo role in the film *Don Juan DeMarco*. Selena started her own clothing line and opened Selena Etc., a boutique established in Corpus Christi and San Antonio. A new record deal with EMI Latin made her a millionaire. Selena was at the height of her career in 1995, with signs of even greater notoriety if she could succeed in solidifying her crossover appeal to American mainstream audiences, but it was not to be. She was shot in the back and killed in Corpus Christi after confronting Yolanda Saldivar, her fan club founder and manager of her Corpus Christi boutique, with evidence that Saldivar was embezzling funds. Selena's death devastated her large fan base. Selena's tragic end, nevertheless, led to greater exposure for Tejano music. When *Dreaming of You* was finally released later that year, it became the first Tejano album to hit number one in the United States. In 1997, the film biography *Selena* told the story of the singer's life and has done much to keep her memory alive. The movie catapulted Jennifer Lopez to stardom for her honest portrayal of the entertainer. That same year, the city of Corpus Christi erected a memorial in her honor, which includes a life-sized bronze statue of the singer.

**The Emergence of a New Texas**

As Texas approached the twenty-first century, the Lone Star State looked very different than most longtime residents were accustomed. The Republican Party became the dominant political institution. After the oil bust, the state's economy became based more on consumer spending and the service sector than from oil production, farming, and ranching. From 1980 to 1995, the state's population grew immensely, became even more urbanized, and reflected unprecedented diversification. With these changes came a myriad of complex problems that Texans continued to confront as the state continued to adjust to the realities of the modern era.

## *Aftermath: Apocalypse in Waco*

*After the initial ATF raid on the Mt. Carmel compound in which Vernon Howell (a.k.a. David Koresh) received a serious gunshot wound, the Branch Davidian leader began to negotiate with the FBI, dragging matters out for over 50 days. Early on during the siege, he promised a surrender if allowed to deliver a message over national radio. After the FBI complied with his request and Howell delivered his address, the cult leader claimed that God told him to remain at Mt. Carmel and await another sign. After 20 children were released, one hundred followers remained, though some would leave during the siege. Howell released a two-hour video in which adults and children testified to their desire to remain at the site with their leader under their own free will.*

*After interviewing many of the released children, the FBI, Attorney General Janet Reno, and President Bill Clinton determined that longstanding physical and sexual abuse continued to take place inside the compound. Howell continued to stall, claiming he needed time to write down various religious messages. Authorities began to believe that he would never peacefully surrender and planned another assault on the complex. On April 19, 1993, an FBI assault came in the form of combat engineering tanks with plans to breach walls and fire tear gas canisters to flush out and capture the occupants. However, fires soon broke out in different parts of the main Mt. Carmel building. Fewer than ten people escaped the building. In all, seventy-six perished; some from suffocation, some from falling rubble as the building collapsed, and some from gunshot wounds, which were either suicides or "mercy killings" as the flames and smoke filled the building. The event made headlines across the country and many were transfixed on the incident as it played out on national television broadcasts.*

*The official government commission's report on the assault showed that the fires were started inside the complex, most likely under Howell's orders to fulfill the leader's apocalyptic teachings (surviving Davidians maintained that the government deliberately or accidentally ignited the tear gas). Some Americans, especially those espousing extreme right-wing political views, have criticized the FBI's assault, blaming overzealous federal authorities for causing the deaths of those at Mt. Carmel. Two years later, one of these anti-government extremists, Timothy McVeigh, sought out his own personal revenge against the federal government. On the second anniversary of the FBI assault on Waco, McVeigh parked a moving truck filled with explosives outside the Alfred P. Murrah Federal Building in Oklahoma City, Oklahoma, and detonated it. One hundred sixty-eight men, women, and children were killed, and hundreds more were wounded.*

# Myth & Legend

## Myth of the Oil Industry

*Many people living outside Texas still believe that oil rigs are the most common feature of the Texas landscape. Some people are surprised to learn that not every Texan has an oil well in his/her backyard. Perhaps today this is a bit of an exaggeration, but the fact remains that the general public's impressions of the Lone Star State have been influenced by vivid stories of wildcatters striking it rich in the oil fields of Texas. It seems only natural that when people think of Texas, they also think of the oil industry.*

*Beginning with Spindletop in 1901, the economy of Texas was undeniably linked to the oil industry. Thousands of people came to Texas seeking jobs in the burgeoning industry. Though many of these jobs seekers worked in the oilfields of eastern and western Texas, a significant number of them worked in oil-related industries, such as refineries and service oriented companies that equipped and maintained the drilling rigs.*

*With the discovery of additional oil fields in West Texas, more people flocked to the high paying jobs the industry offered. During the twentieth century, Texas became so synonymous with oil that one of the longest running soap operas of the late 1970s and 1980s, "Dallas," featured a dysfunctional family that ran an oil company and lived on a large ranch outside of Dallas. This popular show further reinforced the myth that the livelihood of all Texans depended in one way or another on the oil industry.*

*While there are places in Texas where oil rigs and pumps are a common sight, there are also regions where gleaming skyscrapers and parking garages dominate the horizon. It is a myth that all Texans are associated with oil or that Texas's economy is solely based on the oil industry. While oil has been an important factor in the economic stability and prosperity of the state, it should not overshadow the numerous other industries that also exist in Texas. The diversified nature of the Texas economy has allowed the state to weather the boom and bust cycles of the oil industry over the past decade.*

*During the 1970s and again in the early 2000s, Texas enjoyed the economic booms associated with the oil industry. Companies during periods of prosperity provided jobs, paid state taxes, and donated large sums of money to regional charities. But, when oil prices decreased, companies were forced to layoff workers, limit drilling activities, and close down regional offices. Additionally, state revenues collected from oil companies trended downward and charitable contributions dwindled. Despite these economic setbacks, however, the state's economy did not crash, suggesting the success of the Texas economy relies on more than just the oil industry.*

*Today the retail industry, service industry, and tourism dominate the Texas economy, not the oil and gas industry. Approximately 80 percent of jobs in the state are in service industries. Service industry jobs typically do not pay as much as jobs in the oil industry, but they do employ more people. The Texas economy has also benefited significantly from growth in the high-tech industry, in health care, and in the airline industry, especially considering that three major airline companies are headquartered in Texas. Employment in manufacturing has decreased in the twenty-first century, but it represented a significant part of the economy in the last part of the twentieth century.*

*Though oil and gas remain important to the state's economic prosperity, the industry's future remains uncertain. Discussions of global warming and the use of alternative fuel sources have many oilmen worried that their companies will soon go out of business, especially if economic crises, like that witnessed in 2008, continues to threaten their industry. During 2008, crude oil and natural gas prices dropped so precipitously that it created a panic among leading oil companies, resulting in the shutting down of active rigs, laying off oilfield workers, and the closing of subsidiary companies. While the livelihoods of some Texans were definitely affected by this downward trend in the price of oil and gas, most residents, whose jobs were not related to the oil industry, welcomed the lower prices at the gas pump, further illustrating just how far the Texas economy has moved away from the grip of the oil and gas industry.*

**Suggestions for Further Reading**

Bissinger, H.G. *Friday Night Lights: A Town, a Team, and a Dream.* Reading, Mass: Addison-Wesley, 1990.

Cashion, Ty. *Pigskin Pulpit: A Social History of Texas High School Football Coaches.* Austin: Texas State Historical Association, 1998.

Cox, Patrick L. and Michael Phillips, *The House Will Come to Order: How the Texas Speaker Became a Power in State and National Politics.* Austin: University of Texas Press, 2010.

Kumar, Anil. "Did NAFTA Spur Texas Exports?" *Southwest Economy.* Federal Reserve Bank of Dallas, Issue 2, March/April 2006

McCall, Brian. *The Power of the Texas Governor: Connally to Bush.* Austin: University of Texas Press, 2009.

McNeeley, Dave and Jim Henderson. *Bob Bullock: God Bless Texas.* Austin: University of Texas Press, 2008.

Pilkington, Tom. *State of Mind: Texas Literature and Culture.* College Station: Texas A&M University Press, 1998.

Procter, Ben and Archie P. McDonald, eds. *The Texas Heritage.* 4th ed. Wheeling, Illinois: Harlan Davidson, Inc., 2003.

Shropshire, Mike and Frank Schaefer. *The Thorny Rose of Texas: An Intimate Portrait of Governor Ann Richards.* New York: Carol Publishing Group, 1994.

Storey, John W. And Mary L. Kelley, eds. T*wentieth-Century Texas: A Social and Cultural History.* Denton, Texas: University of North Texas Press, 2008.

Texas State Occupational Information Coordinating Committee. *The Texas Economy: There is Nothing So Certain as Change!* Austin, Texas, 1996.

United States Government Accountability Office. *Military Base Realignments and Closures: Estimated Costs have Increased and Estimated Savings Have Decreased.* GAO-08-341T. 12 December 2007.

**IDENTIFICATION:** Briefly describe each term.

S&L crisis
H. Ross Perot
Mark White
Education Reform Act
William Clements
*Edgewood v. Kirby*
Ann Richards
Bob Bullock
oil industry bust
NAFTA
military base closures
Super Conducting Super Collider
Johnson Space Center
Southwest Conference
*Friday Night Lights*
Stevie Ray Vaughan
Selena

**MULTIPLE CHOICE:** Choose the correct response.

1. _____ headed up the Select Committee to develop an educational reform package in the mid-1980s.
   A. Mark White
   B. H. Ross Perot
   C. William Clements
   D. David Ruiz

2. The Texas State Lottery was started when _____ was governor.
   A. Clayton Williams
   B. William Clements
   C. Ann Richards
   D. George W. Bush

3. The catfish farm that presented legal challenges over water pumping rights was located near what major city?
   A. Houston
   B. San Antonio
   C. Beaumont
   D. Austin

4. The "Robin Hood" plan refers to
    A. a plan to change tax rates based on income
    B. a plan to redistribute educational monies
    C. a plan of redistricting for the state legislature
    D. none of the above

5. The first female senator from Texas was _____.
    A. Miriam Ferguson
    B. Barbara Jordan
    C. Irma Rangel
    D. Kay Bailey Hutchison

6. During the mid-to-late 1980s, the price of oil _____.
    A. rose greatly
    B. dropped greatly
    C. remained remarkably stable
    D. went up and down like a roller coaster every month.

7. Which manufacturing area was hardest hit in the 1980s?
    A. Gulf Coast
    B. South Texas
    C. West Texas
    D. Panhandle

8. The Superconductor Supercollider was to be located near which city?
    A. Waxahachie
    B. Wichita Falls
    C. Lufkin
    D. Abilene

9. _____ authored the high school football book *Friday Night Lights* based on his year-long observations in Odessa, Texas
    A. Larry McMurtry
    B. Bob Wettemann
    C. H.G. Bissinger
    D. Molly Ivins

10. The major result of deregulation of the savings and loan industry was _____.
    A. immense growth and prosperity for Texas S&Ls
    B. over-speculation leading to bankruptcy for many Texas S&Ls
    C. government takeover of most S&Ls in Texas
    D. none of the above

**TRUE/FALSE:** Indicate whether each statement is true or false.

1. Republicans Ronald Reagan and George H.W. Bush both won Texas's electoral votes every time they ran for president.

2. Though he lost the 1992 election to Bill Clinton, independent candidate H. Ross Perot won his home state of Texas electoral votes.

3. The Texas governor's office flipped parties every election from 1974 to 1998.

4. Ann Richards served two terms as Texas governor.

5. Governor Ann Richards received criticism for her refusal to appoint many minorities to state government positions.

6. The *Edgewood ISD v. Kirby* case led to significant changes in Texas's funding of education.

7. Carswell Air Force Base and Kelly Air Force Base were both closed in the 1990s by the Department of Defense.

8. The Southwest Conference was a longstanding college sports conference that included mostly Texas teams.

9. The book *Friday Night Lights* painted a glowing portrait of Texas high school football.

10. Selena became the top country music star of the early 1990s.

**MATCHING:** Match the response in column A with the item in column B.

1. Phil Gramm
2. Ann Richards
3. Kay Bailey Hutchison
4. Stevie Ray Vaughan
5. George W. Bush
6. Bill Clements
7. Ronald Reagan
8. H. Ross Perot
9. Mark White
10. H.G. Bissinger

A. author of *Friday Night Lights*
B. legendary blues guitarist
C. defeated Ann Richards' re-election bid
D. only governor of Texas to serve two non-consecutive terms
E. Republican president who supported business deregulation
F. first female U.S. Senator from Texas
G. governor who supported the "no-pass, no play" education reform
H. Republican U.S. Senator from Texas
I. second female governor of Texas
J. billionaire owner of EDS who ran an independent campaign for president

## ESSAY QUESTIONS:

1. Who benefited and who did not benefit from the passage of NAFTA? Why?

2. What problems existed in the state's school financing system and how has Texas sought to address these issues?

3. Discuss the oil bust of the 1980s. What led to the price decrease? How did the downturn in the oil industry affect other industries? How did the crisis lead to a different economy in the Lone Star State?

4. Discuss the emergence of a two-party political system in Texas during the 1980-1994 period. What were some notable successes for the growth of the Republican Party in Texas? Were there any setbacks or was there a direct track to Republican dominance?

# Chapter 20

# The Dawn of a New Century, 1995-2020

*Prelude: A Terrorist Attack in Texas*

Nidal M. Hasan, perpetrator of the 2009 mass shooting at Fort Hood, had been a member of the U.S. military for many years before his rampage. Joining the army after graduating from his Virginia high school in 1988, the American with Palestinian-born parents served eight years as an enlisted soldier while earning a college degree from Virginia Tech. Hasan then attended medical school at the Uniformed Services University of the Health Sciences before completing his residency in psychiatry at the Walter Reed Army Medical Center in Washington, D.C. In July 2009, Hasan, having achieved the rank of major, was transferred to Fort Hood—one of America's largest military installations, serving as a training base and headquarters for numerous U.S. Army units—located outside Killeen, Texas.

Hasan was known among fellow doctors and soldiers as a devout Muslim, often stating his belief that American Muslims should receive conscientious objector status to prevent the possibility of having to fight other Muslims. Agents for the Federal Bureau of Investigation investigated Hasan after intelligence agencies alerted them to intercepted emails between the army psychiatrist and Anwar al-Awlaki, his former radical imam from Virginia known for espousing anti-U.S. government views then hiding out in Yemen (the cleric was later killed in a U.S. Predator drone attack), though nothing specifically threatening was discovered in the correspondence. Those who interacted with him in the days and weeks prior to the shooting apparently had no idea about what he was secretly planning.

Hasan was stationed at Fort Hood only for a few months before the army scheduled his deployment to counsel soldiers in Afghanistan. On November 5, 2009, Major Hasan casually walked into a soldier readiness facility at Fort Hood, ostensibly to complete paperwork for his deployment. Instead, he kneeled down in silence before yelling "Allahu Akhbar!" ("God is Great!" in Arabic), took out a semi-automatic pistol and began firing at the uniformed soldiers in the building. He then ventured outside and continued to shoot at soldiers before exchanging gunfire with civilian base police. Eventually felled by multiple bullets, Hasan lost consciousness *but survived, though one of his wounds left him permanently paralyzed from the waist down. It was all over in ten minutes, with thirteen people dead and thirty wounded.*

At the turn of the twenty-first century, Texas entered an interesting transitional period characterized by a blend of traditional political, social, and cultural beliefs interacting with the new viewpoints. The growth of the Republican Party continued, with its streak of victories in statewide elections effectively remaking Texas into a Republican stronghold even while the Democrats maintained and strengthened control in several pockets within the state. Though large numbers of Texans continued to espouse the maintenance of traditional social values, a growing number (as evidenced by public opinion polls) have come to accept views challenging the majority on such hot button issues as abortion, religion, and gay rights. Economically, Texas witnessed a combination of growth and retraction. The state continued to experience a substantial population increase from both natural births and out-of-state (and international) migration. While many found employment opportunities and a strong housing market at the beginning of the century, various sectors of the Texas economy also began to feel the negative effects of the national "Great Recession," which commenced at the end of the George W. Bush's presidential administration. How Texas would resolve this assortment of important political, social, cultural, and economic issues has yet to be determined.

**Politics During the Bush Years**

Bipartisanship characterized George W. Bush's first term as governor. Facing a legislature controlled by the Democratic Party opposition, Bush worked with Lieutenant Governor Bob Bullock to pass a narrow, but significant, four-point agenda covering education, tort reform, a tougher stand on juvenile crime, and changes to the state welfare system. The governor was able to claim success in all four areas by wooing enough legislators to his point of view with his personable style but also by displaying a willingness to compromise (something critics of his presidency pointed out he often refused to do at the national level).

The hallmark of Bush's education measure provided significant new authority to local school districts but only when their students met minimum standards as indicated by acceptable performance on the Texas Assessment of Academic Skills (TAAS) test administered by state officials. Bush failed in his effort to have the legislature accept a school voucher program, allowing families to use public money to defray the costs of sending their children to private schools. The legislature did approve the governor's call for a state charter-school program thereby creating special public schools exempted from many state rules to enable more educational and administrative experimentation.

Bush's tort reform measures built on efforts already initiated by lawmakers from both major political parties. In 1995 the legislature passed a number of laws limiting punitive damages for businesses, making the level of proof higher for plaintiffs wishing to recoup damages, and limiting a plaintiff's ability to decide where to file a lawsuit (sometimes referred to as "venue shopping"). While the legislation helped to crack down on frivolous lawsuits, critics argued that Texas citizens and businesses who were plaintiffs would have fewer legal rights, insurance companies would have less incentive to settle claims, and efforts to stop the root cause of legal claims—preventable deaths and injuries—would be hampered.

Regarding juvenile crime and welfare reform, the legislature largely followed Bush's lead. The number of beds in juvenile detention facilities increased from 2,500 to 6,300, thus extending the length of incarceration for youthful offenders. The age at which someone could be tried for murder was also reduced from 15 to 14. The legislature also approved the governor's call for welfare reform by imposing time limits and new work requirements on those receiving public assistance but did not approve the governor's desire to end all benefits for parents with more than two children.

Bush enjoyed high approval ratings after the first legislative session commenced. Though social conservatives in his party were upset that he avoided topics important to them, such as school prayer and abortion restrictions, a majority of Texas citizens approved of his limited agenda plus most other bills that he signed into law, including a popular (though controversial) concealed handgun law permitting citizens to carry licensed firearms into public places.

The 1996 elections demonstrated how much the Republican Party had grown in Texas. During the primaries, more Republican than Democratic voters cast ballots. After the general election, the Republicans gained a majority in the State Senate for the first time since Reconstruction. The Republican Party also won two-thirds of the statewide elective positions. The tide reached several major cities including Houston, Dallas, and Fort Worth, with Republicans winning a majority of county offices. Phil Gramm competed for the Republican presidential nomination but dropped out when he did not place well in early contests. Instead, he sought a third-term as a U.S. senator against an unlikely Democratic opponent, Victor Morales. A school teacher with little in the way of campaign funds, Morales nevertheless won a primary runoff against Congressman John Bryant. In the November race, however, Gramm easily defeated Morales by over ten percentage points.

The Republican Party was also deliberately working to appeal to voters (mostly white voters) by emphasizing social issues with positions in line with religious conservatives. Republican candidates touted their opposition to abortion along with their fiscal conservatism. This proved to be a remarkably sound strategy with a majority of white conservative Protestants voting for national Republican candidates including Ronald Reagan and George H.W. Bush. George W. Bush emphasized that he was a "born-again" Christian in his campaigns. The Religious Right (a movement that focused on social conservatism) became more of a player in the political world as the 1990s continued. Exit polls for several elections showed that voters who identified as members of the Religious Right (who might be Catholic or Protestant), heavily voted for Republican candidates.

For people who identify as religious, several surveys conducted in the early 2000s demonstrated that most Protestants belonged to evangelical or conservative denominations. These churches were mostly filled with middle-class parishioners. Some of the churches have transitioned into being mega-churches with thousands of members. Lakewood Church in Houston currently led by Joel Osteen and the Potter's House in Dallas run by T.D. Jakes are such examples. Nearly two hundred congregations in Texas have 1500 or more members. Over thirty have over 5,000 members. The size of these churches allow for a level of charitable outreach to those in need that few can match. It is no wonder that in some cases, members view either federal or state government intervention through social service programs as an unwarranted expense.

In the presidential election, the Democrats re-nominated incumbent President Bill Clinton. The Republicans nominated Senator Robert Dole of Kansas who had served as a congressman for three terms during the 1960s until his election to the Senate in 1968. Ross Perot also ran again as an independent, but this campaign lacked the excitement of his 1992 race. Texans cast nearly 49 percent of their votes for Dole, nearly 44 percent for Clinton, and less than 7 percent for Perot. As in 1992, Clinton won the most electoral votes nationally and returned to the White House for a second term.

During his second legislative session as governor, Bush used some of the political capital acquired from his success during the first session to push for expanded education and tax reforms. Bush also solidified his credentials with his Republican base as a business and social conservative as he sought to position himself for a possible White House run in 2000. The capstone of his efforts was an elaborate plan to take advantage of a budget surplus by cutting property taxes while raising sales and business taxes so the state could pay a higher percentage of school funding. After the effort failed when Republican legislators balked at the proposal, Bush responded by pivoting to support a large tax cut that, along with his lax environmental enforcement record, endeared him to the business community and fiscal conservatives. To woo social conservatives, Bush supported the idea of allowing faith-based Christian groups to receive taxpayer money to provide public services (in addition to proclaiming June 10, 2000, to be "Jesus Day" in the state of Texas, urging all Texans to "answer the call to serve those in need"). He also took a hard line on capital punishment. On his six-year watch, the state executed 152 inmates, more than any previous Texas governor (since surpassed by Rick Perry who oversaw over 200 executions during his time in office).

Of all the death row cases under Bush, the one garnering the most media attention involved Karla Faye Tucker, who had been convicted of murder following a 1983 crime she committed with her boyfriend. High on drugs and alcohol, they murdered a male and female acquaintance during a robbery in Houston, with Tucker using a pick-axe to kill the woman. Soon arrested for these gruesome, bloody crimes, the two assailants were put on trial, convicted, and sentenced to Death Row. While in prison and away from the drugs that she had used on a daily basis, Tucker claimed to be a born-again Christian. By the mid-1990s, she became a symbol for women's rights supporters, the anti-capital punishment lobby, and several Christian groups. Governor Bush received a plea for clemency from Tucker's lawyers as her execution date approached, but based on his understanding of the verdict in the case and the Texas penal code, as well as the fact that he felt more sympathetic toward the victims' families than he did toward Tucker, the governor denied the request for a stay of execution. Tucker was executed by lethal injection in February 1998, becoming the first woman to be executed in the United States since 1984 and the first in Texas since the Civil War.

In the 1998 elections, Democrats hoped to have a full rebound of their electoral fortunes, with some touting Attorney General Dan Morales as a candidate for governor. Morales had received recognition by successfully representing the state in a settlement with the tobacco industry by which Texas received $17 billion to compensate for money spent to provide health care for residents suffering from tobacco-related illnesses, but he declined to run. Instead, the Democrats nominated Land Commissioner Gary Mauro who won only 31 percent of the vote in the race against George W. Bush. (Morales later ran in the Democratic primary for governor in 2002 but lost to Tony Sanchez. The following year his popularity fell when he pled guilty to mail fraud and filing a false tax return that did not report his efforts to profit personally from campaign contributions. He was sentenced to four years in a federal prison.) For the first time in the twentieth century, the Republicans swept all the elections for statewide offices. As many had speculated would happen, Bush soon organized an exploratory committee to pursue the presidency.

Bush did not have an easy run for the 2000 Republican Party nomination, facing stiff competition from Arizona senator John McCain. Though the initial front-runner, Bush lost the New Hampshire primary to McCain. Despite this setback, Bush rallied social and business conservatives to defeat McCain in the South Carolina primary and went on to secure the nomination. In November he easily carried the state of Texas, winning nearly 60 percent of the vote. The election itself was fraught with ballot problems in a few states, most notably Florida, where as matters turned out, the winner of the state's popular vote would receive enough electoral votes to clinch the presidency. Democrats challenged the preliminary results (which showed Bush with a slight lead) based on ballot design discrepancies and alleged errors in machine vote tabulations. The Florida State Supreme Court ordered hand recounts in selected counties, but after Republicans challenged this ruling the U.S. Supreme Court voted by a 5-4 margin in December to halt the recount. Bush, as the state-certified winner of Florida before the recounts began, retained Florida's electoral votes and was inaugurated in January 2001 despite having received over 500,000 fewer national votes than Democratic candidate Al Gore.

Bush became only the second Texan besides Lyndon Baines Johnson ever to serve as president. Bush's father had been born and raised in Connecticut, while the family of Dwight Eisenhower, who had been born in Denison, Texas, moved to Kansas when he was an infant. Bush chose to include many people from his days as governor or his father's term as president to join the White House staff. Karen Hughes, who had served as director of communications during Bush's governorship, served as a close advisor to Bush. Rod Paige, who had worked with the Houston Independent School District, became Secretary of Education and became instrumental in implementation of the No Child Left Behind Act (based on Bush's Texas education reforms) requiring states to develop basic-skills assessments to be given to all students in certain grades in order to receive federal education funds. Also joining the Bush White House were Karl Rove, his political strategist, and Alberto Gonzales, who served as Bush's general counsel while governor and his first presidential term before becoming Attorney General from 2005 to 2007. Bush's vice-president, Dick Cheney, also had lived in Texas before re-locating to Wyoming shortly before the 2000 election to honor an obscure constitutional provision forbidding a president and vice president to reside in the same state.

**Early Twenty-first Century Texas Politics**

When George W. Bush left Austin to take his position as President of the United States, Lieutenant Governor James Richard "Rick" Perry entered the governor's office. Born in the West Texas town of Paint Creek, Perry graduated from Texas A&M University with a degree in animal science. He served in the U.S. Air Force before returning to Texas and winning three terms in the state legislature as a Democrat. In 1989 he switched to the Republican Party and narrowly defeated Jim Hightower in the 1990 race for Agriculture Commissioner. After two terms in that office, Perry sought the position of Lieutenant Governor in 1998 after Bob Bullock announced his retirement. In a close race, Perry defeated Democrat John Sharp by a 50-48 percent margin.

During the early years of Perry's governorship, congressional redistricting became a hot political topic. In 2000, the legislature had redrawn congressional election districts in the state, but following Republican takeover of the state House, and thus the entire state legislature, in 2002 (the same year Perry won election as governor in his own right by defeating Laredo banker Tony Sanchez by a 58 percent to 40 percent margin), Republican Tom DeLay, the U.S. House Majority Leader from Texas, promoted the idea of another round of re-districting. (In 2010, a jury convicted DeLay of felony money laundering charges for illegally channeling $190,000 in corporate donations to Republican state legislature candidates during the 2002 elections to help his party gain control of the legislature.) In 2003 the process began when Governor Perry called the legislature into special session to take up the matter. Opponents charged that the new re-districting was unneeded after only three years of the previous district restructuring and that it was nothing more than gerrymandering by Republican officials. Over 50 Democrats from the Texas House staged a walk-out during the session and stayed in Oklahoma to prevent the legislature from being able to take any actions at all. Texas state troopers were sent after the errant lawmakers, but since they were in Oklahoma, the troopers had no jurisdiction to bring them back to Texas. When another redistricting attempt was made several months later, Democratic senators departed the capital, this time heading for New Mexico. Eventually, after a few Democratic lawmakers broke ranks with their party, a new congressional district map was approved. After the 2004 November elections, which used the redrawn map, Republicans won five additional seats in Congress and Texas's U.S. House delegation had a Republican majority for the first time since Reconstruction. Court challenges were filed, but other than a United States Supreme Court decision to redraw one South Texas district in order to satisfy concerns about possible violation of the Voting Rights Act by diluting Hispanic votes, the redistricting move stood.

As governor, Rick Perry touted his fiscal conservative credentials as evidenced by his record number of vetoes on spending measures while also signing legislation in 2006 that reduced property taxes by over $15 billion. He also resisted any increase in sales taxes or the notion of creating a state income tax, instead favoring increased user fees and the raising of state franchise taxes. In 2001 he proposed the Trans-Texas Corridor—a massive project to construct a 4,000-mile system of multi-lane superhighways, railways, and utility lines from Oklahoma to Mexico and southwestern Texas to southeastern Texas without the use of taxpayer money. Though eventually failing to acquire enough support to move beyond the planning stage, Perry's defeated proposal envisioned the use of private financing (plus the charging of tolls) to cover the estimated $150 billion price tag. Despite these positions on public spending, Perry nevertheless believed the state should actively expend government funds to promote commerce and attract new businesses to Texas. In 2003 he worked with the legislature to create the Texas Enterprise Fund, providing $300 million to attract new business to the state. In 2005, Perry also signed legislation creating the Texas Emerging Technology Fund (TETF), a $200 million investment designed to encourage high-tech research and job creation in Texas.

Governor Perry wooed social conservatives by his positions on many matters of public policy. In 2005, he signed a bill restricting late-term abortions and requiring pregnant girls under 18 to notify their parents before having an abortion. Opposed to gay marriage, Perry also condemned the U.S. Supreme Court's 2003 decision in *Lawrence v. Texas* overturning the state's sodomy law, which made it a crime for gay men or women to engage in private, consensual sexual activity. Regarding the teaching of evolution in public schools, the governor supported teaching creationism and "intelligent design" alongside evolution.

The Republican Party continued to dominate statewide politics during the first decade of the twenty-first century. In the 2006 gubernatorial race, Rick Perry again won the Republican nomination but defeated three general election opponents with only a plurality (39 percent) of the vote. The Democratic nominee, congressman Chris Bell, gained a respectable 30 percent, but he saw many potential anti-Perry votes siphoned away by independent candidates Carol Keeton Strayhorn (a former Republican state comptroller of public accounts who broke with her party over education and tax issues) who garnered 18 percent, and singer, comic-mystery writer, and all-around character Richard "Kinky" Friedman who managed to receive 12 percent.

In 2008, Texas voters were treated to elections as exciting as they proved to be in many other states during that election cycle. The 2008 Democratic Party presidential primary featured a close battle between the last two remaining candidates—Illinois Senator Barack Obama and New York Senator Hillary Clinton. Obama and Clinton both visited the state to give speeches and raise money as they sought Texas's large number of delegates for the Democratic National Convention to be held in Denver, Colorado. In an unprecedented turnout, Clinton eventually carried the popular vote 1,462,734 (50.9 percent) to Obama's 1,362,476 (47.4 percent). Clinton displayed impressive strength among rural white and Hispanic Democrats, while Obama dominated among blacks, urban white liberals and moderates, and the youth of all races. Still, Clinton's performance only gave her 65 delegates to 61 for Obama in the first stage of the Texas Democratic Party's "Texas Two-Step" delegate selection process. State party rules (designed in theory to bolster activism among voters and to reward additional enthusiasm for a candidate), however, dictated that a second round of delegate selection commence to select an additional 67 pledged delegates (party rules also stipulated that Texas would send 35 "superdelegates" from a group of privileged party leaders and elected officials to the national convention). This stage first called for precinct caucuses to be held on election night to select individuals who would later go to county caucuses in order to cast ballots for the supplementary delegates. Obama's campaign took advantage of this process better than Clinton's supporters, resulting in the Illinois senator eventually receiving 38 more delegates to Clinton's additional 29. Though a rather clumsy delegate selection process, the prolonged battle generated more publicity and voter interest for both candidates. Ultimately, Texas sent 193 delegates to the Democratic National Convention, with 99 pledged to Obama and 94 for Clinton, enabling Obama to sustain his momentum and enabling him to secure a historic nomination as the first African-American nominee of a major political party.

The Republican primary proved to be inconsequential because Obama's general election opponent, Arizona Senator John McCain, had all but sealed his party's nomination by the time the primaries reached Texas. McCain easily defeated his last remaining serious rival, former Arkansas governor Mike Huckabee, by a 51-38 percent margin on his way to becoming his party's presumptive nominee. As a result of most polls showing McCain holding a 10-15 percent lead over Obama in Texas (though he trailed Obama nationally throughout the general election campaign), the nominees rarely visited the state, choosing instead to focus on the "battleground states" in closer contention. McCain lost the national election handily, but secured Texas's electoral votes by defeating Obama by a comfortable 55 to 44 percent margin.

Though John McCain won the state and Republicans retained control of all statewide elective offices (plus retained a U.S. Senate seat when incumbent John Cornyn easily defeated Democratic state representative Rick Noriega by 12 percent), signs of possible future electoral change can be found if one looks into the 2008 presidential and local races. In addition to gaining solid South Texas support among the Tejano population who strongly favored Hillary Clinton in the Democratic primary, Barack Obama tallied a majority among liberal and moderate whites, blacks, and Hispanics on his way to carrying all major East Texas cities. Obama won Travis County (Austin) by a 64-35 percent margin, Dallas County by a 57-42 percent, Bexar County (San Antonio) by a 52-47 percent, and Harris County (Houston) by a 50-49 percent. Local Democrats performed well in local races within those metropolitan areas as well as many suburbs surrounding them. The state House races also reflected this shift: Democrats gained three seats, losing one race by less than 100 votes, which would have denied a Republican majority by creating a 75-75 tie. In early 2009, Democratic lawmakers showed some clout when they successfully rebelled against the strong-arm tactics of conservative House Speaker Tom Craddick (the first Republican to hold the position since Reconstruction) by combining with moderate Republicans to force Craddick to drop his bid for a fourth term.

With his re-election in 2006, Governor Perry guaranteed that he would remain in office for at least ten years—the longest tenure of any governor in the history of the state. Because of this long duration in office, he exercised unprecedented control over boards and agencies within the state government, and critics cited a correlation between the governor's appointments and the large amounts those individuals often contributed to his political campaigns.

Early in his second full term, Governor Perry received criticism for his executive order mandating that Texas sixth-grade school girls receive the vaccine for the human papillomavirus (HPV), a common sexually transmitted disease known to cause cervical cancer. The order authorized free vaccinations at state expense (over $300 per child) for those not covered by insurance and allowed parents to opt out of the program entirely, but many citizens groups and politicians from both political parties assailed Perry on moral grounds and safety concerns. News reports also surfaced linking the governor to Merck, the vaccine's manufacturer, in the form of a $6,000 campaign contribution. In June 2007, Perry allowed a bill to become law without his signature rescinding his order.

Perry's approach to the issue of illegal immigration caused less controversy. While opposed to the idea of building a massive fence or wall to divide the Texas-Mexico border, Perry advocated securing the border with an increased number of personnel, calling for 1,000 National Guardsmen to be deployed in South Texas to aid U.S. Border Patrol agents. The governor also advocated increased use of technology to police the border through extensive placement of stationary surveillance cameras and the use of predator drone aircraft.

Senator Kay Bailey Hutchison
Photo credit:
Sen. Hutchison's website,
http://www.hutchison.senate.gov/

When an economic downturn began in 2008, it seemed as if Texas would weather the recession quite well—people continued to move to Texas for jobs, state financing was stable, and property values continued to be strong. However, by 2010 it became apparent that Texas also could not escape its impact. Property values and sales tax collections decreased, and the state legislature faced a ballooning budget deficit. Many state agencies were forced to take a 5 percent decrease in funding in 2009, and the legislature examined the possibility of a 10 percent decrease in funding for state expenditures for the next biennium.

In 2010 Governor Perry sought an unprecedented third full term as Texas governor. Before facing a Democratic challenger in the general election, Perry had to overcome a potentially strong primary contest against Senator Kay Bailey Hutchison. The governor rose to the occasion and defeated Hutchison largely by "moving to the right" and calling himself the only true conservative alternative for Republican primary voters. Portraying Hutchison (a fairly conservative politician) as a moderate-to-borderline-liberal Washington establishment figure, Perry positioned himself well through his occasional refusal to accept federal stimulus money to help combat the recession and even pandering to the extreme right wing of his party when he once famously suggested (incorrectly) that Texas had a legal basis to secede from the union if discontent with federal government policies continued, a position that he conditioned with the statement: "My hope is that America and Washington in particular pays attention. We've got a great union. There's absolutely no reason to dissolve it."

In the fall 2010 election, Perry faced Democrat Bill White, a popular former three-term mayor of Houston who had achieved national prominence in 2005 when in the aftermath of Hurricane Katrina, he welcomed displaced Louisianans to Houston and encouraged them to make a new home in the city. White attempted to win votes largely by pledging to work with Republican legislators in a bipartisan fashion and by accusing Perry of creating a "culture of cronyism" whereby the governor's numerous political appointments rewarded donors to his campaigns. For his part Perry continued his anti-Washington rhetoric, which matched the prevailing mood of the electorate as the recession wore on. Taking advantage of the traditional gains made by minority parties in national mid-term elections, Perry cruised to victory over White by a comfortable 55-42.3 percent margin. In fact, the Texas Republican Party in general turned in a solid performance at the polls, energetically rebounding from its 2008 showing to win back many legislative seats lost during the previous election when Obama's candidacy carried many freshmen Democrats to victory. Republicans also gained fresh control of districts long held by Democrats. Whereas the Republican advantage in the State Senate remained stagnant at 19-12, the GOP's membership in the House ballooned from a slim 77-73 majority to a massive 99-51 margin as even three Republican incumbents with ethical scandals that had dragged their campaigns won re-election. Further, a couple of notable party-switching defections after the election by legislators elected as Democrats gave the Republicans a 101-49 supermajority. Three Democratic congressmen also fell to Republican challengers, including ten-term conservative Chet Edwards of Waco, and Solomon Ortiz, who had served his South Texas district since 1983. To add additional gloom to the results from the Democratic Party's perspective, for the fourth cycle in a row the Republicans swept all statewide races.

In the summer of 2011 with speculation ramping up, Perry decided to throw his hat in the ring and seek the Republican nomination for president. Touting many of the same positions he held as governor, Perry had a rough fall as poor debate performances took their toll on his popularity. He eventually suspended his campaign in January 2012 after a poor fifth-place showing in the Iowa caucuses. A majority of Texas Republican voters supported the Republican Party's eventual nominee, Mitt Romney, throughout the political season. Polls showed he would easily win the state's electoral votes over Barack Obama in the November general election, which he did by a comfortable 57-41 percent margin. (The nation as a whole favored Obama over Romney in 2012, as the president secured a second term by winning 332 electoral votes compared to Romney's 206.) In 2012, former state solicitor general Ted Cruz became the first Tejano elected to the U.S. Senate. Cruz did not have the type of background many had expected from a Hispanic candidate from Texas. Born in Canada, Cruz's ancestry is Cuban, and he emerged victorious in the G.O.P. primary over Lieutenant Governor David Dewhurst due to the strong backing he received from far right "Tea Party" supporters. The results from the state legislative races showed either small Democratic gains or the status quo as the Republican majority in both the Texas House and Texas Senate remained solid.

The 2014 gubernatorial race pitted the popular and long-time state attorney general, Greg Abbott (Republican), against Wendy Davis (Democrat), a member of the Texas Senate. Davis had recently garnered headlines as she filibustered a bill in 2013 that limited the places that could perform abortions in the state. While a "star" in the Democratic Party, Davis failed to fundraise as well as her opponent or to connect with the still large cadre of rural voters. Abbott had solidified his position as a conservative, often by filing lawsuits against President Obama's initiatives for what Abbott described as "federal overreach." Abbott easily won with over 59 percent of the vote. Abbott ran for re-election in

2018 against Democrat challenger Lupe Valdez, the former sheriff of Dallas County. Abbott again won with over 55 percent of the state's votes. The governor strongly supported gun rights including open-carry legislation and the arming of public school teachers.

In the presidential election of 2016, Texas again sided with the Republican Party with Donald J. Trump winning over Hillary Clinton 52 percent to 42 percent. Trump did particularly well in rural areas of the state. The major population centers of Dallas, Houston, Austin, and San Antonio all went for the Democratic candidate, Clinton, as did large areas of South Texas. In the end though only 28 counties voted Democrat to the 226 that voted Republican in this contest.

Issues surrounding gun rights are sure to be in the political forefront in the coming years. Mass shootings have occurred in Texas several times recently. In 2017 a church in Sutherland Springs was the site of an attack by a disgruntled family member of a parishioner. Twenty-six people were killed at the First Baptist Church. In 2018 ten people were killed at Santa Fe High School near Houston when a student brought a weapon to school and commenced firing on his classmates. Then in 2019, at a Wal-Mart in El Paso, a man with a rifle killed twenty-two people before being arrested by law enforcement.

As in 2008, Democrats had to find solace in their continued success in the state's urban areas and pockets of strength in South Texas as evidenced in the 2016 presidential election. (In the 2012 presidential race, Obama won a majority of the vote in Austin, Dallas, Houston, San Antonio, and El Paso as well as the Hispanic-majority counties of the Lower Rio Grande Valley.) Though the Republican Party continues to dominate state-level Texas politics, demographic factors have contributed to local Democratic electoral gains while promising to bolster the party's future statewide chances. The Hispanic population within Texas, often a solid supporter of the Democrats, continued to grow at an accelerated pace. The national results in the 2012 election demonstrated again the potential for Texas's political map to change in the future as Hispanics voted overwhelmingly for Obama (71 percent to 27 percent). (Over 20 percent of Texas's voters in the 2012 general election were Hispanic.) Meanwhile, the youth vote began to emerge as a growing Democratic constituency nationally, as well as in Texas.

In 2018 one of the campaigns watched closely around the state was the U.S. Senate race that pitted incumbent Ted Cruz against challenger Robert "Beto" O'Rourke. O'Rourke was a member of the House of Representatives from the El Paso area and proved to be a dynamic speaker that galvanized supporters throughout the state. Cruz's campaign lacked that same spark in the months prior to November. The final results returned Cruz to the U.S. Senate, but the vote was close at 50.9 percent to O'Rourke's 48.3 percent. Even staunch conservative counties such as Tarrant County (Fort Worth) voted Democrat in this race. It was a sign that the Democratic Party could field compelling candidates who had a real chance at winning elections.

The challenge for Democrats in the future will be to create a new political coalition. Past Democratic efforts to align the state's lower and middle classes against wealthy Republicans failed, due in no small part to Republican policies and tactics designed to appeal to lower- and middle-class white support by dividing the state's electorate along racial and cultural lines. Democrats will try to renew their electoral bond between college-educated, socially liberal upper- and middle-class whites and younger voters while retaining core support among the state's blacks and Hispanics. Republicans will have to continue to address the needs of the same constituents while retaining core support among social and business conservatives or face the possibility of losing control of the reins of state government that its members have fought so long to acquire.

**Public Transportation and Infrastructure**

As the population of the state has continued to grow (Texas ranks second in population among the fifty states), the transportation of people and goods has assumed larger importance. State highways and interstates see more traffic, have more wear and tear courtesy of that traffic, and see more slowdowns as the number of cars and trucks increase. The network of highways in Texas, which was essentially completed decades ago, cannot continue to handle the influx of automobiles.

One option to control traffic is public transportation utilizing buses and trains. The Dallas Area Rapid Transit System (DART) began regional bus service in 1983 and opened its light rail network in 1996. Houston inaugurated its new rail system in November 2003. Other urban areas have begun to explore using their local sales tax money to fund new rail ventures in an effort to ease the stress on the highways. However, some citizens oppose using tax dollars in this manner. The largest city in the nation without an integrated public transportation is the city of Arlington with over 350,000 residents.

Another infrastructure issue is the building of toll roads. An increasing number of important new heavily-used highways opening in Texas are toll roads, such as those in the Dallas-Fort Worth area and the Central Texas Turnpike around Austin. Additionally, proposals exist to enlarge existing highways and possibly convert them to toll roads in the future. The contradiction for many urban Texans remains that while they dislike increased numbers of toll roads because of the added cost to travel, especially in morning commutes, they also dislike the notion of paying higher taxes to offset the costs of constructing and maintaining "free" highways.

A portion of Governor Perry's Trans-Texas Corridor idea reflected an effort not only to promote trade but also to relieve congestion by allowing traffic to bypass major urban areas. The proposed corridor of 4,000 miles of toll roads, utility lines, and rail lines also envisioned separate lanes for trucking and passenger vehicles. Critics argued that the cost of the corridor was too high, objected to Perry signing a contract with a Spanish-based toll road consortium to administer the corridor, and that 500,000 acres would be needed by the state to complete the project. Some of this acreage could only be obtained through the state exercising its right of eminent domain, which is opposed by those who champion the rights of landowners. In the fall of 2009, transportation officials announced that they would not build the corridor due to the immense public criticism. Eminent domain though will come into play as in the proposed plan for a high-speed rail line between Dallas and Houston. Though it would be built by private interests, land would have to be so obtained in the face of much rural opposition to the route.

Making sure that the infrastructure is in place to deliver energy to meet the needs of the state's growing population is another concern in the twenty-first century. Massive changes have also come to the power industry as the growth of wind farms and utilization of wind energy have occurred over the past decade. Large wind turbines with blades in excess of 200 feet dot the skyline in areas of the Panhandle, but they are increasingly appearing in other areas such as Central Texas. Using wind as a power source is important as this is a source of renewable energy. Landowners on whose farms and ranches the turbines are placed receive funds for the area utilized by the structure of the turbines and lease agreements based on their production. The energy manufactured from Texas wind can be sent on transmission lines anywhere in the country as well as providing power to the residents of the state.

## A Home for High-Tech Industries

In the early twenty-first century, Texas continued to be a leading home for the high-tech industry. The Austin area has joined Dallas and Houston as a hub for high-tech research and innovation, in part due to the presence of the Dell Computer Corporation in nearby Round Rock. Michael Dell started the company while attending the University of Texas. Basing his business on providing custom-made computers at a lower cost by the direct sales method rather than purchasing through retailers, Dell assembled computers from surplus parts made to the specifications relayed to him by his clients. The company filled a niche in the market, and consumers responded by buying the products in record numbers. Dell became a multi-billionaire and retired as CEO in 2004 but remains chairman of the board.

Numerous other companies either have headquarters or production facilities in Texas, such as Advanced Micro Devices (AMD), Motorola, Intel, IBM, and Sun Microsystems. Hundreds of computer software companies produce programs for a variety of tasks from managing inventory supplies to construction software. Numerous joint ventures also exist between companies and universities in Texas, such as the Balcones Research Center at the University of Texas at Austin. Many of these labs, which receive both public and private funding, are located in the Houston and Dallas/Fort Worth areas.

The state government of Texas has recently stepped up efforts to further Texas's place as a high-tech leader. Texas is one of more than twenty states that have established economic development funds to nurture start-up technology companies and issue grants to colleges for high-tech research. To receive an award, the applicant's proposal must gain the approval of the governor, lieutenant governor, and House Speaker after receiving recommendations from an advisory committee appointed by the governor. Before the advisory committee considers applications, seven regional boards and one statewide life science board conduct their own reviews. While aiding many Texas businesses and research universities, the fund became embroiled in politics when a *Dallas Morning News* investigation revealed that $16 million of the $160 million dispensed by the Texas Emerging Technology Fund (TETF) went to companies whose investors or officers had donated to Governor Perry's political campaigns. During the 2010 campaign, opponent Bill White accused Governor Perry of using the TETF as a "slush fund" to reward political donors, leading State Senator Florence Shapiro (the fund's Senate sponsor) to contemplate amending the rules to remove the governor, lieutenant governor, and House Speaker from the approval process in order to protect the integrity of the program.

## The Enron Scandal

The bankruptcy of the Enron Corporation in the early 2000s proved to be one of the most spectacular corporate collapses in Texas business history. For a time, Enron was one of the biggest successes of the Texas economy, often billed as one of the most innovative companies in the country. The striking breakdown of this company sent shockwaves throughout the stock exchange and devastation to investors nationwide.

The company that became Enron started in 1931 as a Nebraskan gas company. In 1985 the corporation became known as Enron after changes in ownership and reorganization. Enron opened its new headquarters in Houston in 1986 and became involved in energy-trading, selling electricity and gas from one market to another. As the demand for energy increased throughout the 1990s, Enron was able to earn tremendous profits and became one of the most touted companies in the nation. Reporting annual revenues in excess of $100 billion, Enron was the darling of the stock market. In 1999, the company won the naming rights for the new baseball field of the Houston Astros. The giant rotating "E" outside the company's 50-story headquarters was a symbol of wealth in Houston. However, such wealth and image proved to be achieved largely through smoke and mirrors. By the end of 2001, with its bond-ratings sinking, Enron filed for bankruptcy leaving over 20,000 employees and countless investors wondering what had happened.

What happened was a major accounting scandal. Enron had misreported earnings throughout the 1990s, advertising high profits when, in fact, profits were either minimal or non-existent. Officials at its accounting firm, Arthur Andersen, worked with Enron to ensure that the numbers continued to "look good" and even shredded documents during an audit of Enron. The Securities and Exchange Commission forced Arthur Andersen, at the time one of the largest accounting firms in the country, to surrender its accounting licenses in 2002, and the firm collapsed. As questions into Enron's bookkeeping mounted, so too did questions into the operating activities of Enron. Critics came to blame Enron for recent energy shortfalls in the state of California that had caused rolling blackouts. Tapes emerged of phone calls made by Enron energy traders that demonstrated the traders facilitated and capitalized on California's power crisis.

The top leaders of Enron, including founder Kenneth Lay, chief executive officer Jeffrey Skilling, and chief financial officer Andrew Fastow were put on trial. A jury convicted Lay on ten counts of fraud and conspiracy, but he died before serving any of his sentence. Jeffrey Skilling was found guilty on nineteen counts and sentenced to over twenty years in prison. Fastow agreed to testify for the prosecutors and received a six-year sentence. Fastow now works as a paid speaker at anti-fraud conferences.

Beyond the layoffs that the collapse of the company caused its own employees was the financial nightmare for people who had invested in Enron stock. Employees were regularly encouraged to buy Enron stock as part of their 401(k) portfolios up until the scandal broke. Other large Texas investors, such as the Teacher Retirement System of Texas, had invested heavily in Enron, and the breakdown of the corporation caused billions to be lost. Additionally, Enron had been a substantial contributor to multiple non-profit organizations, such as the arts and the Texas Medical Center, and a major source of donations disappeared when the company collapsed. Any item that had "Enron" on it swiftly became a collector's item on websites such as Ebay and often became worth more than the price of a share of stock. Ultimately, what was left of the assets were sold off to become separate entities and to make payments to Enron's many creditors. This case has become one of the most well-known examples of corporate fraud in the twenty-first century.

Texas Rangers playing at the U.S. Cellular Field, July 22, 2008 against the Chicago White Sox.

## Tourism, Sports, and Entertainment

In the early twenty-first century, tourism, sports, and entertainment venues not only added flavor to Texas culture, they also contributed significantly to the state's economy. The travel and tourism industry is Texas's second-most important "export-oriented" industry (i.e., serving consumers outside of the state), ranking behind oil and gas production. In 2008, the tourism industry's contribution to the gross state product totaled $24 billion, accounting for 2.2 percent of all state earnings and almost 4 percent of the state's jobs. Tourist dollars spent in restaurants, shops, theaters, museums, and amusement parks benefited many local economies, enabling the funding of road and school construction and maintenance projects and providing incentives for the relocation of new businesses. Tourism also benefited Texas via the six-percent state imposed hotel occupancy tax on every hotel or motel room. Over 90 percent of this tax money goes directly into the general fund. Additionally, cities can impose their own hotel tax as high as 7 percent. Hotel tax revenue is often used to fund bond initiatives for income-producing projects, such as the AT&T Center in San Antonio—the home of the San Antonio Spurs.

The official slogan of Texas, "Texas—It's Like a Whole Other Country" has been adopted by the Office of Texas Tourism, the state agency responsible for marketing Texas as a tourist destination. The agency aims not only to position Texas as a travel location for Americans outside the state but also to advertise Texas in Latin America and Europe to attract foreign visitors. Many features draw people to Texas, including the outdoors experience of fishing along the Gulf Coast or hiking in Big Bend National Park. Texas beaches, particularly Galveston and South Padre Island, draw families and young people. The theme parks of Six Flags over Texas at Arlington and San Antonio's Fiesta Texas and Sea World attract millions every year. Historic sites strewn throughout Texas also lure curious travelers. Locales such as the historic King Ranch in South Texas, the plantation tours available in East Texas, and the Sixth Floor Museum of the JFK assassination in Dallas regularly see thousands of annual visitors. San Antonio in particular draws many history-minded tourists, offering the Alamo and numerous other missions in the area among its attractions.

Local economies also benefit from fairs and festivals. The largest fair is the Texas State Fair held every fall at Dallas Fair Park. In 2010, the State Fair broke attendance with a record $37 million spent on rides, games, and food during its 24-day run. Like other parts of the country that have no connection to Renaissance Europe, Texas also hosts two major Renaissance festivals. Scarborough Fair held over several weeks in Lancaster (south of Dallas) each spring and another festival held near Plantersville (northwest of Houston) running for many weeks during the fall feature costumed Renaissance characters engaged in jousting tournaments, comedy routines, musical acts, glass-blowing and blacksmithing demonstrations, and, of course, selling food and trinkets to visitors of all ages.

In 2013, visitors to Texas spent an estimated $56 billion. Among Texas counties, Harris (Houston) saw the most tourist money spent with over $11.2 billion, followed by Dallas with $6.2 billion, Bexar (San Antonio) with $6.5 billion, Tarrant (Fort Worth) with $4.9 billion, Travis (Austin) with $4.4 billion, and El Paso with $1.4 billion. Smaller coastal counties such as Nueces (Corpus Christi) and Galveston are also in the top ten list of Texas counties based on visitor spending. Tourist spending grew significantly in the past several years with some locales seeing over 20 percent increases.

Due to the relatively warmer Texas climate, some people visit for extended periods, such as the "Winter Texans," who escape the winter in northern and mid-western states to travel to Texas, often to the Rio Grande Valley. Many cities, like McAllen, consider the Winter Texans a valuable part of tourism dollars and schedule special events just for them. An online magazine for Winter Texans also promotes opportunities. The growth of tourism in Texas is another example of the growth of the service economy of Texas. For example, amusement parks have had to expand their workforces. More people are needed to work historical sites. People are hired to work at sporting events, and more retail employment is available. More jobs are created to accommodate the influx of people. Between 2006 and 2007 alone, the number of jobs increased by 2.3 percent. The largest service sector to see growth was employment in building and garden supplies where places such as Lowe's and Home Depot are located. This sector saw 5.7 percent growth from adding nearly 5,000 new jobs to the market in Texas. Some service employment is still seasonal, reflecting how the job market has reoriented in Texas. These jobs are increasingly available, but they are not high-paying.

The state's many major league sports franchises, many of them quite successful, attract a myriad of fans whose support provide a source of pride and a vital element to the economies of home cities. In basketball, the Houston Rockets have regularly posted winning seasons and won two consecutive National Basketball Association (NBA) Championships (in 1993-94 and 1994-95). After many years of poor play during its initial years in the NBA, the Dallas Mavericks have risen to be a strong team in the early twenty-first century, regularly making the playoffs and have already made one trip to the championship series. In 1997 the Women's National Basketball Association (WNBA) began operations with a team based in Houston. The Houston Comets won the WNBA Championship in each of the league's first four years. San Antonio got its own WNBA franchise in 2003 when the Utah Starzz relocated to become the San Antonio Silver Stars.

In baseball, the Houston Astros who twice reached the National League Championship Series during the 1980s did so again in 2005, making it this time to the World Series where they lost to the Chicago White Sox. The Astros won the 2017 World Series besting the Los Angeles Dodgers in seven games. In 2000, the Astros left the Astrodome to begin playing at the new Enron Field, which the team renamed Minute Maid Park after the Enron Corporation collapsed. In the Dallas-Fort Worth area, the Texas Rangers relocated in 1994 to the Ballpark at Arlington. After the approval of a new bond initiative, the Rangers take up their new home at a new Globe Life Field in 2020, next to the site of the team's old stadium. Among the favorite players of all time for both Rangers and Astros fans is the pitcher Nolan Ryan, a native of Alvin, Texas, who played for both teams during the 1980s and 1990s and pitched seven no-hitters in his legendary career. In 2010, after a particularly contentious auction of the team, Ryan and a group of investors purchased the Rangers and oversaw the team's first World Series appearance later that same year. The Rangers continued to have playoff success for several years though in 2013 Ryan split from the team.

Football continued to reign as the most popular sport in Texas. To replace the Houston Oilers franchise that left for Tennessee (later to be renamed the Titans), the National Football League awarded the city of Houston a new expansion team, the Texans, which started playing in Reliant Stadium during the 2002 season. In 2009, a new stadium opened in Arlington (located near the Ballpark and Six Flags) to house the Dallas Cowboys who moved from Texas Stadium in nearby Irving. Boasting a normal capacity of 80,000 seats (capable of expansion to over 100,000) and costing over $1.1 billion to build, Cowboys Stadium not only can host football games, but also international soccer tournaments, championship boxing matches, and music concerts. The stadium built for the Texas Rangers in 1994 now known as Globe Life Field will become home to a team in the new XFL, adding a second professional football stadium in Arlington, Texas.

Three other professional sports have a growing fan base in Texas—ice hockey, soccer, and NASCAR. Beginning sporadically before World War II, organized hockey developed a firmer foundation in 1967 when the minor league Dallas Blackhawks and Fort Worth Wings began play as part of the Central Hockey League. The teams remained until the early 1980s before folding. In 1993, however, the Minnesota North Stars of the National Hockey League relocated to Texas and became known as the Dallas Stars. Hosting opponents at the American Airlines Center, the Stars have since made numerous playoff appearances and, in 1999, defeated the Buffalo Sabres to win the Stanley Cup championship. Professional soccer arrived in Texas in 1967 as the Houston Stars and Dallas Tornados began play in the North American Soccer League. The current Major League Soccer (MLS) started competition in 1996 with Texas represented by the FC Dallas franchise. In 2005, MLS added the Houston Dynamo as an expansion team. Meanwhile, NASCAR auto racing has also become an increasingly popular sport in Texas. In Denton County, the Texas Motor Speedway hosts two official NASCAR events per year with over 180,000 fans attending on race days.

Another hallmark of Texas culture that regularly attracts tourists and locals alike is the popularity of public museums and art galleries. Whether they have a narrow or broad focus, museums seek to enhance one's understanding and knowledge while stimulating curiosity and creative thinking. Museums of varying types abound throughout the state of Texas. They archive various periods of Texas history from early colonization to modern events and also feature exhibits reaching beyond the parameters of Texas to feature both American and non-American artists and subjects.

Fort Worth is home to the Kimbell Museum, often described as the best small museum in the nation, which houses an international collection including works of European masters as well as more modern pieces. The museum also showcases two to three major travelling exhibits per year featuring works from topics ranging from ancient Egypt and ancient China to Gauguin and the Impressionists. Next door to the Kimbell is the Amon Carter Museum, named after a prominent twentieth-century Fort Worth businessman and newspaper owner. The museum features western art primarily completed by Frederick Remington and Charles Russell; however, the work of numerous other artists and sculptors are also represented. The Amon Carter also houses rotating exhibits and possesses a photography collection.

One of the more recent additions to the museums of Texas is the Bob Bullock Texas State History Museum in Austin. Named after the long-time lieutenant governor, the museum opened in 2001 and features interactive exhibits and an IMAX theater. Also focusing on Texas history is the Star of the Republic Museum at Washington-on-the-Brazos, which is administered by Blinn College and holds numerous artifacts representing the material culture of the Republic Era. It hosts a Texas Independence Day Celebration each March on its extensive grounds. The National Museum of the Pacific War in Fredericksburg holds a fabulous collection of World War II relics and personal accounts of soldiers and sailors who fought in the Pacific Theater. The Institute of Texan Cultures (ITC) located in San Antonio is the state's premier location for exploring cultural history. The ITC shelters a 50,000 square foot exhibit space devoted to all eras and peoples who have resided in Texas. The state of Texas through the General Land Office is also planning a major change to the area around the Alamo in San Antonio. The project entails closing off roads and closing some nearby businesses to rebuild part of the Alamo complex. The new construction will more closely resemble how the grounds appeared in the early 1800s and will be accessible only through certain access gates. This plan has been controversial as some groups have opposed removing the cenotaph, which now stands in front of the Alamo chapel. The discovery of graves in the area in 2019 has added additional complications. Lawsuits have been filed, and it will be several years before these issues are resolved. Other Texas museums include facilities devoted to women, African Americans, early settlers, the Texas Rangers, railroads, cowboys, the petroleum industry, modern art, and the Holocaust.

Texas boasts a world-class performing arts community offering entertainment to people throughout the state in the form of ballets, symphonies, opera, theatre, and Broadway shows. In Dallas, I.M. Pei served as the architect for the Meyerson Symphony Center, which opened in 1989. It hosts the Dallas Symphony Orchestra along with other groups from the city. It also serves as a venue for tours by musical artists. The nearby city of Fort Worth boasts the Bass Performance Hall, which opened in 1998. Costing $67 million (built entirely with private funds), it is considered part of one of the most successful downtown revitalization efforts in the country, serving as the home of the Fort Worth Symphony Orchestra, the Texas Ballet Theater, and the Fort Worth Opera. Every four years it hosts the Van Cliburn International Piano Competition and Cliburn Concerts. Beginning in 1955, the Houston Grand Opera today performs at the Wortham Theater

Center in the city's Theater District. The Houston Grand Opera has introduced thirty-eight world premieres and six American premieres since 1973 and has received a Tony Award, two Grammy Awards, two Emmy Awards and a Grand Prix du Disques; it is the only opera company in the world to have won all four honors. San Antonio's symphony has a permanent home in the lavish Majestic Theatre in the downtown area. Built in 1929 and renovated in the 1990s, the Majestic features lavish decorations inspired by Moorish and baroque styles. Numerous other smaller venues around the state sponsor community theaters and chorale groups, with some tracing their history back to the late 1800s.

**Education**

The funding of education, whether for public education or higher education, is one area in which Texas has not excelled. Texas regularly ranks in the bottom-half across the nation in terms of money spent on students. According to 2006 statistics, Texas ranks 36th in the nation in academic achievement and 48th in the nation for composite SAT scores. Cuts in funding for higher education at the state level in 2004 necessitated steep tuition increases at public universities and colleges, making higher education out of reach for more and more families. In part due to these costlier tuition rates, community colleges have grown significantly as a lower-cost option for those entering college. In 2007, community colleges across the state enrolled 74 percent of all freshman and sophomore college students.

Efforts to increase student performance through school accountability measures based on standardized test scores also remain controversial. Expanded under Governor Bush, the Texas Assessment of Academic Skills (TAAS), replaced in 2002 with the Texas Assessment of Knowledge and Skills (TAKS), has its share of supporters who believe that the exams can accurately track student learning as well as identify effective schools and educators. Critics of the TAAS and TAKS note that the state places too much emphasis on standardized testing, therefore stifling creative thinking as teachers focus on "teaching to the test" in order to maximize scores. Additionally, critics argue that the test only measures student achievement within the state and that the test is not aligned to national standards. With Texas ranked behind more than half of all the states in regard to academic achievement, they assert that the state exams have minimal educational benefits and only suggest which Texas schools are performing at higher and lower levels of mediocrity.

Some political candidates such as Carol Keeton Strayhorn (independent candidate for governor in 2006) focused on educational issues as a basis of their campaigns for elective office. Strayhorn, a one-time Democrat, one-time Republican, ran as an independent in 2006 and made this topic an important element of her campaign. She lost the race to the incumbent governor, Rick Perry. While many Texans by 2010 wanted changes enacted to the state school system, no serious efforts have gone beyond the rhetorical stage.

The TAKS tests were replaced in 2012 with the STAAR tests, which were supposed to provide more accountability for what was being learned in the classroom. Many criticized the design of the tests and the number of required exams—fifteen separate tests for students to pass. The legislature ended up cutting that number to five, but it is still unclear how successful these exams will be at measuring student knowledge and thinking skills.

At the collegiate level, Texas education has experienced its fair share of controversy. In 1992, a woman named Cheryl Hopwood filed a lawsuit after she was denied admission to the University of Texas Law School. Hopwood contended that she was more qualified than many of the minority applicants who were admitted. Colleges had used affirmative action in admission decisions to help establish diverse student bodies. In 1996, an appeals court ruled in Hopwood's favor and the United States Supreme Court refused to hear a higher appeal requested by the university. *Hopwood v. Texas* effectively banned the use of race as a factor in determining admission to a college and is considered a landmark ruling in the use of affirmative action in education.

**Criminal Justice Issues**

Another area of concern for the future is Texas's growing prison population, which has tripled since 1990. Incarceration rates in Texas exceed the national average by over 40 percent according to some reports. The Texas prison system is a multi-billion dollar operation. The cost of incarceration is staggering, plus the continual need for more prisons to hold an increased number of prisoners will mean high budget costs well into the future.

Conditions at Texas prisons have been under scrutiny for years. In 1972, an inmate imprisoned for robbery, David Ruiz, filed a lawsuit against the Texas Department of Corrections (TDC) and William J. Estelle, head of the TDC, alleging that living conditions in Texas prisons constituted "cruel and unusual punishment." In 1980, the lawsuit finally went to trial. Testimony took nearly a year, and in the end the federal district court agreed with Ruiz. The case, *Ruiz v. Estelle,* resulted in massive changes for Texas prisons. Officials initially tried low-cost options such as early release, but this proved more problematic—violent offenders were released often only having served a small percentage of their time. By the 1990s, Texas decided to begin building more prisons to improve the conditions. Citing the progress that the Texas Department of Corrections had made over the past thirty years, in 2002 a federal judge ordered the end of the U.S. government's oversight of Texas prisons.

Capital punishment in Texas represents another heated issue. In 1972 the U.S. Supreme Court outlawed the death penalty in the case *Furman v. Georgia*, but the Court reversed itself in 1976, and Texas resumed executions. Texas has numerically more executions than any other state. Certainly part of this is attributable to Texas' larger population as compared to other states. But, by 2020, Texas had executed over 560 inmates. The state with the second-most executions is Virginia with just under 100. The Texas totals account for over 36 percent of all executions in the nation since 1976.

In Texas, capital punishment may be applied to cases involving the murder of a police officer or firefighter, murder during the commission of other felonies such as burglary, rape, or arson, or the murder of a child under the age of six. Further, those who commit multiple murders, murder for hire, murder while incarcerated, or murder while escaping prison are also eligible. Texas used the electric chair as its method of execution until 1977 when it switched to lethal injection.

The death penalty may also apply to those convicted of an especially heinous crime. In the final years of the twentieth century, a capital murder case took place in eastern Texas that also made many question just how far Texas had progressed in race relations. In the summer of 1998, authorities discovered the body of James Byrd, Jr., a forty-nine year old African American from Jasper, Texas. Evidence later showed that Byrd had accepted a ride home offered by three white men in a pick-up truck. The men proceeded to murder him by beating him, chaining him to the truck, and dragging him for over three miles. The men, who had ties to white supremacist groups, were arrested soon after the crime. Two of them were sentenced to death while the third received life in prison.

States are coming under increasing scrutiny in light of a moratorium on capital punishment issued by the governor of Illinois in 2000. In 2008 the United Nations specifically mentioned that the state of Texas's practice of capital punishment was problematic in its human rights report. One common criticism is that the application of the death penalty reflects racial prejudice. Currently 40.3 percent of offenders on death row are African American (30.2 percent are white and 28.1 percent are Hispanic) while only 12 percent of Texas residents are African American. The issue of whether capital punishment is humane has become a litigious question in a new way, as well, with many pharmaceutical companies no longer providing the required drugs needed to carry out lethal injections.

In recent years, DNA testing has made possible a reassessment of many criminal cases in the United States. Aware of the new technology and concerned about the possibility of false convictions in the past, the Dallas District Attorney has even given office space to members of the Innocence Project (a non-profit organization dedicated to the use of DNA evidence to free innocent individuals convicted of serious crimes) to pursue instances of wrongful convictions. By 2008, thirty-two individuals in Texas alone have been exonerated through DNA analysis, including eight convictions that resulted in the death penalty.

**Mixing of Cultures**

In its long history, Texas has become home to many cultures. Originally home to various Native American groups, Texas has now absorbed Spaniards, Anglo-Americans, Germans, French, Russian, Polish, Greek, Persian, Hindu, Chinese, Korean, Vietnamese, and many other cultures. This has led to a variety of languages being spoken in Texas, though English remains the most spoken language. Spanish is predominantly spoken in 27 percent of Texas homes. German is still spoken in over 82,000 homes, while French, including Cajun, is spoken in over 65,000 Texas residences

The wide array of ethnicities has led to the promotion of numerous festivals across the state to celebrate these many heritages (and boost local economies). German communities such as Fredericksburg commemorate Oktoberfest, a celebration that originally commemorated a royal marriage that has now evolved into a general fall festivity. The serving of specially brewed beer, traditional German foods, and the variety of festival booths fill several days of merriment The Czech communities, which originated with immigrants arriving during the 1850s, continue to celebrate Czech food and music. Kolaches, a Czech pastry, are found throughout the state. The town of Ennis, southeast of Dallas, hosts the National Polka Festival each May. The small town of West, north of Waco, is home to the Westfest celebration of Czech culture during Labor Day Weekend each year.

Mexican Americans celebrate Mexican holidays and culture in an assortment of ways. In San Antonio every spring there is Fiesta, a ten-day event intended to celebrate the battles of the Alamo and San Jacinto. It features the Battle of Flowers Parade, the Fiesta

Flambeau Parade, and is ruled over by King Antonio and El Rey Feo (the ugly king) bringing together both the Anglo and Mexican cultures. There are also celebrations of Diez y Seis (the beginning of the Revolution of 1810 in Mexico) and Cinco de Mayo (Mexican victory over the French in 1862) in San Antonio, San Angelo, Houston and numerous other communities. Every summer the Texas Folklife Festival is held in San Antonio to commemorate the diverse cultures of Texas and is replete with foods, crafts, and music to represent the ethnic backgrounds of all Texans.

While the Native-American population in Texas had decreased precipitously through much of Texas history, three tribes remain in Texas in the early twenty-first century. The Alabama-Coushattas have been recognized as a legal tribe in Texas for over a hundred years. The state held the trusteeship for their reservation until 1955 when the federal government assumed that responsibility. However, the two entities exchanged responsibilities in 1987, and the state again assumed trusteeship for the reservation. The Alabama-Coushattas actively pursued government assistance on their reservation in Polk County in the following years. For example, the Bureau of Indian Affairs and the Department of Health and Human Services helped with vocational training and health care on the reservation. The Alabama-Coushattas ran a casino for a few months beginning in 2001 before being forced to close the operation. The tribe continues to agitate for a change in state gaming laws that would enable it to re-open the casino and bring more money into the tribe. The Texas tribe is a "sister tribe" of the Louisiana Coushattas who continue to successfully run their own casinos in that state. More recently in 2006 the Alabama-Coushattas filed lawsuits against Washington lobbyist Jack Abramoff and the Christian Coalition's former leader, Ralph Reed, alleging corruption. The tribe argued that Abramoff (who was later sentenced to nearly six years in prison due to tax evasion and bribery charges) promised to obtain federal legislation that would allow the tribe to reopen its casino. The lawsuit was settled out of court in 2007 for an undisclosed amount of money.

The Tiguas of El Paso fought throughout the 1960s to be considered a distinct tribe and eligible for government protection. In the 1980s they petitioned and subsequently were granted federal trust status. This status refers to the federal government's legal commitment to the various Indian tribes. It encompasses the government's responsibility to provide for a tribe after that tribe has turned over its lands to the federal authorities. The U.S. government is responsible for protecting a tribe's right of self-governance and providing basic services. The Tiguas of El Paso also opened a casino when the state-operated lottery began. The casino made millions in profits and employed hundreds of people. After protracted lawsuits filed by the state though, the casino was shut down in 2002. The Tiguas and the Alabama-Coushattas joined forces to push the state legislature to reconsider their gaming enterprises. In the spring of 2007, legislation that would allow these two tribes to resume gaming on their reservations but would restrict any new tribes from opening gaming establishments came up for a vote. The measure failed—vote of 66:66—since it did not gain a majority among the state legislators.

The issue of gaming on reservations has proved to be incredibly complicated and tribe-dependent. The Kickapoo tribe, which currently lives along the U.S.-Mexican border in South Texas, was recognized under a different federal law than the other tribes in Texas, so it is subject to different gaming laws as well. Although the court challenges will certainly continue, the Kickapoos have federal permission to operate a more Vegas-style operation, which has brought slot-machines, craps, and roulette to its reservation casino.

Though the approval came in 2007, no change in operations has yet occurred due to the state government's opposition. This will certainly be a subject of continued legal fights in the future.

**Immigration**

At the turn of the twenty-first century, Texas faces numerous questions regarding border security and immigration. Both issues became national ones by 2007. The movement of illegal immigrants across the border from Mexico became the focus of both state and national politicians as citizens focused on the potential financial burden immigrants can lay on taxpayers. Illegal immigrants can attend public schools and receive medical attention at public hospitals. It is equally evident that the illegal immigrants would not move north if employers did not make jobs available to them. Nevertheless, with income from such jobs, immigrants become consumers in the American economy.

One idea to stem the tide of illegal immigrants was to build a wall or fence along the border. The U.S. Congress approved funding for such a project in 2007 and construction began soon thereafter. The majority of Texas's border, however, had not been fenced and even where fencing exists, people are still crossing. Many South Texans have protested the fence because it will cut through farms, towns, and protected wildlife areas. To combat illegal crossings, the number of U.S. Border Patrol agents in the U.S. has tripled since 1997. The Del Rio Sector in Texas has seen the number of agents climb from approximately 900 to 1600 since 2007 alone.

While illegal immigration has existed for decades, other events south of the Rio Grande have contributed to regional instability. Mexico has suffered through the outbreak of war between various drug cartels as they seek to dominate different regions of the country. The violence in Mexico has led to countless murders of law enforcement officials, military officials, and civilians as the Mexican government attempts to oppose the cartels. Some of the worst violence has been in Juarez just across the border from El Paso. Through the first half of 2010 alone, over 1,000 people were murdered in Juarez. So far the violence has not spread north into Texas, but many live in constant fear of that possibility.

In the 2010s the border region started receiving more national attention as some politicians and President Donald Trump focused more on the issues of illegal immigration. President Trump, as a presidential candidate, began discussing building a "wall" along the border with Mexico to curb illegal immigration. After his election, President Trump continued to voice his support for such construction though Congress did not appropriate all the money that would be needed. Critics of building the "wall" have appeared from both sides of the political spectrum. Many point out the inadvisability of building a wall due to the terrain in some areas. They also point out how such a wall could destroy environmentally sensitive areas and divide communities that have historically existed along the border. U.S. Congressman Will Hurd, a Republican, has represented a district that includes 820 miles of the Texas/Mexico border. He has repeatedly opposed the wall, stating the structure would be ineffective in combating illegal immigration.

Illegal immigration also took center stage in 2019 as large population groups arrived on the southern border planning to enter the U.S. As a result, detention centers opened along the southern border of the United States. These facilities sought to process the thousands of people who were seeking asylum in the United States. The centers quickly became overwhelmed by the numbers of people migrating into the country. Reports of poor sanitary conditions, over-crowding, and children being separated from their parents began to fill media reports. As the number of people pressing for entrance to the U.S. ebbs and flows, this issue will remain a major political issue in subsequent years.

## A Series of Catastrophes

In the early 2000s, a series of tragedies impacted Texas. In 2001, Texans experienced shock, as did the rest of the nation, over the events occurring on September 11 when radical Muslim hijackers took control of four passenger jets and crashed three of them into the twin towers of the World Trade Center in New York City and the Pentagon in Washington, D.C. Approximately 3,000 people died including several native Texans. Locales throughout the state continue to hold memorials and commemorations each year on the anniversary of the attack.

On February 1, 2003, the Columbia space shuttle was heading toward a scheduled landing at the Kennedy Space Center in Florida when it disintegrated upon re-entry over north-central Texas. Debris scattered over several counties in East Texas and Louisiana and authorities arrested some people trying to keep pieces of the shuttle debris as souvenirs or selling them for profit. Investigations later revealed that one of the shuttle's wings was damaged at lift-off by a falling piece of protective foam, leaving the entire craft vulnerable to the excessive heat experienced upon re-entry into the earth's atmosphere.

Mother Nature also delivered a pounding to Texas's coasts in the early twenty-first century. In 2005, Hurricane Rita hit the Gulf Coast affecting such cities as Beaumont and Houston along with coastal Louisiana. Gridlock filled the highways as 3 million people evacuated the Houston area. Flooding was extensive with a storm surge that reached as far as twenty miles inland. This storm came on the heels of the much larger Hurricane Katrina that battered New Orleans just a few weeks earlier. Though the exact number is debated, at least 1400 people died during Katrina and thousands from Louisiana sought shelter and a new home in their western neighbor. The city of Houston, in particular, took in numerous refugees. Then, in 2008, Hurricane Ike hit Galveston. Though Ike did not conjure the destruction of the 1900 hurricane that hit the city, Galveston was severely impacted and power was knocked out to nearly a quarter of the state's population and many parts of the areas remain in ruin nearly three years after the storm made landfall.

In 2017 another hurricane, Hurricane Harvey, approached the Gulf region. A category 4 storm when it arrived on the Texas coast, Harvey delivered not only the expected destruction when it made landfall, but it unexpectedly stalled over the southeast of Texas for days. The city of Houston was inundated with massive rainfall with most areas receiving over 50 inches of rain, and one report of an area receiving 60 inches of rain. Flooding from the rainfall, the overflow of bayous, and the release of water from engineered reservoirs that could no longer cope caused nearly fifty thousand homes to flood. The storm shut down the oil and gas refineries in the region as well leading to instability in that sector. Over 300,000 people had to evacuate the region and thousands more had to be rescued as the flooding continued. The cost of the storm's damage was immense. Over 100 Texans were killed because of the storm, and the state incurred tens of billions of dollars in damage. With the statistics regarding the increased temperature of the earth's oceans, future storms may continue to impact the state.

**Economic Ups and Downs**

In the early 2000s, Texas had to cope with some difficult economic circumstances. A major spike in oil prices during 2007, along with the commensurate rise in gasoline prices up to $4 per gallon, pinched many Texas budgets. There was also a sharp uptick in natural gas prices, leading natural gas companies to begin increased drilling operations especially in the Barnett Shale, which covers thirteen counties in north Texas. While much of the drilling occurred in remote areas, some took place in urban areas such as Fort Worth. Gas companies began paying homeowners signing bonuses for agreeing to lease their mineral rights with some homeowner associations and neighborhood groups able to negotiate as much as $30,000 per acre. Drilling rigs began to pop up on college campuses, golf courses, and along major highways. Critics of this practice point out that if an accident occurs in an urban area, the devastation could be great and that the true environmental impact of all of this drilling, which often uses a process (known as "fracking") based on hydraulically injecting chemical additives in order to fracture the gas-containing rock, remains unknown.

The opposition to "fracking" has grown as numerous earthquakes have occurred particularly in North Texas, home to much of the urban drilling. There have been over 130 earthquakes since 2008. Though often only measuring between 2 and 4 on the Richter scale, the sheer number of the quakes caused questions for residents and geologists. In 2015, a geological survey team determined that they were "most likely" caused by the oil and gas activity in the region, particularly the use of "fracking." The town of Denton voted to ban fracking in a November 2014 referendum, but the state legislature moved in 2015 to limit cities' ability to regulate such activities (thereby undoing the fracking ban), and it was signed into law in May 2015.

Natural gas and oil prices both declined in late 2008 just as a major economic crisis hit the country. Two national mortgage giants sponsored by the federal government, Fannie Mae and Freddy Mac, faced bankruptcy. After underwriting millions of mortgages, the housing market collapsed when many were unable to make their payments, leading entities such as Fannie Mae and other commercial banks to teeter on the brink of insolvency. Other operations that had invested in American mortgages and creative mortgage-backed securities faced similar trials. It became clear that Americans, including many Texans, had been financing their lives through credit at dangerous levels. As bills went unpaid due to lost employment or failure to plan adequately for expenses, creditors got nervous and began revoking credit lines. As the dominoes kept falling, both people and corporations found themselves unable to obtain additional credit. American International Group (AIG), the largest insurance company in the world, received tens of billions from the federal government to remain viable. As the stock market plunged and the full-extent of the credit crisis became evident, other companies such as General Motors faced the financial pinch and applied for federal bailout money to continue operations. Texans saw familiar banks such as Washington Mutual, Guaranty Bank, and Wachovia get taken over by more stable commercial banks before the situation finally stabilized. Meanwhile, the once-booming Texas housing market continued to slump, though not to the extent experienced in California, Nevada, and Florida, which suffered precipitous drops in home sales and prices after years of tremendous growth. High unemployment in Texas continued to hamper recovery. From a ten-year low of 4 percent in April 2008, the unemployment rate reached a twenty-year high of 8.6 percent in January 2010.

Ultimately, Texas must contend with the demographic pressures that its increased population brings. Since 2000, the state is seeing a population jump of nearly 20 percent. Part of this, as mentioned earlier, is due to an increase in the number of people moving to Texas. Some high-profile corporate relocations have brought numerous more individuals to the state such as Toyota Corporation's decision to place their new national headquarters in Plano. While such moves are a testament to the vibrancy of the economy, there are more logistical concerns that the influx of people brings. There will be more automobiles on the highways, more people in need of state aid, and more students in public schools. Texas has benefited from a generally good economy since the mid-1990s, yet funding for many projects is uncertain in the wake of the recession. Issues such as border security and the fate of illegal immigrants cannot be dealt with by Texas alone as these have become national issues. Texas continues to face a host of problems that have not been successfully resolved. The next decades will prove vital as Texas copes with its ever-growing and ever-changing population and attempts to resolve the political, economic, and social issues that emerge from that reality.

## Aftermath: The War Abroad Hits Home

*After the Foot Hood shooting, Major Nidal Hassan was hospitalized before being sent to the Bell County Jail in Belton, Texas to await trial. Hasan's fate will be determined in a military court-martial proceeding. As a soldier accused of crimes committed on a military base, the U.S. Army has complete jurisdiction over the case, including the sentencing phase. If convicted, Hasan faces the possibility of receiving the death penalty. Delays caused by Hasan's changing of counsel and a prolonged dispute over whether the army can compel him to shave a newly-grown beard (U.S. military regulations forbid facial hair) have meant that the trial will not take place until sometime in 2013.*

*Since the terrorist attacks on September 11, 2001, Texas civilians working for military contractors have played a role in the "war on terror" while U.S. soldiers from units based in Texas, especially Fort Hood, have strongly contributed to America's early-twenty-first century military conflicts in the Middle East. Until 2009, Texas soil had avoided exposure to the violence of these conflicts. Increased precautions at Texas airports and the transition of Fort Hood from a base with open access to a closed military post not only reflected the new realities—but had also greatly helped to bolster security at these facilities. Though the Fort Hood shooting demonstrated that Texans were not immune to danger, the countermeasures employed in the wake of the September 11 attacks seem to have minimized the chances of repeating the tragic events of that infamous day.*

# Myth & Legend

## Myth of the Cowboy Culture

*What makes Texas culture unique? The average citizen might answer this question by saying the cowboys. They would not be referring to the famous Dallas Cowboys of football legend, but they are referring to the cowboy culture that seems to permeate throughout the state. Perhaps the center of this cowboy culture is Fort Worth where the slogan of the city is "Where the West Begins." Here, tourists travel to the historic stockyards north of downtown to see the Fort Worth Herd, a group of Texas longhorns that cowboys and cowgirls dressed in late nineteenth century attire drive down Exchange Avenue. This display is supposed to be reminiscent of the days of old when Fort Worth was a bustling cow town. Now the sidewalks of stockyards are crowded with shops filled with cowboy boots, western shirts, and large shiny belt buckles—items necessary for all wanting to participate in the cowboy culture of Texas even if just for a night or two. Of course, these necessary items of cowboy lore are not found just in Fort Worth. All across the state, Texas western stores carry items necessary to transform the ordinary citizen into a lord of the open plains.*

*The image of the cowboy and western culture has been a part of Texas lore since the late nineteenth century. Following the Civil War, many people sought new fortunes in the expanded ranching industry of Texas. The open-range provided people the opportunity to graze large herds of cattle for free, selling them for a huge profit at distant markets within a short period of time. Due to the abundance of land in the western and southern part of the state, the ranching industry grew rapidly. Ranchers in the late 1800s needed workers to round-up the cattle, brand them, and drive them to railheads in Kansas, Missouri, Nebraska, Colorado, and Wyoming. It was during this time that Texas's long association with the popular image of the cowboy was born. Because ranching so dominated Texas's and others' impressions of the state, the cowboys and everything associated with them became the **de facto** culture of the state well through the twentieth century.*

It is a myth, of course, that all Texans are cowboys and embrace the western culture. The number of Texans actively involved in ranching has decreased substantially through the twentieth and twenty-first centuries. In fact, only a small percentage of Texans earn their living through ranching. In fact, more Texans earn a living through farming, yet, the image of the "farmer" is not as romantic as the image of the "cowboy." Even in the 1800s Texas was not solely reliant on the cowboy for its definition of culture. Texas culture was more diversified. For example, the state was home to significant groups of Germans, Czechs, Tejanos, and other ethnic groups who strongly adhered to their culture and values even in Texas. Additionally, most Anglos in the state were farmers, who might have owned one or two milk cows.

In the twentieth century, definitions of culture in Texas have become even more varied as the urban centers of the state grew and embraced ever-changing interests. Museums hold exhibits displaying the paintings and sculptures of old European masters. Performance halls feature ballet, symphonies, and opera. For many Texans, donning a cowboy hat and pulling on boots is a fun thing to do for a couple of days a year, but it not a lifestyle that they follow. Texas literature seems dominated by the cowboy myth; the western is still a popular genre. However, some modern Texas writers are now meandering down new paths and writing stories and poems that have little to do with western lore. While country-and-western music can be found on the radio in virtually every part of Texas, there is also other programming available such as rock, pop, classical, and jazz. Blues' nightclubs in the Dallas area have been legendary in that genre through the twentieth century. Even the stock show and rodeos that are held across the state (a traditional stage for country western musicians/singers) have begun to draw large crowds by booking artists such as Bon Jovi, the Jonas Brothers, and Smokey Robinson. Therefore, any accurate definition or description of Texas culture today has to do more than simply rely on the cowboy past. Perhaps it always did.

## Suggestions for Further Reading

Barkley, Roy, ed., et.al. *The Handbook of Texas Music.* Austin: Texas State Historical Association, 2003.

Cox, Patrick L. and Michael Phillips, *The House Will Come to Order: How the Texas Speaker Became a Power in State and National Politics.* Austin: University of Texas Press, 2010.

*Economic Growth for Texas from Texas: A Report From the Blue Ribbon Economic Task Force.* Austin, Texas: State Comptroller's Office, 2003.

Koster, Rick. *Texas Music.* New York: St. Martin's Press, 1998.

McCall, Brian. *The Power of the Texas Governor: Connally to Bush.* Austin: University of Texas Press, 2009.

McNeeley, Dave and Jim Henderson. *Bob Bullock: God Bless Texas.* Austin: University of Texas Press, 2008.

Office of the Governor. Economic Development and Tourism. *Overview of the Texas Economy.* Available Online at http://www.governor.state.tx.us/divisions/ecodev/bidc/overview/index_html/view

Procter, Ben and Archie P. McDonald, eds. *The Texas Heritage.* 4th ed. Wheeling, Illinois: Harlan Davidson, Inc., 2003.

Rodriguez, Louis J. and Yoshi Fukasawa, eds. *The Texas Economy: 21st Century Economic Challenges.* Wichita Falls, Texas: Midwestern State University Press, 1996.

Storey, John W. And Mary L. Kelley, eds. *Twentieth-Century Texas: A Social and Cultural History* Denton, Texas: University of North Texas Press, 2008.

"Window on State Government." Texas Finances. State Comptroller of Public Accounts. Accessible online at http://www.window.state.tx.us/finances/

# The Dawn of a New Century, 1995-2020   551

**IDENTIFICATION:** Briefly describe each term.

George W. Bush
Texas Assessment of Academic Skills (TAAS)
Karla Faye Tucker
Rick Perry
redistricting
Trans-Texas Corridor
Texas Emerging Technology Fund (TETF)
The Enron Scandal
importance of tourism
*Hopwood v. Texas*
*Ruiz v. Estelle*
James Byrd, Jr.
Innocence Project
Greg Abbott
Alabama-Coushattas
illegal immigration
Hurricane Harvey

**MULTIPLE CHOICE:** Choose the correct response.

1. Which of the following was not a part of the George W. Bush agenda as governor?
   A. education reform
   B. tort reform
   C. a tougher stand on juvenile crime
   D. investing state employees' retirement funds in the stock market

2. Which of the following is not true about the Karla Faye Tucker case:
   A. Bush was almost not re-elected to a second term as governor because he pardoned Tucker
   B. Bush refused to commute her death sentence and Tucker was executed
   C. Tucker was eventually exonerated and released
   D. Bush commuted Tucker's sentence to life imprisonment

3. The state legislators that tried to stop the congressional redistricting in Texas in the early 2000s were members of which party?
   A. Republican
   B. Democrat
   C. Green
   D. Libertarian

4. Which of the following is true about the Trans-Texas Corridor?
   A. It was proposed by George W. Bush
   B. It only took 5 years to complete
   C. The plan received sharp criticism because some land for the project could only be obtained through the state exercising its right of eminent domain
   D. The project was to be funded by creation of a new state income tax

5. The _____ sets aside $200 million to encourage high-tech research and job creation in Texas.
   A. Texas Emerging Technology Fund
   B. Trans-Texas Corridor
   C. Public Works Administration
   D. Job Corps

6. The Teacher Retirement System of Texas lost billions as a result of the _____.
   A. Stock Market Crash of 2001
   B. Enron Scandal
   C. Airline cutbacks following 9/11
   D. Sale of oil-rich land in West Texas at extremely low prices

7. Which of the following are not popular tourist attractions in Texas?
   A. The Kimbell, Sixth Floor, and other museums
   B. the Alamo and other missions in San Antonio
   C. Amusement parks, such as Six Flags over Texas and Fiesta Texas
   D. Civil War battlefields

8. By the turn of the twenty-first century, Texas had major league franchises for all of the following sports except:
   A. football
   B. basketball
   C. baseball
   D. hockey
   E. all of the above are represented in Texas

9. The events involving James Byrd, Jr. demonstrated that _____.
   A. the Enron scandal had reached all levels of society
   B. racism was alive and well in some parts of Texas
   C. deregulation of airline maintenance could cause heinous disasters
   D. significant criticism of the death penalty in Texas

10. Native American groups, such as the Alabama-Coushattas and Kickapoos, have tried to promote economic prosperity on their reservations by _____.
    A. operating gaming casinos
    B. opening banking facilities
    C. creating profitable internet web sites
    D. drilling for oil

**TRUE/FALSE:** Indicate whether each statement is true or false.

1. George W. Bush failed to get any significant portion of his agenda through the Democratic-controlled legislatures during his terms as governor.

2. George W. Bush failed in his second-term effort to increase state government funding for education by cutting property taxes and raising sales and business taxes.

3. Republican governor Rick Perry was originally elected to the state legislature as a Democrat.

4. The Trans-Texas Corridor was endorsed by a majority of Texas voters in a 2004 referendum.

5. Barack Obama won Texas's electoral votes in the 2008 election.

6. The Enron Corporation eventually rebounded from the negative publicity generated by the actions of a few low-level employees that threatened to tarnish the company's reputation.

7. Beto O'Rourke nearly beat Ted Cruz in the 2018 senatorial race.

8. As a result of the Supreme Court's decision in the *Hopwood* case, race cannot be used as a factor in determining admission to college.

9. The death penalty in Texas can be assessed only for the murder of a police officer.

10. The Innocence Project often uses modern DNA testing to help in its efforts to exonerate inmates who have been falsely convicted of crimes.

**MATCHING:** Match the response in column A with the item in column B.

1. David Ruiz
2. Rick Perry
3. Nolan Ryan
4. James Byrd, Jr.
5. Trans-Texas Corridor
6. Michael Dell
7. Kay Bailey Hutchison
8. Karla Fay Tucker
9. George W. Bush
10. Kimbell and Amon Carter art museums

A. convicted murderer at the center of a controversial death penalty case
B. U.S. Senator who lost her bid to unseat Rick Perry in the 2010 Republican primary for governor
C. inmate who sued, alleging that conditions in Texas prisons met the standard of "cruel and unusual punishment"
D. popular Fort Worth tourist destinations
E. longest serving Texas governor
F. murdered in East Texas
G. former pitcher who now co-owns the Texas Rangers
H. proposed infrastructure project never created
I. University of Texas dropout who founded a major computer corporation
J. supported the TAAS test as an educational reform while governor

**ESSAY QUESTIONS:**

1. Describe the state of Texas politics at the turn of the twenty-first century. Which party dominates statewide politics and which party is in the minority? In what geographical areas of the state is each party strong? Among which voter groups is each party strong?

2. Compare and contrast the governorships of George W. Bush and Rick Perry.

3. Describe the importance of tourism, sports, and entertainment to Texas culture and the Texas economy.

4. Identify and describe a major social issue impacting Texas at the turn of the twenty-first century.

# Appendix I

## Texas Governors and Presidents

<u>Governors of Spanish Texas</u>

| | |
|---|---|
| Domingo Terán de los Ríos | 1691-1692 |
| Gregorio de Salinas Varona | 1692-1697 |
| Francisco Cuerbo y Valdez | 1698-1702 |
| Mathías de Aguirre | 1703-1705 |
| Martín de Alarcón | 1705-1708 |
| Simón Padilla y Córdova | 1708-1712 |
| Pedro Fermín de Echevérs y Subisa | 1712-1714 |
| Jaun Valdez | 1714-1716 |
| Martín de Alarcón | 1716-1719 |
| Joseph de Azlor | 1719-1722 |
| Fernando Pérez de Almazán | 1722-1727 |
| Melchor de Media Villa y Azcona | 1727-1730 |
| Juan Antonio Bustillo y Ceballos | 1730-1734 |
| Manuel de Sandoval | 1734-1736 |
| Carlos Benites Franquis de Lugo | 1736-1737 |
| Prudencio de Orobio y Basterra | 1737-1741 |
| Tomás Felipe Wintuisen | 1741-1743 |
| Justo Boneo y Morales | 1743-1744 |
| Francisco García Larios | 1744-1748 |
| Pedro del Barrio Junco y Espriella | 1748-1751 |
| Jacinto de Barrios y Jáuregui | 1751-1759 |
| Angel Martos y Navarrete | 1759-1766 |
| Hugo Oconor | 1767-1770 |
| Barón de Ripperdá | 1770-1778 |
| Domingo Cabello | 1778-1786 |
| Bernardo Bonavía [appointed but never took office] | 1786 |
| Rafel Martínez Pacheco | 1786 1788 |
| [No Governor] | 1788-1790 |
| Manuel Muñoz | 1790-1799 |
| José Irigoyen [appointed but never took office] | 1798-1799 |
| Juan Bautista de Elguézabal [acting governor] | 1799-1805 |
| Antonio Cordero y Bustamante | 1805-1808 |
| Manuel María de Salcedo | 1808-1813 |
| Juan Bautista Casas [revolutionary governor] | 1811 |
| Cristóbal Domínguez | 1813-1814 |
| Ignacio Pérez | 1816-1817 |
| Manuel Pardo | 1817 |
| Antonio Martínez [served after Mexican Revolution] | 1817-1822 |

556    Beyond Myths and Legends

Governors of Mexican Texas
José Félix Trespalacios                                    1822-1823
Luciano García                                             1823


Governors of Cohuila y Texas
Rafael Gonzales                                            1824-1826
José Ignacio de Arizpe                                     1826
Victor Blanco                                              1826-1827
José Ignacio de Arizpe                                     1827
José María Viesca y Montes                                 1827-1831
José María Letona    [died in office]                      1831-1832
Rafal Eca y Músquiz                                        1832-1833
Juan Martín de Veramendi   [died in office]                1833
Francisco Vidaurri y Villaseñor                            1833-1834
Juan José Elguézabal                                       1834-1835
José María Cantú                                           1835
Marciel Borrego                                            1835
Augustín Viesca                                            1835
Miguel Falcón                                              1835
Bartolomé de Cárdenas                                      1835
Rafal Eca y Músquiz                                        1835


Texas Provisional Governors During the Texas Revolution
Henry Smith    [impeached]                                 1835-1836
James W. Robinson [acting]                                 1836


Presidents of the Republic of Texas
David G. Burnet  [interim]                                 March-October 1836
Sam Houston                                                October 1836—December 1838
Mirabeau B. Lamar                                          December 1838—December 1841
Sam Houston                                                December 1841—December 1844
Anson Jones   [governor during annexation]                 December 1844—February 1846


Texas Governors
James Pinckney Henderson                                   February 1846—December 1847
George T. Wood                                             December 1847—December 1849
Peter H. Bell                                              December 1849—November 1853
J. W. Henderson                                            November 1853—December 1853
Elisha M. Pease                                            December 1853—December 1857
Hardin R. Runnels                                          December 1857—December 1859
Sam Houston    [removed from office by                     December 1859—March 1861
               Secession Convention]

| | |
|---|---|
| Edward Clark [appointed by Secession Convention] | March 1861—November 1861 |
| Francis R. Lubbock [Confederate governor] | November 1861—November 1863 |
| Pendleton Murrah [Confederate governor] | November 1863—June 1865 |
| Andrew Jackson Hamilton [provisional governor] | June 1865—August 1966 |
| James Webb Throckmorton [removed from office by by General Sheridan] | August 1866—August 1867 |
| Elisha M. Pease [appointed provisional governor] | August 1867—September 1869 |
| Edmund J. Davis | January 1870—January 1874 |
| Richard Coke | January 1874—December 1876 |
| Richard B. Hubbard | December 1876—January 1879 |
| Oran M. Roberts | January 1879—January 1883 |
| John Ireland | January 1883—January 1887 |
| Lawrence Sullivan Ross | January 1887—January 1891 |
| James Stephen Hogg | January 1891—January 1895 |
| Charles A. Culberson | January 1895—January 1899 |
| Joseph D. Sayers | January 1899—January 1903 |
| S.W.T. Lanham | January 1903—January 1907 |
| Thomas M. Campbell | January 1907—January 1911 |
| Oscar B. Colquitt | January 1911—January 1915 |
| James E. Ferguson [impeached] | January 1915—August 1917 |
| William P. Hobby | August 1917—January 1921 |
| Pat M. Neff | January 1921—January 1925 |
| Miriam A. Ferguson | January 1925—January 1927 |
| Dan Moody | January 1927—January 1931 |
| Ross S. Sterling | January 1931—January 1933 |
| Miriam A. Ferguson | January 1933—January 1935 |
| James V. Allred | January 1935—January 1939 |
| W. Lee O'Daniel | January 1939—August 1941 |
| Coke R. Stevenson | August 1941—January 1947 |
| Beauford H. Jester | January 1947—July 1949 |
| Allan Shivers | July 1949—January 1957 |
| Price Daniels | January 1957—January 1963 |
| John Connally | January 1963—January 1969 |
| Preston Smith | January 1969—January 1973 |
| Dolph Briscoe | January 1973—January 1979 |
| William P. Clements | January 1979—January 1983 |
| Mark White | January 1983—January 1987 |
| William P. Clements | January 1987—1991 |
| Ann W. Richards | January 1991—January 1995 |
| George W. Bush | January 1995—December 2000 |
| James Richard Perry | December 2000—January 2015 |
| Gregory W. Abbott | January 2015— |

# Appendix II

## Population Statistics

<u>Spanish Texas (Estimated Non-Indian Population of the Province of Texas)</u>

| Years | Population |
|---|---|
| 1731-1739 | 1,499 |
| 1740-1749 | 3,203 |
| 1750-1759 | 3,683 |
| 1760-1769 | 3,436 |
| 1770-1779 | 3,050 |
| 1780-1789 | 2,919 |
| 1790-1799 | 3,316 |
| 1805-1809 | 4,329 |
| 1815-1819 | 3,778 |

<u>Mexican Texas (Estimated Non-Indian Population of the Department of Texas)</u>

| Years | Population |
|---|---|
| 1834-1835 | 23,621 |

<u>Republic of Texas (Estimated Non-Indian Population)</u>

| Years | Population |
|---|---|
| 1845 | 125,000 |

<u>State of Texas (Estimated Population)</u>

| Years | Population |
|---|---|
| 1850 | 212,592 |
| 1860 | 604,215 |
| 1870 | 818,579 |
| 1880 | 1,591,749 |
| 1890 | 2,235,527 |
| 1900 | 3,048,710 |
| 1910 | 3,896,542 |
| 1920 | 4,663,228 |
| 1930 | 5,824,715 |
| 1940 | 6,414,824 |
| 1950 | 7,711,194 |
| 1960 | 9,579,677 |
| 1970 | 11,196,730 |
| 1980 | 14,229,191 |
| 1990 | 16,986,335 |
| 2000 | 20,851,820 |
| 2010 | 25,145,561 |

## Estimated Slave Population in Texas*

| Years | Population |
|-------|------------|
| 1783  | 36 |
| 1825  | 443 |
| 1836  | 5,000 (est.) |
| 1840  | 11,323 |
| 1845  | 30,000 (est.) |
| 1850  | 58,161 |
| 1860  | 182,566 |
| 1865  | 250,000 (est.) |

*The exact numbers are from various censuses taken and the estimates are based on the consensus of scholars.

# INDEX

**A**

Abbott, Greg, 530
*ab initio*, 197
Abramoff, Jack, 542
Adaeseños, 37
Adams, Bud, 482
Adamson Act of 1916, 301
Adams-Onís Treaty, 52
Adena, 8
Adobe Walls, Battle of, 284
Advanced Micro Devices (AMD), 508, 533
Affirmative action,
 in education, 540
African Americans,
 as freedpeople, 194–195
 during 1920s, 330–331
 during Reconstruction, 192–194
 in New Deal, 366
 integration of schools and colleges, 445
 in World War II, 391–392, 398
 voter participation in 1960s, 452
Agreda, María de Jesús de, 54
Agricultural Adjustment Act of 1933, 367
Agricultural Adjustment Act of 1938, 362, 370
Agricultural Adjustment Administration (AAA), 367
Agriculture,
 during 1920s, 327–332
 during Post Civil War years, 220–225, 271
 during post-World War II, 414–415
 during World War II, 398
Aguayo, Marqués de San Miguel de, 36
Ahahayo, 11
Aircraft industry, 413
Airline Deregulation Act of 1978, 477, 497
Akokisas, 6
Alabama-Coushatta Reservation, 141
Alabama-Coushattas, 75, 542
Alamo, 35, 78, 90
Alarcón, Martín de, 35
Alfred P. Murrah Federal Building, 513
Alger, Bruce, 444, 456
Alibates National Monument, 4
Allen, Eliza, 127
Allen, Frederick Lewis, 348
Allred, James V., 374, 400

All-Woman Supreme Court, 325–326
Almonte, Juan Nepomuceno, 77
Alta Vista College, 232
Amarillo College, 424
Amarillo, Texas, 327, 362, 398
Amayxoya, 10
Amendment,
 Eighteenth, 316, 374
 Fifteenth, 204, 306
 Fourteenth, 200, 331, 420
 Nineteenth, 314, 325
 Seventeenth, 301
 Sixteenth, 301
 Thirteenth, 197
 Twenty-first, 374
 Twenty-fourth, 451
*America B.C.: Ancient Settlers in the New World* (Fell), 23
American Airlines, 477
American Federation of Labor (AFL), 224, 414
American G.I. Forum, 418
American International Group (AIG), 545
American triad, 9
Ames, Jessie, 315
Amnesty Act of 1872, 207
Amon Carter Museum, 538
Anasazi, 13
Anti-Saloon League, 316
Apaches, 14, 17, 119
Aranamas, 8
Archaic Indians, 4–5
Archer, Branch T., 71, 90
Arciniega, Miguel, 75
Arkansas Post, 172
Arlington Stadium, 484
Armey, Dick, 499
Arredondo, Joaquín de, 50, 94
Arthur Andersen, accounting firm, 534
Article 13 of the 1827 state constitution, 69
Ashby, H.S.P. "Stump," 257
Asphaltum, 7
Astrodome, 445
Astroturf, 484
Asylums, 274
Atakapas, 6
*Atlatl*, 5
AT&T Center, 535
Austin College, 149
Austin, Moses, 63

Austin, Stephen F., 64, 69, 88, 113–115
Austin, Texas, 118, 337
  selection as capital, 234
Australian ballot, 307
Avenger Field, 396

## B

Bailey, Joseph, 308, 339
Baker, Cullen Montgomery, 196, 206, 282
Baker, Jess A, 314
Baker, Mosely, 96
Balcones Research Center, 508, 533
Ball, Thomas H., 310
Balmaceda, José María, 72
Bank Deposit Guaranty Law of 1909, 309
Bankhead Cotton Control Act, 368, 369
Bankhead-Jones Act, 371
Banking industry, 362, 506
Baptist Church, 148, 278
Barker, Eugene C., 290
Barker, Wharton, 261
Barkley, David, 312
Barnes, Ben, 454, 467, 468
Barret, Lyne T., 221
Barrios, 329
Bass Performance Hall, 538
Bastrop, Baron de, 63
Battle, William J., 311
Baum, Dale, 435
Baylor, John R., 169
Baylor University, 118
Bayou Bourbeau, Battle of, 173
Beauchamp, Jenny B., 263
Beaujeu, Taneguy Le Gallois, 31
Beaumont, Texas, 402
Beckworth, Lindley, 429
Bee, Barnard E., 118
Bee, Hamilton, 173
Bell Aircraft Corporation, 413
Bell, Chris, 527
Bell Helicopter, 507
Bell, John, 152
Bell, Peter H., 138
Benavides, Santos, 144, 174, 288
Bennett, Lerone, 157
Bentsen, Lloyd, 470, 498, 499
Bentsen, Lloyd, Jr., 457
Beringia Land Bridge, 1–4
Bernhardt, Sarah, 276
Bernstein, Carl, 467

Bickerstaff, Benjamin F., 196, 206, 282
Bickley, George, 140
Bidais, 6
Big Inch and Little Big Inch, 397
"Big Swing," 329
"Big Thicket," 51
Big Thicket National Preserve, 456
Bimetallists, 257
Bishop College, 441
Bison, 4
Bissinger, H.G., 511
Black bean episode, 124
"Black Chinese," 289
Black Codes, 198
Black, David, 223
Blackland Prairie, 224
Black Power, 452
Blakley, Bill, 444
Bob Bullock Texas State History Museum, 538
Boeing, 413
Bolton, Herbert E., 290
Bonaparte, Joseph, 49, 62
Bonham, James, 92
Bonham, Texas, 361
Booth, Edwin, 276
Border Patrol agents, 543
Borger oil strike, 358
Bourland, James G., 179
Bow and arrow, 5
Bowie, James, 71, 89
Bracero program, 398
Brackenridge, Mary Eleanor, 314
Bradburn, John D., 71
Branch Davidians, 493
Braniff Airways, 477
Brazos Reservation, 141
Brazzil, Ruth, 326
Breckinridge, John, 152
Brenham, Texas, 362
Briscoe, Dolph, 468, 471
Brotherhood of Timber Workers, 303
Brown Power, 453
Brownsville, Texas,
  during Civil War, 177
Bryant, John, 523
Bryan, William Jennings, 261, 335
Buchanan, James, 138, 362
Buena Vista, Battle of, 137
Buffalo Bayou, 115

Buffalo soldiers, 285
Bullock, Bob, 469, 470, 504, 511, 522
Burke-Wadsworth Act, 387
Burleson, Edward, 89, 95
Burleson, Ralph, 338
Burleson, Rufus C., 279
Burnet, David G., 74, 85, 94, 96, 100, 114, 119, 121, 199
Bush, George H.W.,
  election of 1964, 456
  election of 1970, 457
  election of 1980, 495
  North American Free Trade Agreement, 507
Bush, George W.,
  as governor, 522
    concealed handgun law 523
    education issue, 522
    juvenile crime 523
    tort reform measures 522
    welfare reform, 523
  election of 1994, 505
  election of 1998, 525
  election of 2000, 525–527
  second session as governor,
    capital punishment,
      Karla Faye Tucker, 524
    capital punishment support, 524
    faith-based Christian group support, 524
*Bush v. Gore*, 427
Bustamante, Anastasio, 61, 71
Butte, George C., 344
Byrd, James Jr., 540

## C

Cabello, Domingo, 44
Cabeza de Vaca, Alvar Núñez, 15
Cabin Creek, Battle of, 176
*Caddí*, 10
Caddo Mounds State Historic Site, 10
Caddos, 10, 38, 54, 119
Cadillac, Antoine de la Mothe, sieur de, 34
Caldwell, Colbert, 196, 202
Calhoun, John C., 124
Call Field, 312
Call, Woodrow, 479
Camp Bowie, 312
Camp Logan, 312
Camp MacArthur, 312
Camp Travis, 312
Campbell, Earl, 483, 510
Campbell, Randolph B., 210
Campbell, Thomas A., 309
Canahas, 10
Canales, Alma, 472
Canary Islanders, 37
Canby, Edward R., 169, 194
Canion, Rod, 508
Cannibalism, 6
Capital punishment, 540
Carancaguases, 7
Caro, Robert, 434
Carpetbaggers, 204
Carroll, Benajah Harvey, 269, 291
Carr, Waggoner, 454, 457
Cart wars, 143
Casas, Juan Bautista de las, 50
Cass, Lewis, 101
Castañeda, Francisco de, 88
Castro, Fidel, 459
Catholic Church, 148, 278
Cattle drive, 45
Cavalry units, 166
Central Freight Lines, 497
Centralist Conservatives, 63
Chambers, William Morton, 230
Chance Vought Aircraft, 413
Charles III, 43
Charter-school program, 522
Chayas, 10
Cheney, Dick, 525
Chennault, Claire, 393
Cherokees, 52, 119
Chicano movement, 453
Chickamauga, Battle of, 168
Chicken Ranch, 479
Childress, George C., 93
Chittenden, William Lawrence, 289
Christian Coalition, 499
Cisneros, Henry, 498
Civilian Conservation Corps (CCC), 365
Civil rights, 417–418, 444–446
Civil Rights Act of 1866, 200
Civil Rights Act of 1957, 432
Civil Rights Act of 1964, 424, 446, 449
Civil War,
  defending the frontier, 180–181
  dissenters during, 179–181
  Eastern Theater, 166–167
  home front during, 177

New Mexico campaign, 168–169
Trans-Mississippi Theater, 170–175
women during, 178
Civil Works Administration (CWA), 364
Claiborne, William C.C., 48
Clardy, Mary, 260, 263
Clark, Edward, 155, 166
Clark, George, 241, 255, 257
Clarke, Edward, 336
Clay, Henry, 139
Cleburne demands, 237
Clements, William, 347, 469, 499, 500, 502-503
Clinton, Bill,
  election of 1996, 524
Clinton, Hillary,
  election of 2008, 527
Clovis point, 4
Coahuila y Texas, 65
Coahuiltecans, 7, 39
Coapites, 7
Cochran, A. M., 234
Cochran, Jacqueline, 396
Cockrell, Lila, 475
Cocos, 7
Coinage Act, 256
Coke, Richard, 208, 228, 230, 240
Colegio de la Santa Cruz de Querétaro, 35
Colegio de Nuestra Señora de Guadalupe de Zacatecas, 35
Coleman, Ornette, 481
Collinsworth, George M., 88
Collinsworth, James, 117
Colonization Law of 1823, 69
Colonization Law of 1825, 65, 69
Colored Division of the Women's Christian Temperance Union, 281
Colored Farmers' Alliance, 241
Colquitt, Oscar B, 309
Columbia space shuttle, 544
Columbus, Christopher, 14
Comanches, 18, 38, 119, 141, 149, 180, 230
Comfort, Texas, 180
Commission system of city government, 305–306
Community colleges, 539
Compaq Computer, 508
Compean, Mario, 455, 472
Compromise of 1850, 139
Conard, James, 292

Concealed handgun law, 523
Congress of Industrial Organizations (CIO), 372, 414
Connally Hot Oil Act, 372
Connally, John, 444, 446, 454, 456
Connally, Tom, 347, 362, 375, 387, 388, 429
*Connas*, 1
Conner, George, 330
Consolidated Vultee Aircraft Corporation, 396
Constitutional Union Party, 152
Constitution of 1812, 62, 63
Constitution of 1824, 65, 87
Constitution of 1836, 113
Constitution of 1869, 203–204, 206, 219, 228
Constitution of 1876, 229, 234, 471
Consultation of 1835, 90, 114
Continental Airlines, 477
Contract Labor Code, 198
Convict-Lease Code, 199
Copanes, 7
Córdova's Rebellion, 111
Córdova, Vincente, 111
Corn, 9
  during Post Civil War, 224
Cornyn, John, 528
Coronado, Vázquez de, 15
Corpus Christi, Texas, 330, 390
  during Civil War, 177
Cortés, Hernán, 14
Cortina, Juan, 144, 164
Cortinez, Eusebio, 100
Cos, Martín Perfecto de, 76, 87
Cosper, Clyde, 388
Costilla, Miguel Hidalgo y, 49
Cotton,
  and Agricultural Adjustment Administration, 367
  cotton holiday plan, 360–361
  during Civil War years, 177
  during post Civil War years, 225, 249–250, 272
  during post-World War II, 414
  during Progressive era, 302
  during the 1920s, 327
  in Mexican Texas, 68
Cotton Acreage Control Law, 360
Council House Fight, 120

Cowboy Strike, 226
Cox, Jack, 444
Craddick, Tom, 528
Crane, Martin M., 308
Crane, William C., 279
Crockett, Davy, 92
Cronkite, Walter, 356
Crow, John David, 510
Cruz, Ted, 530, 531
Crystal City, Texas, 391, 453, 454
Cuero, Texas, 392
Cujanes, 7
Culberson, Charles, 258, 341
Cuney, Norris Wright, 222, 238, 241
Cunningham, Minnie Fisher, 314, 346
Custer, George A., 196
Custis, Peter, 48

# D

Dabbs, Ellen, 260
Daingerfield, Texas, 398
Dallas Area Rapid Transit System (DART), 532
Dallas Cowboys, 479, 482
Dallas Mavericks, 483, 536
Dallas Stars, 537
Dallas Texans, 482
Dallas, Texas, 273, 337, 364, 446
Dallas Tornados, 537
Daniel, Price, 424, 432, 433, 444
Darrow, Clarence, 336
Daughters of the Republic of Texas (DRT), 134
Davidson, James, 207, 211
Davis, Edmund J., 179, 201, 203, 231, 240
Davis, James H. "Cyclone," 259
Davis, Mollie E. Moore, 290
Davis, Wendy, 530
Deadoses, 6
Dealey, Samuel, 393
"Deep Throat," 467
Dehahuit, 48
DeLay, Tom, 526
De León, Alonso, 32
*Delgado v. Bastrop ISD*, 419
Dell, Michael, 533
Del Mar Junior College, 424
Democratic Party,
  during secession crisis, 150
  in election of 1860, 152
  in Republic, 150
DeMorse, Charles, 165
Denison Dam, 391
Department of Public Safety, 375, 376
DeShields, James T., 290
de Vaca, Cabeza, 15
Dewey, Thomas, 402
DeWitt, Green, 66
Díaz, Porfirio, 309
Dies, Martin, 387, 403, 432
Digital Light Processing (DLP), 508
Dirty Thirty, 466
Disciples of Christ, 278
Diseases,
  brought by Europeans, 16
  in late nineteenth century, 273
Dixiecrats, 426
Dodd City, Texas, 388
Doggett, Lloyd, 498
Dohoney, Ebenezer L., 234
Dole, Robert, 524
Donelson, Andrew Jackson, 125
Donnelly, Ignatius, 261
Dorn, Earl Van, 170
Douglas, Stephen, 139
Dowling, Richard "Dick," 173
Duels, 149
Dugout canoe, 7
Durham, Joseph Idelbert. *See* A. D. "Doc" Lloyd
Dust Bowl, 369
Duwali, Chief, 52, 68, 75, 99, 119

# E

Education,
  in late nineteenth century, 278
Educational Reform Act, 500
Edwards, Chet, 530
Edwards, Daniel, 312
Edwards, Haden, 66
Edwards Underground Aquifer, 510
Eggers, Paul, 457
Eisenhower, Dwight, 393
El Cañon, 41
Election,
  of 1956, 432; of 1914, 310;
  of 1873, 208; of 1876, 254;
  of 1878, 230; of 1880, 231
  of 1886, 234, 254; of 1888, 235;
  of 1890, 255; of 1892, 255, 256, 306;

of 1894, 258, 306; of 1896, 259, 306;
of 1898, 260, 306 of 1900, 261, 306;
of 1902, 306; of 1906, 308;
of 1910, 309; of 1914, 310 of 1918, 311;
of 1920, 309; of 1946, 425
of 1948, 426, 434, 443; of 1952, 429;
of 1954, 430; of 1960, 443; of 1962, 444
of 1963, 453; of 1964, 455;
of 1966, 452, 456, 457; of 1968, 457;
of 1970, 457; of 1972, 468, 472;
of 1974, 469, 472; of 1976, 469;
of 1978, 470; of 1984, 498; of 1986, 500
of 1992, 498; of 1994, 499, 505;
of 1996, 523; of 1998, 524; of 2000, 525;
of 2004, 526; of 2006, 527, 539
of 2008, 527; of 2010, 529;
of 2016, 531; of 2018, 531
Electra oil field, 303
Electronic Data Systems (EDS), 477
Electronics industry, 413
Elm Creek Raid, 163
Elosúa, Antonio, 76
El Paso, Texas, 275, 329, 390
Emergency Banking Act of 1933, 362
Energy-trading, 534
Enron Corporation, 533
Episcopal Church, 148, 278
Equal Legal Rights Amendment, 473
Equal Rights Amendment, 473
Equal Suffrage League of Houston, 314
Estelle, William J., 540
Ethnogenesis, 17
Evans, Hiram Wesley, 340–341
Exxon Company, 317, 476

## F

Fair Labor Standards Act, 372
Fair Play for Cuba Committee, 447
Faith-based Christian groups, 524
Falwell, Jerry, 473, 474
Fannin, James W., 89, 95
Farenthold, Frances "Sissy," 468
Farías, Valentín Gómez, 74, 87
Farm Credit Administration (FCA), 363
Farmers' Alliance, 234, 237, 251–253, 253
Farm Security Administration (FSA), 371
Fastow, Andrew, 534
Federal Communications Commission, 362
Federal Constitution of the United States of Mexico, 63, 65

Federal Deposit Insurance Corporation (FDIC), 361, 496
Federal Emergency Relief Administration (FERA), 363, 370
Federal Employers' Liability Act, 300
Federal Farm Loan Act, 301
Federal Highway Act, 304
Federalist Liberals, 63
Federal Reserve System, 301
Federal Surplus Relief Corporation (FSRC), 368
Federal Theater and Writers' Project, 365
Federal Warehouse Act, 301
Fell, Barry, 23
Felt, Mark, 467
Fence cutting, 226
Fender, Freddy, 481
Ferdinand VII, 62
Ferguson, James, 310, 340–345, 360, 363, 376
Ferguson, Miriam, 343–346, 357, 360, 363, 373, 376
Fiat currency system, 252
Fields, Richard, 64, 67
Fiesta, 541
Fifth Military District, 200
Fifty Cent Law of 1879, 231
Filibusterers, 50
Filisola, Vicente, 75, 95
Fillmore, Millard, 139
Finley, Newton W., 253
Finnigan, Annette, 314
First Congressional Plan of Reconstruction,. *See* Wade-Davis Bill
First National Bank of Midland, 506
First Texas Cavalry (Union), 201
Fisher, William, 122
Fitzgerald, F. Scott, 348
Flake, Ferdinand, 153
Flanagan, James W., 204
Flipper, Henry O., 287
Flores, Manuel, 100
Flour milling, 220
Folsom point, 4
Food processing industry, 414
Food Stamps program, 449
Ford, John "Rip," 164
Foreman, Ed, 444, 456
Fort Bliss, 141, 390, 413
Fort Brown, 141

Fort Hood, 390, 521
Fort Sam Houston, 390
Fort Union, 169
Fort Worth, 141
Fort Worth and Denver City Railroad, 219, 273
Fort Worth Herd, 548
Fort Worth, Texas, 220, 273, 337, 364, 396
Foster, Lafayette L., 255
Franklin, William B., 173
Fredericksburg, Texas, 120, 145, 389
Fredonia Rebellion, 61
Freedmen's Bureau, 193–194
Freedom colonies, 251
Freeman, Thomas, 48
French explorers, 30
*Friday Night Lights: A Town, A Team, and A Dream* (Bissinger), 511
Friedman, Richard "Kinky," 527
Frontier Organization, 180
Frontier Regiment, 180
Fujita, Frank, 385–386
Fundamentalism,
  rise of, 333–335
Funding for colleges and universities, 310
*Furman v. Georgia*, 540
Fusion ticket, 259

**G**

Gaines, Edmund P., 101
Gainesville, Texas, 179
Galveston Bay, 476
Galveston, Houston and Henderson Railroad, 147
Galveston Hurricane of 1900, 305–306, 318
Galveston Island, 53, 192
Galveston Medical Society, 275
Galveston Plan, 305
Galveston Screwmen's Benevolent Association, 222
Galveston, Texas, 122, 177, 232, 274, 275
Gálvez, Bernardo de, 45
Gano, Richard Montgomery, 176
Gaona, Antonio, 95
Garcia, Gregorio N., 288
García, Gus, 419
García, Macario, 393, 418
Garner, John Nance, 361, 375, 399
Garrison, George Pierce, 290
Gay, Bettie, 260

Gay, George, 388
General Dynamics Corporation, 413
General Motors, 477
German Belt, 288
Gibbs, Barney, 260
Giles, Bascom, 432
Gilmer-Aikin laws, 427
Glass, Anthony, 49
Glidden, Joseph, 226
Globe Life Field, 537
Glorieta Pass, 170
Goldbugs, 257
Goldwater, Barry, 449
Gonzales, Alberto, 525
Gonzalez, Henry B., 420, 444, 453
Goodnight, Charles, 226
Goodrich, Chauncey, 149
Goodwin, Sherman, 274
Gore, Al, 525
Gore, Al, Sr., 449
Gould, Jay, 274
Graham, George, 52
Gramm, Phil, 498, 523
Granberry, Jim, 469
Grange (Patrons of Husbandry), 229, 236, 251
Granger, Gordon, 192, 286
Graves, Curtis, 452
Grayson, Peter W., 74, 117
Great Depression, 347
*Great Gatsby, The* (Fitzgerald), 348
Great hanging at Gainesville, 179
Great Recession, 522
Great Society, 449
Great Southwest Strike, 223
Greenback Party, 234, 236, 241, 251, 259
Greenbacks, 256
Greens, 144
Green, Thomas J., 123, 173
Greer, Hilton R., 289
Gregory, Edgar M., 194
Grey, Zane, 349
Grierson, Benjamin H., 285
Griffin, Charles, 192, 194, 200
Griffith, John S., 254
Groce, Jared E., 68, 96
Grover, Henry, 468
Grovey, Richard, 421
Guadalupe-Hidalgo, Treaty of, 137
Guadalupe Mountains National Park, 456

Guadalupe Victoria, 66
Guerra, Dionisio, 288
Guerrero, Vicente, 63, 69, 71
Gulf, Colorado, and Santa Fe Railroad, 219, 275
Gulf Oil Corporation, 317
Gutiérrez de Lara, Bernardo, 50
Gutiérrez, José Ángel, 454, 472

# H

Haley, J. Evetts, 432
Hamilton, Andrew Jackson, 153, 195
Hamilton, Morgan, 202, 230
Hamman, William H., 231
Hampton, Carl, 453
Hardin, John Wesley, 282
Harmon, Leonard Roy, 392
Harris, Jim, 508
Hasan, Nidal M., 521
Hasinais, 12, 38
Hayden, David, 312
Hayes, John L., 179
Hayes, Rebecca Henry, 263, 313
Hays, John Coffee "Jack," 120, 137
Head Start, 449
Hébert, Paul O., 171, 177
Heisman trophy, 510
HemisFair '68, 78
Henderson, James Pinckney, 115, 125, 138
Henry IV, 30
Hepburn Act, 300
Hernández, Pete, 420
*Hernandez v. the State of Texas*, 420
Herrera, Simon, 48, 50
Hewetson, James, 74
Heyerdahl, Thor, 22
Hicks Field, 312
Hidalgo, Father Francisco, 34
High tech industries, 533
Hightower, Jim, 497, 526
Hillbilly Boys, 376
Hill, John, 469
Hispanics,. *See* Texas Mexicans
Hobby, Oveta Culp, 394
Hobby, William, 311, 314, 340, 341
Hogg, James, 241, 253, 257, 279
Hollingsworth, Orlando N., 279
Holly, Buddy, 417
Home Owners Loan Corporation (HOLC), 363

Honey Springs, Battle of, 172
Hood, John Bell, 167
Hood's Texas Brigade, 167
Hoover, Herbert, 347, 356
Hopewell Complex, 8
Hopkins, Harry, 364
Hopwood, Cheryl, 540
*Hopwood v. Texas*, 540
Horse racing, 276, 375
Horses, 17
Horseshoe Bend, Battle of, 126
"Hot oil," 358, 372
House, Edward M., 306
Houston, Andrew Jackson, 399
Houston Astros, 484, 537
Houston Comets, 536
Houston Dynamo, 537
Houston Eagles, 483
Houston, Elizabeth Goode, 263
Houston Grand Opera, 539
Houston Oilers, 482
Houston Rockets, 483, 536
Houston, Sam, 73, 93
    as president of the Republic of Texas, 114–116
    gubernatorial election in 1859, 151
    in election of 1860 and secession crisis, 152–153
    legend of, 126–127
    second administration, 121–122
Houston Texans, 537
Houston, Texas, 113–121, 124–130, 131, 132, 364, 398, 453
    race riots, 315
Houston & Texas Central Railroad, 273
Houteff, Victor, 493
Howard, Oliver O., 193
Howell, Vernon Wayne, 493
Hoyt, Henry F., 274
Hubbard, Richard, 208, 230
Huckabee, Mike, 527
Huddle, William H., 290
Hughes, Karen, 525
Hughes, Sarah, 347
Hughes Tool Company, 372
Human papillomavirus (HPV), 528
Humble Oil Company, 317, 359, 476
Hunt, H. L., 358
Hurd, Will, 543
Hurricane Harvey, 544

Hurricane Ike, 544
Hurricane Katrina, 544
Hurricane Rita, 544
Hussein, Saddam, 476
Hutcheson, Thad, 432
Hutchison, Kay Bailey, 473, 498, 529

**I**

Ibarvo, Antonio Gil, 43, 44
IBM, 508, 533
Ickes, Harold, 364, 397
Immigration,
   illegal, 543
Immigration and Naturalization Service (INS), 391
Imperial Colonization Law, 64
Indentured servants, 65
Industrialization,
   during 1920s, 327–334
   in post-World War II, 412–413
   in World War II, 396–397
Innocence Project, 541
Institute of Texan Cultures (ITC), 78, 289, 538
Intel, 508, 533
International and Great Northern Railroad, 219, 273
Internment camps, 391
Interstate and Foreign Commerce Committee, 362
Ireland, John, 223, 233
Iturbide, Agustín de, 63

**J**

Jack, Patrick, 74
Jackson, Andrew, 113, 115, 126
   West Florida, 52
Jaworski, Leon, 467
Jeffersonian Democrats, 252
Jefferson, Joseph, 276
Jenkins, Charles H., 259
Jennings, Waylon, 481
Jester, Beauford, 426
Jewish population, 278
Jim Crow laws, 238
Jimenez, Flaco, 481
Job Corps, 449
John Sealy Hospital, 275
Johnson, Britt, 163
Johnson, Jack, 276

Johnson, Lyndon, 78, 400, 427
   as president, 449–451
   as vice president, 443–444
   civil rights, 418
   director of NYA, 366
   election of 1948, 434
   Kennedy conspiracy, 458
   Senate Majority Leader, 432
Johnson Space Center, 509
Johnston, Albert Sidney, 167
Joiner, Columbus Marion "Dad," 358
Jolliet, Louis, 31
Jones, Anson, 125
Jones-Connally Act, 368
Jones, F.P., 325
Jones, George, 481
Jones, George W. "Wash," 233
Jones, Jesse, 361, 363
Jones, John B., 283
Jones, Marvin, 362, 369
Joplin, Janis, 481
Jordan, Barbara, 452, 467, 474
Jumanos, 13, 54
Juneteenth, 192

**K**

Kadohadachos, 11, 13
Karankawas, 7, 119
   and Austin, 70
Karcher, John, 413
Kearby, Jerome, 260
Keating-Owen Act, 301
Kelley, Oliver H., 236
Kelly Field, 312, 398
Kenedy, Mifflin, 226
Kenedy, Texas, 391
Kennedy, John F.,
   assassination of, 446–447
   conspiracy theory, 458–459
Kennewick Man, 1
Kichais, 13, 38
Kickapoo, 542
Kiddoo, Joseph, 194
Kilby, Jack, 414
Kilgore, Texas, 358
Killeen, Texas, 390, 394
Killough massacre, 111
Kimbell Museum, 538
King, Billie Jean, 484
King, Larry L., 479

King Ranch, 535
King, Richard, 226
Kiowa, 180, 230
Kirby, John Henry, 220
Kirby Smith, Edmund, 172, 176, 181, 198
Kirby, William, 501
Knights of Labor, 222–225
Knights of the Golden Circle, 140, 154
Know-Nothing Party, 150
Knox, Frank, 404
Kotsotekas, 19
Krueger, Robert, 470
Ku Klux Klan, 204–205, 336–347
Kwahadis, 19

## L

La Bahía, 36
*La Belle*, 31
Labor unions,
   earliest in Texas, 221
"Lady in Blue," 54. *See also* Agreda, María de Jesús de,
Laffitte, Jean, 52
*L'Aimable*, 31
Lamar, Mirabeau Buonaparte, 97
   and education, 118
   annexation of Texas, 113
   in Republic, 117
   land policies, 120
   Native American policy, 119–120
Landry, Tom, 465–466
Lanham, Samuel Willis Tucker, 306
La Raza Unida Party, 455
Laredo, Battle of, 174
Laredo, Texas, 144
   during the Civil War, 177
La Salle, René-Robert Cavelier, sieur de, 31
Laurens, Levi L., 149
Law of April 6, 1830, 61, 71
*Lawrence v. Texas*, 527
Lay, Kenneth, 534
League of United Latin American Citizens (LULAC), 330, 418
League of Women Voters, 314
Leak, Fannie, 260
Lee, Bob, 196, 206
Leftwich, Robert, 74
Lend-Lease aid, 387
Lenenberg, Hattie, 326
León, Martín de, 66

Leon Springs Military Reservation, 312
Letona, José María, 75
Light Crust Doughboys, 376
Lincoln, Abraham, 152
Lipans, 17, 38
Lloyd, A. D. "Doc," 358
Lockheed Martin, 507
Lockridge, Joseph, 452
Long, Huey, 359
Long, James, 52
Longley, Bill, 282
Longoria, Felix, 418
Longview race riot, 315
López, Francisco, 46
López, José Angel, 388
Lost Cause, 206
Lottery, 504
Louisiana, 34
Louisiana Purchase, 51
Louis XIV, 31
Love, Thomas B., 308
Lubbock, Texas, 328, 340
Lumber industry, 220
   during 1920s, 303
Lutcher, Henry J., 220
Lynching, 281, 282

## M

Mackenzie, Ranald S., 284
Macune, Charles W., 252
Magee, William, 50
Magnolia Petroleum Company, 317
Magruder, John B., 172, 177
Majestic Theatre, 539
Malakoff heads, 22
Manford Act, 402
Manned Spacecraft Center, 413
Mann-Elkins Act, 301
Mansfield, Texas, 174
Manufacturing. *See* Industrialization
Marquette, Jacques, 31
Marshall Sit-In Movement, 441
Marshall, Texas, 273
Martin, Albert, 92
Martinez, Antonio, 63
Martin, Wylie, 96
Mason, John T., 101
Massanet, Damián, 52, 54
Mass shootings, 531
Matagorda Bay, 31

Matamoros, Mexico, 113
Matrilineal, 11
Mattox, Jim, 499, 503
Mauro, Gary, 499, 525
Mayfield, Earle, 341, 346
McArdle, Henry Arthur, 290
McCain, John, 525, 527
McClellan, Carole Keeton, 475
McCrae, Gus, 479
McCraw, William, 375
McCulloch, Benjamin, 120, 123, 137, 154, 170
McCulloch, Henry, 164
McDermott, Eugene, 413
McGloin, James, 74
McGovern, George, 467
McKinley, William, 261
McKinney, Collin, 198
McLean, William Pinckney, 255
McLeod, Hugh, 118
McMullen, John, 74
McMurtry, Larry, 479
McNelly, L. H., 283
McPherson, Aimee Semple, 334
McRae, Colin D., 180
McVeigh, Timothy, 513
Medicaid, 449
Medicine Lodge Treaty, 284
Merck, 528
Metcalfe, Nellie, 347
Methodist Church, 148, 277
Mexía, José Antonio, 77
Mexican-American Democrats, 472
Mexican American Legal Defense Fund (MALDEF), 501
Mexican Americans,
  class discrimination, 420
  in the 1960s, 453
  in World War II, 393–394
  segregation of schools, 418
Mexican-American War, 137–138
Mexican American Youth Organization (MAYO), 454, 472
Mexican Farm Labor Program Agreement, 398  *See* Bracero program
Mexican Revolution of 1910, 309
Meyerson Symphony Center, 538
Mézières, Athanase de, 42
Midland Minnie, 3
Midland, Texas, 327

Mier y Terán, Manuel de, 61, 71, 75
Migrant farmers, 250
Milam, Ben, 89
Miller, Doris, 392, 404–405
Mina, Francisco Xavier, 52
Minimum Wage March, 454
Minute Maid Park, 537
Mission Concepción, 89
Mission San Antonio de Bexar, 90
Mission San Antonio de Valero, 35
Mississippian cultural tradition, 9
Missouri Compromise, 135
Mollie Bailey Circus, 277
Moneyhon, Carl, 210
Monterrey, Mexico, 137
Moody, Dan, 339, 344, 345, 357, 360, 400
Moore, G. Bedell, 220
Moore, John H., 88
Morales, Dan, 524
Morales, Victor, 523
Moral Majority, 470
Moscoso, y Alvarado, Luís de, 15
Moss, Fannie, 260
Motorola, 508, 533
Moundbuilding, 10
Mount Carmel, 493
Muñiz, Ramsey, 468, 472
Murchison, Clint Jr., 465
Murphy, Audie, 394
Murto, Bill, 508
Mutscher, Gus, 466
Múzquiz, Ramón, 69, 72

**N**

Napoleon, 49
Narváez, Pánfilo de, 14
NASCAR auto racing, 537
Natchitoches, 11, 38
National Aeronautics and Space Administration (NASA), 413, 508
National Association for the Advancement of Colored People (NAACP), 330
National Colonization Law, 65
Nationalists, 201
National Labor Relations Board (NLRB), 372
National Museum of the Pacific War, 538
National Organization for Women (NOW), 473
National Reclamation Act, 300

National Recovery Administration (NRA), 371
National Reform Press Association, 247
National Urban League, 423
National Women's Conference, 474
National Women's Political Caucus (NWPC), 473
National Youth Administration (NYA), 365–366
Navajos, 14
Naval Air Station, 390
Navarro, José Antonio, 69, 93
Neal, Margie, 347
Neches, Battle of the, 119
Neff, Pat, 309, 335–336, 339–340
Neighbors, Robert S., 138
Neill, James C., 90
Nelson, Willie, 481
Neutral Ground Agreement 48
New Braunfels, Texas, 144
New Deal,
  agriculture programs, 367–368
  evaluation of, 377
  industrial relief, 371–372
  Texas influence, 361–362
  work relief, 362–363
  youth relief, 365–366
New London School Explosion, 355–356, 377
New Mount Carmel, 493
New York Stock Exchange, 356
Ney, Elisabet, 290, 314
Nimitz, Chester, 389, 393
Nixon, Lawrence, 331
*Nixon v. Herndon*, 331
No Child Left Behind Act, 525
Noconis, 19
Nolan, Philip, 47
"no pass, no play," 500
Noriega, Rick, 528
Norris, J. Frank, 333–335
Norris-Rayburn Bill, 371
Norris, S. H., 281
Norteños, 38, 40
North American Free Trade Agreement, 506–507
North Atlantic Aviation, 396
Norton, Seymour F., 259
Nueces, Battle of, 180
Nueces Strip, 136

Nuestra Señora del Refugio, 45
Nuestra Señora del Rosario, 40
Nugent, Thomas, 257

## O

Obama, Barack, 530
  election of 2008, 527
O'Brien, Davey, 510
O'Brien, George W., 299
O'Connor, Dennis M., 226
O'Connor, Thomas, 226
O'Daniel, Wilbert Lee "Pappy," 375, 399, 403, 432, 435
Odessa, Texas, 327, 511
Office of Price Administration (OPA), 394
Ogallala Aquifer, 328
Oil,
  during 1920s, 303, 327–328
  during Post Civil War years, 221
  in post-World War II, 413
  in World War II, 397–398
Oil Industry,
  decline of, 506–507
Old Baylor, 149
Onderdonk, Robert Jenkins, 290
O'Neill, Harriet, 347
Onís, Luis de, 52
*Only Yesterday* (Allen), 348
Oolooteka, Chief, 126
Orbison, Roy, 417
Order of St. Francis, 20
Order of the Star Spangled Banner,. *See* Know-Nothing Party
Ordinance of Secession, 153
O'Reilly, Alejandro, 42
Organization of Petroleum Exporting Countries (OPEC), 466, 506
O'Rourke, Robert "Beto," 531
Orr, Layfette, 165
Ortiz, Solomon, 530
Ortiz, Tadeo de Ayala, 61
Osages, 38
Oswald, Lee Harvey, 446, 458

## P

Pacheco, Rafael Martínez, 46
Pacific Ocean migration theory, 1
Paige, Rod, 525
Painter, Theophilus S., 422
Paleoindians, 3–4

Palmito Ranch, Battle of, 176, 179
Palo Duro Canyon, 284
Panhandle,
　cotton fields, 329
　dust bowl, 369
　oil field, 327
Panic of 1837, 115, 117
Panic of 1873, 226
Park, Milton, 247
Parr, Archer, 315
Parrilla, Diego Ortiz, 41
Patman, Wright, 467
Patrilineal kin, 8
Patrons of Husbandry,. See Grange
Payayas, 8
Peace Party, 179
Pearl Harbor, 387–388
Pease, Elisha M., 144, 151, 198, 200
Peddy, George, 342, 427
Pedraza, Manuel Gómez, 71
Penatekas, 19
Pennybacker, Anna, 315
People's Party, 241, 253. See Populist Party
People's Party II, 453
Permanent University Fund (PUF), 327
Permian Basin oil field, 327
Perot, Ross, 477, 498, 500, 524
Perry, Rick, 498
　as first term governor, 524
　as second term governor, 528
　issue of illegal immigration, 528
Pershing, John J., 312
Petrochemical industry, 413
Petroglyphs, 6
Petty, Elijah P., 182
Phillips Petroleum, 413
Pictographs 6
Pierce, Henry Clay, 308
Pierce, James A., 139
Pilkington, Tom, 479
Piney Woods, 358
Plan de Casa Mata, 63
Plan de Iguala, 63
Plan de San Diego, 310
Planter class, 146–147
Pleasant Hill, Battle of, 175
Plum Creek, Battle of, 120
Political Association of Spanish-Speaking Organizations, 453
Polk, James K., 124, 136

Poll tax, 306, 331, 427, 451
Pope, William H., 239
Population,
　in 1860s, 144
　in 1920s, 302
　late nineteenth century, 271
Populist Party, 236
Populists, 253
　early 1900s, 306
Porter, William Sidney, 290
Portilla, Nicolás de la, 95
Pottery, 8
Potts, L. E., 196
Power, James, 74
Prairie View Normal Institute (Prairie View A & M), 232
Precinct caucuses, 527
Presbyterian Church, 148, 278
Presidio San Antonio de Béxar, 35
Price, Sterling, 170
Prisoners-of-war camps, 390
Progressive Era, 300–309
Prohibition, 234, 252, 278, 316–317, 373–374
Prohibition Party, 234
Provincias Internas, 44
Public Broadcasting System (PBS), 482
Public Works Administration (PWA), 364
Pucek, Ron, 509
Puebloan cultural tradition, 13
Pure Food and Drug Act, 300

**Q**

Quitman, Texas, 253
*Quivira*, 16

**R**

Railroads, 219–222
　during 1920s, 304
Raines, Cadwell W., 256
Rainey, Homer, 425
Ramón, Diego, 35
Ramón, Domingo, 35
Ranchería Grande, 40
Rangel, Irma, 474
Rangers, 484
Ransom, Harry, 445
Rattlesnake Springs, Battle of, 286
Rayburn, Sam, 361, 362, 371, 430, 443
Rayner, John B., 241, 257

Raytheon, 507
Reagan, John H., 255
Reagan, Ronald, 495
Reconstruction Acts, 200
Reconstruction Finance Corporation (RFC), 361
"Redeemers," 271–272
Red River Campaign, 174–175
Red River War, 284
Reed, Ralph, 542
Regulation of 1772, 43
Religious Right, 499
Remington, Frederick, 538
Reno, Janet, 511
Republican Party,
   during Reconstruction, 191–199
   in election of 1860, 152
Republic of Fredonia, 67
Resettlement Administration (RA), 370
Reynolds, George T., 226
Reynolds, Joseph J., 192, 194, 203
Richards, Ann, 475, 499, 503
Richardson, J. P., 417
Richardson, Sam, 166
Riggs, Bobby, 484
Right to work law, 426
Ripperdá, Juan María Vicencio, Barón de, 43
Roaring Twenties, 348–349
Roberts, Meshack, 286
Robertson, Felix D., 342–343
Robertson Insurance Law, 309
Robertson, Sterling C., 74
Roberts, Oran M., 199, 230
Robin Hood Plan, 505
Roden, Benjamin, 493
Roden, Lois, 494
Rodríguez, Johnny, 481
Rodríguez, Thomas A., 288
*Rodriguez v. San Antonio ISD*, 501
*Roe v. Wade*, 474
Romney, Mitt, 530
Roosevelt, Franklin D., 356
Roosevelt, Theodore, 300
Ross, Lawrence "Sul," 234
Rove, Karl, 525
Royal Orders for New Discoveries, 20
Rubí, Marqués de, 43
Ruby, George T., 201, 202
Ruby, Jack, 446, 448, 458
Rudder, James Earl, 388, 393

Ruiz, David, 540
Ruiz, José Francisco, 93
*Ruiz v. Estelle*, 540
Runaway Scrape, 95, 95–97
Runnels, Hardin R., 151
Rural Electrification Act, 362
Rural Electrification Administration (REA), 371
Rusk County, 358
Rusk, Thomas J., 85, 112, 113, 115
Russell, Charles, 538
Ryan, Nolan, 484, 537

S

Saint-Denis, Louis Juchereau de, 34
Salcedo, Manuel, 50
Salt Creek Massacre, 284
Sam Houston Normal Institute (Sam Houston State University), 232
Sampler, Samuel, 312
San Antonio Regional Medical Center, 508
San Antonio Fiesta Texas, 535
San Antonio Silver Stars, 536
San Antonio Spurs, 483
San Antonio State Hospital, 275
San Antonio, Texas, 45, 78, 273, 329, 364, 373, 390
   Sanitarium of the West, 274
Sánchez, Nicasio, 76
Sanchez, Tony, 525, 526
Sanders, Harold Barefoot, 468
San Francisco de los Tejas, 33
San Gabriel missions, 40
San Jacinto, Battle of, 85, 96
San José, 35
San Juan Bautista, 34
Santa Anna, Antonio López de, 63, 73, 113, 87, 122, 73
Santa Fe County, New Mexico, 138
Santa Fe Expedition, 118
Santísimo Nombre de María, 33
Saucedo, José Antonio, 67
Savings and loan associations (S&Ls), 495
Sayers, Joseph, 306, 308
Scalawags, 204
Scarborough Fair, 536
Schlafly, Phyllis, 474
Schnell, Mathis, 234
Scopes, John, 335
Scott, Arthur Carroll, 275

Scott, Winfield, 137
Seagoville camp, 391
Secession crisis, 152–153, 198
Securities And Exchange Commission, 362
Seguín, Juan Erasmo, 65, 69, 96
Seguín, Juan Nepumenco, 72
Selena, 511
Selman, John, 282
Semicolon Case, 208
Serbia, Texas, 145
Shaler, William, 50
Shaman, 6
Shannon, Tommy, 466
Shapiro, Florence, 533
Sharecropping. *See* Tenant farming
Sharp, Frank, 466
Sharp, John, 526
Sharpstown Scandal, 466–467
Sheppard, John Ben, 432
Sheppard, Morris, 341, 362, 399
Sheridan, Philip H., 192, 200
Sherman, Sidney, 97
Shivers, Allan, 424, 428–430, 443
Sibley, Henry Hopkins, 169–170
Sibley, John, 47
Silsbee, Nathan D., 220
Simmons, William J., 336
Siringo, Charles A., 289
Sitton, Thad, 292
Sjolander, John P., 289
Skilling, Jeffrey, 534
Slaughter, C. C., 226
Slavery,
   as issue in annexation, 134–135
   during Civil War, 177
   in early statehood, 142–143
Slidell, John, 136
Smith, Al, 347
Smith, Ashbel, 279
Smith, Henry, 90, 113
Smith, John Lee, 426
Smith, Loonie, 421
Smith, Preston, 457, 466, 468
*Smith v. Allwright*, 402, 420
Social Security Act, 374
Sociedad Benito Juárez, 288
Soil Conservation Act, 362
Soil Conservation and Domestic Allotment Act (SCDAA), 369
Soil Conservation Service, 369

Solutrean theory, 1
Somervell, Alexander, 122
Sondock, Ruby, 347
Soto, Hernando de, 15
Southern Aircraft Corporation, 396
Southern Farmers' Alliance, 252
Southern Lumber Operators' Association, 303
Southern Manifesto, 432
*Southern Mercury*, 247, 253
Southern Methodist University, fooball program, 503
Southern Pacific Railroad, 219
Southern strategy, 469
Southfork Ranch, 480
Southwest Airlines, 478, 497
Southwest Conference (SWC), 510
Southwest Voter Registration Education Project (SVREP), 473
Spanish settlements, 37
Spector, Rose, 347
Spindletop, 302, 303, 358, 514
Stanbery, William, 127
Stance, Emanuel, 286
Star of the Republic Museum, 538
Starr County, 453
State Department of Forestry, 310
State Freight Rate Convention, 255
State Parks System, 340
Steele, Frederick, 174
Steelman, Alan, 468
Stephens, Uriah, 223
Sterling, Ross, 357–358
Stevenson, Adlai, 429
Stevenson, Coke, 401, 427, 434, 443
Stiborik, Joseph, 389
Stock market crash, 347, 356
Stoddard, Helen M., 314
Stone, Oliver, 458
Strayhorn, Carol Keeton, 527, 539
Street Car Barn Convention, 255
Subtreasury plan, 238, 252
Sumners, Hatton, 375, 387
Sun Microsystems, 508, 533
Sun Oil Company, 317
Superconducting Super Collider, 508
Superdelegates, 527
Sutton, William "Bill," 206, 282
Sweatt, Heman, 421
*Sweatt v. Painter*, 423

Sweetwater, Texas, 396
Swenson, S. M., 226

**T**

Taft, William Howard, 300, 309
Tamiques, 8
Tammas, 10
Taovayas, 13, 38
Tarshar, Chief, 100
Tawakonis, 13, 38
Tax-Payers' Convention, 207
Taylor, Creed, 282
Taylor, Richard, 174
Taylor, Texas, 338
Taylor, Zachary, 136
Teacher Retirement System of Texas, 534
Tegener, Frederick "Fritz," 180
Tehuacana Creek, Treaty of, 122
Tejanos, 45, 52, 78–79
  in Civil War, 179–181
  in early statehood years, 143–144
  in the 1920s, 329–330
Telles, Raymond, 453
Temperance movement, 234
Temple Sanitarium, 275
Temple, Texas, 275
Tenant farming,
  by 1880s, 251
  during Reconstruction, 209
  during the 1920s, 328
  in 1930s, 370
  post Civil War, 224
Tenorio, Antonio, 87
Ten Percent Plan, 191
Terán de los Ríos, Domingo, 33
Terrell, Alexander Watkins, 307
Terrell Election Laws, 307
Terrell State Hospital, 275
Terry's Texas Rangers, 168
Texaco, 317, 359
Texarkana, Texas, 398
Texas Advocate, 253
Texas Agricultural and Mechanical College, 230
Texas A&M,
  founding of, 232
  funding of, 256
Texas and Pacific Railroad, 219, 223
Texas Assessment of Academic Skills (TAAS), 522, 539

Texas Association of Nashville, Tennessee, 75
Texas Baptist Educational Society,. *See* Baylor University
Texas Brewers Association, 316
Texas Bureau of Immigration, 271
Texas Center for Superconductivity, 508
Texas Central Railroad, 219
Texas City Disaster, 411–412
Texas City, Texas, 398
Texas Emerging Technology Fund, 526
Texas Enterprise Fund, 526
Texas Equal Rights Association (TERA), 263, 313
Texas Equal Suffrage Association, 311, 314
Texas Farmers' Alliance, 261, 263
Texas Federation of Women's Clubs, 280, 315
Texas Higher Education Coordinating Board, 456
Texas Highway Department, 310
Texas Instruments (TI), 413, 477, 508
Texas League of Professional Baseball Clubs, 276
Texas Local Option Association, 316
Texas Mexican Railroad, 273
Texas Motor Speedway, 537
Texas Mounted Rifles, 137, 164
Texas Mounted Volunteers, 169
Texas Open Records Act, 469
Texas Overland Expedition, 173
Texas & Pacific Railroad, 273
Texas-Padre Island National Seashore, 456
Texas People's Party, 248
Texas Railroad Commission, 255, 304
Texas Rangers, 116, 120–122, 125, 129, 144, 223, 282–283, 309–312, 374, 375, 454, 505
Texas Regulars, 402
Texas Rehabilitation and Relief Commission, 363
Texas Southern University, 427, 445, 453
Texas Stadium, 482
Texas State Bar Association, 338
Texas State Fair, 536
Texas State Historical Association, 290
Texas State Library and Archives Building, 433
Texas State Medical Association, 275
Texas Technological College, 340
Texas Traffic Association, 254
Texas Troubles, 151

"Texas Two-Step" delegate process, 527
Texas Woman Suffrage Association, 314
Texas Women's Political Caucus (TWPC), 473
Thompson, Ben, 282
Thompson, Ernest, 375, 376
Throckmorton, James W., 153, 179, 197, 230
Thurmond, J. Strom, 427
Tidelands oil coastal land, 429
Tiguas of El Paso, 542
Tippit, J.D., 447
Title IX, 474
Tonkawas, 19
  and Austin, 70
Tonti, Henri de, 31
Tower, John, 444, 449, 456, 468, 470, 498
Towery, Roland Kenneth, 431
Towne, Charles, 261
Tracy, Harry, 257
Trans-Mississippi Theater, 166–171
Transportation,
  public transportation, 532
  toll roads, 532
Trans-Texas Corridor, 526
Travis County Medical Society, 275
Travis, William Barrett, 71, 87
Treaties of Velasco, 112, 115
Treaty of Córdoba, 63
Treaty of Paris (1783), 135
Treaty of the Little Arkansas, 283
Treaty of Velasco, 98
Trespalacios, José Felix, 64
Trinity Portland Cement Company, 372
Truman, Harry S, 389
Trump, Donald,
  illegal immigration, 543
Truth In Securities Act, 362
Tucker, Karla Faye, 524
Turtle Bayou Resolutions, 72
Twiggs, David, 153, 164
Twin Sisters, 98
Tyler, Elizabeth, 336
Tyler, John, 124

## U

Ugartachea, Domingo de, 72, 87, 99
Underwood Tariff, 301
Unionists, 179
Union Labor Party, 257
Union League, 196
Union Loyal League, 179
United Airlines, 477
United States Army,
  protection of the Texas frontier, 141–142
University of Texas,
  civil rights activism at, 422
  founding of, 118, 149, 231
  funding of, 256
University of Texas Medical Branch, 275
Upshur, Abel, 124
Urbanization,
  in early twentieth century, 273
  in the 1920s, 332
Urrea, José, 91, 95
Ursúa, Antonio María de Bucareli y, 43
Uvalde, Texas, 361

## V

Vagrancy Code, 199
Valdez, Lupe, 531
Valenzuela, Richie, 417
Valverde, Battle of, 169
Vásquez, Rafael, 122
Vaughan, Stevie Ray, 511
Vehlein, Joseph, 74
Vela, Don Macedonio, 288
Velasquez, Willie, 473
Venue shopping, 522
Vera Cruz, Mexico, 137
Veramendi, Juan Martín de, 75
Veterans' Land Board, 431
Vicksburg, Mississippi, 172
Victorio, 285
Vietnam, 450
Vigilante movements, 149, 281, 311, 338
Vinson, Willie, 402
Von Hartin, Edward, 221
Voting Rights Act of 1965, 451, 456, 473

## W

Waco Medical Society, 275
Wacos, 13
Wade-Davis Bill, 191
Waggoner, William T., 226
Wagner National Labor Relations Act, 372
Walker, Aaron Thibeaux "T-Bone," 417, 481
Walker, Doak, 510
Walker, Edwin, 444, 447
Walker, John George, 173
Walker's Texas Division, 173, 174

Ward, "Chief Justice" Hortense, 326
Wardlaw, Louis, 346
Ware, Andre, 510
War on poverty, 449
Warren, Earl, 448
Warren Report, 458
Washington-on-the-Brazos, Texas, 113
Watergate Affair, 467
Water rights, 509
Waters-Pierce Oil Company, 308
Watie, Stand, 176
Watson, Tom, 259
Waul's Texas Legion, 168
Weaver, James B., 257
Webb, James, 118
Weddington, Sarah, 474
Wells, James B., 315
Western Texas Medical Association, 275
Western, Thomas G., 99
Wharton, William, 73
Whig Party, 150
White, Bill, 529
White flight, 416
White, Mark, 499, 503
White primary, 307, 330
White, Raleigh R., 275
Wichita Falls, Texas, 304, 374
Wichitas, 10, 12, 38
Wigfall, Louis T., 151, 167
Wiley College, 441
Wilkinson, Cary, 275
Wilkinson, James, 48
Williams, Clayton, 503
Wills, Bob, 376, 417
Wilmot, David, 137
Wilson, Woodrow, 300, 309
Wind farms, 532
Winter Texans, 536
Woll, Adrián, 122
Wolters, Jacob, 359

Women,
   and job discrimination, 365
   during early statehood, 148
   farm life of, 328
   in Farmers' Allliance, 260
   in World War II, 394, 398
   urban jobs in 1920s, 332
   "Women of the Klan," 337
Women Accepted for Volunteer Emergency
   Service (WAVES), 394
Women's Airforce Service Pilots (WASPs),
   396
Women's Army Corps (WACs), 394
Women's Christian Temperance Union
   (WCTU), 234, 262
Woodland Era, 6
Woodmen of the World, 325
Woodward, Bob, 467
Woolly mammoths, 2
Workmen's Compensation Act, 301
Works Progress Administration (WPA), 364
World War I, 311–316
World War II, 387–396
Wright Amendment, 478

# X

Xinesí, 10

# Y

Yamparikas, 19
Yarborough, Don, 444, 456
Yarborough, Ralph, 428–429, 432, 449, 456, 468
Yellow Dog Democrats, 469
*Yellow Stone* (steamboat), 96
Youngblood, James E., 330
Young, William C., 169, 179

# Z

Zavala, Lorenzo de, 74, 77, 94
Zimmermann, Arthur, 312